HISTORY OF THE AMERICAN CINEMA

Volume 7

1950–1959

Audrey Hepburn and Fred Astaire in FUNNY FACE *(1957).*

HISTORY OF THE AMERICAN CINEMA

CHARLES HARPOLE, GENERAL EDITOR

7
TRANSFORMING THE SCREEN
1950 ~ 1959

Peter Lev

CHARLES SCRIBNER'S SONS®

THOMSON

GALE

New York • Detroit • San Diego • San Francisco • Cleveland
New Haven, Conn. • Waterville, Maine • London • Munich

History of American Cinema, Volume 7
Peter Lev

LIBRARY OF CONGRESS CATALOGING-IN-PUBLICATION DATA

Lev, Peter, 1948–
Transforming the screen, 1950-1959 / Peter Lev.
p. cm. — (History of the American cinema ; v. 7)
Includes bibliographical references and index.
ISBN 0-684-80495-6 (hardcover : alk. paper)
1. Motion pictures—United States—History.   I. Title.   II. Series.
PN1993.5.U6L445 2003
791.43'0973'09045—dc21   2003001988

Printed in the United States of America
10 9 8 7 6 5 4 3 2 1

Advisory Board

The Cinema History Project and the
History of the American Cinema
have been supported by grants from the
National Endowment for the Humanities and the
John and Mary R. Markle Foundation.

For Yola Lev, Divi Lewin, and Shirley Lev

Contents

Acknowledgments

Writing and coordinating a book for the History of the American Cinema series has certainly been my largest and most interesting research endeavor. I think of it as a "three-year sprint"; as with a sprint, it has been at some times exhilarating, at other moments exhausting. My sincerest thanks to the many individuals and organizations that helped me along the way.

Paul Monaco recommended me for the 1950s volume and advised me on some early decisions. At Scribners, John Fitzpatrick was a wonderful editor with a remarkable knowledge of film history. John often pointed me in the right direction with a phone call or a few lines of e-mail. Sarah Turner expertly guided the manuscript through the final editorial stages, and Sonia Benson did a fine, thoughtful job as copy editor. Charles Harpole, General Editor of the series, was especially helpful in the area of film technology. The five contributors of individual chapters were a joy to work with: Brian Neve, University of Bath; Janet Wasko, University of Oregon; Victoria O'Donnell, Montana State University; Jack C. Ellis, Northwestern University; and Greg S. Faller, Towson University.

Over the past three years I have frequented a number of research libraries and special collections. I benefited greatly from several visits to the Margaret Herrick Library of the Academy of Motion Picture Arts and Sciences, the single best resource I know for the study of film history. Barbara Hall, head of Special Collections at the Academy Library, was enormously helpful. Thanks also to the Library of Congress and the libraries of Brigham Young University; Georgetown University; Stanford University; University of California, Los Angeles; University of Southern California; and Wisconsin Center for Film and Theater Research. In my home state of Maryland I consulted numerous university and public libraries, and became perhaps the best customer of the Albert S. Cook Library, Towson University.

My colleagues at Towson have been consistently helpful and enthusiastic. Thanks to William Horne (1946–2002), Maravene Loeschke, Barry Moore, Greg Faller, and Keith Tishken. Bill Horne loaned me numerous DVDs and tapes from his personal collection, the last one a few weeks before his untimely death. Thanks as well to Dean Esslinger, Luz Mangurian, and the Faculty Research Committee at Towson University for their support of my work.

My love and gratitude to Yvonne and Sara cannot easily be expressed, but I will try. Thanks for everything.

Introduction

In 1950 Darryl F. Zanuck, vice president in charge of production at Twentieth Century–Fox, was described in a *Time* magazine cover story as the preeminent Hollywood executive of his generation. "Since the war," said *Time*, "Zanuck's 20th Century-Fox has consistently led the field in the quality of its films." Fox had won a Best Picture Oscar for GENTLEMAN'S AGREEMENT in 1947, and would add another for ALL ABOUT EVE in 1950. At the box office, Fox had been consistently successful, with profits of more than $10 million each year from 1942 to 1949. Since film is a thoroughly collaborative medium, credit for Fox's achievements should be given to the studio's producers, directors, writers, actors, composers, cinematographers, and other creative personnel, as well as to the head of production. However, *Time* noted (and Zanuck's biographers would concur) that each Fox film was "shaped in large measure—for better or worse—by the taste and imagination of Cinemogul Zanuck." In recognition of his great value to the company, Zanuck had been given a ten-year contract with a base salary of $260,000 per year. [1]

The American film industry faced serious challenges in the early 1950s, notably the divorcement of production companies from theater chains (forced by an anti-trust decision) and the growth of television, but Zanuck's Fox remained both profitable and innovative. Zanuck moved the studio from topical and controversial subjects to more entertainment-oriented fare, based on his analysis of the public mood. Fox was fortunate to develop one of the 1950s' most important young stars, Marilyn Monroe. Also, Zanuck and Spyros Skouras, Fox's New York–based president, were both heavily involved in Fox's introduction of CinemaScope, the most commercially successful widescreen process of the 1950s. The first CinemaScope films buoyed Fox's profits in 1953 and 1954 and positively affected the entire Hollywood film industry.

It was therefore shocking when Darryl Zanuck quit his executive job in 1956 to become an independent producer. Zanuck's decision was impelled to some extent by personal reasons. He had been having an affair with an actress, Bella Darvi, and when his wife, Virginia, discovered the affair, she threw Zanuck out of the house. Publicly embarrassed, Zanuck left Fox for Europe to become a Paris-based producer. Fox would finance and release his films under generous provisions that reflected his reputation as a filmmaker and his status as the company's single largest stockholder. Beyond the immediate embarrassment, it is likely that Zanuck was going through a period of "middle-aged craziness." After years of demanding, stressful work, he probably wanted to enjoy the hedonistic lifestyle of the stereotypical Hollywood producer.

But there were professional reasons as well for Zanuck's departure from Los Angeles. Between 1950 and 1956 the Hollywood film companies had moved fairly rapidly from a "studio system" of production to an emphasis on individually "packaged" films, in which a "package" consisting of a story and a group of creative personnel was generally put together by a producer or a talent agency.[2] The studio system was characterized by vertical integration, with one company owning production, distribution, and exhibition businesses, as well as by division of labor, long-term contracts, and hierarchical management. This was an efficient way to produce and release large numbers of films. However, the Paramount anti-trust decision of 1948 made vertical integration illegal. At the same time, the film audience was eroding year by year because of the influence of television. In these conditions, it made more sense to organize the film business around individual productions, thus cutting corporate overhead. Independent producers like Sam Spiegel, Otto Preminger, Stanley Kramer, and Hecht-Hill-Lancaster (Burt Lancaster's company), who might make only one film per year, were rapidly becoming the creative center of the film industry. By the late 1950s, studios, though still important, were mainly providing financing and distribution for the independents. Twentieth Century–Fox and Metro-Goldwyn-Mayer (MGM) resisted this trend for several years, but with Zanuck's resignation in 1956, followed by the firing of Dore Schary (MGM's production head) in 1957, the victory of the independents was clear.

Darryl Zanuck was keenly aware that the power of the studio bosses was waning. Producer Kenneth MacGowan reports Zanuck's complaint that the head of the studio was no longer in charge; he was becoming "a negotiator, an executive, a peacemaker." Zanuck added that "everyone was becoming a corporation," reacting to the trend in which directors and actors were becoming independent producers and forming corporations so that earnings would be taxed at the corporate rate.[3] Financially, Zanuck resented that an independent producer with one big success could make far more money than a studio executive. For example, Frank Ross, who produced Fox's CinemaScope blockbuster THE ROBE (1953), earned more money on that film than studio boss Zanuck would make in several years.[4] Ross's most important decision regarding THE ROBE was buying the screen rights in the 1940s; this eventually entitled him to a percentage of the profits.

One of the problems Zanuck faced at Fox was a blurring of lines of responsibility between himself and Skouras. In the studio system of the 1940s, the New York office (Skouras) handled distribution and exhibition, whereas the Los Angeles office (Zanuck) took full responsibility for production. However, Fox had no exhibition business after September 1952 because of compliance with the anti-trust decision, and so Skouras's activities as president of Twentieth Century–Fox began to overlap with production. (Skouras was in theory Zanuck's boss, though in practice the two men had more of a peer relationship.) For example, it was Skouras and not Zanuck who negotiated with French inventor Henri Chrétien for the anamorphic lens technology that became CinemaScope.

With all these changes in process, it is little wonder that Zanuck felt "trapped," and that he told writer-producer Philip Dunne "I'm in the wrong business."[5] The intensely competitive Zanuck saw himself as a producer, not a corporate executive, and the creative scope of his job was diminishing. Independent producing was a more creative and

*Darryl F. Zanuck during the filming
of* The Sun Also Rises *(1957).*

more autonomous job, which offered in addition the chance of a huge financial windfall. So Zanuck became an independent producer and moved to Europe—in part for personal reasons and in part for professional reasons (subsidies, cheap production costs, unique locations). His first efforts were generally ineffective. Spyros Skouras, commenting on a couple of failures, told Zanuck in 1958 that he was out of touch with the American market and that he had to decide if he was an "adventurer" (this was a veiled reference to Zanuck's personal life) or a dedicated filmmaker.[6] However, in 1962 Zanuck produced the critically acclaimed and financially successful The Longest Day. This earned him the respect of the Hollywood community as well as a substantial monetary return. Zanuck then returned to Fox as its president, avoiding the head of production job that he had handled so well in previous years.

The story of Darryl Zanuck presents in microcosm several key themes of the history of the American film industry in the 1950s: the challenge from television, the decline of the studio system, the rise of independent production, the introduction of new technologies, the importance of overseas production. This period is often and correctly described as "transitional." The Hollywood of 1950 was essentially conservative, very much a part of the "studio" or "classic" era which began in the 1920s. The major studios were organized as they had been for decades (though independent production was beginning to make inroads); the star system and the genre system were very strong; the Production Code Administration (industry-run) and the Legion of Decency (affiliated with the Catholic Church) kept a tight control on screen morality. By 1959 this industry profile had greatly changed: independent production had become the order of the day; the genre system was in rapid flux (with some genres declining, others coming to prominence, and a few films not fitting into one genre); screen censorship had loosened, though not disappeared.

Though cultural historians often consider the 1950s a bland and conservative time—
"the new car, the TV dinner and your new program on the sofa"[7]—there was actually a
surprising diversity among the American films of the period. Yes, many 1950s films were
conservative in aesthetics, politics, and the representation of gender roles, but this was
also the era of beatniks, Method Acting, film noir, teen films (as expressions of a unique
teenage culture), films about minority groups, and even a bit of gender-bending (for
example, Pillow Talk and Some Like It Hot, both 1959). Long-established male stars
such as John Wayne, Bing Crosby, James Stewart, Bob Hope, William Holden, and Gary
Cooper enjoyed continued popularity, but 1950s films also featured a wide range of new
stars, including Marlon Brando, Montgomery Clift, Marilyn Monroe, Grace Kelly, Burt
Lancaster, Rock Hudson, Doris Day, Audrey Hepburn, Elvis Presley, and James Dean.
Behind the camera, veteran directors Cecil B. DeMille, John Ford, Alfred Hitchcock,
John Huston, Joseph L. Mankiewicz, Billy Wilder, and William Wyler flourished,
whereas "young Turks," including Robert Aldrich, Richard Brooks, John Cassavetes,
Stanley Kubrick, and Sidney Lumet, were just beginning to become known. There is no

Tony Curtis and Marilyn Monroe in Some Like It Hot *(1959).*

simple way to summarize the range of feature films in this period, but the distance between DeMille's lavish, backward-looking THE TEN COMMANDMENTS (1956) and Cassavetes's spare, hipsterish SHADOWS (1959) gives some sense of the possibilities. Documentary and experimental film add further variations, from sponsored films to semi-abstract city symphonies (documentary), and from abstract expressionism to dance film to computer-generated imagery (experimental).

This volume of the History of the American Cinema series emphasizes both industrial and aesthetic film history. Chapters 1 and 9 describe the changing structure of the Hollywood film industry, focusing on such topics as major and minor studios, independent producers, talent agencies, exhibitors, and labor disputes. Chapters 2 and 10 discuss the feature films of the period, using genre rather than auteurism as the guiding principle. Within this organizing framework, several chapters (some by the lead author, others by guest contributors) analyze specific topics of great importance to the film business and/or to film as a cultural force. Chapter 3 by Brian Neve discusses anti-communism, the Hollywood Blacklist and the resulting lack of a social or progressive cinema in the Hollywood of the early and mid-1950s. Brian uses as a case study the career of Elia Kazan, who was simultaneously a witness who cooperated with HUAC (the House Committee on Un-American Activites) by naming associates as former Communists and a director who tried to retain a commitment to socially progressive causes in such films as VIVA ZAPATA! (1952), ON THE WATERFRONT (1954), and A FACE IN THE CROWD (1957). Chapter 4 summarizes a very active decade of local censorship, industry self-censorship, and pressures on film content (or unofficial censorship) from special interest groups such as the Legion of Decency. In some cases political censorship, usually associated with anti-communism, was added to the moral censorship that had become a customary part of Hollywood film production.

Chapters 5 and 6 deal with the film industry's varied responses to the threat of television. Chapter 5 discusses the many 1950s image and sound technologies that differentiated the filmgoing experience from television. The most significant of these new technologies were Eastman Color, Cinerama, 3-D, CinemaScope, stereophonic sound, VistaVision, Todd-AO, and Panavision. In Chapter 6, Janet Wasko presents Hollywood's several attempts to create synergies with television, including failed strategies (theater TV, subscription TV) and more successful alternatives (series television produced on film, the beginnings of media conglomeration). Case studies for this chapter include Disney, a small animation company which added live-action films, television, and an amusement park in the 1950s; and MCA, a talent agency that became a major TV production company and then began the process of acquiring a film studio (Universal).

Chapter 7 delineates Hollywood's increasing internationalism, with about 40 percent of distribution income coming from abroad and a lower but still significant percentage of production moving to foreign studios and locations. Two very different "waves" of production abroad are described: first, the activities of Hollywood exiles (most of them blacklisted writers and directors) who re-established careers in such places as France, England, Greece, and Mexico; second, producers and directors like Darryl Zanuck, who went abroad because of favorable production conditions and who had distribution contracts with the Hollywood studios. This chapter also includes a case study on the production and the marketing of THE TEN COMMANDMENTS, Hollywood's most successful international release of the period.

Chapter 8, by Victoria O'Donnell, describes the science fiction film, which became a major genre in the 1950s, and its relationship to fears of the atomic bomb and the Cold

War. Audiences and critics have an enormous affection for 1950s science fiction, even though only a few of the films (perhaps THE THING, 1951, THE DAY THE EARTH STOOD STILL, 1951, and INVASION OF THE BODY SNATCHERS, 1956) can be considered among the very best Hollywood work of the decade. The explanation seems to be that the science fiction of this era turns shared but hard-to-articulate anxieties into indirect narratives. The process is more or less transparent, so the spectator can actually perceive the transformation of history into myth.

As is typical of the History of the American Cinema series, this volume ends with chapters on documentary and experimental film. Chapter 11 by Jack C. Ellis presents the many uses of documentary in the period—UN films, USIA films, Disney True-Life Adventures, corporate documentaries, anthropological films, mental health films, city symphonies, and television documentaries. Documentary, like the fiction film, was in a period of transition. Theatrical screenings, fairly common during World War II, were declining in the 1950s, but television offered new opportunities for documentary production and distribution. Chapter 12 by Greg Faller opposes the "orthodox" view that Stan Brakhage's abstract expressionism was the key development of the period and shows the tremendous diversity of 1950s experimental films. Of special interest in Greg Faller's chapter is the detailed attention paid to dance films (a frequently neglected genre), including work by James Broughton, Shirley Clarke, and Ed Emshwiller.

This book is a reference history of a decade of American film, but it does not attempt to discuss every film, or even every high-quality film. Instead, it tries to balance an overview of the film industry with a discussion of representative films—not all the great melodramas, but a reasonable sample (ALL ABOUT EVE, SUNSET BOULEVARD, WRITTEN ON THE WIND, SOME CAME RUNNING); not all the Westerns, but selected films of John Ford, Anthony Mann, Howard Hawks, Fred Zinnemann, and others. Comprehensiveness is actually a danger, for a work of cinema history should not become an annotated list of thousands of films. For those seeking information on individual titles, many of the 1950s' most important films are indeed discussed in some detail. For those seeking more general knowledge, look to the pattern of the book as well as to its facts.

Peter Lev
10 August 2002

1

The American Film Industry in the Early 1950s

Industry-Wide Problems

The Hollywood film industry of 1950 was threatened on several different fronts. Television broadcasting was rapidly becoming the dominant entertainment medium in the United States. The Paramount anti-trust consent decree requiring separate ownership for production companies and theater chains had gone into effect on 1 January 1950. Large numbers of young men and women were marrying, having children, and moving to the suburbs, which affected the viability of downtown first-run movie theaters. Foreign revenues were endangered by protectionist tactics including quota systems, high taxes, and blocked funds. Finally, the morality and patriotism of Hollywood films and filmmakers were under attack from government, religious, and citizens' groups.

One quick way to get a sense of the film industry's declining fortunes in the early 1950s is to consider box-office statistics. Unfortunately, all such data is approximate. Table 1 presents three versions of the average weekly motion-picture attendance in the United States. The most widely quoted source, the U.S. Census Bureau, shows that weekly attendance dropped from 80 million in 1940 and 90 million in 1946 to 60 million in 1950 and 40 million in 1960. Another, possibly more precise, set of figures comes from the Theatre Owners of America (TOA), and covers only 1946–1956. Here, the 1946 peak is lower at 82.4 million per week, but the drop-off starts sooner and is more severe. A third set of figures, derived from U.S. Department of Commerce and Bureau of Labor Statistics data, shows almost a bell curve for 1940–1950. Though the three versions differ, the general trend is the same. Admissions rose from 1940 to 1946, and then dropped fairly rapidly so that by 1956 attendance was down almost 50 percent from the 1946 peak.

The decline in motion-picture admissions from 1946 to 1960 can be most productively studied in two segments. First, in the late 1940s the drop-off was largely a readjustment after some unusual wartime and postwartime conditions. During and just after World War II, people had money to spend and relatively few ways to spend it. Gasoline was rationed, many commodities were reserved for the war effort, and the movies "enjoyed a virtual monopoly of the entertainment business."[1] But with the end of wartime scarcities Americans turned to big-ticket purchases. Many bought new homes in the suburbs, which meant they were far away from the downtown movie theaters.

TABLE 1: ESTIMATED AVERAGE WEEKLY MOTION-PICTURE ATTENDANCE IN THE U.S. 1940–1960 (IN THOUSANDS)[2]

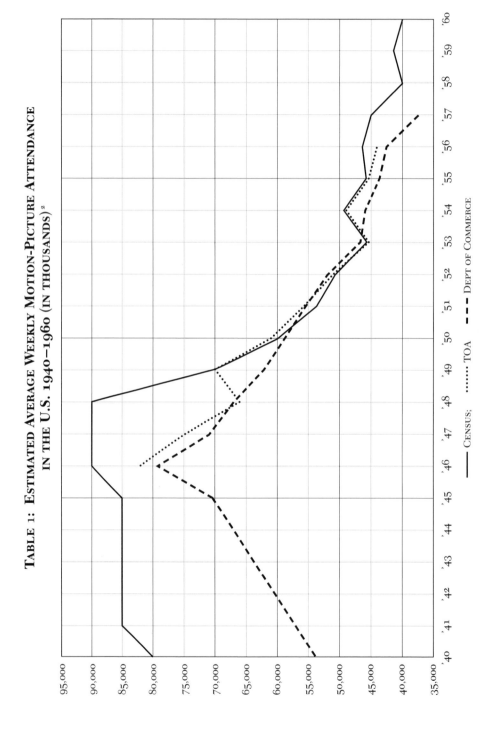

Television had not been a major factor in the 1940s. On 1 April 1948, only twenty commercial television stations were broadcasting in the United States. There was no television broadcasting in the southern states, and very little west of the Mississippi. Only 300,000 television sets had been sold. *Fortune* estimated that "90 per cent of the citizenry has not yet seen a television program."[3]

But television was, by all accounts, the key factor in the steady decline of American film audiences in the 1950s. By 1 January 1950 there were 98 commercial VHF television stations in the United States, by 1954 there were 233, by 1960 there were 440.[4] In the early 1950s the Sunday editions of big-city papers were crammed with full-page ads pushing the sales of the various models of TV receivers. In 1950 more than 7.3 million TV sets were sold in the United States, and U.S. TV sales were never less than 5 million in the years 1950–1959.[5] Poll results released by Paramount in 1950 revealed that families with television in the home decreased their film-going by 20–30 percent; Paramount assured the press that these figures were more accurate than a previous poll, which found a 46–74 percent drop.[6] A Warner Bros. poll in 1951 found that television ownership was already responsible for a 3–4 percent drop in the overall U.S. film audience, with further declines on the way.[7] Changes in living patterns (as in the trend toward suburbanization) and competition from other leisure activities (such as sports and travel) also affected film attendance in the 1950s.

The anti-trust case which ended vertical integration in the film industry did not directly hurt movie attendance, but it did have a profound effect on film industry stability and profitability. The case began when the government accused the eight largest Hollywood companies—Paramount, Metro-Goldwyn-Mayer (MGM), Twentieth Century–Fox, Warner Bros., RKO, Columbia, Universal, and United Artists—of monopolizing film distribution and exhibition through ownership of first-run theaters and of participating in a variety of collusive practices. Paramount, MGM, Fox, Warner, and RKO—often referred to as the "five major studios"—owned about 65 percent of the first-run theaters in the United States. In many cases, they did not compete head-to-head with one another. Instead, they offered each other favorable terms and divided up the major markets into stable configurations of first-run and subsequent-run theaters. MGM's parent company, Loew's, was very strong in New York, Paramount in Chicago, Fox on the West Coast, and so on. Columbia, Universal, and United Artists, the "three minors," did not own theater chains, but they did benefit from the nationwide cartel.[8] Distribution and exhibition were structured so that films from the established Hollywood studios could count on a profitable release pattern, and well-connected theaters (usually first-run houses owned by the majors or by local chains) could count on a steady supply of good-quality films. However, producers outside the Hollywood system and independent exhibitors would have a difficult time breaking into the established release patterns.

The federal government won its case in the late 1940s and entered into a series of consent decrees with the eight affected studios. For the five majors, the government required the divorcement of production and distribution from exhibition; also, large stockholders would need to divest their holdings in one of the newly formed companies within two years of the divorce. The idea was that a breakup of the studios would end the cozy control of exhibition and lead to greater competition throughout the film industry. The government also required the sale of some theaters (in monopoly areas), the exhibition of a percentage of films from non-major companies, and a looser, more competitive approach to runs and exclusivities. Block booking, the licensing of films in "blocks or indivisible groups,"[9] had been outlawed since 1946.

These changes did end a set of monopolistic practices. However, their effects on an already struggling film industry went well beyond encouraging competition. By cutting the link between production and exhibition, the consent decrees made film production a much less stable undertaking. Every film became a risk, for both producer and exhibitor. While in the past the risk had been cushioned by the activities of a large, integrated company (so that a loss in production, for example, could be compensated for by a profitable year in exhibition), after the anti-trust suit producer and exhibitor were no longer natural allies, and oversupply and undersupply became very real possibilities. Further, the FCC was skeptical about awarding television station licenses to companies found guilty of anti-trust violations. An absolute ban was not declared, but the FCC declared "a strong presumption" that monopolists would not be "qualified to operate a broadcast station in the public interest."[10] This greatly limited the film industry's attempts to expand into television.

The uncertainty of foreign markets was of great concern to the Hollywood companies in the late 1940s. U.S. allies, such as Britain and France, and former enemies, such as Germany and Japan, were facing enormous rebuilding costs after World War II. American movies were popular in all of these countries, but Britain and France in particular were concerned about precious foreign exchange going to amusements rather than necessities. (Germany and Japan, as occupied nations, had less freedom of action.)[11] They therefore imposed a series of restrictions on the American film industry, including tariffs, blocked funds, and quota systems. International commerce was potentially a growth sector for the Hollywood industry, because television was much slower to gain a foothold abroad than in the United States. But if currency was blocked from export, then foreign earnings could not be counted on to make up for a domestic slowdown. Through intensive negotiations and some creative deal-making, the Hollywood companies had managed to free up most foreign earnings by 1950.[12] However, part of the deal-making was to use blocked funds to produce an increasing number of films abroad, and this had the effect of decreasing jobs in Hollywood.

Yet another danger to Hollywood in the early 1950s was a set of assaults from Congress and various citizens' groups centering on patriotism and morality. The House Un-American Activities Committee (HUAC), investigating communism in the United States, had interviewed ten unfriendly witnesses from the film industry in 1947; "unfriendly" here means uncooperative and suspected of Communist activity. The Hollywood Ten refused to answer questions and were found guilty of Contempt of Congress; their appeals exhausted, all ten went to jail in 1950. In 1951, HUAC returned to Hollywood for lengthier hearings on communism in the film industry. At the same time, an industry-wide blacklist of suspected leftists meant that hundreds of people (many of them screenwriters) lost their jobs. HUAC's efforts were supplemented by the American Legion and other veterans' groups and by the state of California's Tenney Committee. Also in 1950, Senator Edwin C. Johnson of Colorado complained about Hollywood's morality and called for a Federal licensing of motion pictures.[13]

It is difficult to quantify the effect these highly publicized problems had on film industry earnings. Studio attorneys responding to civil suits brought by several of the Hollywood Ten (all of whom had been fired) were unable to prove that the release of any film had been injured by publicity about the Ten.[14] On the other hand, the 1952 U.S. release of LIMELIGHT, by actor-director Charlie Chaplin, was hurt by a pressure campaign led by the American Legion. (Chaplin had been accused of both immorality and Communist sympathies.)[15] Sporadic picketing of other films in the early 1950s scared the studios, especially since the American Legion declared that local chapters could decide to picket on their own.[16] However, such picketing remained small-scale and probably had a minimal effect on box-office returns. In broader terms, it is clear that the political uproar of the early 1950s—with Senator Joseph McCarthy brandishing lists of Communists in government and HUAC investigating communism in many aspects of American life—led to restrictions on subject matter in Hollywood studio films. Social issue films, concern for minorities, or criticism of big business were suspect; even sympathy for the underdog was problematic. Director Elia Kazan commented in 1952 that the studios were trying so hard not to offend that "Actors are afraid to act, writers are afraid to write, and producers are afraid to produce."[17] Critic Robert Sklar (writing in 1975) concurred, saying that Hollywood in the late 1940s and the 1950s lost some of its appeal because of extreme caution.[18] This new caution must have affected the box office, but it is impossible to know how much.

Hollywood's leading figures were frequently asked to comment on the industry's problems in the early 1950s, and to suggest solutions. Producer David Selznick felt that filmmakers were "struggling desperately to make ends meet," and that the audience had "drastically changed."[19] Selznick's proposed solutions were, first, to rely on younger producers (since his generation might now be out of touch with the audience); and, second, to shift some production to Europe, where production costs were lower.[20] Director Howard Hawks suggested that Hollywood needed to make "pictures with imagination that sustain interest," because "Television is taking over the trivia."[21] Producer Samuel

Howard Hawks (left) and Jane Russell on the set of Gentlemen Prefer Blondes *(1953).*

Goldwyn thought that the key to future prosperity was a pay-TV technology called "phonevision," which would present Hollywood movies on home television sets.[22] Paramount executives Barney Balaban and Y. Frank Freeman called for sustained efforts to cut costs, with Freeman pointing to a $50 million gap between major studio spending and income in 1949.[23]

All these proposed solutions were put into practice in the 1950s. Young producers such as Stanley Kramer and the team of Harold Hecht–Burt Lancaster became important figures in the film industry. Hollywood put greater emphasis on "A" productions, and eventually on color and widescreen, to differentiate itself from television. Pictures may actually have gotten "better," as well, to meet the less loyal and more demanding audiences of the 1950s—certainly directors John Ford, Alfred Hitchcock, Billy Wilder, Elia Kazan, Fred Zinnemann, Vincente Minnelli, Gene Kelly, Stanley Donen, and Joseph Mankiewicz did some of their best work in this decade. Samuel Goldwyn's movies-at-home solution proved commercially unfeasible in the 1950s, but some accommodation with television was clearly needed. Finally, cost-cutting proceeded through the late 1940s and early 1950s. The studios cut overhead principally by saving on personnel costs. Both creative and technical staff were laid off, and those who remained were often required to take pay cuts.

The numerous challenges of the early 1950s had a powerful impact on the Hollywood film industry, but each company was affected differently. Among the major studios, for example, the consent decree presented an immediate problem for Paramount, which was required to quickly divest its theater chain, and less of a problem for MGM and its parent company Loew's, which held onto a vertically integrated company for some years. For the minor studios—principally Columbia, United Artists, and Universal—the changing conditions of the 1950s created dangers but also opportunities. The declining audience was clearly a problem for everyone. On the other hand, with the end of the vertically integrated majors, the Hollywood minors suddenly had the opportunity to compete for space in first-run theaters. Columbia and United Artists both seized this opportunity, making some of the most prestigious and successful films of the 1950s. Since the multiple changes of the early 1950s affected different studios in different ways, it is useful to discuss how each of the Hollywood majors and minors fared during this period.

Major Studios

Metro-Goldwyn-Mayer (MGM) had been for many years a high-budget, high-prestige film company. MGM was known for its lavish production values, its many stars under contract, and its mastery of the musical genre. With its East Coast parent Loew's Inc., MGM had been the dominating film company of the 1930s and had remained solidly profitable in the 1940s. The Loew's theater chain was relatively small, approximately 140 houses, but it included a number of well-placed first-run theaters. Loew's was particularly strong in New York City. The leaders of the company were Nicholas Schenck, president of Loew's, and Louis B. Mayer, studio head of MGM. Schenck had been with Loew's since 1907 and had served as president since the death of founder Marcus Loew in 1927. Mayer had been running the studio since it began (as a merger between three smaller production companies) in 1924.

Though MGM appeared to be a profitable and stable company, its top-heavy management structure interfered with adjustments to the new economic conditions of the late 1940s and early 1950s. Mayer's official position was vice president in charge of production. Under him were several other vice presidents and more than forty producers. Decisions were made, very cautiously, by committee. Thomas Schatz notes that Irving Thalberg, MGM's legendary production executive who died in 1936, had turned out forty-five films in 1927 with six supervisors; twenty years later MGM was making slightly fewer pictures with an enormous increase in high-level managers.[24] The executives at MGM and Loew's were older men who had been in their jobs a long time. For example, vice presidents Eddie Mannix and Benny Thau had been with MGM since the mid-1920s. Arthur Freed, producer of MGM's most prestigious musicals, had started in show business as a writer of song lyrics, but his association with MGM went back to 1927 (the beginning of sound film). He had been an MGM producer since 1939. Not surprisingly, managers with such long tenure were resistant to change. Lillian Ross in her book *Picture* presents the executives of MGM and Loew's as aging "yes men," following the lead of their respective chiefs Mayer and Schenck.[25]

Nicholas Schenck, in an attempt to revitalize the company, had in 1948 asked Mayer to find an executive to take charge of all of MGM's productions. Mayer eventually recommended Dore Schary, at age 43 already a distinguished writer, producer, and executive. Schary had been a supervisor of "B" pictures at MGM in the early 1940s. He produced I'LL BE SEEING YOU for David Selznick in 1944, and then moved to RKO as head of production. At RKO he supervised such films as THE SPIRAL STAIRCASE (1946), CROSSFIRE (1947), and THEY LIVE BY NIGHT (1949). Schary's liberal politics posed a potential conflict with the "archconservatism" of Mayer and Schenck,[26] but Schary had already shown a willingness to cooperate with the prevailing anticommunism. He promised to bring a more contemporary sensibility to MGM without unduly affecting the studio's traditions. Schary joined MGM as vice president in charge of production on 1 July 1948. Mayer's official title became vice president in charge of the studio.

In practice, Schary's ability to change MGM's output was fairly limited. Nicholas Schenck strongly backed Schary, but MGM's veteran staffers were fiercely loyal to Mayer. Arthur Freed, for example, reported only to Mayer, even though Schary was in theory his boss.[27] The power struggle was resolved only in June 1951, when Mayer retired from MGM under pressure from Schenck. Even at this point, though, the MGM studio had a momentum of its own that Schary could only gradually change. With its roster of stars, its high-quality but expensive departments, and its veteran producers, MGM was committed to a certain type of production. Schary could have drastically cut staff and relied on independent producers in the early 1950s—if the Loew's board of directors would have gone along. MGM did not follow that path. Instead, it kept to a program of expensive, in-house productions. Musical productions, for example, though far more expensive than the average film, remained about 25 percent of the studio's output. This was necessary to justify and maintain MGM's large number of musical specialists—producers, arrangers, supervisors, singers, and dancers, to name a few.[28]

MGM's financial situation can be analyzed in unusual detail thanks to a large bound book known as the "Eddie Mannix Ledger," which was found in the papers of MGM head of publicity Howard Strickling.[29] Eddie Mannix was the general manager and one of the administrative vice presidents for MGM. His ledger gives basic financial data for every film distributed by MGM between 1924 and 1962, including production cost, overhead days, domestic earnings, foreign earnings, and profit or loss. Interestingly, total earnings minus production costs do not equal profit or loss in Mannix's accounting; profit is always much smaller than this simple equation might suggest. The explanation seems to be that distribution and publicity costs are subtracted from earnings, though there is no column for such costs.[30] There are other unknowns about the ledger as well: how data was compiled and how the document was used. Nevertheless, even if Mannix's data is more trustworthy in the comparative than in the absolute sense, the ledger still gives us a wealth of information on specific films, specific years, and multiyear trends.

TABLE 2: MGM PRODUCTION DATA, 1949–1950 TO 1953–1954 (IN THOUSANDS)[31]

YEAR	FILMS PRODUCED	COST	DOMESTIC EARNINGS	FOREIGN EARNINGS	PROFIT
1949–1950	38	53,702	63,452	30,580	3,910
1950–1951	37	48,477	57,691	35,997	8,143
1951–1952	40	61,019	60,204	40,131	1,438
1952–1953	44	57,506	58,672	44,721	1,349
1953–1954	29	43,833	51,701	38,940	6,375

The data in table 2 reveal that MGM's output increased slightly between 1949–1950 and 1952–1953. This is consistent with the rest of the film industry, and it suggests that film production did not immediately adjust to the decline in audiences. The number of films distributed by the majors and minors actually peaked in 1951, before declining sharply in 1954. Although this seems like an odd response to an industry-wide crisis, Michael Conant comments that the studios were under pressure from exhibitors to raise the total number of films in distribution in the years around 1950. Conant's explanation is that with declining audiences, theaters needed to change their programs more often. After the divorcement required by the consent decree, producer/distributors would have had less incentive to help exhibitors in this way.[32] The rise in production may also have been an attempt to exploit the industry's instability by taking theater bookings from competitors. MGM had an additional reason to keep production levels high, for this studio was not facing the imminent loss of its theater chain. Loew's theaters remained profitable well into the 1950s, and Loew's and MGM did not split until 1954 (ownership was not completely divested until 1959!).[33] So the "business as usual" of the MGM studio was matched by a continuation of a vertically integrated Loew's, Inc.

MGM's cost per film was high, but not out of line with the costs of its competitors. Using the Eddie Mannix Ledger's figures, the average production cost per film can be calculated as $1,413,000 in 1949–1950, $1,310,000 in 1950–1951, $1,525,000 in 1951–1952, $1,307,000 in 1952–1953, and $1,511,000 in 1953–1954. By comparison, Paramount's production cost per film was $1,428,000 in 1949, and Fox's was a very high $1,787,700.[34] In a period of marginal profits, the control of spending could be crucial to determining success or failure in a particular year. For example, the difference between MGM's balance sheets for 1949–1950 and 1950–1951 is not a matter of gross earnings—they are almost identical. But profits doubled in 1950–1951 because of a 7 percent reduction in costs. In 1953–1954, MGM went in a different direction—reducing output but not the average cost per film. This was at least modestly successful, because yearly production costs dropped 24 percent and earnings dropped only 12 percent.

The Mannix Ledger suggests that foreign earnings had become more and more important to MGM's operation. Domestic earnings, under pressure from television and other factors, declined slightly from 1949–1950 to 1952–1953. Foreign earnings increased substantially in the same period, from $30.58 million to $44.72 million. Note that in Europe, only England had an extensive television industry in the early 1950s. In France, Italy, Germany, and Spain television was still in its infancy, and therefore motion pictures remained the leading form of mass media entertainment. However, the dramatic increase in foreign earnings may be misleading because the totals include blocked funds. Many countries that imported American movies restricted the export of a percentage of the profits to the United States. These funds needed to be spent within the country in which they were generated. Given such restrictions, it is very difficult to know how much of MGM's foreign earnings were immediately available to MGM/Loew's in the United States.

One surprise revealed in the individual film entries of the Eddie Mannix roster is that musical films are not the studio's most profitable productions in the early 1950s. AN AMERICAN IN PARIS (1951), winner of several Academy Awards, cost $2,754,000 (about twice the cost of an average MGM feature) and earned an estimated profit of $1,361,000. By contrast, the Spencer Tracy–Elizabeth Taylor comedy FATHER OF THE BRIDE (1950) cost $1,215,000 and had an estimated profit of almost $3 million. MGM's most expensive film of the period, QUO VADIS? (1951) also did extremely well. The cost was $7,623,000, earnings were an estimated $21.2 million (with foreign earnings almost 50 percent of this total), and profit was estimated at $5,562,000. As for other celebrated musicals of the period, SINGIN' IN THE RAIN (1952) cost $2,593,000 and had eked out an estimated profit of $693,000 by 1957. THE BAND WAGON (1953) cost $2,873,000 and took an estimated loss of $1,147,000. BRIGADOON (1954), IT'S ALWAYS FAIR WEATHER (1955), and SILK STOCKINGS (1957) all lost more than $1,300,000, and INVITATION TO THE DANCE (started production 1952, released 1957) was an almost complete write-off, with a cost of $2,822,000 and a loss of $2,523,000. These figures certainly explain MGM's greatly curtailed production of musicals in the late 1950s.[35]

Famous as the studio of the stars, MGM had numerous high-profile stars in its films of the late 1940s and early 1950s. The list includes Spencer Tracy, Clark Gable, Robert Taylor, Robert Young, Gene Kelly, Van Johnson, and Red Skelton among the men, plus female stars Katharine Hepburn, Esther Williams, Lana Turner, Myrna Loy, Jane Powell, Elizabeth Taylor, June Allyson, Debbie Reynolds, and Cyd Charisse. Most of these were under long-term contracts, and MGM was slower than some of the other studios (e.g., Paramount, Warner Bros., Columbia) to move to short-term deals with top stars. Judy Garland, a popular MGM star of the 1940s, was released by the studio in 1950 after a history of illness and substance abuse.

Producers at MGM included Arthur Freed, Joe Pasternak, Jack Cummings, Sam Zimbalist, Pandro Berman, and John Houseman. Among the directors were Richard Brooks, Clarence Brown, George Cukor, Mervyn Le Roy, Vincente Minnelli, Gene Kelly, Stanley Donen (first as co-director with Kelly, eventually going off on his own), John Sturges, Charles Walters, and William Wellman. This was a strong and veteran group of filmmakers.

The challenge to any film company in the 1940s and 1950s was to adjust and keep adjusting to rapidly changing conditions. Paramount, Twentieth Century–Fox, and Warner Bros. all managed the adjustments fairly well. Paramount Pictures was, by the mid-1940s, the largest and most profitable of the major studios. Its theater chain of about 1,400 houses was the largest in the United States, and it also had a strong position in Canada. However, Paramount split into two separate companies in 1950, following the terms of the consent decree. The theater chain became United Paramount The-atres (which later merged with the ABC Radio and TV network), and the production/distribution branch Paramount Pictures was on its own. Paramount Pictures kept the Canadian and overseas theaters (318 in all), which were not affected by the consent decree. Paramount also had a minority interest in the Dumont television company (equipment manufacturer and broadcasting network) and owned a television station in Los Angeles.

Paramount Pictures' top managers were President Barney Balaban in New York and studio head Y. Frank Freeman in Los Angeles. Freeman's background was in film exhibition (as was Balaban's), but he had been managing Paramount's West Coast operations since 1938. Under Balaban and Freeman, Paramount had emphasized "A" pictures and long runs in the 1940s and had made excellent profits—$39.2 million in 1945 and $28.2 million in 1946. This was by far the best showing of any Hollywood studio. However, it should be remembered that Paramount had the largest theater chain, so in boom years it would do particularly well. In the late 1940s, as the overall film audience declined, Paramount cut its average cost per film from $1,512,000 (1946) to $1,144,000 (1950).[36] The "new" Paramount production and distribution company averaged profits of about $6 million between 1950 and 1953, but of course the company itself was much smaller than in the 1940s.

Paramount had a strong group of stars and a number of capable filmmakers under contract. The two biggest stars were Bing Crosby and Bob Hope, both of whom were ranked in the top ten list of Hollywood stars for eleven consecutive years, 1943 to 1953.[37] Other Paramount stars circa 1950 were Alan Ladd, William Holden, Betty Hutton, Jerry Lewis, Dean Martin, Dorothy Lamour, and Charlton Heston. Even more impressive were the producers and directors associated with Paramount. Cecil B. DeMille, a producer *and* director, was the most successful filmmaker (in box-office terms) in the film industry. DeMille, born in 1881, had helped to found Paramount's West Coast studio in 1913 and had worked with Paramount for most of his career. In his later years he was still producing a series of high-grossing epics—SAMSON AND DELILAH (1949), THE GREATEST SHOW ON EARTH (1952), and THE TEN COMMANDMENTS (1956). DeMille's films were so important to the studio that he was charged a lower overhead than anyone else.[38] Hal Wallis, another industry veteran, moved from Warner Bros. to Paramount in the mid-1940s. Wallis produced 3 to 4 pictures per year at Paramount as an independent producer who received a percentage of the profits for the films he made. Wallis also prided himself on finding new talent—two of his coups were multi-film contracts with Burt Lancaster and Elvis Presley. Other high-quality filmmakers at Paramount were Leo McCarey, George Seaton, George Stevens, Billy Wilder, and William Wyler.

Twentieth Century–Fox, like its competitors, had prospered during World War II and the immediate postwar period. Taking advantage of the long theatrical runs characteristic of the period, Fox made fewer but more expensive films in the 1940s. Fox's average cost per film in 1947 was an astoundingly high $2,328,600. The strategy paid off with profits of $22.6 million in 1946 and $14 million in 1947. As audiences dropped in the late 1940s, Fox reduced its average cost per feature, and thus maintained profitability. Only in 1951 and 1952 did profits fall dramatically ($4.3 million in 1951, $3.7 million in 1952).

Fox's top management consisted of Spyros Skouras in New York and Darryl Zanuck in Hollywood. Skouros, basically a film exhibition man, had been organizing and managing theater chains since the 1920s. Skouras responded to film's declining audience circa 1950 by looking for technological, exhibition-based solutions. He first turned to theater TV,

Cecil B. DeMille, Samuel Goldwyn, and Adolph Zukor, three pioneers of the Hollywood film industry.

touting a system known as Eidophor. When that generated little enthusiasm, he bought a widescreen process based on anamorphic lenses and called it "CinemaScope." Beginning with the blockbuster 1953 release THE ROBE, CinemaScope became the most successful technological innovation of the 1950s. When the production/distribution end of Fox split from the theater chain in September 1952, Spyros Skouras stayed with the production company while his brother Charles (also a veteran theater man) headed the theater chain. This led to claims from independent exhibitors that the two companies were still setting common policy and that the intent of the consent decree was not being met.[39]

Unlike Y. Frank Freeman at Paramount, who was basically a manager, Darryl Zanuck at Fox was a hands-on creative producer. Zanuck had been a writer, producer, and production executive at Warner Bros. from 1926 to 1933. He left Warners to found an independent company, Twentieth Century Productions, with partner Joseph Schenck. In 1935 Zanuck and Schenck merged Twentieth Century with Fox, and Zanuck became the new company's West Coast studio head—a position he held until 1956. Zanuck personally produced a few films each year at Fox, and he made creative contributions to many more. In the late 1940s, Fox under Zanuck produced and distributed several prize-winning films on controversial issues, including GENTLEMAN'S AGREEMENT (1947), THE SNAKE PIT (1948), and PINKY (1949). Zanuck also supported a switch to shooting crime films on location, taking advantage of the audience's new postwar familiarity with documentary immediacy. But Fox in the late 1940s also made many conventional entertainment films, including a series of Technicolor musicals starring Betty Grable.

Zanuck noted in the early 1950s that audiences seemed to be interested in escapist entertainment, and he turned Fox's production schedule toward musicals, comedies, and adventure stories.[40] Two of the biggest Fox stars, Gregory Peck and Susan Hayward, were teamed successfully in the Biblical story DAVID AND BATHSHEBA (1951). Other stars of 1950–1952 were Richard Widmark, Victor Mature, Anne Baxter, Gene Tierney, Clifton Webb, Jean Peters, Dan Dailey, Dana Andrews, and Jeanne Crain. Among the top film-makers working for Fox from 1949 into the early 1950s were Joseph Mankiewicz, Howard Hawks, Elia Kazan, Jules Dassin, writer-producer Nunnally Johnson, Otto Preminger, and Robert Wise. Fox's most important new star of the period was Marilyn Monroe, but the studio did not immediately understand her box-office power. For example, in HOW TO MARRY A MILLIONAIRE (1953), Monroe receives third billing, behind Lauren Bacall and Betty Grable.

Warner Bros. in 1950 was a publicly owned but family-managed company. Harry Warner, the oldest brother, was president of the company, based in New York. Albert Warner, the treasurer of Warner Bros., was also in New York. Jack Warner was vice president in charge of production, and therefore the top executive at Warner Bros.' Burbank studio. (A fourth brother, Sam Warner, had died in 1926.) This management team had been in place since the 1920s. Like its competitors, Warners had stunningly profitable years in 1946 and 1947. Unlike Paramount, MGM, and Fox, Warner Bros.' biggest year was 1947, with a profit of $22 million. The company's profits then gradually declined to $11.8 million in 1948 and an average of about $10 million between 1949 and 1951. The divorce of the theater chain (which became Stanley Warner Theatres) took place on 28 February 1953. After divorcement, Warner Bros.' profits were only $2.9 million in 1953.

Jack Warner, always a budget-conscious executive, responded to the less favorable conditions of the late 1940s and early 1950s by slashing costs. Many of the Warner stars were released from their long-term contracts—the list includes James Cagney, Humphrey Bogart, Bette Davis, Barbara Stanwyck, Olivia de Havilland, and George Raft. Only a few Warner stars—notably Errol Flynn and Ronald Reagan—were kept on into the early 1950s. In 1951, department heads were laid off, the publicity staff was reduced, and the story department was closed.[41] Prolific producer Jerry Wald left for RKO (which paid $150,000 for his contract). Henry Blanke, another top Warners producer, endured several salary cuts, and even Jack Warner's assistant Steve Trilling was eventually dismissed. Thomas Schatz notes that the various cuts sustained Warners' profits at the highest level in the industry in 1950 and 1951, but "the potential for future profits was diminished considerably."[42] However, one could also suggest that Jack Warner was quickly moving the company toward a future of distributing independent productions. Distribution agreements were made with producer/director Alfred Hitchcock, and with producer/stars such as James Cagney (the former Warners contract star) and Burt Lancaster.

Warner Bros. had been known for its noir films in the 1940s, many of them starring Humphrey Bogart, Edward G. Robinson, and/or John Garfield. In the early 1950s, Warners (like Fox) switched its emphasis to musicals, comedies, and adventure films. Doris Day quickly became the studio's biggest star, appearing in a series of musicals including TEA FOR TWO (1950), LULLABY OF BROADWAY (1951), ON MOONLIGHT BAY (1951), and CALAMITY JANE (1953). Gordon MacRae appeared opposite Day in many of these films. Another star of Warner musicals in the early 1950s was Virginia Mayo. Warners also made short-term agreements with some of Hollywood's top talents: Gary Cooper, John Wayne, Jane Wyman, Gregory Peck, Patricia Neal, and Randolph Scott.

Warner Bros. was the first major studio to invest in 3-D production, and scored a big success with the 3-D horror film HOUSE OF WAX (1953). Warners also worked with such prestigious directors as Hitchcock, Elia Kazan (A STREETCAR NAMED DESIRE, 1951), and Michael Curtiz (who had been a Warners contract director since the 1930s).

RKO was the weakest and most erratic of the five major studios. The RKO theater chain was relatively small (124 theaters) but it was well situated with first-run houses in New York, New Jersey, and Ohio. However, the production end of the business had struggled through several different managements in the 1930s and 1940s, with consistent profitability only in the boom years of 1943–1946. In 1947–1948 RKO was trying to build up in-house production under controlling owner Floyd Odlum, president Peter Rathvon, and studio head Dore Schary. Schary was particularly proud of the young directors he had under contract, including Edward Dmytryk, Nicholas Ray, Joseph Losey, and Mark Robson.[43] At this point Odlum, who viewed RKO as an investment rather than a vocation, sold his interest in RKO to one of the strangest figures in twentieth-century American history: Howard Hughes.

The young Howard Hughes produced a few important films (HELL'S ANGELS, 1930; SCARFACE, 1932) while building his fortune in non-film-related businesses. In 1948, Hughes purchased a controlling interest in RKO, one of the five largest Hollywood studios.

The fabulously wealthy Hughes already controlled three enormous corporations: Hughes Tool Company (oil-drilling equipment), Hughes Aircraft (a defense contractor), and Trans-World Airlines. He had worked intermittently in Hollywood as an independent producer, with credits including Hell's Angels (1930), Scarface (1932), and The Outlaw (1943). His films had been expensive and controversial, often flouting conventional morality, but some of them had been successful as well.

Hughes promised Rathvon and Schary that he would be a hands-off owner, giving studio management more freedom than they had under Odlum. He broke this promise in about a month, ordering Schary to fire Barbara Bel Geddes from the cast of Bed of Roses and to take Battleground (one of Schary's favored projects) off the RKO production schedule. Schary resigned on 30 June 1948; he eventually bought Battleground for his next employer, MGM (it was a big hit in 1949). Rathvon soon resigned as well. Management of the studio was given to a three-man executive committee including veteran producer Sid Rogell. In the summer of 1948, Hughes fired several hundred RKO employees, and he canceled work on four expensive pictures.[44] One of these was The Robe, a novel set in New Testament times that would become one of the biggest hits of the 1950s.

Howard Hughes tried to personally manage RKO, paying obsessive attention to certain films. However, Hughes was not an experienced motion-picture executive and he had other business interests. He therefore neglected long-range planning while attempting to be both owner and creative producer. Hughes did agree in 1949 to divest RKO's theater chain from the production business—the studio became the first to go along with the government's remedy in the Paramount case. But Hughes held onto the production side of RKO for several more years, even though no one was really running the business. Hughes almost never set foot on the RKO lot,[45] yet he insisted on approving story properties, casting, agreements with producers, and other things that could have been delegated. Often decisions were delayed, and therefore RKO could not compete with the other studios for talent and properties. Hughes did ask at least a few of the top Hollywood producers and executives to come to work at RKO (Hal Wallis declined),[46] and in 1950 he succeeded in bringing producer Jerry Wald and his partner, writer Norman Krasna, to RKO as independent producers. The Wald-Krasna team was supposed to make twelve films per year for RKO over a five-year period, which would be a huge help in generating product for the studio's distribution system. However, Hughes retained approval over stories and casting, and Wald-Krasna struggled to get anything approved in 1951. Wald and Krasna left RKO in 1952, having produced only four pictures (two complete, two in process).

RKO was involved in a long series of scandals during the Hughes years. Hughes was often in court, sometimes with RKO stockholders. Among the scandals were: 1) an attempt to exploit Ingrid Bergman's affair with Roberto Rossellini, and the birth of their illegitimate child, in the ad campaign for Stromboli (1950); 2) the favorable deals Howard Hughes as an individual made with RKO, the corporation, for films Hughes had produced or was producing; 3) a dispute with producer Jack Skirball, who had negotiated a deal with RKO for a big-budget film with Gregory Peck (Hughes maintained there was no deal; Skirball won in court); 4) the denial of screen credit to blacklisted screenwriter Paul Jarrico for The Las Vegas Story (1952), which caused a dispute with the Screen Writers Guild and eventually a civil suit.

In September 1952 Hughes found a buyer—actually a syndicate of buyers—for his scandal-ridden studio, but this touched off the biggest scandal of all. The *Wall Street*

Journal revealed, in a series of articles starting 16 October 1952, that some of the buyers had histories of mail order fraud, high-stakes gambling, and association with organized crime.[47] Because of this unwanted publicity, the buyers backed out of the deal, forfeiting their down payment. Hughes was back in control of RKO.

During these crisis years, RKO production slowed but did not stop. According to *Fortune*, RKO's in-house production decreased from twenty-eight films in 1947 to ten in 1952.[48] The quality of RKO's films was sometimes good. Directors Fritz Lang and Nicholas Ray stayed with the studio well into the 1950s, as did actors Robert Mitchum, Robert Ryan, and Jane Russell (Russell's contract was originally with Hughes, not RKO). But there simply were not enough films to justify the overhead of running a major studio. RKO's distribution network limped along thanks largely to contracts with independent producers, including Samuel Goldwyn and Walt Disney.

As might be imagined, the mismanagement of RKO led to consistent financial losses and to the destruction of the studio's reputation. Losses on the production side totaled more than $20 million between 1948 and 1953.[49] It is possible that RKO would not have flourished under any management in the film industry downturn of the 1950s. However, since all the other leading studios managed to stay afloat through the decade, the decline and fall of RKO must be blamed first and foremost on Howard Hughes.

Minor Studios

Columbia and Universal were considered minor studios because their production and distribution businesses were not complemented by ownership of a theater chain. Without the muscle of their own theaters, Columbia and Universal did not in general try to rival the star power and high production values of the five major studios. Both of these companies specialized in "B" movies or "programmers" through the mid-1940s; in Tino Balio's words, they "were useful to the majors in supplying low-cost pictures to facilitate frequent program changes and double features."[50] Columbia did produce a few high-budget, high-prestige films in the 1930s, notably the comedies of Frank Capra. When "A" movies became predictably successful at the end of World War II, both studios raised the budgets of some films, while continuing to make less expensive Westerns, series (e.g., Universal's Francis the Talking Mule films), and serials. Columbia benefited from having Rita Hayworth under contract—she was one of the top stars and sex symbols of the 1940s. Universal had no star with this kind of drawing power until Rock Hudson hit his stride in the mid-1950s.

Columbia was founded by the Cohn brothers, Harry and Jack, but this was not an equal partnership. Harry, based in Los Angeles, was after 1932 both president and head of production for the studio, while Jack, based in New York, was executive vice president. Harry Cohn was a legendary Hollywood figure, crude, petty, penny-pinching. Producer Stanley Kramer, who had a multi-picture deal at Columbia between 1952 and 1954, describes Cohn as "vulgar, domineering, semi-literate, ruthless, boorish and some might say malevolent."[51] He was also a shrewd Hollywood executive with a good "eye for commercial prospects," as Kramer admits.[52] Harry Cohn supervised the entire Columbia studio as well as occasionally serving as de facto producer on a film.

In the early 1950s, Cohn's strategies were to raise output and to challenge the dominance of the majors with a number of high-prestige films. Columbia led the film industry with fifty-nine releases in 1950 and sixty-three in 1951, though the cost-per-picture would not have compared to MGM, Paramount, Fox, or Warner Bros. Columbia was still making Westerns and other low-budget genre films (as well as Three Stooges shorts), but was mixing in a surprising number of top-quality films. Many of the "A" pictures were independent productions from Stanley Kramer Productions (DEATH OF A SALESMAN, 1951; THE MEMBER OF THE WEDDING, 1952; THE CAINE MUTINY, 1954). Columbia was also making excellent films in-house, for example the George Cukor–directed BORN YESTERDAY (1950), and the Academy Award–winning FROM HERE TO ETERNITY (1953). Harry Cohn believed in short-term contracts, so it is difficult to compile a list of Columbia stars in the early 1950s. Judy Holliday, Rita Hayworth, and Broderick Crawford were clearly associated with Columbia. Humphrey Bogart and Randolph Scott worked at Columbia among other studios. Burt Lancaster, Glenn Ford, Gloria Grahame, Gale Storm, William Holden, Kirk Douglas, Donna Reed, Lucille Ball, Charles Boyer, Loretta Young, Robert Cummings, Mel Ferrer, and Anthony Quinn all made at least one Columbia film.

Universal Pictures' production output in the late 1940s was a strange amalgam of low-budget series (Ma and Pa Kettle, Abbott and Costello), crime films (THE KILLERS, 1946; THE NAKED CITY, 1948), Technicolor exoticism (NIGHT IN PARADISE, 1946; BAGDAD, 1949), and adaptations of leading playwrights (ANOTHER PART OF THE FOREST and ALL MY SONS, both 1948), plus musicals, comedies, and Westerns. Production heads William Goetz (Louis B. Mayer's son-in-law) and Leo Spitz had raised production budgets to compete with the majors, but their prestige pictures lost money and so they had to cut back on overall spending.[53] In 1952, Decca Records bought a controlling interest in Universal, and Milton Rackmil became president of both Decca and Universal. Goetz and Spitz were replaced by Edward Muhl, who had previously been studio manager. The Decca-Universal combination was an early example of media conglomeration. Decca had been releasing records featuring Universal stars and Universal properties for more than a decade, but these arrangements were based on individual deals, not a blanket contract.[54] In the early 1950s, Decca's taking control of Universal suggested that further links were likely. Milton Rackmil told the press that certain functions of the two companies might be combined and that a joint approach to producing for television was possible.[55]

Under Muhl and Rackmil, Universal added glossy entertainments, often in Technicolor, to its genre movies and serials. These included exotic, Arabian Nights–type stories (FLAME OF ARABY, 1951), conventional melodramas (ALL I DESIRE, 1953), and Technicolor Westerns (THE REDHEAD FROM WYOMING, 1953, starring Maureen O'Hara). Universal had directors Anthony Mann, Budd Boetticher, Raoul Walsh, and Donald Siegel making Westerns in the early 1950s—an impressive lineup. Anthony Mann's black and white WINCHESTER '73 (1950) was noteworthy because star James Stewart was given 50 percent of the profits. This approach, designed by Stewart's agent Lew Wasserman, could be used to lure top talent away from the major studios. WINCHESTER '73 was a hit, according to writer Dennis McDougal, and "Stewart eventually earned more than $600,000 from a movie it cost Universal $917,374 to make."[56] Universal stars of the period included Stewart, Rock Hudson, Tony Curtis, Yvonne De Carlo, Maureen O'Hara, Donald O'Connor, and Piper Laurie.

United Artists, the smallest of the "little three," was founded in 1919 to distribute the films of its owners Mary Pickford, Douglas Fairbanks, Charlie Chaplin, and D. W. Griffith. Thirty years later, Pickford and Chaplin were still the owners, but the studio was in desperate trouble. Pickford had retired from the movies, Chaplin was producing one

James Stewart and Shelley Winters in WINCHESTER '73 *(1950),
directed by Anthony Mann for Universal.*

film every four or five years, and United Artists was having difficulty attracting independent producers to its distribution setup. A number of studios were trying to sign independent producers around 1950, and United Artists was hindered by a lack of funding and an inefficient management scheme. UA President Grad Sears had to get approval from owners Pickford and Chaplin on proposed deals, whereas executives at other companies had much more freedom of action.[57] United Artists, like RKO, had too few films for its distribution pipeline, and therefore UA was losing $100,000 a week by 1951.[58]

United Artists was saved from bankruptcy and/or dissolution via an unusual offer from Arthur Krim and Robert Benjamin, both successful New York lawyers with considerable film industry experience. Krim and Benjamin offered to take over operation of United Artists for ten years "on the condition that if UA earned a profit in any one of the first three years, the Krim-Benjamin team would be allowed to purchase a 50 percent interest in the company for a nominal one dollar a share."[59] This arrangement was accepted in February 1951. The "new" United Artists took over the film inventory of Eagle-Lion Pictures (Krim and Benjamin had worked for this short-lived company in the late 1940s) to get distribution moving again. It then made distribution agreements with Horizon Pictures for THE AFRICAN QUEEN (1951) and with Stanley Kramer Pro-

Arthur Krim, president of United Artists, in a 1958 photo.

ductions for HIGH NOON (1952); both turned out to be major hits. United Artists was modestly profitable in 1951, so the terms of the Krim-Benjamin agreement with Pickford and Chaplin went into effect almost immediately. Krim and Benjamin then built on their early success to design a new strategy for independent production (which will be discussed later in this chapter).

A step down from Universal, Columbia, and United Artists were the "Poverty Row" studios, principally Monogram and Republic. These production-distribution companies provided extremely inexpensive genre films (primarily Westerns) to fill out the programs of smaller theaters. They were badly squeezed in the late 1940s and early 1950s by the downturn in film receipts and the closing of many theaters. Television became a factor in the 1950s, because set owners could now stay home and watch formula entertainment. Republic experimented with a few "A" productions, including John Ford Westerns (FORT APACHE, 1948; RIO GRANDE, 1950) and Nicholas Ray's JOHNNY GUITAR (1954). Monogram changed its name to Allied Artists in 1953 and concentrated on medium-budget production.

Independent Production

"Independent production" is a much-used but rarely defined phrase in the American film industry. In historical context, the phrase refers to a move away from a factory-like system where all aspects of a production are handled by studio employees, and toward a flexible, free-lance system where the personnel and other elements of a production are assembled for each individual film. Janet Staiger describes independent production as a "package-unit system," meaning that the key unit of organization is the individual film rather than the studio's yearly production schedule.[60] We must add a caveat here, because the film studio remained an important economic presence even after the increase in independent production of the 1950s. Studios no longer control every aspect of a film's production, but they do generally provide the crucial elements of financing and distribution. Also, to protect their investments, studios have generally retained some oversight of the production process itself—for example, cost and schedule guarantees and right of final cut—as well as control of advertising and distribution.

Though Hollywood in the 1930s and 1940s was dominated by the big studios, a few producers such as Samuel Goldwyn, David Selznick, and Walter Wanger chose to make their films independently, negotiating distribution contracts with the major or minor studios. Goldwyn, Selznick, and Wanger had stars and directors under contract and owned high-prestige story properties, all of which enhanced their negotiations with the studios. Selznick, for example, bought the rights to the enormously popular novel, *Gone with the Wind*, a property any of the studios would have been delighted to own. However, because Selznick wanted Clark Gable in the leading role of Rhett Butler, he made a distribution deal with MGM, offering the studio a substantial chunk of the profits. Independent production was never entirely independent; it was always a negotiation.

In the early to mid-1940s, producers, directors, and a few stars formed their own production companies to make films for studio distribution. The list includes Alfred Hitchcock Productions; Liberty Films (Frank Capra, William Wyler, and George Stevens); International Pictures (Gary Cooper); Argosy Productions (John Ford and Merian C. Cooper); and Cagney Productions (James and Bill Cagney). There were three basic reasons for creative people to form a production company instead of working on a studio contract: 1) Independent producers were entitled to a share of a film's profits, and therefore could make huge sums from a major success; 2) Personal income taxes were very high, and corporate taxes were much lower, so film people derived immediate benefits from "becoming a corporation"; 3) Some creative people were tired of studio bureaucracies and wanted to guide their own careers.

During the boom years of the mid-1940s, banks provided easy credit to independent producers on the theory that "a feature film—any feature film—would always return at least 60 percent of its negative costs at the box office."[61] Major banks such as Bank of America, Security First National Bank, and Guaranty Trust were therefore willing to advance up to 60 percent of negative cost with the film-in-process as its own collateral. Other loans and salary deferments provided the remaining 40 percent of funding. This liberal approach to credit naturally stimulated the growth of independent production. Janet Wasko notes that there were forty independent companies producing features in 1945, and 100 (including the major studios) in 1947.[62]

With the downturn in film industry receipts starting in 1947, the "60 percent rule" proved to be unduly optimistic. Numerous films were not making back even the 60 percent of the primary bank loan. Even the independent efforts of important filmmakers like Frank Capra (IT's A WONDERFUL LIFE, 1946) and Preston Sturges (MAD WEDNESDAY, 1947) were box-office flops. Major banks had to foreclose on motion-picture loans and to laboriously try to regain their investments through foreign distribution and other strategies. At this point the banks cut back on financing individual pictures, preferring to loan money to larger corporations with tangible assets—the major distribution companies.[63] Instead of negotiating directly with a bank, an independent producer now needed a distribution agreement, a completion guarantee, and perhaps a loan guarantee from a leading distributor. So, paradoxically, independent production became more and more dependent on the judgment and oversight of the major and minor Hollywood studios.[64]

Independent productions did not diminish or disappear with the new restrictions on bank lending, mainly because they suited the needs of the studios. With audiences declining and the consent decrees adding considerable uncertainty to the film business, the studios had an immediate need to cut overhead. By sponsoring independent production, they could eliminate the need for large permanent staffs. A studio could be reduced to management, accounting, sales, advertising, and publicity departments, plus a skeleton crew to maintain the physical facilities. In practice, this happened gradually, over a period of years or even decades. The process of cutting permanent staff can be highlighted by some estimates from *The Film Daily Yearbook*. In 1945 the major studios had 804 actors under contract, in 1950 the number had decreased to 474, and in 1955 to 209. As for writers, there were 490 under contract at the major studios in 1945, 147 in 1950, and only 67 in 1955.[65] In this same period, the members of craft unions were also moving from year-round contracts to free-lance work, but with far less publicity.

For creative people, the new working conditions were a mixed blessing. Those most in demand could now require princely salaries plus a percentage of the profits. And by forming their own production companies, actors, directors, and other filmmakers could be taxed at the 52 percent maximum for corporations instead of the confiscatory 75 to 92 percent for personal incomes over $100,000.[66] A number of actors, including Humphrey Bogart, Ida Lupino, Burt Lancaster, and Danny Kaye, formed production companies around 1950. However, profit participation meant nothing if a film was not successful, and those stars who invested in their own projects could actually take a loss. For marginally employed actors and other creative types the end of a studio contract meant uncertainty, likely periods of unemployment, and possibly the search for a new career. Membership in the Screen Actors Guild dropped 19 percent between 1947 and 1951 (it was later to rebound, because of Los Angeles–based television production).[67] The *New York Times* put this statistic into human terms in a profile of character actor Gino Corrado. Corrado, who had specialized in waiter and headwaiter roles (his credits include TOP HAT, 1935; GONE WITH THE WIND, 1939; and CASABLANCA, 1942) was by 1949 out of show business and working as a real-life headwaiter at a restaurant in Beverly Hills.[68]

The trend toward independent production accelerated in 1950 and 1951. *Variety* reported in early 1950 that much of the support for independent production was coming from the smaller, more marginal studios. RKO, Columbia, Republic, Monogram, and the small distributors Eagle Lion and Film Classics were all offering financial assistance to in-demand producers.[69] In some cases prestigious producers went to minor studios because of favorable financing as well as the autonomy and profit participation of indie production. For example, Louis de Rochemont signed with Columbia, and John Ford and Merian C. Cooper reached agreement with the Poverty Row studio Republic. Later in 1950 Paramount was actively recruiting independent producers and was changing to an emphasis on "semi-autonomous production units" rather than "salaried house producers."[70] RKO and Warner Bros. were moving in the same direction, with only MGM and Twentieth Century–Fox among the majors sticking to in-house production. By February 1951, Columbia was assembling a high-profile group of independent producers, Warners was working with Cagney Productions and Milton Sperling, and Fox had a three-picture deal with Joseph Bernhard.[71]

The films made as the studio system gradually dissolved should probably be called "semi-independent productions." The studio did far more than rent space to production companies. It arranged financing, approved story and budget, monitored production, and controlled marketing and distribution. Also, since studios in the early 1950s retained many of their contract personnel and technical departments, independent producers were encouraged (and in some cases required) to use studio crews and facilities. Independent production was really a partnership between producers and studios, with much depending on contract provisions and working relationships between the principals. Everything was open to negotiation, so that even regular studio contracts for top talent began to include profit participation and the ability to do outside films.

United Artists, traditionally the distributor of Hollywood's handful of top independent producers, had not prospered when the other studios began competing for this same talent. However, after the fortunate successes of THE AFRICAN QUEEN and HIGH NOON, the new management team of Arthur Krim and Robert Benjamin moved UA in a radically new direction. UA had no studio facilities or contract personnel to support, and therefore could provide more autonomy to the creative producer. Krim and Benjamin realized that the key element determining success in the "new Hollywood" of 1950 was the relationship between distributor and producer. By carefully choosing successful and reliable independent producers and establishing long-term relationships with them, United Artists could compete for talent with the biggest major studios. Further, United Artists was willing to forgo the day-to-day monitoring of production that had been standard in the studio system and had been taken over by the banks and then by studios sponsoring semi-independent production. For experienced producers, United Artists was willing to make a deal based on story, budget approval, and a completion guarantee. The producer was then free to organize and shoot the film on his own (female producers were at this time very rare), turning over the finished product to United Artists for distribution. This relationship of trust was a significant change in studio/talent relations, and it helped United Artists assemble a high-quality group of affiliated independent producers.[72]

One important effect of the move toward independent production was the increasing power of talent agencies. Under the studio system, agents negotiated for their clients, but the major studios had the upper hand. Stars, directors, and writers had relatively few potential employers, and the standard Hollywood contract lasted seven years, with the studio holding all the options. A star at the peak of popularity might have some room for negotiation, but in a famous case Bette Davis found that she could not get out of her Warner Bros. contract. However, with the studios laying off employees and independent productions taking over, agents suddenly gained considerable power as potential packagers of motion pictures. Previously most personnel decisions (casting, key crew members) had been based on who was available on a studio lot. Loan-outs from one studio to another were possible, but studio executives always looked to their own personnel first. Now independent producers could hire from an increasing pool of free-lance talent as well as negotiating for studio contract personnel. Large talent agencies were uniquely situated to put together interesting film projects based on people they represented (such as actors, directors, writers, and cinematographers), and to pitch them to studios. The packaging of successful projects generated increased income for the agency and its clients, and this, in turn, led to more clout in the agency's future negotiations with the film studios.

Charles Feldman of Famous Artists represented a number of the top stars in Hollywood in 1950: Tyrone Power, Marlene Dietrich, Fred MacMurray, Randolph Scott, Ida Lupino, Susan Hayward, Ava Gardner, William Holden, Lauren Bacall, Charles Boyer, and John Wayne; also directors Howard Hawks, Edmund Goulding, Jean Negulesco, and Otto Preminger.[73] He used this roster of talent to enhance his own moneymaking activities, as well as maximizing opportunities for those he represented. In addition to being an agent, Feldman became a producer. He received a waiver from the Screen Actors Guild to produce an occasional picture, and agreed in return not to take his 10 percent agent's fee when he was also functioning as producer. The waiver was necessary because serving as agent and producer was perceived (correctly) as a conflict of interest—the producer might wish to limit salaries of the very actors whom he was representing as an agent. Feldman was the producer or co-producer on some of the top films of the 1940s and 1950s: RED RIVER (1948), A STREETCAR NAMED DESIRE (1951), and THE SEVEN YEAR ITCH (1955). He generally served more as a packager than as a line producer, often buying a story property and re-selling it to a studio, usually with a director and/or actors attached.

Lew Wasserman of MCA (Music Corporation of America) was the most important agent of the dominant Hollywood talent agency. MCA had been founded by Dr. Jules Stein to represent musicians of the big band era, but had quickly moved beyond this focus to other aspects of show business. By 1950, Stein was semi-retired, and Wasserman was running most aspects of the business. MCA represented Clark Gable, Marilyn Monroe, Joan Crawford, Rita Hayworth, Marlon Brando, Burt Lancaster, Tony Curtis, Dean Martin, Jerry Lewis, Ronald Reagan, Lana Turner, Gregory Peck, Cary Grant, and Jane Russell; also directors such as Alfred Hitchcock, Billy Wilder, and Nicholas Ray; writers such as Tennessee Williams, William Inge, and Arthur Miller; and British talent including Peter Ustinov, Michael Redgrave, Rex Harrison, Christopher Lee, Alec Guinness, Claire Bloom, and Audrey Hepburn.[74] MCA would offer package deals of its stars to producers of the highest-profile Hollywood projects, including film adaptations of Broadway musicals. For example, for Samuel Goldwyn's production of GUYS AND DOLLS, MCA offered Betty Grable, Clark Gable, Bob Hope, and Jane Russell.[75] Though this package from the early 1950s did not work out, Goldwyn did end up using MCA client Marlon Brando in the lead role of the 1955 film.

Wasserman's MCA had become by the early 1950s a major center of power in the rapidly changing Hollywood film industry. One index of this power was a visit made by Arthur Krim, president of the re-energized United Artists, to Los Angeles in 1952. Krim was trying to attract top talent to his studio and was offering stars partial ownership of the films they would appear in. He went to Los Angeles specifically to meet with Wasserman about MCA clients Gregory Peck, Marlon Brando, Alan Ladd, Cary Grant, and James Stewart.[76] Remarkably, no producer was involved in the discussions—or, to put matters slightly differently, Wasserman was acting as de facto producer. Another, harder to pin down aspect of Wasserman's power is that he seems to have had considerable success in keeping clients off of the blacklist. Liberal Wasserman clients such as Burt Lancaster and Nicholas Ray were rarely troubled by accusations of Communist sympathies.

Independent or semi-independent production was very much shaped by individual contracts, and therefore differed from case to case. Nevertheless, the experience of a few prominent independent producers in the early 1950s can suggest some of the general directions of this trend.

Samuel Goldwyn was the dean of American independent producers. He had entered the film business in 1912, at age 28, and by 1916 had formed his own production company. (Goldwyn was never associated with Metro-Goldwyn-Mayer; that studio had absorbed one of his former companies.) Goldwyn released his films primarily through United Artists (1919 to 1939) and RKO (1939 to 1952). An energetic, combative producer, he bought excellent story properties (including many novels and Broadway plays) and hired top writers, directors, actors, cinematographers, and art directors to realize his projects. Goldwyn managed to compete with the big studios because of the quality of his stories and the box-office clout of his stars. In the 1940s, he had some of Hollywood's top talent under contract, including Gary Cooper (early 1940s), Danny Kaye (a Goldwyn discovery), director William Wyler, and cinematographer Gregg Toland. Goldwyn won the Academy Award for Best Picture in 1946, for THE BEST YEARS OF OUR LIVES.

By 1950, however, Goldwyn (at age 66) was slowing down. The flow of excellent story properties had stopped, and Goldwyn was making an undistinguished run of films: A SONG IS BORN (1948), with Danny Kaye; ROSEANNA MCCOY (1949), a retelling of the Hatfield-McCoy feud; EDGE OF DOOM (1950), a crime film directed by Mark Robson. HANS CHRISTIAN ANDERSEN (1952) was better, a big-budget musical starring Danny Kaye. Objections from Denmark that the story was not biographically accurate caused only temporary embarrassment. Though the film business was moving rapidly toward independent production, Goldwyn, a pioneer in this area, was not able to profit from the change. His practice of putting actors under contract and then loaning and trading with the major studios was out-of-step with the current arrangements that involved using a pool of free-lance talent. Goldwyn star Farley Granger, for example, complained that he simply did not have enough work in the early 1950s, and that he was able to make a name for himself only via loan-outs to RKO (THEY LIVE BY NIGHT, 1949) and Alfred Hitchcock (ROPE, 1948, and STRANGERS ON A TRAIN, 1951).[77]

For Walt Disney, another veteran independent producer, the 1950s were a period of expansion and innovation. The Walt Disney Company, managed by Walt and his brother Roy, had been in Hollywood since the late 1920s, specializing in animation. Although Disney characters and the Disney name were known around the world, Disney was a very small and marginal company before 1950. Disney had won several Academy Awards in the 1930s, including a special achievement award for the animated feature SNOW WHITE AND THE SEVEN DWARFS (1937), but the company had struggled in the 1940s. A bitter strike by Disney animators in 1941 disrupted operations and cost the company some of its most creative people. Disney survived the war years only because of commissioned projects from various branches of the federal government.

After World War II, Disney cartoons were in a poor position because less money and fewer bookings were available to short subjects. Feature-length animation was still viable, but this was a lengthy and cost-intensive type of filmmaking. The Disney Company therefore expanded the types of films it was making in two different directions. First, the company produced a series of medium-length and feature-length nature documentaries, labeled Disney *True-Life Adventures*. Such films cost far less than feature-length fiction or animation, yet they were popular box-office attractions. Disney also began to make feature-length fiction films. The first few were made in England, to take advantage of blocked funds—TREASURE ISLAND (1950), and THE STORY OF ROBIN HOOD (1952), for example. These low-budget adventure films aimed at children and families were modestly profitable, and so Disney was encouraged to make more live-action films. In fact, twenty-four live-action features were produced between 1950 and 1961.[78] These features often appeared on Disney's TV show ("Disneyland"), and in one unusual case a wildly popular TV series on Davy Crockett was recycled as the theatrical movie DAVY CROCKETT, KING OF THE WILD FRONTIER (1954).

The Disney Company made a major move when it established its own theatrical distribution company, Buena Vista Film Distribution Company, in 1953. With its stock of animated films, documentaries, and live-action features, Disney now had enough prod-

*Walt Disney with animation camera. The Disney Company
expanded from its core animation business to documentary and
live-action features in the early 1950s.*

uct to support a distribution network of its own. The company announced that one of its
reasons for leaving RKO was that the *True-Life Adventures* needed special handling.
Additionally, a Disney executive explained in 1954 that Disney was already handling "our
own music, merchandise, and accessories," and so it was logical to "take over the selling
of our own pictures."[79] Not mentioned, but undoubtedly a factor in the new enterprise,
was a series of scandals associated with RKO when an ownership group that briefly took
over the studio in 1952 became known to be involved in organized crime and gambling.
Disney, with its appeal to the family trade, would have been damaged by the association.
After several years of losses, the stability of RKO as a company was also in question. Disney's defection was a further blow to RKO, for Disney product had played an important
role in supplying RKO's distribution system.

Director Howard Hawks is emblematic of the top-ranking Hollywood directors and
actors who took advantage of the trend toward independent production without founding companies of any lasting impact. Hawks, like Goldwyn and Disney, had begun making movies in the silent film era. An original thinker with a knack for making excellent
genre films, Hawks preferred short-term contracts to longer studio commitments. His

first attempt at independent production was RED RIVER (1948), produced by Monterey Productions and distributed through United Artists. The shareholders of Monterey were Hawks, his wife, Slim, and his agent, Charles Feldman; the working capital came mainly from a group of private investors. RED RIVER was an excellent film that drew large audiences, but it did not make a profit for Monterey because Hawks went wildly over budget. Hawks did not begin to see his deferred salary until 1952.[80] Independent production often carried a high degree of risk.

In the early 1950s, Hawks divided his time between a studio contract at Twentieth Century–Fox and various independent ventures. Even the studio contract shows how the industry climate had changed, for it provided the director with profit participation, story approval, and the right to make one film per year elsewhere. At Fox, Hawks directed the comedies I WAS A MALE WAR BRIDE (1949) and MONKEY BUSINESS (1952), the musical GENTLEMEN PREFER BLONDES (1953), and an episode for the omnibus film O. HENRY'S FULL HOUSE (1952). However, Hawks biographer Todd McCarthy notes that when it became clear that Darryl Zanuck wanted Hawks to make Zanuck films, rather than vice versa, Hawks lost interest in his Fox contract.[81] He established another production company, Winchester Pictures, and began working on a three-picture, semi-independent deal for RKO. Two Winchester films were ultimately made: THE THING (1951, produced by Hawks and directed by Christian Nyby); and THE BIG SKY (1952). Hawks next made a deal with Warner Bros. and founded yet another company, Continental Company Ltd., to produce LAND OF THE PHARAOHS (1955). In all cases, Hawks's production companies were short-term vehicles intended to maximize his autonomy and compensation.

Actor Burt Lancaster became an actor-producer very early in his career and used these dual roles to create a significant body of work. On the basis of appearing in one Broadway play in late 1945, Lancaster was offered several Hollywood contracts. He chose to sign with Hal Wallis, who also had young stars Lizabeth Scott and Kirk Douglas under contract. Lancaster's contract was a relatively conventional seven-year deal, with a gradually increasing salary, and all renewal options held by the producer. It did, however, allow for one outside (non-Wallis) film per year.

Since Wallis had nothing for Lancaster to do, the young actor went to work for producer Mark Hellinger in the Hemingway adaptation THE KILLERS (released 1947). This picture made Lancaster a star, which changed the Wallis-Lancaster dynamic. Lancaster and his agent Harold Hecht insisted on re-negotiating the contract, adding an option for a second outside film.[82] Quickly using this new freedom, Lancaster and Hecht founded their first production company, Norma Productions (named after Lancaster's wife) in 1947. Their debut film as producers was KISS THE BLOOD OFF MY HANDS (1948), co-produced by Joan Fontaine's Rampart Productions. By 1950, Lancaster had independent production deals with Warner Bros. and Columbia plus the Wallis contract. In 1953 Lancaster switched to a new agent, the ubiquitous Lew Wasserman, who negotiated a favorable contract with United Artists. The non-exclusive Wallis contract was still in force until 1956, but by 1953 Lancaster was himself one of the leading producers in Hollywood. Via first Norma Productions and then Hecht-Hill-Lancaster (story editor James Hill was added as a third partner), Lancaster was to make a series of important films at UA, including APACHE (1954), VERA CRUZ (1954), MARTY (1955), SWEET SMELL OF SUCCESS (1957), and ELMER GANTRY (1960).

For Samuel Goldwyn, the independent productions of the late 1940s and early 1950s were simply "business as usual." For Howard Hawks, independent production offered

Hal Wallis and Burt Lancaster in 1949.

more risk and more potential reward, but not dramatic changes in the way he made films. However, the examples of Burt Lancaster and Walt Disney show that the independent production trend of the 1950s could foster greater creativity and flexibility in the film industry. A star could become a producer and establish a creative identity as a film-maker, not just as "talent." An animator could expand into documentary and live-action features, then to distribution, and on to television, establishing in the process a new creative identity. The changes of the late 1940s and early 1950s in Hollywood brought a share of instability, unemployment, even panic; but they also pushed the industry toward a different, more entrepreneurial, model of filmmaking.

2

Genres and Production Trends, 1950–1954

In social/political terms, the 1950s can be summarized as a period of half-war, half-peace. In the Korean War, which began in 1950 and ended in 1953, the United States entered into military engagement not only with Communist North Korea but also with the far stronger People's Republic of China. More than 30,000 American servicemen died in this undeclared war. However, the Korean conflict was a faraway engagement that did not immediately threaten the stability of the United States or its European allies. A greater threat to the United States was the Cold War with the Soviet Union and its allies, with its complex issues of diplomatic and economic competition, border disputes (Berlin, Korea, Hungary), nuclear gamesmanship, espionage, and internal subversion. Competition with the Soviet Union led to a quick buildup of U.S. nuclear forces in the late 1940s and early 1950s, which was countered by the Soviet development of both atomic and hydrogen bombs.

Hollywood films responded to these sociopolitical tensions in a variety of ways. Korean War films were rushed into production, with the strong support of the Department of Defense. Among the first to reach the theaters were THE STEEL HELMET (1951) and ONE MINUTE TO ZERO (1952). Occasionally films plumbed the almost-unthinkable subject of nuclear war (ON THE BEACH, 1959), while many others indirectly invoked the concept of nuclear threat by focusing on a fear of new or alien technology (as was the case in science fiction films like THE THING, 1951; THE DAY THE EARTH STOOD STILL, 1951; and FORBIDDEN PLANET, 1956). Internal subversion and the threat of communism at home was another theme pursued in films both directly, via the anti-Communist cycle of films and indirectly, in science fiction and other genre films. A general set of themes in the time period was distrust, hatred, and anxiety among humans, explored in such varied genres as suspense thriller, film noir, Western, and even love story. One cultural critic has declared that virtually all the anxieties of popular culture in this period are ultimately nuclear anxieties.[1]

However, for many Americans the early 1950s was an era of peace and prosperity. Americans were marrying and having babies at a record rate. New suburban towns modeled on Long Island's Levittown were springing up around the major cities. Homebuilding, automobiles, and electric appliances were the foundations of a very strong consumer economy. With a political move toward the Right came an attempt to shake off the internationalism of the New Deal and to return to the insularity of the pre–World War II period. In domestic terms, the move to the Right meant a suspicion of unions, minorities, and liberals and a return to such basic concerns as family and community. Many Hollywood films of the period stayed away from political causes and delineated the values of a prosperous and increasingly suburbanized society.

The description of film genres in this chapter is not intended to be complete. It includes about thirty representative films, but leaves out entire genres (such as romantic comedy) as well as many fine pictures. Science fiction films will be considered later (in Chapter 8). This chapter does, however, hope to suggest some of the richness and diversity of Hollywood cinema in the early 1950s. The film industry was suffering in economic terms, but its output was surprisingly accomplished.

Musicals: The Freed Unit

A widely quoted poll of the 1940s found that the Hollywood musical was the genre most appreciated by American audiences.[2] Following this indication of their audience's taste in movies, the studios turned out a steady stream of musicals through the 1940s and into the 1950s. Because of the requirements of the genre—music, choreography, art direction, costumes—musicals were substantially more expensive than the average Hollywood film. Therefore, it was the four largest studios, Metro-Goldwyn-Mayer (MGM), Paramount, Fox, and Warners, that produced most of the musicals of the period. Columbia, Universal, RKO, and Goldwyn made an occasional effort.

MGM was the studio most identified with the musical genre, and producer Arthur Freed supervised MGM's most elaborate and ambitious musicals. Freed was largely responsible for the development of the "integrated musical"—a seamless combination of music, dance, narrative, art direction, and camera movement. Freed's efforts as producer were supported and realized by an impressive array of talent, sometimes known as the Freed Unit, including associate producer Roger Edens; designers Cedric Gibbons, Cecil Beaton, Irene Gibbons, and Irene Sharaff; arrangers Conrad Salinger, Johnny Green, Saul Chaplin, Adolph Deutsch, and André Previn; directors Vincente Minnelli, Gene Kelly, and Stanley Donen; and musical stars Gene Kelly, Fred Astaire, Cyd Charisse, Leslie Caron, Frank Sinatra, Debbie Reynolds, and Donald O'Connor.[3]

AN AMERICAN IN PARIS (1951) was the Freed Unit's most acclaimed success of the 1950s, winning six Academy Awards including Best Picture. This brilliant collaboration featured pre-existing songs by George and Ira Gershwin, a script by Alan Jay Lerner, direction by Vincente Minnelli, and costumes by Irene Sharaff. Gene Kelly, then at the peak of his career, was both star and choreographer. The plot features Kelly as Jerry Mulligan, an American painter trying to make a name for himself in Paris. He is torn between two women, Milo (Nina Foch), a rich American who can help his career, and Lise (Leslie Caron), a French shopgirl whom he loves. Following the musical genre's pursuit of the "perfect couple" and the "perfect society,"[4] Mulligan chooses Lise and an idealistic rather than materialistic view of art.

AN AMERICAN IN PARIS is known for its dance numbers, and particularly for the Artists' Ball and the ballet scenes that conclude the film. In the former, Jerry (Kelly) and Lise (Caron) play out a bittersweet drama of misunderstanding while clinging to their "logical" but emotionally wrong partners, Milo (Foch) and Henri (Georges Guetary). Costumes and sets for the Artists' Ball are entirely in black and white (though color film is still employed), which suggests both the artistic daring of bohemian Paris and the main characters' repression of their true feelings. The idea to use black and white evidently came from Vincente Minnelli, a director with a wonderful visual flair. After Lise leaves the ball, Jerry has a daydream represented by a long ballet sequence—seventeen minutes long! Here the pursuit of Lise mingles with Jerry's need to find himself as an artist, which is represented in a series of decors based on French Impressionist painters. The ballet unfolds a revelation that Jerry's identity as an artist connects him to Lise, France, and painting. After this revelation, Lise reappears at dawn outside the ball. The couple embrace, without words.

These final scenes are an ambitious attempt to link American popular culture with an older, more artistic European tradition. It is easy to see why both Vincente Minnelli, a director with a painterly sensibility, and Gene Kelly, a dancer seeking artistic recognition, would be attracted to such a project. The success of this project can be gauged from the 1952 response of a French critic, Claude Mauriac. Mauriac, writing in the conservative arts weekly *Le Figaro Littéraire*, said that Paris "includes Gershwin as much as Utrillo," and that this film "gives evidence" of a love of the city. He found the sequence based on French painting inconsistent—lauding the Toulouse-Lautrec and Rousseau scenes, questioning those starting from Dufy and Renoir. However, Mauriac praised the dancing and choreography of Gene Kelly and found the studio sets to be interesting and respectful transpositions of Paris. Overall, Mauriac described this French-American hybrid as an exciting new development in the arts.[5]

The next Arthur Freed–Gene Kelly collaboration, SINGIN' IN THE RAIN (1952), was less successful at the Academy Awards and the box office than AN AMERICAN IN PARIS, but in the last half-century it has become one of the most beloved American films. Set in Hollywood in the late 1920s, the film follows Don Lockwood (Kelly), a silent film star, as he negotiates the difficult transition from silence to sound. Don's on-screen love interest in a series of silent films, dumb blonde Lina Lamont (Jean Hagen), wants to extend their relationship to real life. However, Lina is crude, petty, and uneducated; she will never make it in sound films. Don is attracted to a young would-be actress, Cathy Selden (Debbie Reynolds). In a clever ending, Cathy dubs Lina's singing voice onstage at a movie premiere, and Don reveals the artifice by opening the curtains. We presume that Don and Cathy will be the new Hollywood couple, combining talent and a genuine love for each other.

This project began with a catalog of songs written by Nacio Herb Brown (music) and Arthur Freed (lyrics), in the days before Freed became a producer. Writers Betty Comden and Adolph Green were brought in from New York to build a script around the songs. They eventually hit upon the Hollywood-based plot described above, which would respect the period-specific qualities of the songs. Comden and Green describe working in a comfortable and supportive atmosphere; they were sheltered from the film industry's economic and political turbulence by Arthur Freed.[6] Gene Kelly once again was star and choreographer, and for this film he added the title of co-director. The other co-director was Stanley Donen, a young protégé of Kelly who was soon to be a fine director in his own right. Kelly successfully lobbied for Donald O'Connor, a strong dancer, rather than non-dancer Oscar Levant as his male co-star. The female lead, Debbie Reynolds, was an MGM starlet without singing or dancing experience; however, she was a hard worker who, in Kelly's words, "proved able to master the basics of dancing" via "long hours of demanding physical effort."[7]

The artistic tone of SINGIN' IN THE RAIN is quite different from the "high art" aspirations of AN AMERICAN IN PARIS. Here the emphasis is on the traditions of American dance, vaudeville, and musical theater. The pretentiousness of high art is parodied in an early scene where Don Lockwood speaks ironically to an interviewer about the "Dignity!" of silent movies, and a better indication of the film's artistic values comes from Donald O'Connor's solo number "Make 'em Laugh." (Freed more or less plagiarized this song from Cole Porter's "Be a Clown." Stanley Donen had asked Freed for a "'Be a Clown' type number," and Freed responded with an almost exact duplicate.) "Make 'em Laugh" becomes the basis for a wild celebration of pratfalls and acrobatics, including a dance up the wall and onto the ceiling. Even the long and lavish ballet that ends the film, featuring Cyd Charisse rather than Debbie Reynolds, is simple and unpretentious in theme. Titled "Gotta Dance! Gotta Dance!," it shows a young rube coming to New York to be in the theater. When, after many adventures, he finally establishes himself as a Broadway dancer, the sequence ends as another talented hayseed arrives in the city.

SINGIN' IN THE RAIN is a remarkably integrated musical, with the musical numbers presenting the thoughts and feelings of the characters as the story progresses. The "Singin' in the Rain" number itself is a Gene Kelly solo which expresses his character's joy

Gene Kelly and Cyd Charisse in the "Gotta Dance!" finale to SINGIN' IN THE RAIN *(1952).*

over falling in love with Cathy and being loved in return. The rain and the puddles add naturalness as well as novelty to the situation. Stanley Kubrick's twisted homage to this number in A CLOCKWORK ORANGE does not negate the power of the original. Another lovely representation of the lovers' feelings occurs in a deserted sound studio where Don sings to Kathy ("You Are My Lucky Star") and manipulates lights, props, and wind machines to create a romantic atmosphere. The theme here is that song, dance, and visuals can create a kind of transparency, an artificial but perfectly re-created version of human emotion.

Beyond its celebration of romantic love, SINGIN' IN THE RAIN can be considered as a commentary on the film industry. The explicit subject is the difficult change from silent to sound films in the 1920s; symbolically, it may also make a statement about Hollywood's troubles of the early 1950s. If so, the message is that these troubles will pass, that Hollywood's language of image, music, story, and dance is still in touch with the audience.

Gene Kelly, MGM and Hollywood's most prominent musical star, abruptly left for England in late December 1951 and stayed away until August 1953. Biographer Claude Hirschhorn explains that Kelly went to Europe for tax reasons, and that his agent Lew Wasserman had originated the plan of spending eighteen months abroad and thus avoiding U.S. income taxes.[8] Critic/filmmaker Peter Wollen has suggested an alternate motivation: that the liberal Kelly went abroad with MGM's blessing to avoid being connected with the second wave of blacklisting in 1951–1952. Kelly's wife, Betsy Blair, *was* blacklisted between 1949 and 1955, but she was able to find work in Europe. As for Kelly himself, he had been threatened with blacklisting by an article in the *American Legion Magazine*, and he may have decided to leave the country rather than face further harassment.[9] Kelly's own explanation for the long stay in Europe was that "Metro-Goldwyn-Mayer is my employer. They decide what I am to do."[10] His statement is not inconsistent with Wollen's intriguing theory.

With Kelly in Europe, the next big production of the Freed Unit was THE BAND WAGON (1953), starring Fred Astaire and Cyd Charisse. (Kelly had been tentatively slated for a musical version of *Huckleberry Finn*, which was never made.) It is interesting to speculate on the change in tone between leading male roles, from Kelly starring in SINGIN' IN THE RAIN to Astaire starring in THE BAND WAGON. Kelly was a hot-blooded, physical dancer who, if cast in THE BAND WAGON, would have created a stronger romantic bond with Cyd Charisse. Astaire's cooler, more ironic persona distracted attention from the theme of the couple—also, at age 53, Astaire was twenty-two years older than Charisse. With Astaire in the lead, THE BAND WAGON became a brilliant musical evocation of unusual moods, via such numbers as "By Myself" and "Triplets" ("We hate each other very much, We hate our folks"). It also presents an interesting conflict between high-art elements represented by Jeffrey Cordova (Jack Buchanan), an actor/director performing *Oedipus Rex* on Broadway, and unpretentious American entertainment. THE BAND WAGON is a fascinating moment in the careers of Astaire, director Vincente Minnelli, and producer Freed, but it was not a hit in 1953.

As for Gene Kelly, he made two mediocre non-musicals in Europe, then launched into the ambitious ballet film INVITATION TO THE DANCE. This was originally planned as a four-part film spotlighting the talent and stylistic diversity of European ballet. Only three parts were ever filmed, and Kelly was prevailed upon to appear (as a recognizable Hollywood star) in all three. Without the support of the Freed Unit's behind-the-scenes talent, production was difficult; as costs rose, MGM worried about the commercial possibilities of the film. INVITATION TO THE DANCE was not released until 1957, and at that point it did almost no business. It is a beautiful film, but far outside the Hollywood mainstream.

When Kelly finally returned to Hollywood in 1953 to star in Brigadoon, both his personal prestige and the prestige of the Freed Unit had diminished. Kelly found himself working for director Vincente Minnelli in a film planned for Scotland but eventually shot, for economic reasons, in Hollywood. Kelly probably could not have greatly affected the changes sweeping through MGM and all the studios in the 1950s had he remained in the United States after Singin' in the Rain, but with Huckleberry Finn or other projects he might have protected the Freed Unit for a few more years.

Doris Day and Marilyn Monroe

Doris Day's musicals at Warners were typically conservative in both theme and approach. In By the Light of the Silvery Moon (1953), for example, the subject is coming of age in a well-off Indiana family circa 1920. The story is taken from Booth Tarkington's "Penrod" stories, but there is clearly a strong debt to the film Meet Me in St. Louis (a Minnelli-Freed musical from 1944) as well. Both films center on a marriageable daughter, with comic relief provided by a younger sibling. In both films the father threatens the stability of the home—in the earlier film, he plans to move the family to New York; in the later one, he seems to be romantically involved with an actress. To clinch the connection, the father in both films is played by the same actor, Leon Ames.

Marjorie (Doris Day) in By the Light is having problems with her boyfriend William (Gordon MacRae) as well as her father. William, just back from the army, will not marry before he has a good job, and Marjorie feels she is becoming an old maid. At another moment in the story, Marjorie stalls on marriage because she is embarrassed about her father. Both complications are easily resolved, and the father turns out to be blameless, but the film has more substance than this. Marjorie is a competent and intelligent young woman, but she needs to learn how to trust the men in her life (that is, to take a woman's traditional role). This is sometimes hard for her to do. For example, in one funny vignette Marjorie and William are driving on a snowy night and the car breaks down. The mechanically gifted Marjorie gets under the car and solves the problem. Then William announces "I got her going," and Marjorie responds with a resentful "Yeah." More generally, the Doris Day of this film is a full-figured woman trying to fit into modest, girlish clothes. The contrast between her mature 1950s look and the "appropriate clothing" of 1920 suggests that she is being constrained here by a limited role.

Stylistically, By the Light is a well-made period piece in color with a number of songs but only a few dances. Doris Day's big dance number involves an onstage parody of being a farmer. Its childlike tumbling and baggy costume are a way to stress Marjorie's lack of sophistication (playing once again with the woman/girl theme). A more successful musical number is the ice-skating rendition of the title song that closes the film. Here all problems have been resolved and happy couples skate hand-in-hand in the moonlight. The harmony of the couple, the community, and nature suggest the wonderful benefits of following convention.

The Marilyn Monroe–Jane Russell musical Gentlemen Prefer Blondes (directed by Howard Hawks, Twentieth Century–Fox, 1953) gives a different view of women and sexuality in the 1950s. Here Lorelei Lee (Monroe) and Dorothy Shaw (Russell) are

Leon Ames, Doris Day, and Rosemary DeCamp in the Warner Bros. musical BY THE LIGHT OF THE SILVERY MOON *(1953).*

showgirls and best friends. Their livelihood and social status are entirely due to their attractiveness to men, but they enjoy a surprising amount of independence. Though Lorelei acts like a dumb blonde, she carefully chooses and manipulates her ideal man, Gus Edmond (Tommy Noonan), a docile and generous rich man's son. Dorothy also carefully chooses her man. While she doesn't care about money, she does care about sincerity. Both women are strong, active, aggressively sexual characters (very different from Doris Day), and the men in the film are curiously passive. Director Howard Hawks was known for playing with role reversals in his comedies, and here neither Gus, nor Dorothy's romantic interest Malone (Elliott Reid), nor the elderly rich man Piggy (Charles Coburn) is able to exert the traditional masculine control. The theme of female independence is made most strongly in the musical number "Is There Anyone Here for Love?," set on an ocean liner taking Lorelei and Dorothy to France. Dorothy strides through a workout of the U.S. Olympic Team (they are en route to a competition in Europe), singing in thinly described terms about her appetite for sex. The athletes in tracksuits are handsome but interchangeable, without personality—one could label them "beefcake"—whereas Russell is powerful, controlling, and appreciative of the masculine physique.

Jane Russell gets first billing in the film, but Marilyn Monroe is its revelation. With her blonde hair, red lips, curvy figure, and shiny costumes, she is the embodiment of male fantasy. GENTLEMEN PREFER BLONDES made Monroe a star in 1953, and in the same year she appeared on the cover of the first *Playboy* magazine. Yet Monroe is cer-

Marilyn Monroe and Jane Russell in GENTLEMEN PREFER
BLONDES *(1953).*

tainly more than a body in this film. She has a childlike side (though it may be consciously put on), as when she sings "Bye Bye Baby" to the hapless Gus. She can be
charming, attentive, and deferential to men, and she is careful not to appear too smart.
Critic Richard Dyer suggests that the secret to Monroe's appeal is that she is sexual without being threatening. Her innocent persona breaks the link between sex and guilt, thus
reassuring a still-conflicted audience.[11] Supporting Dyer's argument is the fact that most
audiences pick out the innocent and deferential Monroe rather than the more aggressive
Russell as the star of the film.

GENTLEMEN PREFER BLONDES does give an interesting view of the early 1950s'
woman, and it has been praised as a proto-feminist film, but in some respects it remains
traditional in its woman-as-spectacle approach. Like the Jean Harlows, Marlene Diet-
richs, and Betty Grables of previous eras, Monroe and Russell are paraded before the
male gaze. On occasion they are framed in profile, from the waist up or the knees up, to
emphasize breast size—this might be called the exploitation shot, borrowed from the
world of the pin-up. They are also verbally demeaned: One athlete asks "If you were in a
shipwreck, which one would you save?" and the reply (based on the women's generous
figures) is "Those two couldn't drown." Finally, although the men are weak and the
women strong, this film ends with the most conventional of comic denouements—a
double marriage. Women's independence does not threaten the established social order.

Film Noir

American film noir, which flourished in the 1940s and 1950s, is distinguished by dark visuals and stories of corruption, betrayal, and violence. Many scenes are set at night, and characteristic shots show deep shadows broken by undiffused pools of light. Other visual motifs include unusual camera angles (high angle, low angle, canted angle), diagonal compositions, deep focus shots, and repeated use of stairways, mirrors, and prison-like bars. The stories present crime, paranoia, and severe tensions between men and women.

THE ASPHALT JUNGLE (directed by John Huston, MGM, 1950) is a caper movie, a detailed study of the planning, execution, and ultimate failure of a jewel robbery. It takes place almost entirely within the criminal milieu, showing us a gallery of unique characters: the brilliant planner Doc (Sam Jaffe), the hooligan Dix Handley (Sterling Hayden, in the starring role), the socially prominent but corrupt lawyer Emmerich (Louis Calhern), the bookie Cobby (Marc Lawrence), plus the safecracker, the driver, the corrupt cop, and so on. Two women with supporting roles are Jean Hagen as Dix's girlfriend and Marilyn Monroe (three years before GENTLEMEN PREFER BLONDES) as Emmerich's mis-

Director John Huston in a publicity photo for THE RED BADGE OF COURAGE *(1951).*

tress. The film is so focused on the underworld that criminals become more or less the norm, and most of the characters are viewed sympathetically. Only at the end of the film do we find a police commissioner re-establishing the point of view of law-abiding society, and his remarks are undercut because he calls Dix Handley "a man without human feelings or human mercy." Viewers have seen by this point that Dix has complex human feelings, and so they may choose to ignore the commissioner's message.

Visually, THE ASPHALT JUNGLE mixes carefully composed, expressionistic images with a more realistic, documentary look. Many of the night exteriors have a lustrous quality, with very dark blacks broken by occasional gleams. Interiors are carefully composed, with strong shadows and a few deep focus images. But at least some of the exteriors show realistically worn urban buildings, and the interiors vary from Emmerich's lavish surroundings to the modest apartments of Dix and the other crooks. Director Huston and cinematographer Harold Rosson did a nice job of giving noir a documentary feel, following the lead of such earlier films as CALL NORTHSIDE 777 (1948). The withholding of music until the last few scenes adds to the sense of realism. Huston and producer Arthur Hornblow had wanted to go further in this direction, identifying the setting as an actual American city (e.g., Kansas City), but they were overruled by MGM's legal department.[12]

IN A LONELY PLACE (directed by Nicholas Ray, Columbia, 1950) is about a murder and a love affair. Dixon Steele (Humphrey Bogart), a Hollywood screenwriter, is the prime subject in the murder of a hat-check girl. Though Dixon is innocent, his potential for violence ends a romance with Laurel (Gloria Grahame), an aspiring actress who is his neighbor. This is an unusual film noir, since the murder happens off-screen and the on-screen violence consists of a couple of fistfights. However, it is at least as threatening and anxiety-producing as THE ASPHALT JUNGLE or other films about criminality and corruption, because here the danger comes from within the smart, witty, sympathetic hero. The "lonely place" may be the capacity for violence within ourselves.

The film noir visuals of IN A LONELY PLACE come primarily at the end of the film. Dixon, furious with Laurel, drives through the night like a maniac. A mix of objective and subjective shots shows Dixon's anger, the careening of the car, and Laurel's brave acceptance of whatever happens. Dixon scrapes another car, then picks a fight with the young driver and almost kills him. A bit later, Laurel has a dream, shown in expressionistic double exposures, of Dixon as a murderer. Laurel can no longer trust Dixon, and the love affair is over. All that remains is regret.

The Hollywood setting adds a few more levels to the film. The disaffected view of Hollywood from a screenwriter's position is hardly unique. However, the film noir stylistics of IN A LONELY PLACE may evoke the specific anxieties of 1950—the experience of World War II, the Cold War, and the mistrust between men and women. The absence of glamour and success in a film about Hollywood also suggests the film industry's grim prospects in 1950. Finally, Nicholas Ray's biographer Bernard Eisenschatz proposed that the mood of IN A LONELY PLACE derives at least indirectly from the blacklist period. Like a blacklisted Hollywood writer, Dixon is isolated by the film industry and pursued by the law.[13]

Director Fritz Lang was one of the German émigrés who brought the expressionist film style to Hollywood, but in THE BIG HEAT (Columbia, 1953) he is working with limited resources. Compared to THE ASPHALT JUNGLE or IN A LONELY PLACE, THE BIG HEAT looks like a threadbare "B" film. Character and theme provide most of the interest. Glenn Ford plays Dave Bannion, a police detective trying to solve a murder in a thoroughly corrupt town. When Bannion persists in his investigation, his wife is killed by a car bomb intended for him. Bannion, a representation of the average American, becomes completely taken over by his impulse for revenge. This is a familiar theme for Fritz Lang; to quote the song from Lang's Western RANCHO NOTORIOUS (1952), he tells stories of "hate, murder and revenge."[14] Bannion eventually solves the murder and returns to his desk at the police department (normal life), but doubts and insecurities remain. Bannion is a homicide detective, which means that his job is based on the human propensity for violence.

There is only one extraordinary visual motif in THE BIG HEAT. Debbie (Gloria Grahame), a gangster's girlfriend, breaks rank with the criminals and pays a visit to Bannion. Her reason seems to be personal attraction, not informing, but nevertheless she is punished by having scalding-hot coffee thrown in her face. Debbie is permanently disfigured, and from this point she wears a mask of bandages over half her face. Lang later noted that the film conveniently ignores the option of plastic surgery.[15] Debbie is confused about moral responsibility: Is she just an innocent bystander, or does she share the guilt for Mrs. Bannion's murder and other crimes? The half-mask hauntingly suggests the duality, and this is reinforced by Debbie's crazed musings about her "good side" and her "bad side." The scenes involving the half-mask aptly present a "beauty and the beast" symbolism; one imagines Lang devoting a great deal of energy to this motif.

KISS ME DEADLY (United Artists, 1955) is based on a novel by Mickey Spillane, whose violent and misogynist detective fiction was enormously popular throughout the 1950s. The film adaptation, written by A. I. Bezzerides and directed by Robert Aldrich, departs from the novel in important ways. The female characters are given more substance, and a wonderful new character, the auto mechanic Nick (Nick Dennis), is added. Most crucially, whereas the novel's first-person narration strongly involves the reader with Spillane's hero Mike Hammer, the film's third-person approach allows some distance. In an early scene, Christina (Cloris Leachman) tells Mike that he loves only himself, and this charge of narcissism seems to hold true throughout the film. Mike has his secretary/girlfriend Velda (Maxine Cooper) seduce men as part of divorce investigations, and when asked to assist law enforcement agencies he responds "What's in it for me?" Of the several innocent victims killed during the film, he mourns only his friend Nick. Mike is aggressive, independent, and sexy, but not necessarily sympathetic.

The world of KISS ME DEADLY is kinetic and unstable. Mike Hammer is usually in motion—driving, walking, running—and is often accompanied by a moving camera. Even in static close-ups, Mike seems to be straining toward the camera. He is an always-threatening presence. Nick adds to the frenetic mood by moving very fast and punctuating his speech with motor sounds: "va-va-voom!" Instability, typical of film noir, here reaches a peak as various male authority figures—a gangster, a doctor, and Mike Hammer himself—appear to be in control but are not. False or hidden identities are everywhere, indeed for most of the film Mike's leading antagonists are a pair of shoes (glimpsed when Mike is tied to a bed) and a voice on the telephone. Numerous characters in the film, including the protagonist, are at one time or another shot, beaten up, or kidnapped.

Whereas most noir films suggest an existential anxiety, not reducible to a simple plot, in KISS ME DEADLY this anxiety is ultimately linked to the atomic bomb. Mike spends most of the film looking for "the great whatsit," something of great value that no one seems willing or able to define. When he finally learns the secret in indirect terms ("Manhattan Project . . . Los Alamos . . . Trinity"), Mike keeps looking for the "whatsit" and ultimately finds a bomb in an unrealistically small, lead-shielded box. Another character opens the box at a beachfront house and creates a fire and a powerful explosion.

The film ends with this nuclear apocalypse, but even here there is ambiguity. For many years, prints of KISS ME DEADLY concluded with the opening of the box and then an explosion in exterior longshot. However, a restored version of the film includes a sequence of Mike and Velda escaping from the house and wading into the ocean as the explosion occurs. Robert Aldrich insisted that this was the only correct ending of the film, adding that "Mike was left alone long enough to see what havoc he had caused, though certainly he and Velda were seriously contaminated."[16]

War Films: World War II

World War II has been a subject of continuing fascination for the Hollywood film industry for more than sixty years. In American popular memory, this is the "good war"—a global conflict between good and evil that the United States and its allies clearly won. After a lull in war films from 1946 to 1948, a new cycle of World War II movies began in 1949, including such titles as TASK FORCE, BATTLEGROUND, SANDS OF IWO JIMA, and TWELVE O'CLOCK HIGH. These films redefine the American World War II experience in ways colored by contemporary needs and values.

SANDS OF IWO JIMA (1949) is the film most responsible for creating John Wayne as *the* American military hero. A medium-budget film by the Poverty Row studio Republic, it was shot primarily at Camp Pendleton in southern California, with some documentary footage added from island landings in the South Pacific campaign. Allen Dwan was the director. The film shows its Poverty Row origins in the performances of a few supporting actors (officers with no trace of presence or authority), but overall this is a well-scripted and well-performed film.

John Wayne plays Sergeant Stryker, an experienced marine drill sergeant who knows just when to be tough with his men and when to take it easy. Stryker has some personal problems, notably a wife who has left him, taking their son with her, but when on duty he is an exacting teacher and a good role model. His teaching methods include physical contact (he hits one clumsy soldier with a rifle and has a fistfight with another), thus giving obvious meaning to the name "Stryker." Stryker can also be unorthodox. For example, he teaches the footwork needed for bayonet drill via a folk dance. The film follows Stryker's platoon from training to the landings at Tarawa and Iwo Jima. Stryker requires some risks, forbids others, and bonds with even those marines who were against him during training. Then Stryker dies in combat on Iwo Jima. His men read his inspirational letter to his son, and carry on.

SANDS OF IWO JIMA clearly includes a mythic dimension. The title of the movie echoes the cadence of the Marine Corps hymn, adding a famous World War II engagement to "the halls of Montezuma" and "the shores of Tripoli." Stryker's final mission is the raising of the U.S. flag on Mount Suribachi overlooking Iwo Jima, a moment which has become emblematic of the entire U.S. war effort in World War II. Though Stryker himself dies on the way up, his men continue to the summit and raise the flag in a shot closely based on the Pulitzer Prize–winning photograph by Joseph Rosenthal of the raising of the flag atop Mount Suribachi. Emotionally, the sense is that John Wayne, American hero, dies in the course of this mission and hands off the responsibility to the Everyman figures of his platoon—that is, to us.

Given this mythic dimension, it is not surprising that SANDS OF IWO JIMA has attracted continuing attention, both pro and con, as a portrait of the marines. Historian Lawrence

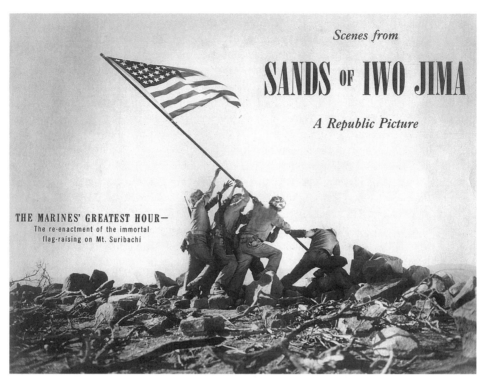

Publicity photo for SANDS OF IWO JIMA *(1949).*

Suid commented in 1978 that for both the marines and the American public, John Wayne in this movie "remains the symbolic Marine."[17] He quoted Marine General David Shoup, a hero of the Tarawa landing, who said that Wayne represents the "hell for leather, go and get 'em attitude" of the Marine Corps. On the other hand, Ron Kovic's memoir *Born on the Fourth of July* views the John Wayne military hero image as a distorting and unrealistic representation of war which contributed to America's debacle in Vietnam. Kovic, a paralyzed veteran of the Vietnam War, specifically mentions SANDS OF IWO JIMA as a film which profoundly impressed him in childhood.[18] He also calls himself "your John Wayne come home" in the short, bitter poem that opens his book.[19]

OPERATION PACIFIC (1951) is a John Wayne–starring war movie from Warner Bros. involving two central issues: when should the life of one man be sacrificed for the good of many?; and when (if ever) should a woman abandon a man who is a single-minded soldier? Duke Gifford, the John Wayne character, puts himself under a cloud of suspicion by ordering a submarine to submerge even though Pop Perry (Ward Bond), the badly wounded captain, is on the conning tower. Gifford later resolves this issue by heroically saving a navy pilot—who is Captain Perry's younger brother—despite substantial risk to his men and his submarine. The pilot also happens to be his rival for the affections of his ex-wife, Mary Stuart (Patricia Neal, playing a navy nurse). Having proved himself to be the bravest and biggest-hearted man around, Wayne is re-united with Mary, who is now willing to make great sacrifices for her man, even if he neglects her. OPERATION PACIFIC is formulaic entertainment, but it does present exciting scenes of submarine warfare.

At Twentieth Century–Fox, the war films were more complex and more reflective than the gung-ho John Wayne movies. Bernard F. Dick, in his history of the American war film, attributes this to the experience and personality of studio production head Darryl Zanuck. Zanuck made training films as a colonel in the Signal Corps during the war, and he became friendly with General Eisenhower, Lord Mountbatten, and other military leaders. According to Dick, Zanuck continued making World War II films through THE LONGEST DAY (1962) in part because of his own need to "rethink and relive" this war.[20] A further index of the Fox studio's interest in military matters is that Frank McCarthy, who had been secretary to General George C. Marshall during World War II, was hired as a Fox executive in 1949. McCarthy was, naturally, involved in the planning of war films; he was also in charge of censorship matters. McCarthy eventually became the producer of PATTON (1970) and MACARTHUR (1977).

TWELVE O'CLOCK HIGH (directed by Henry King, 1950), one of the very best Fox war movies, concerns a hard-luck squadron of American airmen stationed in Britain. After many losses, a new commander, played by Gregory Peck, is brought in to restore morale. Peck makes the pilots believe in themselves, and establishes the squadron as an excellent fighting force, but eventually cracks psychologically because of the strain of sending men to their deaths. The squadron continues on, succeeding in a crucial mission without the commander. The film is presented in moody black and white and in flashback. It honors Peck as a hero without glossing over the terrible stress of leading men into war. This film is as patriotic as SANDS OF IWO JIMA, yet more nuanced in its treatment of the day-to-day realities of war.

HALLS OF MONTEZUMA (1950), directed by Lewis Milestone for Fox, is similarly complex in its attitudes toward war. Here Richard Widmark, as Lieutenant Carl Anderson, leads a group of marines in an assault on a Japanese-held island in the Pacific. Widmark suffers from debilitating migraine headaches, but he forces himself into battle because of loyalty to the seven men who have been with him for some time. He depends on pills supplied by Doc (Karl Malden) in order to keep going. At the film's end, most of Anderson's cherished comrades are dead or wounded, but the lieutenant himself fights on. HALLS OF MONTEZUMA offers no resolution and no patriotic victory, but simply a view of dedicated men in combat. Though supportive of the American military, this film also has an undercurrent of despair.[21] It is probably not irrelevant that Lewis Milestone was the director of the antiwar classic ALL QUIET ON THE WESTERN FRONT (1930).

THE DESERT FOX (another film from Fox, directed by Henry King, 1952) tells an unusual story in a pedestrian style. It includes some documentary combat footage, but most of the film is studio-shot material about headquarters officers. The interest of this film is ideological: it focuses on the German general Edwin Rommel (James Mason), and presents him as both a great soldier and a leader of an anti-Hitler conspiracy. Since West Germany was clearly a U.S. ally by 1952, this film seems to be an attempt to create a German past that is not defined solely by Nazism. Dick comments that Zanuck was "mildly revisionist" in his view of the Axis.[22]

The most important war film of the 1950s came not from Darryl Zanuck's Fox but from Harry Cohn's Columbia Pictures. As part of his strategy to compete with the five major studios after the Paramount case, Cohn bought the rights to James Jones's controversial best-seller *From Here to Eternity* in 1951. There was some doubt that this huge, sprawling novel could ever be fashioned into a Hollywood film since it featured prostitution, homosexuality, venereal disease, an affair between an enlisted man and an officer's wife, several instances of brutality within the peacetime U.S. Army, and a general lack of reverence for the rules and the hierarchy of the army. On the other hand, the novel had been both a critical and a popular success, and it offered wonderful characters, picturesque Hawaiian settings, and a dramatic ending—the Japanese attack on Pearl Harbor.

Screenwriter Dan Taradash pitched his ideas for adapting *From Here to Eternity* to producer Buddy Adler and then to Harry Cohn, and was hired immediately. Homosexuality—the contacts between G Company's enlisted men and rich Honolulu "queers"—was entirely excised. Many other controversial points were toned down. Taradash retained three centers of interest: the conflicts between Private Prewitt (Montgomery Clift), Private Maggio (Frank Sinatra), and the army; the romance between Prewitt and Lorene (Donna Reed); and the romance between First Sergeant Warden (Burt Lancaster) and Karen Holmes (Deborah Kerr), the wife of Warden's boss, Captain Dana Holmes.[23] Though Taradash was frustrated by Harry Cohn's insistence that the finished film *must* run less than two hours (final running time was 1:58), he managed to protect all three narrative strands through pre-production.

The stellar cast outlined above was signed for the film, and Fred Zinnemann, fresh from the success of HIGH NOON (1952), was brought in to direct. The creative team of Taradash, Zinnemann, Adler, and Cohn next had to contend with two very different oversight agencies. First, the Production Code Administration of the Motion Picture Association of America looked at every Hollywood film in order to enforce a consistent set of moral standards. The PCA was concerned about a lack of "recognition of the immorality of the relationship" between Karen and Warden. The relationship could exist (without it, a big chunk of the book would be lost), but only if a "voice for morality" said it was wrong. Second, the PCA wanted to be very sure that the New Congress Club where Lorene works could not be identified as a brothel in the film.[24] The filmmakers conceded on the second point; the New Congress Club in the film is a rather sanitized social club, and Lorene's job becomes dance hostess. On the first objection, however, Taradash, Adler, Zinnemann, and Cohn held firm. Karen announces near the end of the film that her romance with Warden would never have worked, but she does not say it was wrong.

The second oversight agency was the United States military. Any film requesting assistance from the Department of Defense (DOD) was required to submit a script to the Pictorial Branch, Office of Public Information, Office of the Assistant Secretary of Defense (Legislative and Public Affairs), the office supervising film industry/DOD cooperation. This was not exactly censorship, since filmmakers were never obliged to use DOD equipment, personnel, footage, or expertise. However, many war films would be difficult or even impossible to produce without Department of Defense resources. The DOD's policy on cooperation was that films would be supported if they were "accurate and authentic"; complied with "the highest standards of propriety and dignity"; were not "detrimental to Department of Defense policy regarding operations, morale, or discipline"; and benefited the DOD and the "Public good."[25] Officials within the DOD were skeptical about to whether FROM HERE TO ETERNITY met these conditions. However, Don Baruch of the Pictorial Branch felt that the DOD should offer assistance and work with the filmmakers to revise some of the more questionable aspects of the film.[26] This point of view eventually prevailed.

A memo from Buddy Adler responding to the DOD's objections to the script shows that the military was mainly concerned with toning down the scenes of brutality. Adler and Taradash agreed that Fatso's (Ernest Borgnine) brutality toward Maggio (Frank Sinatra) should be presented as a personal thing, not as standard army procedure. Taradash and Adler also agreed that the lazy, vindictive, and incompetent Captain Holmes should not be promoted (as in the book), but should be removed from the army for his persecution of Prewitt. Taradash and Adler did not agree to add a rollup credit saying that FROM HERE TO ETERNITY shows a special case, and that "these conditions CAN NOT and DO NOT exist today."[27] In general, the Department of Defense showed respect for Taradash's script and tried mainly to contextualize the brutality (which Taradash had already greatly reduced from the book). As to Captain Holmes's forced resignation rather than promotion-for-incompetence, this was not a central part of the script.

Under the direction of Fred Zinnemann, FROM HERE TO ETERNITY became one of the very best films ever made about the American military. Location shooting was done at Schofield Barracks in Hawaii, the setting for James Jones's book. The performances are remarkable. Montgomery Clift as the stubborn Prewitt gives an original and haunting twist to the soldier-as-outsider. Burt Lancaster is, if anything, even better as the ultra-competent but also passionate Sergeant Warden. Frank Sinatra is thoroughly believable as the hot-headed Maggio, and Deborah Kerr catches some of the bitterness and yearning of Karen Holmes. As to Donna Reed, her cool and calculating Lorene suggests that her range as an actress went well beyond the role for which she is most remembered, the suburban mom she played in the TV sitcom *The Donna Reed Show* (1958–1966). The scene between Warden and Karen on the beach, which combines several scenes from the book, is deservedly known as one of the most erotic moments in American cinema (even

Donna Reed and Montgomery Clift in a production still for FROM HERE TO ETERNITY (1953). Director Fred Zinnemann is in the center background.

Burt Lancaster and Deborah Kerr in FROM HERE TO ETERNITY.

though both actors wear modest bathing costumes). And, despite the many romantic scenes, this really is a film about the military, about the complicated men who serve in the army and the system that supports them and at times abuses them. Both Adler and Taradash pointed out, in defending the film from DOD criticism, that Prewitt is basically a good soldier and Warden is a great soldier.[28] They could have added that G Company in the film, as in the book, responds quickly and effectively to the Japanese attack on Hawaii on 7 December 1941—at this level, at least, the system works.

Korea

Korean War films are patriotic but also surprisingly ambivalent about the importance and impact of that war. ONE MINUTE TO ZERO (RKO, 1952), directed by Tay Garnett, was one of the first films about Korea to appear. Like OPERATION PACIFIC, it blends combat scenes with a love story, in this case involving Robert Mitchum as an army colonel and Ann Blyth as a United Nations relief worker. As in OPERATION PACIFIC, the male lead's dedication to duty is vindicated and the female lead's reservations are swept away. But the moral problem raised by ONE MINUTE TO ZERO is not only difficult but still unresolved—almost fifty years after the Korean War ended! In a key scene, Mitchum orders artillery fire on a column of refugees approaching American positions because there are North Korean troops among the refugees. Ann Blyth's character is horrified because her suitor is killing innocent people, the very people she is in Korea to help. However, in the terms of the film Mitchum's action is correct—his troops really were in danger. Ann Blyth eventually sees the justice of this point of view, and welcomes Mitchum back into her arms.

Part of the drama of ONE MINUTE TO ZERO occurred behind the scenes. The script RKO submitted to the Department of Defense as a condition of cooperation did not include the controversial scene of Americans firing on the refugee column. The scene was filmed without the prior knowledge or approval of the DOD—this is another example of Howard Hughes not following through on agreements he had made. When the DOD discovered the problem, they requested that the scene of firing on the refugee column be removed. Hughes carefully inquired if the dispute over ONE MINUTE TO ZERO would affect the major defense contracts held by Hughes Aircraft. When told this would not affect his business interests, Hughes refused to cut the offending scene.[29]

A fascinating aspect of this film is that the controversial scene bears some resemblance to a still-disputed historical incident. In July 1950 American troops fired on Korean refugees at No Gun Ri and killed many civilians (the South Korean government says that 248 died). Very little is known about the circumstances of the attack, which is why President Clinton in January 2001 offered a statement of regret rather than a formal apology to the South Korean government.[30] ONE MINUTE TO ZERO seems to be alluding to and even justifying an incident similar to No Gun Ri. However, as Lawrence Suid comments, "the Army felt it did not want to be associated with a film that showed its men killing innocent civilians."[31] Since production was complete, the DOD Office of Public Information had little leverage, but it did announce that it would not aid the release of the film.

The most commercially successful Korean War film was THE BRIDGES AT TOKO-RI (Paramount, 1954; directed by Mark Robson), based on a novel by James Michener. It centers on navy pilot Harry Brubaker (William Holden), a World War II veteran recalled to action in Korea. In the first two missions we see, Brubaker is: 1) fished up from the sea by a rescue helicopter; and 2) forced to make an emergency landing on an obstructed carrier deck. He is a physically and psychologically worn-out flyer, and in a dialogue scene with Admiral Tarrant (Fredric March) he questions both his personal need to be in the war and the rationale of the Korean War in general. Tarrant replies with an early statement of the domino theory: "That's rubbish, son, and you know it. If we did [withdraw from Korea] they'd take Japan, Indochina, the Philippines. Where would you have us make our stand, the Mississippi?"

Further dramatizing Brubaker's problems, as well as the pull between wartime and peacetime values, is a long sequence of Brubaker on leave in Japan with his wife, Nancy (Grace Kelly), and two daughters. The interweaving of combat and romance is a familiar part of war films—see, for example, OPERATION PACIFIC and ONE MINUTE TO ZERO— but here we find an unusual juxtaposition of domestic bliss and wartime mission. Indeed, Rick Worland considers THE BRIDGES OF TOKO-RI a blending of the war film and the family melodrama. According to Worland, the film questions the war effort and "creates an off-balance combination of resolve and regret" through its contrast of "family relationships with their inevitable ties to individual, domestic concerns" with "the military mission described in global, strategic terms."[32] The casting of Grace Kelly, whose film persona is romantic, smart, and competent (here and in other films such as REAR WINDOW, 1954), adds to the main character's dilemma.

Brubaker tears himself away from his family and returns to the carrier to face a dangerous mission—the bombing of the bridges at Toko-Ri. As squadron leader, he carries out this mission successfully, but is forced to bail out over enemy territory. Brubaker and the helicopter pilots sent to rescue him are then killed on the ground by North Korean soldiers. This is a grim conclusion to a patriotic war movie. In the final scene, Admiral Tarrant is left to reflect on the character of Brubaker, a reluctant fighter who performed heroically. Tarrant looks out at the choppy sea and gives a brooding speech beginning "Where do we get such men?" The film cuts to a short action sequence of planes taking off from the carrier deck. Then we see a calmer Admiral Tarrant, his spirits restored because there is still a job to do. The film ends.

The BRIDGES OF TOKO-RI could be taken as a relatively formulaic war movie, with the scenes of Brubaker and family on leave demonstrating the values Americans are fighting for. But as Rick Worland suggests, this film with its melancholy tone also embodies the doubts and regrets many Americans felt about the Korean conflict.[33]

Anti-Communist Films

From 1948 to 1954, the Hollywood studios released between thirty-five and forty films on the dangers of domestic and international communism.[34] Most of these films were unsuccessful at the box office, and they may have been made primarily for political rather than commercial purposes. If Hollywood's loyalty to the United States was under question during the McCarthyist period, what better way to demonstrate that loyalty than through specifically anti-Communist films? However, there was a problem: the writers of films about domestic communism seemed to have great difficulty finding an effective storyline.

In RKO's I MARRIED A COMMUNIST (1950), Brad Collins (Robert Ryan) is a reformer trying to clean up a corrupt union. This reformer has a hidden past; under another name he once belonged to the Communist party and even committed a murder under Communist direction. When confronted by local Communists, he drops all anti-corruption activity until his brother is killed. Then he courageously reveals his past to his wife (Laraine Day) and fights against Communist domination of the union. Despite being the hero, Collins must die at the end as punishment for: 1) his previous crime; and 2) his previous adherence to communism. Aside from connecting communism with union corruption, I MARRIED A COMMUNIST has absolutely nothing to say about Communist ideas or values. In this film, Communists are thugs, pure and simple.

BIG JIM MCLAIN (Warner Bros., 1952) has similar problems. Here John Wayne plays the title character, a House Un-American Activities Committee investigator assigned to Hawaii to search out Communist activity. McLain discovers a cell of Communists led by Dr. Gelster (Gayne Whitman), and also begins a romance with Gelster's secretary Nancy Vallons (Nancy Olson). When McLain eventually uncovers a plot to sabotage American shipping, he teams up with the police to raid a Communist meeting and thoroughly enjoys the ensuing fistfight. That HUAC's charge was not law enforcement but rather to lay the groundwork for legislation is entirely forgotten by the makers of this film. BIG JIM MCLAIN, like I MARRIED A COMMUNIST, has nothing to say about Communists except that they are bad. John Wayne was very good in a number of Westerns and war films of the 1950s, but in BIG JIM MCLAIN he does not rise above the mediocrity of the film.

Leo McCarey's MY SON JOHN (Paramount, 1952) is probably the American film which best dramatizes anti-communism in the early 1950s. McCarey and screenwriter John Lee Mahin present their anti-communist theme within the framework of a family

Robert Walker, Helen Hayes, and Dean Jagger in MY SON JOHN *(1952).*

melodrama blended with some comic elements. Lucille and Dan Jefferson (Helen Hayes and Dean Jagger), an Irish Catholic couple, have three sons: Chuck and Ben, former high school athletes who are in the army and leaving for Korea, and John (Robert Walker), an intellectual who has a desk job in Washington. When John returns home after a year's absence he is in constant conflict with his father, a member of the American Legion, and uneasy even around his mother, who loves and admires him. John turns out to be part of a Communist spy ring, and his mother, her health destroyed, after much hesitation cooperates with the FBI to expose him. John tries to turn himself in but is killed (presumably by a Communist gunman) en route. He leaves a speech on tape in which he confesses to Communist activities and tells others not to follow his example.

John's major "crimes" through most of the film are that he disrespects his father, lies to his mother, and cannot meet the gaze of his parish priest. The parents' simple faith in God and country is presented as correct and not open to question. The parents do have their flaws—for example, the father drinks too much, which triggers one of the humorous scenes. But John's alternate values—he is an intellectual, an internationalist, a reformer—do not measure up to the traditional values of the family. MY SON JOHN's political position is reductive and carries the implication that any deviation from the norm is subversive. John's taped speech makes this explicit, saying that he started as a liberal do-gooder and found himself pursuing more radical (indeed treasonous) solutions. But at least there is a position here. I MARRIED A COMMUNIST and BIG JIM McLAIN are about nothing at all.

Anti-Communism and Film Noir

According to James Naremore, noir films of the 1940s often had a liberal or progressive slant, recognizing the unequal power relationships in society and favoring the less privileged.[35] However, in the early 1950s this correlation between a style and a political position broke down. Film noir became either apolitical or an expression of the anti-Communist hysteria of the time. I MARRIED A COMMUNIST, already discussed in this chapter, could be considered a film noir because of its dark images and crime-film plot. It is, however, thoroughly undistinguished in visual style. On the other hand, PICKUP ON SOUTH STREET (Twentieth Century–Fox, 1953), written and directed by Samuel Fuller, is a stylistically exciting film which deals—somewhat bizarrely—with domestic communism.

In Fuller's film, the pickpocket Skip McCoy (Richard Widmark) steals a woman's wallet on the New York subway. It turns out that she, as a favor to a boyfriend, is couriering some stolen microfilm for the Communists. Skip hides the microfilm and refuses to cooperate with the Communists or the police. Candy (Jean Peters), the woman on the subway, becomes his accomplice and romantic interest. When the Commies kill Skip's friend Mo (Thelma Ritter), Skip solves the case himself, tracking down the Communists, beating them up, outwitting the police and the FBI. And, naturally, he gets the girl. All this is shown in an exaggerated film noir style, with tight close-ups, canted angles, low key lighting. Skip is presented as an anarchist loner who lives in a poetic setting—a wooden shack on a pier at 66 South Street in Manhattan. He and Candy (very sexy in low-cut outfits) are cartoonish rather than realistic characters, but they do suggest the dangerous sexuality of urban outlaws in film noir.

The explicit theme of the film is that even American criminals hate Communists. Skip, Candy, and Mo, three mostly amoral characters, all despise communism and resolve to fight against it, though Skip's action might be revenge more than anything else. This rather silly premise allows Fuller to make a fast-moving crime movie with no attention to defining or describing communism. However, an implicit theme can be found in the style of the film, with the film noir mood creating an impression of America under threat of internal subversion. Communists could be anywhere; they might be next to you on the New York subway at night.

STRANGERS ON A TRAIN (Warner Bros., 1951) is usually discussed as a well-constructed Alfred Hitchcock thriller. Guy (Farley Granger) meets Bruno (Robert Walker) on a train; Guy expresses frustration with his wife, Miriam; Bruno takes this as an invitation to murder Miriam, which he does. Then Bruno asks Guy to return the favor by murdering Bruno's father. Guy has done nothing wrong, but he feels guilty; at some level he wanted to kill Miriam. This is the famous Hitchcock "transfer of guilt."

Critic Robert Corber has added to contemporary understanding of STRANGERS ON A TRAIN by pointing to elements of homosexuality and politics. First, he says that Bruno is homosexual, and thus the encounter with Guy involves not only murder but also a threat to sexual identity. Guy is attracted to Bruno, Guy is like Bruno, Guy's sexuality is therefore fluid and changeable rather than fixed. Corber also points to an interesting change between Patricia Highsmith's novel and Hitchcock's film—the film adds the setting of Washington, D.C., where Guy is the assistant to a senator and in love with the senator's daughter. The Washington setting allows the threat of homosexuality to connect with threats to political security, for in the McCarthyist period both gays and Communists were investigated and at times were lumped together.[36] In one memorable image Guy walks by the Jefferson Memorial with a policeman and sees Bruno on the steps of the Memorial. Bruno's "dark silhouette" seems very out of place on the "gleaming white marble" of the monument, and this suggests not only Guy's personal troubles but also Bruno's threat to the Republic.[37]

Homosexual and political elements are present, but they do not entirely explain STRANGERS ON A TRAIN. Bruno is not explicitly a homosexual in the film—indeed, the Production Code allowed no presentation of homosexuality. The spectator can intuit this character's sexual orientation through such clues as Bruno's dependence on his mother and his exaggerated attention to personal grooming. Political symbolism is even more hidden than sexual identity. The Washington setting is never explained, except perhaps by showing that Guy as a would-be politician has much to lose if he is involved in any scandal. STRANGERS ON A TRAIN is not primarily about anti-Communist and homosexual panic, but it uses these elements to help create the background of anxiety so characteristic of film noir and of Hitchcock films in general.

Westerns

The late 1940s and early 1950s were an important time of transition for the Western film. The simple, formulaic Westerns of the early sound period were no longer attractive to audiences. Westerns of the 1950s had to provide something more: in theme, in setting, and in technique. French critic André Bazin referred to this moment of change as the era of the "superwestern," meaning that a successful Western had to be innovative in "aesthetic, sociological, moral, psychological, political, or erotic" terms. (Bazin's essay on the Western distinguishes between "superwesterns," where something extrinsic has been added to the genre—examples are HIGH NOON and SHANE—and "novelistic" Westerns, where traditional themes are treated with more complexity than in previous decades, in cases such as Anthony Mann's films. This discussion of the Western considers both trends under the heading of superwesterns).[38] The Westerns of the late 1940s met this challenge to be innovative with such memorable films as DUEL IN THE SUN (1947), PURSUED (1947), and RED RIVER (1948). In the early 1950s the period of experimentation continued, and a number of excellent films were made.

John Ford, a celebrated director of both silent and sound Westerns (THE IRON HORSE, 1924; STAGECOACH, 1939; MY DARLING CLEMENTINE, 1946), was still working in a fairly traditional vein in the early 1950s. RIO GRANDE (Republic Pictures, 1950), the third film in Ford's Cavalry trilogy, was about efforts to defeat the Apaches in the 1870s. In the film, bands of Apaches have been raiding the United States and then retreating across the Rio Grande to sanctuary in Mexico. With the support of General Sheridan and the immediate stimulus of the abduction of children, a U.S. Cavalry force led by Colonel Kirby York (John Wayne) crosses the Rio Grande, attacks the Apaches, and rescues the children. The film does present a conflict between father and son—Colonel York and Trooper York (Claude Jarman)—and it gives unusual importance to Mrs. York (Maureen O'Hara). This begins to suggest the psychological complexity of many "superwesterns." However, in RIO GRANDE these conflicts are quickly resolved and the film ends with a show of family, military, and national unity.

RIO GRANDE is highly traditional in its treatment of the Apaches. They are the Enemy, dangerous adversaries who can strike at any time. Their history and motivations are not discussed, and they are rarely given names. The film does avoid some negative stereotypes—the Apaches have no bizarre or bloodthirsty customs, and they do not harm or even greatly frighten the children. But Ford's emphasis is very strongly on the Cavalry and its bonds of family, friendship, and military regulations. He is simply not interested in the Indians (or Native Americans);[39] however, in a few years this would change.

BROKEN ARROW (Twentieth Century–Fox, 1950), set in Arizona in 1870, takes a different view of the conflict between the army, the settlers, and the Apaches. In this film prospector and army scout Tom Jeffords (James Stewart) helps a wounded Chiricahua Apache teenager in the desert and as a result he is well treated after he is captured by the Apaches. Stewart's unique experience allows him to assist in the signing of a treaty between the U.S. Army and the Apache chief, Cochise. A younger Apache, Geronimo, refuses the treaty and leads a group of dissidents into exile and banditry. Stewart's experience of the Apaches as human beings results in his marriage to an Apache woman. However, his bride is killed by white settlers, implying the film's point of view on the imperfect nature of the accord between Caucasian Americans and Native Americans. Though BROKEN ARROW is described as historically accurate in an opening voiceover narration, critic and historian Frank Manchel has found numerous inaccuracies. For example, the film shows Native Americans unfamiliar with prospecting for gold, but by 1870 prospectors had been illegally exploring Indian lands for many years. The story of Geronimo is falsified, because Geronimo remained with his people on the reservation until after Cochise's death in 1874. Most troubling of all, the film does not show the results of the treaty, the horrible conditions on the Chiricahua Apache reservation including malnutrition, disease and harassment by government authorities.[40] Clearly, BROKEN ARROW is an idealized version of history. However, within the traditions of the Western genre, it takes an innovative position. It humanizes the Apaches, presents Cochise as a great leader, and includes a marriage between a Caucasian American and a Native American. If historical films address both the present and the past, then BROKEN ARROW suggests the possibility of reconciliation between the white Americans of 1950 and a variety of minority groups (including, but not limited to, the African American community). This line of argument is developed further in Chapter 9.

Director Anthony Mann was one of the key figures in the 1950s reworking of the Western genre. Mann's Westerns were notable for psychological complexity and bleakness of tone. THE FURIES (Paramount, 1950), centers on a conflict between father and daughter. T. C. Jeffords (Walter Huston), owner of a huge ranch in New Mexico called "The Furies," rules his domain "like a feudal lord" (quoting the opening credits of the film). T. C. is strong, passionate, impulsive, generous; he is also proud, petty, violent, and often blind to the emotions of others. Daughter Vance Jeffords (Barbara Stanwyck) has most of her father's vices and virtues. Their conflict comes to a climax when Vance stabs T. C.'s fiancée with a scissors, mutilating her face, and T. C. responds by hanging Vance's friend Juan Herrera (Gilbert Roland) as a horse thief. The Herreras have lived as squatters on the ranch for generations, and by custom they take what they need—so Juan and his family are an affront to T. C.'s self-image as lord and master. Vance breaks with her father, and eventually schemes successfully to buy out the ranch, revealing her identity only at the last moment. T. C. takes his daughter's victory in good grace, but just after their reconciliation he is shot dead by Mrs. Herrera, Juan's mother.

When it presents drawing rooms, banks, and city folks, THE FURIES is a very ordinary film. However, the family and clan conflicts, often shown in day-for-night exteriors, have an extraordinary power. T. C. is a kind of demigod, a force of nature; he can rescue a calf

from mud or throw the strongest bull. His cowboys make him a legend in his own lifetime via a campfire song. Vance also has a half-mythic status; entirely comfortable on
horseback even at night, she is born to power on the ranch. Vance is often shown from
low angles (like her father) to emphasize strength. The Herreras are equally elemental, a
part of the land, as their rocky fortress suggests. Thus when T. C. hangs Juan, breaking
his promise of safe conduct for the Herreras to leave the ranch, nature has been violated. The moonlit hanging scene, with the actual deed inferred from Vance's reactions
and Mrs. Herrera's screams, has an astonishing emotional charge.[41] THE FURIES is not
quite Greek tragedy (*The Furies* is the name sometimes given to the third play of the
Oresteia, by Aeschylus) but the reference is far from trivial.

THE FAR COUNTRY (1955) is similarly shocking and violent, but with the element of
color spectacle added. This film starts in Seattle, with Jeff Webster (James Stewart)
and his partner Ben Tatum (Walter Brennan) boarding a boat for Alaska. Most of the
film takes place in the gorgeous scenery of Skagway, Alaska, and the Yukon Territory,
where the visual beauty contrasts powerfully with the depths of human cruelty. James
Stewart here plays somewhat against type as a nasty, selfish cowboy accused of two
murders. He is, however, less venal than the corrupt judge and businessman Mr. Gannon, played by John McIntyre, who rules the frontier North by both legal and illegal
terror. With his partner killed and the mining town in shambles, the selfish Stewart ("I
look after me") finally turns on Gannon and saves what is left of the community. The
hero's concluding change of heart resembles the final scenes of CASABLANCA (1942),
but with far less uplift. Even in a "happy ending" film, Mann focuses on human weakness and cruelty.

Alan Ladd in SHANE *(1953).*

Alan Ladd and Brandon de Wilde in SHANE.

SHANE (1953), directed by George Stevens, is another superwestern of visual spectacle, shot in the high plains of Wyoming. It is also an innovative Western in its emphasis on the narrative position of a young boy, Joey, who makes the film's conflict between homesteaders and ranchers seem larger-than-life. Joey mythologizes the gunslinger-turned-farmhand named Shane (Alan Ladd), who in the iconography of the film becomes almost a Messiah figure. In Joey's vision of the story, the conflicts between adults are overcharged with emotion, creating exhilaration and terror. Even little things take on power and beauty, as in the scene where Shane and Joe Starrett (Joey's father, played by Van Heflin) uproot an enormous stump. The attraction between Shane and Joey's mother (Jean Arthur) is also interesting—Joey feels it but never quite understands it. The film's narrative strategy is apt because Westerns are, in large part, a genre intended for young boys. By placing an "ideal spectator" within the text and having this spectator to some extent create the text, Stevens and his scriptwriters create a meta-Western, a Western about the experience of Westerns.

HIGH NOON (United Artists, 1952), directed by Fred Zinnemann, is an innovative Western in both theme and narrative structure. Like THE FAR COUNTRY, HIGH NOON questions the effectiveness of community in the face of evil. Marshal Will Kane (Gary Cooper) can find no one to help him in a noon showdown with four notorious gunmen, the Miller gang. No citizen of the prosperous town of Hadleyville is willing to risk his life to protect law and order. Kane faces the gunmen himself, though he does get a last minute assist from his new bride, Amy (Grace Kelly). Kane prevails, then throws down his sheriff's star and leaves the town in disgust.

The structural innovation is that HIGH NOON takes place in "real time"—one minute of screen time equals one minute of time within the story. The film diegesis starts a bit after 10 A.M. and finishes just after noon. This rarely used approach adds greatly to the tension and narrative drive of HIGH NOON. Decisions must be made; the crisis looms at twelve o'clock. The simple premise of the film is clearly established over the first hour and a half, and then the last fifteen minutes becomes an almost wordless montage. Here every camera angle and every cut serves to heighten the drama—with the clock ticking, only the most essential actions can be shown.

Many commentators on the film, including the filmmakers, agree that it makes a political statement. However, they disagree on exactly what is being said. For screenwriter Carl Foreman, HIGH NOON is a political allegory stemming from his personal experience with HUAC and the blacklist (an ex-Communist, Foreman testified as an unfriendly witness before HUAC in 1951). Foreman said that the film was about "Hollywood and no other place but Hollywood."[42] For producer Stanley Kramer, it is a film about "a town that died because no one there had the guts to defend it."[43] Kramer also stresses the simplicity of the film, calling it "a story about right versus wrong."[44] For director Fred Zinnemann, "it was the story of a man who must make a decision according to his conscience."[45] Zinnemann adds that the hero is old and tired, *not* a mythical hero, and that the town is a "symbol of a democracy gone soft."[46]

One aspect of the film that is not much discussed is Amy Kane's shooting of one of the Miller gang, despite her Quaker (and therefore pacifist) beliefs. In the context of the film, it seems that she, like her husband, has made a difficult decision. One could also say that the filmmakers so mistrust human reactions to crisis that they are confident only of the husband-wife bond. More generally, this might be a comment on the need for violence in certain situations—as in the fight against Hitler, or against communism.

Melodrama

"Melodrama" in the American cinema defines a film genre that centers on tensions within an intimate group. It involves extremes of emotion and often but not always privileges a feminine point of view. In melodrama, the protagonist works through conflict and suffering to find her or his place in the social world. Though the surface message confirms traditional social patterns, this genre can also have a subversive charge, because it explores the tensions and contradictions within gender roles and families. Melodrama has therefore become a favorite genre of feminist critics.

ALL ABOUT EVE (written and directed by Joseph Mankiewicz, Twentieth Century–Fox, 1950), takes place in the world of the Broadway theater. There are many fascinating characters—a critic, a director, a producer, a writer, the writer's wife—but the film centers on an aging star, Margo Channing (Bette Davis), and her young, theater-obsessed protégé, Eve Harrington (Anne Baxter). In the first part of the film, Eve is attentive and adoring to Margo and her circle. In the second half, she manages by unethical means to supplant Margo and become a Broadway star herself. The tempestuous Margo realizes she is past her prime and accepts the decline of her career with a surprising generosity and grace. She affirms her identity as woman first, actress second, and strengthens her bonds to a fiancé (Gary Merrill, who plays the director) and friends. On the other hand, Eve wins a prestigious award but has no friends to share it with—except for a star-struck young woman who wanders into her hotel room, thus perpetuating the cycle which began with Margo and Eve.

ALL ABOUT EVE lends itself to two quite different interpretations. The first and most direct would be that Margo is a wise woman with a sense of proportion, whereas Eve is

Bette Davis as Margo Channing and Gary Merrill as her fiancé in ALL ABOUT EVE *(1950).*

a monster. By accepting a woman's place in society, Margo can look forward to a life beyond her acting career. But this interpretation does not adequately present the excitement and possibility of life in the theater. A second interpretation would stress that in the world of theater, women are the approximate equal of men. Certainly, Margo is the strongest and most successful character in the film, but there are other strong women as well: Eve Harrington, Karen Richards (the playwright's wife, played by Celeste Holm), and Birdie Coonan (Margo's dresser, played by Thelma Ritter). The theater milieu is filled with private and public intrigues, and the women negotiate them at least as well as the men.

SUNSET BOULEVARD (directed by Billy Wilder, Paramount, 1950) is a hybrid film, part melodrama, part film noir, part black comedy. The black humor begins with the choice of narrator—a man whom we see floating face down in a swimming pool. The dead man, Joe Gillis (William Holden), then tells us in flashback how he got to this point. A struggling screenwriter, Gillis comes by accident to the door of an aged and reclusive Hollywood silent film star, Norma Desmond (Gloria Swanson). Norma thinks that she is still the ultimate screen star: "It's the pictures that got small." He becomes her script collaborator, then her lover, filling the role once taken by her butler and ex-husband Max (Erich von Stroheim). Joe is so humiliated by this that he turns away a beautiful young woman (Nancy Olson) who tries to rescue him from Norma's bizarre mansion. When Joe does start to leave, Norma shoots him (thus the swimming pool scene). As the police arrest her, she parades down the mansion stairs for columnists and newsreel cameramen, content that her stardom has returned.

SUNSET BOULEVARD is far more bitter than ALL ABOUT EVE about the contradiction between stardom and aging. Norma Desmond has nothing to substitute for the glamour of the studios—though wealthy, she is literally insane. Adding to the cruelty of this presentation, director Billy Wilder has cast actual silent film stars in a number of parts. Gloria Swanson was a first-rank star of the 1920s, Erich von Stroheim was an enormously important director and actor, and they are joined by Buster Keaton, Anna Q. Nilsson, and H. B. Warner in bit parts. There is a certain amount of pathos to Norma's situation, but she does not attain Margo Channing's philosophical acceptance of a change of life.

SUNSET BOULEVARD can also be seen as a pessimistic and bitter comment on contemporary Hollywood. It shows that Hollywood is an unstable, rapidly changing place, where creative giants may be forgotten within their lifetimes. Unlike SINGIN' IN THE RAIN, which presents Hollywood entertainment as flourishing despite technological change, in SUNSET BOULEVARD Hollywood may be a "haunted house," crippled by the emergent medium of television. Cecil B. DeMille plays himself in Wilder's film, working on a Paramount soundstage, but others of his generation have been abandoned by the industry. The implication is that this could happen again—today's stars could be tomorrow's Norma Desmonds.

HARD, FAST, AND BEAUTIFUL (RKO, 1951) is a film directed and co-produced by Hollywood's only female director of the 1950s, Ida Lupino. Lupino (better known as an actress) and her husband, Collier Young, were the principals of Filmakers, a company which released a series of films through RKO. The Lupino-Young films were well-made and intelligent and cost only about $350,000 per picture. In HARD, FAST, AND BEAUTIFUL, an ambitious mother takes advantage of her daughter's tennis skills to move to a different social level. Millie Farley (Claire Trevor), the mother, and Florence Farley (Sally Forrest), the daughter, leave a modest neighborhood in Santa Monica, California, to tour the United States and Europe. Millie essentially abandons her husband Will (Kenneth Patterson), though without getting a divorce, and throws herself into the social whirl of the tennis circuit. She is encouraged by Fletcher Locke (Carleton G. Young), her daughter's socially prominent coach. The daughter wins two U.S. Open championships at Forest Hills, but after the second championship she immediately quits tennis for love of her hometown boyfriend. The mother is abandoned by everyone.

This film uses both narration and visual storytelling to indicate shifting emotional loyalties. Millie's narration, which occasionally punctuates the first half of the film, suggests empathy for her daughter and husband and a willingness to be critical of herself. The visuals here also present Millie's point of view: difficult decisions, surprising success, motherly devotion. Later on, the narration disappears and Millie's view of things is more open to question. For example, Will is suddenly taken ill and Millie thinks the next day's tennis match is more important than a visit home. Wife and daughter do visit a dying Will, who takes the occasion to bond with Florence and berate Millie for her selfishness. Then Millie gets involved with exploiting Florence's fame and keeping her on the tennis tour and away from the boy she loves. When Florence finally quits and Fletcher goes off to speak to another young player, Millie is left alone and devastated.

So, is Millie a sympathetic mother trying to give her daughter opportunities, or a nasty and selfish character prone to self-delusion (as presented in the voiceovers)? The film gives no explicit answer, but it does maintain a sense of balance. Florence's life is certainly not ruined; her independence and her common sense are ultimately affirmed. Millie has made serious mistakes, and Florence breaks away from her. This may be as much the normal separation of adolescent from parent as a response to Millie's selfishness. There are no female monsters here, no episodes of hysteria, no use of violence to ratchet up emotions. The spectator is free to decide whether Millie is destroyed by the final scene or whether she is lonely and hurting but still whole. One is tempted to ascribe the subtlety of the final moments to the presence of a woman behind the camera.[47]

A STREETCAR NAMED DESIRE (directed by Elia Kazan, Warner Bros., 1951), based on the hit play by Tennessee Williams, is a brutally honest melodrama about desire and illusion. The central characters are Blanche Dubois (Vivian Leigh), a former schoolteacher; her sister, Stella (Kim Hunter); and Stella's husband, Stanley Kowalski (Marlon Brando). Blanche leaves the family plantation, lost because of debts, to stay with Stella and Stanley in their small New Orleans apartment. She is a dreamer and a romantic, someone who hides the truth from herself and others. She prefers shadows, makeup, elaborate flirtations, anything that allows her to escape from the realities of an unhappy life. Stanley, on the other hand, is direct and physical, and his relationship with Stella is based on sexual satisfaction. Stanley eventually discovers that Blanche lost the family plantation, had a scandalous relationship with one of her students, and left her small town in disgrace. When Stella is in the hospital having a baby, Stanley rapes Blanche (this could not be shown or even talked about in the Hollywood of 1951, but Kazan does manage to suggest it). After Stella returns home, there is tension and hostility between husband and wife, but also an agreement that the delusional Blanche must go. Stella, Stanley, neighbors, and friends collude to send Blanche to a mental asylum (as with the rape, this destination is only suggested).

If melodrama is about accepting the limits of society, A STREETCAR NAMED DESIRE fits the definition, but in a cruel and extreme way. Blanche is weak and full of illusions;

Vivian Leigh as Blanche Dubois in A STREETCAR NAMED DESIRE *(1951), based on the play by Tennessee Williams.*

she is destroyed. Stanley and Stella fulfill one of the basics of marriage, they produce a baby. And though Stella punishes Stanley by withholding herself and the baby from him, this seems to be temporary. The sexual attraction is still there. Desire is a streetcar that runs over people. A STREETCAR NAMED DESIRE is an astonishing film to be made in Hollywood in the early fifties. Though it contains no nudity or profanity, its powerful and transgressive view of sexuality is far outside the period's norms—the norms of the screen, that is. Part of STREETCAR's attraction (play and film) is that it describes real but generally unspoken matters.

Conclusion

In general, the early 1950s was a period of high-quality films made within socially and aesthetically conservative parameters. As producer John Houseman explained in 1950, the movies had to be good, because audience loyalties were waning. In the mid-1940s customers would line up to see almost any film; by the 1950s movie spectators were much more selective.[48] But this did not immediately translate into creative innovation for a couple of reasons. For one thing, the major studios with their thousands of employees and extensive physical plants were set up to make a certain kind of film. MGM, for example, had the resources and the expertise to make top-quality musicals according to traditional patterns. The blacklist and related pressures also encouraged conventional thinking: war films were expected to be patriotic (though TWELVE O'CLOCK HIGH, HALLS OF MONTEZUMA, and THE BRIDGES OF TOKO-RI all introduced a degree of complexity) and even film noir invoked anti-communism (as in PICKUP ON SOUTH STREET).

Some films fled social controversy by situating stories in a nostalgically remembered past. For example, SINGIN' IN THE RAIN is set in the 1920s and features Arthur Freed–Nacio Herb Brown songs from that period. BY THE LIGHT OF THE SILVERY MOON is set in approximately the same period. Even GENTLEMEN PREFER BLONDES, a brassy contemporary film, is based on a novel from the 1920s. Other films stuck determinedly to a small, enclosed context with little sense of a broader social world; consider, for example, the theater in ALL ABOUT EVE, the movie business in IN A LONELY PLACE, Norma Desmond's mansion in SUNSET BOULEVARD. Sometimes this emphasis on a small, tight universe becomes mannered; both ALL ABOUT EVE and SUNSET BOULEVARD have a comic, campy element because they insist on the crucial importance of their respective "worlds" (though Margo Channing in ALL ABOUT EVE has a healthy ability to move on from the life of a Broadway diva).

Paradoxically, it is the Western, among the most traditional of American film genres, which shows the greatest capacity for innovation in the early 1950s. The superwestern described by André Bazin involves experimentation with both film form and film content. Films such as SHANE and THE FAR COUNTRY redefine the Western's visual scope for color and widescreen. SHANE adds the narrative innovation of privileging the Brandon de Wilde character's youthful point of view. Anthony Mann's THE FURIES invests the Western with elements of Greek tragedy. HIGH NOON provides both a formal innovation, the identity between narrative (or on-screen) time and real time, and a strategy for indirect social criticism. BROKEN ARROW revises the Western's traditional account of the relationship between Caucasian American and Native American communities.

With hindsight it seems clear that the Hollywood films of the early 1950s needed to change, but that both film industry conditions and broader social factors mitigated against change. Hollywood was, for example, late to respond to teenagers as a crucial audience segment. Later periods showed that teens wanted to see films about their own generation, but the film industry's traditional structure and aging personnel circa 1950 were ill-equipped to make such films. Hollywood also shied away from films about social issues and changing sexual morality, even though both subjects (especially the latter) had been film industry staples in the past. Here the logical explanation must be social pressures (the blacklist, threats from Congress, censorship), even though the exact mechanisms of influence are not always clear.

The result of this need to change/blockage of change was a form of "High Classicism"—well-made but conventional films. Both the musical and film noir were relying on the styles and the creative personnel of the 1940s. Melodramas insisted on conventional morality, and a fairly large cycle of films dramatized (and supported) McCarthyist anticommunism. More critical social commentary was largely limited to indirect expressions in adventure genres such as the Western and science fiction (see Chapter 8), and to the mood (more than the narrative) of film noir. The films of the period do sometimes have a "timeless" quality—and certainly the Freed musicals and films like GENTLEMEN PREFER BLONDES, ALL ABOUT EVE, SUNSET BOULEVARD, SANDS OF IWO JIMA, HIGH NOON, and SHANE have retained an enthusiastic audience, but this has both positive and negative aspects. The positive element is the familiar set of themes, styles, and narrative patterns that make these films easy to understand. The negative element is that films from this era maintained an isolation from what Robert Sklar calls "the changes and movements in the dominant culture at large."[49] A STREETCAR NAMED DESIRE and GENTLEMEN PREFER BLONDES suggest a new frankness about sexuality, KISS ME DEADLY begins to criticize the macho male, and HIGH NOON may be describing the anti-Communist panic (depending on how one interprets the film), but overall the films of the early 1950s are curiously detached from the issues of their time. In the later 1950s, films connected to social, political, and cultural issues reappear, as Chapter 10 will demonstrate.

3

HUAC, the Blacklist, and the Decline of Social Cinema

BRIAN NEVE

The Origins of the Blacklist

The Hollywood Blacklist had its origins in the 1947 decision of the House Committee on Un-American Activities (HUAC) to hold hearings on communism in Hollywood. The committee had been formed in 1938, but only became a standing committee of the House of Representatives in 1945, at the prompting of notorious anti-Semitic Congressman John Rankin of Mississippi. Thereafter, in the years of an emerging Cold War politics, HUAC became a vehicle for politicians who opposed the New Deal tradition of social democracy and reform. The committee followed the example of the Joint Fact-Finding Committee of the California legislature (the Tenney Committee), which had held hearings on Communist influence in Hollywood since 1943. The November 1946 elections had returned Republican majorities to both houses of Congress, while the ground for ideological conflict within the film capital had already been prepared by the founding in 1944 of the Motion Picture Alliance for the Preservation of American Ideals (Motion Picture Alliance).[1]

The Motion Picture Alliance, which included such figures as Sam Wood, Walt Disney, and Lela Rogers (mother of Ginger Rogers), drew attention to what its members saw as left-wing propaganda in wartime film and the left-leaning influence of, in particular, Hollywood screenwriters. Many key members had strong associations with William Randolph Hearst, who had used his media outlets since the mid-1930s to publicize his anti-Communist position, while the Alliance also included veterans of the conservative fight against studio recognition of the Screen Writers Guild (achieved in 1940). The emergence of the Cold War and President Truman's executive order of March 1947, establishing a loyalty program for the executive branch, established an image of domestic subversion within government, while bitter industrial conflicts of 1945–1946 further polarized Hollywood politics. There was union-related violence at Warner Bros. and other studios as the Conference of Studio Unions (CSU) became involved in a prolonged dispute with both the studios and the International Alliance of Theatrical Stage Employees (IATSE). The CSU strike of 1946 was countered by a studio lockout, and by December 1946 IATSE had taken firm control of the Hollywood crafts unions. With the defeat of the CSU, Roy Brewer, the new West Coast head of IATSE, emerged as a powerful Motion Picture Alliance figure. He testified to HUAC in 1947 about what he saw as Communist responsibility for the labor disturbances.[2]

Not only Alliance members encouraged the House Committee to investigate Hollywood communism. During the first year of J. Parnell Thomas's chairmanship of HUAC, 1947, the Committee developed a close relationship with the FBI, which had collected extensive information on Hollywood communism with the aid of numerous informers. Amongst the studio moguls it was Jack Warner who stoked the fires of the anti-Communist crusade by providing the committee, meeting covertly in Los Angeles in May 1947, with horror stories of Communists working at his studio. Warner Bros. had been the most socially conscious of the Hollywood companies, but Jack Warner had been strongly influenced by the picket line violence at his studio in 1945.

It was in October 1947 that the formal hearings took place in Washington, D.C. In the first week there was testimony from "friendly" witnesses, mainly from the Motion Picture Alliance, as well as from defensive studio bosses, of whom the most cooperative was again Jack Warner. The second week was reserved for the testimony of nineteen more witnesses who were, for the most part, both screenwriters and Communists. (Edward Dmytryk and Adrian Scott seem to have been included at the last minute because of their responsibility, as director and producer, for the recently completed film attacking anti-Semitism, Crossfire, 1947).

With widespread liberal and industry fears of a blacklist, there was strong general support for the principle of the First Amendment on which these initial nineteen witnesses had agreed to stand. In particular, liberals Philip Dunne, William Wyler, and John Huston had organized the Committee for the First Amendment, and arranged for a planeload of stars to visit Washington prior to the second week of hearings. Yet the First Amendment strategy was implicit rather than explicit in the testimony of the ten "unfriendly" witnesses—Alvah Bessie, Herbert Biberman, Lester Cole, Edward Dmytryk, Ring Lardner Jr., John Howard Lawson, Albert Maltz, Samuel Ornitz, Adrian Scott, Dalton Trumbo—who were called on to testify before the hearings were unexpectedly suspended. Several of them became involved in a shouting match with Chairman Thomas, and all followed the example of the initial witness, screenwriter John Howard Lawson, in refusing to answer questions as to their membership in the party. The Hollywood Ten were each cited for contempt of Congress. HUAC publicized apparent evidence of their Communist affiliations (for example, Lawson's leadership role in the party was widely known), and therefore liberal support for the unfriendly witnesses' First Amendment rights collapsed in a few weeks. Some liberals were shocked at the performance of the Ten, while others—for example, Humphrey Bogart, who had travelled to Washington with the Committee for the First Amendment—came under fierce studio pressure to publicly denounce communism.

Eric Johnston, president of the Motion Picture Producers Association (MPAA), and spokesman for the producers and their boards of directors, had originally resisted any blacklist, but with the committee producing evidence of Communist membership, he quickly came to terms with the strength of the opposition. On 24 November the House of Representatives voted overwhelmingly for the citation of the Hollywood Ten for contempt of Congress. On the same day Johnston convened a meeting of studio producers and executives at the Waldorf-Astoria Hotel in New York. Their discussions led to the drafting, by a committee of five including Dore Schary, of the so-called Waldorf Statement, declaring that the studios would dismiss those of the Hollywood Ten under contract and would not re-employ any of them "until such time as he is acquitted or has purged himself of contempt and declared under oath that he is not a Communist." The statement continued: "We will not knowingly employ a Communist or a member of any party or group which advocates the overthrow of the Government of the United States by force or by any illegal or unconstitutional methods."[3] This statement essentially instituted a blacklist, although the full implementation would have to wait three years for the appeals of the Ten to be exhausted. (It is interesting to note, that although much discussion of the blacklist centers on the "Hollywood Ten," an eleventh man, Bertolt Brecht, also testified, denied being a Communist, and immediately left the country for Europe. Additional "unfriendly" witnesses who agreed not to cooperate with the committee but who were not called to testify in 1947 were Richard Collins, Gordon Kahn, Howard Koch, Lewis Milestone, Larry Parks, Irving Pichel, Robert Rossen, and Waldo Salt.)

There were soon indications that in the wake of this decision the studios were becoming more wary of social topics. Eric Johnston argued in 1947 that "We'll have no more films that show the seamy side of American life," while the same year William Wyler suggested that in the "current climate" he would no longer be allowed to make THE BEST YEARS OF OUR LIVES (1946).[4] Yet the late 1940s saw various forms of social cinema, from the much celebrated social problem films CROSSFIRE (1947) and GENTLEMAN'S AGREEMENT (1948), to the cycles of films that would later be classified as semi-documentary and film noir. Location shooting allowed inexperienced but ambitious directors a degree of freedom from traditional studio supervision and also contributed to a greater sense of real life being recorded on film, while crime thrillers often allowed a political critique to be expressed in a disguised (and deniable) form. The unexpected re-election of Harry Truman in November 1948 was even taken as evidence that "liberal days were here again," encouraging studio heads to give the go-ahead to a group of films that raised and articulated (however belatedly) a set of liberal positions and ideas on race. What is more difficult to assess is the impact of the darkening national and international political situation, with the emergence of a Cold War agenda and an international specter of "Red Fascism" at the expense of the dominant concerns of the long Roosevelt era. With a series of economic and other shocks to the established studio system, including the decline in audiences from 1947 and the culmination of the administration's anti-trust action in 1948, it was increasingly clear that the established industry leaders and producers had to plan for change.[5]

Writers were notoriously low in the Hollywood pecking order, yet subsequent scholarship has done much to establish the impact of liberal and left-wing writers in important areas of film in the Depression years, during the war, and for a time after the war. The broad agreement of liberals and radicals on an anti-fascist and progressive agenda (especially during the late thirties and the war years, when the American Communist Party encouraged such an alliance) was seen as a "Popular Front." By the late forties this unity was in rapid decline (symbolized by the collapse of rank and file support for the Committee for the First Amendment), but the left-wing writer and director Abraham Polonsky referred to this time in the changing Hollywood system as providing "interesting" opportunities for a "thirties" generation of socially minded artists. This group of Depression era writers and especially directors were gaining a tentative foothold in the industry. Their distinctive social and aesthetic goals constituted a perceived threat to the producer-dominated studio system with its "pure entertainment" ethic. The search for postwar subjects, the wartime experiences of filmmakers, the trend toward independent production, and the opportunities for location shooting had all seemed to increase the range of issues and images in postwar cinema. Yet the deepening association in the public mind of the American Communist Party with a Soviet Union that was now a key international enemy of the United States meant that the days of the Popular Front alliance between radicals and liberals were numbered. Albert Maltz's appeal to John Huston in 1949, calling for an alliance against the forces of reaction on the basis of "common Jeffersonian principles," was in vain. Arthur Schlesinger, standard bearer for a new anti-Communist liberalism, a "vital center," was nearer the dominant current of intellectual thought, while those in Hollywood with radical associations were increasingly looking over their shoulders. When in 1950 the Supreme Court declined to review the cases of Dalton Trumbo and John Howard Lawson, appealing on behalf of the Hollywood Ten, the blacklist already implicit in Eric Johnston's statement was ready to be implemented.[6]

While some key social problem films, from CROSSFIRE to GENTLEMAN'S AGREEMENT and PINKY (1949) were successful at the box office, not all of them were seen as suitable for the increasingly important foreign market, either in economic or public relations terms. The decline in domestic audiences placed greater emphasis on the maintenance and expansion of foreign markets for American films. As Richard Maltby points out, the industry's need for State Department help in exploiting these markets hindered Hollywood's "social conscience" by obligating an increasingly "optimistic portrayal of the American way of life." Frank Capra, who had used radical and liberal writers in constructing his ultimately affirmative vision of America, commented in 1947 that: "Our job will be to make all criticisms expressed add up to praise—and I say it's going to be tough."[7] Only three weeks before the Waldorf Statement Dore Schary had called for renewed thought to be given to the "effect of our pictures abroad."[8] By the early 1950s, with the involvement of the CIA in America's international image, this would become an even more important consideration.

HUAC, McCarthyism, and the Blacklist

The effect of the new Cold War agenda on Hollywood can be seen in terms of the decision by the Supreme Court in 1950 not to review the appeal by Hollywood Ten members Dalton Trumbo and John Howard Lawson against the 1947 "contempt of Congress" conviction. In 1949 Justices Frank Murphy and Wiley B. Rutledge had died within two months of each other. With two other justices, they had been seen as a solid voting bloc on the Court in favor of civil liberties, giving First Amendment issues preferred status in their deliberations. Yet by 1949 the pressures on President Truman were such that he filled the two vacancies on the Court by appointing conservative justices who were prepared to give more weight to issues of national security. In May 1950 the refusal of the reconstituted Court to review the case brought on behalf of the Ten led to them all serving prison sentences of six months to a year during 1950–1951. In a speech in New York in June 1950, before serving his sentence, Ring Lardner Jr. had commented that a Court with "Murphy, Rutledge, Douglas and Black could be counted on to slap down the demagogues." The next year, in the Dennis case, the same Court upheld the conviction of the leaders of the American Communist Party under the Smith Act for advocating the overthrow of the United States government. This case virtually outlawed the Communist Party, as well as legitimating the "anti-communist crusade" that was to follow.[9]

By 1950 the country was in the grip of something like a national panic over what was seen, at all levels of society, as a plausible domestic and international threat of communism. By February, when Senator Joseph McCarthy began his period in the limelight with his notorious speech in Wheeling, West Virginia, he was in part reacting to the conviction of Alger Hiss, the former State Department official and Roosevelt aide who had been accused by HUAC in 1948 of passing secrets to a Communist spy ring. To cultural historian Richard Pells, the conviction of Hiss lent credence to "the theory that all communists should be regarded as potential foreign agents." Later in 1950 the war in Korea began and Ethel and Julius Rosenberg were arrested on a charge of conspiracy to commit espionage, further fueling the obsession of the FBI and professional blacklisting organizations with Communists as actual or potential spies.[10] Indeed by this time domestic communism was seen largely in terms of an actual or potential Soviet threat to the interests of the state, rather than as a movement of radicals with varying degrees of relationship with the national Communist leadership.

In May 1950 the Motion Picture Alliance called for a "complete delousing" of the film industry. Its new president, John Wayne, felt that producers had not delivered on the commitments of the Waldorf Statement, and Alliance members welcomed what seemed to be an impending second wave of Congressional intervention. In June a booklet on the left-wing affiliations of television and radio personnel, *Red Channels*, was published, while in September Harry Warner addressed 2,000 Warner Bros. employees and executives on a sound stage about the Communist threat, making it clear that he wanted no Communists at the studio. In the summer there was also a protracted battle between liberal and conservative factions of the Screen Directors Guild over a plan, urged on the Guild membership by arch anti-Communist Cecil B. DeMille during the absence from the country of Guild President Joseph L. Mankiewicz, to introduce a mandatory oath for existing and new members affirming non-adherence to the Communist party. To DeMille, who was finally forced to back down in an epic membership meeting, the "question we are asking is, are you on the American side or on the other side."[11]

As anticipated, in March 1951 the House Committee resumed its Washington hearings on communism in the film industry. In effect, in the period from 1951 to 1953, the blacklist that was announced in 1947 was enforced. The core group of those who then found themselves unemployable by the main studios were those known by the authorities to have been Communists, and who, on being subpoenaed, declined to cooperate with the committee. Given the fate of those who pleaded the First Amendment in 1947, those unwilling to cooperate with the committee by naming names, were advised to invoke the Fifth Amendment against self-incrimination. While the committee and the FBI knew the names of present and past Communists, the naming of names by former members of the Communist party, together with a recantation of past beliefs, was a ritual required of those who wished to return to work. While witnesses may have left the party many years before, most still regarded their public identification of previous friends and colleagues as Communist party members as a process of informing that was morally repugnant. Many ultimately took part in what historian and journalist Victor Navasky later called "degradation ceremonies," or the naming of names, because this is what was required for them to be able to work again in the film industry, using their own names.

Those who declined to answer questions on the party membership of others invoked the Fifth Amendment. But in effect such a stance was taken as evidence that the individual had something to hide—in terms of present or past party membership—and they found themselves unemployable in the studios that were a party to the Waldorf Statement. Those who cooperated added names to the blacklist, unless the individuals concerned could clear themselves either before the committee, or through other clearance mechanisms soon to be established. In the hearings held in Washington from 1951 to 1953, over 200 Communists were named. In the first two years of the new bout of hearings Larry Parks, Richard Collins, Budd Schulberg, Edward Dmytryk (reversing his position as one of the original Hollywood Ten), Elia Kazan, Clifford Odets, and Sterling Hayden (who later declared himself ashamed of his testimony) were among those who became "friendly" witnesses, while Howard Da Silva, Abraham Polonsky, Paul Jarrico, Carl Foreman, and Lillian Hellman were among those who took the Fifth in the same period. Robert Rossen testified in 1951 about his own party membership but declined to name others, but in 1953 he returned to the committee as a friendly witness. The blacklisted actor Mickey Knox remembers Rossen telling him at the time that: "I did a terrible thing. I named my friends. But I have to work." Some blacklisted writers continued to work covertly, usually at a fraction of the salary, and often on unpromising assignments, while others moved abroad. Using fronts was not an option for directors (or actors), and an important group of directors interested in social or political themes, a number of whom had begun to develop reputations in the late forties, also looked for work abroad. The group included Joseph Losey, Jules Dassin, John Berry, Bernard Vorhaus, and Cy Endfield.[12]

While the studios' blacklist was generated essentially by the House Committee, with the complicity of those who gave it names, a number of private organizations exploited and expanded the process in the early 1950s for a mixture of commercial and ideological motives. American Business Consultants, formed in 1947 by ex-FBI men, marketed books and newsletters, in particular *Red Channels* (1950) and *Counterattack*, to employers and advertisers interested in the leftist associations of those in the entertainment industry. Other muckraking publications, including *Alert* ("A Weekly Confidential Report on Communism and How to Combat It"), available from 1951, and organizations including Aware ("An organization to combat the Communist conspiracy in the entertainment world"), set up in 1952, also touted sensational allegations. But by far the most influential organization in this period in expanding the blacklist and helping to create a wider "graylist" was the American Legion. The Legion with its 3,000 branches produced the most credible threat to picket theaters playing non-conforming movies, and its leadership and publications, including *Firing Line*, had a direct effect on the studios and their hiring policies.

In addition to the blacklist of over 200 Communists or ex-Communists, a graylist of a hundred or more artists with left or liberal associations operated in the early fifties. For example, Lewis Milestone, a "Popular Fronter" but not a party member, and a director who had bemoaned a state of "No pictures with messages" in 1949, spent the first half of the fifties in Europe in part because his presence on such a list made it difficult or impossible to get work. An issue of *Alert* in January 1951 referred to Milestone and Michael Blankfort, director and writer of HALLS OF MONTEZUMA (1950) as "two notorious participants in Communist fronts and causes." The director Vincent Sherman was also on a graylist for eighteen months in the early fifties, in part because the magazine *Counterattack* was sending out confidential letters to his studio heads detailing his associations with alleged Communist fronts. The tenor of *Counterattack*'s campaign can be judged from other statements in their typewritten reports. One refers to "Isadore Scharf (pardon me, I mean Dore Schary)," an anti-Semitic reference to the studio head's full name, which was Isidore Schary. Another, in April 1951, suggests that the only way to "clear up the hundreds of Communists and pro-Communists" in the industry is to "get a boycott rolling against those producers and Moscow maggots in their casts."[13]

The American Legion never authorized a national boycott, although a number of right-wing groups further weakened industry resistance to the blacklist by picketing theaters that were showing suspect films. A group called Catholic War Veterans picketed BORN YESTERDAY (1950) when it opened in New York. According to the film's star, Judy Holliday, whose political associations had been publicized by *Red Channels*, the placards read "While our boys are dying in Korea, Judy Holliday is instead defaming Congress." DEATH OF A SALESMAN (1951) was picketed by a group called the Wage Earners Committee, calling attention not only to the supposedly subversive nature of Arthur Miller's original play, but to producer Stanley Kramer's "Record of coddling Reds and pinkos." Also picketed was Joseph Losey's last-but-one American film, M (1951), presumably because of the left-wing associations of Losey and Waldo Salt, who contributed additional dialogue. (Salt was one of the Hollywood Nineteen. He had been subpoenaed by HUAC in 1947 but was not called to testify.) In addition, Ayn Rand's "Screen Guide for Americans," a pamphlet which in particular encouraged favorable screen treatment of business, was published by the Motion Picture Alliance. Blacklisting organizations were particularly hostile to what was seen as social realism. *Firing Line* ("Facts for Fighting Communism"), for example, warned its readers against the film version of DEATH OF A SALESMAN: this "realistic picture of American Life," it argued, "will naturally be welcomed by Stalinists all over the world," and will give an "unflattering portrait of American life" to millions of foreigners. *Firing Line* also warned its readers about other distinctive if disparate films, including VIVA ZAPATA! (1952), SATURDAY'S HERO (1951), Chaplin's forthcoming LIMELIGHT (1952), and the liberal science fiction fable, THE DAY THE EARTH STOOD STILL (1951).[14]

The American Legion significantly increased the pressure by publishing an article by J. B. Matthews, "Did the Movies Really Clean House?," in December 1951. (Matthews, a fellow traveller turned anti-Communist, had been a star witness for HUAC in its first incarnation under the chairmanship of Martin Dies in 1938. A longtime Hearst associate, his voluminous study of the left-wing affiliations of Hollywood personnel had helped prompt Rankin's interest in a new investigation in 1945.) The studios and their financial backers were particularly frightened by the threat of American Legion picketing of theaters explicit in the Matthews article. There followed a reported "fruitful" meeting between the American Legion, Eric Johnston, and representatives of the key producing companies in March 1952. Out of this meeting, clearance procedures were established. These procedures involved the blacklisted artists writing explanatory letters to the American Legion, where "experts," including the veteran Hearst columnist George Sokolsky, actor Ward Bond, and union boss Roy Brewer, would separate the "liberal lambs from the Communist wolves." One studio that developed its own political screening program at this time was RKO Radio Pictures, with studio head Howard Hughes closing down production for three months in 1952 for this purpose.[15]

This pressure added to the woes of an industry already laying off workers in response to declining audiences and foreign markets. Yet in 1952 a group of anonymous screenwriters suggested that the continued investigations were seen by film executives as a mixed blessing, as not only were workers and unions "pacified, but the industry was enabled to 'slash employees pay-checks.'"[16] This argument seems to support the later interpretation that the blacklist was, at least in part, "good business" for the studios, enabling them to regain control over the entertainment marketplace after the economic and other "shocks" after the war. Jon Lewis has discussed the blacklist as a postwar business strategy adopted by an industry threatened by political regulation, declining audiences, and anti-trust decisions, and he also sees anti-Semitism as a weapon used against both Hollywood Communists and the old-style studio moguls. The number of Hollywood liberals and radicals who were Jewish, and the fear of Jewish moguls that the investigations might encourage a wider anti-Semitism from WASP politicians in Washington, was a distinctive element of this era.[17]

Of those not called before the House Committee, many writers and directors were put under pressure to "clear" themselves by writing a formal letter to their studio employers. In July 1950 W. R.Wilkerson, in his "Trade Views" column in the *Hollywood Reporter*, wrote scathingly of "foreigners," including Billy Wilder and William Wyler, who had criticized the treatment of the Hollywood Ten. He argued that this "is no time for such claptrap and something should be done to muzzle them in the future." In his reply (published two days later) Wyler pointed out that open criticism of government was, "according to the principles on which our republic is founded," not only permitted but encouraged. Yet Wyler was finally pressed to write to the president of Paramount, Frank Freeman, in May 1954, making clear his "basic feelings and loyalties" and his "position in regard to the worldwide conflict between the Free World of the Democracies and the Slave States of the Soviet System." He drew attention to his sworn statement in the files of the Screen Directors Guild, showing that he had never been a member of the Communist party. He had supported an amici curae brief for Trumbo and Lawson in 1951, but by 1954, in a way that suggests the growing pressure on liberals to disassociate themselves from Communists, he was critical of the Hollywood Ten: "I was one of a group that urged them to deny or affirm membership in that party. I did that in the mistaken belief that members of the group were not members of that party."[18]

While Lillian Hellman (who herself took the Fifth Amendment) and Victor Navasky have written of the blacklist in terms of a simple moral distinction between those who named names and those who resisted, others have suggested a more complicated picture. Certainly many friendly witnesses mentioned disillusionment with the Communist party in their testimony—and party membership in the early fifties was in rapid decline. This may have weakened the resistance of some who went on to cooperate with HUAC. Most current and dedicated party members had little doubt as to what to do, but others, especially those who had been out of the party for some time, clearly balanced the unpleasantness of informing with a reluctance, to paraphrase Edward Dmytryk's words, to sacrifice career and family for a cause they had grown to dislike. Hellman's and Navasky's perspective has rather over-simplified the moral dynamics of the period, or at least under-examined the political dimension of the moral choices that artists faced at the time. The issues always appeared more morally clear-cut to those—the great majority of resisters—who were still committed to the party. Paul Jarrico, a screenwriter who was prominent in the Communist party and who was himself blacklisted, argued that, "for those who were generally pissed off at the party but reluctant to name names, the choice must have been difficult. For a person like me, a true blue red, the choice was easy."[19]

Social Content in Film

While inferences can be made from their previous credits about the effects of the times on some key blacklisted writers, directors, and actors, it is difficult to separate out the

effects of the darkening Cold War atmosphere, the blacklist, and other changes in industry and society that were affecting the type of film being made. The concern with the
image of America in foreign markets was certainly a factor that influenced the studios, as
was the threat of picketing by the American Legion and other organizations. In a survey
of the content of American films in the period 1947 to 1954, Dorothy Jones notes in particular a marked decline in social problem films from 1949 to 1952, with more emphasis
on "pure entertainment," and in particular more anti-Communist films and war films of
the "sure-fire patriotic variety." Jones also points to the Oscar winners of 1950–1952,
ALL ABOUT EVE, AN AMERICAN IN PARIS, and THE GREATEST SHOW ON EARTH, as indicative of the type of product most favored by the Hollywood establishment.[20]

Other interpretations are generally consistent with this analysis, stressing a shift in
the early fifties to Westerns, war films, and biblical epics, and to a perspective that was
more often psychological than social. To blacklisted writer Walter Bernstein, psychology
was in, social criticism was out, and Hollywood was becoming increasingly concerned to
reflect the perspectives of a growing younger audience. At the time, the critic Manny
Farber pointed to another development, a wave of "art or mood" films including A
STREETCAR NAMED DESIRE, A PLACE IN THE SUN, and SUNSET BOULEVARD (all 1951); to
Farber these "Freud-Marx epics" represented the social significance of the 1930s gone
sour. Lary May, in his own study of what he sees as a cultural reconstruction of American
national identity in the Cold War period, uses an analysis of thousands of film plots from
the trade paper the *Motion Picture Herald* as a source of evidence on the key changes in
theme from the 1930s to the 1950s. He charts a decline in unhappy (what he calls Noir)

Blacklisted writer Michael Wilson won an Academy Award for his work on the script for
A PLACE IN THE SUN (1951), based on Theodore Dreiser's novel An American Tragedy.
Montgomery Clift and Shelley Winters starred in the film, along with Elizabeth Taylor.

endings in the fifties, a rise in the focus on youth as an alternative to the adult world over the same period, and a fall in the incidence of depictions both of the rich as a moral threat and of big business as villainous.[21]

Certainly the early 1950s saw a tailing-off of the crime dramas now classified as part of the film noir cycle. Thom Andersen has written of a sub-group of noir films—he labeled them "films gris"—which was characteristic of the period 1947–1951. These films shared some of the stylistic features associated with film noir but dealt in particular with social issues and exhibited an awareness of class as a critical factor in American life. Such films looked back to the 1930s in their politics, and were increasingly viewed with suspicion by those concerned that Hollywood films affirm America to a global market. The writers and particularly the directors who were most responsible for this cycle of films were those most affected by the second wave of Congressional investigations. Jules Dassin, for example, directed THIEVES HIGHWAY (1949) and NIGHT AND THE CITY (1950) before becoming a victim of the blacklist and moving permanently to Europe. Nicholas Ray avoided the blacklist, but his work in the late forties, including THEY LIVE BY NIGHT (1949) and KNOCK ON ANY DOOR (1949), dealt with the problems of youth in a way that clearly relates, in retrospect, to Andersen's notion of work and the "psychological injuries of class." Ray also worked in part in Europe in the fifties, and was reportedly on a graylist for a time, while arguably making metaphoric reference to the blacklist in IN A LONELY PLACE (1950) and JOHNNY GUITAR (1954). The youthful rebels of the fifties became cultural icons, but were rarely linked to broader social forces. THE WILD ONE (1954) appeared shorn of most of its criticism of business following PCA pressure, while the James Dean persona in Kazan's EAST OF EDEN (1954) and Ray's own REBEL WITHOUT A CAUSE (1955) is primarily defined in terms of conflicts within the family.[22]

Two other directors associated with some form of social drama who left America for Europe for political reasons were Joseph Losey and Cy Endfield. THE PROWLER (1951), from a script mainly written by Dalton Trumbo, certainly fits the main contours of Andersen's model. To Losey the film was about "false values": "'100,000 bucks, a Cadillac, and a blonde' were the sine qua non of American life at the time and it didn't matter how you got them—whether you stole the girl from somebody else, stole the money, and got the Cadillac from corruption." In an early scene a policeman, Webb Garwood (Van Heflin) is called to a baroque Los Angeles house to investigate a suspected prowler. He there begins a relationship with a lonely woman, Susan Gilvray (Evelyn Keyes), attracted to the lifestyle and social status that she represents. Class envy and sexual passion are blended, and writer and director, sharing a social perspective on the material, both contribute to what becomes, with a little help from the PCA, a social morality tale. Soon after the film's release Losey, anticipating the imminent delivery of a subpoena, left for London, while Trumbo began a period in exile in Mexico.[23]

Cy Endfield also moved to London, and one of his last American films is characteristic of the perspective and approach that was being marginalized by the politics of the time. TRY AND GET ME! (THE SOUND OF FURY) (1951) was one of the last of the socially pointed noir films of the late forties and early fifties. Within a study of yellow journalism, crime, and mob violence, the film sets out a notion of false values, as family man Howard Tyler (Frank Lovejoy), desperate to find work, strays into petty crime and ultimate victimhood. The PCA suggested its usual "voice for morality," and warned against "any philosophizing that might seem to relieve your murderers of the blame for their crimes and put this blame on society generally." Yet the film still provides an unusual view of the pressures of unemployment on family and breadwinner, and it represents a dimension of

Elia Kazan (left), a visiting Marlon Brando, Julie Harris, and James Dean in a publicity photo for EAST OF EDEN *(1955).*

film that Endfield and others might have explored further had circumstances been different.[24]

Perhaps the core figures of this small body of work, however, were the actor John Garfield and the radical writer-director Abraham Polonsky. Garfield received his training as an actor within the legendary Group Theatre in New York in the thirties, gaining prominence following his role in Clifford Odets's *Awake and Sing* in 1935. The actor had helped to set up Enterprise Pictures on leaving Warners in 1946, and had appeared in two key late-forties films with political significance, the upbeat BODY AND SOUL (Robert Rossen, 1947) and the dark FORCE OF EVIL (Polonsky, 1948), both from Polonsky scripts. It was Garfield who had insisted on the reinstating of Hemingway's black character in THE BREAKING POINT (Michael Curtiz, 1951), providing what Thomas Cripps calls a "bold stride towards a humane portrayal of interracial comradeship." Although the FBI knew Garfield was not a Communist, he was subpoenaed in March 1951 and then harassed further when he talked of his own political affiliations but refused to discuss others'; he was pushed into a magazine recantation of his political views before he died of a heart attack in May 1952. Polonsky, writing about Garfield, said that the "Group trained him, the movies made him, the Blacklist killed him." The director of FORCE OF EVIL had written a typically witty and politically informed script for I CAN GET IT FOR YOU WHOLESALE (Michael Gordon, 1951)—informed in particular by his concern with sexual double standards and the pervasive effects of capitalist values—before returning from a trip to France to face HUAC. Tracked and wiretapped by the FBI, Polonsky took the Fifth Amendment in April 1951 at a hearing at which the chair, the conservative Republican Harold Velde of Illinois, described him as " a very dangerous citizen." In the mid-fifties Polonsky worked anonymously on a number of scripts, as well as writing a series of "You Are There" teleplays for CBS television, and a novel, *A Season of Fear*,

FORCE OF EVIL (1948), written and directed by Abraham Polonsky. John Garfield is on the right.

dealing with the blacklist. His banishment from film following the hearing raises questions about how his highly integrated art and politics might have developed in 1960s absence of a blacklist. As it was, Polonsky remained on the blacklist until late in the sixties when he received screenplay credit (his first since 1951) for MADIGAN (Don Siegel, 1968) and returned to directing with TELL THEM WILLIE BOY IS HERE (1969).[25]

A cycle of films released in 1949 and 1950 brought a new and liberal perspective to the question of race prejudice in America. The so-called "message cycle," including PINKY (Elia Kazan, 1949) and INTRUDER IN THE DUST (Clarence Brown, 1949), came to an end more because it had run its course than because of any pressure on producers in this area. Joseph Mankiewicz's NO WAY OUT (1950), with Sidney Poitier in his first feature film role, was the most forthright of the cycle. Thomas Cripps has suggested that the "central metaphor of integrationism" in these films influenced the later themes of the civil rights movement.[26]

After 1950, according to film historian David Eldridge, the changed political atmosphere made it "difficult for politically and socially sensitive films to get made in this period." CIA monitoring of the social content of the movies, certainly in 1953, shows the U.S. government's strong concern with America's movie image (and especially with foreign perceptions of America).[27] From different positions, reactionaries, conservatives and "corporate liberals" influenced the blacklist and the movie agenda in the early fifties. As Jonathan Munby argues, Eric Johnston's desire for an end to Depression memories and for affirmative images of a new America of economic abundance and class consensus all too easily aligned with the distinct resentments and agendas of the Motion Picture Alliance and HUAC.[28]

Throughout the 1950s, studios and producers were wary of scripts that might attract the attention of the professional blacklisters. Bernard Vorhaus, soon to be blacklisted, remembers trying to interest two studios in a social problem story and finding that such topics, unpolitical but "critical of certain conditions," were seen at the time as "suspect." Cy Endfield felt that the box-office success of darker "social" films, including his own TRY AND GET ME! and Billy Wilder's ACE IN THE HOLE (also called THE BIG CARNIVAL, 1951) was damaged by a change of public mood at the onset of the Korean War. The studios were particularly sensitive about American social content in films pitched at foreign markets, while in any case, by the middle of the decade the relative prosperity was throwing up problems that seemed quite distinct from those of the 1930s and the war years.[29]

Another blacklisted writer, Michael Wilson, who wrote the script for SALT OF THE EARTH (1953), contributed several articles to *Hollywood Review* on the impact of the contemporary political mood on screen content. Into the vacuum created by the collapse of the humanist strand in filmmaking, Wilson argued, had come a series of films set in World War II that glorified the services. In 1954 he complained that not only had anything even remotely resembling the Mr. Deeds character (in Frank Capra's MR DEEDS GOES TO TOWN, 1936) vanished from the screen, but also that the "fascist personality" was replacing the romantic hero. Capra's decline in the fifties may indicate the natural eclipse of a career, but it may also reflect the problem of marketing his populist fables in a Cold War era which was sensitive to anything that looked like social criticism. Only the Western retained some ability to criticize, with HIGH NOON (1952) and SILVER LODE (1954) making oblique reference to contemporary politics, and Anthony Mann's THE FAR COUNTRY (1954), presenting serious social reflection in a story from America's mythic past.[30]

Those who cooperated with HUAC and returned to filmmaking after a time away frequently found it difficult to re-engage with familiar genres. The agenda had moved on, as can be seen in the different tones created by Fred Zinnemann, in his film based on James Jones's best selling novel *From Here to Eternity* (1953) and by Edward Dmytryk in THE CAINE MUTINY, a major box-office success of 1954. Dmytryk had served his six-month jail term as one of the Hollywood Ten, but had then "cleared" himself by reappearing as a cooperative witness before HUAC in April 1951, denouncing the Communist party. THE CAINE MUTINY establishes a situation in which the audience supports the naval rebellion, but then the conclusion reverses the whole tone of the story and affirms the principle of obeying authority as a primary obligation. National security undercuts the notion of justified opposition to a tyrant. Another writer-director returning to Hollywood, Robert Rossen, had been a key figure in socially relevant filmmaking since the late thirties, with key credits including his script for Warners' THEY WON'T FORGET (1937) and his direction of ALL THE KINGS MEN (1949). He returned to filmmaking after his 1953 cooperative testimony with the melodrama MAMBO (1955) and the epic ALEXANDER THE GREAT (1956), but only really returned to the social milieu of his pre-HUAC film career with THE HUSTLER, in 1961. As Thomas Schatz argues, the shift in Hollywood themes can be judged by the return of Howard Hawks and John Huston to Warner Bros. as producer-directors in the mid-fifties, nearly a decade after THE BIG SLEEP (1946) and KEY LARGO (1948). Hawks returned to make LAND OF THE PHARAOHS (1955) while Huston, a key figure in the early resistance to HUAC, made MOBY DICK

(1956). Huston's films following The Asphalt Jungle (1950), in which crime is examined in class terms, lack the social and political implications (and associations) of virtually all his early work.[31]

The Case of Elia Kazan in the Early 1950s

Elia Kazan was one of a number of artists who arrived in Hollywood from outside, very often from New York theatrical and/or political circles. An extraordinary template for such a career development had been set by Orson Welles at the beginning of the 1940s, with his unprecedented contract at RKO and renowned opening production (Citizen Kane, 1941). Later in the decade Abraham Polonsky, Jules Dassin, Joseph Losey, Nicholas Ray, and Elia Kazan also embraced a film industry in which the old studio controls were beginning to weaken. Kazan established a reputation at Twentieth Century–Fox in the late forties by successfully directing both prestigious social problem films and semi-documentary productions. As the 1950s dawned there were signs that Kazan had begun to downplay any overt political associations, but there was every indication that he wanted to work on more independent and ambitious film projects.

Kazan's goals for this new phase in his career were artistic more than explicitly political, but he was conscious that his political associations—his two-year Communist party membership in the mid-1930s—made him vulnerable to any renewed Congressional investigation. Like Welles and others of his generation, Kazan was conscious of the ways in which working in Hollywood involved a conflict between notions of film as art and film as entertainment. For example, the conservative editor of the *Hollywood Reporter*, W. R. Wilkerson, had welcomed the Waldorf Statement as a means of purging the industry of a "thirties" generation of well-educated and serious-minded filmmakers who favored "realism" and felt that entertainment was not enough. In a 1951 letter to Jack Warner, Kazan noted that "from the thinly veiled hints to us in some of Billy Wilkerson's editorial remarks, I gather that his opinion is that Streetcar is not the kind of picture he thinks the industry should be making."[32] With Viva Zapata!, his "Mexican horse epic," Kazan was again subject to industry pressure via Darryl F. Zanuck's overall supervision, although the location shooting and his own relationship with John Steinbeck as writer were consistent with the director's striving for greater independence.

The intense sensitivity at this time of Zanuck and his studio to the political meanings that might be attached to films is well demonstrated by the debates on the script of Viva Zapata! in early 1951. At the time there were political threats to two of Kazan's projects. While Zanuck was asking whether this was "the moment to tell the story of a Mexican revolutionary hero?," another figure in Kazan's immediate social and political milieu, Arthur Miller, was withdrawing from a planned project based on events on the New York waterfront, following political interference and cold feet at Columbia Pictures. Kazan seemed to feel that with Viva Zapata! he could handle the studio and make an acceptable compromise, and that the finished film would be broadly consistent with Steinbeck's—and his own—notion of the Mexican revolution. The political pressures of the time clearly led to changes in the script, though the notion of a repudiation of power by the peasant leader can be found in early drafts, and "opposition to communism" remains only a secondary sub-theme in the final version of Viva Zapata![33] In December 1950 Zanuck was worried that audiences (and professional anti-Communists) would associate Zapata with communism: "I hope people don't get the impression that we are advocating

Marlon Brando and Jean Peters in Viva Zapata! *(1952),*
directed by Elia Kazan and produced by Darryl F. Zanuck.

revolt or civil war as the only means to peace." The most noticeable of the later script changes was the enlargement of the role of the professional revolutionary, Fernando, in order to balance the sympathy for a revolutionary leader with an explicitly anti-Stalinist motif. The composer Alex North, whom Kazan had brought to Hollywood to score A Streetcar Named Desire, wrote critically to his friend that Darryl Zanuck seemed to be the "'strong' man in this version," and that the latest script suggested to him a "post Korean War version with all the not too subtle innuendoes."[34]

Politically, as Richard Slotkin suggests, Steinbeck and Kazan defended a populist idea of the people of Morleos against both the "strong man" dictatorships of Diaz and others and the "left-wing" opportunism of Fernando. However one resolves the debate which any historical reconstruction invites, the film does make the Mexican peasantry a key part of the drama, at times invoking Eisenstein, in ways that are unusual in American cinema.[35]

Viva Zapata! was completed but unreleased by the time that Kazan first appeared before the House Un-American Activities Committee, in January 1952. He answered questions on his own Communist party membership, but refused to give the names of others. The film was released in February, and in a letter in the *Saturday Review of Literature* in early April Kazan discussed how the "political tensions of the present time bore down on us—John Steinbeck, and Darryl Zanuck and me—as we thought about and shaped a historical picture." He pointed out the significance of the "Communist mentality" of the Fernando character, and referred to Zapata as "a man of individual conscience," who led his people "out of bondage and did not betray them." A week later Kazan returned to the House Committee, this time naming eight former members of the Group Theatre as Communists. In an unprecedented paid advertisement in the *New York Times* he argued that those in possession of facts concerning "a dangerous and alien conspiracy" had an obligation to let the facts be known "to the public or to the appropriate Government agency." He supplied the committee with a self-serving account of his career and productions, a list that ended with a reference to VIVA ZAPATA! as an "anticommunist picture."[36]

There are those, including historians of the period, who see the film's portrayal of Zapata and his movement as "still subtle, powerful and true." Yet at the time, and in particular in the light of Kazan's testimony, some saw the film as conservative in its implications about the possibility of successful popular revolt. John Howard Lawson, for example, critiqued the film's conservative message as follows: "If power is an absolute source of corruption, if it must be renounced by every honest leader, the people are doomed to eternal submission."

Zanuck was disappointed with the box-office returns for VIVA ZAPATA!, and the episode strengthened his resolve to move towards a policy of "strictly entertainment films." Concerned with foreign revenues, Zanuck stressed the importance of color productions and also the new medium of CinemaScope—both of which were arguably less suitable for social realist subjects. Kazan, in his first film after his testimony, and arguably as part of his "clearance," accepted a studio assignment from Zanuck, going to Germany to make MAN ON A TIGHTROPE (1953), a drama about the efforts of a traveling circus to escape to the "West" from Communist Czechoslovakia. Unsatisfactory to mainstream audiences, to his peers, and to Zanuck, who cut the film, MAN ON A TIGHTROPE represented Kazan's lowest point before the resurgence represented by ON THE WATERFRONT (1954).[37]

The raw material for Kazan's next film was provided by events on the New York waterfront in the early 1950s. The inequities of the hiring and employment methods on the docks, including the notorious "shape up" (in which longshoremen were daily forced to assemble before a union hiring boss, who would only choose a portion of them to work the shift), had been widely documented by journalists and commissions, as had the corrupt practices of unions and employers. After Kazan's project with Arthur Miller fell through, Kazan's wife had urged him to contact screenwriter and novelist Budd Schulberg.

Molly Day Thatcher, daughter of a Wall Street lawyer and granddaughter of the president of Yale, had married Kazan in 1932, and their relationship centrally affected his work and career decisions. It was Molly Kazan who had, by the 1950s, developed a principled anti-Communist critique, and who wrote her husband's notorious *New York Times* advertisement. As Navasky shows, family circumstances impinged on how people reacted to the challenge of HUAC. The lasting relationship between Schulberg and Kazan was also an example of the way the politics of the time reshuffled artistic associations and alliances. Schulberg had himself been in the Communist party in the late thirties and chose to appear before HUAC as one of the first of the new round of friendly witnesses in 1951, having been named before the committee by screenwriter (and former member of the Nineteen) Richard Collins. Schulberg presented himself as a strong "premature anti-Stalinist" (to use a phrase he used later, in talking to Navasky), pointing

Arthur Keegan and Marlon Brando in ON THE WATERFRONT, *Academy Award–winner for Best Picture in 1954.*

to the silence of American Communist Party members in the face of the injustices in the Soviet Union and Communist Eastern Europe.

The script that Schulberg produced with Kazan, based on close relationships with the real rebels on the New York waterfront and the Catholic priests who supported them, was rejected by Twentieth Century–Fox and the other studios before Sam Spiegel agreed to an independent, New York–based production.[38]

Kazan had used the phrase "man of individual conscience" in relation to VIVA ZAPATA!, but the term is also central to ON THE WATERFRONT. For all Schulberg's committed research (including his work with those who testified to the New York State Crime Commission) and the use of real New York locations (in the bitterly cold winter of 1953), the film drifts, under Kazan's direction and with Marlon Brando's central performance, from the sociological to the personal and even existential. In preparing for the film Kazan made it clear that he saw the film not as a documentary but as Terry Molloy's story, a subjective account of a personal journey toward redemption and dignity. The intensity of this perspective, Brando's ability to internalize and represent it, and the effectiveness of Schulberg's overall contextualization of this story, are what distinguish the final film.

While Schulberg has denied the intent to make the film a metaphor for the "naming names" ritual that both he and Kazan had taken part in, Kazan has at various times suggested that his own approach to the material was in part influenced by this traumatic experience. (Steinbeck had referred to "'the Congress thing' having torn him apart").

Kazan at the time refuted the idea that the film represented an apology or defense, suggesting that "if we'd been trying for that, we wouldn't have had Brando's brother killed. Brando gave his evidence because he was angry. How's that an apology for us?" On the other hand, he admitted that "any experience the artist goes through he uses in his work."[39]

Kazan's work with Brando—and for all the actor's "genius" one cannot but give credit to this focused direction, to what later in his career Kazan called his own "transference of emotion" to the character—helped give the film an impact that even those who bitterly opposed its politics were forced to recognize. Here was a film, and a hero, that drew on the thirties traditions of class and the common man while also constructing an interior sense that was suggestive of a new and more uncertain politics. The film was a commercial success and swept the Academy Awards, although there were those who were quick to denounce what they saw as the "informer as social hero" motif for the times. John Howard Lawson wrote of the film's "anti-democratic, anti-labor, anti-human propaganda," and saw it as emblematic of the "influence of McCarthyism on American film production." The British critic and director Lindsay Anderson devoted an article in a British film journal to what he called the unconsciously fascist implications of the film's ending, while Navasky's notion that the Waterfront Crime Commission was an "analog for HUAC" also pegs the film back to this issue.[40]

For all the self-serving behavior of this period—and Kazan has broadly admitted that he essentially named names because the cost of his continued silence, in terms of his career prospects in film, became too great for him—commentators sometimes underplay the gathering force of the liberal discontent with the Communist party and the autonomy of elements of anti-Communist feeling. Kazan's friend Joseph L. Mankiewicz spoke in 1950 of the liberal as an additional victim of McCarthyism, being "slandered, libeled, prosecuted and threatened with extinction."[41] It is common to talk of the turning of film from social to psychological themes in the fifties, and to see Kazan's work as a key example of this trend, although the centrality of psychology in dominant notions of acting in the thirties progressive theaters is clearly as important an influence on Kazan's early career as radical politics. There is little doubt that his testimony and contribution to ON THE WATERFRONT, in some combination, dramatize his newfound Americanism, and his new distance from the immigrant outsider's perspective that had first led him to politics in the thirties.

In EAST OF EDEN (1955) Kazan retreated into history, although James Dean's role and performance had a contemporary social and cultural resonance, suggesting the way postwar economic and social change was producing new icons and identities. BABY DOLL (1956), Kazan's second film collaboration with Tennessee Williams, is arguably more socially pointed than his first. Often seen as a trifling black comedy of sexual jealousy, the fierce reaction of the Catholic Legion of Decency and of Cardinal Spellman indicated that the washed clean, post-testimony Kazan was still provoking anger. Viewing the film now it is certainly possible to see background as foreground, and to make a case that the watching, amused black characters are indicative of the civil rights revolution that was still to come on the film's release. As for A FACE IN THE CROWD (1957), with Kazan reunited with Schulberg, this satire starts with the 1930s common man but then shows his manipulation and destruction in an emerging marketing culture in which celebrity sells toothpaste and right-wing politics alike. There are echoes of 1930s and 1940s progressivism, but no credible vision of change; the people eventually see through the co-opted and corrupted Lonesome Rhodes (Andy Griffith), but there will be others to take his place.[42]

A Fight Back: SALT OF THE EARTH

SALT OF THE EARTH (1954) was a remarkable attempt by blacklisted artists to fight back through the medium of film. While in the short term the film reached only a small general audience, in the longer term it successfully reached specialized audiences—people who knew the film was ahead of its time. Paul Jarrico, Herbert Biberman, and Adrian Scott (the producer of CROSSFIRE) were involved in the formation of the Independent Productions Corporation (IPC), in September 1951. (Jarrico, a leading figure in Hollywood Communist Party circles in the early 1950s, had pleaded the Fifth Amendment before HUAC earlier that year; Biberman and Scott were members of the Hollywood Ten.) Simon M. Lazarus, who had himself taken the Fifth Amendment before HUAC, became the corporation's president, seeing the possibility of good financial returns by tapping into the considerable talents of blacklisted artists.[43]

While the producers at IPC at first considered several projects, they soon focussed their attention on one particular set of events as a suitable subject for their opening production. In the fall of 1950, Local 890 of the International Union of Mine, Mill, and Smelter Workers (Mine-Mill), based in Bayard, New Mexico, went on strike against the Empire Zinc Corporation, a subsidiary of New Jersey Zinc, the largest zinc producer in the United States. A distinctive feature of the strike was the fact that Mexican Americans constituted an overwhelming majority of the strikers; the union was viewed as supportive of their civil rights. Affiliated with the Communist party, Mine-Mill had (in 1950) been one of a series of left-wing unions recently expelled by the CIO. James J. Lorence has documented the process that led IPC to base its film on the protracted strike in New Mexico, and also the unique way in which the members of the Local became part of this creative process. Another feature of the strike which impressed producer Paul Jarrico was the key role played by the women. He may also have seen parallels between the strikers and blacklisted film workers. Jarrico saw the project as a "crime to fit the punishment" (of being blacklisted) and defined the crime as an effort to depict the "dignity of women, labor and a racial minority." The filmmaking process was from the beginning closely monitored by the FBI, "for whom the progress of SALT OF THE EARTH became an obsession."[44]

Writer Michael Wilson had been successful in the early fifties with his shared (Academy Award winning) screenplay for A PLACE IN THE SUN (1951) and his script for FIVE FINGERS (1952), but by 1952 he had been blacklisted. Director Biberman and Jarrico considered but finally disregarded a critical assessment of Wilson's script by John Howard Lawson.[45] The union, Mine-Mill, became the producer, with the members of the Local being widely consulted on the script and production process. Biberman rejected the notion of Anglos in key roles, in this sense making the film a challenge to dominant Hollywood conventions concerning the representation of ethnicity. Five professional actors were used, including Mexican actress Rosaura Revueltas in the key role of Esperanza Quintero, and Will Geer, one of the first actors to take the Fifth and face the blacklist, as the Sheriff. For all the other roles, including Esperanza's husband Ramon, local non-professionals were used.

Shooting began in early 1953, and the production immediately led to political controversy. On 24 February 1953, on the floor of the House of Representatives, Congressman Donald Jackson suggested that the picture was "deliberately designed to inflame racial

Juan Chacon and Rosaura Revueltas in SALT OF THE EARTH *(1954).*

hatreds and to depict the United States of America as the enemy of all coloured people." The film, he continued, would "do incalculable harm" if shown abroad, and so should be suppressed.[46] This declaration produced an enthusiastic response from Howard Hughes on how the industry could and should ensure that the film was never shown. Columnists were quick to point out that this Communist movie plot was taking shape not far from Los Alamos, where the atomic bomb had been tested, and the film's production and subsequent distribution were subject to sustained harassment. Near the end of shooting Revueltas was arrested by the Immigration and Naturalization Service, with the result that the only shots of the film's main character in the climax of the film were close-ups shot in Mexico and smuggled across the border.[47] Roy Brewer refused Lazarus's request for a studio crew, and IATSE pressure made it difficult for the company to obtain a good theater for the New York premiere. The film played in only thirteen movie theaters out of the nation's 13,000 before its last first-run theatrical showing in September 1954.

The script contains some rather undigested chunks of political rhetoric ("This instalment plan, it's the curse of the working man") and Juan Chacon, as Ramon, cannot quite convey the increasing importance of the domestic struggle in the Quintero household to the resolution of the general conflict over class and ethnicity. The script offers an unfolding dialectic during the extended strike, as the women, and particularly Esperanza, overcome setbacks and gain in confidence and social power. Revueltas underplays a key line to her screen husband: "I'm going to bed now. Sleep where you please, but not with me." Striking images are the exception, but include the first view of the women as a collective force, gathered on a hilltop like "Indians" in a John Ford Western, and the recurring and defiant circles of the picketing miners and their wives. There is also a pointed intercutting between Ramon and Esperanza, with the husband being beaten by the police and the wife in labor. The film provides a moving and stirring celebration of the ideals of its creators, and the issues (from sanitation and hot running water to Mexican identity, sexual politics, and class solidarity) are remarkable for their time.

The emphasis on class in SALT OF THE EARTH is perhaps most forced, while the involvement of the Anglo organizer is underplayed, but it was certainly unfair to argue, as Pauline Kael did in her contemporary review, that the film was "as clear a piece of Communist propaganda as we have had in many years." The American Legion echoed this view, attacking the film in its newsletter as one of the most "vicious propaganda films ever distributed in the United States," seeing it as designed for a "hate America" campaign in Latin America.[48] The film, with its rousing score by blacklisted composer Sol Kaplan, reads now as more of a timeless moral fable than a semi-documentary. The Esperanza role is perhaps over-reverent and stylized, but the film does record an otherwise unreported area of postwar life, untouched by the growth of a consumer society. Its energy, commitment, and sensitivity to ethnic, class, and feminist issues, which were either marginalized or below the level of consciousness in 1950s America, make it a crucial icon of the blacklist era.

Conclusion

By the mid 1950s the political climate was beginning to moderate, and the cycles of anti-Communist and Korean war films were in decline.[49] The blacklist as an institution also began to crumble in the late 1950s, with Dalton Trumbo's efforts in particular contributing to its demise. Trumbo's Academy Award for THE BRAVE ONE in 1957, under the assumed name Robert Rich, helped demonstrate the absurdity of the blacklist, given the vibrant black market in scripts, many of them made into films by King Bros. and released through United Artists, which was never a signatory to the blacklist. Yet lives were ruined and changed forever, and for some, such as Abraham Polonsky, the effects of the blacklist carried on into the late 1960s. Script credits were even more tardily adjusted; it took thirty years or more for Michael Wilson and Carl Foreman to receive proper public credit for their script for THE BRIDGE ON THE RIVER KWAI (1957).

The blacklist was part of an intense period of history in which American national identity was adapted for a new era of American Cold War leadership, and in which, in Arthur Miller's phrase, the oxygen "went out of the air" for certain ideas. The languages of class, populism, and social criticism became suddenly suspect, and all sorts of artists decided, like the actress Judy Holliday before the McCarran (Internal Security) Sub-Committee in 1952, to no longer say "Yes" to anything "except cancer, polio, and cerebral palsy."[50] For a particular 1930s generation of ambitious and talented artists, liberals or radicals, the dream had been one of greater artistic autonomy in terms of both the process and content of filmmaking. This collective dream was badly weakened by the events of the early 1950s.

Other factors changed the film agenda, including the decline of the "B" picture, the growing importance of the foreign market, and the industry's shift to forms and spectacles designed to repulse the threat of television. The language of cultural individualism was also becoming as relevant as any class agenda to many in the audience, especially as economic growth and suburban spread proceeded and the reconstituted film industry stumbled towards niche marketing. Yet the blacklist process ruined lives, silenced voices, and tarnished many survivors, and it contributed to the decline of a democratic and cosmopolitan strain in American popular culture. Depression memories dimmed, class consensus replaced class conflict, and authority and domesticity became new watchwords. Even Orson Welles, perhaps the most shining of Popular Front stars, and whose independent leftism left him unscathed by HUAC, if not by the FBI, failed to find an accommodation with the industry.[51] His TOUCH OF EVIL (1958), with its dark, morally complex perspective on the ordinary corruptions of public life, now seems to echo some of the forms and concerns that the blacklist helped to marginalize from the new and affirmative consensus in American cinema and life.

4

Censorship and Self-Regulation

Censorship of the American film industry in the 1950s can best be regarded as a complex series of negotiations among several parties. The Production Code Administration (PCA), the film industry's self-censorship group, worked with studios and producers to ensure that Hollywood films met consistent moral standards. The PCA had been established in 1934 in order to minimize the dangers of outside censorship. The Catholic Church's Legion of Decency, often working in concert with the PCA, was an important force for conservative morality on screen. Government was involved at several levels, via state and local censorship boards, judicial oversight, and pressures from the U.S. Congress. The film studios responded to all of these conflicting groups, as well as to a rapidly changing audience.

The Production Code

The Motion Picture Production Code was written in 1929 by the Jesuit priest Daniel J. Lord and the publisher Martin J. Quigley (owner of film industry trade papers, and a Catholic). This was a code regulating the moral content of feature films, designed so that Hollywood could police itself and thus avoid or minimize outside censorship. It was adopted by the Motion Picture Producers and Distributors Association (MPPDA), the film industry trade association, in 1930. The Code begins with the following "General Principles":

1. No picture shall be produced which will lower the moral standards of those who see it. Hence the sympathy of the audience shall never be thrown to the side of crime, wrongdoing, evil, or sin.
2. Correct standards of life, subject only to the requirements of drama and entertainment, shall be presented.
3. Law—divine, natural or human—shall not be ridiculed, nor shall sympathy be created for its violation.[1]

The Code then lists a number of "Particular Applications," including treatment of crime, brutality, sex, vulgarity, obscenity, costumes, religion, etc. The Code also provides a few pages of explanation for the general principles and the applications.

The Code was advisory at first, but quickly became more obligatory thanks to outside pressures plus corrective actions taken by MPPDA Chairman Will H. Hays. In 1934 the Production Code Administration was formed as a branch of the MPPDA. The major and minor distributors belonging to the trade association agreed to submit scripts and finished films to the PCA. No film from these distributors was to be released without a "PCA Seal of Approval." The first head of the PCA was Joseph Breen, one of Hays's assistants. This choice embodied the intricate politics that was always a part of the PCA, because Breen, a Catholic layman, had been orchestrating Catholic pressure on the MPPDA while working for Hays.

PCA employee Albert Van Schmus, speaking long after the PCA's demise, had two explanations for the Catholic Church's influence on a supposedly independent and nonsectarian organization. First, Catholics were concentrated in the big cities that were the film industry's crucial audience. Second, Catholics were far more organized and therefore more capable of pressuring the film industry than the numerically superior Protestants, who were split into many denominations.[2] The Council of Churches of Christ (an umbrella group of Protestant churches), was occasionally consulted by production companies and/or the PCA when Protestantism was portrayed on screen. For example, the Los Angeles office of the Council was asked for comments on the church scene in HIGH NOON. However, the Protestant churches of the United States had no film industry lobbying organization that could compare to the Legion of Decency.

Breen, Jack Vizzard, and other Catholics involved in the self-censorship process did try to establish a broad, ecumenical tone for the PCA in the 1950s. This philosophy is nicely outlined in correspondence between Martin Quigley (still an unofficial advisor to the PCA in the 1950s) and historian/columnist Arthur Schlesinger Jr. in 1954. Schlesinger had written a piece in the then-liberal *New York Post* attacking the Production Code. Quigley replied that the principles of the Production Code "derive wholly from the Ten Commandments, the basic moral charter of all of the religions of the Judean-Christian civilization."[3] When Schlesinger objected to the "niggling detail" of the Production Code, not implied, in his opinion, by the Ten Commandments, Quigley pointed to the general principles of the Code and not the specific details as central.[4] Schlesinger, somewhat mollified, replied "I do not disagree with many of the general rules," but continued to question their narrow application.[5]

There has been some debate about whether the Production Code had a specifically Catholic orientation. Jack Vizzard, writing about Martin J. Quigley's beliefs, described what he called the Catholic Church's "jaundice about human nature": Man lives under "the blight of Original Sin," in a "state of exile." Therefore, humanity must be protected not only from obvious immorality, but from too much enjoyment of "the enticements of the world."[6] Historian Stephen Vaughn finds a similar viewpoint in Father Daniel J. Lord's "traditional Catholic interpretation of postlapsarian man."[7] When applied to the photographic medium of film, this attitude becomes a fear of the physical and of the body. Many PCA rules, from the ban on indecent dancing to the restrictions on costuming, were designed to limit the appeal of the physical world. This policy does link up with Catholic doctrine, but it also matches the beliefs of many Protestant denominations. It is consistent with the Jewish religion as well (though the reasons for distrusting the body may differ between Judaism and Christianity)—an important point, for a majority of the studio bosses (but not Zanuck, Skouras, or Hughes) and many of the creative personnel were Jewish. The Catholic influence on the PCA had more to do with the politics of decision-making than with the Code itself.

Joseph Breen had headed the Production Code Administration since the 1930s. He felt that the PCA had broad powers to ensure the morality of Hollywood films, and he refused to limit himself to the written provisions of the Code. He once told a new staff member not to waste time reading over the written Code, explaining "Just you listen to *me. I* am the Code!" Jack Vizzard explained that Breen was technically correct, since at least one of the Code's General Principles—the section on "divine, natural and human" law—was so broad as to include almost anything.[8] Nevertheless, Breen and his staff frequently had to negotiate with the Hollywood studios, which were at least indirectly their employers. For those films that had Code problems, the PCA would work with the producers (usually at script stage, occasionally after filming) to suggest solutions. The producers would accept some changes, contest others, and eventually agreement would be reached. The PCA and its parent organization, the MPAA (successor organization to the MPPDA), were financed by the studios, so the PCA's authority (indeed, its very existence) was dependent on the companies it was censoring/regulating. On the other hand, the studios needed PCA approval to show various sectors of the public—the government, the churches, the press, the exhibitors, and the paying customers—that Hollywood films were following accepted standards of morality and good taste. Both sides had considerable incentive to make the system work. The PCA could refuse a Seal of Approval to a particular film if negotiations with the producer and distributor were unsuccessful, but this very rarely happened.

During the early 1950s, the film industry's PCA-enforced morality gradually came into conflict with audience interests and industry conditions. For one thing, Americans were more worldly after the shocks and dislocations of World War II, with millions of men stationed abroad and millions of women in the workplace. There was also a great emphasis on sexuality in 1950s America, sexuality as both the cause and the solution of problems. The Kinsey reports (published in 1947 and 1952) and the popularization of psychoanalysis may have contributed to this emphasis. Also, the film industry's internal problems provided a reason for filmmakers to challenge the status quo. With the number of North American movie spectators consistently dropping, studios and independent producers were under pressure to find new, more sensational subjects and thus revive audience interest. They pushed against the restraints of the Production Code in a variety of ways: with more revealing costumes for women (THE FRENCH LINE, 1954); franker attitudes toward adultery (FROM HERE TO ETERNITY, 1953); and well-made treatments of previously forbidden subjects (THE MAN WITH THE GOLDEN ARM, about drug addiction, 1955; TEA AND SYMPATHY, about the fear of homosexuality, 1956).

THE MOON IS BLUE (directed by Otto Preminger for United Artists, 1953) provided an early test of how the PCA would react to changing attitudes about sexuality. This was the adaptation of a very popular stage play that featured no revealing costumes or immoral behavior but a great deal of dialogue about sex. A young woman named Patty O'Neill (Maggie McNamara) meets architect Don Gresham (William Holden) on top of the Empire State Building and goes home with him for drinks and dinner. Joined at times by Holden's upstairs neighbors, aging playboy David Slater (David Niven) and his daughter Cynthia (Dawn Addams), they have a lively conversation about seduction, virginity, and marriage. For example, when Patty asks what's bad about the phrase "professional virgin," Don answers "People who advertise are anxious to sell something." After many misadventures, Patty angrily leaves in the early morning, but Don finds her the next day (again on top of the Empire State Building), and proposes.

The PCA reviewed the play script, then the film script, then the finished film, and

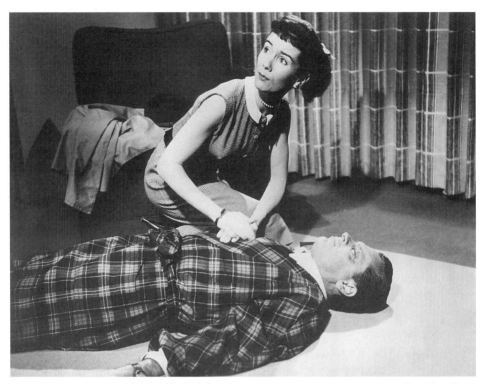

Maggie McNamara and William Holden in The Moon Is Blue *(1953), produced and directed by Otto Preminger.*

consistently found The Moon Is Blue unacceptable. A 10 April letter from Breen to Preminger summarized the PCA's attitude as follows: "The picture contains an unacceptably light attitude towards seduction, illicit sex, chastity and virginity."[9] Preminger and United Artists decided to release the film without a seal, with United Artists temporarily dropping out of the MPAA to avoid paying a fine. The film's reception was interestingly mixed. Many reviewers endorsed it, with Bosley Crowther of the *New York Times* exclaiming, "The theme of this confection is as moral as a Sunday school book. It is that virtue triumphs. The good little girl gets the man."[10] On the other hand, *Showmen's Trade Review* said that it was "a shock even for the most sophisticated" to hear words like "virgin" and "seduce" in a motion picture.[11] The Legion of Decency condemned the film, but this action was primarily aimed at supporting the PCA.[12] Three state censorship boards banned The Moon Is Blue, but four approved it.

Largely because of the various censorship controversies, The Moon Is Blue became a big hit. Film historian Tino Balio reports that it "was shut out of many theaters, but where it did play it broke box-office records."[13] United Artists and Preminger had won their gamble of releasing a film without a Code Seal. This suggested that the Production Code, written in 1929, was no longer a good fit with audience expectations and needs in the 1950s. The PCA responded by being more flexible, and eventually by revising the Code.

During the early 1950s, Joseph Breen gradually gave up his responsibilities to the PCA's deputy director, Geoffrey Shurlock. Shurlock, an Englishman and a Protestant, was less dogmatic and less confrontational than Breen. Albert Van Schmus describes Shurlock as an intellectual who "was responsible for innovations over the years that would permit the creative people" to get more of their ideas across.[14] Shurlock was also a pragmatist who saw his job as protecting the film industry from outside criticism and intervention. Breen understood this as well, but Breen had his own moral and ideological agenda. The transition to Shurlock's point of view was already in process when the MPAA announced Breen's retirement on 15 October 1954. Shurlock took over as director, with Jack Vizzard as his deputy (thus continuing the Catholic influence in PCA management).

One example of the PCA's new pragmatism under Shurlock was the three-year effort to adapt TEA AND SYMPATHY for the screen. This play by Robert Anderson, directed on Broadway by Elia Kazan, was a huge hit in the fall of 1953. Set in a New England prep school, it presents the story of Tom, an eighteen-year-old student, who is ridiculed by his peers for shunning team sports, liking folk music, and playing the female lead in the school play. He is comforted and defended by Laura, the wife of his housemaster Bill. After Tom is thoroughly humiliated and his expulsion seems imminent, Laura sleeps with him just once to show he is heterosexual and to give him confidence. Laura also comes to understand a problem with her own husband—he has an unacted-upon attrac-

TEA AND SYMPATHY (1956) *portrays the troubled marriage of Bill (Leif Ericson) and Laura Reynolds (Deborah Kerr).*

tion to boys and therefore spends all his time with the students (and avoiding her). This insight also suggests that Tom is persecuted because his odd behavior makes the prep school students and masters uncomfortable about themselves.

Martin Quigley wrote to Joseph Breen (still director of the PCA in 1953) saying that TEA AND SYMPATHY might be a "major problem." Sex perversion, the term used for homosexuality in the Production Code, could not be presented or implied in a motion picture. The "solution" to the drama, Laura's seduction of Tom, was equally objectionable, for the Code insisted that adultery must be shown as morally wrong. Quigley's letter commented that he did not see a way to change this theme of adultery as solution.[15] Yet a third troubling theme was Laura's insight that many men, including those who persecute homosexuals, may have homosexual desires.

Breen sent two of his assistants, Shurlock and Vizzard, to New York to see the play. They agreed that TEA AND SYMPATHY could not be adapted for film maintaining either the homosexual theme or the concluding adultery. Shurlock and Vizzard then communicated their decision to a long list of Hollywood figures who expressed interest in the play: Samuel Goldwyn, Elia Kazan, and playwright Robert Anderson (this group was planning an independent production); Dore Schary, William McKenna, and Robert Vogel of MGM; Jack Warner of Warner Bros.; Frank McCarthy and Julian Blaustein of Fox; Luigi Luraschi of Paramount; and several others. Harry Cohn of Columbia had been the first to inquire about the play— he sent the PCA a synopsis before Shurlock and Vizzard's New York trip.[16] The PCA told all these executives and filmmakers that TEA AND SYMPATHY had serious Code problems and that they could not see a solution. However, Vizzard's memo on the 29 October 1953 meeting with Schary, McKenna, and Vogel shows interest in a change proposed by Schary: suppose that Tom proves his manhood by defending Laura from her husband rather than sleeping with her? Schary's alteration would make Tom unconventional but still reassuringly masculine.[17] Shurlock and Vizzard remained worried about homosexuality and adultery.

In 1955 Shurlock, as director of the PCA, was under pressure to resolve the dispute over TEA AND SYMPATHY. Playwright Robert Anderson, now working with Schary, turned in a treatment for the film adaptation on 13 January 1955. Shurlock responded to Schary on 25 March that Anderson's treatment was still in violation, because of the two original problems. (The delay itself suggests a special case; the PCA usually responded in a few days.)[18] Schary appealed to MPAA President Eric Johnston and scheduled a formal appeal to the MPAA Board of Directors. Though Shurlock told Johnston he saw "no solution," he resumed negotiations with Schary. Meanwhile, in mid-1955 the independently distributed British film I AM A CAMERA was released without a Code seal, and Otto Preminger and United Artists had announced their plan to release THE MAN WITH THE GOLDEN ARM (objectionable because of its portrayal of drug addiction) without a seal. Historian Jerold Simmons speculates that because Shurlock was threatened by an erosion of PCA authority, he compromised with Schary and approved TEA AND SYMPATHY in August 1955.[19] The word "queer," used several times in the play, had disappeared from the film script, and Laura's recognition of her husband's latent homosexuality was absent. Also, the script adds a "voice for morality" (a favorite PCA device) when an older Tom returns to school and finds Laura's letter saying their brief sexual encounter was wrong. However, the suspicion of Tom's homosexuality remains vital to the script, and Laura does still begin to seduce Tom (the cut after one kiss leaves no doubt about what will happen).

Though the PCA was satisfied, the Legion of Decency was not. In August 1956 the National Office of the Legion reviewed a finished print of TEA AND SYMPATHY and found

TEA AND SYMPATHY: the famous kiss between Deborah Kerr and John Kerr. This kiss "proves" that the prep school boy played by John Kerr is heterosexual.

it still unacceptable. Father Thomas Little of the National Office wanted a stronger letter from Laura showing that adultery was wrong. Deborah Kerr, who played Laura, was called back by MGM to record a new version of the letter (spoken in voiceover). Father Little was still unhappy, but because of the mixed reactions of Bishop William A. Scully (head of a committee that supervised the Legion) and a special panel of reviewers, the Legion did not condemn the film.[20] After three years of negotiations, TEA AND SYMPATHY was ready for release.

On 11 December 1956 the MPAA announced a revision of the Production Code. Such controversial matters as abortion, childbirth, and drug addiction, all formerly prohibited, could now be presented (with important restrictions) in Hollywood movies. Miscegenation, defined as a "sex relationship between the white and black races," was prohibited in the 1929 Code but not even mentioned in the new Code. The Code language on brutality had been beefed up—it now said "Excessive and inhumane acts of cruelty and brutality shall not be presented. This includes all detailed and protracted presentation of physical violence, torture and abuse." A brief section on cruelty to animals was included in the Code proper—it was based on a special resolution of the

MPAA Board of Directors from 1940. One portion of the Code that did not change was the prohibition of "sex perversion" (homosexuality).

Response to this fairly modest revision of the Production Code was mostly positive, with Samuel Goldwyn seeing "a considerable step in the right direction," whereas Martin Quigley stressed a continuity with the previous Code.[21] Thomas Pryor of the *New York Times* correctly saw that interpretation, rather than Code language, was crucial: "It is doubtful that the alterations in the Code will bring about any noticeable change in the pattern of movie entertainment, for interpretation of the old Code, adopted in 1930, has become more and more liberal in recent years."[22]

In 1959, the Code was still around, but interpretation was increasingly loose. Jack Hamilton of *Look* summarized the situation as follows: "Many producers now evade, while claiming to uphold, the Code's musty restrictions. The good-behavior rule book is allowed to exist for only one reason: It serves as a buffer against outside, and more troublesome, censorship." To support his point, Hamilton mentions such films as SOME LIKE IT HOT (1959, with a scantily clothed Marilyn Monroe and jokes about sex and gender) and ANATOMY OF A MURDER (1959, a courtroom drama including very specific discussion of rape). Shurlock explained to Hamilton that any subject except homosexuality could be presented in PCA-approved films, as long as a "moral conflict" provided the "proper frame of reference."[23] TEA AND SYMPATHY, a film passed by Shurlock, suggests that even this last forbidden area could be presented in acceptable ways in a Hollywood film.

Screenwriter James Poe proposed to Hamilton that the "national preoccupation with sex" meant that the MPAA should consider some kind of a classification system separating films for children and films for adults.[24] The rating system idea had come up occasionally in the mid-1950s,[25] but it was a hot topic in 1959. The PCA and the film industry in general felt squeezed by conflicting demands: (1) Audiences wanted to see more "adult" treatments of sexuality; and (2) religious and civic groups were increasingly upset by lax enforcement of the Production Code. Classification of movies as appropriate for certain age groups offered a possible solution to this dilemma, since it would create opportunities for adult viewing while also protecting young moviegoers. Ratings by age group were already in effect in Great Britain, France, and other countries, and both the Legion of Decency and the "Green Sheet" (a periodical sponsored by the MPAA, intended primarily for parents) were publishing advisory ratings in the United States. However, many film industry people, especially exhibitors, were strongly opposed to any system of classification. Though they complained about classification as censorship, their "motivating reasoning," said a *Variety* editorial, was clearly "loss of revenue."[26] How could a struggling industry possibly benefit from restricting its customer base? Why should the film industry turn away teenagers, who were more likely than their parents to go out to a movie? The MPAA studied a classification system in the fall of 1959,[27] but took no action on this controversial notion for several years.

The Legion of Decency

The Catholic Legion of Decency was the most successful pressure group in the history of American cinema. Founded in 1934, the Legion was designed both to influence the newly formed Production Code Administration and to directly pressure the film companies. Originally, the Legion was a campaign in which millions of Catholics signed pledge cards agreeing not to attend immoral movies. Pledges were administered in church on a yearly basis. This was supplemented in 1936 by a National Legion of Decency office in New York, which published a biweekly ratings sheet on films in release. Films were rated (primarily by a group of women volunteers) according to the following categories:

A-I   Morally Unobjectionable for General Patronage
A-II   Morally Unobjectionable for Adults
B   Morally Objectionable in Part for All
C   Condemned

The "A-II" category was actually something like the MPAA's later "PG" or "PG-13" ratings—guidance from parents and others was encouraged, but no specific age limit was given.

The majority of studio films were sent to the Legion office in New York for preview, and many films were re-cut to meet Legion objections. In those few cases when the Legion's objections were not resolved, filmmakers risked not only a C rating but also denunciations from the pulpit, organized picketing and boycotts, and efforts to dissuade theaters from booking a film. The Catholic Church was not always unanimous in its view of an individual film, but certainly Hollywood took its threat of organized action seriously. The church also offered consultants to smooth out any script problems for films dealing with Catholic subject matter. Most commonly, the script consultant was Father John Devlin, head of the Los Angeles Legion of Decency. Father Devlin was involved, for example, in the plot problem posed by I CONFESS (directed by Alfred Hitchcock, 1953), where a priest played by Montgomery Clift cannot reveal a murderer's confession. Father Devlin was not paid for his consulting work, but the film companies generally made a donation to his Los Angeles parish.[28]

The close collaboration between the Legion of Decency and the PCA, established in the 1930s, continued into the 1950s. This was partly a matter of history and demographics, but it also stemmed from some shrewd political decisions. The Catholic Church consistently supported the authority of the PCA and joined the MPAA in opposing federal government censorship. It was willing to go along with even questionable PCA objections to specific films. In return, the Legion and the church expected access and influence. Martin Quigley frequently served as intermediary between the Legion and the PCA; he was in constant contact with the administrators of the National Legion of Decency, and he often visited and corresponded with Breen, Vizzard, and other PCA staffers.[29] Jack Vizzard became the PCA's "specialist" in Catholic Church relations. For example, he was sent to St. Louis to consult with Archbishop Joseph Ritter about the opening of THE FRENCH LINE (1954), a Howard Hughes film which had been denied a PCA seal; and he was location consultant on HEAVEN KNOWS, MR. ALLISON (directed by John Huston, 1957), a film about a nun and a marine corporal marooned on a desert island.[30]

The influence of the Legion of Decency gradually declined in the 1950s when it became clear that Legion objections might not hurt a film at the box office. When "The Miracle," part of the three-part film WAYS OF LOVE (1950), was declared blasphemous by the Legion and the Catholic hierarchy, the ensuing publicity almost certainly improved the box-office prospects of this foreign language film. THE FRENCH LINE was also helped, if anything, by the condemnations of the Catholic Church, as Father Little admitted in his annual report.[31]

However, the Legion did have a negative impact on the release of BABY DOLL, a 1956 film produced and directed by Elia Kazan based on a script by Tennessee Williams. The film describes a bizarre triangular relationship between middle-aged Archie Lee Meighan (Karl Malden), who owns a cotton gin in the deep South, his nineteen-year-old bride, Baby Doll (Carroll Baker), and the handsome immigrant Silva Vacarro (Eli Wallach), who owns another local cotton gin. Archie Lee has agreed not to consummate the marriage until Baby Doll's twentieth birthday; he is relishing and Baby Doll is dreading the imminence of that date. Meanwhile, Silva is hanging around Archie Lee's ruin of a house, and Baby Doll seems far more interested in him than in her husband. One suggestive scene presents Silva sleeping in Baby Doll's crib upstairs; this implies a seduction, although Kazan joked that the cramped space made lovemaking impossible.[32] Note that a beautiful nineteen-year-old blonde sleeping in a crib is already kinky; Baby Doll also sucks her thumb. At any rate, Silva seems less interested in Baby Doll than in confirming that Archie Lee is the arsonist who burned down his (Silva's) cotton gin. At the end of the film Archie Lee is taken away to jail and Silva abandons Baby Doll.

In 1952, the PCA strongly objected to an early script draft of BABY DOLL, complaining about a "low and sordid tone" and an unacceptable treatment of adultery.[33] However, by 1956 the Shurlock-led PCA was more accommodating; it accepted the film's tone and negotiated with Kazan on a number of specific points. Catholic figures including Martin Quigley were furious at what they perceived as major violations of the Production Code.[34]

The Legion of Decency condemned BABY DOLL and the Catholic Church mounted a strong campaign against the film. Cardinal Francis Spellman of New York spoke out against it from the pulpit of St. Patrick's Cathedral. He denounced the film as "evil in concept" and "certain to exert an immoral and corrupting influence on those who see it," adding that it was "astonishing and deplorable" that such a film had been passed by the PCA. Cardinal Spellman hadn't seen the picture; his speech mentions that it had been

Child-woman Carroll Baker in her crib in BABY DOLL *(1956).*

"responsibly judged."[35] Other members of the Catholic hierarchy called for a boycott of the film. Theater owners were pressured not to show BABY DOLL, and in some cases a six-month boycott was threatened for theaters that exhibited the film.[36] Despite some criticisms of the anti–BABY DOLL campaign, notably from Dean James A. Pike of the Episcopal Cathedral of St. John the Divine in New York, Catholic groups did succeed in limiting the release of this film. According to Kazan, press releases trumpeting its box-office success were false. Kazan admits in his autobiography that "the cardinal's attack hurt us," and that BABY DOLL "never made a profit." (At least one observer, writer Gregory Black, makes the intriguing suggestion that BABY DOLL lost money because it was a mediocre film.)[37]

In the late 1950s the Legion began to change from a stern moral judge of Hollywood entertainment to a more flexible and appreciative critic of the industry. This was a response to liberalization within the Catholic Church as well as to the changing tastes and expectations of American audiences. In 1957, the Legion shifted its categories: "A-II" became "Acceptable for Adults and Adolescents" and a new "A-III" category, "Acceptable for Adults," was added. The existence of the new category allowed the Legion to approve films with "truly adult subject matter."[38] This reduced the number of films rated "B" (objectionable though not condemned), and therefore smoothed relations between the Legion, the studios, and the film audience. The new category allowed the Legion to approve such films as PEYTON PLACE (1957), which had been carefully crafted by Twentieth Century–Fox to meet PCA and Legion guidelines while retaining the adult appeal of Grace Metalious's novel.

Government Censorship

Seven state censorship boards and several dozen local boards were operating in the early 1950s with the specific task of regulating movie content.[39] Major population centers such as New York State and the city of Chicago were included. The institutional setup of these boards varied greatly. In New York, the censorship authority was the Motion Picture Division, supervised by the State Board of Regents, an educational oversight group. In Maryland, the State Board of Motion Picture Censors was appointed directly by the governor. In Chicago, the censorship mechanism included both the Film Review Section (part of the Police Department) and a Motion Picture Appeal Board (an independent office within city government).[40] The state censorship boards were actually supported by fees paid by film producers. State and local censors were empowered to require cuts, or to ban a film outright. In Maryland, the films banned were generally pictures from small distributors not part of the MPAA that featured "sensational treatment of sex and narcotics"—for example, GIRLS' CLUB, FRENCH WHITE CARGO, WILD WEED, and SINS OF THE FATHERS.[41] However, the United Artists film THE WELL (1951) was never released in Baltimore because the Maryland Board requested fifteen cuts, effectively destroying the film's theme of racial conflict in a small town. Major Hollywood films which were released with important cuts included A PLACE IN THE SUN (Paramount, directed by George Stevens, 1951) and A STREETCAR NAMED DESIRE (1951). In STREETCAR, the Maryland board cut most of the crucial scene between Blanche and Stanley where rape is implied.[42]

The legal standing of state and local censorship boards was greatly limited by a landmark Supreme Court decision, *Burstyn vs. Wilson* (1952), usually known as "the *Miracle* decision." This case involves a forty-minute Italian film titled "The Miracle," directed by Roberto Rossellini, from a story idea by Federico Fellini, and starring Anna Magnani. This medium-length film was joined to two others of similar length ("A Day in the Country" by Jean Renoir and "Jofroi" by Marcel Pagnol) and presented in the United States in 1950 under the title WAYS OF LOVE.[43] The distributor was Joseph Burstyn, a small independent specializing in foreign films. "The Miracle" told the story of a simple (perhaps feeble-minded) peasant woman, played by Anna Magnani, who believes she has been impregnated by Saint Joseph. It takes a half-ironic, half-believing attitude to the story, and treats the main character with great sympathy. This kind of ambiguous art film would normally have reached a very small American audience. However, after attacks by Catholic literalists, "The Miracle" became a battleground for pro-censorship and anti-censorship forces, and the unexpected notoriety helped its box-office performance.

WAYS OF LOVE was approved by the Motion Picture Division of the New York State Board of Regents and opened at the Paris Theater in midtown Manhattan. Then "The Miracle," one segment of the film, was banned from theaters in New York City by Edward McCaffrey, Commissioner of Licenses for the city, who found the Rossellini segment to be "a blasphemous affront to a great many of our fellow citizens."[44] At this point the Legion of Decency, New York's Cardinal Spellman, and other Catholic authorities launched attacks on the film. McCaffrey's ban was overturned in court, and WAYS OF LOVE (including "The Miracle") began a very profitable run in Manhattan. Then the New York State Board of Regents overruled its own Motion Picture Division, revoking the license for WAYS OF LOVE. Per the *New York Times*, the Regents' report "declared that the mockery or profaning of religious beliefs sacred to any portion of the public is abhorrent to the laws of the state."[45]

The right of the Regents to ban the film was upheld by the New York State Appeals Court, but then overturned by the United States Supreme Court. The Court based its unanimous decision on the simple but powerful principle that "expression by means of motion pictures is included within the free speech and free press guaranty of the First and Fourteenth Amendments."[46] Movies had since the *Mutual* case of 1915 been considered as a "business pure and simple" and not as "part of the press of the country or as organs of public opinion."[47] The opinion in the *Miracle* case, written by Justice Tom C. Clark, carefully stated that First Amendment protection did not mean "absolute freedom to exhibit every motion picture of every kind at all times and places." However, the opinion did find that "sacrilegious" was not an adequate standard for censorship, and that government should not be called on "to suppress real or imagined attacks upon a particular religious doctrine, whether they appear in publications, speeches, or motion pictures."[48]

The principle that motion pictures were a protected form of speech meant that all state and local censorship was open to question. Statutes governing censorship had to make a compelling case for an exception to First Amendment protection. Over the next several years, both the U.S. Supreme Court and a variety of state courts used the *Miracle* decision to limit the appropriate grounds for film censorship. The Supreme Court invalidated criteria such as "immoral" or "would tend to corrupt morals" (*LA RONDE* case, New York, 1952; reversed by the Supreme Court, 1954); "other than moral, educational, amusing or harmless" (*M* case, Ohio, 1953; reversed by the Supreme Court, 1954); "of such character to be prejudicial to the best interests of the people of said City" (*PINKY* case, Marshall, Texas, 1952; reversed by the Supreme Court, 1952); and "cruel. obscene, indecent, or immoral, or such as tend to debase or corrupt morals" (*THE MOON IS BLUE* case, Kansas, 1955; reversed by the Supreme Court, 1955).[49] State courts in Ohio (*RKO v. Dept. of Education,* 1954) and Massachusetts (*Brattle Films v. Commissioner of Public Safety,* 1955) ruled that licensing of motion pictures was illegal because "prior censorship itself violated the First Amendment."[50] However, in 1961 the U.S. Supreme Court in *Times Film v. Chicago* did affirm, by a 5–4 vote, that prior censorship of motion pictures was in some circumstances justified. The majority opinion by Justice Clark specifically mentioned obscenity as a possible ground for limiting free speech.[51] State and local censorship was not dead, but it had been severely limited in scope. According to the MPAA, by 1965 only four state and ten local boards were actively involved in the censoring of motion pictures.[52]

At the same time that the Supreme Court was dramatically curtailing the grounds for film censorship, the legislative and executive branches of the federal government were pressuring Hollywood in a variety of ways in order to control film content. The most sustained pressure was brought by the HUAC hearings on communism, which are usually described as attacks on individuals but which had a chilling effect on film content as well (see Chapter 3). However, the federal government also tried to influence and control film content in other ways. In 1950 Senator Edwin C. Johnson (Democrat of Colorado), chairman of the Interstate Commerce Committee, threatened Hollywood with a bill that would "require Government licensing of all actors, actresses, producers and films and would deny or revoke licenses in cases of immoral behavior or content."[53] Johnson's anger was evidently fueled by the love affair between Ingrid Bergman and Roberto Rossellini (Bergman was married to Dr. Peter Lindstrom at the time), and the outrageous advertising campaign for the Bergman-Rossellini film STROMBOLI (U.S. release 1950) which exploited that affair. It should come as no surprise, given the many scandals associated with Howard Hughes, that STROMBOLI was distributed by Hughes's RKO. Johnson's proposed bill, with its sweeping regulation of off-screen as well as on-screen conduct, was probably never intended as serious legislation. It was, instead, a way of pressuring Hollywood toward stricter self-regulation. Johnson called off his investigation when film industry leaders announced that they would amend the MPAA Advertising Code to prohibit "exploitation of misconduct" of actors and other film personalities.[54] The MPAA board of directors approved such an amendment on 21 June 1950.

Throughout the 1950s, both the government and the press were very concerned about the distribution of American films abroad: Did they contribute to a positive or negative image of America? This was an urgent question because of the Cold War struggle for world dominance. Though the United States did not routinely censor or control the content of exported films, there were some federal government attempts to influence film exports. In 1953, Cecil B. DeMille became a special consultant to the Motion Picture Service (MPS), a branch of the United States Information Service (USIS). The MPS's main activity was producing and distributing documentary films that would be shown in USIS posts in 87 countries, but it also recommended films for showing in Eastern Europe and "regulated American participation in film festivals abroad."[55] C. D. Jackson, who was President Eisenhower's Special Adviser for Psychological Warfare, met with DeMille on how best to use American films abroad.[56] A 1959 Congressional hearing revealed a further USIS role—it "blacklisted" certain films from distribution in twelve countries (Burma, Chile, Indonesia, Israel, Pakistan, the Philippines, Poland, Spain, Formosa, Turkey, Vietnam, and Yugoslavia) by excluding them from a program which expedited payments to American companies. Among the eighty-two films denied participation in this program (presumably because they presented negative images of the United States) were ALL QUIET ON THE WESTERN FRONT, ALL THE KING'S MEN, THE JAMES DEAN STORY, and SWEET SMELL OF SUCCESS.[57] Also, Luigi Luraschi, Director of Foreign and Domestic Censorship for Paramount, was recruited by the CIA as a confidential informant on the Hollywood industry; Luraschi's reports from 1953 focus on the international implications of Hollywood movies.[58] On the legislative side, Senator Alexander Wiley (Republican of Wisconsin), ranking Republican member of the Senate Foreign Relations Committee, gave a 1955 speech blasting Hollywood for the export of films that show "an America of sex, sin and sadism, of gangsterism, corruption, filth and degradation." He added, "Such films—few in number—but powerful in effect, have literally been poisoning the minds of some people in the world against us. These films are causing the very opposite of the friendly effect which should be created, if we are to defeat Soviet propaganda."[59] Senator Wiley's proposed solution was not federal censorship but heightened self-regulation.

In 1955, Senator Estes Kefauver (Democrat of Tennessee) chaired hearings of the Juvenile Delinquency Subcommittee of the Judicial Committee on the influence of television, comic books, motion pictures, and pornography on juvenile delinquency. From 15–17 June the Kefauver subcommittee met in Los Angeles with psychiatrists, the critic William Mooring (of the Catholic publication *Tidings*), studio heads, MPAA officials, and other Hollywood figures including the actor Ronald Reagan (former head of the Screen Actors Guild).[60] Kefauver's biographer notes that the subcommittee found no clear answers on "the link between juvenile delinquency and the crime, violence, and sex dramatized in movies, radio, books and TV."[61] However, the subcommittee did recommend "consultation of behavior experts by the code agency and modernization of both the industry's film and advertising codes." Kefauver later announced that he was pleased by the revised language on brutality in the December 1956 revision of the Production Code.[62]

Yet another instance of the federal government influencing film content was the Department of Defense cooperation agreement with the film and television industries.[63] Any filmmaker who wanted to use DOD personnel, equipment, or facilities was required to submit a script for approval. In practice, this meant that almost every film involving recent U.S. military history would need script approval from the DOD's Pictorial Branch, Office of Public Information. The DOD's "stipulations for extending cooperation" included not only accuracy but also adherence to DOD policy and "best interest."[64] In the 1950s, the great majority of film industry-DOD collaborations were friendly and noncontroversial. In a few cases (for example, STRATEGIC AIR COMMAND, 1955), the scripts for war movies were actually written by retired military officers. When the source material for Hollywood films was critical of the military, as in FROM HERE TO ETERNITY (1953), MR. ROBERTS (1955), and ON THE BEACH (1959), there was considerable give-and-take between the military and the producers as to what would be acceptable in the film version. The only studio film which was refused cooperation during the 1950s was ATTACK! (1956), directed by Robert Aldrich for United Artists release. Lieutenant Colonel H. D. Knight of the Army's Public Information Division found the script of this film to be "a very distasteful story and derogatory of Army leadership during combat," and therefore he recommended denial of any form of cooperation.[65] Director Aldrich and his partners (their independent company was called The Associates and Aldrich) decided to make ATTACK! without DOD aid instead of drastically changing the script.

Censorship and Anti-Communism

Both the Production Code Administration and the Legion of Decency were set up to evaluate movies based on moral criteria. The Production Code contains no discussion of politics except for the catch-all provision on "divine, natural and human law" and brief mentions of respecting the flag and fairly portraying all nations. However, the anti-communism of the 1950s was so pervasive that the wall between moral and political regulation largely disappeared. Kenneth Clark of the MPAA, responding to a charge that BORN YESTERDAY (1950) was a Marxist satire, announced that the PCA would not approve a film hostile "to the purposes of our democracy." The *New York Times* added that Joseph Breen had been quietly recommending changes to screenplays "that he feels contain or seem to contain anti-capitalistic sentiments."[66] Meanwhile, the unofficial and official representatives of the Catholic Church had a tendency to blur moral and political arguments. Thus, Martin Quigley in the *Motion Picture Herald* denounced "The Miracle" as Communist (though Roberto Rossellini was a supporter of the Christian Democrats in Italy), and Cardinal Spellman objected to BABY DOLL as both a religious leader and "a loyal citizen" of America.[67] Several Catholic critics (but not the Legion of Decency) actually referred to the film MARTIN LUTHER (1953) as communistic, even though their basic objection stemmed from religious doctrine rather than secular politics.[68]

One way to examine the influence of anti-communism on film censorship is to look at the Hollywood films that attempt a critique of the excesses of McCarthyism. In the early 1950s there simply were no films which directly addressed this issue. However, at least three films from the second half of the decade did take up the topic of extreme anti-communism—TRIAL (1955), STORM CENTER (1956), and THREE BRAVE MEN (1957). The censorship histories of these films reveal a good deal about the limits of expression in 1950s Hollywood.

TRIAL, produced by MGM, is based on a novel by Don Mankiewicz (son of screenwriter Herman Mankiewicz, nephew of director Joseph L. Mankiewicz) which critiques the Communist party *and* small-town conservatives *and* McCarthyist investigating committees. David Blake (played by Glenn Ford in the film), a naive law professor, is hired by lawyer Barney Castle (played by Arthur Kennedy) to defend Angel Chavez, a teenaged Hispanic boy accused of killing a white girl his own age. With the help of Castle's secretary Abbe Klein (the film changes her name to Abbe Nile, or Nyle, perhaps to avoid the stereotype that Communists are Jewish), Blake develops a convincing argument for Angel's innocence. However, Blake is hindered by Barney Castle, because Castle is a Communist who wants to create a martyr. And even though Abbe and David are falling in love, she gives him no warning about Castle's background because she is a former Communist herself. Meanwhile, Blake is subpoenaed by a state committee investigating communism. Angel is convicted and executed in the novel, but Blake manages to clear his own name.

At the insistence of Dore Schary, the ending of the script (written by Don Mankiewicz, adapting his own novel) was changed so that Angel gets off with a light sentence to a juvenile work farm and the true villain, Barney Castle, is charged with contempt of court. An unhappy tale of how American justice could punish the innocent becomes a demonstration of how right will prevail.[69] Nevertheless, Jack Vizzard of the PCA had major concerns about the script for TRIAL. Vizzard's "Memo for the Files" of

30 March 1955, summarizing a meeting with Schary, producer Charles Schnee, and Mankiewicz, noted that the project brought up a "policy problem" as well as Code issues. The "policy problem" was that the film, though *purportedly* an anti-Communist story," could be construed as "Communist Party line propaganda." Some objectionable elements had already been omitted, but Vizzard was still worried about "a plea for kindness" for former Communists, and about the critique of the State Investigating Committee, which was used by its head, Senator Carl Baron Battle, "as an instrument to build himself up to the title of 'King of the Anti-Communists.'" Vizzard worried that a film like this could discredit the entire industry. He concluded that TRIAL would be denied a Code Seal until the policy matter had been resolved by MPAA President Eric Johnston.[70]

Vizzard's autobiography reveals that he was terribly concerned about Schary's loyalties—was the MGM studio head a Stevenson liberal or a Communist sympathizer? Vizzard was greatly relieved when Schary agreed to change the script and remove anything that could be construed as Communistic. Schary commented (according to Vizzard) "This is a risk that everyone encounters when he tries to make a picture about a social injustice, on the side of the underdog."[71] It is extraordinary that Dore Schary, who had co-written the Waldorf Declaration of 1947 (inaugurating the blacklist) and had enforced the blacklist at RKO and MGM, could be suspected of communism in 1955. However, Vizzard's paranoia about Schary may have been widely shared. This same attitude was expressed by Luigi Luraschi, who told his CIA contact that "Metro" (MGM) is "the Company we must do something about." The only reason given was: "It is felt that he [Dore Schary] leaned very much to the left."[72] Evidently, being a liberal and making films about underdogs and minorities were suspicious matters in Cold War Hollywood.

TRIAL's various objectionable points were changed and the film was released to good reviews and solid business. Most of the reviewers described TRIAL as a hard-hitting anti-Communist film, though some also found it controversial. For example, the *Los Angeles Mirror-News* stressed the anti-Communist angle. According to *Variety*'s reviewer, "the film says a lot of fairly grim and unpretty things about human nature" but leaves the viewer with a good feeling. *Boxoffice* commented that the film presented "racial bigotry, rabble rousing and a Communist rally," which are "rarely shown on the screen."[73] Almost all of the book's discussion of the Battle committee disappeared in the film, and Abbe no longer has a Communist past (she was only a fellow traveler). TRIAL is a fascinating example of how liberal ideas were limited and channeled in the Hollywood of 1955: it retains the theme of minority rights, but must give up (because of PCA objections) the critique of investigating committees.

In the early 1950s Daniel Taradash and Elick Moll wrote a script for producer Stanley Kramer about a small-town librarian who loses her job because she will not remove a book titled *The Communist Dream* from the library collection. The film project got a publicity boost when Mary Pickford agreed to appear in it (she had not made a film for many years), but at the last minute Pickford withdrew. The film, with an explicitly anti-McCarthyist theme, was, according to Taradash "a terribly difficult picture to make because it ran counter to the entire mood of the country."[74] However, in 1955 Taradash convinced Columbia Pictures to finance the film for Phoenix Corporation, an independent company formed by Taradash and producer Julian Blaustein. Bette Davis would star, Taradash would direct, and Taradash and Blaustein would take no salaries but would share in the profits (if any). Harry Cohn personally supported this film, despite the objections of other Columbia executives.

The Librarian, the working title for the film, obviously would not do, so in 1956 the title was changed to STORM CENTER. It is an uneven film, with an excellent role for Davis but also less-than-satisfying subplots about a disturbed young boy who burns down the library and an ambitious, Red-baiting city councilman. The burning of the library is not well connected to the rest of the plot, but emotionally it suggests that removing a book from the shelves is the equivalent of burning it. Davis's character is ultimately rehired, and she vows never to allow another book to be removed.

The censorship history of STORM CENTER is interestingly mixed. The PCA approved it with minimal fuss, asking only that caution be used in presenting children playing with matches.[75] The MPAA actually participated in a First Amendment–oriented publicity brochure for the film, with Arthur DeBra, MPAA Director of Community Relations, writing about "the untrammeled right to read."[76] On the other hand, the Legion of Decency found STORM CENTER disturbing and objectionable. The film had no profanity, nudity, brutality, or other moral problems, so the Legion gave it a Separate Classification (rather than a "C" rating), explaining that "the highly propagandistic nature of this controversial film (book-burning, anti-communism, civil liberties) offers a warped and strongly emotional solution to a complex problem of American life."[77] Father Little of the Legion actually called Columbia Pictures to discuss possible Communist affiliations of producer Julian Blaustein, who had been investigated by the Tenney Committee in California in 1948. Columbia ignored Father Little's implicit threat.[78] The Legion was evidently unwilling to accept any criticism of anti-communism in 1956, and this included Taradash's very specific and limited argument for free speech.

Bette Davis as the small-town librarian in STORM CENTER *(1956).*

In 1957, Twentieth Century–Fox released THREE BRAVE MEN, a dramatic film about a real-life mistake made by the U.S. Navy's internal security program. The film was based on Pulitzer Prize–winning articles by Anthony Lewis, who reported on the case of Abraham Chasanow. Chasanow, a civilian employee of the navy with almost twenty-three years of service, was declared a security risk and suspended without pay on 29 July 1953. He was charged with Communist associations and with being part of a radical group in Greenbelt, Maryland. Chasanow's friends rallied around him, and an official hearing endorsed his good character and suggested that the charges arose from an emotional dispute about housing in Greenbelt. Nevertheless, Chasanow was fired by the navy in 1954. A few months later, a new, more thorough investigation requested by Assistant Secretary of the Navy J. H. Smith Jr. found no Communist affiliations and no radical group. Chasanow was cleared and reinstated.[79]

Chasanow's story was adapted for the screen by Philip Dunne for Twentieth Century–Fox; Dunne also directed. The "three brave men" of the title are Bernie Goldsmith (the Chasanow character), played by Ernest Borgnine;[80] his lawyer, played by Ray Milland; and the assistant secretary of the navy, played by Dean Jagger. Philip Dunne's script was found uncontroversial by the PCA. However, the final script was shaped by intensive collaboration between the filmmakers and the U.S. Navy.

Twentieth Century–Fox sent the script of THREE BRAVE MEN to the navy in July 1956. Though Fox did want navy help with props and locations, this story involved no combat scenes and it could have been shot without cooperation. Nevertheless, Fox submitted to a kind of voluntary censorship (which was, of course, common practice for American films about the military). Fox most likely wanted the navy's advice and also its approval—to avoid any controversy after the film's release. Thomas S. Gates Jr., acting secretary of the navy, found Philip Dunne's script inaccurate and misleading.[81] In response, Dunne quickly wrote a new draft, relying on navy sources for accuracy and emphasizing "that the Chasanow case was far from being a typical case and that under current procedures it could not happen again." Dunne's script also stresses the necessity for security procedures and eliminates "direct reference to the anti-Semitic aspect of the case."[82] Albert Pratt, assistant secretary of the navy, upon receiving the new draft, replied that the film still needed to make clear that the "Communist internal threat" was responsible for new security procedures and that the navy was working hard to meet this threat "while at the same time preserving the traditional rights of the individual."[83] The film company and the U.S. Navy must have reached an understanding, for a later memo announces that the DOD was generally satisfied by the finished film.[84]

Philip Dunne's autobiography expresses disappointment with THREE BRAVE MEN. The original idea was to tell "a story (the true one) of unseen terror, of a man fighting in the dark against unknown enemies." Chasanow is "accused of disloyalty, fired, disgraced and ruined," and he is not allowed "to avail himself of any of the protections supposedly guaranteed by the Constitution." However, the film was rewritten, following the navy's recommendations, so that the emphasis was on "the Navy's point of view, not the victim's."[85] The basic theme of the finished film is that the navy's internal security program made a mistake and later corrected its mistake. This theme is powerfully presented by the closing lines of the film, spoken by the assistant secretary: "A free country learns from its mistakes. I offer you the Navy's apology for the grave injustice you've suffered." Philip Dunne was hoping for more—for a Kafkaesque tale of the denial of human rights—but he does note that "no other picture had even feebly attacked the witch-hunters."[86] He is correct in his assessment, with the exception of STORM CENTER.

Conclusion

The Hollywood film industry of the 1950s faced a confusing pattern of government censorship and "voluntary agencies" that "exercise some measure of surveillance, judgment and even control" over the film medium.[87] Many different censoring and influencing organizations had to be considered, and the "rules" of what was morally and politically acceptable were rapidly changing. State and local censorship became much less active after the *Miracle* decision of 1952, but the federal government tried to influence movie content in various ways. Among the "voluntary agencies," the most important were the Production Code Administration (the "internal censor" of the film industry), and the Catholic Church's Legion of Decency. These two organizations, which often but not always worked in complementary ways, had a firm grip on film content in the early 1950s but gradually loosened that grip as the decade progressed.

It must be stressed that the PCA and the Legion did not simply make judgments on finished films, they worked with the filmmakers to set the moral and, in some cases, political tone of 1950s Hollywood (as with THREE BRAVE MEN, the Defense Department could also be involved in this process). Consensus emerged in a give-and-take between the filmmakers and the regulators. In many cases there was no controversy about a film's content. In a few highly publicized cases—THE MOON IS BLUE, BABY DOLL, TEA AND SYMPATHY, and a few others—there was a great deal of controversy, and decisions made regarding them set future parameters for both the film industry and the regulating agencies. However, the influence of the audience must also be considered. For example, both the PCA and the Legion opposed THE MOON IS BLUE, but audiences flocked to it and critics endorsed it. This weakened the voluntary agencies and speeded the trend toward more explicit treatment of sexuality in Hollywood films.

5

Technology and Spectacle

One response of the Hollywood studios to the rapid audience loss of the late 1940s and the 1950s was to emphasize the motion picture's capacity for spectacle. Television was limited by a small screen, poor visual definition, black and white (rather than color), and mediocre sound quality. Film could do better in all these areas. Further, with the increased affluence of the 1950s, people were buying automobiles, taking vacations, and experiencing the sights and sounds of the United States and foreign lands. Film was capable of bringing these experiences to the local theater, albeit in a passive and not completely satisfactory way. Several popular genres stressed the power of the image in the early 1950s: the musical (AN AMERICAN IN PARIS, 1951; GENTLEMEN PREFER BLONDES, 1953), the Western (SHANE and THE NAKED SPUR, both 1953), the Biblical epic (QUO VADIS?, 1951; DAVID AND BATHSHEBA, 1951), the exotic adventure film (KING SOLOMON'S MINES, 1950; THE CRIMSON PIRATE, 1952), even the suspense film (NIAGARA, 1953; TO CATCH A THIEF, 1955). Though the musical was, in general, bound to soundstages for a few more years, other spectacle-oriented movies derived much of their power from location shooting. Thus, many Westerns took advantage of harsh and majestic landscapes of the Western states, and NIAGARA never strayed far from the awesome spectacle of Niagara Falls.

Color

A key aspect of the new interest in spectacle was a gradual shift to color filming. Since the early 1930s, color film production and laboratory work in Hollywood had been dominated by the Technicolor Corporation. Technicolor had introduced the first practical three-strip color system in 1932; prior to that color systems had been either very cumbersome or limited to a partial color spectrum. Three separate negatives were exposed by the Technicolor camera (one for each primary color), and these three images were eventually printed onto positive film stock by a dye transfer process known as "imbibition printing." This process, similar to color lithography, produced bright, pure colors that worked especially well for high key interiors (as in musicals or historical dramas). Technicolor's equipment and industrial processes were zealously guarded, and every film that used Technicolor cameras was required to employ a Technicolor-approved color consultant. (Often the color consultant was Natalie Kalmus, the ex-wife of Technicolor President Herbert Kalmus.)

In the early 1950s, the demand for color filming in the United States increased, and Technicolor was unable to keep up with the Hollywood industry's needs. Technicolor had always been a small company that serviced a limited number of high-quality films; for example, in 1952 Technicolor could supply cameras to only fifteen films shooting simultaneously.[1] This allowed other processes, such as Ansco, Cinecolor, and Trucolor, to gain a foothold in the market. Though it has been suggested that Technicolor limited its capacity to keep prices high, a more likely explanation is that Technicolor's expansion was limited by war-related shortages, postwar strikes, and the expectation that three-strip Technicolor would soon be replaced by a tripack film stock.[2] "Tripack" in this context means placing three layers recording the primary colors onto one strip of film. Technicolor had experimented with tripack in the 1940s, but the results were not satisfactory.

Hollywood's approach to color filming changed significantly with the introduction of Eastmancolor tripack negative film—announced in 1950, with the first feature films released in 1951 and 1952. A few of the early Eastmancolor features were HURRICANE ISLAND (Columbia, 1951), THE SWORD OF MONTE CRISTO (Fox, 1951), SUNNY SIDE OF THE STREET (Columbia, 1951) and CARSON CITY (Warners, 1952). The color processes for these films were credited as "Super Cinecolor" and "Warner Color."[3] Eastman Kodak's one-strip process meant that the cost of color film stock was greatly reduced, and special camera equipment was no longer needed when shooting color rather than black and white. Also, Eastman Kodak was willing to license its processing technology to other companies, so that film companies could use their in-house facilities for color laboratory work. Warnercolor, for example, is Eastmancolor film developed with Eastmancolor technology in Warner Bros.' own laboratory. Color filmmaking was suddenly more affordable (as well as more competitive), though costs were still higher than black and white. In response to this technological breakthrough, plus the need to compete with television, color production rose from about 15 percent of Hollywood's output in 1950 to about 50 percent in 1955.[4]

Technicolor Corporation responded to the new, more competitive environment of color technology by rapidly phasing out its production component and adapting its laboratory operations for tripack film. The last American film photographed with Technicolor cameras was FOXFIRE, produced by Universal in 1954. However, Technicolor did succeed in making its imbibition printing compatible with the tripack Eastmancolor negative. Therefore, Technicolor became a high-quality (and high-cost) lab for color processing in the 1950s. In 1955, Technicolor further modified its lab processes to improve the image quality of widescreen projection.[5] Though the specialized Technicolor cameras disappeared, "Color by Technicolor" (meaning all processing done by Technicolor) was a credit found on many of the important films of the 1950s.

Despite the new technologies, the percentage of Hollywood films made in color actually dropped between 1955 and 1958, before recovering in 1959 and 1960. Film historian Gorham Kindem gives two explanations for the decline. First, attendance dropped sharply in this period, and producers, budgeting for the decrease in revenue, could reduce costs by using black and white. Second, it became clear in 1956 that Hollywood films would soon derive much of their income from sales to television (before this, the major studios held out against selling to a competitor). Since television was in black and white, color filming added no value to a potential TV sale.[6]

One could add that the film industry may have gone too far in the early 1950s in its enthusiasm for color, because some types of film are better suited to black and white. Twentieth Century–Fox, for example, declared in 1953 that all of its films would henceforth be in color and CinemaScope. Fox was accentuating the "special event" quality of CinemaScope, but its all-color policy still seems excessive, since the Best Picture Oscars for 1953 (FROM HERE TO ETERNITY), 1954 (ON THE WATERFRONT), and 1955 (MARTY) all went to black and white films. By 1959, Fox had figured out that black and white works well with certain subjects; it allowed George Stevens to make THE DIARY OF ANNE FRANK in black and white and CinemaScope.

Eastman Kodak made a further contribution to color motion pictures in 1959 with the introduction of the Eastmancolor 5250 35 mm. negative film. This was a high-speed, low-grain film stock, meaning that it could provide excellent results with less lighting than other color films. Previous color stocks had required very high light levels, which increased production costs in comparison with black and white filming. Eastman 5250 reduced the cost differential, and also made it easier to film high-quality exteriors. Barry Salt, a historian of film technology, says that Eastmancolor 5250 "completely eliminated competition in the U.S.A. by its superiority."[7]

One unintended consequence of the switch to Eastmancolor was a shortened lifetime for color prints—not a problem for first and second runs, but a terrible dilemma for film preservation. Three-strip Technicolor printing creates a more-or-less permanent image, although the film stock itself deteriorates over time. Eastmancolor, however, can fade in a matter of years to a purplish red, with blue and green highlights disappearing (since the mid-1970s, Eastman Kodak has been marketing slower-fading stocks).[8] This problem can be remedied by making separate black and white negatives for each of the three primary colors. However, the solution is so expensive that in practice film archives cannot save all of their films, and so must make agonizing choices.

3-D

The introduction of Eastmancolor in the early 1950s was a technological change which fit extremely well with the established standards and practices of the Hollywood film industry. Eastmancolor made the expensive Technicolor cameras unnecessary, and did not change projection equipment or other aspects of film exhibition. The basic structure of the film industry remained unaltered, except that the importance of one supplier (Technicolor) declined, and the importance of another supplier (Eastman Kodak) increased.

However, in 1952 the film industry was rocked by two other technological changes: 3-D and Cinerama. These inventions changed production equipment, exhibition equipment, and the experience of the viewer. Further, since both inventions were controlled (at least at first) by companies outside the studio system, they threatened to finish the work of the Paramount anti-trust consent decrees that went into effect on 1 January 1950 by curtailing the market power of the major and minor studios.

Stereoscopic motion pictures can be traced back to William Friese-Greene's experiments of 1889. The basic principle is simple—in human vision, depth perception results in part from the separation of the two eyes, resulting in two slightly different views of an object. This can be simulated in photography by using two cameras with lenses a few inches apart, or using a system of mirrors to produce the correct image separation. Then the two images are projected on a screen, either using a two-color system (for instance, red-green) or opposite polarization of light. When the images are viewed through glasses or filters so that the left eye sees only one color or polarity, and the right eye sees the other, a three-dimensional effect is achieved. Stereoscopic

motion pictures work in the same way, except that there are additional projection problems. Either the image is produced by two projectors, in which case precisely matching
registration is essential, or both images are printed by a lab onto one strip of film. In the
second case, registration should not be a problem, but viewing the film absolutely
requires the special glasses. (In a two-projector system, turning off one projector creates a conventional, 2-D film image).

Stereoscopic film was essentially an amateur pastime as the 1950s began. There was
favorable press coverage for a program of stereoscopic shorts presented in London in
1951, and the *New York Times* respectfully reviewed a three-dimensional short by two
UCLA graduate students in January 1952.[9] However, the organization that made stereoscopic motion pictures an important part of the film industry in 1952–1953 was Natural
Vision, a company controlled by screenwriter Milton J. Gunzburg and his family. Using
equipment developed by cinematographer Friend Baker, who had experimented with
stereoscopy as a hobby for many years, Gunzburg showed samples of 3-D production to
a film industry audience in June 1951. Twentieth Century–Fox took a six-month option
on the Natural Vision process, but decided not to commit to production. According to
Gunzburg, Spyros Skouras of Fox was obsessed with finding a way to present 3-D "without glasses," and Natural Vision could not do this.[10] With no offers from the studios,
Gunzburg agreed to provide Natural Vision equipment and expertise to independent
producer Arch Oboler (known mainly as a radio producer) for a film that was eventually
called BWANA DEVIL. Gunzburg also negotiated an exclusive contract for polarized viewers from the Polaroid Corporation; Polaroid would supply viewers to theaters for 10
cents a pair, with Natural Vision receiving 3.3 cents for every pair sold. Though in effect
only until 15 July 1953, this contract earned Natural Vision more than $2.5 million.[11]

BWANA DEVIL (1952) was a "B" movie about the building of a railroad in Africa and
the disruption and terror caused by two lions. *Variety* commented that Oboler's "script
and direction are very poor," and that the 3-D technique and the glasses both need
improvement.[12] The film did, however, present some interesting depth effects via wide
angle close ups of monkeys, lions, and people; deep focus shots featuring objects in several planes and diagonal movements; and a spear which seems to be thrown right at the
audience. The center of interest in BWANA DEVIL was the delight in a new kind of
motion-picture vision; the mediocre plot was beside the point. When it opened at two
theaters in Hollywood in November 1952 as an independent release, BWANA DEVIL was
an immediate box-office hit. Based on this success, Arch Oboler negotiated a distribution contract with United Artists that guaranteed him $1,750,000. Natural Vision was
entitled to 20 percent of Oboler's profit on the film.[13] BWANA DEVIL went on to earn several million dollars, even though its distribution to theaters was limited by Polaroid's
inability to keep up with the demand for glasses.[14]

3-D filmmaking was suddenly the craze in Hollywood. The major and minor studios
feverishly prepared to shoot and release films. Warner Bros. signed a two-picture deal
with Natural Vision and announced that HOUSE OF WAX (1953), a remake of the horror
film MYSTERY OF THE WAX MUSEUM, would be its first 3-D production. Other studios
were interested in using Natural Vision equipment, but Natural Vision had only one 3-D
camera, with another on order. Therefore, a number of Hollywood studios and independent companies quickly devised their own 3-D systems. The technology was relatively
simple and not covered by patents, but by rushing into production the various companies may have sacrificed quality control. Columbia Pictures actually beat Warners into
distribution with the low-budget MAN IN THE DARK, which was released on 8 April 1953.

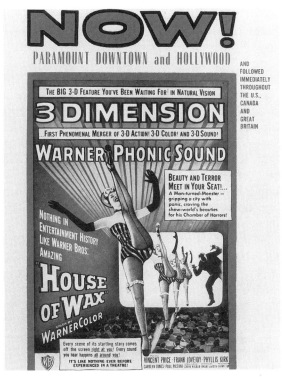

Poster for HOUSE OF WAX *(1953), emphasizing the three-dimensional quality of the image.*

Warners followed with the Natural Vision HOUSE OF WAX at the end of April. This was a much better film than BWANA DEVIL, with "an exciting story, lush production trappings, perfect photography, color, a slight widescreen," and even "four track WarnerPhonic sound" (multitrack sound was also a feature of Cinerama and the slightly later Cinema-Scope).[15] Strangely enough, André de Toth, the director of HOUSE OF WAX, had only one eye and so was incapable of seeing stereoscopic effects. Despite the director's handicap, HOUSE OF WAX was a tremendous success.

It is widely believed that the 3-D films of 1953 and 1954 were mostly low-budget genre films, but R. M. Hayes, author of a history of 3-D, maintains that these films were of equal or better quality than the 2-D films made by the same companies at the same time.[16] Certainly, 3-D was used for low-budget features and shorts, but a surprising number of higher budget and high-prestige features were also shot (though not necessarily released) in 3-D processes. The list includes HOUSE OF WAX, THE CHARGE AT FEATHER RIVER (Warners, 1953), KISS ME KATE (MGM, 1953), TAZA: SON OF COCHISE (Universal, 1954), MISS SADIE THOMPSON (Columbia, 1953), HONDO (Warners, 1953), and DIAL M FOR MURDER (Warners, 1954). THE FRENCH LINE (RKO, 1954), starring Jane Russell, was also in 3-D; this poorly written, poorly acted film is nevertheless interesting for its challenge to censorship standards and its salacious advertising campaign (for example, "Jane Russell in 3 Dimensions—and what dimensions").[17] And one of the 3-D features without big stars, CREATURE FROM THE BLACK LAGOON (directed by Jack Arnold, Universal, 1954), is often mentioned as a horror film classic.

Alfred Hitchcock's DIAL M FOR MURDER is the only film on this list which has recently been presented to audiences in 3-D. In 1954 it was released primarily in a 2-D (or flat) version, though there were several 3-D engagements. A 1999 theatrical re-release in 3-D was surprisingly successful.[18] Though Hitchcock professed a dislike of the 3-D technique, his approach to it in this film was unusual but effective. The film was based on a stage play, and most of it takes place in the living room of a London flat. Hitchcock carefully controlled composition and movement, so that the first half hour is static but full of lamps, chair arms, and other items jutting out in front of the actors. Then actors and camera begin to move as Tony (Ray Milland) sketches out the perfect murder. The only 3-D action shot involves Tony's wife, Margot (Grace Kelly), killing an intruder with a pair of scissors—even here there is restraint, as the movement goes away from the camera rather than toward camera and audience. J. Hoberman of the *Village Voice*, writing in 1999, praised the film's "minimalist" approach, adding that "Hitchcock's canny restraint allows the stereo image to assert its own uncanny characteristics."[19]

In March 1953, an article in *American Cinematographer* announced "All Hollywood Shooting 3-D Films." However, by December 1953 the same magazine's lead article asked "Is 3-D Dead . . .?"[20] 3-D by this point had encountered a great deal of criticism from distributors, exhibitors, critics, and audiences. There were complaints about the polarized glasses: they were uncomfortable and poorly made; they were not always available from suppliers; and they cost too much (10 cents a pair). There were complaints about projection: the image was shaky; the image was too dark; the 3-D illusion was reduced or absent for patrons sitting to the side. There were also complaints about production quality and the choice of subjects.

By early 1954 the boom was over. Studio heads had decided that 3-D was a novelty without lasting importance; they quickly released films already made (often in 2-D rather than 3-D engagements), and started no new 3-D productions. The Polaroid Corporation had improved viewing glasses and projection systems, but no one was interested.[21] Producers and exhibitors moved on to other technical innovations, involving wider screens and sharper images.

Cinerama

Cinerama was a process using three cameras and three projectors to create a panoramic image that was projected on a large, curved screen. The cameras and projectors used 35 mm. film, but with "the height of the frame extended over 6 sprocket holes rather than the usual 4."[22] Cinerama's aspect ratio (the width divided by the height of the film image) was 2.72 to 1, or about twice the width of the "Academy Ratio" of 1.33 to 1 which had been standard in American movies for many years. The film speed was 26 frames per second, slightly higher than the standard 24 fps in order to improve image stability. Cinerama also used a multitrack sound system involving eight microphones and eight speakers (five behind the screen, three in the back of the theater). Via peripheral vision and stereo sound, this system created a powerful effect of audience participation.

As with 3-D, multi-projector processes had a long history; there had even been a Cinéorama using 10 projectors demonstrated in Paris in 1900. Cinerama (the name is apparently unrelated to "Cinéorama") was developed in the United States over a period of fifteen years by Fred Waller, who had at one time been the head of special effects photography at Paramount. Waller was responsible for two multi-projector and curved

Publicity for THIS IS CINERAMA *(1952): an audience watching the famous roller coaster scene.*

screen exhibits which were part of the 1939 New York World's Fair. Then during World War II he created an aerial gunnery simulation using five projectors and a huge spherical screen. After the war, Waller worked on adapting his multi-screen concept for civilian use with backing from Laurence Rockefeller, Time, Inc., and sound engineer Hazard E. Reeves. With the Hollywood studios showing no interest in the process, Rockefeller and Time, Inc. dropped out in 1950, but Reeves persevered.

The first entertainment figure to become excited about Cinerama was theatrical producer Michael Todd (who at this time had no film experience), and Todd involved radio and newsreel commentator Lowell Thomas. Between 1950 and 1952, Michael Todd and his son Michael Todd Jr. shot the European travelogue material that became the first act of THIS IS CINERAMA. It was Mike Todd Jr. who shot the roller coaster footage that so memorably introduced the new Cinerama process. (The idea for this sequence came from test footage shot by Fred Waller.) In 1952, Michael Todd Sr. ended his association with Cinerama; he was replaced by film industry veteran Merian C. Cooper, whose background included documentary filmmaking in the 1920s, the production of KING KONG in 1933, and a partnership with John Ford in the independent company Argosy Pictures in the 1940s and 1950s. Cooper shot the American scenes for Act 2 of THIS IS CINERAMA and edited the film for its 30 September 1952 debut in New York City. Both Michael Todd Sr. and Cooper deserve credit for the artistic side of the film; Lowell Thomas, co-producer (with Cooper) and narrator of the film's prologue, was less involved with the creative decisions.

The music for THIS IS CINERAMA was composed primarily by Max Steiner, uncredited and uncompensated because in 1952 he was music director for Warners. Lowell Thomas had tried to borrow Steiner for the film, but Jack Warner declined. Steiner decided to go ahead anyway, working on Warners' SPRINGFIELD RIFLE (1952) and THIS IS CINERAMA at the same time. Composer and musical director Lou Forbes, one of Steiner's close friends, was sent to New York to work with the Cinerama people. Steiner wrote the music and supervised the orchestrations in Hollywood. Forbes conducted the orchestra in New York. Forbes and Steiner together figured out how to adapt click tracks (a way to match musical compositions to film shots and scenes) to Cinerama's 26 frames per second. Steiner later wrote that he had taken on this job "because of my admiration and affection for my friend Merian Cooper."[23] Cooper, summing up THIS IS CINERAMA in 1954, thanked "a great musical genius who cannot be named, but who contributed hugely to the music for this picture."[24] The story of the music illustrates that THIS IS CINERAMA was an oddly marginal venture, far outside the Hollywood mainstream.

Cinerama was an enormous success in its premiere engagement, with critics comparing its importance to the introduction of sound movies in the late 1920s.[25] *Time* magazine (no longer financially involved in the process) spoke of a "Movie Revolution" and talked about Cinerama as a "'three dimensional' sensation to eyes & ears," even though the optical basis of Cinerama was not stereoscopy but peripheral vision.[26] Merian C. Cooper and other Cinerama officials confidently predicted that widescreen filming on the model of Cinerama would "replace most flat screen movies."[27]

Cinerama was consciously planned as a one-of-a-kind system that would provide an experience far different from that of normal motion pictures. This approach had both positive and negative consequences. On the positive side, Cinerama was able to promote itself as a new entertainment experience and to charge premium prices for reserved-seat engagements. But the choice to remain apart from established film industry standards also limited the impact of Cinerama in a variety of ways. To begin with, Cinerama productions could not be adapted for regular 35 mm. showings, because of the three projectors, the 26 frames per second, the 6 sprocket holes per frame, and the multitrack magnetic sound (in the 1960s, technical adjustments made Cinerama compatible with conventional film and television screenings). The cost of transforming a theater for Cinerama presentation was an estimated $75,000 to $140,000 per screen.[28] Theater owners were unwilling to advance such a large sum, so Cinerama remodeled or built its own theaters, one market at a time. And Cinerama projection was so labor intensive that about 50 percent of box-office receipts went to operating expenses.[29] In production, the visible lines between the three projected images were a constant irritation; filmmakers had to learn to mask or minimize them. Also, Cinerama close-ups were so large as to be disquieting. However, Cinerama was very good for what Merian C. Cooper called "true environmental effect"; it could hold the attention of the audience with only landscapes (or seascapes) and music.[30]

Cinerama's complex financial arrangements caused additional difficulties. Ownership of the process was split between three companies: Vitarama, which owned the patents; Cinerama, Inc., which owned the production and exhibition equipment; and Cinerama Productions, which produced the films. Key figures like Fred Waller, Hazard E. Reeves, Lowell Thomas, Merian C. Cooper, and Louis B. Mayer (who was chairman of the board for a few years) were given blocks of stock and also stock options. The arrangements favored early owners such as Reeves and hurt other owners—including those who had bought publicly traded shares of Cinerama, Inc.[31] The Stanley Warner theater chain (formerly a branch of Warner Bros.) invested in Cinerama in mid-1953, a welcome development. However, Stanley Warner was unwilling to support a major expansion until it could acquire a controlling interest in Cinerama Productions, which finally happened in 1958.[32] The Byzantine financial situation meant there was little money for new films *or* new theaters. Cinerama produced only five films—all travelogues—in the 1950s: THIS IS

CINERAMA; CINERAMA HOLIDAY (1955); SEVEN WONDERS OF THE WORLD (1956); SEARCH FOR PARADISE (1957); and SOUTH SEAS ADVENTURE (1958). As to theaters, in November 1954, THIS IS CINERAMA was screening in thirteen cities; but by 1959 there were still only twenty-two Cinerama theaters in the world.[33]

Cinerama had ironically lost its technological edge before Stanley Warner's accelerated theater-building program began in the early 1960s. By the mid-to-late 1950s a variety of widescreen formats with excellent picture and sound quality was available: Todd-AO, Super Panavision 70 mm., Ultra Panavision 70 mm., and others. These formats used one camera and one projector and therefore got rid of the irritating frame lines. Cinerama stuck with its three-camera, three-projector setup through HOW THE WEST WAS WON (1962), but switched to the one camera, one projector Ultra Panavision 70 for IT'S A MAD MAD MAD MAD WORLD (1963). From this point on "Cinerama" became a prestigious brand name rather than a distinctive approach to film production and exhibition.

CinemaScope

With the stunning debuts of 3-D and Cinerama in 1952–1953, the Hollywood film industry found new hope in the struggle with television. The Polaroid Corporation sold 60 million pairs of polarized glasses in 3-D's first year, and Cinerama earned more than

Poster for HOW TO MARRY A MILLIONAIRE *(1953). The three female costars create a horizontal composition that matches the CinemaScope frame. Marilyn Monroe gets first billing in the poster, but third billing in the film credits.*

$14 million in its first two years despite being in only thirteen theaters by the end of that period.[34] However, these successes created some difficult choices for the Hollywood studios. Would widescreen and 3-D transform the motion-picture industry? Should the studios invest in one of the currently available formats? Or, since the underlying concepts of 3-D and widescreen were not patentable, should the individual studios strive to develop new formats of their own?

The studios responded to these issues in several different ways. Some of them invested heavily in 3-D, but Twentieth Century–Fox and Republic showed little interest. All the studios tried to do something with "widescreen," but sometimes this meant only that a standard 35 mm. image had been cropped so that the familiar 1.33 to 1 aspect ratio became 1.66 or 1.75 or 1.85. Paramount, for example, promoted SHANE as the first major studio release in widescreen because a film shot in 1.33 to 1 was presented on the big screen at Radio City Music Hall in 1.66 to 1.[35] This masking of the image was by no means a radical change in film technology. However, there was a significant widescreen process pioneered by a major studio in 1953: CinemaScope from Twentieth Century–Fox.

CinemaScope was Fox's attempt to create 3-D without glasses and Cinerama without high costs. It was based on Henri Chrétien's Hypergonar lenses, which had been demonstrated but barely used in France in the 1920s. Chrétien's lenses were "anamorphic," meaning that they could stretch or squeeze one dimension (in this case the width) of an image. The camera lens squeezed a wide image into the standard 1.33 to 1 film frame, and the projector lens stretched this image into a much wider aspect ratio—as much as 2.66 to 1. CinemaScope was an inexpensive process because the lenses were attached to existing cameras and projectors, and no changes were made to film stock. The major costs were in exhibition—a large and slightly curved screen, and audio equipment that would play four track magnetic sound.

Fox president Spyros Skouras, production head Darryl Zanuck, and research head Earl Sponable had this long-forgotten invention ready for mass diffusion within an astonishing nine months. Skouras purchased an option on the lenses from Chrétien in December 1952—all patents had expired, but by acquiring working lenses Fox gained an important lead on its competitors. In the last week of January, Fox had already chosen the name "CinemaScope" and was demonstrating the process to its own personnel and the heads of other studios. On 1 February 1953 Fox announced that its entire output of films would move to CinemaScope, color, and stereo sound.[36] This bold gamble was necessary to convince theater owners to invest in CinemaScope equipment—there would be little incentive to change for one or two films. Darryl Zanuck did hedge the studio's bet by arranging for several non-CinemaScope pictures to be filmed by independents but distributed by Fox.[37]

Fox then arranged for producers and exhibitors to see a 50-minute demonstration reel of CinemaScope in Hollywood, beginning 18 March 1953 (coinciding with Academy Awards week). The demo reel included scenes from the first two CinemaScope films in production, THE ROBE and HOW TO MARRY A MILLIONAIRE (both 1953); the "Diamonds Are a Girl's Best Friend" number from GENTLEMEN PREFER BLONDES (which Fox was to release that year in the traditional, non-CinemaScope format); and travelogue footage of Sun Valley, Idaho, New York harbor, and other locations. Also, on 18 March MGM announced that it would produce films in the CinemaScope format. By 23 March, Fox had commitments from more than 1,200 theaters to install CinemaScope equipment.[38] Spyros Skouras had prepared for this rush of business by signing contracts with Bausch and Lomb and other manufacturers to ensure an adequate supply of lenses. In April the

CinemaScope reel was shown to exhibitors and critics in New York. Bosley Crowther of the *New York Times* found it "similar to Cinerama" and praised the "commendable fidelity and naturalness" of the images. He was surprised by the fluid cutting, including close-ups, in the excerpt from THE ROBE. Crowther also noted the effective use of directional sound in a scene featuring a rehearsal of the Fox symphony orchestra.[39]

THE ROBE then premiered at the Roxy Theater in New York on 16 September 1953 before an enthusiastic crowd of 6,500 people. The film quickly became an enormous success, and those exhibitors who had signed up for CinemaScope in March profited from their foresight. THE ROBE, based on a best-seller by Lloyd Douglas, brings together scenes of early Christianity with Roman spectacle and a love story. It is at its best in the first hour, where the story elements blend seamlessly and the new Cinema-Scope process contributes to a sense of awe. The film follows the life of a Roman tribune, Marcellus Gallio (Richard Burton), who leads the soldiers who crucify Jesus and then becomes a Christian himself. Following a tradition of modesty before the sacred, we never see Jesus' face, and he speaks only one line: "Father, forgive them, for they know not what they do." But with composition, framing, sound effects, and music (the score is by Alfred Newman), director Henry Koster does create emotionally powerful sequences. In the film's second half there are many two-character dialogue scenes, and much of the religious meaning attaches to a relic (the robe of the title) rather than to Jesus and his teachings. Here THE ROBE sometimes feels like just another film.

The CinemaScope process itself was both a critical and an audience success. W. R. Wilkerson of the *Hollywood Reporter* commented that the picture looked perfect from all parts of the theater and the sound was also perfect, even though the stereo effects

Jean Simmons and Richard Burton in THE ROBE *(1953).*

took a few minutes to get used to. Perhaps inspired by the Biblical subject, Wilkerson concluded that CinemaScope was the "Moses" that would lead Hollywood "out of a film wilderness."[40] *Variety*'s review was similarly effusive, comparing THE ROBE's release to the impact of THE JAZZ SINGER (the first Hollywood "talkie") in 1927.[41] According to Darryl Zanuck, Fox decided not to present THE ROBE as a roadshow (a reserved-seat attraction in a limited number of theaters) before general release because people were too eager to see it.[42] Also, though Zanuck did not say so, a quick general release put pressure on wavering theaters to purchase CinemaScope equipment. THE ROBE cost $4.5 million and earned $30 million, justifying Fox's gamble on the CinemaScope process.

HOW TO MARRY A MILLIONAIRE, starring Marilyn Monroe, Lauren Bacall, and Betty Grable, was the second CinemaScope film. As critic Lisa Cohen suggests, the success of this slight romantic comedy showed that CinemaScope could convincingly present domestic spaces as well as the huge scale of the epic.[43] The use of three female stars may in itself be a response to CinemaScope's shape, for it takes at least three figures in a line to fill the long, rectangular frame. HOW TO MARRY A MILLIONAIRE earned $7.5 million, nowhere near the return of THE ROBE but an excellent result for 1953. These two films, plus the commitment of Fox and MGM to future releases, established CinemaScope as a new (but by no means exclusive) standard for motion pictures.

However, Spyros Skouras did face a revolt from theater owners regarding some of CinemaScope's new technology. The wide aspect ratio, which required only anamorphic lens attachments, was accepted and even welcomed. But exhibitors strongly objected to Fox's policy of requiring a Miracle Mirror screen (which avoided the problem of unwanted reflections) and four-track magnetic sound. Fox yielded to exhibitor pressure about screens in December 1953 and allowed small theaters to use whatever screens

Judy Garland sings "The Man That Got Away" in A STAR IS BORN *(1954).*

James Mason and Judy Garland in A STAR IS BORN. *Note the substantial difference in aspect ratio between this image (CinemaScope) and the image on the facing page (which is slightly wider than the traditional 1.33 to 1).*

they wished. Zanuck and Skouras were both strong advocates of stereo sound, especially the surround track, so they held out on this point a few more months.[44] After a May 1954 meeting with exhibitors hosted by Skouras, Fox reversed itself on stereo sound as well and agreed that future CinemaScope films would be released in three different sound formats. An exhibitor could choose four track magnetic, or four track optical, or one track optical. The optical tracks slightly reduced the width of the CinemaScope image, so that the 2.66 to 1 aspect ratio became 2.55 to 1. Eventually, CinemaScope was standardized at 2.35 to 1 for all audio formats.[45]

The uncertainties of this period for production companies can be exemplified by Warner Bros.' experience with the musical version of A STAR IS BORN. This comeback film for Judy Garland was planned as Warners' big release for 1953–1954. An exceptionally talented group of creative participants was assembled: George Cukor as director; Moss Hart as screenwriter; Harold Arlen and Ira Gershwin as songwriters; James Mason as costar with Garland. However, Jack Warner had no idea what film format would be appropriate for a high-budget musical in 1953. A STAR IS BORN was first announced as a film in 3-D. Then, as 3-D's novelty waned, the format was changed to WarnerScope (also known as WarnerSuperScope), which was the studio's attempt to develop its own anamorphic lens (similar to CinemaScope) without paying royalties to Fox. This was perfectly legal, but the test lenses manufactured for Warners by the German lensmaker Zeiss were obviously inferior to Fox's anamorphic lens.

Jack Warner changed his mind again and declared that A STAR IS BORN would be shot in 1.75 widescreen (but not anamorphic) and three-strip Technicolor. A few weeks of filming were done in this format beginning 12 October 1953. However, after the huge success of THE ROBE (which opened in September 1953) Albert and Harry Warner in New York pressured their brother Jack to switch over to CinemaScope. Jack Warner vis-

ited the Twentieth Century–Fox studio to have his first look at CinemaScope and immediately finalized the deal for Fox's process. So, A Star Is Born was now revamped for
CinemaScope and Eastmancolor. Released in September 1954, it became one of the
more prestigious of the early CinemaScope productions, thanks to a wonderful performance by Garland and Cukor's fluid, long-take style. Unfortunately, the film went enormously over budget (due in part to Jack Warner's indecision, in part to Garland's
frequent absences) and did not make a profit.[46] At any rate, Warner Bros.' switch to CinemaScope in late 1953 further enhanced Fox's pre-eminence in widescreen.

VistaVision, Todd-AO, and Other Formats

The brilliant debuts of Cinerama and CinemaScope touched off an intense period of
technological development and entrepreneurial activity. Many new widescreen systems
were introduced: Cinemapanoramic, CinemaScope 55, Dyaliscope, MGM Camera 65,
PanaScope, Panavision, Super Panavision 70, SuperScope, Technirama, Techniscope,
Todd-AO, Ultra-Panavision 70, Vistascope, VistaVision, and Vistarama.[47] Of these, the
most important were VistaVision, Todd-AO, and Panavision.

VistaVision was Paramount's answer to Fox's CinemaScope. It used 35 mm. film stock,
but ran the film through the camera horizontally and recorded a much larger frame area
(eight perforations rather than four). Films could be exhibited with horizontal movement
and larger frame, or reduced to standard 35 mm., or shown with a slight anamorphic
process. In all three cases, the VistaVision system with its increased frame area offered
more visual detail and greater depth of field than CinemaScope or the suddenly outdated
1.33 to 1 format. VistaVision could be presented at aspect ratios ranging from 1.33 to 1 to
2 to 1, but Paramount recommended 1.85 to 1. Paramount's publicity stressed that CinemaScope's screen was uncomfortably wide, and that in the VistaVision alternative "height
is as important as width."[48] VistaVision was also exhibitor-friendly: it could be shown in
standard 35 mm., though more expensive alternatives were available; it required no special screen; and it used optical sound. The sound was recorded in a system called "Per-
specta," which allowed for playback in mono or in a sort of stereo (via cues encoded on
the optical track).[49]

The first VistaVision film was White Christmas (1954), a musical starring Bing
Crosby and Danny Kaye, which showed off the process's visual quality, depth of field,
and image height. The film often creates depth by presenting a narrow stage viewed
from the audience area—such compositions would have been hard to fit into Cinema-
Scope's elongated image. White Christmas was a creditable introduction to the new
process, but it lacked the spectacular impact of This Is Cinerama or The Robe. VistaVision was used by Paramount for a number of high quality films of the 1950s including
Strategic Air Command (1955), To Catch a Thief (1955), The Man Who Knew Too
Much (1956), The Ten Commandments (1956), Funny Face (1957), Vertigo (1958),
and L'il Abner (1959). Though never attaining the acceptance of CinemaScope, it was
also adopted by other studios for films including High Society (MGM, 1956), The
Searchers (Warner Bros., 1956), Auntie Mame (Warner Bros., 1958), The Vikings
(United Artists, 1958), and North by Northwest (MGM, 1959).

VistaVision became technologically obsolete because of the introduction of the fine-
grained, more light-sensitive 5250 color film stock by Eastman Kodak in 1959.[50] Image
sharpness on this stock was so good that VistaVision's larger negative and reduction

Bing Crosby, Vera-Ellen, Rosemary Clooney, and Danny Kaye in WHITE CHRISTMAS
(1954), the first VistaVision production.

printing were no longer necessary. VistaVision did, however, help to establish 1.85 to 1 as a favored aspect ratio for widescreen films. Since the mid-1950s, the two most common aspect ratios for Hollywood films have been 1.85 to 1 (the VistaVision ratio) and 2.25-2.35 to 1 (the CinemaScope ratio).

Theater producer and entrepreneur Michael Todd had supervised many of the scenes of THIS IS CINERAMA, but he had been frustrated by Cinerama's join lines and other technical limits. When Cinerama became a huge success, Todd was no longer affiliated with any of the Cinerama companies. He resolved to make a "better Cinerama," even though he had no technical training and almost no film industry experience. In October 1952 Todd recruited a leading optics expert, Dr. Brian O'Brien, who was vice president for research at American Optical Corporation, and gave him the job of developing a superior widescreen movie process. Todd gave his new partnership with O'Brien the name "Todd-AO," meaning "Todd-American Optical."

Within a few months, O'Brien and his team had settled on a wide film solution—the use of a 65 mm. camera negative and a 70 mm. release print. Todd-AO's wider film would have about four times the frame area of a 35 mm. film.[51] Wide film formats had been tried in the late 1920s (the 70 mm. Grandeur process, for example) but had been abandoned because of lack of studio interest. Todd-AO added to the wide film concept an enormous wide-angle lens, a film speed of 30 frames per second, six track magnetic stereo sound, and a projection system which corrected for distortion on the sides of the image.[52]

Magna Theatre Corporation was established as the new firm that would produce and

*Alfred Hitchcock in front of a VistaVision camera. Hitchcock
used this new technology in* To Catch a Thief *(1955),*
The Man Who Knew Too Much *(1956),* Vertigo *(1958),
and* North by Northwest *(1959).*

distribute Todd-AO films. As investors and partners, Todd brought in Joseph Schenck
and George P. Skouras of United Artists Theaters, producers Arthur Hornblow Jr. and
Edward Small, and renowned theatrical producers Richard Rodgers and Oscar Hammerstein II. (Schenck was formerly a top executive at Fox and brother of Nicholas
Schenck, chairman of Loew's, Inc.; George Skouras was the younger brother of Spyros
Skouras.) For the first Todd-AO film, Todd wanted the rights to Oklahoma!, Rodgers
and Hammerstein's Broadway musical, which they had withheld from Hollywood for ten
years. After viewing a Todd-AO demonstration in mid-1953, Rodgers and Hammerstein
agreed to sell Magna the film rights to Oklahoma! for $1,020,000.[53] Fred Zinnemann
would direct, Hornblow would produce, and Rodgers and Hammerstein would retain
artistic control.

Charles Skouras had an extraordinary suggestion for the opening scenes of Oklahoma!, which he thought would add $10 million to the film's gross. He described (in a
memo to Rodgers and Hammerstein) the cast of the film boarding a DC-7 and beginning an aerial tour of the United States: New York City, Philadelphia, Washington, D.C.,

the Mississippi River, and on to Oklahoma City and a transition to the musical OKLA-HOMA![54] Rodgers and Hammerstein opposed this suggestion, clearly based on THIS IS CINERAMA; they insisted that the film be shot without visual pyrotechnics.

OKLAHOMA! was filmed in both Todd-AO and CinemaScope, a necessary precaution in case Todd-AO broke down (at the start of production, for example, there was only one Todd-AO lens, no backup).[55] Fred Zinnemann considered casting the then-unknown James Dean as the male lead, but settled on an established musical star, Gordon MacRae.[56] Other leading roles were filled by Shirley Jones, Gloria Grahame, and Rod Steiger. The film version of OKLAHOMA! was stylistically cautious, but it nevertheless attracted a broad public. Shown on a roadshow basis, it became a major event, like THIS IS CINERAMA and THE ROBE. Only a handful of Todd-AO installations existed in 1955, so most of the country saw the CinemaScope version. Even the London premiere of OKLA-HOMA! in 1956 was presented in CinemaScope.[57]

The next Todd-AO picture was produced by Michael Todd: AROUND THE WORLD IN EIGHTY DAYS (1956), directed by Michael Anderson and starring David Niven, Cantin-flas, and Shirley MacLaine. This long and spectacular film based on the novel by Jules Verne combined a travelogue, a comic adventure, and cameo appearances by a long list of stars: Ronald Colman, Noel Coward, Marlene Dietrich, Buster Keaton, Beatrice Lil-lie, George Raft, Gilbert Roland, Frank Sinatra, and Red Skelton, among others. It was

George Raft, Marlene Dietrich, and David Niven in AROUND THE WORLD IN EIGHTY DAYS (1956).

based in part on Todd's work with Orson Welles on a 1946 Broadway musical version of Verne's novel (Alexander Korda replaced Todd as producer of the Broadway show a few weeks before the opening).[58] AROUND THE WORLD IN EIGHTY DAYS was even more successful than OKLAHOMA!, and it won the Academy Award for Best Picture in 1956.

In 1958, Twentieth Century–Fox invested $600,000 in Todd-AO for the right to produce three Todd-AO films plus an option to take over 51 percent ownership of the company. Donald A. Henderson of Fox explained that CinemaScope had lost most of its impact, and with Todd-AO Fox hoped to re-establish its widescreen competitive advantage.[59] However, by this time the value of exclusive processes was ending, because the Hollywood film industry was rapidly standardizing its widescreen formats. In the late 1950s and early 1960s a film could be shot in 35 mm. anamorphic or non-anamorphic, or in 70 mm. anamorphic or non-anamorphic, or in Cinerama. Todd-AO reduced its film speed to 24 frames per second so that it could become interchangeable with other 70 mm. processes. Only sixteen feature films were released in Todd-AO, and only four in the 1950s: OKLAHOMA!, AROUND THE WORLD IN EIGHTY DAYS, SOUTH PACIFIC (1958), and PORGY AND BESS (1959).

Panavision was (and is) a company that made lenses and other equipment for the film industry. The company began in the early 1950s as a manufacturer of anamorphic lenses for theater projection. When Twentieth Century–Fox decided to cease supplying CinemaScope lenses to theaters in 1954, Spyros Skouros specifically endorsed Panavision lenses as a high-quality alternative, thus giving the fledgling company a boost. Another important early Panavision product was a laboratory printer designed for Columbia Pictures which could print an anamorphic CinemaScope negative as a non-anamorphic 1.85 to 1 release print, thus eliminating the need to shoot a film in two versions (anamorphic and non-anamorphic). In the second half of the 1950s, Panavision worked with MGM to develop a variety of wide-film (65 or 70 mm.) formats. Two films were made in MGM Camera 65: RAINTREE COUNTY (1957) and BEN-HUR (1959). Ironically, RAINTREE COUNTY was released in 35 mm. only, because in 1957 all theaters equipped for 70 mm. were playing AROUND THE WORLD IN EIGHTY DAYS. BEN-HUR, however, was an enormous success, which helped to establish Panavision as the leading supplier of wide film equipment. Panavision then developed Super Panavision 70, a wide-film system with technical specs identical to Todd-AO. This system was used for EXODUS (United Artists, 1960), WEST SIDE STORY (United Artists, 1961) and LAWRENCE OF ARABIA (Columbia, 1962). Though Panavision invented no revolutionary formats, it improved the visual quality and the flexibility of 35 mm. and 70 mm. widescreen cinema. Panavision lenses therefore became the de facto Hollywood standard.[60]

Widescreen Revolution

The key question to be asked about the widescreen processes of the 1950s is this: How much of a difference did they make in the history of Hollywood? For critic/historian Andrew Dowdy, their impact was minimal. The "CinemaScope rebound," he says, lasted only about two years, from late 1953 to late 1955, so widescreen was a novelty only slightly more successful than 3-D. Movie admissions declined alarmingly in 1957 and 1958, despite all the new image technologies.[61] John Belton, author of the excellent *Widescreen Cinema*, gives a more nuanced view. On the one hand, he agrees that the various widescreen processes did not create a revolutionary change in cinema. They offered an aesthetic of participation, but it was only a false participation, which has "atrophied into an almost programmatic stimulus and response."[62] On the other hand, Belton feels that Cinerama, CinemaScope, Todd-AO, and the other widescreen processes offered a model of cinema flexible enough to please many kinds of spectators in many different viewing situations. He explains that "spectators were confronted with a variety of viewing situations from which they could choose, each of which engaged them in a different way, depending upon theater size and design, projection aspect ratio, and the dramatic content of the film. The cinema became a host of different cinemas; its traditional mass audience became, in turn, an assortment of highly diverse viewing groups."[63] This fragmentation of the film-viewing experience has, of course, accelerated since the 1950s.

A further claim could be made for widescreen's historical impact. In the early 1950s there were serious questions about whether film could survive at all as a form of mass entertainment. The successes of THIS IS CINERAMA, THE ROBE, HOW TO MARRY A MILLIONAIRE, THERE'S NO BUSINESS LIKE SHOW BUSINESS (Fox, 1954), WHITE CHRISTMAS, OKLAHOMA!, AROUND THE WORLD IN EIGHTY DAYS, and THE TEN COMMANDMENTS showed that spectators would visit the theaters for the right kind of attraction. Producers needed to adjust, and continue to adjust, to audience needs—the "bigger is better" approach worked for only a few years. But at least the "CinemaScope rebound" demonstrated a basis for continuing to make movies for the theaters. The Hollywood film industry would not become a mere adjunct to television.

6

Hollywood and Television in the 1950s: The Roots of Diversification

JANET WASKO

The film and broadcasting industries have shared a "symbiotic relationship" since the 1920s, with the major Hollywood companies attempting to develop and control television as a new distribution outlet. In the 1950s, the film companies produced programming for much of the prime-time TV schedule, and they also experimented with alternatives to broadcast television. By the end of the 1950s diversification was well under way—the Hollywood film companies were becoming media companies.

The importance of television for the film industry during the 1950s cannot be overstated. It has been argued that television was the primary factor affecting the dramatic plunge in ticket sales, box-office receipts, and company profits in Hollywood between 1947 and 1957 (see Chapter 1).[1] However, the film industry's relationship with television in the fifties must be understood in the context of social and economic changes (suburbanization, changes in demographics, and consumer spending habits) and political tensions (McCarthyism and HUAC). In addition, Hollywood was experiencing structural changes due to the Paramount decrees, the growth of independent production, trade barriers in foreign markets, and the demise of the Production Code, as well as changes in movie-viewing habits. While these developments are discussed more fully elsewhere in this volume, the current chapter focuses on the connections between the film industry and the television industry during this critical decade.[2]

Early Interactions Between the Film Industry and Television

Many historians have discussed the majors' involvement with broadcasting as early as the 1920s. For instance, Christopher Anderson argued that "the studios wanted not merely to participate in electronic communication but to *control* the radio and television industries"[3] (emphasis in the original). During this early period, the major studios were involved in radio in numerous ways. A few of their activities included the ownership of stations (Warner Bros. opened two radio stations, KFWB, Los Angeles, and WBPI, New York); investments in networks (Paramount was involved with CBS in the late 1920s); and relationships with radio interests (RKO was a subsidiary of RCA). While the Depression limited the studios' direct interests, Hollywood still utilized the airwaves for promotion as well as providing talent and programming.[4]

A few of the Hollywood studio executives demonstrated keen interest in television experiments during the 1930s. For instance, the Warner brothers followed the technological evolution of television quite closely, even attempting to attract Vladimir Zworykin away from RCA in the late 1930s. Meanwhile, David Selznick, a successful independent Hollywood producer, became involved with the early television inventor Philo T. Farnsworth.[5]

There is further evidence that the industry as a whole was not only watching the development of television technology, but saw opportunities in the new technology. As early as the 1920s the Motion Picture Producers and Distributors Association (MPPDA), the industry's trade organization, was preparing reports on television, followed by investigations in the 1930s of the film industry's role in the forthcoming television business.[6] Mortimer Prall, son of the FCC chairman, was hired by the MPPDA to prepare one report, in which he noted that "the motion picture industry has its greatest opportunity for expansion knocking on its door."[7]

In 1938, the Academy of Motion Picture Arts and Sciences requested its research council to study the film industry's preparation for the inevitable introduction of television, while numerous articles appeared that discussed the subject. One of the recommendations from the Academy was for the industry to pursue theater television, which will be discussed below.[8] Furthermore, both the MPPDA and the Academy formed ongoing committees to monitor television developments.

After World War II, there was a good deal of attention to the potential for the film industry to provide programming for the emerging television business, especially in light of the declining box office. Hollywood film producers and labor organizations, in particular, anticipated a new market for filmed products and employment opportunities in television production.[9]

Beyond the general industry interest in television, a few of the major studios had grand plans to control television through the ownership of distribution outlets, both individual stations and networks. Paramount was especially active in the evolution of television through its ownership of television properties, and, as outlined in the following sections, through attempts to innovate alternative television systems. In 1938, Paramount purchased substantial ownership interests in the Alan B. DuMont Laboratories Company. Over the next ten years, DuMont operated two experimental television stations in New York and Washington.[10] Paramount also was involved in another experimental license in Chicago around 1940 through its theater subsidiary, Balaban and Katz, as well as forming a subsidiary called Television Productions, Inc.

By 1948, Paramount owned four out of the first nine TV stations in the United States and had applied for licenses in six additional cities. Paramount owned KTLA, Los Angeles's first television station, and WBKB in Chicago, while DuMont owned and operated WABD in New York, WTTG in Washington, D.C., and WDTV in Pittsburgh. By the end of the 1940s, Paramount was distributing filmed television programs to a few stations through its Paramount Television Network, with plans to develop a full-fledged network. Although additional station ownership was planned, the FCC denied Paramount and DuMont's claim that they were separate companies and they were forced to adhere to the FCC limit of five stations.[11]

But Paramount wasn't the only film studio interested in television outlets.[12] MGM, Warners, Disney, and Twentieth Century–Fox actively vied for early TV outlets. Several of these companies applied for licenses in the Los Angeles area, but lost out to Paramount, probably because of the Paramount–DuMont connection.

Interestingly, some theater exhibitors in addition to Balaban and Katz also were interested in station ownership. Several theater chains applied for licenses in 1945, and the majority of stations owned by film interests in 1956 were held by theater owners.[13] Mitchell Wolfson, for example, owned a chain of South Florida theaters and the first TV station in Miami. He apparently felt that TV was not a threat and told fellow exhibitors that closed theaters should be converted to TV studios.[14]

However, Hollywood's bid to own television outlets mostly failed at this point, impeded chiefly by forces outside the film industry, especially the U.S. government. The government's hostility towards the film industry was apparent as early as 1940, when the FCC held hearings on technical standards for television. Another example of the government's attitude was evident at a meeting held in spring 1945, when the chairman of the FCC warned a group of Hollywood executives not to count on control or extensive ownership in the developing television business.[15] Furthermore, the FCC freeze on licensing new television stations (September 1948 to April 1952) for the announced purpose of establishing allocation policies and technical standards had the additional effect of preventing ownership of television stations by the Hollywood studios.

But most importantly, many of the studios' applications (especially Paramount's) were denied or withdrawn after the government's successful anti-trust suit against the majors. The FCC's policy was established in the Communications Act of 1934, which authorized the agency to refuse licenses to individuals or companies convicted of monopolistic activities. In addition, numerous statements by the agency confirmed a hostile attitude towards applicants with connections to the film industry.

Although the Hollywood studios most often were thwarted in their attempts to own broadcast outlets at this time, some companies still managed to own a few stations or align with networks. Several decades later, corporations associated with the film industry gained full control over television networks, as well as numerous cable channels and systems.

Meanwhile, during the 1940s and 1950s Hollywood also was trying to influence television's development through the innovation of two alternatives to TV broadcasting: theater televison and subscription television.

Theater Television

Theater television was one of the ways that Hollywood tried to "fight television with television."[16] The process involved screening television programming in motion picture theaters using two different systems: direct projection (television transmission projected onto screens) or "instantaneous projection" using a film intermediary (in other words, television signals transferred to film in less than a minute and then projected).

All of the major Hollywood companies were interested and active in developing theater television during the late 1940s and early 1950s; however, Paramount (again) was the most heavily involved. Hollywood's enthusiasm over theater TV was not surprising, since the Big

Five studios owned extensive theater chains at the time. But theater television also provided the opportunity to control distribution, as well as offering a way to differentiate Hollywood's products from broadcast television. Theater TV could feature more costly programming and a larger format than provided by "free" television viewed in homes.[17] In addition, exhibitors were interested in theater television, feeling that it might compete well with home television systems. In 1946, *Film Daily* reported that over half of the 350 theater owners participating in a survey were anticipating using theater television.[18]

Theater television can be traced back to the 1930s when RCA developed a large screen system utilizing a tube similar to those in home receivers, but with greater light output. The company demonstrated the system in 1930 at RKO-Proctor's 58th Street Theater in New York City.[19] By 1941, RCA's system had been installed in a few test theaters at a cost of $15,800 per theater.

Paramount and Fox invested in theater television as early as 1941, using an intermediary film system produced by Scophony, a company owned by Paramount. The Scophony system involved the use of 35 mm. film and an installation cost of $25,000. According to film historian Douglas Gomery, Scophony Ltd. (as well as Baird Television) had experimented with theater television technology in Great Britain, but without too much success. Paramount helped organize the Scophony Corporation of America in 1943 to "protect its position vis-a-vis RCA."[20] However, in 1945, an anti-trust suit claimed that Paramount and Fox, through control of Scophony patents, were conspiring to prevent the development of television technology.[21] From this point on, then, Paramount focused on its Paramount Intermediate Film System, an expensive system (around $35,000) that produced a 35 mm. print that could be edited and reused.[22]

After World War II, Warner and Fox aligned with RCA and arranged several demonstrations in 1948 and 1949. The relationship turned out to be short-lived, but Fox later became involved with several other systems. General Precision Laboratories, one of Fox's main stockholders, developed a method that used 16 mm. film and cost $33,000 to install. Fox also was associated with direct projection systems, including one produced by General Precision for $15,600, as well as a Swiss system called Eidophor that used carbon arc lights to project color images and cost around $25,000 to install. In 1951, Fox arranged with General Electric to produce equipment for use with the Eidophor system. Although the system could not compete with RCA's lower-price equipment, Fox did not give up on theater TV until the late 1950s.[23]

While theater television technologies attracted the interest of many production companies and theater chains before World War II, there was little development during the war. As noted above, activities continued in the late 1940s. The time seemed right: few television sets were in homes, the FCC freeze prevented expansion of television stations, and the studios were withholding films from television.

Paramount introduced its system in New York at the Paramount Theater in 1948 and continued to feature political news coverage, prizefights, and other sporting events through 1951. Paramount introduced theater TV in Chicago and Los Angeles in 1948 and 1949. In Chicago, Paramount's Balaban and Katz experimented with live programming at its theaters in Chicago in 1949 and 1950, but found that it was too expensive. Although Balaban and Katz had given up on theater television by mid-1951, other theaters were still adding the technology.

By the end of 1952, over one hundred theaters nationwide had installed or were installing theater television, with RCA controlling 75 percent of the market. A network called the Theater Television Network had formed, featuring sports events (such as boxing and collegiate games), public affairs, and entertainment events. During 1952, the Walcott-Marciano prizefight was presented in fifty theaters in thirty cities, with revenues totaling more than $400,000.[24]

However, by 1953, the high hopes for theater TV had faded. Paramount finally abandoned the project that year with losses at many of the theaters that had been equipped with its system.[25] Theater television's ultimate failure involves many interrelated factors that were identified by some industry sources at the time and have been discussed more recently by film and broadcast historians.

First, there were ongoing issues involved in securing effective and cost-efficient methods of transmission. Both telephone wires and the broadcast spectrum were used, but there were problems with both approaches. Initially some systems used telephone wires, or more specifically, intercity links from AT&T. However, the wire transmission system proved to be too expensive and insufficient for video transmission. Theater owners requested a hearing from the FCC in 1948 to review the issue of costs, but the petition was denied. Meanwhile, requests had been made to the FCC for radio frequencies to use for theater TV experimentation. In 1944, the Society of Motion Picture Engineers applied for space, and, though some frequencies were provided in 1945, they were deleted by 1947. From 1947 to 1949, Paramount and Fox were temporarily awarded frequencies for experimentation.[26]

Then, in 1949, exhibitors filed another FCC petition requesting 10 to 12 channels in the UHF spectrum for a "movie band." Hearings were held October 1952 through 1953, but the FCC decided to deny special frequencies, suggesting that the petitioners use common-carrier services or reapply. For various reasons, the companies did not reapply.[27] If these frequencies had been allocated, future development of film, cable, and television industries might have been quite different. However, without spectrum space, theater TV systems were forced to use expensive telephone lines, which affected the quality as well as the cost of operation.

Thus, another general problem was the FCC's resistance. Historical evidence indicates that the government did not share the film industry's enthusiasm for theater television. As film and radio historian Michele Hilmes noted, "the FCC, with an unerring eye for the maintenance of the status quo, rejected this vision. . . ."[28] The rejection in many ways was connected with the film industry's monopolistic tendencies, exemplified in the Paramount decrees, as well as the anti-trust suit dealing with the Scophony patents involving Paramount and Fox.

It is important to note that the broadcasting industry had similar inclinations, as evidenced in the case against the radio networks in the late 1930s, as well as a later anti-trust suit against the television networks for monopolizing program supply and distribution (1972).[29] Nevertheless, at this point it was clear that the government favored the "public interest" orientation of the broadcast industry against the "crass commerical" interest of Hollywood companies.

Meanwhile, other developments contributed to the doomed theater television project. With the lifting of the FCC's freeze in April 1952, television exploded on the scene, as millions of Americans turned to "free" television in the convenience of their homes. By 1954, there were 233 commercial stations and 26 million TV homes.[30] In addition, the size of home screens increased and color standards eventually were established. With these changes it became nearly impossible for theater television to compete.

During this time period, the industry was undergoing profound structural changes that ultimately separated production and distribution from exhibition. Thus, the interests of the studios (or the production/distribution companies) at times were different from those of exhibitors. This became even more significant when it came to selling products to the newly developing television industry, but also ultimately affected the support for theater television by the different sectors of the film industry. For instance, several unions were against theater television, especially the International Alliance of Theatrical Stage Employees (IATSE), but also trade organizations representing actors and musicians.[31]

In the end, the major studios and theaters shifted their focus to new formats or gimmicks that would compete with home television rather than continuing to pursue theater television. Various widescreen systems were adopted, as well as experimentation with 3-D. Theaters with financial problems found that these systems were less expensive, yet more profitable, than the equipment needed for theater television. Gomery concluded, "if theater television had proven profitable, it no doubt would have spread quickly to all parts of the United States."[32]

Meanwhile, the Hollywood companies were exploring another alternative television system through their active interests in developing subscription TV. Although there was some discussion of theater and subscription television co-existing, in the end, theater television was abandoned and the subscription TV battle began.

SUBSCRIPTION TELEVISION

Various experiments with subscription or pay television in the 1940s and 1950s involved companies connected to the film industry in one way or another. But it also must be noted that some film interests were involved in introducing pay systems, while others opposed those efforts. Though theater television was (at least, initially) welcomed by exhibitors, pay television was another thing altogether. Exhibitors not only feared it, they vigorously fought against it.

Again, Paramount took the lead in attempts to develop a viable pay television system. Timothy R. White pointed out that Paramount had a form of subscription TV in mind when it bought Scophony in 1942, and continued these efforts with DuMont. In the mid-1940s, Paramount planned to form a mobile system using DuMont equipment to transmit programming to theaters. However, these ideas ultimately were abandoned.[33]

By the late 1940s, three competing pay-TV sysems had been introduced, which then were tested in the early 1950s. Zenith's Phonevision was introduced in 1947, using telephone lines to unscramble a broadcast signal. Indeed, Zenith was the first company to ask for FCC permission to experiment with pay television in 1949, and tested its system in Chicago in 1950. After 1954, the company shifted to using a coin box or punch card system, but still was having problems obtaining programming. Paramount became involved with a system that used a scrambled broadcast signal through its 50 percent ownership of International Telemeter. Films were viewed by placing coins in a box on a television set, which then descrambled the picture. By 1957, Telemeter's system featured three channels using either wires or broadcast signals.[34] The Skiatron Corporation owned by Matthew Fox, an entrepreneur with some connections to the film industry, developed yet another system. Fox received the help of IBM to develop a system called Subscribervision, which used a punch card and a scrambled broadcast signal. RKO became involved with this system when a Chicago television station, WOR-TV, tested the Subscribervision system in 1950.[35]

Again, there was a good deal of enthusiasm by some Hollywood companies for a pay television system as an alternative to the advertiser-supported system adopted by broadcasters. (For instance, see Chapter 1 for references to Sam Goldwyn's opinions.) However, there were only a few actual experiments with pay systems during the 1950s.

The system that attracted the most attention was Telemeter in 1953, when it provided a community antenna system, plus special programs for extra fees, to 274 homes in Palm Springs, California. Charges included a $150–$450 installation fee, plus additional fees for cable and coin box use, plus program charges. In addition to sporting events and other live programming, the service offered the same film that was playing at the local theater for a slightly higher fee.

Apparently, the aim was to attract viewers who never went to theaters, and some theater owners even cooperated with the experiment. However, one of the Palm Springs theater owners charged that Paramount was in violation of the recent anti-trust suit against the majors. Although Telemeter claimed to be a success with over 2,500 subscribers, the system apparently buckled under the threat of governmental restriction. And despite the connection to Paramount, the system seemed to be unable to procure an adequate inventory of Hollywood films.[36]

Meanwhile, Southwestern Bell Telephone and Jerrold Electronics in Bartlesville, Oklahoma, introduced another system, called Telemovies. This featured a first-run movie channel and a rerun movie channel. First-run movies were shown concurrently at the local theater chain, thus avoiding one potential source of opposition. But even though the experiment received a good deal of press attention, the service apparently had financial problems. The use of telephone lines was costly, the flat monthly fee to customers was very high, and the company had some difficulties developing a system for paying Hollywood companies for the use of their films.[37] The Southwestern Bell system ceased operation in 1958.

Meanwhile, Paramount maintained its faith in pay TV, increasing its interest in Telemeter to 88 percent by 1958 and announcing that it would open systems in New York, on the West Coast, and in Canada. The company operated a service near Toronto, Canada, for a few years, but had lost $3 million by 1965, when Paramount's subscription TV activities ended.[38]

Despite the enthusiasm expressed for "pay-see" and "toll-video" (as *Variety* called them), most of these experiments had failed by 1965. One might wonder why a direct pay system of television that became successful two decades later failed at this time. Again, the reasons are multi-faceted, interrelated, and similar to the reasons that theater television failed. First, systems that relied on phone lines found that the costs were prohibitive. However, it seems possible that such technical problems eventually could have been overcome. Even more problematic was the attack on pay-TV that came from the theater sector of the film industry, as well as broadcasters and other groups, especially after the Paramount/Telemeter Palm Springs experiment in 1953. Ironically, Paramount Pictures was attacked by United Paramount Theaters, which had recently been divested from Paramount and merged with ABC television in 1953.

While additional experiments were carried out in the early 1960s, broadcast and theater forces continued to lobby extensively to defeat pay television. A statewide referendum specifically directed at former NBC President Pat Weaver's Subscription Television was passed in California in 1964.[39] Although the referendum was eventually declared unconstitutional, the extensive publicity around the ballot measure and its success seemed to seal the fate of pay television, at least during this period in history.

There were also serious obstacles due to delay and resistance from the federal government. Hilmes argues that pay television failed because of "slow strangulation by federal regulation."[40] It seems clear that the FCC understood its mandate was to protect the existing broadcast system, and it found encouragement as well from those who lobbied against pay-TV, namely broadcast and exhibition interests. Congressional representatives who had broadcast investments joined the anti–pay television movement as well. In fact, at least six bills were introduced to ban pay television, with hearings held on the topic by the FCC, the Senate, and the House.[41] Although the FCC agreed to a temporary subscription TV trial in 1957, during the next year the Senate and House requested a delay and finally forbid the commission to allow such trials.[42] Undoubtedly, the film industry's efforts to establish pay-TV suffered from anti-trust litigation, not only the Paramount decrees, but other cases as well.

Another huge problem was the competition from "free" TV. It might be argued that the film industry mostly moved in the wrong direction with early subscription experiments. Perhaps it was too early for pay systems that did not offer a regular schedule of special programming for which audiences would pay an extra fee. But the idea of paying for television programming also suffered notably from the campaign to save "free" TV. Pay television succeeded in later decades when the systems merged with cable television and offered programming not available on over-the-air broadcasting.

In addition, Hilmes has pointed out that "the FCC's public interest mandate, adopted and reinterpreted by broadcast television and theater interests, became equated in the public mind with the unchallengeable supremacy of the 'free TV' system."[43] For example, an article in *Consumer Reports* from 1949 made a case against the film industry's involvement in television, citing the large size and monopolistic tendencies of the film industry and the likely deterioration of public service with Hollywood's involvement in television programming.[44] It might be noted that both industries exchanged barbs relating to the quality of their products, as can be seen in this quip from *Variety*: "Television is only indirectly show business. Mostly it's advertising business."[45] And during testimony by an NBC executive at a government hearing, the "film-come-latelys" were accused of conspiring to unleash on television, "the lowest common Hollywood denominator . . . a continuing flow of stale and stereotyped film product."[46]

In summary, then, it is indisputable that Hollywood actively attempted to become involved in the evolving television system in the United States. Despite its inability to own or control broadcast outlets at an early stage or to develop successful alternative systems, the film industry eventually was able to profit from television in other ways.

Strategies for Coexistence with Television

While the events surrounding theater television and pay television unfolded, Hollywood was developing specific strategies for selling its products to the emerging television industry. By the 1950s, the film industry had firmly established a key role in the supply of the majority of television programming. Before discussing these developments, it is important to establish the backdrop for Hollywood's eventual triumph.

The evolving economic structure of television programming had shifted rather quickly from commercial sponsorship controlled by advertising agencies, with one main sponsor per program, to a magazine format with different sources of advertising controlled by the networks. As Mullen explained: "The degree of flexibility telefilm and videotape production techniques brought to television programming complemented the flexibility of magazine-format sponsorship. By the 1960s, virtually every component of the television schedule was both interchangeable and recyclable."[47]

The transition from live to recorded programming was another important factor in the evolution of television programming. The networks clung to live television, which was one way of maintaining control. (Live television meant that stations had to receive live feeds from the networks according to a specific schedule. Taped or filmed programs could be aired by stations whenever they chose to run them.) The networks and their critics also insisted that live television programming was creatively superior to filmed fare.[48] Nevertheless, the lower cost and reliability of recorded programs finally prevailed. As Hilmes explained: "by breaking down their own restrictions against the use of recorded programs, the major networks paved the way for the gradual disappearance of unwieldy and unpredictable live programming and the rapid rise in the use of film, as Hollywood wedged a toe in the door by means of syndicated film series."[49]

The ongoing structural changes within the film industry due to the Paramount decrees meant that the interests of producers eventually became different from those of exhibitors. Additional changes included the decline of studio-produced feature films and the growth of independently produced films, as well as fewer, more expensive films with increased promotion costs. Generally, the production-distribution companies benefited from these developments, while exhibition mostly suffered. In a 1985 article on Hollywood and television, William Boddy concluded: "The cumulative effect of these changes within the theatrical film industry in the early 1950s was a shift of power from exhibition to production-distribution. . . ."[50] In an overview of the industry in the late 1950s, a *Variety* writer echoed these sentiments:

> TV has had a terribly divisive effect on the film industry. It has accomplished what even divorcement could not really accomplish, i.e. a split between Hollywood (in the production sense of the word) and exhibition-distribution. It is simply a fact that, today, with the TV mart looming so importantly and the electronic medium advancing ever further, the basic interests of the Coast and the rest of the industry are not necessarily the same.[51]

HOLLYWOOD TELEVISION PRODUCTION

As indicated by the numerous investments in production companies in the late 1930s and 1940s, the major studios clearly intended to become involved in television programming. As new stations opened, the demand for filmed programs increased. However, some of the studios delayed production for broadcasting, as they hoped to develop the alternative television systems discussed above. In addition, it wasn't until the late 1950s that the major integrated companies were fully divorced from their theater chains. Thus, during much of the decade, they were forced to avoid conflict with theater owners and moved ever so cautiously into television production, as well as resisting sales of their new theatrical films to television. (In fact, Boddy noted that in 1950 the FCC actually issued a warning to the Hollywood studios for withholding talent and products from broadcast television.)[52] This is undoubtedly one of the reasons why many observers have concluded that Hollywood was hostile to television.

Nevertheless, a relatively large number of Hollywood independent producers created programming for broadcast television during the late 1940s and early 1950s. Jerry Fairbanks seems to have been the first Hollywood producer to sell a series to television when he marketed *The Public Prosecutor* to NBC in 1948.[53] Other programs that followed were mostly low-budget shows, including numerous Westerns (*Hopalong Cassidy, Roy Rogers, The Lone Ranger,* and *Cisco Kid*, to name a few), as well as crime, mystery, science fiction, and situation comedies. The business was highly competitive, with over 800 producers claiming to be involved during this early period, which came to be known as the "gold rush" period of television production. However, the business involved high speculation and slow paybacks on programs that averaged $12,000 to $15,000 per half-hour episode. Even at this early stage, a distinct financing system was emerging, with programs usually produced at a deficit and profits emerging in syndication, international distribution, and other products.[54]

By 1952, the production costs were rising (up to $20,000 per program) and the competition declining. The most successful telefilm production companies were those that had resources available and could provide commercially oriented, profitable productions. Among the few surviving independents were Fairbanks's company, Bing Crosby Productions, Hal Roach Studios, Ziv Television, and a few others.[55] Thus, early television production provides another example of an industry that moved through an initial period of robust competition to a concentrated market structure. As Dennis Dombkowski concluded:

> "Efficiency" and industry stability were thus gained at the cost of variety in program sources. It should be pointed out that it was no economic law that made this necessary for the television program supply industry, but rather the

The Lone Ranger *was one of many popular Western shows on 1950s television.*

inevitable requirements of a commercial system which was being designed for a nationwide service of networks and their correspondingly greater capital requirements, rather than a decentralized and less "efficient" system.[56]

Initially, the networks resisted filmed programming, aiming to control program supply and national advertising distribution. The networks insisted that their live, dramatic programming was higher quality than the cheaply made action-adventure shows and situation comedies produced by film companies. At this point, relatively low prices were offered for TV programming, even though high costs were anticipated for Hollywood-produced programming.[57]

However, even at the networks, filmed programming ultimately prevailed. The market for subsequent release of television programming (reruns, syndication, and foreign sales) was a major factor in the acceptance of filmed TV programming by the networks and the entrance of the Hollywood majors into telefilm production.

Only a few of the major companies produced television series, commercials, and news during the late 1940s and early 1950s. By 1952, television subsidiaries were formed by Columbia (Screen Gems), Universal (United World Films), and Monogram (Interstate Television). It might be noted that none of these companies were major integrated studios that owned theaters.

Most historians agree that the other major studios became much more active in television production after 1953. The reasons often cited are the lifting of the freeze in 1952, the increase in advertising money, the decline in the theatrical box office, and the actual divorcement of production/distribution from exhibition.[58]

At first, the majors offered programs that were designed to promote their film products or that featured their own names: *Disneyland, Warner Bros. Presents, MGM Parade*, and *Twentieth Century–Fox Hour*. They also tended to draw from their film resources for some program ideas (for instance, *RinTinTin*, a series of movies since the 1920s that became a popular TV series in the mid-1950s). But the studios moved on to produce a wide range of programs, including prestigious dramatic shows (such as *Playhouse 90*) and especially half-hour series that were quite profitable in network and syndicated markets.

Each major company moved into television at a somewhat different pace. In 1956, Columbia produced thirteen half-hour series and one ninety-minute program, with television representing one-quarter of the company's revenues. Around the same time, Twentieth Century–Fox produced four half-hour shows and one one-hour series. Meanwhile, Warner Bros. received nearly one-third of its profits from television by the end of the decade. Paramount was much slower than the other studios, and it wasn't until the 1970s that television production became important. By 1964, six Hollywood companies represented 45 percent of the domestic market for syndicated TV series.[59]

Although Hollywood had to make adjustments for television production, the pattern had been set. Commercially oriented filmed programming became the main staple of American television and the large Hollywood studios came to dominate the market. Erik Barnouw identified more than 100 Hollywood-produced television series on the air or in production by the end of 1957.[60] By the end of 1959, 78 percent of network evening programming originated in Hollywood and over 88 percent of that was filmed.[61] And, although a 1956 congressional study of the film industry found that 170 producers were involved in making television programs of various lengths,[62] a handful of well-endowed Hollywood companies dominated the program supply. At the beginning of 1959, *Variety* estimated that $105 million would be dedicated to telefilm production during the year.[63]

Anderson concluded: "By the end of the 1950s, with the fates of the networks and studios deeply entwined, filmed television series emerged as the dominant product of the Hollywood studios and the dominant form of prime-time programming—a pattern that has remained unchanged for more than thirty years."[64]

FEATURE FILMS ON TELEVISION

Hollywood's major line of business—feature-length films—would seem to have been an obvious program source for television, with its insatiable need to fill airtime. Paramount actually televised some of its films in the early 1930s, but through an experimental station in Los Angeles that only reached few receivers.[65] A number of British films were sold to television stations as early as 1948, followed by features from small Hollywood companies such as Republic and Monogram. Yet, the major studios held their films back for various reasons, including their relationship with exhibitors and talent unions, their involvement in alternative exhibition schemes such as theater and subscription TV, and their dissatisfaction with the prices offered by the networks for quality films. Based on information from government documentation, Dombkowski argued that low prices offered by the networks was the primary reason. (Statements in the trade press confirm this point. For instance, in 1952, Spyros Skouras stated that TV, "can only pay us buttons for our old films, and certainly can't even begin to compete for the new product.")[66]

By 1955, the divorcement of exhibition freed the distributors from their commitments to theaters and broadcast television had become more established and profitable. Thus, the major studios began releasing their older films to television. An agreement between the producers and trade unions required negotiation for the licensing of films produced after 1948. Thus, pre-1948 films were the first ones sold to television stations. The majors either sold their films to other companies or set up their own television distribution divisions. RKO started the licensing deluge in 1955 when it sold its features and shorts to C. and C. Television. Meanwhile, Columbia sold its own feature films through its Screen Gems subsidiary, which also handled Universal's older films. Fox sold its films to National Telefilm Associates, but then purchased 50 percent of the company in 1956. Eventually, Paramount sold its library to an affiliate of the Music Corporation of America (MCA), which later was to merge with Universal. (White notes that Paramount delayed the sale of pre-1948 films until much later than the other studios because of their hope that pay television would succeed.)[67]

In his 1960 book, Michael Conant cited government documentation claiming that in 1954 there were eighty motion picture exchanges dedicated to the distribution of films to television, with total receipts of $24 million. He further estimated that by February 1958, around 3,700 pre-1949 feature films had been sold or leased to television for an estimated $220 million.[68] As predicted, the appearance of feature films on television ate into the theatrical box office. A specially commissioned study by the theater owners found that towards the end of 1957, one-quarter of television programming represented recycled movies.[69] Independent stations (not affiliated with the networks) found feature films to be a major source of programming, sometimes providing up to 48 percent of their schedules.[70]

But the licensing of feature films was still predominantly to individual television stations, not to the networks. Even though over thirty prime time network programs consisted of feature films between 1948 and 1957, these offerings were sporadic and inconsistent.[71] The networks resisted the regular use of feature films in their schedules, but also were unable (or unwilling) to pay enough to satisfy the majors. Meanwhile, the studios found the syndication market for pre-1948 films to be quite profitable, but resisted issuing newer films because of the potential loss of revenues from theater reissues.

Of course, the networks eventually came around to featuring Hollywood films in their prime time schedules. But it wasn't until the early 1960s, after a new labor agreement had been negotiated with the talent unions, that the majors began seriously releasing their newer films to television. When they did, however, there was a plethora of post-1948 films on the market. In fact, so many newer films were licensed by the majors during 1961 that some feared supplies would be exhausted in only a few years.[72] This was one of the factors that influenced the evolution of Hollywood-produced made-for-TV movies and mini-series that started emerging in the mid-1960s.[73]

By 1960, television had become the hot new medium; 90 percent of American homes were equipped with sets. And a good deal of the televised programming came from Hollywood. By this time, over 40 percent of network programming was produced by the Hollywood majors.[74]

It is nearly impossible to estimate the actual revenues that film companies earned from television during the 1950s, as few companies specifically identified television revenues in their annual reports.[75] An overview of the diversification trends in *Variety* at the end of the decade included estimates of television's contributions to total revenues for a few companies for 1958: Columbia, 25 percent, Disney, 20 percent, Loew's, 11 percent, and Warners, 30 percent.[76]

It is clear that, at least by the mid-1960s television was heavily dependent on Hollywood-produced programming and Hollywood had become dependent on television as a crucial source of revenues. This relationship continued to grow through the 1970s, as documented by Thomas H. Guback and Dennis J. Dombkowski in a 1976 article, and indeed through the end of the century.[77] Even though the major studios were not able to control television or develop alternative forms, they eventually found television to be a valuable new market for their old products, and they also developed new products for the expanding new medium.

The New Diversification

By the late 1950s and early 1960s, the Hollywood majors represented newly diversified corporations, reporting sizable profits. The next two sections will look more closely at two companies that were particularly successful with these new diversification strategies: Walt Disney and Universal. The Walt Disney Company was an independent production company that benefitted greatly from diversification in the 1950s. At the same time, Universal was a "second rank" studio through the 1940s, but through its alliance with MCA in the late 1950s it became one of the Hollywood majors by the mid-1960s. Both companies moved into television during the 1950s, thus setting the foundation for their roles as diversified entertainment conglomerates at the end of the century.

WALT DISNEY PRODUCTIONS

As briefly noted in Chapter 1, the Walt Disney Company was a relatively small independent that mainly produced animated cartoons from the early 1920s, adding animated features in the 1930s. The extensive merchandising campaigns accompanying these films contributed to the company's revenues and made it possible to continue production of cutting-edge animation. However, Disney did not represent the kind of integration and diversification typical of the major studios until the 1950s.

Walt Disney is often acknowledged as the first executive in Hollywood to recognize the potential of television. While this claim ignores other film companies' ongoing attempts to get into the television business in various ways, Disney still deserves credit for recognizing television's potential value in promoting and diversifying the film business. Disney explained, "Through television I can reach my audience. I can talk to my audience. They are the audience that wants to see my pictures."[78] It seems likely that the Disney company had television in mind for its products from the mid-1930s, when it changed from United Artists to RKO as distributor; the crucial factor was United Artists' refusal to allow Disney to retain television rights to films.[79]

At first, the Disney Company produced a few Christmas specials, beginning with "One Hour in Wonderland," broadcast on NBC in 1950. Apparently, all three of the networks tried to convince Disney to produce a weekly series. Finally, in October 1954 the weekly series *Disneyland* appeared on ABC, moving to NBC seven years later as *Walt Disney's Wonderful World of Color*. The television series allowed the studio to recycle its

Walt Disney is congratulated by Joan Crawford as the Academy Award nominations are announced for 1953.

already released products, similar to the technique of continuously re-releasing its animated features in theaters every few years, thus reaping further profits with little additional cost.

But television also proved helpful in several ways for Disney's most cherished project—an amusement park that would appeal to adults as well as children. The arrangements with ABC for the Disney television series apparently were prompted by Disney's need for capital to build Disneyland, which eventually opened in Anaheim, California, in 1955. ABC invested $500,000 in the park and became a 35 percent owner, plus guaranteeing loans of up to $4.5 million. Walt Disney apparently received little support from the Disney Company itself, but managed to raise the funds from the ABC deal and loans on his insurance policies. In 1952, he formed a separate company called Walt Disney Inc., later to become WED Enterprises, to develop the park without involving company funds. Disneyland ultimately cost $17 million, but was an instant success with one million visitors during its first seven weeks of operation.

In addition to providing financial backing, *Disneyland,* the television series, became a terrific promotional vehicle for the park even before it opened. The show was organized around the same four divisions as the park—Fantasyland, Adventureland, Frontierland, and Tomorrowland—and constantly featured updates on the new park. Of course, new content also was developed for the show. For instance, Davy Crockett started as a three-part episode, inspired a national merchandising sensation, and was then recycled as two feature films.(The company obviously underestimated the success of the series, as Disney explained: "We had no idea what was going to happen to 'Crockett.' Why, by the time the first show finally got on the air, we were already shooting the third one and calmly killing Davy off at the Alamo. It became one of the biggest overnight hits in TV history, and there we were with just three films and a dead hero.") [80] However, a good deal of the show featured the studio's recycled cartoons and feature films. The Davy Crocket phenomenon—with coonskin caps purchased by young boys all over the country—was another reminder of the Disney Company's successful merchandising business, which had been established in the early 1930s.

In 1955, the company introduced a daily afternoon television show designed exclusively for children and proclaimed as a "new concept in television programming." *The Mickey Mouse Club* featured the mouse-eared singing and dancing Mouseketeers, plus other segments that involved Disney's products (such as Disney cartoons and news about Disneyland). Despite its enormous popularity in 1955–1956 (at one point, reaching 75 percent of the television sets in the United States and attracting lots of advertising), and the endurance of its theme song, *The Mickey Mouse Club* only lasted four seasons. The main reasons for its cancellation were: 1) the high cost of producing the show; 2) a significant drop in ratings from 1955 levels; and 3) a dispute between Disney and ABC over control of *The Mickey Mouse Club* and another series, *Zorro.*[81]

In addition to these developments, the company also finally decided to distribute its own films, creating Buena Vista Distribution (as noted in Chapter 1). The move was attributed to Walt Disney's deep concern about maintaining control over his own products, as had been seen in an earlier incident when the Disney character, Oswald the Lucky Rabbit, was "stolen" by another company. To a large extent, the move into distribution signaled the Disney Company's transition from a marginal independent film company to one of the Hollywood majors.

Even though the company may have been slow to control its own film distribution, it might be argued that Disney led the way in the diversification that would characterize the industry for the next few decades. As writer Richard Schickel argued, the Disney Company had a head start on the rest of the industry. While the larger, integrated majors were dealing with the rising competitive threat of television, as well as the loss of their theaters due to the Paramount decrees, the Disney Company was diversifying its film products, as well as its over-all business.[82] For instance, in 1960 Disney reported the following income sources: film rentals, $18.4 million, amusement park, $18.1 million, television, $4.9 million, and other (publications, comic strips, licensing cartoon characters and music), $4.9 million.[83] Furthermore, by the beginning of the 1960s, the company was integrating these businesses, thus laying the foundation for the Disney synergy that blossomed in the 1980s and 1990s. In addition, the Disney Company was especially successful at selling and promoting its products globally. By 1954, it was estimated that one-third of the world's population had seen at least one Disney film.

By the end of the 1950s, the company was recognized by *Variety* as one of the "ideal diversified amusements setups."[84] And by the end of the century, the Disney Company was one of the largest entertainment conglomerates in the world, including substantial investments in network television (ABC), cable television (ESPN, A&E, Lifetime, the Disney Channel, and other stations), as well as motion pictures, theme parks, real estate, and merchandising.[85]

MCA/UNIVERSAL

Another current major entertainment conglomerate to develop important diversified activities (especially in television) during the 1950s was MCA/Universal. The story involves two different companies that came together during this decade.

Universal Studios is one of the oldest film companies in the United States, dating back to 1906 when Carl Laemmle opened the White Front Theatre in Chicago. The same year, the Laemmle Film Service was established as a film distribution company that by 1919 was servicing a majority of cinemas in the Midwest and Canada. In 1909, the Independent Moving Picture Company of America (IMP) was formed to produce films. Universal Film Manufacturing Company as founded in 1912, was the result of a merger of IMP and several other film companies. In 1915, the company established studio facilities at a 230-acre ranch in southern California called Universal City.[86] Although Universal produced and distributed a range of films over the years, the company produced mostly "B" pictures that supplemented the major studios' "A" films.

Universal began diversification activities in 1951 when Decca Records acquired a 38 percent share and soon thereafter controlled the company. Universal had encountered serious losses from a few expensive independent films from 1946 to 1949. Thus, the new management attempted to cut costs and increase revenues through low-budget productions, including situation comedies such as the Ma and Pa Kettle series, and a number of science fiction films, including CREATURE FROM THE BLACK LAGOON (1954) and THE INCREDIBLE SHRINKING MAN (1957).

The company had moved into television production in the late 1940s in hopes of attracting revenues, but also in an effort to keep its facilities open during production lulls. Universal's subsidiary, United World Films, was especially active in producing television commercials and had produced over 5,000 commercials that attracted $3 million in annual revenues by 1958.[87] The company also was releasing theatrical films to television, with *Variety* dubbing United World "a dominant factor in the home movies field" in 1958.[88]

Decca/Universal's relationship with Music Corporation of America (MCA) began in December 1958, when Universal sold its 367-acre studio lot for $11.25 million to MCA, then leased back studio space at $1 million a year.

MCA dates back to 1924, when Dr. Jules Stein and William R. Goodheart Jr. founded it as a talent agency for live music and later radio. (See Chapter 1.) In 1935, in addition to Lew Wasserman joining the company, MCA received a "blanket waiver" from the American Federation of Musicians, permitting the agency to act in a dual capacity as talent booker and program producer, and allowing it to package radio shows with its own bands. MCA added live show production in 1943 through a subsidiary called Revue Productions. The company also expanded its agency business with the addition of Hayward-Deverich Agency in Beverly Hills and the Leland Hayward Agency in New York. New clients included top Hollywood stars such as Greta Garbo, Fred Astaire, Jimmy Stewart, Henry Fonda, and Gregory Peck. The company gained a reputation for taking care of its clients, arranging lucrative contracts and creative financial deals. For instance, in 1950 Wasserman negotiated a percentage deal for Jimmy Stewart to receive 50 percent of the net receipts for WINCHESTER '73 from Universal—a deal that was said to have revolutionized the film business, since before that time stars had rarely received a share of the box office.

MCA client Alfred Hitchcock displayed his macabre sense of humor as host of Alfred Hitchcock Presents.

As the company grew to become a dominant force in the entertainment industry, it began attracting the attention of the federal government for anti-trust violations. In the first of many suits filed against the company, a judge found MCA guilty of restraint of trade in 1946, calling the agency "the Octopus . . . with tentacles reaching out to all phases and grasping everything in show business." However, what followed during the 1950s extended the Octopus's reach much further than the judge might have imagined.

MCA, as the largest talent agency in the business, began its move into television production in 1952. Revue Productions re-emerged as the company's television subsidiary, with a TV version of radio's *Stars over Hollywood,* called *Armour Theatre.* The series was recorded on film, which increased the production expense, but MCA arranged for its clients to appear on the programs for minimum scale.

As Revue continued to produce other television series, the issue of conflict of interest again emerged. And, again, the agency was able to obtain a "blanket waiver" from the talent guilds that enabled it to gain a considerable advantage in television production. The unprecedented and exclusive waiver from the Screen Actors Guild allowed Revue to produce television shows and simultaneously represent talent in those shows. The Writers Guild granted MCA a similar waiver, allowing it to represent screenwriters and to produce TV programs through Revue.

By 1954, MCA was earning 57 percent of its revenues from television programming. During the 1950s, Revue Productions became incredibly successful in television, with such high-ranking shows as *Wagon Train, Alfred Hitchcock Presents, The Jack Benny Show, Ozzie and Harriet, Dragnet, This Is Your Life, Leave It to Beaver,* and many, many others. By most accounts, MCA was the dominant force in television by the end of the decade, with 85 percent of its revenues from television sales and producing more programming than any other company, including the television networks themselves.

Although MCA produced programs for every network, the company developed a special relationship with NBC that was similar to Disney's with ABC. One report cited an NBC executive showing an MCA vice president plans for its 1957 season, saying, "here are the empty spots, you fill them." An assortment of MCA programs was featured on NBC that year, including *M Squad, Wagon Train, Tales of Wells Fargo,* and others.[89] Meanwhile, MCA also produced a number of shows directly for syndication, including *Mike Hammer, Biff Baker, U.S.A.,* and *Famous Playhouse.*

MCA expanded in other areas of the entertainment business, as well. In 1958, the company purchased Paramount Studios' pre-1950 sound film library for $50 million, the richest television syndication deal to date. The same year, the company incorporated as MCA Inc., a neatly diversified enterprise encompassing film and television production and distribution, talent management, music production and distribution, and a variety of other entertainment fields. By this time, it also had moved into the tourist/theme park business through a deal with Grey Line Bus Tours called "Dine with the Stars." Buses drove around the lot with visitors, who would then have lunch in the commissary. By 1964, the Universal Studios Tour opened in conjunction with Glamour Trams, including two drivers, two guides, and one ticket seller; the price of admission was set at $6.50 for two adults and a child

While these diversification activities were proving to be quite lucrative, at the end of the decade the government again began to focus attention on MCA. One of the problems was the blanket waiver that was issued in 1952 (and extended in 1954), while Ronald Reagan (an MCA client) was president of SAG. Although some argued that the waiver was issued to encourage employment, the government alleged that it was a con-

Ricky, David, and Ozzie Nelson in HERE COME THE NELSONS *(1951), a Universal film that became the basis for the Revue Productions television show* Ozzie *and* Harriet.

spiracy that allowed MCA to monopolize talent and television program production. (Other agencies had not been given such waivers.) Reagan's involvement as both SAG negotiator and MCA client suggested a conflict of interest. Reagan remembered few of the details during government hearings, but it seems that a year after MCA's waiver was granted, he had become the host and star (and later, producer) of Revue's General Electric Theater on CBS. The program contributed to Reagan becoming a multi-millionaire by the time the show closed nine years later.

Other allegations involved MCA's restraint of trade, extortion, discrimination, blacklisting, and use of predatory business practices. One of MCA's practices was to develop television programs or motion pictures as "packages" of the agency's clients. The agency received a commission on the sale of the package to various outlets. While other agencies used this technique, MCA was particularly successful in its implementation, and had become known for its practice of refusing to let a company employ one of its clients unless a complete MCA "package" was involved.

Around the same time as the government investigations, MCA announced plans to purchase Decca Records, which included Universal Pictures. Interestingly, the growth of Universal Pictures into a major studio was due to sizable profits from increasingly bigger films that were put together as "MCA packages." Examples included three of Universal's biggest moneymakers of 1959: OPERATION PETTICOAT ($18.6 million), IMITATION OF LIFE ($13 million), and PILLOW TALK ($15 million).

Although the government initally moved to block the purchase of Decca and Universal, MCA finally agreed to a consent decree with the Justice Department in 1962, clearing the way for the merger. The company chose to divest its talent management activities, but gained even more clout in the lucrative film and television business, as well as in the music industry. Though the company continued to pursue other forms of diversification during subsequent years, these developments during the 1950s were consequential in the rise of MCA/Universal as a significant player in the entertainment industry at the end of the twentieth century. [90]

Conclusion

Although the film industry failed to dominate the emerging television industry in the 1950s, Hollywood actively participated in television's evolution during the decade and established a strong relationship that eventually led to the integration of these two industries. It is clear that Hollywood companies kept a close watch on the evolving television technology and even became involved in its early growth. However, strategies that involved hardware development and ownership of broadcast outlets were mostly unsuccessful. Station and network ownership, as well as alternative systems, such as theater television and early forms of pay-TV, were thwarted, especially by government protectionism, but also by resistance from exhibitors and other factors. Notably, the Hollywood majors' monopolistic tendencies proved detrimental to some of their efforts to expand into the newly emerging television industry.

However, Hollywood did succeed in becoming involved in the television business through program supply. During a period of box-office decline, the newly emerging television industry provided the opportunity for the major studios to draw upon their expertise and resources to create new products (like prime-time series and made-for-TV films) for the growing television market. In the end, the majors were able to dominate that market. In addition, the film industry was able to recycle and profit yet again from feature films that had already produced sizable profits. Eventually, television also served as another market for newly produced theatrical films.

These activities ultimately led to the diversification of the film industry, as well as the eventual integration of the film and television industries later in the century. As Anderson fittingly concluded:

> Since the movie studios began producing television, the diversification of media corporations into related fields and the consolidation of capital through corporate mergers have produced an environment in which media industries are increasingly interwoven. Although these tendencies existed before the 1950s, the impulse toward integration rose markedly during that tumultuous decade and has become more pronounced in subsequent years.[91]

In other words, television provided the film industry with new opportunities that laid the groundwork for the diversification and concentration that characterized the entertainment industry at the end of the century.

7

Hollywood International

The economic strength of the American film industry has depended since the 1920s on two essential components: first, a large and homogeneous national market; and second, an extensive international distribution network. The national market (sometimes described as North American, including Canada) of a billion or more spectators each year allows for production of hundreds of films per year with good production values and a relatively high average cost. International distribution adds a further chance for films to earn back their costs and return a profit. Further, because the primary cost of making a film lies in producing the first copy, it makes economic sense to distribute American films to small as well as large markets. For most countries, it is far cheaper to import American films than to support a competitive film industry of their own.

During World War II, Hollywood's earnings were strongly based on North American distribution, with England being the only important overseas market. This changed fairly rapidly in the twenty years after the war. National sales declined and international sales increased until, in the early 1960s, international income was substantially greater than income from the U.S. market. Great Britain remained the best foreign customer for Hollywood films, but income from Western Europe, Latin America, and Japan also contributed strongly to the American film industry's earnings.

Media historian Jeremy Tunstall described the period 1943–1953 as "the high tide of American media" in the world because of American military, political, and economic power.[1] In the film industry, the Hollywood companies after World War II had undamaged facilities plus a backlog of hundreds of films not yet shown in Europe or Japan. They therefore had enormous advantages over the struggling, often war-damaged film industries of England, France, Italy, and other European countries. Further, countries receiving Marshall Plan aid after World War II were encouraged to accept American films for political and ideological reasons, and in West Germany and Japan, American occupation forces had considerable control over the national economy.

One factor making foreign markets more and more crucial to Hollywood was the American industry's problems at home. Television and other leisure time activities were cutting into the film audience throughout the 1950s. The same thing happened in England, albeit a few years later. But in continental Europe, television was much slower to get started, and so the larger countries of Western Europe (mainly Italy and France) became important customers of the Hollywood film industry. Italian government statistics show that for the years 1950–1959 American films took in gross box-office receipts of $925 million in Italy, with the high point being $116.7 million in 1956.[2]

European Protectionism and Working Abroad

Western European countries including Great Britain responded to Hollywood dominance by enacting legislation aimed at limiting their outflow of currency and protecting national film industries. Protectionist laws included import quotas, screen quotas (reserving a certain number of weeks at every theater for national productions), fees and taxes on imports, subsidies for national film companies, and blocked funds. The "blocking" of funds or currency meant that a portion of the income earned in film distribution could only be spent in the country in which it was earned. Economic film historian Thomas Guback lists three alternatives for American film companies faced with blocked funds: they could leave funds in frozen accounts until restrictions were lifted; invest in foreign goods and import them to the United States; or make films abroad.[3]

Accounting materials for STRANGERS ON A TRAIN (Warner Bros., 1951) provide a useful snapshot of the extent of international distribution and the problem of blocked funds. This film was produced at a cost of $1,568,246 and released in the United States in 1951. As of 27 February 1954 it had earned $1,691,213 in the United States and $86,541 in Canada.[4] At this point, STRANGERS ON A TRAIN had been distributed by Warners in thirty-five countries or territories. England was by far the largest foreign market, with income of almost $365,000, but the film had earned at least $20,000 in each of the following countries: Argentina, Australia, Belgium, Brazil, France, Germany, Italy, Japan, Mexico, and Sweden. The film had also been released by local distributors to a variety of small markets including Bermuda, Gibraltar, Greece, Iran, Iraq, and Jamaica. "Free" (that is, unblocked) funds taken from international distribution were $871,715, or slightly more than half of U.S. earnings. However, some funds were blocked in fourteen countries, and this amounted to more than $150,000.[5] By early 1954, the film's foreign earnings (including Canada and the blocked funds) had been about 40 percent of total earnings. Note that in 1954 the film had not yet been distributed in Spain, and it may still have been playing in some international markets.

Clearly STRANGERS ON A TRAIN would have been in dire straits without foreign earnings. The film barely made back its production cost in the U.S. market, which meant it had not repaid distribution expenses (prints, sales offices, physical distribution, and advertising). These expenses are often figured as roughly equal to production costs,[6] meaning that STRANGERS ON A TRAIN would have to earn $3,136,000 to break even. However, if one assumes that both production overhead and distribution costs include a certain amount of studio profit, a more realistic break-even point might be 1.6 to 1.8 times production cost. Because of foreign earnings, STRANGERS ON A TRAIN had, by 1954, earned about 1.8 times its production budget and therefore had recovered its costs with the chance of a small profit.[7] And even though the blocked funds are a relatively small part of the film's earnings ($150,000+ out of $2.8 million), they are crucial to its balance sheet. It was certainly in Warners' interest to pursue the blocked funds.

Although some Hollywood companies engaged in elaborate schemes to repatriate blocked funds, most of these funds were used to produce films abroad. The Hollywood studios were producers and distributors of films, not general import-export companies, so it made sense to stick to their core business. By employing frozen earnings to produce films, the studios served the interest of the "host" countries (those holding the blocked funds), but also their own interests. For host countries, Hollywood-sponsored productions added to the national economy, decreased foreign exchange problems, helped the national film industry (work for actors and technicians, rental for studios and equipment), and even added long-term benefits such as prestige and tourist activity. For the Hollywood studios, production abroad allowed them to invest otherwise unavailable funds in films that could then be shown in American and international markets.

The Hollywood studios quickly found that international productions had other advantages. Labor was often much cheaper in overseas locations; this was important to all pictures, but it could be crucial to epic films requiring elaborate sets and thousands of extras. Filmmakers also benefited from the visual possibilities of shooting in famous world capitals or regions known for natural beauty. And the Hollywood companies found that by creating subsidiaries in various countries they could benefit from the same subsidies and protectionist rules that were supporting local filmmakers. Thomas Guback commented that the first wave of productions abroad benefited from blocked funds, but the second wave was more interested in subsidies.[8]

Despite the advantages, production abroad was hardly a risk-free operation. The internationally produced films emphasized exteriors (why go abroad to shoot in a studio?), but this meant that weather became a factor. One reason that Los Angeles had long been established as the center of American film production was its dependable weather—more than 300 days of sunshine per year. Locations on other continents were far less predictable, indeed journalistic accounts of production abroad often recorded complaints about endless rain. American companies filming abroad were also subject to local customs and local censorship. In Venice, the crew for SUMMERTIME (1955) found that it was difficult and expensive to film from barges, especially since they could be moved only at certain times of day (according to the tides). On this same production, filmmakers learned that they were expected to reimburse storeowners for "loss of business" whether or not any real losses had occurred.[9] For WAY OF A GAUCHO (1952), filmed in Argentina, writer-producer Philip Dunne discovered that the followers of President Juan Perón "had made the legendary gaucho, then almost extinct, a national hero and symbol of their own aggressive nationalism."[10] The film's script had to be rewritten to correspond with official policy, and the entire production was carefully monitored by Perón's minister of information, Raul Apold.[11]

Runaway Productions

The trend toward filming abroad had serious consequences for California-based film workers. Employment had already been hurt by the decreasing number of films made by the major and minor studios each year. For example, the Production Code Administration approved 429 features in 1950, but only 305 in 1955.[12] However, these figures do not adequately show the drop in Los Angeles area employment, because many "Hollywood" pictures were being produced in other countries. A *New York Times* reporter's unofficial estimate of Hollywood activity in 1953 reported that thirty-four features were made abroad and eight more were shot partly in foreign locations and partly in California.[13] A more detailed study of "American-interest" films made abroad was written by labor historian Irving Bernstein for the Hollywood AFL Film Council in 1957. An

"American-interest" film is defined as "a picture financed in whole or in part by an American company," but shot in a foreign country and with foreign labor except for stars, director, and perhaps a few other key creative personnel. Bernstein found that 314 features had been made abroad by Hollywood companies between 1949 and 1956, with 55 for the most recent year (see Graph 1).[14] This translated to unemployment or under-employment for thousands of Hollywood-based workers. Film industry labor organizations were naturally concerned about this development, which they labeled "runaway production." The term took on a pejorative force ("American-interest film" is a more neutral synonym), suggesting that the Hollywood studios were acting irresponsibly when they did not protect the California-based labor force. Of course, the studios had a responsibility to their stockholders as well.

The runaway productions of the 1950s were mostly filmed in Europe, but they also reached Africa, Asia, South America, and various islands. Dozens of films were made in Italy, including QUO VADIS? (1951), ROMAN HOLIDAY (1953), BEAT THE DEVIL (1953), SUMMERTIME (1955), MAMBO (1954), A FAREWELL TO ARMS (1957), THREE COINS IN THE FOUNTAIN (1954), SEVEN HILLS OF ROME (1957), and BEN-HUR (1959). France was represented by THE LAST TIME I SAW PARIS (1954), TO CATCH A THIEF (1955), TRAPEZE (1956), FUNNY FACE (1957), and THE VIKINGS (1958; filmed in part on the coast of Brittany). Egypt was the setting for VALLEY OF THE KINGS (1954), THE EGYPT-IAN (1954), LAND OF THE PHARAOHS (1955), and THE TEN COMMANDMENTS (1956), and sub-Saharan Africa hosted KING SOLOMON'S MINES (1950), THE AFRICAN QUEEN (1951), THE SNOWS OF KILIMANJARO (1952), MOGAMBO (1953), and THE ROOTS OF HEAVEN (1958). India was represented by ELEPHANT WALK (1954), THE RAINS OF RANCHIPUR (1955), and BHOWANI JUNCTION (1956); Hong Kong by LOVE IS A MANY-SPLENDORED THING (1955). A Hollywood company even visited Fiji for the film HIS MAJESTY O'KEEFE (Warners, 1953), starring Burt Lancaster. For many of the colonial or ex-colonial locations, blocked funds and/or subsidies could be obtained from the colonizing country.

GRAPH 1: AMERICAN-INTEREST FEATURES, 1949–1957[15]

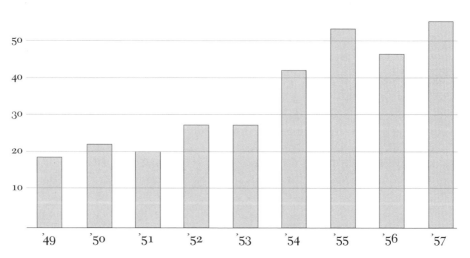

The Trevi Fountain in Rome, one of the locations used in THREE COINS IN THE FOUNTAIN
(1954).

Among directors, John Huston was the most traveled filmmaker of the period. He made THE AFRICAN QUEEN (1951) in Belgian Congo; MOULIN ROUGE (1952) in Paris; BEAT THE DEVIL (1954) in Italy; MOBY DICK (1956) in Ireland, Madeira, and the Canary Islands; HEAVEN KNOWS, MR. ALLISON (1957) in Tobago; THE BARBARIAN AND THE GEISHA (1958) in Japan; and THE ROOTS OF HEAVEN (1958) in French Equatorial Africa, Uganda, and Belgian Congo. In addition to location shooting, some of these films involved studio work in London, Paris, or Rome. Huston had established residence in Ireland in 1952, in part for tax reasons, and so he rarely set foot in Los Angeles. Nevertheless, he was considered one of the top "Hollywood" directors.

Huston and producer Darryl Zanuck were involved in the most disastrous overseas production of the 1950s, THE ROOTS OF HEAVEN. The novel *The Roots of Heaven*, by Romain Gary, tells the story of a Frenchman named Morel who is trying to protect the elephant herds of French Equatorial Africa at some point after World War II.[16] Morel feels that the survival of wild creatures is absolutely essential to human freedom and dignity, but he is laughed at in a colonial society that is closely bound to the ivory trade. Nevertheless, Morel does bring together a band of misfits and malcontents to pursue his quixotic goal of protecting the elephants. He interferes with the hunting process by attacking male hunters with buckshot and publicly flogging a female hunter at a dinner party. Morel receives extensive press coverage and generates worldwide sympathy for his cause, but he does not succeed in stopping the slaughter of elephants.

This subject, with its blend of adventure, exoticism, philosophy, and ecological awareness, could have made a fine film, but the difficulties of production overwhelmed the project. THE ROOTS OF HEAVEN was rushed into location shooting to beat the rainy season. The heat in Chad (then part of French Equatorial Africa) was intolerable; local food and water could not be consumed; malaria and other diseases slowed production; sunstroke, mental illness, and alcoholism were additional hazards, due to the extreme conditions of the location. The 160 cast and crew members amassed several hundred sick calls. The script, written by Huston's friend Patrick Leigh Fermor, a travel writer, was not very good according to Huston, but there was no time to work on it.[17] Indeed, the location company just barely filmed the most needed scenes before the rains came.

Unfortunately, the finished film shows all of these problems. It begins with slow and talky expository scenes made almost entirely at Boulogne Studios near Paris. The match between studio and location is poor, and the film lacks action until the last half hour. The leading cast members—Trevor Howard as Morel, Juliette Greco as Minna, Errol Flynn as Colonel Forsythe—are unimpressive until the climactic scenes. Though the novel insists on Africa as a magically wild place, full of exotic birds and mammals, the film shows only a few minutes of an elephant herd. Darryl Zanuck admitted to biographer Mel Gussow that the beleaguered filmmakers omitted many location scenes that should have been shot: "We took the quickest and easiest way out."[18] THE ROOTS OF HEAVEN cost more than $4 million (despite an absence of major stars), and was a box-office disaster. This film was defeated by its location.

By the late 1950s, Hollywood companies were pursuing subsidy and co-production deals as well as blocked funds. British subsidiaries of Hollywood companies could qual-

Jean-Pierre Kerien, Gina Lollobrigida, and Tony Curtis in TRAPEZE *(1956), a $4 million film shot on location in Paris.*

Producer Darryl Zanuck and female lead Juliette Greco during the filming of ROOTS OF HEAVEN *(1958).*

ify fairly easily for the generous Eady funds given to British filmmakers. The Eady Pool of funds (named for Sir Wilfred Eady, a civil servant who helped to shape Great Britain's post–World War II motion picture policy) was generated by an entertainment tax on all movies. Rebates were then given to those films considered "British," and this included a substantial number of films financed by Hollywood companies. For example, among the officially British films for 1957 were THE BARRETTS OF WIMPOLE STREET (MGM), SAINT JOAN (United Artists), THE PRINCE AND THE SHOWGIRL (Warner Bros.), ISLAND IN THE SUN (Twentieth Century–Fox), THE STORY OF ESTHER COSTELLO (Columbia), THE BRIDGE ON THE RIVER KWAI (Columbia), and BITTER VICTORY (Columbia).[19] Irving Bernstein notes that American companies made 105 films in England between 1950 and 1957, and that the Eady Pool "was of decisive importance in persuading U.S. producers to shift operations from Hollywood to London."[20] France and Italy had similar, but less generous, subsidy programs. Though the original intent had been to support national film producers, Great Britain, Italy, and France were willing to subsidize Hollywood film companies as well in order to stimulate film industry investment and employment.

The "American-interest" films resulting from the subsidy programs were also called "mid-Atlantic," because they combined American and European influences. Many such films were uncomfortable compromises, but a few achieved excellent quality. For example, THE BRIDGE ON THE RIVER KWAI (1957) is primarily a British film—directed by David Lean and featuring Alec Guinness, James Donald, and Jack Hawkins. How-

GRAPH 2: AMERICAN-INTEREST FILMS MADE IN THE UNITED
KINGDOM OR CONSIDERED "BRITISH NATIONALITY," 1949–1957[21]

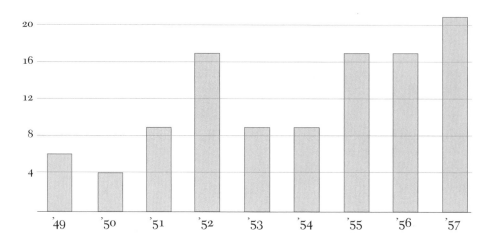

ever, production funds came from the British subsidiary of Columbia Pictures, the producer was Sam Spiegel, and one important role went to Hollywood actor William
Holden. The two screenwriters were American—Carl Foreman and Michael Wilson—
but they were uncredited because of the blacklist. (Sole credit for the script went to
Pierre Boulle, author of the original novel, who did not speak or write English.) In this
film, the American and British elements mesh beautifully, with Holden's simple, direct
characterization of an American officer contrasting with Guinness's Colonel Nicholson
(the highest-ranking British prisoner) and the other British officers, with their host of
moral dilemmas. THE BRIDGE ON THE RIVER KWAI won the Academy Award for Best
Picture in 1957, and it was recently voted one of the ten best British films of all time.

A co-production is a film made by companies from two or more nations and governed
by specific, government-to-government agreements between those nations. In Europe,
co-production is a commonly used means for achieving higher budgets, higher subsidies,
and greater potential audiences for films. (Co-productions now exist in other parts of the
world, but in the 1950s they were primarily a European phenomenon.) Strictly speaking,
American companies are not a part of co-productions, because the U.S. government
does not intervene in the film business to the extent that European governments do, but
loosely, all sorts of collaborations are called "co-productions." In practice, via foreign
subsidiaries, Hollywood companies can invest in co-productions as they invest in single-
nationality films. And American-financed films can therefore enjoy subsidies from two
or even three countries. Columbia and United Artists were probably the studios most
actively using foreign subsidiaries in the late 1950s.

One of the more fascinating co-productions of the late 1950s was BITTER VICTORY
(1958), directed by Nicholas Ray and financed primarily by Columbia Pictures. This
film was considered a French-Italian-British co-production even though the French
and Italian elements seem underrepresented. The director was American; the stars
were Welsh (Richard Burton), German (Curt Jurgens), and American (Ruth Roman);
many of the featured players were British; and the location for exteriors was Libya. As a

Alec Guinness as a British officer in a Japanese prison camp in THE BRIDGE ON THE
RIVER KWAI, *which won the Academy Award for Best Picture in 1957. Though financed
by Columbia Pictures, it is often considered a British film.*

co-production, the film would have been eligible for French and Italian subsidies plus
the Eady levy. With money from an American studio plus three governments, producer
Paul Graetz could pay himself a large producer's fee and profit financially whether or not
the film made back its cost. He also paid his wife a salary, as location producer. These
conditions, which are fairly common in European production, often produce mediocre
films. But for BITTER VICTORY, they meant that the producer left Ray essentially unsu-
pervised on all matters except budget. Commercial success was not so important, and
therefore Ray was able to make a haunting film about cowardice, heroism, and lack of
self-knowledge.[22] This was one case where "mid-Atlantic" production conditions created
a degree of freedom for the filmmaker, instead of imposing crippling compromises.

The Blacklist and Overseas Productions

At the same time that the Hollywood studios were expanding their operations overseas,
a number of blacklisted, graylisted, or otherwise estranged American filmmakers were
also working abroad. Some of these individuals found a place in a non-Hollywood
national film industry. Others lived in Mexico, England, France, or Italy, far from the
American Legion and the investigating committees, but worked in secret for American

Curt Jurgens (left) in BITTER VICTORY *(1958), a French-Italian-British co-production directed by Nicholas Ray.*

film companies. A few managed to make films as independent producers despite being cut off from Hollywood distribution. Hundreds of people—writers, directors, actors, and others—were blacklisted, at tremendous personal and professional cost. However, a few dozen of these were able to find work abroad.

Dalton Trumbo, one of the original Hollywood Ten, was the most prolific of the blacklisted screenwriters. Upon finishing his prison sentence for contempt of Congress (refusal to cooperate with the House Un-American Activities Committee, or HUAC) in 1951, he moved to Mexico City and wrote several scripts using fronts and pseudonyms. His most frequent employers were the King brothers, low-budget film producers in Los Angeles. One of Trumbo's scripts for the King brothers, "The Boy and the Bull" (written in 1953), eventually became the film THE BRAVE ONE (1956), which won an Academy Award for the screenwriter "Robert Rich" (Trumbo's pseudonym). Robert Rich never came forward to claim this award, which embarrassed the Academy of Motion Picture Arts and Sciences. Trumbo returned to the Los Angeles area in 1954 because he found it difficult to negotiate sales and ensure payment for scripts while in Mexico.[23] In 1959–1960 Trumbo "broke" the blacklist by receiving screen credit for writing SPARTA-CUS for producer Kirk Douglas and EXODUS for producer Otto Preminger.

Other blacklisted individuals who relocated to Mexico in the early 1950s included writers Ring Lardner Jr., Albert Maltz, Gordon Kahn, Ian McLellan Hunter, and Hugo Butler, as well as producer George Pepper. Most of them stayed only briefly; Ring Lardner Jr., for example, moved to Connecticut after six months. However, Hugo Butler and George Pepper established themselves in the Mexican film industry, notably working with the director Luis Buñuel (himself an exile from Francisco Franco's dictatorship of Spain).[24] Butler wrote two English language films for Buñuel, ADVENTURES OF ROBINSON CRUSOE (1954) and THE YOUNG ONE (1960), working under pseudonyms so as not to affect United States distribution. Butler also worked with director Robert Aldrich on AUTUMN LEAVES (1956, using a front) and with blacklisted director Joseph Losey on films made in England.

A number of blacklisted writers and directors found work in Europe. Carl Foreman, the screenwriter for CHAMPION (1949) and HIGH NOON (1952), was blacklisted in 1951 after appearing before HUAC as an unfriendly witness. He moved to England in 1952, where he worked in television and film writing and as an assistant to producer Alexander Korda.[25] Foreman appeared before HUAC in executive session in 1956, and was cleared of all wrongdoing. After this he wrote and produced THE KEY (1958), a high-budget British movie with financing from Columbia Pictures. By 1978, when he was honored by a retrospective at the Museum of Modern Art, Foreman had become the president of the Writer's Guild of Great Britain, a founding governor of the British Film Institute, a fellow of the Royal Society of Arts, and a commander of the British Empire.[26]

Donald Ogden Stewart and Michael Wilson also maintained screenwriting careers while living in Europe. Stewart had co-written a number of high-budget Hollywood comedies in the 1930s and 1940s, including DINNER AT EIGHT (1933), HOLIDAY (1938), and THE PHILADELPHIA STORY (1940). He was less active in Europe, but he did manage to contribute to scripts for ESCAPADE (1955) and SUMMERTIME (1955) and to write the English language dialogue for Roberto Rossellini's EUROPA 51 (1952). Stewart and his wife, Ella Winter, also made their house in England a kind of salon for American expatriates. Michael Wilson had won a pre-blacklist Academy Award for the screenplay of A PLACE IN THE SUN (1951). In the early years of the blacklist, he wrote SALT OF THE EARTH (1953) and collaborated on several low-budget Hollywood scripts with Dalton Trumbo (neither could be credited, of course). In 1954 Wilson moved to Europe, making his home in Paris. He was co-scriptwriter (without credit) on two prestigious films directed by David Lean, THE BRIDGE ON THE RIVER KWAI and LAWRENCE OF ARABIA (1962), and he also co-scripted the Italian film LA TEMPESTA (directed by Alberto Lattuada, 1958).

Hannah Weinstein, an American producer based in London, became an unlikely "angel" for many blacklisted writers. Weinstein had moved to Paris from New York after a divorce. (Ally Acker, in her 1991 book on women in film, said that Weinstein moved to Europe because of the blacklist. She had been active in liberal politics in New York.)[27] With no experience in the film business, Weinstein produced and successfully marketed a low-budget French film, FAITS DIVERS A PARIS (1950). She then moved to London and produced a television series, *Colonel Dorner of Scotland Yard*. Though talented people were involved, including blacklisted Americans Abraham Polonsky and Walter Bernstein, the series lasted only one year. Weinstein's next series, *The Adventures of Robin Hood*, starring Richard Greene, was produced in partnership with agent Lew Grade (soon to be a media tycoon) for the fledgling ITV network. It was a tremendous hit in Britain and also in the United States, where it was picked up by ABC. The American network and its sponsors would have been surprised to learn that the pilot for *The Adventures of Robin Hood* was written pseudonymously by Ring Lardner Jr. and Ian McLellan Hunter (both blacklisted), and that Weinstein employed other blacklisted writers as well.[28] Lardner suggests light-heartedly in his autobiography that *Robin Hood*,

NEVER ON SUNDAY (1960), directed by Jules Dassin, starred Melina Mercouri (left) and Jules Dassin (right, standing behind table).

with its emphasis on equality and fairness, may have subverted "a whole new generation of young Americans."[29]

Blacklisted directors had great difficulty finding work, because film directing is such a public occupation. A writer can communicate with only one person, a film's producer, but a director must interact with dozens (in some cases hundreds) of actors and crew. Nevertheless, both Joseph Losey and Jules Dassin managed to work steadily and impressively during the 1950s. Losey was in Europe in 1951 to direct STRANGER ON THE PROWL (1953) when he was subpoenaed to appear before HUAC. He settled in London rather than returning to Hollywood, and he gradually established himself in the British film industry via a series of crime films: THE SLEEPING TIGER (1954), FINGER OF GUILT (1956), TIME WITHOUT PITY (1957), and CHANCE MEETING (1959). Though these are modest genre films, Losey did manage to inflect them with themes of class and power. Also, Losey first worked with the actor Dirk Bogarde on THE SLEEPING TIGER; Bogarde would later be the star of Losey's brilliant collaborations with writer Harold Pinter, THE SERVANT (1963) and ACCIDENT (1967).

Jules Dassin's post-Hollywood career took him first to France and then to Greece. In France, he directed a superb crime thriller, RIFIFI (1954), which is clearly influenced by American film noir (and especially by THE ASPHALT JUNGLE). However, the characters, dialogue, and setting also seem to be thoroughly French. Dassin's best-known film in Greece, NEVER ON SUNDAY (1960), was about an American intellectual abroad. It featured Dassin himself as the expatriate American and Melina Mercouri as the prostitute who teaches him to appreciate the material reality of modern Greece. This film in English and Greek was financed by United Artists (despite the blacklist) and was a commercial and critical success. Melina Mercouri, Dassin's wife, was named Best Actress at Cannes and was nominated for an Academy Award.

Charlie Chaplin was not exactly blacklisted: as a wealthy producer and part owner of United Artists, he could hardly be denied access to film production. However, Chaplin was harassed by anti-Communist groups, including the American Legion, throughout the 1950s. He was not a Communist, but he was part of various peace groups and public events that involved Communist participation. Chaplin was also under attack, in the press and the courts, for personal reasons. In the mid-1940s he had been charged with a Mann Act violation (transporting a woman across state lines for immoral purposes) and a paternity suit, both involving a young would-be actress named Joan Barry. Chaplin won the Mann Act case but lost the paternity suit—even though a blood test showed he could not be the father of Barry's daughter!

When Chaplin sailed from New York to England in September 1952, the U.S. Attorney General notified him that he would not be re-admitted to the United States without an official hearing. This action was based on a section of U.S. law that allowed aliens to be barred for moral and/or political reasons (Chaplin had retained his British citizenship).[30] Chaplin chose to remain in Europe; he established residence in Switzerland for tax purposes, but spent much of his time in London. He did not return to the United States until 1972, when he was given a special Academy Award.

Buster Keaton (left) and Charlie Chaplin appeared together on screen in LIMELIGHT *(1952).*

LIMELIGHT (1952), the last film Chaplin made in the United States, tells the story of an aging London vaudeville comedian, Calvero (Chaplin), who helps and eventually marries a beautiful young dancer (Claire Bloom). Of special interest is a scene on stage featuring both Chaplin and Buster Keaton (the only time they appeared on screen together). LIMELIGHT is an explicitly non-political film whose theme is the mortality and rebirth of the artist—an older performer (Calvero) dies, and a young performer (the dancer) becomes a star. Nevertheless, LIMELIGHT was picketed by the American Legion and had a disappointing commercial career in the United States. The Legion was evidently responding to Chaplin's reputation rather than to the film's content.

A KING IN NEW YORK (1957), made in England, is about the dapper, white-haired King Shahdov (Chaplin), who settles in New York after being dethroned by a revolution. With no money, Shahdov finds himself pitching a variety of products on American television. He also befriends a young boy, Rupert Macabee (played by Chaplin's son Michael) whose parents are in trouble with HUAC. Rupert, who can spout Marxist and anarchist ideas like a much older person, eventually is questioned by committee investigators and names some of his parents' friends without understanding what he is doing. Young, naive Rupert becomes representative of those who have suffered from McCarthyism and the blacklist. Both Chaplin the writer/director and Shahdov the character distance themselves from Rupert's ideas, but the film shows great sympathy for the boy's personal

Charlie Chaplin as King Shahdov in A KING IN NEW YORK (1957).

Orson Welles directed and played the leading role of Gregory Arkadin in MR. ARKADIN *(1955).*

problems. As for King Shahdov, he decides that the American mixture of commercialism and political intolerance is not for him, and so he returns to Europe. A KING IN NEW YORK was respectfully received in England, though some critics acknowledged flaws. Those American reviewers who saw the film in London rejected it both politically and artistically.[31] A KING IN NEW YORK did not play in American theaters until 1973.

Orson Welles, like Chaplin, spent most of the 1950s in Europe. Welles had several reasons for living abroad. He owed a substantial tax bill to the I.R.S.—this was the announced reason for his going abroad in 1948, and it was still a problem in 1959. His directing efforts on THE MAGNIFICENT AMBERSONS (1942), IT'S ALL TRUE (1942, never finished), THE LADY FROM SHANGHAI (1948), and MACBETH (1948) had all ended in bitter disputes with the studios and were box office failures. Welles was still in demand as an actor, but his Hollywood career as a director appeared to be over. Welles may also have been concerned about the anti-Communist mood in the United States in the late 1940s and early 1950s. As a high-profile liberal who had spoken out on international issues during World War II, Welles could have been blacklisted or graylisted had he stayed in the United States.[32] Finally, Welles may have relished the personal and professional challenges of living as an itinerant artist (biographer Barbara Leaming uses the phrase "glorious gypsy"): constant travel, constant struggles for money, frenetic activity in film, theater, and other media.[33]

Welles directed two major films in Europe in the 1950s, OTHELLO (1952) and MR. ARKADIN (also known as CONFIDENTIAL REPORT, 1955). OTHELLO was shot over a period of four years in a variety of locations, with filming halted whenever Welles ran out of money. This OTHELLO is visually stunning but also fragmented (reflecting its production history); biographer David Thomson calls it "fascinating as a sketchbook for a great movie."[34] Nevertheless, the film shared the Palme d'Or at Cannes in 1952. MR. ARKADIN, with story, script, and direction by Welles, describes an investigation into the early career of financier Gregory Arkadin (Welles), who claims amnesia before 1927. The not-too-bright detective figure (Robert Arden) hired by Arkadin makes it possible for the financier to find and murder all those who remember his early days. In structure, the film is a cynical and perverse remake of CITIZEN KANE. Unfortunately, the style is so fragmented and the characters so distant that this film soon runs out of narrative energy. The best Orson Welles film from the 1950s is clearly TOUCH OF EVIL (1958), which was filmed in Los Angeles for a Hollywood studio (see Chapter 10).

The studio-sponsored runaway productions and the unsponsored (often blacklisted) expatriates were factors contributing to a new cosmopolitanism in world cinema in the 1950s. Hollywood cinema was no longer "made in Los Angeles"; instead, there was an expectation that large-scale productions would film in authentic locations worldwide. Meanwhile, American exiles such as Hugo Butler, Carl Foreman, Joseph Losey, Jules Dassin, and Orson Welles added to the cultural mix of non-Hollywood film industries.

Case Study: THE TEN COMMANDMENTS As International Epic

Cecil B. DeMille's THE TEN COMMANDMENTS (1956) is a good example of a Hollywood film shaped in pre-production, production, and distribution by international politics and economics. The epic genre, with its combination of spectacle, action, and familiar story, was a characteristic and successful product of 1950s Hollywood largely because its appeal stretched beyond national borders. The epic's grand scale attracted a broad, unsophisticated audience, which would generally be less interested in social drama or comedy of manners. It also provided a good showpiece for the new visual technologies of the 1950s (CinemaScope, VistaVision, 70 mm.). And the epic's culturally sanctioned subject matter allowed for a level of sexual display—scanty costumes and suggestive scenes—which would have otherwise encountered censorship problems in the United States and many other countries.

Producer-director DeMille's first crucial decision was to film much of THE TEN COM-MANDMENTS in Egypt. DeMille's silent version of THE TEN COMMANDMENTS (1923) had been made in California, but for the remake there were several compelling reasons to go abroad. First, blocked funds could be used to support at least some of the production budget. Second, labor and materials were available at extremely reasonable rates, and DeMille proposed to build a huge city and to film a three-mile-long procession of the Exodus. Third, Egyptian scenes would offer the visual spectacle of famous places and international travel. Fourth, large-scale photography in Egypt would provide a wonderful showcase for Paramount's new VistaVision process. Fifth, for religious viewers a film shot in authentic locales would be much more convincing than a re-creation in Hollywood. The major drawbacks of filming in Egypt were logistical: the need to send all rushes back to Hollywood; language problems; availability of resources, and so on. However, DeMille was known for his ability to organize large-scale productions, and he and his assistants enthusiastically set to work on this one.

The political situation in Egypt was also cause for concern. In the early 1950s, the monarchy of King Farouk ended with a military coup. DeMille was invited to film in Egypt by General Naguib, the new head of state, but when his location company arrived in Egypt Naguib was being eased out by a younger officer, Colonel Gamal Abdel Nasser. Fortunately, Nasser also welcomed the film production—according to DeMille's long-time associate producer Henry Wilcoxon, Nasser and his military colleagues admired DeMille's film THE CRUSADES (1935).[35] Kenneth Clark, vice president of the MPAA, sent DeMille a three-page political briefing on Egypt, including comments on the Suez situation, attitudes toward Israel and Jews, Moses' status as a prophet of Islam, and knowledgeable Americans in Cairo.[36] DeMille and Paramount were fortunate that their location work in Egypt was concluded in 1954. In 1956 a dispute between Egypt and Britain over the Suez Canal escalated into war and world crisis.

The screenplay for the film (by Jesse L. Lasky Jr., Jack Gariss, Aeneas McKenzie, and Frederic M. Frank) closely follows the Biblical account, but with a long and interesting addition to fill the thirty years between Moses' infancy and adulthood which is not covered in Exodus, Chapter 1. Relying on Roman and Jewish authors as well as archeological clues, the screenwriters posit that Moses became a general and a prince of Egypt during the reign of Sethi I. Royal succession at this time descended through the female line, so the script has Moses vying with Rameses (Sethi's son) for the hand of Princess Nefertiri. Moses is then disgraced by the revelation that he is a Hebrew, which explains (according to DeMille and his writers) why he has been excised from the written and visual records of ancient Egypt.[37] The addition to the story is ingenious and dramatically exciting, but it remains a speculation. After many scenes of palace intrigue, the film returns to the Biblical account of the Exodus, including Sinai, the crossing of the Red Sea, and the final scene of Moses viewing the Promised Land.

In visual style, THE TEN COMMANDMENTS is eclectic. According to Katherine Orrison's book on the 1956 production of THE TEN COMMANDMENTS, De Mille was specifically aiming for a visual design "that would resonate with the color, pageantry, and detail of the pre-Raphaelite painters."[38] The film uses a color scheme of reds, greens, and blues based on medieval painting as reformulated by the Pre-Raphaelite painters of nineteenth-century England. In particular, the work of Dante Gabriel Rossetti (1828–1882) seems to be a source, not only for colors but for compositions and costumes as well.[39] The film also draws on the work of American painter Arnold Friburg, who is best known for his scenes from the Bible and the Book of Mormon.[40] Friburg was part of the creative team for THE TEN COMMANDMENTS—he worked on the costumes, on the "'Stages of Moses'" for the makeup department," and on "paintings of each big scene" which after production were assembled in the film's souvenir program.[41] Friburg's work helps to add a Christian iconography to the story of Moses, so that, at least subliminally, the story becomes an anticipation of Christianity. A third major visual element in THE TEN COMMANDMENTS is the influence of ancient Egyptian design on the costumes, jewelry, architecture, painting, and sculpture. It bears repeating that the film is eclectic, therefore one should not expect a strict authenticity of Egyptian design. Finally, THE TEN COMMANDMENTS certainly uses Hollywood visual conventions, including three point lighting, soft lighting for female faces, high key lighting in the Egyptian court (except during the ten plagues), balanced compositions, close-ups for emotional scenes, and so on.

In addition to its religious dimension, the 1956 version of THE TEN COMMANDMENTS clearly has a political message. The film's prologue states that it is about whether humanity will be ruled by a dictatorship or by the laws of God. By implication, the Pharaoh's reign can be viewed as a representation of Russian Communism, and the Hebrews as the free and democratic West. The key freedom being presented is religious freedom, but DeMille also casts the Exodus as an allegory for political freedom. Moses' last, prominently featured speech in the film is "Go, proclaim liberty throughout the lands, unto all the inhabitants thereof" (Leviticus 25:10), which is the inscription on the Liberty Bell in Philadelphia. In its biblical context this line is not a statement by Moses, but rather part of the description of the Jubilee year, when debts are to be forgiven and people are to return to their ancestral property. By inserting this line into the scene when Moses views the land of Canaan, the film provides an allegory of American democracy.

The scale of THE TEN COMMANDMENTS can in itself be viewed as an advertisement for American economic and technological power. John Belton has described how the United States and the Soviet Union competed in a series of World's Fairs to show who had the most spectacular motion-picture technology.[42] This competition extended into the commercial marketplace as well, with the Soviets providing their own widescreen technologies, including approximate versions of Cinerama and Todd-AO. The Soviet Union could not, however, match the worldwide reach of Hollywood distribution. THE TEN COMMANDMENTS was intended to show off Paramount's VistaVision technology, but it was also a demonstration of American power and American values. Any film epic communicates (among other things) the power, wealth, and skill of its makers. In fact, writer Michael Wood commented that "the ancient world of the epics was a huge, multi-faceted metaphor for Hollywood itself."[43] THE TEN COMMANDMENTS, with its near-legendary director and studio and its quote from the Liberty Bell (and Leviticus), presented itself to the world as not just a corporate but an American product. As to values, the emphasis on freedom and the blending of religious and political discourses are both characteristic of Cold War America.

The political positioning of THE TEN COMMANDMENTS is subtly modified by the film's casting. The positive characters in the film are played by white Anglo-Saxon Americans, notably Charlton Heston as Moses and John Derek as Joshua. The English actor Cedric Hardwicke playing Pharaoh Sethi has an in-between status—kindly disposed toward Moses but still somewhat foreign, therefore suspect. The two villains of THE TEN COMMANDMENTS are very interesting. Yul Brynner as the cruel Rameses is an exotic (or orientalist) figure—sexy, powerful, of unknown and probably mixed racial heritage. Though DeMille and Brynner evidently had a good personal relationship, Brynner's casting as Rameses creates an unfortunate "Us versus Them" stereotype. To prove the point, imagine a TEN COMMANDMENTS with Brynner as Moses and Heston as Rameses—the meaning changes substantially.

The second villain is Dathan, overseer for Pharaoh and traitor to his own Hebrew people, who is played by Edward G. Robinson. Here we encounter a complex tangle of Cold War ideology. Robinson, a big star of the 1930s and 1940s, had been blacklisted (or perhaps graylisted) in the early 1950s because of his work for liberal causes and so-called "fellow-traveler" organizations. Robinson struggled to clear his name, but he could not recant because he was never a Communist and he remained proud of his liberal activities.[44] Finally, the politically conservative DeMille cast him as Dathan, breaking the blacklist and restoring Robinson's credibility in the film industry. Robinson in his autobiography praises DeMille's fairness and his "sense of decency and justice."[45] However, there seems to be a regrettable stereotype here as well. The liberal Jewish actor, accused of communism, plays a villain and a traitor in a film where Charlton Heston plays a Jewish hero.

Yul Brynner as Rameses and Charlton Heston as Moses in Cecil B. DeMille's production of THE TEN COMMANDMENTS (1956).

The scenes of THE TEN COMMANDMENTS shot in Egypt concentrated on visual spectacle: enormous stone cities and endless lines of people and animals. Charlton Heston, speaking in 1990, called the Egyptian scenes "essentially a second-unit shoot";[46] this is an exaggeration, because the vast Egyptian tableaux were essential to the film. DeMille, an excellent director of spectacle, was present for the duration of the location shoot. Of the major actors, only Charlton Heston and Yul Brynner made the trip to Egypt. The huge exterior sets were built by Egyptian workmen under the supervision of architect Anis Serag El Dine. Four VistaVision cameras shipped from the United States beautifully photographed the cities, pyramids, and sphinxes, aided by the brilliant desert sun. The only near-catastrophe of location shooting was a heart attack suffered by the seventy-three-year-old DeMille, who was, however, able to continue working.

THE TEN COMMANDMENTS does an excellent job of matching the exteriors shot in Egypt with the dialogue scenes and dramatic set pieces (such as the golden calf and the parting of the Red Sea) filmed in Hollywood. In the scenes of Moses building Sethi's city, the film cuts fluidly between images taken in Egypt and images taken in California, with a few shots combining Egypt and California in composite images (as when Charlton Heston as Moses opens a curtain to show the city as it is being built to Cedric Hardwicke as the Pharaoh). In the Mount Sinai sequence, the blend of images is less impressive, with the long shot location images not matching the studio-shot close-ups. For strictly visual values, the entire sequence might better have been shot in California. But the filming on Mount Sinai fulfilled a promise to religious viewers. The film presents itself as a pilgrimage (the opening credits announce that "Those who see this movie . . . will make a pilgrimage over the very ground that Moses trod more than 3,000 years ago"), and

Mount Sinai is by far the most sacred site in the picture. Therefore, DeMille, Heston, and the crew spent several days on Mount Sinai filming in difficult conditions (with no road to the top and no electricity).

The acting in the film is a mixture of standard Hollywood and something less familiar. There is no doubt that the star power of Charlton Heston, Yul Brynner, Anne Baxter, and Edward G. Robinson gives the film much of its cachet. But THE TEN COMMAND-MENTS also has a unique and curious acting style—simplified, a bit larger than life, but consistent and usually dignified. With this acting style plus the eclectic costumes and

Moses (Charlton Heston) descends from Mount Sinai in THE TEN COMMANDMENTS.

settings, DeMille was somewhat successful in creating a defamiliarized context for ancient Egypt. Unlike Howard Hawks, who blamed the failure of LAND OF THE PHARAOHS (1955) on not knowing how a Pharaoh talks,[47] DeMille and company had actually imagined a compelling, though not authentic, version of pharaonic Egypt.

The most questionable performances involve the leading actresses, Anne Baxter as Nefertiri and Yvonne de Carlo as Sephora (who becomes Moses' wife). Anne Baxter's performance is intense and sometimes over the top. She is not helped by unrealistic dialogue, for example "Oh Moses, Moses, Moses, you stubborn, splendid, adorable fool." Baxter as Nefertiri wears loose tunics which nevertheless emphasize her breasts (she looks a bit like 1950s pinup Bettie Page). Her scenes with Yul Brynner—two sexual predators vying for dominance—are fun but campy. As for Yvonne de Carlo, she is very much the American girl next door rather than a member of a desert tribe. Sephora is modestly dressed, well-groomed, and well-spoken—a properly brought up young woman of the American middle class. The problem here may be that DeMille was working with stereotypes from the 1920s—Nefertiri as the Vamp, Sephora as the Virgin—but his audience was no longer comfortable with this dualism. Debra Paget as Lilia is a more complex and more modern female character. Courageous, loyal, faithful to her beloved Joshua, she is forced into concubinage by Baka (Vincent Price) and Dathan, in one of the film's many vignettes of sexual domination. But when Lilia is liberated, she overcomes her shame and becomes Joshua's wife.

THE TEN COMMANDMENTS was promoted as a special event, attempting to attract spectators who would not ordinarily come to the theater. DeMille and Paramount aimed particularly to attract religious audiences. Priests, ministers, and rabbis were invited to preview screenings in the United States and then asked for their comments. The *Hollywood Citizen-News* of 22 October 1956 contained a sample of such comments: Cardinal James Francis McIntyre of the Catholic Church called the film "a great mission given to Mr. DeMille;" David O. McKay, president of the Mormon Church, described it as "truly great—the greatest picture ever made"; Rabbi Edgar F. Magnin of Los Angeles declared "I don't know when I have been so moved and inspired."[48] Paramount used similarly favorable comments by clergymen to publicize the film in Europe and South America. The studio also tried to attract Muslim audiences, by quoting, for example, the prime minister of Pakistan, Mohammed Ali.[49]

Another marketing strategy was to emphasize the name "Cecil B. DeMille." In 1956 DeMille was the most widely known American director (Alfred Hitchcock's peak of popularity came a few years later, via the success of his television show). DeMille's two previous films, SAMSON AND DELILAH (1949) and THE GREATEST SHOW ON EARTH (1952) had been huge box-office successes, and THE GREATEST SHOW ON EARTH had won the Oscar for Best Picture. DeMille himself represented the entire history of American cinema, including both silent and sound pictures; indeed, his silent version of THE TEN COMMANDMENTS had been a worldwide hit in 1923. Though DeMille had made a variety of films, he was associated with the large-scale historical epic, and his works included some of the biggest, most spectacular movies of all time. The director's fame was so great that THE TEN COMMANDMENTS was almost always identified as "Cecil B. DeMille's THE TEN COMMANDMENTS," even though this phrase could be construed as borderline blasphemous. One further strategy connecting director and film was the use of DeMille as narrator. He appears on-screen in the very first scene to introduce the film, and then provides occasional voice-over narration for the next three and a half hours. DeMille is thus literally telling us the story.

When DeMille visited Europe to personally publicize his film, he was treated as a celebrity, and also as an important, though unofficial, representative of the United States. DeMille was, in fact, active in the Republican Party (the party of President Dwight D. Eisenhower) and he had publicly spoken out on Cold War issues. In London, DeMille met Queen Elizabeth and Sir Winston Churchill and was interviewed at length on BBC Television. In Paris, he received a medal at the Hotel de Ville, met President René-Jules-Gustave Coty, and spoke with Catholic, Protestant, and Jewish leaders. In Rome, DeMille was blessed by Pope Pius XII and spoke with President Giovanni Gronchi. In Germany, he met Chancellor Konrad Adenauer of the Federal Government and Berlin mayor Willy Brandt, and he delivered a speech before the Berlin League of Human Rights.[50] It is difficult to imagine a contemporary American director receiving such a reception. In promoting himself, DeMille promoted his film, and he also promoted America.

Critical reaction to THE TEN COMMANDMENTS in the United States was no better than mixed. Bosley Crowther of the *New York Times* thoroughly appreciated the film, declaring that "it is a moving story of the spirit of freedom rising in a man, under the divine inspiration of his Maker," and that "it strikes a ringing note today."[51] W. R. Wilkerson of *The Hollywood Reporter* was effusive in his praise. Both *Variety* and *Newsweek* were more cautious, praising the film's large-scale spectacle but questioning the script and the acting.[52] Arthur Knight of *Saturday Review* found the film "one-dimensional," and John McCarten of *The New Yorker* described it as "high, wide, occasionally handsome, and full of coarse special effects."[53] *Time* magazine was savage in its criticism, accusing DeMille of vulgarity and perhaps blasphemy. A typical comment from *Time's* reviewer is "the Exodus itself seems almost a sort of Sexodus—the result of Moses' unhappy (and purely fictional) love life."[54]

On the other hand, public reaction to the film, as expressed by the box office, was incredibly positive. After one year THE TEN COMMANDMENTS had grossed $26.5 million in the United States, with almost 10 percent of that figure coming from one Manhattan theater, the Criterion.[55] It eventually took in more than $100 million worldwide, which easily surpassed the previous record set by GONE WITH THE WIND (1939). More than half of this income came from foreign distribution. But THE TEN COMMANDMENTS did not play in President Nasser's Egypt, which had moved toward Arab nationalism after the 1956 Suez war. Censors in the United Arab Republic (Egypt plus Syria) banned the film because they felt it favored the Jews over the Egyptians.[56]

For the twenty-first century spectator, THE TEN COMMANDMENTS is an amazing mixture of spectacle, drama, religion, politics, commerce, and self-aggrandizement. Brilliant visual feats blend uneasily with Cold War ideology. The huge scale of the film is itself a statement, an embodiment of American wealth and power and a challenge to the Soviet adversary. THE TEN COMMANDMENTS reaches out to audiences of various religions and nationalities, but it retains an aggressively American point of view.

The most perceptive modern critique of the film comes from director Martin Scorsese in his compilation film A PERSONAL JOURNEY THROUGH AMERICAN MOVIES. Scorsese describes the film as a "sumptuous fantasy," in which "the marvelous supersedes the sacred." He adds praise for "the tableaux vivants, the colors, the dreamlike quality of the imagery, and of course the special effects." What Scorsese implies, but tactfully does not say, is this: One can respect and enjoy THE TEN COMMANDMENTS without accepting the film's tangle of social, political, and religious motifs.

8

Science Fiction Films and Cold War Anxiety

Victoria O'Donnell

Science fiction films became a major Hollywood genre in the 1950s. Through imaginative narratives and special effects, hundreds (by one estimate, five hundred film features and shorts were produced between 1948 and 1962)[1] of science fiction films presented indirect expressions of anxiety about the possibility of a nuclear holocaust or a Communist invasion of America. These fears were expressed in various guises, such as aliens using mind control, monstrous mutants unleashed by radioactive fallout, radiation's terrible effects on human life, and scientists obsessed with dangerous experiments. Although both government and private groups discouraged criticism of U.S. policies and expressions of fear about national security during the Cold War, the producers of science fiction films were generally left alone by government regulators and the private groups that tried to shape public opinion. Controversy over the development of atomic weapons and potential consequences had been repressed in public debates and in other film genres,[2] but it could be recast in stories about mutant ants and grasshoppers, pods that took over people's minds, space travel, and the nuclear destruction of civilizations on other planets. By dislocating the narratives to different times and/or different worlds, the science fiction genre catered to public anxiety about the bomb and communism. In most of the films, scientists and/or the military managed to vanquish the enemy, offering reassurance that these threats could be overcome. In films where destruction had already taken place, the endings offered hope and redemption. Thus the science fiction films of the Cold War era may be generally interpreted as advocating the idea that Americans would be able to cope with external threats to their security.

The science fiction film came into its own as a genre in American cinema in the 1950s with an enormous production rate. According to Joyce A. Evans, "This rapid proliferation [of science fiction films] presents one of the most interesting developments in post–World War II film history, for never in the history of motion pictures has any other genre developed and multiplied so rapidly in so brief a period."[3] Hollywood science fiction had been mostly limited to serials in the 1930s and 1940s, for example *Buck Rogers* (1939) and *Flash Gordon* (1940). The feature-length THINGS TO COME (1936), based on the novel by H. G. Wells, was a notable exception. But the genre did not really "take off" until 1950, for a variety of reasons. First, if the Hollywood science fiction genre was largely a response to nuclear anxiety, that anxiety received a huge boost when the Russians successfully tested an atomic bomb in 1949. Second, science fiction literature, as represented by such figures as authors Robert Heinlein and Ray Bradbury and editor John W. Campbell, was booming in the early 1950s. Third, the box-office success of science fiction films in 1950 and 1951 led to increased production in future years, as is typical of Hollywood cycles. Fourth, the very successful re-release of KING KONG (1933) in 1952 further demonstrated the public's appetite for science fiction—and it may have inflected 1950s sci-fi toward the mutants and monsters subgenre.[4]

The resulting "wave" of science fiction films addressed thematic concerns of the 1950s and was limited by the technology of the period. However, though dated in many ways, these films have had surprising staying power. They continue into the twenty-first century to be shown on cable television, sold on VHS and DVD, critiqued in popular and scholarly books, and discussed in university classes. Several have been remade, including INVASION OF THE BODY SNATCHERS (twice), THE THING, THE BLOB, THE FLY, INVADERS FROM MARS, and RED PLANET MARS. There also have been frequent sequels such as REVENGE OF THE CREATURE (1955), THE CREATURE WALKS AMONG US (1959), WAR OF THE COLOSSAL BEAST (1958), THE RETURN OF THE FLY (1959), and BEWARE THE BLOB (1972).

First and foremost, science fiction is about scientific possibility that explores the unknown. It consists of a story that, in the words of sci-fi literature critic Eric Rabkin, "both warns against and applauds the advance of science and technology [while] it consistently considers the problems and possibilities posed by meeting the new, the unexpected, the alien. Science fiction draws its considerable entertainment value from deep mythic or social wells. . . . science fiction is a phenomenon that arises wherever modern science and technology make people aware of new problems or cause them to view old problems in new ways."[5] Film scholar Vivian Sobchack adds, "If science fiction is about science at all, it is not about abstract science, science in a vacuum. In the SF film, science is always related to society, and its positive and negative aspects are seen in light of their social effect."[6]

While science was both implicit and explicit in the science fiction films of the 1950s, it was explained simplistically. Scientists were often represented as troublesome idealists or obstructionists because they wanted to save a destructive species or phenomenon in order to study it. Scientists were either represented as responsible for the problems that arose, or they were responsible for finding solutions to whatever was threatening the planet. Government officials and the military were often represented as heroes who fought the enemy; or, conversely, they were portrayed as ignorant of the peaceful intentions of the invaders and often as hotheads who just wanted to obliterate the threat. Aliens were frequently portrayed as superior to earthlings in intelligence and technology, perhaps representing what Americans feared in the Soviets. Likewise, mutants that resulted from atomic radiation, such as gigantic ants and locusts, were represented as socially organized and conforming in ways that many Americans perceived the Bolsheviks to be. A further essential theme was secrecy: scientists, or government officials, or the military, or all three, were hiding from the public the amazing events ultimately revealed in these films.

Many science fiction films were low budget, with a visual style that resembled the semi-documentary look of crime and espionage films of the 1940s and early 1950s. Although the science fiction films had extravagant stories about sensational events, their style tended to be restrained and visually bland. They were usually shot in black and white with flat lighting that gave them a gray tone, and some were in 3-D. As a rule, sci-fi actors were not well known, and some, such as Richard Carlson, Kenneth Tobey, and Jeff Morrow, appeared in several of the decade's films. As leading men, they were not particularly handsome and because of their similarity in physical characteristics and acting styles, they could have been interchangeable in their roles. A few films, such as FORBIDDEN PLANET (1956), had big budgets and famous actors, and were shot in color and CinemaScope.

Science fiction films created spectacles of the present and the future with sets, models, paintings, costumes, makeup, types of action, documentary footage, and special effects. Some studios hired famous science fiction illustrators to do the scenic backdrops. High quality films, such as THE THING and THE DAY THE EARTH STOOD STILL (both 1951), used authentic scientific equipment borrowed from universities and tanks and machine guns on loan from the National Guard. Sets were often simple, but for some films they became quite elaborate. During the filming of THE INCREDIBLE SHRINKING MAN (1957), for example, the sets were closed to keep secret the techniques employed to make the lead character look smaller and smaller. Under the direction of special effects man Clifford Stine, objects were built to super scale, twenty-five to one hundred times larger than normal; for example, a common straight pin was twelve feet long and a pair of scissors was twenty-five feet long. Every time the man shrank, new sets had to be constructed.[7] As with the treatment of science, the use of spectacle was generally simplistic. Viewers could distinguish the use of effects: the models and miniatures, the sets based on 1950s modern architecture, and the human actors playing aliens and mutants. Yet this transparency is part of 1950s science fiction's paradoxical charm; the simplicity of the effects highlights the process of turning contemporary fears into indirect narratives or myths.

The key historical point to be made about the science fiction films of the 1950s is that they came about "in direct relationship to the increasing public concern about communism and the fear of a nuclear disaster."[8] Phil Hardy, editor of the *Overlook Film Encyclopedia*: *Science Fiction*, wrote "Lurking behind every frame of fifties Science Fiction . . . is the fear of nuclear Armageddon. So much so that by the end of the decade monsters of all shapes and sizes were introduced with nothing but a muttered comment about radiation as the justification for their appearance."[9] The near deluge of 1950s science fiction films was part of a fearful and anxious American cultural climate. As historian Paul Boyer said, "for all its exotic trappings, science fiction is best understood as a commentary on contemporary issues."[10]

The contemporary issues were, of course, anxiety over the spread of communism and the consequences of a nuclear disaster and radioactive fallout. As Susan Sontag wrote in her famous essay about science fiction films, "The Imagination of Disaster": "there is a historically specifiable twist which intensifies the anxiety. I mean, the trauma suffered by everyone in the middle of the 20th century when it became clear that, from now on to the end of human history, every person would spend his individual life under the threat not only of individual death, which is certain, but of something almost insupportable psychologically—collective incineration and extinction which could come at any time, virtually without warning."[11]

Although most Americans were euphoric when atomic bombs were dropped on Hiroshima on 6 August 1945 and Nagasaki on 9 August 1945, bringing about victory in World War II, it was not long before the advent of the atomic bomb drastically affected the American perception of life and culture. At first, popular culture representations of the bomb were positive and prevalent in songs, cereal box prizes, jewelry, and language. For example, the American public blithely gave the "bikini" bathing suit its name from the atomic tests on 1 and 25 July 1946 at Bikini Atoll in the Marshall Islands. Months later, the public learned that the Bikini tests had caused death from radiation sickness among the hundreds of mice, rats, goats, pigs, and guinea pigs aboard the test ships and the fish in surrounding waters. Publications such as the *Bulletin of Atomic Scientists*, which developed the "doomsday clock," and David Bradley's *No Place to Hide* (1948), a best-seller by a physician, publicized the grave threat of nuclear weapons and radioactive fallout. Fear and speculation about fallout, genetic mutation, and radioactive sickness were widely discussed in government and the media. Subsequent events, including the Soviet test of an atomic bomb in 1949 and both American and Soviet tests of the hydrogen bomb a few years later, added to the "age of anxiety."

The era was also haunted by the threat of communism. The threat was rooted in reality, for the Soviet Union had subsumed Eastern Europe, violently squashing resistance wherever it arose. At home, Alger Hiss, who was suspected of being a Communist spy, was convicted for perjury and imprisoned in 1951; Julius and Ethel Rosenberg were executed for espionage in 1953; Senator Joseph McCarthy emerged as a powerful demagogue in the early 1950s, creating a widespread "Red Scare." Legislators, judges, military officers, university administrators, clergy, journalists, and politicians joined the cause of trying to exorcise communism. Many science fiction films of the 1950s present allegorical treatments of communism as a plague, a form of mind control, an invasion, or a loss of identity.

Other contemporary events that inspired science fiction filmmakers were UFO sightings and the beginnings of space travel. UFOs were reported as early as 1947 near Roswell, New Mexico, and in Washington State, and the sightings continued throughout the fifties. A feature-length "documentary" on the subject, UNIDENTIFIED FLYING OBJECTS (released by United Artists, 1956), stated that 15 percent of the sightings were unexplained. Travel in space became a reality on 4 October 1957 when the Soviet Union launched *Sputnik*. This demonstration of scientific and technological prowess by the Soviets began a new wave of panic and paranoia in the United States. It also suggested that in some areas, at least, the line between science fiction and science fact was relatively narrow. Space travel was possible, and therefore the many dreams and nightmares of science fiction deserved serious consideration.

The popularity of science fiction was also influenced by the activities of the scientists' movement. The Federation of Atomic Scientists (FAC), the organization established by scientists to halt further development of atomic weaponry, played a large role in molding the public's fearful attitudes toward the bomb and the consequences of a nuclear war. The FAC advocated an international movement to control atomic weapons and attempted to educate the public through magazine and newspaper articles, radio broadcasts, cartoons, information packets, and lectures. Historian Alan Winkler believed that the Federation of Atomic Scientists inspired artistic creations, including the fifties science fiction movies.[12] Science fiction writers, said Isaac Asimov, were "salvaged into respectability" as science fiction stories, books, and films were propelled into popularity.[13] Film producers responded to the popularity of science fiction. For example, when in 1950 the number of science fiction magazines increased from eight to twenty, Howard Hawks decided that the time was right to make THE THING, one of the first major science fiction films of the fifties.

Because the Hollywood industry had suffered economic reverses due to anti-trust decisions and the popularity of television, smaller studios and independent production companies found it easier to raise finances for the relatively small-budget projects. Although big budget science fiction films such as THE DAY THE EARTH STOOD STILL were marketed to adults, low-budget films were aggressively marketed to teenagers and drive-in movie theaters. More science fiction films were shown in drive-in theaters than any other genre.[14] Independent filmmakers like Roger Corman identified teens as the primary audience, releasing science fiction films as double features. Although Hollywood's historic audiences no longer patronized movie theaters, a new and specific teenage audience for science fiction films emerged. Samuel Z. Arkoff, a producer at American International Pictures, understood the tastes of this new teenage audience and made science fiction films to both cater to and form those interests.[15] The Motion Picture Association of America (MPAA) survey conducted in 1957 found that 21 percent of movie audiences were between the ages of fifteen and nineteen. Fifteen percent were between ten and fourteen. Teenagers were the primary audience for drive-in movie theaters.[16] The teenage culture after World War II was characterized by suburbanization, disposable income, and consumerism. According to Barry R. Litman, "In the 1950s, as drive-ins sprang up across the country, the "B" picture was adapted to its new audience, which included older teenagers who had access to the family car. Instead of horse operas, science fiction films became the standard "B" movie fare at drive-ins. [The science fiction films] included content that attracted this older, teenage audience."[17] Reviewers also noted that science fiction films catered to teenage tastes. A 1956 *Variety* review of IT CONQUERED THE WORLD referred to teenagers as "moppets" who "loved the gore, and continually shrieked avid appreciation."[18] The same publication noted in 1958 that THE BLOB had dialogue "tailored to the teenage set."[19]

Four major themes can be seen in the science fiction films of the fifties: (1) Extraterrestrial travel, (2) Alien invasion and infiltration, (3) Mutants, metamorphosis, and resurrection of extinct species, and (4) Near annihilation or the end of the Earth. Each of these themes related, at least indirectly, to the world events of the 1950s and reflected the fear and anxiety of the atomic age and the Cold War. The themes were Hollywood's version of a nation coming to grips with its postwar knowledge that humanity could destroy itself as well as the paranoia that had resulted from the red scare, in which Communists appeared to be infiltrating and subverting normal American life and values. Victorious in World War II, Americans now feared failure in the face of atomic and nuclear energy in the hands of the enemy. Science fiction films tended to merge the fear of a Communist takeover with the fear of annihilation, particularly in the form of invasion from outside forces.

The low-budget science fiction films of the 1950s tended to be about terrible threats and workable solutions; whereas, the more ambitious science fiction films presented a range of attitudes toward the perils of the new era and the human ability to cope with them. The more expansive productions presented the conflicting views of the military and scientists, federal and local government, and hope and despair. Many of the films were set in America's heartland, often in small Western towns where local law officers may or may not be able to overcome the difficulties of invasion by mutants or aliens. The desert was frequently used as a setting, perhaps because this was the actual setting for atomic testing. Expeditions, whether to the jungle or to other planets, were inevitably dangerous; disaster lurked in the unfamiliar. Life on Earth was presented as more desirable than life on other planets, but the problems experienced on other planets provided lessons to be learned about protecting civilization on Earth. When the films' settings were urban, buildings, bridges, streets, automobiles, and people were destroyed in plots about disastrous mutant invasion or cataclysmic destruction from a nuclear holocaust. Another inherent theme was tampering with nature, which led to threatened or realized catastrophe. Religion, if included at all, tended to be quite subtle, with a belief in God assumed on the part of the audience.

Extraterrestrial Travel

Two of the pioneer science fiction films released in May and June 1950 were ROCKETSHIP X-M, produced by Robert Lippert and co-produced, written, and directed by Kurt Neumann, and DESTINATION MOON, a Technicolor film produced by George Pal and directed by Irving Pichel that won an Academy Award for its art director, Ernst Fegte. The two films could not have been more different although both had the theme of space travel.

DESTINATION MOON, loosely based on a Robert Heinlein story, "Rocketship Galileo," is about three men, a military general, an engineer, and a scientist who, along with a radio engineer, take a privately funded trip to the Moon in a rocket ship fired by atomic energy. Pal employed physicists and engineers as consultants for authenticity and the noted science illustrator Chesley Bonestell for the scenic backdrop. Pal wanted documentary realism for the film, thus it is highly technical and quite prophetic of the actual Moon landing in 1969. In the film, Walter Lantz's Woody Woodpecker explains the theory of rocket travel in an animated sequence. Heinlein, a major science fiction writer, was given credit as one of the writers, but his story was changed so much it is doubtful that he wrote much of the screenplay. Nevertheless, the film's premiere was held at the Hayden Planetarium in New York for science fiction writers and editors as a tribute to Heinlein.[20]

DESTINATION MOON was atypical of the science fiction films of the decade in that it was optimistic. The film contains a strong reference to the Cold War, when the General points out that although it is peacetime, there will be a need for a rocket ship one of these days: "We're not the only ones who know the moon can be reached. . . . The race is on! . . . The first country that can use the moon for the launching of missiles will control the earth." This comment was not lost on the press, where reviews of the film had headlines such as, "Must America engage in a race to the moon in self-defense?"[21] and references to "iron-curtain jitters."[22]

ROCKETSHIP X-M was the first science fiction film of the fifties to emphasize that humanity could annihilate itself in a nuclear war; however, in this case, humanity was on Mars. An American expedition on its way to the Moon is diverted by meteors to Mars where the crew discovers that a civilization has been wiped out by atomic weapons. The surviving Martians, blind, horribly disfigured, and crazed, have reverted to the Stone Age. The Martians kill half of the crew while the others return to Earth to die in a crash landing, but not before they radio in their discovery. The original script portrayed a different Mars, one that had not had an atomic war, but Neumann changed it to a grim story to capitalize on a topic that was on the minds of the public, the consequences of a nuclear

The lunar landscape in Destination Moon *(1950), designed by visual effects artist and science illustrator Chesley Bonestell.*

war.[23] The film cost $95,000 and made a million dollars in the first few months after its release. The *Los Angeles Times* reported, "The scientific thriller probably will be a regular part of the program from now on. Rocketship X-M and Destination Moon have proved how successful that type of feature can be."[24] The Steven Spielberg film E.T. (1982) contains a similar acknowledgement of the importance of the film: when E.T. turns on the television set, the images on the screen are from Rocketship X-M.

In November 1951, another extraterrestrial flight took place in Cinecolor in Flight to Mars, produced by Walter Mirisch and directed by Lesley Selander. This time four scientists and a newspaperman, played by Cameron Mitchell, make a crash landing on Mars, where the Martians live a luxurious life underground. Although they seem friendly at first, the Martians want the earthlings' spaceship after it is repaired in order to preemptively destroy the Earth because they fear invasion. They speak English as the result of monitoring radio broadcasts from Earth. Three of the Martians warn the visitors of the plot, thus the Earth people escape, taking two of the friendly Martians with them. It was not surprising that Mars, the red planet, would be the home of enemies who feigned friendliness and who knew English from monitoring broadcasts. "Red," of course, was the buzzword for Communists throughout the fifties, and, like the Martians, the "Reds" were different from Americans. The Martians were represented as cold, devious, ruthless, and dangerous, characteristics commonly associated with the Soviet Communists.

Other extraterrestrial travel films were made throughout the decade, but the most lavish and well-made was Forbidden Planet from MGM, in CinemaScope and Eastman Color. Released in 1956 and starring Walter Pidgeon, Anne Francis, and Leslie Nielsen, it was directed by Fred McLeod Wilcox, famous for LASSIE COME HOME. Special effects were by Disney's Joshua Meador, and it may have been the first film to use an all-electronic score, composed by Bebe and Louis Barron.[25] Based on Shakespeare's *The Tempest* and written by Cyril Hume, FORBIDDEN PLANET takes place in the twenty-second century on the planet Altair-IV, where an American military mission arrives in a palatial flying saucer, the C-57D, to search for survivors of a previous flight from twenty years before. The only survivors on the planet are Dr. Morbius (Pidgeon) and his daughter Altaira (Francis), also known as Alta, who live in a beautiful, high-technology home with an amazing robot named Robby, who has superhuman strength, keeps the house in perfect order, and designs Altaira's clothing. The Americans learn that a super race, known as the Krel, had inhabited Altair-IV but its members were destroyed when their own subconscious ids turned on them. Furthermore, an invisible monster lurks on the planet, killing some of the Americans. The monster, it seems, is a projection of the jealous Morbius's id: a separate creature, his evil self who is stirred into a rage by the commander's attention to Altaira. To protect his daughter, Morbius blows up Altair IV (and

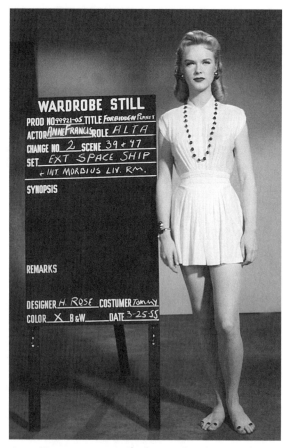

Anne Francis in a wardrobe test for FORBIDDEN PLANET *(1956).*

himself) while the Americans escape with Altaira and Robby. As Robby pilots the flying saucer, the commander and Altaira watch the exploding planet on their viewing screen. Dr. Morbius represents untrustworthy science, an intellectual destroyed by his own brilliance and abilities who loses to the military. The film ends with the American commander's moralistic words, "We're all part monsters in our subconscious, so we have laws and religion . . . it will remind us that after all, we're not God." He is essentially saying that our real enemy is not out there but inside ourselves.

Robby the robot was one of the most elaborate robots ever built for a film. Although there were 2,600 feet of electrical wiring in him to operate his flashing lights, antennae, and other gadgets, Robby was inhabited by an actor who was inside the robot case all the time. Unlike the monster robots of other science fiction films, Robby was programmed not to harm a human or let a human be harmed. He was a much-loved figure, and appeared in THE INVISIBLE BOY in 1957, partly because the robot had been so expensive to build that MGM felt obliged to use him again.[26] He also appeared on several television shows in the fifties.

The films with extraterrestrial travel themes became a major trend in science fiction films for decades to come, fascinating audiences with stories about space and other planets. While some of these films had a semblance of accuracy about space travel, others offered wildly imaginative scenarios about life on other planets. The lessons these films imparted were that Martians were to be feared; it was important for the United States to be first in space; and humans needed to recognize their own imperfections, especially regarding the use of atomic technology.

Alien Invasion and Infiltration

Invasion films were common[27] in the 1950s featuring a variety of aliens portrayed as superior to earthlings both in intelligence and technology. In these films, aliens represent what some Americans feared about the Soviets. Invaders, friends or enemies, and often with the help of robots, either come to warn earthlings or to destroy them with superior technology. Sometimes the invaders use the strategy of infiltration, taking over the minds of the people, making slaves of them, or appropriating their bodies, thus making war unnecessary. Infiltration usually starts with authority figures such as community leaders or parents, who, once taken over by aliens, look just like their former selves but lack emotions and souls. The result of the infiltration is loss of free will, loss of identity, and disintegration of the family and community. The takeover represents what many Americans believed would occur in a Communist invasion.

The invasion films ranged from serious drama such as THE DAY THE EARTH STOOD STILL (1951) to drive-in movie fare such as THE BLOB (1958). Regardless of their quality, most invasion films opened with scenes of civic or domestic calm, with an emphasis on order and certainty that is disrupted by the arrival of something or someone, usually from the sky. A hero (or heroes) discovers the invader and seeks to understand or destroy it. The people doubt the hero's story, resist his or her efforts to organize action, and confusion or panic occurs. If the hero succeeds in eliminating the threat, there is a reaffirmation of the old order coupled with warnings about the future.

Two of the most notable science fiction films opened in 1951. The *Los Angeles Times*, on 8 April 1951, anticipated the opening of THE THING and THE DAY THE EARTH STOOD STILL with a headline claiming, "Scientific Thriller to Be Regular Studio Fixture."

The Thing (from Another World),[28] an RKO/Howard Hawks production, was the "first to link inhuman, devouring, alien beings with the Red Menace."[29] Hawks had wanted to produce a Class-A science fiction film for years but waited until the public was ready for such a film. He had purchased a story, "Who Goes There," by John W. Campbell Jr. in 1949 as the basis for the screenplay. For fourteen months, he and a team of researchers verified the story points with electronic engineers, scientists, and university professors. After 400 readings and seventy screen tests, Hawks cast twenty-three little-known actors, including James Arness as the creature, otherwise known as "The Thing." When he budgeted the film at $1.3 million, his colleagues were aghast because he had cast no well-known names. It took the makeup artist, Lee Greenway, five months and eighteen sculptures of the creature before Hawks was satisfied; however, five insurance companies turned him down when he tried to get insurance for the creature. Insurers refused because "The Thing" had to be frozen in a block of ice, hacked by axes, attacked by dogs, set afire, and electrocuted.

The Thing was set in the Arctic Circle to suggest American surveillance of the Soviet nuclear threat,[30] but because daylight was available only two hours a day at the North Pole, location work began in Cut Bank, Montana, about fifty miles south of the Canadian border, where the scenery was similar and eight hours of daylight enabled longer work days. Sub-zero temperatures, however, created hardships for the cast and crew, who wore fur-lined pants and parkas as well as fur-lined aviation boots and had to cope with sets destroyed by high winds and frozen equipment.[31] Finally, the company relocated to the RKO Ranch in the San Fernando Valley where the most famous scene, the crew

James Arness as the title character in The Thing *(1951).*

forming a ring around the submerged flying saucer, was shot in 100-degree weather. Christian Nyby, a film editor, was given credit for the film's direction, although various sources[32] suggest that either Hawks directed or he guided Nyby very closely, for he was on the set every day. The film has Hawks's trademarks—ensemble acting, overlapping dialogue that is at times humorous, and a sharp, assertive woman.

THE THING is about an air force captain and his men, a journalist, a group of scientists, and a secretary, at the North Pole who discover the traces of a spacecraft in the form of a very large circle in the ice. One of the men says, "We finally got one," and the journalist Scotty says, "We found a flying saucer." The aircraft burns and explodes, but there is a "man" about eight feet tall frozen in the ice. He turns out not to be a man at all, but a huge, irradiated, humanoid vegetable ("a giant carrot," quips Scotty) that drinks blood and is able to propagate itself with seedpods. The scientist, Dr. Carrington, marvels at the creature's superiority and begs the captain not to harm it. The creature, however, kills the sled dogs and two of the men while Carrington nurtures its growing seedpods with blood plasma in the base greenhouse. Since bullets do not harm it, the men consider how to kill it. When the captain asks, "What do you do with a vegetable," Nikki, the secretary, says, "Boil it, stew it, bake it, fry it." Burning it with kerosene and a flame gun, however, does not work, so working as a team, they successfully electrocute it, but not before Carrington tries to be friends with it. He rushes up to the creature and gets thrown across the room for his trouble. Scotty sends out his story and ends it with, "Tell the world. Tell this to everyone wherever they are: Watch the skies! Watch everywhere. Keep on looking. Watch the skies!"

Instead of using special effects, the film frightens because the creature is only seen in shadows and claustrophobic darkness, leaving details to our imagination. It resembles a man but has no emotions, no personality. The eerie musical score of Dimitri Tiomkin adds to the chills. The teamwork of the military men defeats the malevolent invader, but they also have to resist the scientist who wants to preserve it for study "because it has so much to teach us." Carrington the scientist, wearing a goatee, a Russian-style fur hat, and, at other times, a silk dressing gown and ascot, looks different, somewhat like Lenin. The men identify him as a Nobel Prize winner and a participant at Bikini, thus linking him with the atomic bomb. He is pitted against the military men because he is soft on the alien, and even helps to propagate it in the base greenhouse. In the end, however, he apologizes for his lack of caution. Scotty, the journalist, has to wait for the captain's permission to take a picture and must withhold his story until he is allowed to release it at the end of the film, thus the press is more or less controlled by the military. The military men save the day despite interference from the scientist, reaffirming the old order but leaving the audience with a stern warning to "watch the skies," suggesting that evil invaders are still out there.

THE DAY THE EARTH STOOD STILL, a Twentieth Century–Fox production, had a cast of established actors that included English actor Michael Rennie, Patricia Neal, Hugh Marlowe, and Sam Jaffe. The director was Robert Wise and the producer Julian Blaustein. The *Los Angeles Times* noted two firsts: Twentieth Century–Fox's first science fiction film and the first science fiction film to feature well-known actors.[33] Based on a 1940 short story by Harry Bates, "Farewell to the Master," THE DAY THE EARTH STOOD STILL was "earthbound" in that it did not have scenes in space. Darryl Zanuck was pleased because that made the film less costly, although it came in at $1.2 million.[34] Dr. Samuel Herrick, a UCLA astronomer, was the technical advisor, and the tanks and machine guns were borrowed from the National Guard.[35] Blaustein said, "We ourselves have rockets, jet propulsion, atomic energy. So everything in the picture will really be an extension of known facts."[36] Further realism was provided by using the actual location of the Mall and monuments in Washington, D.C., and the voices of four well-known radio commentators, Drew Pearson, Elmer Davis, H. V. Kaltenborn, and Gabriel Heatter. Special effects were limited to the robot's ray vision (a light emanating from his eye slots) and the spaceship, a two-foot miniature with a traveling matte. Two foam rubber suits covered in metallic spray paint were designed for the robot, one with a zipper in the back for the approach scenes and one with a zipper in the front for the retreat scenes. Locke Martin, a seven feet, seven inches tall doorman at Grauman's Chinese Theater, wore the suits as Gort, the robot, but he could only stay in a suit for forty-five minutes at a time, thus a statue was constructed for the scenes in which he did not move. The musical score was written by Bernard Herrmann, using electric violins, bass, and theremins.

THE DAY THE EARTH STOOD STILL begins with radio reports of a UFO spotted flying over various parts of the world. It is a pleasant spring day in Washington, D.C., where children peacefully play ball and people have picnics on the grass. A spaceship descends upon this scene, flying low over the monuments of the Mall, landing on a baseball field and causing panic. Almost immediately it is surrounded by soldiers, tanks, and artillery. The spaceman, a scientist named Klaatu, emerges, announcing, "We have come to visit you in peace and good will," but when he reaches into his spacesuit for a gift for the president of the United States, a frightened soldier reacts, shooting him in the shoulder. Gort, a huge robot, appears, melting the weapons with a beam from his eye slot. The soldiers are unable to enter the spaceship or even analyze it.

After Klaatu is taken to Walter Reed Hospital, the president's emissary visits him. When Klaatu asks for a meeting of all the world leaders, the emissary replies, "Our world at the present moment is full of tensions and suspicions. In the present international situation, such a meeting would be quite impossible." Klaatu escapes, and because he looks like a human in ordinary clothing he is able to mingle with the people. He befriends a widow, Helen Benson, and her young son Bobby, who takes Klaatu on a tour of Washington, D.C. and the monuments commemorating great men. Bobby tells him about Professor Barnhart, an Einstein look-alike scientist. Barnhart understands Klaatu's warnings of Earth's imminent destruction if spaceships are developed to threaten other planets and arranges a meeting of the world's scientists and intellectuals. Meanwhile, Barnhart suggests that Klaatu demonstrate his powers, but dissuades him from leveling Manhattan. Klaatu's compromise is nonviolent—he stops everything that depends on electricity all over the world, except hospitals and airplanes in flight, for thirty minutes. Thus the world stands still, not for a day, but for half an hour. Klaatu is shot and killed on his way to the big meeting, but Gort resurrects him. The reborn Klaatu leaves with this message: "If you threaten to extend your violence, this earth of yours will be reduced to a burned-out cinder. Your choice is simple: join us and live in peace or pursue your present course and face obliteration."

Producer Blaustein said of Klaatu's desire for an international meeting: "This is a plea for a stronger United Nations with an effective police force. Our man tells us we must do this or the world will be destroyed."[37] The Barnhart character, unlike Dr. Carrington, the scientist in THE THING, is a sympathetic and convincing representation of scientists and the scientists' movement. The military represent fear and paranoia, attempting to kill Klaatu rather than to give him a chance to promote peace in the world. The woman and her son represent ordinary people who, together with the scientist, see Klaatu as a superior being who wants to save humanity; whereas, the military is myopic in its quest

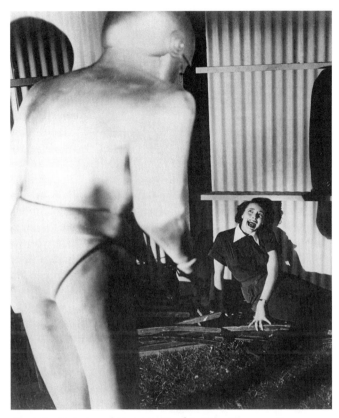

Gort the Robot and Patricia Neal in THE DAY THE EARTH
STOOD STILL *(1951).*

to destroy him. The media spreads fear and panic without trying to get the real story. Although Klaatu is a messianic figure who assumes the name "Mr. Carpenter" and is killed and resurrected, Robert Wise said he did not intend any religious symbolism: "We were not trying to say that this is a version of Christ's return."[38]

THE DAY THE EARTH STOOD STILL was a success with movie audiences and critics alike. *Variety*'s critic Frank Scully liked the film because of its intelligence, with its "scientists who try to think their way out instead of generals who try to fight their way out."[39] The *Los Angeles Times* liked its "newsreelish realism" and "the triumph of mind over matter."[40] THE THING and THE DAY THE EARTH STOOD STILL were the two most important invasion films of the fifties, both for their success at the box office and for their quality. They also started a trend of invasion films that lasted throughout the decade.

The invasion films that followed tended to be more frightening, with alien invaders threatening the American way of life. The invaders were often dangerous Martians or monsters with superior intelligence or strength. Even if they meant no harm, the aliens were able to control humans for their own advantage. When they meant harm, they were capable of mass destruction.

IT CAME FROM OUTER SPACE was director Jack Arnold's first science fiction film for Universal. It premiered in 1953 and was the first 3-D film on a wide screen with stereophonic sound. Arnold said, "I think science fiction films are a marvelous medium for telling a story, creating a mood, and delivering whatever kind of social message should be delivered."[41] Based on *The Meteor* by Ray Bradbury, the film features a crash landing near a small town in the Arizona desert of a spaceship that looks like a meteor. John Putnam, an astronomer played by Richard Carlson, is the lone witness, but because a landslide has covered the spaceship in a crater, the townspeople refuse to believe him. The aliens are xenomorphs, ectoplasmic beings who are able to assume the identities of others, but in their natural state they look like giant, peeled eyeballs floating inside plastic globes, lunging out of the screen and into the audience in 3-D. Shots of the townspeople are from the point of view of the aliens, thus the people appear on screen through a shimmering, eyelike bubble. The aliens assume the identities of the townspeople so they can repair their spaceship unnoticed but they mean no harm. They just want to fix their spaceship and be on their way after returning the citizens to their original forms. They take other identities because they are afraid of what humans will do to them. Eventually the townspeople catch on and attempt to destroy the aliens, but Putnam protects them in the final confrontation, explaining, "They don't trust us because what we don't understand we destroy."[42] At the end, the people gather round Putnam, who says, "It wasn't the right time for us to meet, but there'll be other nights, other stars for us to watch; they'll be back." This film is somewhat unusual in that there are no military forces, only a sheriff, to fight against the invaders, who leave the Earth unharmed.

The aliens in INVADERS FROM MARS, a Twentieth Century–Fox Eastmancolor release in 1953,[43] meant to do harm, for they implanted radios in the citizens' necks, turning them into cold, emotionless pawns used to destroy U.S. weapons and research stations and stop atomic rocket testing. The film is seen through the eyes of a child, a twelve-year-old boy named Jimmy, who lives in a small California town, and who awakens at night to see a Martian spaceship land on a nearby sandpit into which it disappears. The Martians are green and eight feet tall, with rigid, unemotional faces and bulbous eyes. They are controlled by a disembodied supreme intelligence in the form of a head in a glass globe. It represents humankind developed to its ultimate intelligence. Jimmy, unable to convince the townspeople that Martians have landed and are taking over people, convinces a psychologist, a scientist, and an army officer; the officer then destroys the Martians and their spaceship with explosives. At the end of the film, Jimmy awakens and we learn that this has all been a dream, and then he sees a spaceship land in the sandpit. . . . Jimmy is forever trapped in a nightmare world of Martian invaders, atomic rockets, and dehumanized automatons, a life of fear of atomic attack and invasion by brutal and emotionless Martians/Communists.

IT CAME FROM OUTER SPACE and INVADERS FROM MARS were set in small towns where aliens penetrated the very heart of America. The apparently secure environment of the small town was no safer than the urban areas where atomic attacks could occur. The invaders were able to assume the identity or control the minds of the townspeople, thus making it impossible to tell the difference between genuine Americans and the enemy. Those who knew about the enemy, whether they were scientists or an innocent child, had a difficult time convincing others of the truth. Each of these themes represents the social and political paranoia of the Cold War era.

THIS ISLAND EARTH, a 1955 Universal Studios film directed by Joseph Newman, featured realistic special effects and Technicolor. Aliens from the planet Metaluna, which is millions of light years from Earth, capture nuclear scientists and transport them back to their home planet, which is disintegrating. A new source of atomic energy is needed to set up an isolation layer around Metaluna to protect it from the continuous attack of the more powerful planet Zagon; however, the aliens and the American scientists arrive too late, for the enemy has exploded nuclear warheads on Metaluna. The Metalunans, though technologically and intellectually more advanced than earthlings, had a regimented social system ruled by a dictator who expected complete obedience. Dissenters were lobotomized, and there was no religion. The devastation of their planet serves as an example of the need for a strong nuclear arsenal as deterrence. The message is "Peace Through Strength," for the kidnapped scientists return to Earth dedicated to the American political system and a belief in a strong nuclear defense capability. The planet Metaluna lacked a strong defense system and was thus ill-prepared to ward off an enemy nuclear attack. The scientists, recognizing the importance of nuclear deterrence, affirm the United States policy of weapons build-up to thwart attack from the Soviet Union.

WAR OF THE WORLDS, a George Pal production directed by Byron Haskin, came out in 1953. It won an Academy Award for Gordon Jennings for special effects. Once again, Chesley Bonestell did the astronomical art. Based on the well-known H. G. Wells novel, the film was located in California instead of England and in 1953 instead of 1890. A spaceship that looks like a meteor falls near a small community, but a famous nuclear physicist named Clayton Forrester guesses that it is a Martian spaceship. Actually, the ship is part of a mass invasion, for meteors fall all over the world, opening up to release flying machines with attached death rays. Forrester, who seems to be pro-military, sends for the army, but no matter how much armament is used against the Martians they are invincible. Martians inside the spaceships control the death rays that vaporize humans and buildings. After trying conventional warfare, the military resorts to atomic bombs, although there is a fear of "radiation danger," but the Martians are unharmed by them. Images of cities in ruins and fleeing refugees are seen, while Forrester and others pray for God to intervene. Religious symbols abound, and the resolution seems to be God-sent, for the Martians begin to die from exposure to the Earth's bacteria. As the Martians fall dead, Sir Cedric Hardwicke, the narrator, says, "After all that men could do, victory came through the littlest things [the bacteria] which God in his wisdom had put on this Earth." *Variety* commented that "Viewers take vicarious pleasure in the terror loosed in the film—then walk out of theatres relieved to find the world still as it was."[44]

Some of the teenager/drive-in invasion films were ROBOT MONSTER (1953), KRONOS (1957), and THE BLOB (1958). In ROBOT MONSTER, a 3-D production from Three Dimensions Pictures, Ro-Man, an actor in a gorilla suit and diving helmet, comes from an unknown planet to invade Earth. He wipes out the entire population save six people, a scientist and his family, who have taken a serum. All sorts of prehistoric monsters come to life in the mayhem, but they fight among themselves.[45] KRONOS, a Twentieth Century–Fox/Regal Films production directed by Kurt Neumann, features a 100-foot-tall electronic monster, which scours Earth for fresh supplies of energy to replenish the resources of his own planet. Newscasters in the film dubbed the monster "Kronos" after the Greek giant who rose out of the sea. The army attacks with atomic missiles and H-bombs to no avail as Kronos sucks up energy from atoms. A scientist figures out how to short-circuit the invader, which absorbs its own energy and disappears. THE BLOB from Paramount was sure to appeal to teenagers as the actor Steve McQueen, in his first movie role, leads fellow teens into battle to save their small town from a giant glob of gelatin from outer space that engorges people. Leaking through doorsills and vents, it could devour the entire continent, but the teens save the day by putting it out with a fire extinguisher.

Films with an infiltration theme emphasized paranoia because endless vigilance was required to protect oneself from an enemy capable of subversively controlling minds and bodies. Family members, lovers, and best friends were not to be trusted, for they could be the enemy operating within the self of another. Invasion of the Body Snatchers, directed by Don Siegel for Allied Artists/Walter Wanger production in 1956, was the best of the infiltration films. This film presents the enemy as giant pods that, as a result of atomic radiation, come to Earth to take possession of human bodies in a small California town. The result is a community of people who are calm but emotionless, affecting an aura of normalcy. Friends and relatives who have not yet been infiltrated see that others are not what they used to be, but soon they too are taken over until only two people are left, Dr. Miles Bennell and his sweetheart, Becky Driscoll. Because the victims are still alive but no longer in control of their own minds, alien invasion here is similar to brainwashing, as it occurred in Communist political prisons during the Korean War. Miles and Becky must fight or hide from the aliens, but they also must not sleep, for that is when the pods take over human bodies. Becky does sleep when Miles leaves their hiding place to check on what he thinks is another "real" human. When he comes back and kisses her, her eyes open with a vacant stare, and he recognizes that she too is a pod person. He runs to the highway, trying to flag down cars, but they ignore him. He shouts, "You're next, you fools! You're in danger!" Because the studio thought the film too pessimistic, a prologue and conclusion were added with Miles telling the story in flashback and finally getting authorities to respond to the threat.

Dana Wynter, who played Becky, said that she, Kevin McCarthy, who played Miles, and others assumed they were making an anti-Communist movie: "We took it for granted that's what we were making, but it wasn't spoken about openly on the set or anything like that."[46] Siegel said, "This is probably my best film. I think that the world is populated by pods and I wanted to show them."[47] Siegel, however, did not confirm Wynter's assumption, for he left the question of whether pods were anti-Communist conformists or invading Communists unresolved. The political Right saw the film as the denunciation of Communist mind-control; whereas, the Left saw it as McCarthyites inducing and/or reinforcing stifling conformity on society. A *Los Angeles Weekly* review (published in 2000) stated, "The result dryly lampoons the spirit of conformity that dominated American life in the Eisenhower era; the menacing sense that one is being invisibly ganged up on can be read as an explicit attack on McCarthyism [or] a rebellion against totalitarianism of any kind."[48]

Invasion of the Body Snatchers was shot in nineteen days and cost $300,000, with only $15,000 spent on special effects.[49] Most of the scenes are at night, in the dark, in enclosed physical spaces, in small rooms, empty nightclubs, closets, and abandoned caves—suggesting isolation and paranoia. The actors are framed in doorways from low angles creating a sense of claustrophobia. It is an important film that visually and narratively represents the loss of identity and the fear that one's closest friends and relatives are not who they appear to be. What defined humans in the film was emotion, for in other respects the pod people looked like anyone else. This film mirrored the prevalent fear of an enemy within, and it contributed memorable images to American visual culture of the 1950s, especially the image of Kevin McCarthy running down the highway shouting, "You're next!"

I Married a Monster from Outer Space (1958) is a strong film despite its outlandish title. A bridegroom-to-be witnesses the landing of a spaceship on the night before his wedding and is taken over by one of the aliens who assumes his shape. On the honeymoon night, Marge, the bride, senses that something is wrong. Directed by Gene

Dana Wynter and Kevin McCarthy in INVASION OF THE BODY SNATCHERS *(1956). This low-budget film created an aura of fear despite the almost complete absence of special effects.*

Fowler in 1958, the film can be seen as a feminine analogue to INVASION OF THE BODY SNATCHERS.[50] The wife writes a letter to her mother saying that "Bill isn't the man I fell in love with," and, after following him into the woods where she see his true self emerge from its human shell, realizes that he is an alien. When she turns to the police chief for help, he suggests she go to an asylum because he is also an alien in a human shell. The alien husband and police chief prevent her from contacting higher authorities and keep her from leaving town; thus she is powerless. It turns out, however, that the aliens are impotent, thus the real humans are the men who have become fathers. Marge turns for help to the men with children (note the affirmation of conventional family values) and is able to save humanity and be reunited with her real husband.

Mutants, Metamorphosis, and Resurrection of Extinct Species

The terrible effects of atomic radiation became known after 1952 when both the United States and the Soviet Union began atmospheric tests of multi-megaton thermonuclear bombs. A hydrogen bomb test in March 1954 spread radioactive debris over 8,800 square miles of the Pacific, carrying radioactive poison to the crew of a Japanese fishing boat eighty-five miles away. The Atomic Energy Commission kept this particular instance a secret from the public until the spring of 1955, when the Federal Civil Defense Administration revealed that radioactive fallout was "invisible, insidious, and uniquely dangerous."[51] Scientists and physicians announced studies that exposed the hazards of radioactive substances, including leukemia, bone cancer, and long-term genetic damage.[52] Panic over the negative effects of radiation provided fodder for many science fiction films. Small insects mutated into huge monsters, people became impossibly large or incredibly small, and creatures long extinct came to life. Scientists in the films were often to blame for experiments that resulted in dreadful changes. Alternatively, atomic explosions released extinct creatures from icecaps or underwater caves, or radiation from the explosions caused the mutation of harmless creatures into terrifying monsters. People in these films were often depicted as bewildered or hysterical, while the FBI and the military remained organized and ready to take on new threats.

A few films featured mutated insects that had become prowling monsters. Them!, a 1954 film from Warner Bros., directed by Gordon Douglas in a semi-documentary style, had an intelligent script written by Ted Sherdeman.[53] The film's specific content was kept secret during production, but the pre-release posters featuring gigantic ants suggested the story line. It became Warner Bros.' highest grossing film of 1954.[54] Them! was originally planned to be in 3-D and color, but Jack Warner, who did not care for the story, cut Douglas's budget and forced a switch to black and white. It was one of the few films to successfully use a full-scale working model, a twelve-foot monster ant mounted on a boom. Another model with only a head and forequarters was used for close-ups.

Them! takes place in the New Mexico desert near Los Alamos, where the atomic bomb was developed. Several years after the World War II era research, two state troopers find a general store destroyed, the shopkeeper killed, and a six-year-old girl, whose parents are missing, in shock. One officer goes for help, bringing an FBI agent (James Arness) back to the site where they find the other officer dead and a strange footprint in the sand. Two entomologists from the Department of Agriculture (Edmund Gwen and Joan Weldon) arrive on the scene and learn that sugar is missing from the store, and that the storekeeper's and state trooper's bodies are full of formic acid. They recognize the print as that of a giant ant. Also, when one of the entomologists holds formic acid under the little girl's nose, she comes out of shock and screams, "Them! Them!" At that point, a giant ant appears. Together the scientists and the military destroy the New Mexico ant nest, but two queen ants escape, one to a navy ship, where it destroys the crew and sinks with the ship, the other to the huge storm drains under Los Angeles[55] where the finale occurs. Two children are being held by the ants, but one of the state policemen (James Whitmore) dies saving them, and the ants are gassed and wiped out.

The genetic mutation of the ants had been caused by lingering radiation from the explosion of the first atomic bomb. Had the ants continued to propagate, they would have taken over the world. Joan Weldon said in an interview, "Them! was an anti-war, anti-nuclear message [that] was very intentional. Ted Sherdeman . . . decided he was going to write . . . about how these kind of warheads were going to discombobulate the Earth."[56] Reviewers of Them! recognized that the ants were a projection of fear of atomic bombs. For example, the *Hollywood Reporter* said of the film: "A natural exploitation piece that, from the viewpoint of timeliness, fits in perfectly with the current fears over possible effects of hydrogen bomb explosions. . . . The story closes with the pleasant thought that there's no telling what further mutations might evolve from subsequent A-bomb explosions."[57] The ants could also have been a symbolic enemy, the Soviet Union, for in one scene, the entomologist says that ants are "savage, ruthless, and courageous fighters." He also tells how ants use slave laborers in their colonies, evoking images of a totalitarian society.

An over-the-shoulder shot suggests the menace of a giant ant in THEM! *(1954).*

TARANTULA, a 1955 Universal International film in color directed by Jack Arnold and produced by William Alland, continued the cycle of giant insect films. It is a film about a scientist who injects a tarantula with an atomic mixture that causes it to grow to one hundred feet tall. The creature then proceeds to destroy everything in its path until it is killed by napalm dropped by the air force. Other cinematic mutants of the decade include: radiation-swollen grasshoppers that invade Chicago in BEGINNING OF THE END (1957), giant snails affected by radiation that creep into the Los Angeles Naval Station to eat navy personnel in THE MONSTER THAT CHALLENGED THE WORLD (1957), an octopus turned monster by radioactivity that nearly destroys San Francisco in Roger Corman's IT CAME FROM BENEATH THE SEA (1955), and enormous crabs, genetically altered by hydrogen bomb fall-out, that absorb the knowledge and voices of the people they eat in Corman's ATTACK OF THE CRAB MONSTERS (1957). In each case, atomic blasts or radiation have brought to life a monster which was, in turn, destroyed by some use of atomic energy. Normalcy returns as science and technology solve the problems they helped to create.

The films with metamorphosis themes were about people or creatures which completely change their form or structure. THE FLY, directed by Kurt Neumann and filmed in CinemaScope for Twentieth Century–Fox with a budget of $700,000,[58] premiered in June 1958. A scientist for the Air Defense Ministry experiments with a teleportation machine and has his molecules mixed with that of a fly. Now he has become half human, half fly and is unable to change back to his normal self. He has the head of a fly, and the fly has his head. He realizes that he must destroy his research and equipment and that he will die, sacrificing himself for the good of humanity. He has tampered with the unknown and paid for his efforts. A press release from Twentieth Century–Fox indicated that Dr. Lee De Forest had actually worked on a similar project prior to his death. The *Los Angeles Mirror News* picked up on this in its review: "How farfetched is this idea of disintegration and reassembling elsewhere? Not as much as you might think. Dr. Frank Creswell, formerly with the Atomic Energy Commission in the flight research program of the Air Force and technical advisor on the film, says the transmitting of matter will probably be accomplished within the next decade. . . . This was a necessary step toward utilization of atomic energy and, theoretically, can be extended to all solids."[59] Advertising copy for the film claimed, "The first time atomic mutation of humans has been shown on the screen."

Yet, the prior year saw at least three films in which humans were metamorphosed, two to giant proportions, the other to minuscule dimensions. ATTACK OF THE 50 FOOT WOMAN (1958), an Allied Artists release of a Bernard Woolner production, directed by Nathan Hertz, is the story of a woman who is seized by an alien in the desert and irradiated by his touch. She grows to enormous proportions and squeezes to death her philandering husband before she is shot by the sheriff. This film was a double bill with WAR OF THE SATELLITES.[60] THE AMAZING COLOSSAL MAN (1957), an American-International release directed and produced by Bert Gordon and double-billed with CAT GIRL, was about an army colonel who is burned in a plutonium explosion, regenerates his skin, and grows ten feet a day until he is seventy feet tall and weighs thousands of pounds. His heart, however, does not expand at the same rate, thus he has a mental collapse and causes pandemonium in Las Vegas. He is pursued to Boulder Dam where he is riddled with bullets, plunging over the side of the dam. Neither of these films, however, could match the poignancy of Jack Arnold's THE INCREDIBLE SHRINKING MAN (1957), a Universal release from Albert Zugsmith Productions. This is the story of an average American man, Scott Carey, who while out boating is exposed to nuclear fallout from a cloud that leaves shimmering white particles on him. This causes him to shrink uncontrollably because his molecules have been rearranged and his growth is reversed. There are no monsters or aliens in the film, only everyday animals and objects such as a cat, a leaking faucet, a sewing box with needles and pins, and a spider, all of which become menacing and dangerous to Scott. Unable to be a normal husband, he is humiliated and filled with self-loathing, yet when he shrinks to one inch and is still shrinking he maintains, "I exist." This is a powerful moment in the film, for even though Scott has become infinitesimal in size, he is still human and aware of his own existence. Critics saw the message that human beings were being diminished by their own atomic technology. Philip K. Scheuer wrote, "it leaves you with at the last—two thoughts, really. One is that we had better look to our survival in an Atomic Age. The other is that even 'the least of these' remains one of God's creatures."[61]

THE INCREDIBLE SHRINKING MAN captures the emotional experiences of Cold War America with its themes of the paranoia, fear, and distrust. It opens with the image of a dwindling human outline as a mushroom cloud grows. Yet, the ending of the film suggests that one can find philosophical and spiritual growth in a difficult time. Arnold, who said he never made a picture without a message, resisted Universal's preference for a happy ending with doctors finding a serum to reverse the shrinking process because he wanted a metaphysical ending with the man accepting his fate.[62]

An extinct creature brought back to life, usually by an atomic explosion, was the basis for films such as THE BEAST FROM 20,000 FATHOMS (1953). Produced by Hal Chester and Jack Dietz of Mutual Pictures of California, a small independent company that was

Grant Williams as the small and still shrinking protagonist in THE INCREDIBLE SHRINK-
ING MAN (1957).

purchased by Warner Bros., and directed by Eugene Lourie, the film was an adaptation
of a Ray Bradbury story. A rhedosaurus, a fictional Mesozoic beast, is loosed from an arctic icecap by an atomic blast. It is mean, disorderly, and ill-tempered, invading New York
City, crushing cars, leveling buildings, devouring people, and creating panic among the
crowds as it stomps into Times Square. Buildings are destroyed, communications are
flooded, and many lives are lost. The National Guard bombards the rhedosaurus with
bazookas, cannons, and machine guns, but it disappears, seriously wounded. When the
soldiers track it by following large pools of blood, they become very sick and collapse.
After blood samples from the beast are analyzed, it is discovered that it contains toxic
bacteria resistant to antibiotics. This is the film's metaphor for radiation sickness. An
atomic scientist in the film concludes that they must use a radioactive isotope to kill the
rhedosaurus. The soldiers then confront the beast at Coney Island where, while the
creature is tearing apart a roller coaster, a sharpshooter fires the isotope and kills it.
Thus, although scientists created the atomic bomb that unleashed the destructive monster in the first place, a scientist had the knowledge to destroy the beast as well.

Perhaps the most unforgettable prehistoric creature in a fifties science fiction film
was CREATURE FROM THE BLACK LAGOON, a 1954 Universal International 3-D film produced by William Alland and directed by Jack Arnold, two men who became major contributors to the 1950s science fiction films. The film is about the Gill Man, a half fish,
half human, who is discovered by paleontologists in the Amazon jungles. While trying to
study him, several members of the expedition are killed, but the Gill Man is attracted to

Kay (Julia Adams), and tries to prevent the scientists from leaving. The underwater scenes in which the Gill Man swims beneath Kay, attempting to touch her legs, are both frightening and erotic, creating sympathy and identification with the creature. Arnold said, "He's a living, breathing organism. All he wants is to be left alone. When he's disturbed, he fights back."[63] Ricou Browning, a student at Florida State University, was chosen to be the Gill Man in the water because he could hold his breath for long periods of time underwater. Makeup artist Bud Westmore sculpted a full-body mold (reportedly inspired by the Oscar statuette)[64] for Browning and stuntman Gil Chapman, who played the creature on land. Two men are suitors to Kay—Richard Carlson plays an ichthyologist, a scientist interested in knowledge that will help people to adapt when they travel to other planets (or in the aftermath of a nuclear holocaust), while Richard Denning is his boss, obsessed with the economic windfall the capture of the creature would bring. Denning's character is killed by the Gill Man, who drags him into the depths of the Black Lagoon. The Gill Man subsequently captures Kay, who may actually be attracted to him, taking her to a cave. Carlson saves her and shoots the Gill Man, who staggers to the water and slides in. (Since the creature did not die, there were two sequels, THE REVENGE OF THE CREATURE, in 1955, and THE CREATURE WALKS AMONG US, in 1957.)

The Creature himself in a scene from CREATURE FROM THE BLACK LAGOON *(1954).*

Although the 3-D appeared awkward at times, the film was a success. Critic Sara Hamilton wrote, "[It is] the scariest apparition since 'Frankenstein' . . . the underwater scenes are fantastic and the direction smartly placed."[65] The film brought out the fear of exploring the unknown and of awakening primordial forces that could not be controlled.

GODZILLA, KING OF THE MONSTERS reflected the nuclear anxiety of both the Japanese and the Americans. Made originally in Japan as GOJIRA in 1954, the Japanese film was re-edited under the direction of Terry Morse for Embassy Pictures (the distribution company of exhibitor Joseph E. Levine) and released in 1956. Much of the dialogue was dubbed into English, and scenes featuring Raymond Burr as narrator were added. The story unfolds as Burr, playing a newspaper reporter named Steve Martin, witnesses the destruction caused by a once-dormant prehistoric monster that has been given radioactive powers as the result of nuclear weapons tests in the Pacific. Godzilla, named after a legendary Japanese monster, is four hundred feet tall and nasty. He devastates Tokyo, spewing flames from his mouth and trampling down skyscrapers, and he is impervious to gunfire and high voltage. The government response is headed by a paleontologist, his daughter, a naval officer (the daughter's boyfriend), and several other scientists. Godzilla finally succumbs to a secret weapon developed by one of the scientists. The film was a box-office success, and therefore Godzilla returned again and again in Japanese-made sequels as well as a cheaply made update of the original film, again with inserts of Burr, made in 1985.

Near Annihilation or the End of the Earth

The most pessimistic theme of the fifties science fiction films represented the fear that nuclear bombs would blow up the Earth. Yet most of the films also expressed optimism about survival. Some films suggested redemption, usually Christian in character.

The first science fiction film to deal with nuclear holocaust and its survivors was FIVE, a Columbia Pictures release of Arch Oboler Productions in April 1951. Written and directed by Oboler, FIVE is about the last five survivors on Earth after an atomic blast. One by one, three of the characters are eliminated until there remains only one man named Michael, after the archangel who drove Adam and Eve out of Eden, and one woman, Roseanne, who is pregnant with her husband's child, left to build a new world in an agrarian utopia. They return to the city to confirm Roseanne's husband's death and discover a gruesome scene of empty buildings and corpses in cars. Rather than talk about the destruction, the characters debate about humanity regenerating itself in a community where all people can live together in peace and harmony.

WHEN WORLDS COLLIDE, a 1951 Paramount release of a George Pal production, was based on the H. G. Wells novel and also on a novel by Edwin Balmer and Philip Wylie, with the script written by Sydney Boehm. The story concerns a scientist who finds that the planet Zyra will pass so close to the Earth in one year's time that tidal waves, volcanoes, and fires will occur, and then the star Bellus will collide with what remains of the world. With a "Noah's Ark" twist, a rocket ship is constructed to transport forty-four people, animals, and plants to a new planet. The United Nations refuses to support the project, but a wheelchair-bound millionaire offers to pay for it if he can go on the rocket. The travelers are the six people who originated the idea and nineteen men and nineteen women selected by a drawing. The disaster occurs, leaving New York City completely underwater, and, as the rocket ship is loading, mobs rush it. The rocket takes off and the passengers see on a television screen the collision of Earth and Bellus. When they land on the new planet, they see it is like Earth and they are pilgrims beginning a new life. This adult and well-made film was a box office success.[66] Pal said that he believed the success of the new science fiction movies was due to World War II rocket and atomic bomb developments. He said, "the subject is the thing, the stars or players are secondary."[67] Rudy Maté, who directed the film, said his scenes had "almost newsreel quality. I tried to be as realistic as I could. The story is so incredible that if the audience doesn't believe every word it won't believe anything."[68] A sound crew, carefully screened by the FBI, was allowed access to the jet testing building at Lockheed. Under armed guard, they recorded the sound of a jet engine, but Lockheed officials and the U.S. Army would not allow the crew to see what they were recording.[69]

RED PLANET MARS, a 1952 film directed by Harry Horner and produced by Anthony Veiller and Donald Hyde, concerns the safety of the free world and directly references domestic fears about international tensions in the world. The characters say things like, "The whole world's scared; it's become our natural state." There is also a lot of talk about science and religion. Scientists in a laboratory "alive with hydrogen" make contact with Mars via a television transmitter. The Martians are ruled by a "Supreme Authority," a Christ-like deity who taught them to love goodness and hate evil. The Martians have no invasion plans, but an evil scientist tries to take over the laboratory in order to use the knowledge conveyed by the Martians. The scientists blow up the laboratory, killing the evil scientist and themselves. Meanwhile Christian rebels overthrow communism in the Soviet Union, establishing a pre-revolutionary theocracy. Although this film did not depict annihilation, it expressed the fear of it and proposed a Christian solution, for the president of the United States does away with the separation of church and state and creates a Christian government. RED PLANET MARS also was unusual in that it directly rather than allegorically presented Soviet communism in the plot.

Roger Corman's 1956 film THE DAY THE WORLD ENDED is about the near destruction of the Earth by a giant atomic bomb. Seven survivors, one of whom has a bomb shelter big enough for three people, struggle for scarce food and water and worry about mutants outside. Finally all but two die. The survivors, a man and a woman, go out to see if anyone else is still living. A three-eyed mutant threatens them, but they overcome it. A *Los Angeles Times* review listed the formula for such films: "Any horror film that hopes to achieve any self-respect must have three elements: A creature—preferably an atomic mutation—a pretty girl and a handsome man. The mutation must pursue the fair damsel but must be thwarted, either by the Lothario or the elements, or by both."[70]

In 1959, two films took up the theme of nuclear apocalypse in a quietly realistic way, stressing the experience of ordinary individuals rather than mutations, aliens, or other fantasy elements. THE WORLD, THE FLESH, AND THE DEVIL, released by MGM in black and white CinemaScope, was directed by Ranald MacDougall from his own script. It presents a post-nuclear war New York City inhabited by only three survivors. Ralph Burton (Harry Belafonte), a miner who was underground when the bombs hit, escapes from the resulting cave-in after several days and makes his way to New York. He eventually meets a second survivor, a blonde woman named Sarah Crandall (Inger Stevens). She is attracted to him, but he insists that they live in separate buildings because "People might talk." Racism and its relation to sexuality thus persists after the apocalypse. Eventually a third survivor appears—Benson Thacker (Mel Ferrer), who had been at sea when the bombs fell. An uncomfortable romantic rivalry ensues, culminating in Benson insisting on armed conflict with Ralph to see who gets Sarah. Sarah, who maintains she is not an object to be possessed, intervenes and brings about a reconciliation. In the end, she takes their hands and all three walk away. The ending is ambiguous; perhaps the love triangle has turned into a threesome, or alternatively Benson and Ralph may be fighting again tomorrow. This film's one glaring implausibility is a complete absence of corpses after carnage of unthinkable dimensions.

ON THE BEACH (1959), produced and directed by Stanley Kramer and released by United Artists, was a realistic and very sad look at the end of the world via nuclear exchange. Based on the book by Nevil Shute and adapted for the film by John Paxton, it depicts the impact of a nuclear war upon ordinary people who will soon die of radiation poisoning. With a stellar cast headed by Gregory Peck, Ava Gardner, Fred Astaire, and Anthony Perkins, the film was widely anticipated. Kramer acquired expertise from officials at the Department of Defense about how nuclear conflict with the Soviets should be presented. Advice as well as some equipment and personnel was given on the condition that the military be presented in a positive way and that the Soviets bear the onus for the tragedy, although it is not clear that Kramer agreed to such limitations.[71] The submarine in the film was modeled after the real atomic submarine *Sargo*, but what we see in the film is a British submarine revamped to look like the new atomic subs. The State Department had refused Kramer's request to photograph an American one.[72] Joseph Keyerleber, in his essay on the film, said that the government refused to let Kramer use the real submarine because the assistant secretary of state disagreed that everyone in the world would die. He believed that there would be survivors if a nuclear war occurred, insisting that casualties would be limited to eight or nine million.[73] ON THE BEACH had simultaneous premieres on 17 December 1959 in Amsterdam, Berlin, Caracas, Chicago, Lima, London, Los Angeles, Madrid, Melbourne, Moscow, New York City, Paris, Rome, Johannesburg, Stockholm, Tokyo, Toronto, Washington, D.C., and Zurich.[74] It is interesting to note that in Russia, the general public did not see ON THE BEACH. A select group of 1,200 Russians, some foreign guests, and Gregory Peck and his wife attended a private screening at the Soviet Filmworkers Union.[75]

ON THE BEACH did not detail a nuclear holocaust with bombed-out cities and far-reaching destruction, but instead it presented the effects of fall-out and the resulting feelings of hopelessness. Stanley Kramer wanted the film to be quietly unhysterical, revealing the real tragedy of war in the faces of healthy young people.[76] The story begins after nearly all the people of the world have died. An American submarine comes to Australia where the survivors await death as a lethal cloud of atomic dust slowly drifts toward them. As they wait, they cling to what they love in life—friends, children, spouses, and lovers. People talk about the unfairness of their fate: as one woman says, "It's not fair. No one in the Southern Hemisphere ever dropped a bomb. . . . We had nothing to do with it. Why should we have to die because other countries nine or ten thousand miles away from us wanted to have a war?" The film openly challenges the illusions of nuclear supremacy. The war came about, as Julian, the cynical scientist (Astaire), says, "When people accepted the idiotic idea that peace could be maintained by arranging to defend themselves with weapons they couldn't possibly use without committing suicide." When he is asked to justify the role that scientists played in bringing about a nuclear holocaust, Julian, in a reference to the scientists' movement, answers, "Every man who worked on this thing told you what would happen. The scientists signed petition after petition, but no one would listen." The submarine commander leaves Australia, looking for evidence of life elsewhere. Through the periscope he sees the deserted city of San Francisco, eerily empty streets, hauntingly quiet—no life anywhere. Following a Morse code signal coming from near San Diego, the crew hopes to find life but instead discovers a telegraph key caught in a window shade. It is a horrifying moment that convinces them that the world is doomed. Back in Australia, the submarine captain (Peck), who has lost his wife and children, has a fling with the beautiful Moira (Ava Gardner), and the people begin to line up for suicide pills. The crew of the submarine decides to die in the places they know best, so they set off on their last voyage. In Australia, papers blow in the empty streets, while the wind flaps a banner that says, "There is still time."

Direct, prophetic, technically outstanding, the film was unsettling and controversial. Kramer said, "I only hoped that the emotional impact of what we were presenting would convince people that we'd damn well better do something to assure our survival."[77] Nonetheless, the film lost $700,000, which *Variety* attributed to its "preachy quality."[78] The *Mirror News*, in a story about the disputes over ON THE BEACH, reported that Senator Wallace Bennett of Utah spoke against the film in Congress saying, "In my opinion it paints a distorted picture of what a nuclear war probably would be like." The head of the New York State Civil Defense, Lieutenant General Clarence R. Huebner, said the film "does not do justice to the theory that there is a 'relatively simple defense against radioactive fall-out' and that the end of the war as pictured is not inevitable." In rebuttal, the *New York Post* editorialized: "That is precisely the point of the movie, except that the producer is suggesting that the best way to avoid the end is to prevent the beginning of the end."[79] Bosley Crowther, film critic for the *New York Times*, also took issue with both Senator Bennett and Lieutenant General Huebner in his column because he said not only were the film's audiences profoundly affected by it, but also the film "has been hailed by various statesmen and scientists" (including Linus Pauling and Freeman Dyson, well-known physicists).[80] ON THE BEACH was a more direct and serious treatment of the perils of the Atomic Age than anything that Hollywood had done before.

Conclusion

The number of American science fiction films made in the 1950s and the degree of variation among these films suggest the establishment of an important genre. The films ranged from scientific accuracy to sheer fantasy, from low-budget views of Middle America to elaborate creations of alternate worlds, from simple plots of threat and retaliation to more ambitious variations on the theme of humanity responding to invasion and disaster. The four major types of science fiction films profiled above—space travel; alien invasion and infiltration; mutants, metamorphosis, and long-extinct creatures; near annihilation or the end of humanity—all echoed American anxiety about the Cold War. However, many of the films based on these motifs also offered reassurance and hope for survival. The low-budget films, marketed to teens and preteens and distributed to drive-ins, stressed monsters and giants and suspenseful action plots. Other, more thoughtful films of the period such as THE DAY THE EARTH STOOD STILL, INVASION OF THE BODY SNATCHERS, THE INCREDIBLE SHRINKING MAN, and ON THE BEACH, became classics suitable for both teenage and adult audiences.

One way to chart the surprisingly diverse ideological positions of 1950s science fiction is via the presentation of scientists and the military, stock figures in most of the films. Scientists are sometimes heroic, sometimes misguided; military men either save the world or rashly put it at risk. In THE THING, a scientist (perhaps misguided, perhaps temporarily mad) helps the invading creature to reproduce itself. The soldiers have no illusions about the invader, and they successfully destroy it. This film obviously favors extreme suspicion and the use of force in dealing with the unknown. THE DAY THE EARTH STOOD STILL, made in the same year as THE THING (1951), takes the opposite position. Here the scientist Dr. Barnhart is a wise and sympathetic character and the military is trigger-happy. Dr. Barnhart arranges for the alien Klaatu to bring his message of nuclear disarmament to the world; this film is anti-military, pro-scientist, and pro-United Nations. Scientists are foolish and untrustworthy in obvious ways in THE FLY and TARANTULA; the military comes to the rescue by napalming the spider in the latter film. A more complicated version of the untrustworthy scientist is Dr. Morbius in FORBIDDEN PLANET. This brilliant man cannot control his instincts or emotions (described in the film as the Freudian id), which are magnified by alien machinery until they threaten both the military expedition and the entire planet. Here it is the human personality in general, with its aggressive instincts, which threatens annihilation—an impressively broad theme. However, the military does solve the immediate problem by evacuating the planet so that Morbius (sacrificing himself) can blow it up. FORBIDDEN PLANET can be seen, therefore, as both a philosophical allegory and a simple threat/response film.

Though scientists and the military are often in conflict, it is just as common for them to work together. The entomologist Dr. Medford in THEM! is so prestigious that he can call on the full resources of the government, meeting with the president, lecturing top officials, and being flown around the country by a general in an air force plane. Dr. Medford provides the knowledge and the military (along with the police) provide the weapons to destroy the giant ants. A scientist and an army officer work together to destroy a spaceship in INVADERS FROM MARS. Two scientists and one military officer join together to track and destroy the giant octopus in IT CAME FROM BENEATH THE SEA; as an added bonus, the female scientist and the officer fall in love. In THIS ISLAND EARTH, the kidnapped scientists are unable to help the Metalunans, but they return to Earth with a firm belief in the necessity of American nuclear deterrence, the favored military strategy of the 1950s.

Although the locale for invasion and disorder in the science fiction film was often a small town or the desert, help was usually sought from without. Scientists, the military, law enforcement personnel—all are brought in to repel the alien invaders or destroy the mutated monsters. Most of the films place tremendous emphasis on teamwork and consensus. INVASION OF THE BODY SNATCHERS was originally designed as a film that would critique the need for consensus—Miles Bennell cannot trust the other residents of his town because they are all pod people. But Allied Artists evidently found this theme too disturbing, for a framing story was added to show that Miles had found help.

In the great majority of 1950s science fiction films, the solution to the problem comes from America's scientific, military, and political resources. However, a few films give a religious rather than a secular explanation of problem and/or solution. In THEM!, Dr. Medford says of the invading giant ants, "We may be witnessing a biblical prophecy come true . . . The beast will reign over the Earth." When the main character in THE INCREDIBLE SHRINKING MAN shrinks to a tiny inch, he still exists for he is one with God. In WAR OF THE WORLDS, the bacteria that kill the invading Martians are attributed to God's wisdom and foresight. RED PLANET MARS combines religion and politics as a solution to the threat of alien science: Christian governments are established in both the United States and the Soviet Union.

Most films found a way to defeat the alien or monstrous threat, but even when civilization was destroyed a message of hope remained. In FIVE humanity is given a chance to regenerate itself with a new Adam and Eve. In WHEN WORLDS COLLIDE, the survivors of Earth's destruction are able to start again on a new, Earthlike planet. THE DAY THE EARTH STOOD STILL does not solve humanity's problems, but it does urge a doctrine of peaceful coexistence. ON THE BEACH might seem an exception to the rule, because all humans are doomed by nuclear fallout, but a banner in the deserted streets of Melbourne breaks from the film's plot to directly address the spectator. "There is still time," it says.

If science fiction is, as Eric Rabkin has stated, about "the problems and possibilities posed by meeting the new, the unexpected, the alien," then American science fiction films of the 1950s are a very focused and topical version of this general definition. Whether realistic or fantasy-oriented, these films revolve around fears of nuclear weapons and Communist domination. The films are not all the same, they vary markedly in story, symbolism, and attitude toward the threat, but they are certainly aimed at specific political and scientific problems. The appeal of the 1950s cycle of science fiction films lies mainly in the outpouring of imaginative renderings of simple and specific fears.

9

The Film Industry in the Late 1950s

By 1955 the film industry's attempt to overcome the challenge of television and re-establish its dominance in audio-visual entertainment had clearly failed. Many excellent films had been made in the first half of the decade, but the downward trend of cinema admissions continued. Technological innovation had lifted the fortunes of a few companies, with Twentieth Century–Fox's CinemaScope providing the broadest stimulus. However, even the "CinemaScope rebound" lasted only a year or two. New film content might have enticed spectators back into the theaters, but the conservative political mood plus the various censoring groups such as the PCA and the Legion of Decency limited the possibilities for change. Pay-TV experiments featuring movies and other content had failed, at least for the moment (they would be revived, with great success, in the 1980s). Though filmmakers satirized and scolded commercial TV in such films as IT'S ALWAYS FAIR WEATHER (1955), THE GIRL CAN'T HELP IT (1956), WILL SUCCESS SPOIL ROCK HUNTER? (1957), and A FACE IN THE CROWD (1957), this adversary would not go away.

There were a few positive signs for the film industry at mid-decade. Films from the 1930s and 1940s, probably considered worthless in the studio account books, suddenly had value as programming for television. Recent pictures had greater value, though the film companies were reluctant to sell them. Sales or leases to television would help most of the studios survive the hard times of the late 1950s. The film companies were also beginning to produce original programming for TV—this was a lower budget, lower profit margin business than film, but at least it did keep people and facilities working. In feature film production, the foreign market was still welcoming American films; foreign sales became increasingly important as U.S. sales declined. And there were opportunities to make profitable films for the more segmented audiences that were still going to the movies.

Decline of the Majors

The five "major" Hollywood studios (MGM, Paramount, Fox, Warners, and RKO) went through a difficult period in the late 1950s (1955 to 1959). These were large, well-established organizations with traditions of success. It was hard for them to change, but the new conditions of the period made change imperative. Some of the studios were sold; others changed management; a few went through proxy fights. All of the large studios survived, except for Howard Hughes's RKO.

MGM went through four years of management turmoil between 1955 and 1959, with the board of directors constantly fighting over who would control the company and what direction it would take. Nicholas Schenck, longtime president of Loew's Inc. (MGM's parent company) resigned under pressure in December 1955 and was replaced by Arthur Loew, son of the company's founder. Arthur Loew in turn resigned in late 1956, and was replaced by Loew's Inc. career employee Joseph Vogel. Vogel struggled to cut costs at MGM and started making deals to finance independent productions (MGM was far behind its competitors in courting the top independents). Meanwhile, some members of the Loew's board were promoting a number of aggressive initiatives: outright sale of MGM's film library to television; liquidation of all highly valued Loew's assets; replacement of the current management team (one scenario had Louis B. Mayer returning to power); divestiture of the film production/distribution business, with retention of the theater chain and the music, radio, and TV businesses; even a possible merger with United Artists.[1]

Vogel managed to survive all threats to his authority. He pushed through a plan to divest the theater chain, not the film business, which was probably the right decision. With a shrinking motion-picture audience the theater chains, which had large, underperforming real estate holdings, were more at risk than the production companies. When MGM finally did split off from the Loew's exhibition chain on 12 March 1959 (Loew's had delayed this for several years based on the difficulty of getting fair value for the theaters), Vogel became the president of MGM, Inc.

MGM production head Dore Schary had been hired in 1949 to solve all the problems of the postwar era and restore the studio to commercial and artistic pre-eminence. However, Schary was not given the authority to clean house and restructure, and he was always resented by the studio old guard. Further, Schary was a liberal, and MGM was the most politically conservative of studios—many of its employees belonged to the Alliance for the Preservation of American Ideals. Schary did sponsor a few social problem films at MGM in the mid-1950s, including BAD DAY AT BLACK ROCK, BLACKBOARD JUNGLE, and TRIAL (all 1955). These films were more successful than MGM's traditional offerings, indeed BLACKBOARD JUNGLE was a box-office hit. Nevertheless, when Schary was fired (by Vogel) in 1957 his adversaries joked that he had "sold the studio for a pot of message."[2] Schary was replaced as production head by Benny Thau, an MGM executive since the 1920s.

Though it survived threats of takeover and dismemberment, MGM's film business was in poor shape from 1956 through 1958. Joseph Vogel labeled MGM's 1957 releases (all inherited from Schary's management) "the worst collection of pictures in its history,"[3] and the figures bear him out. According to the Eddie Mannix Ledger, of MGM's twenty in-house productions in the 1956–1957 season, an astonishing nineteen took losses. Only THE TEAHOUSE OF THE AUGUST MOON earned a profit, and the overall loss of this group of films was $15,775,000. Earnings from MGM's other businesses (including sales to television) cut this loss to an acceptable $455,000 in 1957.[4] By 1957–1958, MGM's slate of ten in-house productions and twenty-four films by outside producers recorded a profit of almost $5 million; "outside producers" included MGM veterans such as Pandro Berman and Arthur Freed, who were being financed as independents (or "semi-independents") by the studio.[5]

Emmet John Hughes's 1957 *Fortune* article on MGM twice mentions a planned production of BEN-HUR as the great hope of the company.[6] This was a remake of MGM's 1925 silent epic set in Judea and Rome during the time of Christ. It was also a shrewd attempt to reprise the enormous success of THE TEN COMMANDMENTS: like Cecil B. DeMille's Paramount hit, BEN-HUR would combine religion, spectacle, and melodrama in a superproduction starring Charlton Heston. William Wyler, one of Hollywood's top producer-directors, was put in charge. Location shooting was set for Rome (where Wyler had previously made ROMAN HOLIDAY), and BEN-HUR's budget of $10 million eventually grew to $15 million. The film was an enormous success upon its release in 1959. It won Best Picture and numerous other Academy Awards, and its substantial earnings put MGM firmly in the black for the next couple of years (for critical discussion of BEN-HUR, see Chapter 10).

RKO, the weakest of the Hollywood majors, experienced a series of dramatic changes in the late 1950s, and eventually went out of business. Howard Hughes had unsuccessfully tried to sell the studio in 1952 (see Chapter 1). On 31 March 1954 he bought up all outstanding shares of stock in the studio for $23.5 million; this was a prelude to selling RKO to General Tire and Rubber Company for $25 million on 18 July 1955. General Tire's successful broadcasting subsidiary, General Teleradio, owned five television stations, six radio stations, and three radio networks. Thomas F. O'Neil, president of General Teleradio, admitted that he was mainly interested in RKO's film library, which would have considerable value when sold or leased to television. However, O'Neil added that his company intended to operate RKO as a film production and distribution company, and that neither he nor Hughes wanted to see the company liquidated.[7]

O'Neil followed through on his promises for RKO. The film library of 740 pictures and 1,000 shorts was sold to C & C Super Corporation for $15.2 million on 26 December 1955. General Teleradio retained the right to package 150 of the films for a one-time national TV

Hugh Griffith and Charlton Heston in BEN-HUR *(1959). Both won Academy Awards, Griffith for Best Supporting Actor and Heston for Best Actor.*

showing before they went into C & C Super's hands. General Teleradio also retained the right to show RKO Pictures on its own TV stations—there were now six of them, in New York, Los Angeles, Boston, Memphis, Hartford, and Palm Beach.[8] And the "new" company, RKO Teleradio, with O'Neil as president, moved quickly into film production.

RKO had been a skeleton operation during Hughes's last few years, with only a few in-house productions and distribution limited mainly to low-budget independents. To get some high-quality films into the distribution pipeline, O'Neil made a deal with David O. Selznick for re-release of several films (REBECCA, THE ADVENTURES OF TOM SAWYER, THE THIRD MAN, SPELLBOUND, and THE PARADINE CASE) plus financing for an unspecified number of new Selznick-produced films. By 1956, RKO was busy with new productions and had even signed several promising actors, including Anita Ekberg and Rod Steiger, to appear in RKO films. However, it was difficult to attract the best producing, directing, and acting talent, especially since O'Neil preferred the no-frills production model of the television industry, and so the RKO pictures were at a competitive disadvantage. RKO ceased production in January 1957 and agreed to have some of its pending releases distributed by Universal. RKO's studio facilities were sold to Desilu Productions later in the year, suggesting in microcosm the problems of film and the triumph of television. By October 1958 all that was left of RKO was a small international sales operation, plus two made-for-television films in production in Cuba.[9]

At Twentieth Century–Fox, Darryl Zanuck abruptly resigned as head of production in 1956. Zanuck became an independent producer with a contract to deliver one to four films per year for Fox release. Management of Fox was to be shared by New York–based president Spyros Skouras and head of production Buddy Adler (Zanuck's replacement). Skouras was an excellent businessman whose most notable recent achievement had been the successful introduction of CinemaScope. However, he was not skilled or experienced in the supervision of individual productions, and Zanuck had consistently kept him away from this part of Fox's operations. Buddy Adler was an experienced producer who was hired away from Columbia by Fox in 1954. Adler's reputation as a first-rank producer rested primarily on one film, FROM HERE TO ETERNITY (1953). That film was very much a team effort, with Adler as producer relying heavily on a strong writer (Daniel Taradash), a strong director (Fred Zinnemann), and a studio head who made many production decisions (Harry Cohn). Adler at Fox turned out to be cautious and uncommunicative, which disturbed such veteran Fox producers as Nunnally Johnson and Philip Dunne.[10] Skouras filled some of the resulting power vacuum, sending long memos to Adler about Fox's production program.

In 1956 Fox released a number of successful films, including THE KING AND I, BUS STOP, and LOVE ME TENDER (the first Elvis Presley film), and recorded a profit of $6.2 million. Profits stayed at approximately the same level for the next two years, with the studio's biggest successes being PEYTON PLACE (1957) and SOUTH PACIFIC (1958). However, the studio balance sheet is deceiving, because it depends on the sale or lease of pre-1948 films to television. In 1956, Fox leased fifty of its films to N.T.A. (a television distributor) for between $2 and $3 million. Fox then extended this deal so that fifty to sixty-eight pre-1948 films would be leased to N.T.A. annually, for a return of $75,000 per film, or $3.75 to $5.1 million annually.[11] Fox also became a producer of original material for television, with its first successes being *My Friend Flicka* and *The Twentieth Century–Fox Hour.*

By 1959, despite the new streams of income from television, Fox was in trouble. Buddy Adler's production program of bland and glossy pictures, many of them shot on

Poster for TOP HAT *(1935), one of several hundred RKO features that were sold to television in 1955.*

the studio lot, resulted in a year when only two of twenty major releases earned significant profits.[12] These were JOURNEY TO THE CENTER OF THE EARTH (big-budget science fiction) and BLUE DENIM (medium-budget teen film), both aimed at younger audiences. Fox had also been successful with films starring Pat Boone (BERNARDINE, 1957; APRIL LOVE, 1957), so the studio seemed to be edging into pictures for the teenage market. Darryl Zanuck as independent producer was a surprising disappointment in the late 1950s. DELUXE TOUR, after a very expensive pre-production, never became a feature film; THE ROOTS OF HEAVEN (1958) was a huge failure. Only ISLAND IN THE SUN (1957) was a successful Zanuck production. Twentieth Century–Fox sold off a portion of its back lot in 1959 in a highly profitable transaction, but nevertheless the studio earned only $4.9 million in 1959. This was followed by a modest loss ($2.9 million) in 1960 and more substantial losses in 1961 and 1962.

Unlike Fox, which maintained a good deal of in-house production in the late 1950s, Warner Bros. had transformed itself into a company that financed and distributed independent productions. Some of the best Warner films of the period, including GIANT (produced and directed by George Stevens, 1956) and THE SEARCHERS (produced by Merian C. Cooper, directed by John Ford, 1956), were controlled by the filmmakers with little oversight by the studio. Jack Warner's only response to the cost overruns on GIANT was to plead with George Stevens to be more careful. Meanwhile, Warner Bros.

had established a very successful lineup of television series, including the Western hits *Cheyenne, Maverick,* and *Lawman,* and the youth-oriented *77 Sunset Strip.*

Warners film releases of the period included a mix of big-budget epics (HELEN OF TROY, 1956), musicals (AUNTIE MAME, 1958; DAMN YANKEES, 1958) and dramas (MAR- JORIE MORNINGSTAR, 1958; THE NUN'S STORY, 1959), with lower budget war films, sci- ence fiction and suspense films, and even a few British imports. Warners did invest in contracts with young talent, including James Dean, Tab Hunter, and Natalie Wood, but most of the studio's attention went to pre-sold properties (films based on best-sell- ing novels or popular plays) and short-term deals with independent producers. In addition to George Stevens and John Ford/Merian C. Cooper, Warners worked with producer/directors Elia Kazan (A FACE IN THE CROWD, 1957), Laurence Olivier (THE PRINCE AND THE SHOWGIRL, 1957, co-produced by Marilyn Monroe), Billy Wilder (THE SPIRIT OF ST. LOUIS, 1957), Stanley Donen (THE PAJAMA GAME, 1957 and DAMN YANKEES, 1958) and Howard Hawks (LAND OF THE PHARAOHS, 1955, and RIO BRAVO, 1959).

Warner Bros.' change of ownership in 1956 involved a bizarre family drama. Studio president Harry Warner and treasurer Albert Warner, both based in New York, had been trying to sell the studio since 1951. However, Harry Warner had feuded with Los Angeles–based Jack Warner for decades, and he was unwilling to leave Warner Bros. in his younger brother's hands. In mid-May 1956, the press announced that all three of the surviving Warner brothers would sell their stock to a syndicate headed by Serge Semenenko of First National Bank of Boston. The new studio president would most likely be Sy Fabian, a veteran film exhibitor. However, Fabian would have to either leave his current job as head of Stanley-Warner Theatres or obtain an anti-trust exemp- tion. A few weeks later, it became clear that Fabian would not be moving to Warner Bros., and that Jack Warner (who bought back a substantial portion of stock) would be taking over leadership of the company. The transaction had been a ruse to get Harry Warner to sell out.[13] Jack Warner became president and remained in that post for eleven more years.

The participation of banker Semenenko suggests that, aside from family politics, Warner Bros. was a sound investment in 1956, and financial results bear this out. Warner Bros. was modestly profitable from 1955 to 1957. It took a loss of $1 million in 1958, when other studios were also struggling, and rebounded to an impressive $9.4 million profit in 1959.

Paramount Pictures pursued a "semi-independent production" strategy through the 1950s. Top producers paid an overhead charge to the studio in return for financing, technical support, distribution, and publicity. Producers were linked to Paramount by contract, but they were partners—with profit participation—rather than simply employ- ees. The leading producers at Paramount under this arrangement in the late 1950s were Alfred Hitchcock, Cecil B. DeMille, and Hal Wallis. Some of Paramount's top stars of the period, like Bing Crosby and Bob Hope, also took a share of film profits.

Paramount was consistently profitable in the late 1950s, thanks to a strong group of feature releases plus a favorable sale of older films to television. Profits ranged between $9.4 million in 1955 and $4.4 million in 1959. In 1958, Paramount sold its pre-1948 film library to MCA for $50 million, including a $10 million down payment, $25 million in installments, and $15 million to be paid from future grosses. As Dennis McDougal com- mented, "the terms were by far the richest that any studio had yet been able to get from a TV syndicator."[14]

*Jack L. Warner, who became president of Warner Bros.
in 1956, with Lauren Bacall. Jack Warner bought out his
brothers Harry and Albert in a bizarre transaction.*

Cecil B. DeMille completed only two films as producer-director in the 1950s, yet he was tremendously important to Paramount's success during this period. THE GREATEST SHOW ON EARTH (1952) recorded North American rentals of $12.8 million, making it the studio's number two box-office attraction of the decade. Number one was DeMille's THE TEN COMMANDMENTS (1956), with $34.2 million in North American rentals and a larger figure earned abroad. DeMille had begun another production in 1958, THE BUCCANEER, starring Yul Brynner as the pirate Jean Lafitte. However, since his health was failing, DeMille made Henry Wilcoxon producer and Anthony Quinn (DeMille's son-in-law) director. Quinn turned out to be an inadequate director, and the film was a failure. DeMille died on 21 January 1959, as THE TEN COMMANDMENTS was still setting box-office records around the world. One wonders if a healthy DeMille could have made THE BUCCANEER a blockbuster as well.

Alfred Hitchcock made several films for Paramount between 1954 and 1960, including REAR WINDOW, TO CATCH A THIEF, THE MAN WHO KNEW TOO MUCH, VERTIGO, and PSYCHO. The first four are high-budget films benefiting from the surprising complementarity of clear, crisp color photography and Hitchcock's dark, psychological themes. REAR WINDOW (1954) was an excellent commercial success, with a cost of $1 million and

North American rentals of $5.3 million. VERTIGO (1958), on the other hand, was a break-even film, but it is now regarded by many as Hitchcock's masterpiece. PSYCHO (1960) was a black and white, modestly budgeted film which turned out to be Hitchcock's biggest success of all time. Beginning in 1955, Hitchcock was also the producer (and occasional director) of *Alfred Hitchcock Presents*, a hit television series produced by MCA, not Paramount.

Hal Wallis produced a few dozen films for Paramount in the 1950s and introduced an amazing roster of new talent. Among his discoveries of the late 1940s and the 1950s were Burt Lancaster, Kirk Douglas, Charlton Heston, Lizabeth Scott, Jerry Lewis, Dean Martin, Shirley MacLaine, and Elvis Presley. The consistently popular Martin and Lewis made twelve films for Wallis and Paramount in the 1950s, after which Lewis made four additional Wallis films. Like many of Wallis's stars, Martin and Lewis had non-exclusive contracts—they were required to make a certain number of films per year for Wallis at Paramount, but had the option to do outside productions (usually one per year) as well. Wallis's autobiography, written with Charles Higham, is aptly titled *Starmaker*.

In addition to the Wallis stars, Paramount introduced Grace Kelly and Audrey Hepburn in the 1950s, and presented multiple films starring Bing Crosby, Bob Hope, Danny Kaye, James Stewart, William Holden, and Sophia Loren. Perhaps more than any other studio, Paramount managed to sustain an atmosphere of continuity and glamour in the tumultuous 1950s.

Smaller Studios

The 1948 Paramount anti-trust decision created new opportunities for smaller studios to compete with the five majors. By the late 1950s, the theater chains that had made Fox, MGM, Paramount, RKO, and Warners such dominant powers in the North American marketplace had all been divested (except for straggler MGM). The large, well-equipped studio lots of the majors often became a drag on profits because fewer films were being made. Also, exhibitors were looking for new sources of product, because the majors were naturally interested in their own profits and therefore wanted a larger share of receipts. Columbia, Universal, and United Artists all moved aggressively into "A" pictures to exploit this new opportunity.

Meanwhile, the market for low-budget or "B" pictures was troubled. Prime-time television was by 1955 competing successfully with theatrical motion pictures by supplying filmed series for home viewing. This was particularly true of Westerns, which had made up much of the output of Columbia and of the Poverty Row studios Republic and Monogram. Original, one-hour Western dramas were now plentifully available in prime time, and pre-1948 feature-length Westerns were also appearing on TV. With so much Western drama on television, the demand for "B" Westerns in the theaters quickly dried up. Other "B" movie genres, such as horror, science fiction, and teen films, still had a theatrical audience, but this segment of the film market was now changeable and uncertain.

Columbia had always made a few prestigious, high-budget movies to go along with its more modest "programmers." In the mid- to late 1950s, this part of the business expanded. Three films distributed by Columbia won Academy Awards for Best Picture in the 1950s—FROM HERE TO ETERNITY (1953), ON THE WATERFRONT (1954), and THE BRIDGE ON THE RIVER KWAI (1957). However, only FROM HERE TO ETERNITY was an in-house production; the latter two were produced by independent producer Sam Spiegel and had little artistic input from Columbia Pictures. Columbia's president, Harry Cohn, did make the decision to finance and release ON THE WATERFRONT after Darryl Zanuck of Fox had turned it down. Columbia also made a number of in-house "A" pictures between 1955 and 1958. For example, PICNIC (1955) and PAL JOEY (1957) both featured Columbia contract star Kim Novak, as well as William Holden in PICNIC and Frank Sinatra and Rita Hayworth in PAL JOEY. After Harry Cohn's death in 1958, Columbia moved quickly to an emphasis on independent productions. According to *Variety*, Columbia had deals with twenty-eight independents in early 1959, while only three staff producers remained under contract.[15] ANATOMY OF A MURDER (produced and directed by Otto Preminger) and SUDDENLY, LAST SUMMER (produced and directed by Joseph L. Mankiewicz) were two of the top quality independent films released by Columbia in 1959.

Columbia was expanding in a number of different directions in the late 1950s. "B" movie producer Sam Katzman (an independent producer with long-term ties to Columbia) was one of the first to specialize in the teen market. He made ROCK AROUND THE CLOCK (1956) to exploit the success of MGM's BLACKBOARD JUNGLE (1955), and followed up with DON'T KNOCK THE ROCK (also 1956). Columbia's television subsidiary Screen Gems, headed by Harry Cohn's nephew Ralph Cohn, was involved in everything from TV commercials to series production to the syndication of features and shorts. And Columbia had aggressively moved into production in England and France, financing films for local distribution (via a Columbia subsidiary) as well as the occasional high-budget international film. Columbia also acquired an art-house distributor, Kingsley Productions, which it used for U.S. distribution of the sexy and wildly popular films of Brigitte Bardot.

Universal Pictures, owned by Decca Records since 1953, struggled to find an identity in the 1950s. Universal had stuck with its "B" movie series in the early 1950s, including Abbott and Costello, Ma and Pa Kettle, and Francis the Talking Mule. The studio also made "A" pictures, notably the Westerns of Anthony Mann (often starring James Stewart) and the glossy melodramas and comedies of staff producer Ross Hunter. Hunter-produced melodramas directed by Douglas Sirk and starring Rock Hudson, like MAGNIFICENT OBSESSION (1954) and ALL THAT HEAVEN ALLOWS (1955), were known in the 1950s as superior "women's pictures"; they are now valued for the stylistic depth and social criticism of director Sirk. The Ross Hunter–produced PILLOW TALK (1959) has no such depth; it is a glamorous and glossy comedy directed by Michael Gordon and starring Rock Hudson and Doris Day.

United Artists (UA) is a great success story of the 1950s. Almost bankrupt in 1950, UA prospered under the new management team of Arthur Krim and Robert Benjamin, who took over in 1951. Company profits increased from $314,000 in 1951 to $4,111,000 in 1959. United Artists had always been a company that distributed independent productions, so the company's turnaround is linked to the increasing clout of the independents in the 1950s. However, Krim and Benjamin deserve credit for creating a strategy that would attract and retain some of the leading independents, despite competition from the majors. Unlike Paramount or MGM, UA charged independents little or no production overhead, because it did not have sound stages, post-production facilities, or a large permanent staff. Also, UA gave its producers a great deal of freedom after creative ingredients and budget were approved.[16] United Artists provided production financing and was repaid from a film's earnings. For successful films, the studio and the producer would divide the profits, with the exact shares varying from contract to contract. United Artists did not need to earn a profit on every film because the studio made most of its money on distribution fees, which ranged from 30 percent in the domestic market to 45 percent overseas.

For this strategy to work, it was essential to run a high volume of pictures through the company's distribution network. United Artists released an average of forty-two films per year between 1951 and 1960, with a high of fifty-four in 1957. Many of these were low-budget films (including some British imports), but the company did finance and release several big-budget spectaculars between 1955 and 1959. UA also became known for the quality of its releases, in all budget categories. MARTY (1955), for example, won the Oscar for Best Picture despite a modest $300,000 budget. UA followed up with a number of low-budget prestige pictures, including THE BACHELOR PARTY (1957), TWELVE ANGRY MEN (1957), and PATHS OF GLORY (1957). In 1956, United Artists won another Best Picture Oscar, but this time for a widescreen extravaganza, AROUND THE WORLD IN EIGHTY DAYS.

Another indication of United Artists' success was its contracts with leading stars. The United Artists of 1952 was fortunate to have HIGH NOON, with Gary Cooper and Grace Kelly, on its release schedule; otherwise the company was presenting low-budget movies with second- or third-rank stars. However, by 1958, with its newfound prestige plus the lure of shared profits, United Artists had non-exclusive contracts with Burt Lancaster, Kirk Douglas, John Wayne, Frank Sinatra, Henry Fonda, Rita Hayworth, Bob Hope, Yul Brynner, Susan Hayward, Cary Grant, Gregory Peck, and Tony Curtis, among others. These were independent producer contracts which could include 30–75 percent of a film's net profit for an individual star. Of course, many films never made a profit.[17]

United Artists was slow to diversify. Its emphasis in the late 1950s was building up its film business rather than moving into television production. UA did not produce a network series until 1959–1960, and did not have a significant presence in series TV until 1963–1964. Also, unlike the majors, United Artists had the rights to only a small group of pre-1948 pictures. These were sold to a TV syndicator in 1951, when the company was desperate for operating money.[18] In the absence of television revenues, UA's success was entirely dependent on film production and distribution.

The traditional Poverty Row studios did not fare well in the late 1950s. Republic Pictures, traditionally associated with Westerns, was badly hurt by the competition of Western series on TV. Republic halted production temporarily in 1956, and then announced in 1958 that it was getting out of the film business.[19] The Republic Corporation (the name was changed in 1960) continued to exist in the 1960s and 1970s, but at this point its primary film-related business was a film-processing laboratory. Monogram, a studio quite similar to Republic, changed its name to Allied Artists in 1953 and tried to move into medium-budget pictures. The company made modest profits from 1951 to 1956 but took losses from 1957 to 1959. In these later years, Allied Artists cut expenses by returning to more low-budget films, this time aimed at the drive-in market.

The most important development in low-budget pictures was the birth of a new company, American International Pictures (AIP). This production and distribution company was formed by lawyer Samuel Z. Arkoff and sales manager James H. Nicholson as American Releasing Corporation in 1954; the name was changed to AIP in 1956. The idea was to make a series of extremely low-budget pictures and release them as double-bills to sub-distributors in the United States, Canada, and England. Even if the films played for only a week or two, AIP would make money. Special attention was paid to advertising and to the changing tastes of the teenage audience. Sometimes the advertising was created before the picture; if the ad looked strong, a picture would be made (note that this approach anticipates the "high concept" "A" movies of later years).[20] Sometimes the advertising and the title were downright misleading. THE BEAST WITH A MILLION EYES (1955), for example, turned out to be a small alien creature with perhaps three eyes.

Nicholson, Arkoff, and their most prolific producer-director, Roger Corman, had a very good sense of what the teenage audience wanted. They quickly abandoned the Western and concentrated on science fiction, horror, juvenile delinquency, and rock movies. By 1957–1958, AIP was releasing about twenty films per year, and Arkoff could boast that thirty-nine of his last forty-one pictures had been profitable.[21] However, in 1958 and 1959 there was a great deal of competition for low-budget exploitation movies from Allied Artists and other low budget specialists plus Columbia, United Artists, and Universal. Even Corman was competing with AIP—he also worked for Allied Artists and for his own company, Filmgroup. AIP responded by raising the budgets on its movies and by launching a "prestige" series of horror pictures, beginning with the Corman-directed HOUSE OF USHER in 1960.

Independent Producers

The preceding discussion of major and minor studios gives a good overview of industry conditions in the late 1950s: all the studios were struggling with important industry changes, and some were adapting more quickly than others. An alternate way to survey this same period would be to discuss the leading independents, because independent production was gradually becoming the standard way of making Hollywood films. According to Tino Balio, about 20 percent of films released by the eight top studios in 1949 were independent productions; this had risen to 58 percent in 1957.[22] Also, the Best Picture Academy Award winners for 1954 through 1957 were all independent productions: ON THE WATERFRONT, MARTY, AROUND THE WORLD IN EIGHTY DAYS, and THE BRIDGE ON THE RIVER KWAI. The Best Picture Oscar reverted to MGM and Arthur Freed for GIGI in 1958, but by this time even Arthur Freed was an independent producer!

Of course, "independent producer" could mean many things in Hollywood. An independent producer could be an actor (John Wayne), a director (Alfred Hitchcock), a packager (Charles Feldman), a wealthy investor (C. V. Whitney), a former studio executive (Darryl Zanuck), or even someone whose background was in producing (Sam Spiegel). In some cases, the "independent" label was primarily a way to share profits and risks with talent; in other situations, the producer ran the show with minimal oversight by the studio. United Artists offered a range of options for its independents, from leaving the producer alone to providing extensive management services. Those UA-affiliated producers needing help with the business side of filmmaking were encouraged to work with the three Mirisch brothers, who charged a weekly production fee plus a percentage of the profits and/or the distribution earnings.[23] The Mirisch Brothers company became a partner as well as a service provider to producers—it thus provided yet another model of "the independent producer."

The actors who tried their hand at independent production had very different experiences. John Wayne produced a number of films (primarily Westerns) for Warner Bros. with a partner, Robert Fellows. Wayne did not star in all of them, yet undoubtedly Wayne's agreement to act in several Warner releases was a vital part of the arrangement. Wayne also had a production deal at United Artists, where his first film was CHINA DOLL (1958). Bing Crosby Productions was originally a way to give Crosby better financial terms at Paramount, where he had been a fixture for many years. Crosby's company eventually made films at other studios, such as HIGH SOCIETY (1956) at MGM and SAY ONE FOR ME (1959) at Fox, and also expanded into television. Kirk Douglas started Bryna Productions in association with United Artists, but he moved on to make SPARTA-CUS (1960) at Universal and STRANGERS WHEN WE MEET (1960) at Columbia. Marilyn Monroe Productions was formed for two purposes—to leverage a better contract from Fox, and to give the star greater control over the choice of subject. Monroe's one independent project, THE PRINCE AND THE SHOWGIRL (1957), co-produced with Laurence Olivier Productions, largely accomplished both of these aims. Even though Monroe was legally bound by a long-term Fox contract, her popularity led the studio to allow the independent film (which was distributed by Warners) and to renegotiate salary.

Frank Sinatra used his Academy Award of 1953 (for Best Supporting Actor in FROM HERE TO ETERNITY) to revive a movie career that had been lagging. Instead of affiliating with one studio, he worked in the 1950s for Columbia, Goldwyn, MGM, RKO, Paramount, Warner Bros., United Artists, and Universal. Sinatra's contracts generally involved a salary plus either partial ownership of the picture or a percentage of the profits. Like other independents, he was willing to negotiate on salary in order to enhance his profit participation. Although Sinatra rarely took a "producer" credit in the 1950s, he sometimes originated and packaged a film via his own Kent Productions. For example,

Laurence Olivier and Marilyn Monroe were co-stars and co-producers of THE PRINCE AND THE SHOWGIRL *(1957).*

for THE JOKER IS WILD (1957) he bought the property, recruited the director, and sold the project to Paramount.[24] Sinatra is remembered today primarily as a singer and a recording artist, but most of his income in the late 1950s came from film and television.

Burt Lancaster's production company, first called Norma Productions, then Hecht-Lancaster and then Hecht-Hill-Lancaster, went through an astonishing rise and fall. Lancaster's deal at United Artists, signed in 1953, was an important step for both the studio and the actor. UA needed the prestige of a major star on its release schedule, and Lancaster wanted more control over the films in which he appeared. Lancaster soon expanded his activities as a producer. In 1955 Lancaster and Harold Hecht convinced UA to put $300,000 into MARTY, based on a teleplay by Paddy Chayefsky (this film does not feature Burt Lancaster the actor). Both the subject matter (working-class Brooklyn) and the source (television) were highly unusual for a Hollywood film, yet MARTY won the Academy Award for Best Picture. Hecht-Lancaster followed it with the European-made TRAPEZE (1956), which cost $4 million and earned $20 million, thanks in large part to its foreign popularity.

Lancaster, Hecht, and new partner James Hill (a former story editor) then launched into a frenzied period of developing new properties, charging millions of dollars in expenses to UA. One of their films from this period was SWEET SMELL OF SUCCESS (1957), a dark film about a New York gossip columnist (loosely based on Walter Winchell), which was a box-office disaster but has since become a cult favorite. Lancaster and his partners were by this time spending wildly on their Beverly Hills office and going over budget on every film. By late 1959, Hecht-Hill-Lancaster owed UA almost $3 million. The once-proud independent dissolved in February 1960, and Lancaster agreed to partially compensate UA by acting in four future films at a relatively low salary ($150,000 per picture).[25]

There is a little-known coda to the last few years of Hecht-Hill-Lancaster, told by Lancaster biographer Kate Buford. In 1957 and 1958, at the very moment that Hecht-Hill-Lancaster was foundering, Loew's head Joseph Vogel was seriously negotiating for the three partners to take over management of MGM. Vogel, faced with a poor slate of pictures and a rebellious board of directors, wanted the cachet of hiring the producers of MARTY. Part of the deal was that Lancaster would play the title role of BEN-HUR, for the princely sum of $1 million. Hecht, Hill, and Lancaster were not enthusiastic about the proposed deal, and neither was the MGM board. Still, Vogel's proposition is an indication of how far power in Hollywood had shifted—a few years earlier, it would have been inconceivable to offer management positions at MGM to young independent producers.[26]

Many of the producers and directors who became independent producers have already been mentioned in this chapter, via their affiliations with specific studios. One group not sufficiently discussed is the array of producers and directors who worked with United Artists. This distinguished group included Otto Preminger, Billy Wilder, William Wyler, Stanley Kramer, Joseph L. Mankiewicz, Edward Small, and the partnership of James B. Harris–Stanley Kubrick. Preminger was a producer-director who prided himself on taking complete charge of his films. He even orchestrated publicity, for example when he challenged the Production Code (THE MOON IS BLUE, 1953; THE MAN WITH THE GOLDEN ARM, 1955) or when he launched a talent search for the title role in SAINT JOAN, 1957 (Jean Seberg won the part). Billy Wilder, one of Hollywood's leading writer-directors, preferred not to handle production chores himself; he used Edward Small and Arthur Hornblow as producers on his first film at UA (WITNESS FOR THE PROSECUTION, 1957) and the Mirisch brothers thereafter. William Wyler and Joseph Mankiewicz were much-in-demand filmmakers who moved from studio to studio, depending on the project; Wyler made one film for UA in the 1950s (The Big Country, 1958), and Mankiewicz made two (The Barefoot Contessa, 1954, and The Quiet American, 1958). Stanley Kramer became a director as well as a producer in 1958. Responding to a gradual easing of the Cold War and the blacklist, he made such controversial films as The Defiant Ones (1958) and On the Beach (1959). Edward Small generated a great number of low-budget productions for UA, and thus kept the distribution business working. Like other low-budget producers, Small moved gradually from Westerns to horror and science fiction in the late 1950s. He also produced a few higher budget productions: Witness for the Prosecution (directed by Billy Wilder, 1957) and Solomon and Sheba (directed by King Vidor, 1959). The young director Stanley Kubrick and his co-producer James Harris were making inexpensive but stylistically distinctive films for UA release. The Killing (1956) lost money but impressed the Hollywood community. The anti-war Paths of Glory (1957) might be considered a "Hollywood art film."

Tony Curtis and Sidney Poitier in The Defiant Ones *(1958), a social message film produced and directed by Stanley Kramer.*

Crisis in Exhibition

The Paramount decision of 1948 produced a number of unexpected consequences for the exhibition end of the film industry. Exhibitors had hoped to gain better terms and a more competitive working environment by breaking the dominance of the major studios. Instead they found themselves in a business that was unstable and at risk. Declining attendance caused by television and other factors hurt the exhibitors most. Production companies could adjust their yearly output, but theater owners (both large chains and smaller companies) had fixed investments that were often heavily mortgaged. Any downturn in business would result in theater closings. Also, with the required split between studios and theater chains, producers no longer had a strong incentive to make enough product for a full year's schedule. Indeed, by limiting production the major studios could force up the rental terms for their films. In 1956, Leonard Goldenson of ABC-Paramount Theatres summarized the effects of the Paramount consent decrees as follows:

> The decree placed the balance of power in the hands of the producers. It brought about the product shortage, the multiple runs, the exorbitant film rentals, over-extended playing times and competitive bidding.[27]

Another serious problem was that the production companies no longer had a strong incentive to withhold their film libraries from television. When production companies and theater chains formed integrated companies, it was self-evident that the studios would protect the interests of their exhibitor-partners. But in the late 1950s, after divestment, production companies began to view television companies differently, as another set of potential customers rather than enemies of the film business.[28] Production companies still had to consider the needs of exhibitors, who were their primary source of income, but they could begin to supplement theatrical income with an incremental release of films to television. The federal government was actually pushing the studios in this direction, via a claim that withholding films from television constituted restraint of trade.

To some extent, the problems of smaller audiences and reduced Hollywood output were self-correcting. As audiences declined, unprofitable theaters would go out of business, and the remaining theaters would have a better chance to survive. Diminished output from the main Hollywood studios might hasten this process along. But if Hollywood's reduced output was an artificial limitation (aimed at forcing better terms), then other producers could step in to fill the need for product. In the late 1950s this did happen as AIP and Allied Artists provided low-budget films and foreign producers found a variety of American markets. Many urban theaters turned to European "art cinema," often with a strong erotic content, as an alternative to going out of business. For example, in Minneapolis, Brigitte Bardot's breakout hit AND GOD CREATED WOMAN (1956) played at five theaters in the summer of 1958, while two other Bardot pictures, LA PARISIENNE (1957) and MAM'ZELLE PIGALLE (1956), were doing good business at one theater each.[29] Another type of import, the sword and sandals "epic," was pioneered by Boston exhibitor Joseph L. Levine. The Italian-made and English-dubbed HERCULES, promoted by Levine and distributed by Warner Bros., was a huge hit in 1959, earning $5 million. According to Balio, Levine's promotional campaign cost $1 million and "combined a media blitz and saturation booking,"[30] tactics that were then innovative and are now taken for granted.

Yet another set of problems stemmed from the locations of theaters. Americans were deserting the cities and moving to the suburbs, but first-run theaters were in big-city downtowns and second-run theaters were mostly in urban neighborhoods. As Richard Brandt, president of a small theater chain, said in 1958: "The trouble today is that so many houses are in the wrong places. This country is mis-seated, not over-seated."[31] Brandt's remarks were prescient, but since theater owners were strapped for capital it took many years to develop the suburban multiplexes that would serve middle-class viewers. In the meantime, the number of traditional, "hardtop" theaters in the United States declined from 16,904 in 1950 to 12,291 in 1960. Some of this decline was counteracted by an increase in the number of drive-in theaters, which rose from 2,202 to 4,700 in the same ten years.[32] Drive-ins required less investment than hardtops and were well suited to newly developed suburban areas where open land was still available.

The changing technologies of cinema, such as 3-D, widescreen, and stereo sound, were a mixed blessing to exhibitors. On the one hand, these new approaches to spectacle were a way to get viewers back into the theaters. On the other hand, each of the competing technologies required new equipment, and few exhibitors had money to spend. The great attraction of CinemaScope was that it required only add-on lenses and a new screen, *not* new projectors. Stereo sound was originally required for CinemaScope exhibition, but this requirement was quickly dropped because of complaints from exhibitors.[33] Cinerama was expensive to install and expensive to operate, and so it never reached more than a few dozen theaters. Other systems such as 3-D, VistaVision, and Todd-AO had their own pluses and minuses. Given the several choices, it is not surprising that in 1952 theater owners talked about forming a research consortium to evaluate and perhaps even standardize new technologies.[34] This attempt at collective action did not get very far, and the various technologies were left to compete for exhibitor adherence in the marketplace.

A Changing Workplace: Musicians and Actors

Though Hollywood motion-picture production declined in the late 1950s, the employment picture was surprisingly positive. Television production was more and more based in Los Angeles, rather than New York, and TV was making up for a shortfall in film production. In mid-1959, for example, the *New York Times* reported that all of Warner Bros.' twenty-three sound stages were busy, even though only one feature film was being shot. Television work, including commercials as well as series, was generating thousands of hours of filmed material. June 1959 employment in the film-TV industry was up 12 percent over June 1958.[35] However, the employment situation varied according to how closely a job category was linked to theatrical film. For example, employment was booming for editors, makeup artists, and costumers (all skills which could transfer from film to television), but studio publicists were being laid off.[36] The decline in feature film production also created interesting recruitment problems—with so few films being made, it was hard to hire and train new actors, directors, and technicians. Therefore, film industry personnel were getting older even as the audience was getting younger.

The move away from the studio system entailed a more uncertain employment situation. In the 1930s and 1940s, both creative personnel and technicians had been linked to the studios via long-term contracts. But in the 1950s, with independent production and a new emphasis on shooting films abroad, neither studios nor employees could count on a steady flow of production work. Long-term contracts were much less common and Hol-lywood employment, while still lucrative, was far from guaranteed. Also, the studios and the Hollywood unions had different positions on how personnel should be compensated when their work appeared on television. These issues will be explored via consideration of two groups of studio employees: the musicians and the actors.

At the height of the studio system, the major Hollywood companies had needed large and stable music departments to service thirty to fifty productions per year. Composers, arrangers, copyists, musicians, sound recordists, and sound editors were all required, sometimes at short notice—the studios had a habit of rushing post-production (includ-ing music) to get films into release. Some music supervisors were management employ-ees, but the musicians in the studio orchestras belonged to a union, the American Federation of Musicians (AFM). By the early 1950s Hollywood musicians had a favor-able and secure contract, ensuring that they would be available when needed for record-ing. When a new employment contract came up for negotiation in 1958, the musicians naturally wanted to extend their job security, whereas the studios (who had slashed employees in other areas) wanted to hire musicians on a free-lance basis. The union and the studios were also far apart on television issues. The union wanted its members guar-anteed employment on all studio television productions, and it also demanded residuals whenever films were played on TV. The studios flatly rejected both demands. Since the two sides were so far apart, the union went out on strike on 20 February 1958.

It quickly became evident that the studios had the upper hand in this dispute. Activity on the studio lots was not disrupted, because the musicians did not picket and other Hollywood unions did not join a work stoppage. Films needing music were inconve-nienced, but studios found they could hire competent orchestras in Mexico or Europe to record movie soundtracks. In one famous case, the score for VERTIGO was recorded for two days in England and then stopped, because the British union had a reciprocal agree-ment with the American Federation of Musicians. Paramount simply moved the record-ing process to Vienna, where the music for VERTIGO was completed. The studios also considered using pre-recorded "track music" as an alternative to live recordings. The Screen Composers Association (not part of AFM) took no position on the use of foreign orchestras, but it did come out strongly against track music, which would hurt the job security of composers as well as musicians.[37]

The union was further weakened by an internal conflict stemming from disputed trust funds. Under long-standing contracts, the AFM was being paid a small royalty for all music (not just music for films) recorded in the United States; this was to compensate musicians who had lost income when recordings replaced live performances. Hollywood musicians resented the fact that 53 percent of these royalties came from their record-ings, but they received only 4 percent of the payouts. Additionally, between 1952 and 1955 film companies had paid a small royalty to individual musicians when pre-1948 films they had worked on appeared on television; in June 1955 the AFM's international board decided that these royalties should go into the general trust fund.[38] Many Holly-wood musicians also felt that the AFM's position on a new studio contract was unrealis-tic, and that it was important to get back to work.

Based on these grievances, a new locally based union, the Musicians Guild of Amer-ica, won the right to represent film studio musicians in a National Labor Relations Board election held on 10–11 July 1958. Cecil Read, president of the new union, quickly nego-tiated a settlement with the Hollywood studios. Union members were able to return to work after twenty weeks, but they lost most of their demands. The union conceded that film work would henceforth "be on an individual freelance basis operating within the economic-reality window of supply and demand."[39] This meant the end of studio orchestras. The union also lost its bid for royalties when films were released on television. The union did win a raise in the minimum salary for a three-hour recording session, and a concession that there would be at least one recording session per thirteen episodes of a TV series.[40]

The Screen Actors Guild had closely watched the musicians' strike, because actors (as well as other Hollywood employees) were enormously concerned with TV residuals. Actors, like musicians, felt that the recycling of old movies on TV was taking work away from current film industry employees; in essence, they were competing with themselves, and without compensation.[41] However, actors had much more power in Hollywood than musicians: stars were crucial to both feature film and series television production, and on-camera actors could not readily be replaced.

The Screen Actors Guild began contract negotiations with the studios in late 1959 with two primary issues: residuals for films appearing on TV, and health and pension plans for SAG members. The studios threatened to counteract a strike by moving all productions abroad, an extension of the tactic that had worked in the musicians' strike. The shift to production abroad—which was instituted to some degree by Twentieth Century–Fox and other studios—also shows how comfortable the studios were with runaway production.[42] Early discussions with the studios were not productive, so on 7 March 1960 the actors went out on strike. Unlike the musicians, the actors did succeed in shutting down several feature film productions, thus putting pressure on the studios to settle. The actors and the production companies eventually agreed on a compromise: no royalties would be paid on pre-1960 movies, but royalties for actors would commence with films released in 1960. The actors also won health and pension plan coverage. The compromise established the principle that film producers would share income from television screenings with creative personnel, and it was therefore an important moment in the history of Hollywood labor relations.[43]

Finding Audiences

At the height of the studio period, producers and studio executives assumed that a broad general audience would support Hollywood's menu of genres. Women might prefer musicals and men Westerns, but either genre could attract a large and dependable audience. In the 1950s this comfortable relationship among studio, exhibitor, and audience broke down, and therefore producers and exhibitors needed to look much more closely at who was going to the movies. Market research and film industry experience suggested two vitally important facts about the late 1950s audience. First, the film audience was now primarily young people: a 1957 survey showed that 72 percent of the audience was under the age of thirty.[44] Second, according to film historian John Izod, "the better educated and paid went to the movies more than others, paying more for their tickets."[45]

The practical world of film production and exhibition translated this simple profile of movie audiences into a more complex set of movie types and moviegoing experiences. By the late 1950s, there were at least four distinctive (though at times overlapping) film audiences in the United States. "Road show attractions" played in elaborate downtown theaters to an audience of affluent viewers, tourists, and families or couples who rarely went to the movies. These were generally visual spectaculars, elaborate epics, or adaptations of Broadway shows. They were shown at twice-daily screenings with advance tickets—the idea was that viewers would pay handsomely for the very best and most lavish films. The term "road show" is borrowed from theater, and this type of exhibition tried to reproduce the special event quality of going to live theater. In mid-1958, five "road show" attractions were playing in first-run Broadway cinemas: WINDJAMMER (the first film made in Cinemiracle, a widescreen process similar to Cinerama); SOUTH PACIFIC; THIS IS CINERAMA (a revival of the 1952 film); THE BRIDGE ON THE RIVER KWAI; and AROUND THE WORLD IN EIGHTY DAYS.[46]

The traditional first-run/second-run audience for Hollywood pictures had been diminished by television, but it was still the crucial support for a nationwide network of theaters. This group of spectators was attracted by popular stars, high production values, and often a well-known source (novel, play, or historical event). The first-run/second-run audience had become more selective in its tastes. Veteran producer Jerry Wald, writing in 1959, declared that only a dozen stars (all of them male) influenced the box office. Wald suggested "superior film making" as a complement or an alternative to the star system.[47] Beyond such traditional strategies as the star system, adaptations of novels and plays, and Wald's "superior film making," high- and medium-budget Hollywood films reached out to younger audiences with intergenerational stories, like the love stories of adults and teens in IMITATION OF LIFE and A SUMMER PLACE (both 1959), and some stories that privileged the teen point of view, such as REBEL WITHOUT A CAUSE (1955) and BLUE DENIM (1959). Late 1950s Hollywood films also reached out to well-educated viewers via stories that explored controversial topics, including infidelity, abortion, drug addiction, race relations, and nuclear war.

A third distinctive audience was the big city and university town spectators who favored art movies. A few art theaters had existed since the 1920s, but by the 1950s there were hundreds in the United States. One of the reasons (as mentioned above) was a lack of Hollywood product to support small urban theaters. But there were other reasons as well: a frustration with Hollywood's simplistic themes; a strong interest in films with a frank and adult sexual content; a curiosity and sophistication about other cultures.[48] The art film is usually assumed to be foreign (and often subtitled) in the United States, and indeed the new art film audience supported films from Great Britain, France, Italy, Scandinavia, and Japan. However, art theaters often played American films as well, as long as there was some kind of adult or artistic theme. For example, on 1 October 1958, some of midtown Manhattan's art theaters were playing French imports, including LA PARISIENNE and LE ROUGE ET LE NOIR (THE RED AND THE BLACK), but the Little Carnegie was screening THE MATCHMAKER (Paramount), and the Fine Arts was showing ME AND THE COLONEL (Columbia). In other cities these American films probably would have played in traditional first-run theaters, so there was some overlap between first-run and art house exhibition.[49]

A fourth type of audience was the working class, small town, and teenage spectators who had traditionally supported action films and low-budget comedies. Many small-town theaters closed, so demand for this kind of product declined. A new market for low-budget pictures was the drive-in, but the spectators here were interestingly split. Drive-ins attracted the family trade (because of convenience and price), but were even more attractive to teenage audiences.[50] So drive-in programming ranged from Westerns and comedies to the more youth-oriented horror, science fiction, and teen films.

Conclusion

The American film industry experienced wrenching changes in the late 1950s. Two studios, RKO and Republic, went out of business; most of the others suffered through management changes or proxy fights. Independent production became more and more the norm, which diminished the power of the major studios (now reduced to four, with the demise of RKO). Employment in Hollywood motion pictures continued to shrink, which affected the studios' ability to find and prepare new talent. Overall employment in the Hollywood entertainment business was up, however, thanks to the rapid growth of filmed television. This mixed employment picture meant that those professions closely tied to film experienced job losses and/or worsening employment conditions, whereas professions that were needed for film and TV enjoyed booming employment. Film exhibition suffered even more than production, as thousands of traditional theaters closed. The loss of traditional theaters was partially balanced by an increase in the number of drive-ins.

One encouraging sign was that producers and exhibitors were beginning to make films and design theatergoing experiences for the spectators who were still coming to the movies. By 1958 and 1959, at least four important strategies for attracting and sustaining audiences had been developed: the road show, the traditional first-run, the art movie, and the drive-in movie (which might also attract small town and working class viewers). Much more remained to be done: for example, Hollywood's aging personnel needed a better understanding of the rapidly changing teenage culture. But at least the American feature film industry had moved on from the strategies of the mid-1940s.

10

Genres and Production Trends, 1955–1959

The changes that occurred in American film industry structure during the later 1950s—with the five major studios in continuing decline and independents on the rise—had a significant effect on the kinds of films that were made. Hollywood filmmaking began to evolve toward a broader spectrum of film types and spectator choices. Under the studio system of the 1930s and 1940s, dominated by the "Big Five" studios, the entire yearly output of Twentieth Century–Fox or Warner Bros. had to meet the expectations and preferences of the studio production head (Darryl Zanuck at Fox, Jack Warner at Warner Bros.). Under the independent production system of the late 1950s, a far larger group of decision-makers had more leeway (though certainly not total freedom) to attract and entertain movie audiences in new ways. The independents also had less loyalty than the studio moguls to industry traditions and to homogenizing institutions such as the Motion Picture Production Code.

Genres are always changing; indeed, the very notion of "film genre" relies on a tension between continuity and variation. The audience for a genre film expects both a familiar narrative experience and an increment of innovation. However, the late 1950s does seem to be the beginning of an important shift away from a relatively stable system of film genres (reflecting the studios' sense of the audience) and toward more variety and experimentation (reflecting the range of interests of the independent producers interacting with a changing, fragmenting audience). The period of increased variation in film genre is sometimes called "postclassical Hollywood": an era marking the end of the studio system and the beginning of something new. Critic/historian James Harvey described the "postclassical movie" as one that "emphasized and aestheticized" genre, "using the familiarity not to reassure but to astonish and even discomfit us."[1] As Harvey suggested, individual films became more self-conscious and more complex in this period; two of his examples are TOUCH OF EVIL (1958) and VERTIGO (1959). Genres considered in overview also changed in postclassical Hollywood, with Westerns, for example, becoming more divergent from one another. And some of the best films of the late 1950s do not fit comfortably into any one genre.

Though internal film industry conditions account for much of the shift described above, external sociopolitical conditions also had a strong influence on the films of 1955–1959. By the mid-1950s, the Cold War had eased, though not disappeared, both internationally and domestically. The Korean War ended in 1953 with disengagement and the armistice of Panmunjom. After Stalin's death in 1953 and the ascension of Nikita Khrushchev, the United States and the Soviet Union reached an uneasy "peaceful coexistence." Within the United States, the anti-Communist crusade gradually subsided. Joseph McCarthy was censored by the Senate in 1954, though various mechanisms of domestic anti-Communism, including the Hollywood Blacklist, continued through the decade. The return to relative normalcy allowed Hollywood to move beyond the paranoia and conformity of the early 1950s and to consider a wider range of subjects and themes.

The economic boom fueled by housing and consumerism continued into the late 1950s. Though the film industry itself was not particularly prosperous, the lavish homes, big cars, and stylish wardrobes shown on the cinema screen were a manifestation of American wealth and power. This "background" material, rather than film plots and themes, may have been the most influential message that Hollywood exported to the world. American films certainly charted the dynamics of the middle-class family, the pleasures of the wealthy, and the dating rituals of teenagers and urban professionals. The working class was under-represented but not completely absent. Hollywood also presented the many landscapes and subcultures of the United States and the world, often in color and widescreen and with an emphasis on the picturesque and the touristic.

Historian Elaine Tyler May has suggested that the emphasis on the family in 1950s America was not something separate from Cold War anxieties, but rather an attempt to find security in threatening times. In the 1950s American couples married earlier, had families earlier, and had larger families than in other decades of the twentieth century. Further, suburban families lived according to conservatively defined gender roles (husband as breadwinner, wife as homemaker) that were quite different from the prevailing attitudes of the World War II years, when women were encouraged to work.[2] Thus, in focusing on the family and on intimate relationships the movies were actually presenting rather than avoiding (or presenting as well as avoiding) social issues of great currency. Many films described tensions within the couple and the family and were at least moderately critical of the status quo. This criticism was, however, undercut by the genres chosen to explore family and personal life: melodrama and romantic comedy. Both genres may posit alternative ways of living in society, but they conclude with a reaffirmation of social order. (Occasionally the reaffirmation is ironic; see the discussion of Douglas Sirk, below.)

In the 1940s and the early 1950s the American film industry generally presented teenagers as either miniature adults or children. It was in 1955, with the release of BLACKBOARD JUNGLE and REBEL WITHOUT A CAUSE, that the teenage years began to be shown as a separate stage of life. Though the movies may claim some credit (or blame) for spreading this idea of the teenager, Hollywood films were largely reacting to a new youth culture made possible by a booming economy, technological advances (from inexpensive automobiles to the 45 rpm record player), and cultural blending (like the mixture of the popular music of both black and white culture, which produced rock and roll). Hollywood teenagers did not, however, fit into a narrow stereotype—they ranged from well-behaved rich kids (BERNARDINE, 1957) or surfers (GIDGET, 1959) to troubled teens (EAST OF EDEN, 1955) and juvenile delinquents (BLACKBOARD JUNGLE).

The subject of race relations was considered too liberal or even Communistic for Hollywood films at the height of the blacklist period (though NO WAY OUT, 1950, and THE WELL, 1951, are exceptions to this rule). However, by the second half of the decade race relations, once again on Hollywood's agenda, were explored in a number of ways. Some films directly discussed black-white or Hispanic-white relationships—notably THE DEFIANT ONES (1958) and TRIAL (1955). Other films indirectly broached the subject; for example, in THE SEARCHERS (1956), TROOPER HOOK (1957), and other Westerns, white-Indian relationships (often involving marriage, mixed-race children, and questions of mutual acceptance) can be seen as metaphorical explorations of white-black relationships. Race issues were handled in several different genres—melodrama, war film, teen film, prison film (if that is a genre), and Western.

The discussion of Hollywood genres here is not intended to be encyclopedic or to cover all of the "best" films. Rather, a sample of thirty-five films has been chosen to show the range of artistic accomplishments in the period and to highlight several characteristic concerns. Some major films have been omitted—for example, Hitchcock is represented by VERTIGO (1958), but TO CATCH A THIEF (1955), THE MAN WHO KNEW TOO MUCH (1956), and NORTH BY NORTHWEST (1959) are left out. The advantage of this strategy is that the chosen films can be examined in detail.

Musicals

The Freed Unit at MGM—a highly successful group of musical comedy actors, directors, choreographers, composers, and arrangers supervised by producer Arthur Freed—cut back on production in the late 1950s but did continue to create a few original musicals (not based on a Broadway show). IT'S ALWAYS FAIR WEATHER (1955) was a sequel to ON THE TOWN (1949), the idea being that the three GIs from that movie would meet ten years later in the same New York bar. As with ON THE TOWN, the script was by Comden and Green and the star was Gene Kelly, but in a few important respects the latter movie is a step down in quality. Whereas the earlier film featured Kelly *and* Frank Sinatra, in IT'S ALWAYS FAIR WEATHER Kelly dominates his male co-stars, Dan Dailey and Michael Kidd. ON THE TOWN has a superb musical score by Leonard Bernstein, but André Previn's songs for IT'S ALWAYS FAIR WEATHER are, by the composer's own admission, not strong.[3] There is also a youthful exuberance to ON THE TOWN that is sadly lacking in the sequel. The three ex-soldiers have led very different lives, and each brings personal and professional problems to the meeting at the bar. Their resumed friendship takes a strange detour through a TV show (a version of "reality TV," based on the 1950s show *This Is Your Life*), which actually broadcasts part of their story. This leads to a satire of live TV and also complicates several strands of the plot. The film ends in a comic reunification—the perfect couple and the perfect friends—but it labors mightily to get there.

SILK STOCKINGS (1957) is not an original. Indeed the story had been previously presented at least three times: as a play by Melchior Lengyel, as the Hollywood film NINOTCHKA (1939), and as a Broadway musical. The story behind all of the productions is that a serious, even grim, female bureaucrat from the Soviet Union travels to Paris on business where she is courted and converted to capitalism by a Western and therefore decadent man. The 1939 film version, directed by Ernst Lubitsch from a script by Billy Wilder and Charles Brackett, is a sly and gentle satire of communism and a validation of the capitalist and hedonist West. The Soviet official was beautifully played on screen by Greta Garbo. In reprising this story, MGM was betting that the anti-Communist panic of the early 1950s had subsided enough so that audiences could appreciate a comic treatment of Communist-capitalist differences.

The 1957 film version of Cole Porter's musical *Silk Stockings*, directed by Rouben Mamoulian, features Fred Astaire as Steve Canfield, a gallant American film producer, and Cyd Charisse as Nina Yoshenko (Ninotchka), a pragmatic and suspicious Soviet envoy. Much of the conflict between political and economic systems is presented via singing and dancing, which is entirely appropriate for a film starring Astaire and Charisse. The title calls attention to Charisse's legs as well as to the frankly consumerist appeals of capitalism. The title specifically refers to a wordless dance solo in which Charisse replaces her dowdy underthings with stockings and lingerie—an early indication of her seduction/conversion. An amusing element of the musical is a trio of male commissars (Peter Lorre, Jules Munshin, and Joseph Buloff), who have preceded Ninotchka to Paris and have been seduced by Western life. These three oddballs slither through a couple of dance numbers, suggesting Russian "difference" and perhaps homosexuality. After many plot complications, the male commissars open a Russian nightclub in Paris, and Ninotchka accepts (by implication at least) a proposal of marriage from Steve.

SILK STOCKINGS is neither serious nor fair in its consideration of Cold War issues, but it does have the virtues of a well-made film. The score, the star performances, the art direction, and the blend of dancing and drama all confirm that MGM was still making excellent musicals late into the 1950s.

FUNNY FACE (1957) started out as another Freed Unit production, but moved from MGM to Paramount for two reasons: 1) the desired stars, Audrey Hepburn and Fred Astaire, had contractual commitments to Paramount; and 2) MGM's top executives were not enthusiastic about the project.[4] So, a number of MGM creative personnel, including producer Roger Edens, director Stanley Donen, writer Leonard Gershe, arranger Adolph Deutsch, vocal arranger Conrad Salinger, music supervisor Lela Simone, and choreographer Eugene Loring, moved to Paramount to make this film. According to Hugh Fordin, the personnel plus the story plus the Gershwin score were sold to Paramount as a "package."[5] A third star, Kay Thompson, had once worked with the Freed unit as a vocal arranger, but she had been pursuing a singing career in New York for several years.

In FUNNY FACE Astaire plays a fashion photographer—modeled on Richard Avedon—who works primarily for Maggie Prescott (Kay Thompson), the tyrannical editor of *Quality* magazine. Hepburn, an intellectual who wears dark, baggy clothing, is "discovered" by Astaire in a Greenwich Village bookstore. Astaire persuades Thompson that Hepburn's "funny" face, though not conventionally beautiful, is just what the magazine needs for a Paris spring fashion article, and Hepburn agrees to go to Paris because of her passion for a French philosophical movement, Empathicalism (a parody of existentialism). In Paris, Hepburn slips away to spend time in an Empathicalist cellar club; she is a less-than-devoted fashion model. However, she eventually realizes that Professor Flaustre (Michel Auclair), leader of the Empathicalists, is a phony, and that Astaire is the man who truly has empathy and love for her.

Unlike AN AMERICAN IN PARIS, which did a good job of stylizing Paris on a studio set, FUNNY FACE shows us the lyricism of the real Paris. A montage set piece, "Ici Paris," presents the three characters (each one alone in the frame) rushing around Paris and exulting in its tourist sights—the Arch of Triumph, Champs Elysées, Montmartre, Palace of Trocadero, the Seine, Luxembourg Gardens, and so on. Concluding the song, they all arrive at the Eiffel Tower. Later Astaire and Hepburn are together in the frame but

Fred Astaire on location in Paris for Funny Face *(1957), a Paramount film made with the participation of Roger Edens, Conrad Salinger, and other key personnel borrowed from MGM's Freed Unit.*

exploring Paris as the backdrop for a fashion shoot. At the end of the film, they have connected with Paris as passionate human beings—they are married at dawn in the picturesque little church that they first encountered as a setting for photos.

The explicit theme of the film is that the beatnik/existentialist aspect of the Hepburn character must be tamed by American culture and values so that she can find true love. Beatnik characteristics, as portrayed in Funny Face, include the lack of feeling, culture, and good judgment. This is demonstrated by a scene where Astaire and Thompson, dressed as pseudo-beatniks, talk their way into an Empathicalist party and captivate their French hosts with a dreadful parody of American folk/country/rock music. Astaire is then able to rescue Hepburn from the unwanted romantic advances of Professor Flaustre, and to provide her with a picture-perfect romantic wedding.

However, the very presence of beatniks—wearing black, sitting in cellar clubs, listening to jazz, the males bearded, the females sexually aggressive—suggests a youthful rebellion against the conformity represented (and disseminated) by Thompson and Astaire. This rebellion is beautifully embodied by Hepburn midway through the film when she rejects an over-protective Astaire and expresses her feelings via a solo jazz dance (she is eventually joined by two male beatniks). The asymmetrical, unpredictable, sensual dance with rhythmic accompaniment is a powerful rejection of conventional Hollywood musical styles—and of Fred Astaire, a central figure in establishing those styles. The rejection of Astaire and romance is quickly recouped by a narrative that brings the two main characters together. But one can still dream of a FUNNY FACE in which Audrey Hepburn abandons Fred Astaire and remains in Paris with the Empathicalists.

GIGI (1958), based on a novel by Colette, is another Freed Unit film set in Paris, this time early twentieth-century Paris. The title character (played by Leslie Caron) is a spirited teenager being raised by her grandmother and great-aunt to be a courtesan, a mistress of rich men. Both the handsome Gaston Lachaille (Louis Jourdan) and his jaded uncle Honoré (Maurice Chevalier) are captivated by her youth, simplicity, and joie de vivre. Gaston works out an arrangement with the grandmother for Gigi to become his mistress. Gigi refuses, then accepts. But Gaston reconsiders, and asks the grandmother for Gigi's hand in marriage. The film concludes with Chevalier singing "Thank Heaven for Little Girls." Despite the conventional denouement, this film's content would not have been acceptable under Production Code censorship even a few years earlier.

Stylistically, GIGI is different from the other top MGM musicals of the 1950s—it is a singing musical, an operetta, rather than a dancing musical. Film historian Gerald Mast complained that GIGI has the feel of a Broadway show rather than a movie (although it was not adapted from a play). He added that "Leslie Caron doesn't even dance—the one musical thing she knows how to do."[6] Nevertheless, the film does achieve some of the synergy of the best Freed musicals because of the integration of story, music, and visual style. Director Vincente Minnelli, production designer Cecil Beaton, and cinematographer Joseph Ruttenberg marvelously evoke a period Paris (shot on location) with rich colors and a gliding camera. The use of CinemaScope, which usually mandates shallow focus, here allows for composition in depth as well as width. GIGI won Arthur Freed his second Best Picture Oscar of the decade.

SOUTH PACIFIC (1958), based on the Broadway show by Richard Rodgers and Oscar Hammerstein II, was released in 70 mm. Panavision in 1958. Though listed as a Buddy Adler production for Twentieth Century–Fox, this film was actually owned and controlled by Rodgers and Hammerstein with distribution by Fox. Despite wonderful songs, important themes, and breathtaking scenery, SOUTH PACIFIC is a disappointing film. The images are often static and shallow, with spectacular vistas presented as picturesque backdrops instead of lived-in realities. The production is very respectful of the Broadway original, with good performances by Mitzi Gaynor, Rossano Brazzi, John Kerr, and Ray Walston. Yet this film somehow lacks a spark—it has not been re-imagined for the screen. Mast commented that SOUTH PACIFIC and other Rodgers and Hammerstein films of the fifties (OKLAHOMA!, 1955; CAROUSEL, 1956; THE KING AND I, 1956) are "reverential attempts . . . to hang decorative sights on important music."[7]

The original film musical as a staple of Hollywood programming was essentially finished as of 1958. Arthur Freed produced only one more musical, BELLS ARE RINGING (1960), after GIGI; his last film was the non-musical LIGHT IN THE PIAZZA (1962). Stanley Donen quickly followed FUNNY FACE with two more musicals, THE PAJAMA GAME (1957) and DAMN YANKEES (1958), but these were adaptations of Broadway shows and they did not presage a continuing commitment to musical production. After 1958 Donen moved to non-musical films. Causes of the demise of the original musical have been much debated, but two main factors were probably involved: 1. original musicals were far more expensive than the average Hollywood film; 2. musical tastes were changing, particularly among the young people who now constituted Hollywood's most dependable audience.

Comedy

In the late 1950s, many romantic comedies responded to America's changing sexual mores by considering the idea that adventurous but otherwise normal people might have sex outside of marriage. Often such comedies feature a playboy looking for casual love affairs who is eventually pushed toward marriage by the love of a beautiful and morally traditional woman. Or the playboy might lose the woman to a less exciting but more reliable man. In either version, the arc of the plot allows for both the thrill of a "new" morality and the security of the old ways.

Judy Holliday was a kind of throwback—an entertainer whose working class persona succeeded because of common sense and a good heart. She could have been a heroine of 1930s screwball comedy; in the 1950s her populist leanings seemed a bit out of place. It is probably not coincidental that Holliday worked for Columbia, which had produced IT HAPPENED ONE NIGHT (1933), MR. DEEDS GOES TO TOWN (1936), and other populist fables directed by Frank Capra. In IT SHOULD HAPPEN TO YOU (1954), Holliday's character Gladys Glover loses her job and buys space on a billboard in Manhattan's Columbus Circle to advertise her name (no other message). This is a simple and direct way to say "I exist" and it is also eccentric in the tradition of screwball comedy. Gladys's self-advertisement brings her to the attention of Evan Adams III (Peter Lawford), who needs the billboard space for his soap company. Adams, a would-be playboy, expects that his money, power, and favors will convince a grateful Gladys to go to bed with him, but she rejects him. Instead, she winds up with a poor but honorable documentary filmmaker (played by Jack Lemmon), who has admired her without forcing a romantic relationship. Lemmon's slice-of-life documentary work allows this Hollywood movie to make a not entirely convincing comparison between the falsity of advertising and the honesty of film.

AN AFFAIR TO REMEMBER (1957) is about two very experienced, even jaded, socialites (expertly played by Cary Grant and Deborah Kerr) who meet on a transatlantic liner, flirt at length, agree not to fall in love, and fall in love anyway. The film concludes with a series of melodramatic flourishes: the couple agree to meet at the top of the Empire State Building, but Kerr doesn't get there because of a car accident. Exactly one year later, Grant and Kerr both travel to the rendezvous point in the desperate hope that the other will be there; they meet and declare their love. AN AFFAIR TO REMEMBER was introduced to a younger generation by the hit romantic comedy SLEEPLESS IN SEATTLE (1993), where it is presented via dialogue and film clips as the perfect romantic movie. This is an odd "afterlife" for a film that spends much of its time debunking the clichés of courtship and seduction.

SOME LIKE IT HOT (1959), directed by Billy Wilder and starring Marilyn Monroe, Tony Curtis, and Jack Lemmon, is undoubtedly the most screened and most written-about romantic comedy of the 1950s. It was based on the 1951 German film comedy FANFAREN DER LIEBE, in which two male musicians dress in women's clothes and play in a female band. Wilder and co-scriptwriter I. A. L. Diamond changed the setting to Chicago and Florida in 1929 so that everyone would be in costume and the men in drag would stand out less. Casting for SOME LIKE IT HOT was a lengthy process, with Bob Hope, Danny Kaye, Frank Sinatra, and Tony Curtis among those considered for the male leads.[8] The film was finally cast with Curtis and Jack Lemmon as the men in drag, and Marilyn Monroe as the female lead.

Two unemployed musicians, saxophone player Joe (Curtis) and bassist Jerry (Lemmon), hide from the Chicago mob by dressing as women and taking a job with a touring all-female jazz band. Joe becomes "Josephine" and Jerry "Daphne." The two befriend Sugar Kane (Monroe), the band's beautiful singer, on a train going to Florida. During the band's long engagement at a luxury hotel, Joe begins courting Sugar, disguising himself as a millionaire playboy while at the same time using his female persona to become her close friend. At the same time, Jerry/Daphne resists the amorous advances of aging millionaire Osgood Fielding III, played by Joe E. Brown. At the film's end Joe reveals himself to Sugar as a penniless musician and she accepts him. Meanwhile, Osgood proposes to Daphne, who in desperation reveals that she is a man. Osgood then serenely delivers the film's ending line: "Nobody's perfect."

SOME LIKE IT HOT's virtues include wonderful casting and excellent comic timing. Curtis nicely juggles three personae, Joe, Josephine, and the mild-mannered million-

The supposedly all-female orchestra of SOME LIKE IT HOT *(1959), including Tony Curtis (with saxophone, left), Jack Lemmon (with bass), and Marilyn Monroe (with ukulele, center).*

aire, and it is the last character's diffidence that allows the usually aggressive and con-niving Joe to connect with Sugar. Lemmon's Jerry is the sidekick here, aware of the craziness of Joe's schemes and yet deferring to his friend. Jerry also seems to enjoy the masquerade of drag, and this morphs into a willingness to take on the feminine role in courtship.

Billy Wilder was the director who best understood Marilyn Monroe's movie persona. Wilder's THE SEVEN YEAR ITCH (1955) was a wonderful vehicle for Monroe, the film that established her natural, naive, all-American sexuality. By the time of SOME LIKE IT HOT, Monroe was looking older and had put on a few pounds. So Wilder and Diamond cre-ated a character that was thirtyish and a bit dissipated, but still beautiful and sexy. This character is also warm and compassionate, accepting her own weaknesses and those of others. Monroe adjusts her performance so that she can convincingly be Josephine's sin-cere, intimate friend and at the same time a somewhat calculating (but not cold) woman angling to land a rich bachelor. Further, Monroe can be aggressive because the million-aire is shy, and this makes the relationship exciting and unpredictable.

SOME LIKE IT HOT's enduring popularity derives in part from star power, but it also involves themes of sympathy and understanding between men and women. Many romantic comedies of the 1950s present seduction as a game or even a war between men and women (as exemplified by titles such as THE TENDER TRAP, 1955). Certainly the romance of Sugar and Joe is among other things a game, with each character trying to highlight certain things and hide others. But the comic device of putting men in drag allows the film to show women as warm, funny, interesting human beings instead of stereotyped objects of desire. Joe and Jerry get past many of the physical and social bar-riers that typically separate unmarried men and women. The result is at times titillating, but more importantly it reveals that despite appearances, the opposite sex is very much like us (whether "us" is male or female).

The romance between Daphne and Osgood stretches this sympathy between the sexes even further. If the other sex is like us, then why shouldn't Daphne remain a woman, as culturally if not physically defined? Her elderly suitor, it seems, would be quite content. This is a bombshell of an idea which Wilder and Diamond deftly throw into a madcap comedy.

Epics

The epic film was a staple of Hollywood in the 1950s, but "epic" can have a few different meanings. First, it can simply describe a large-scale film, which means one could have epic war films, or Westerns, or perhaps even melodramas (like GIANT, 1956). More typi-cally, "epic story" or "epic film" refers to a well-known story about a hero set in the past. Further, epics such as the *Iliad* or the *Divine Comedy* are founding or defining stories about a people, a nation, or a religion; readers or film viewers would therefore experi-ence some part of their cultural identity in the content and symbolism of an epic. But a film epic need not be so ambitious in its reach; sometimes it is simply an adventure film set in a familiar era of the past.

THE VIKINGS (directed by Richard Fleischer, 1958) was a film produced by and star-ring Kirk Douglas. United Artists had established a relationship with Douglas's Bryna Productions in the mid-1950s, and this film with its $3.5 million budget signaled UA's confidence in him. THE VIKINGS is a beautiful film to look at, photographed in Technirama (Technicolor's widescreen process) by British cinematographer Jack Cardiff. The many scenes of eighth-century Viking ships on the water or hugging a rocky coast are absolutely breathtaking, and interiors in the Viking banquet hall are impressive as well. Douglas himself is an excellent swashbuckler in the role of Einar, son of the Viking leader Ragnar (Ernest Borgnine). Unfortunately, the film has story problems; as the *New York Times* put it, THE VIKINGS is a "scrambled saga."[9] The plot includes a complex intrigue about the succession to a small British kingdom, with Eric (Tony Curtis), whom we first meet as a Viking slave, as a possible heir to the throne. Another chunk of the plot involves the Welsh Princess Morgana (Janet Leigh), who is torn between three men: the evil King Aella, Einar, and Eric. Even though Douglas is by far the most charismatic presence in the film, it is the less impressive Curtis (Brooklyn accent and all) who gets the girl.

THE VIKINGS does not have that extra dimension of epic-as-founding-story mentioned above. Possible connections to British history or the Viking exploration of North America are not pursued. So the film becomes an adventure story, with good visuals and lots of action scenes. The film earned $6,000,000, but after distribution expenses it did not return a profit.[10]

BEN-HUR (directed by William Wyler, 1959) was the single most popular film released in the 1950s, surpassing even DeMille's THE TEN COMMANDMENTS (for a detailed discussion of THE TEN COMMANDMENTS, see Chapter 7). This film was a "founding story" of Western culture and the Christian religion, since the life of the fictional Judah Ben-Hur (Charlton Heston) connects at several points with the life and death of Jesus Christ. MGM put $15 million into the project; such a large budget is always a gamble, but the silent BEN-HUR had been a huge hit in the 1920s and the success of THE ROBE and THE TEN COMMANDMENTS suggested a continuing interest in biblical epics. Also, the 1880 novel *Ben-Hur* by General Lew Wallace had been popular for many decades.

Filmed in Italy, BEN-HUR was a colossal undertaking, a 220-minute film involving three production units. William Wyler and cinematographer Robert L. Surtees headed the first production unit, which had the primary responsibility of filming the dialogue scenes. A second unit led by director Andrew Marton, cinematographer Piero Portalupi, and legendary stuntman Yakima Canutt filmed the film's major set piece, the eleven-minute chariot race. The huge set for the race extended over eighteen acres and took more than a year to build. The third unit led by director Richard Thorpe and cinematographer Harold E. Wellman filmed a sea battle and helped out on the chariot race.[11]

Judah Ben-Hur is a Jewish prince who lives in Jerusalem at the time of Jesus of Nazareth. He is arrested and enslaved by the Romans, serves several years as a galley slave, and eventually makes his way back to Jerusalem. Ben-Hur defeats his boyhood friend, now enemy, Messala (Stephen Boyd), the man who arrested him, in the spectacular chariot race. Then Ben-Hur and his family are redeemed (his mother and sister cured of leprosy) at the moment of Jesus's trial and crucifixion.

BEN-HUR was shot in MGM 65, a wide film process developed by Panavision. Like Todd-AO, this process used a 65 mm. negative to make a 70 mm. print. Image quality was much sharper than 35 mm. CinemaScope, but MGM 65 had an extremely shallow depth of field. The directors and cinematographers struggled mightily with this drawback, with many images composed in diagonals and in depth even if the backdrop was not entirely sharp. For example, in the early scene where Ben-Hur meets Messala, the two characters approach from opposite ends of a long hall, prefiguring their conflict.

However, close-up scenes do become a problem, with the lead actors typically positioned in one plane across the foreground rather than in more varied arrangements.[12]

The film suggests at times that Judah Ben-Hur's suffering and redemption mirror the life of Christ. Ben-Hur is the same age as Jesus; in one scene he is almost mistaken for Jesus, while in another scene he is bound with a wooden pole to form a rough cross. But it is equally plausible that the story simply is about a man named Ben-Hur, with no allegory. This understanding supports one of the film's themes—that religion is the encounter between ordinary people and the divine. Judah Ben-Hur, a strong, passionate, angry man, lives through a series of troubles and adventures. He and his family are saved by Christ's death on the cross.

There are also some political ideas in BEN-HUR. First and foremost, the film comes out strongly against tyranny, as represented by the Romans, and for the liberty of conquered peoples. This has a Cold War resonance and may also refer to the Nazi conquest of Europe during World War II. A second idea is the independence of a Jewish state, only a dream for thousands of years but a reality since 1948 and the founding of Israel. Ironically, the film shows Jew and Arab working together for independence from Rome; such cooperation has not been part of the recent history of the Middle East.

Critical reaction to BEN-HUR was generally positive, and the film swept an unprecedented eleven Academy Awards, including Best Picture, Best Actor, Best Supporting Actor (Hugh Griffith), Best Color Cinematography, and Best Musical Score (Miklos Rozsa).

War Films

With the Korean War over and World War II receding a bit in memory, the war films of 1955–1959 do not cluster around a single theme or setting. Korean War and World War II dramas are most numerous, but also characteristic of the period are war comedies (MR. ROBERTS, STALAG 17, OPERATION PETTICOAT), war love stories (THE HUNTERS and KINGS GO FORTH), and contemporary Cold War films.

STRATEGIC AIR COMMAND (1955), one of the Cold War films, is about a bomber unit of the U.S. Air Force, America's primary deterrent force in the nuclear standoff with the Soviet Union. This film is notable for an unusually close collaboration between the Department of Defense and Hollywood. Screenwriter Beirne Lay Jr., a colonel in the U.S. Air Force Reserve (and co-scriptwriter of TWELVE O'CLOCK HIGH, 1950), wrote the script at the prompting of Air Force General Curtis LeMay, head of the Strategic Air Command (SAC). The Department of Defense had some security concerns about publicizing SAC, but Paramount's request for cooperation was approved thanks to LeMay's strong support.[13] A technical advisor was sought who would have "complete understanding of SAC mission, familiarity with B-36 and B-47 aircraft, inherent sense of public relations, and ability to work closely with demanding civilians and defend Air Force interests."[14] The advisor chosen, Colonel Dick Lassiter, helped director Anthony Mann get everything he needed and even flew a B-47 himself to expedite a difficult scene.[15]

STRATEGIC AIR COMMAND is about a major league pitcher who is recalled to active duty flying a bomber for SAC. (The part was played by James Stewart, who had been an air force pilot and was, like Beirne Lay, a colonel in the Air Force Reserve.)[16] The pitcher and his wife (June Allyson) go willingly on this assignment. After the Stewart character is injured in a plane crash, he is offered a choice: return to baseball as a coach or stay with

SAC in a desk job. He chooses to continue serving his country. Though the story is quite conventional the film was a hit, probably because audiences were fascinated by the planes and the organization which constituted so much of America's military power in the Nuclear Age. Beirne Lay had anticipated this in his story outline, saying "Visually . . . the streaking jet bombers and the newest operational techniques of the Strategic Air Command—in other words the airplane—may be the star of the piece."[17]

MISTER ROBERTS (1955) is a war comedy, based on a hit Broadway play, that shows, among other things, the monotonous routine of military service. The title character, played by Henry Fonda, is the cargo officer of the freighter *Reluctant*, which is stationed in the South Pacific. Roberts frequently defends the ship's crew from the captain (James Cagney), a petty and tyrannical officer who cares only for his own record of delivering cargo on time. Roberts requests, on a regular basis, transfer to a combat ship, and the captain regularly refuses. The film includes a number of comic set pieces but ends on a serious note, as Roberts finally succeeds in transferring to combat duty and is killed by a kamikaze pilot in the last days of the war.

Despite its skeptical view of the navy, MISTER ROBERTS was approved for Department of Defense cooperation because of the participation of veteran director John Ford. Ford had made World War II documentaries for the navy, he was a retired rear admiral, and his support and affection for the armed services were beyond question. However, Ford left the production long before completion, because of quarrels with Fonda, heavy drinking, and an inflamed gall bladder. Doubts about the material may have been the underlying problem—Ford tried to change the film's humor, but Fonda and others resisted. Mervyn LeRoy finished the film, sticking closely to the play, and Joshua Logan (director of the Broadway version) also directed a few scenes. The resulting film is competent but visually bland.

Stanley Kubrick's PATHS OF GLORY (1957), based on the novel *Paths of Glory* by Humphrey Cobb, is a savage indictment of military organizations and modern war. United Artists was skeptical about this project and agreed to finance it only if a top Hollywood star could be cast. Director Kubrick and producer James Harris responded by signing Kirk Douglas.[18] The film was shot outside of Munich, and it has the look of an inexpensive, black and white European art film.

In the trench warfare of World War I, French General Mireau (George Macready) sends the battle-weary men of his regiment into battle in search of a promotion for himself. When the attack fails, General Mireau has three men, chosen more or less at random, court-martialed for cowardice. Colonel Dax (Douglas) pleads for their lives, both at the court-martial and in a private interview with Mireau's superior, General Broulard (Adolphe Menjou). The three soldiers are nevertheless killed by a firing squad. General Broulard then cynically offers to promote Dax as Mireau's replacement. Dax declines, and Broulard sends Dax and his troops back to the front.

This film's primary point is that the military enterprise is fatally flawed by its strict, inflexible hierarchy. The world of the officers is amazingly different from the world of the men, as shown by visual contrasts and by the commanders' complete authority. The top officers live in a spacious palace, the ordinary men in dark, cramped barracks or trenches. Colonel Dax tries to be a good officer, but even he can do little against the system. By undercutting Dax's heroism and letting innocent men be convicted and shot, Kubrick makes a simple, clear anti-military statement—a highly unusual stance for American war films of the 1950s. However, the film mutes its critique to some degree by singling out the French rather than the American military.

PATHS OF GLORY was not a popular film in 1957–1958. *Variety* called it a "grim story" and summarized its marketability as "prospects dim."[19] It was banned in France for many years, and was shown in Belgium only after a disclaimer was added calling the story "an isolated case in total contrast with the historical gallantry of the vast majority of French soldiers."[20] However, the film was made for a relatively low budget ($850,000, of which $350,000 went to Kirk Douglas), and according to Balio it managed to break even.[21]

PORK CHOP HILL (1959) presents a situation much like that in PATHS OF GLORY, but comes to different conclusions. In the last hours of the Korean War, American soldiers are ordered to take a hill of no particular value to show the enemy that the United States remains willing to fight. The commanding officer in the field (played by Gregory Peck) and the rank-and-file soldiers know that peace is imminent, and yet they follow their orders and take Pork Chop Hill despite heavy casualties. One difference between this film and PATHS OF GLORY is that here the staff officers understand the grim irony of the situation and agonize over the inevitable casualties. PORK CHOP HILL minimizes the differences (of worldview, or social class, or privilege) between officers at headquarters and soldiers at the front. Also, PORK CHOP HILL is ambivalent about whether the sacrifice was necessary.

Sy Bartlett, producer of PORK CHOP HILL, thought that the film was a "very, very anti-war" story, but it can also be seen as a realistic film about American soldiers carrying out an unusually difficult mission.[22] Director Lewis Milestone, here as in HALLS OF MONTEZUMA (1950), has balanced a sense of war's futility with a generally supportive picture of the American military.

Film Noir

Film noir was in decline in the late 1950s. Many films were being made in color and widescreen, and film noir depends on low key black and white. ("Neo-noir," a style that uses desaturated color to suggest film noir effects, was some years away.) Thematically, film noir's romantic pessimism and decaying urban settings were out of fashion; audiences were more interested in comedy, melodrama, and teen films.

However, the film noir style did not entirely disappear. Fritz Lang continued making low-budget noirs at RKO, like WHILE THE CITY SLEEPS and BEYOND A REASONABLE DOUBT (both 1956) until the studio closed in 1957. Mark Robson directed THE HARDER THEY FALL (1956), starring Humphrey Bogart in his last screen role. And Orson Welles contributed the last great film noir—TOUCH OF EVIL (1958).

Orson Welles had not directed a Hollywood film for ten years when he was invited to write and direct TOUCH OF EVIL (based on the novel *Badge of Evil*, by Whit Masterson) for Universal. Both star Charlton Heston and producer Albert Zugsmith take credit for convincing Universal to hire Welles, and both may be correct.[23] The medium-budget film was made on location in Venice, California, a West Los Angeles neighborhood that worked admirably as the script's Southwestern border town. Welles, who was by this time feared as a profligate, out-of-control director, finished production on time and on budget. Then he spent several months on the editing but left for Mexico before it was finished. Universal completed post-production and did not allow Welles to significantly alter the studio's cut.

Mike Vargas (Charlton Heston), a high-ranking Mexican narcotics investigator, and his American bride, Susie (Janet Leigh), are crossing the border to the USA when a car

Director-actor Orson Welles, in character as Hank Quinlan, steps behind the camera during the filming of TOUCH OF EVIL *(1958).*

bomb explodes, killing wealthy rancher Rudy Linnekar and his young girlfriend. Vargas sends Susie to a hotel and joins the murder investigation. He finds himself in conflict with a hard-boiled police captain, Hank Quinlan (Orson Welles), who seems to rely on intuition and unethical shortcuts. Meanwhile, Susie is being threatened (first at the hotel, then at a rural motel) by a group of Hispanic juvenile delinquents trying to pressure her husband into abandoning a case. Quinlan's admiring sidekick, Sergeant Menzies (Joseph Calleia), proves that his boss has planted evidence; both Menzies and Quinlan are then killed in a shootout. Vargas rushes to the motel to save his wife.

TOUCH OF EVIL is a film noir, in both plot and style, but it is also a complex, ambitious, many-layered work. The film begins with a three-and-one-half minute crane shot, which follows Linnekar and his girlfriend (driving) and Vargas and Susie (walking) from Mexico through a border checkpoint and into the United States. This bravura piece of filmmaking, one of the most famous single shots in the history of film, ends with the car bomb exploding. Throughout the film, Welles combines the wide-angle, deep focus cinematography developed in CITIZEN KANE (1941) and THE MAGNIFICENT AMBERSONS (1942) with the poetic use of darkness and shadows characteristic of film noir. As in CIT-

IZEN KANE, characters compete for dominance of the frame—an interesting struggle, because Vargas is tall and charismatic and Quinlan is disheveled but enormous (he is typically filmed from low angles to enhance this effect). There is a strong "B"-movie element in TOUCH OF EVIL, seen especially in the stereotyped young delinquents and the snatches of rock and roll on the soundtrack. But there is also a Shakespearian nobility to the film, for example in Menzies's love for the boss he must sorrowfully betray. Quinlan himself is a complex character, "hateful" but very human, and Marlene Dietrich and TV star Dennis Weaver are unforgettable in minor roles.[24]

The 1998 revised version of TOUCH OF EVIL, edited by Walter Murch, uses an extraordinary fifty-eight-page cutting memo from Orson Welles (responding to the studio cut) as the basis for reshaping the film.[25] The new version is perhaps more dynamic in a formal sense, but it does not drastically change TOUCH OF EVIL. Instead, the 1958 and 1998 versions can be seen as two variations on the same great work (just as a piece of music can be interpreted in more than one way). For example, in the 1958 version the famous opening shot is the credit sequence and is heavily overlaid with Henry Mancini's musical theme. The new version gets rid of the credits and uses rock music blaring from bars to give this shot a much more three-dimensional feel. So, the 1958 opening is a bit reductive and depends on Mancini's music to set the tone—but Mancini's music is very good! Throughout the film, the studio cut may be more stereotyped and simplified than Welles had desired. To give another example, Welles's memo asks Universal to tone down the entrance of the delinquents, male and female, when Susie is drugged at the motel. But such over-the-top moments are part of TOUCH OF EVIL's charm—it is both high art and exploitation fare.

Akim Tamiroff and Orson Welles in TOUCH OF EVIL.

Westerns

The Western genre, once the dependable mainstay of Hollywood film production, was by the late 1950s a mainstay of network television. Numerous prime-time Western series were being made by Warner Bros., MCA, and other Los Angeles–based companies. Older Western films were also constantly appearing on television. Nevertheless, top-quality Western films continued to be made, in surprising numbers. This chapter can only suggest a few of the high spots, leaving out such films as THE MAN FROM LARAMIE (1955), TROOPER HOOK (1957), FORTY GUNS (1957), THE LEFT-HANDED GUN (1958), THE BIG COUNTRY (1958), and LAST TRAIN FROM GUN HILL (1959).

Director Budd Boetticher, producer Harry J. Brown, and star Randolph Scott collaborated on six modestly budgeted Westerns for Columbia. All of them have fairly limited action but an interesting set of moral choices. According to writer Jim Kitses, the hero played by Scott has "a great serenity, the knowledge that we are fundamentally alone, that nothing lasts, that what matters in the face of all this is 'living the way a man should.'"[26] In RIDE LONESOME (1959), this hero must contend with a young killer, the killer's more experienced brother, two outlaws who want to go straight, a beautiful widow (not a threat but a responsibility), and a band of Mescalero Apaches. With intelligence and nerve, he balances all the problems and saves his anger and passion for the older brother, who many years earlier had killed his wife. Boetticher's films of this period are simple, clear, and unpretentious.

The most notable Westerns of 1955–1959, however, are the "superwesterns"—meaning large-scale films which in some way redefine the genre. This redefinition can be political (as in HIGH NOON), sociological (as in SHANE), psychological (as in WINCHESTER '73), or formal (as in THE FAR COUNTRY), and there are surely other possibilities.[27] The self-conscious reshaping of a genre suggests that simpler formulae have lost their power, and thus the genre is entering a baroque or ironic period. However, a few films of the late 1950s manage to create a believable set of Western conventions (such as character or landscape) while at the same time complicating the themes and/or forms.

John Ford's THE SEARCHERS (1956) is a film in which Ford, the master of the genre, dramatically changes and deepens his ideas about the Western hero and the Indians/Native Americans. (Ford had been making important Westerns since THE IRON HORSE, 1924.) The story, based on a novel by Alan Le May, starts with former Confederate Ethan Edwards (John Wayne) returning to his brother's ranch in Texas in 1868. Almost immediately, Ethan's brother, sister-in-law, and older niece are killed by a Comanche war party. The younger niece, Debbie, is kidnapped. Ethan sets off to look for Debbie along with Aaron's adopted son Marty (Jeffrey Hunter)—a third "searcher," the older niece's boyfriend Brad, is killed almost immediately by the Comanches.

Ethan and Marty spend years tracking the Comanche band led by Chief Scar (Henry Brandon). Much of the film explores their difficult relationship—Marty is one-fourth Cherokee, which to Ethan means he is a "breed." Marty also proves to be the voice of moderation, whereas Ethan is consumed by hatred of Scar and all things Indian. Late in the film, Ethan recognizes Marty's loyalty and makes Marty his heir. When they find the Comanches, Marty kills Scar, and Ethan scalps him. Marty considers Debbie (now played by Natalie Wood) his sister, but Ethan has announced his intention to kill her, because she has become one of Scar's wives. But at the last minute Ethan pulls her up onto his horse and says "Let's go home, Debbie."

Natalie Wood, at this point one of the wives of Chief Scar, displays settlers' scalps for John Wayne and Jeffrey Hunter in THE SEARCHERS *(1956).*

The John Wayne character is not portrayed in a kind or heroic light in THE SEARCHERS, even though then as now John Wayne represented the archetypal Western hero. Ethan is an extremist, stubborn enough to ignore the surrender at Appomattox and remain a Confederate in 1868. He is very much like Chief Scar, indeed they are equivalent in their hatred (Scar's family was killed by whites, Ethan's by Comanches). In one memorable scene, Ethan and Scar meet in a parley; they are the same size in a two shot, they glower at each other and exchange insults. Ethan and Scar both have enormous determination and strength, but their values lead to endless revenge. Marty is equally determined, and yet he is able to see ways for the two communities, white and Native American, to come together.

In 1956 THE SEARCHERS was greeted by critics as an excellent John Ford/John Wayne Western.[28] Later critics have seen the film as a passionate re-examination of race relations in America. According to Brian Henderson, who started this line of criticism in 1980, THE SEARCHERS is a metaphor for African American/white relationships in the era of *Brown vs. Board of Education*, the Supreme Court's 1954 school desegregation case. The message, per Henderson, is that assimilationist blacks (represented by Marty) will be accepted by the dominant community, but separatist or rebellious blacks (represented by Scar) will not be tolerated.[29] Perhaps the best evidence that Ford really was thinking about race relations in 1956 is the series of films that he made a few years later: SERGEANT RUTLEDGE (1960) is about a black cavalryman who is charged with raping a white woman and found innocent; TWO RODE TOGETHER (1961) is, like THE SEARCHERS, a film involving captives and race prejudice; CHEYENNE

AUTUMN (1964) is the story of an Indian tribe which is deceived and abused by the United States government.

MAN OF THE WEST (directed by Anthony Mann, 1958) is a summation of the Western genre, as the title suggests. It begins with Link Jones (Gary Cooper), a reformed outlaw, catching a train to Fort Worth to hire a schoolteacher for his small frontier town. The train is ambushed by robbers, so Link and two other passengers—Billie (Julie London), a singer, and Beasley (Arthur O'Connell), a gambler—find themselves on foot a hundred miles from civilization. Link takes them to an isolated ranch where they find the train robbers, led by Dock Tobin (Lee J. Cobb). Beasley is killed, and Link and Billie are threatened. Link eventually kills all the gang members, but not before Dock rapes Billie—the rape is strongly suggested, but not shown or discussed. As the film ends, Link and Billie are driving a covered wagon back to society.

MAN OF THE WEST takes place at a moment when civilization is replacing the frontier, but lawlessness is still a threat. Dock Tobin is old and half-crazy, his outlaws an unreliable bunch, but they still have guns and they still kill people. The film's originality lies in giving the frontier/civilization tension both familial and psychological dimensions. Link is the hero and Dock is the villain, but Link and Dock are also family—Dock raised Link as his "son." They once committed daring and outrageous crimes together. Dock is Link's past, and even his violent, amoral double. (This doubling is more apparent in Mann's WINCHESTER '73, where hero and villain are brothers.) But the duality of goodness and violence also exists *within* Link. He is Billie's selfless protector but at the same time a brilliant, ruthless killer. After wiping out Dock's gang, will he be able to meekly return to civilization? And should he deny the "dark side" that was necessary for his (and Billie's) survival?

Visually, MAN OF THE WEST's CinemaScope color images show a beautiful Western landscape—town, decaying ranch, ghost town, desert. The images are classic, but also in a sense wild, because civilization does not intrude too much. The town and the train disappear early. Though the frontier may be ending as a historical period, the complexities of human nature remain, and MAN OF THE WEST is ultimately a psychological Western.

RIO BRAVO (1959) supposedly originated from director Howard Hawks's disgust with HIGH NOON (1952). In that film, the marshal played by Gary Cooper asks a cowardly town for help but is refused; in RIO BRAVO Hawks substituted a sheriff who is reluctant and choosy about accepting help. Hawks may have objected to HIGH NOON's liberal bias, and to its reliance on abstractions such as "the citizens" or "the town."[30] At any rate, in RIO BRAVO Sheriff John Chance (John Wayne) takes on an outlaw gang without support from the town but with a group of friends: an old man (Walter Brennan), a drunk (Dean Martin), a hotelkeeper (Pedro Gonzalez-Gonzalez), a teenage gunman (Ricky Nelson), and a saloon girl (Angie Dickinson).

RIO BRAVO's strength is also its weakness. The film displays an incredible grace and ease as it refines the Western down to a few characters and a few stock situations. The characters fill iconic roles yet interact with a great deal of warmth and individuality. However, the film's concentration and grace lead to a loss of context. Nothing exists except for the Hawksian group doing a difficult job on a Western street. RIO BRAVO is so self-consciously a John Wayne/Howard Hawks Western that it loses credibility as a film about the nineteenth-century American West. There is a strange emptiness beneath its attractive surface.

A related problem is that RIO BRAVO seems to be a studio lot Western. It was shot on one exterior set, the Western Main Street at Old Tucson, Arizona (the equivalent of a

Western street on a studio back lot). The interiors were filmed at Warner Bros.' Burbank studio. In earlier periods, a studio Western would be normal and expected. But by
1959, after many fine Westerns had been shot on location, RIO BRAVO seems artificial
and limited.

Melodrama

Thomas Schatz has defined "melodrama" as a type of film "that depicted a virtuous individual (usually a woman) or couple (usually lovers) victimized by repressive and
inequitable social circumstances, particularly those involving marriage, occupation, and
the nuclear family."[31] In the late 1950s this genre flourished, probably because American
culture was so focused on the nuclear family and on sexuality. New themes including
male anxieties, mental illness, homosexuality, and racism were added to the melodrama's
traditional concerns. Schatz lists eighteen important melodramas of 1955–1959, noting
that his list is not complete: THE COBWEB; EAST OF EDEN; REBEL WITHOUT A CAUSE;
THERE'S ALWAYS TOMORROW; PICNIC; ALL THAT HEAVEN ALLOWS; GIANT; BIGGER THAN
LIFE; TEA AND SYMPATHY; WRITTEN ON THE WIND; THE LONG, HOT SUMMER; PEYTON
PLACE; CAT ON A HOT TIN ROOF; THE TARNISHED ANGELS; TOO MUCH, TOO SOON; A
SUMMER PLACE; SOME CAME RUNNING; and IMITATION OF LIFE. Among the films he
leaves out are THE MAN IN THE GRAY FLANNEL SUIT and THE THREE FACES OF EVE.
Such a list is far too extensive for this chapter (even if REBEL WITHOUT A CAUSE is placed
in another category, the teen film), so only a handful of films will be discussed here.

GIANT (directed by George Stevens, 1956) is based on a large, sprawling novel by
Edna Ferber. Novel and film chronicle the lives of a wealthy Texas family from 1925 to
the early 1950s. Like THE SEARCHERS, the film has a subtext involving race relations.
Bick Benedict (Rock Hudson), a Texas cattleman, courts and marries Leslie Lynnton
(Elizabeth Taylor), an aristocrat from the Maryland hunt country. It's a stormy marriage,
with Bick's sister Luz (Mercedes McCambridge) slow to accept the bride from the East,
and Leslie and Bick arguing about treatment of the ranch's Hispanic workers. This argument comes to a head when son Jody Benedict (Dennis Hopper) marries a Hispanic
woman. In another subplot, Bick refuses to join the oil boom sweeping Texas, but Jett
Rink (James Dean), formerly a Benedict family employee, strikes oil on adjacent property. Jett is infatuated with Leslie from his years on the ranch, and as a newly rich oilman
he thinks that a romance with her will affirm his social standing. But problems between
husband and wife are smoothed over, and by film's end Bick comfortably accepts his
daughter-in-law and his grandchildren.

Visually, this film constructs three different landscapes for its three main characters.
Bick is the Texas patriarch, and the vast dimensions of the ranch reflect his power. Leslie
comes from the upper-class horse farms of Maryland, so she brings a different culture
and a more genteel tradition of wealth to the marriage. She is also an intelligent and
independent woman, who at one point moves back to Maryland out of frustration with
her husband. Jett Rink is the outsider, socially disadvantaged but with a tremendous
energy and passion. His Texas landscape involves oil rigs and trucks, as opposed to Bick's
cattle and wide-open spaces. The moment when Jett strikes oil and bathes in the gusher
may be the film's emotional high point. Jett ends up as a lonely, embittered drunk; as
Kevin Thomas notes, the film seems to be punishing him for his threat to the family.[32]

*Elizabeth Taylor and Rock Hudson as the married couple at
the center of* GIANT *(1956).*

WRITTEN ON THE WIND (1956) is another film set in Texas, but this time traditional
wealth lies with the oil tycoons. Jasper Hadley (Robert Keith), head of Hadley Oil, has two
spoiled children—drunken playboy Kyle Hadley (Robert Stack) and nymphomaniac
Marylee Hadley (Dorothy Malone). Mitch Wayne (Rock Hudson), a geologist for the firm,
is almost another son to Jasper Hadley, though Hudson is always deferential and tries to
keep the "real" children out of trouble. Kyle and Mitch meet Lucy Moore (Lauren Bacall)
at Hadley Oil's advertising agency in New York; Kyle courts her and marries her. The film
dramatizes at length Kyle's fears of inadequacy and his sister Marylee's promiscuity (which
triggers her father's fatal heart attack). The action reaches a fever pitch when Lucy
announces she is pregnant, Kyle strikes her (causing a miscarriage), and Mitch defends
her. Then Kyle comes home drunk with a pistol, struggles with Marylee, and shoots himself. Mitch is tried for murder. At the trial, a subdued and lucid Marylee exonerates Mitch.
Mitch is now free to marry Lucy, and Marylee will take over the oil business.

The reputation of Douglas Sirk, the director of WRITTEN ON THE WIND, has strikingly
changed over the last half century. In the 1950s, Sirk was known as a superior director of
women's pictures. Now he is considered an ironist or perhaps a "hyper-realist"[33]—one
whose films are so intense in their use of melodramatic convention that they ultimately
explode conventional meanings. In WRITTEN ON THE WIND all the main characters are

stereotypes, but the film suggests complexities beyond the stereotypes. Kyle Hadley is a frightened man presenting the facade of a millionaire playboy, and the root of his problem seems to be impotence—producer Albert Zugsmith later commented on the novelty of a Hollywood film dealing with impotence, even though it had to be played "down, down, down."[34] Mitch Wayne really is attracted to Lucy Moore and vice versa, but the attraction must remain below the surface because of social convention. Marylee Hadley is much more aggressive than her brother, she is the father's true heir, but this manifests itself as drunkenness and promiscuity until her brother dies.

As an example of Douglas Sirk's visual style, consider the image at the end of the film of Marylee Hadley in a well-tailored suit sitting at her father's desk and playing with an oil well statuette. Behind her is a portrait of Jasper Hadley with the same statuette. The denotative meaning is that Marylee is now in charge, she will be conducting the family business. Superficially, at least, order has been restored. There is also a sexual connotation, that the female sibling is more potent than the male, therefore she deserves to possess the phallus (WRITTEN ON THE WIND is often lurid in its symbolism). Beyond these two obvious levels, director Douglas Sirk points to a third implied meaning of the oil well statuette, the undercurrent of loss it represents. Marylee has lost her father, her brother, and the man she loves (Mitch); all she has left is the family oil business.[35] She is fighting back tears as the movie ends.

CAT ON A HOT TIN ROOF (directed by Richard Brooks, 1958) is an adaptation of a Tennessee Williams play. Like most of Williams's work the film revolves around a dysfunctional southern family. Big Daddy (Burl Ives), a wealthy landowner, is seriously ill, and his family gathers around him on his birthday. Big Daddy reaches out to his younger

James Dean as a young ranch hand and Elizabeth Taylor as the boss's wife in GIANT.

son Brick (Paul Newman), but Brick rejects any family interaction and stays in his room, drinking. Brick also wants nothing to do with his wife, Maggie (Elizabeth Taylor), whom he calls "Maggie the Cat." He refuses Maggie's sexual advances and accuses her of having slept with his best friend Skipper, who then committed suicide. Maggie denies that this got beyond a kiss. Big Daddy and Brick have a long, violent heart-to-heart talk. Big Daddy tells Brick to grow up; Brick tells his father that the illness is cancer (though this word is never spoken). The two men create a bond by honestly confronting their fears. Brick then transforms another important relationship when he forgives Maggie's lie about being pregnant and says he wants to make a baby with her.

From a modern standpoint, it is surprising that such a talky and static film was a popular success for MGM. Director Richard Brooks added a few outdoor scenes, but this still feels like a filmed play. However, Tennessee Williams's dialogue (with some adjustments by Brooks and co-screenwriter James Poe) is so intense and so dynamic that the pace never lags. Big Daddy is tyrannical and bombastic, thoroughly used to having his own way, and he is out of control because of pain and fear. Brick is passive yet stubborn, unwilling to yield anything and certainly unwilling to be polite. These two collide, literally and figuratively, in memorable ways. Maggie is yielding but also scheming, and her frank discussion of sexuality would have shocked viewers in 1958. A key issue, never resolved, is Brick's intimate friendship with Skipper, which he evidently preferred to his marriage. Much discussion of Williams's play centered around whether Brick was homosexual. This is toned down in the movie, but Brick and Skipper's friendship still seems unusual. With or without the homosexual element, CAT ON A HOT TIN ROOF has a verbal directness verging on brutality that goes far beyond the 1950s norm. It is still a melodrama, however; it describes sympathetic people victimized by illness, death, and family quarrels who find their way to a positive conclusion.

SOME CAME RUNNING (directed by Vincente Minnelli, 1959), adapted from a long novel by James Jones, features Dave Hirsh (Frank Sinatra), newly discharged from the army, returning to his (fictional) home town of Parkman, Indiana. Dave drinks, gambles, and gets in fights, but he is also a published novelist. Dave wanders between respectable Parkman society and the demi-monde of bars and poker games. He finds his brother Frank (Arthur Kennedy), a businessman and pillar of the establishment, to be hypocritical, but develops a warm friendship with professional gambler 'Bama Diller (Dean Martin). In particular, Dave is emotionally pulled between Ginny Moorhead (Shirley MacLaine), a sweet and surprisingly naive tramp who follows him to Parkman, and Gwen French (Martha Hyer), a schoolteacher who admires his writing but distrusts his morals. Rejected by Gwen, Dave marries Ginny, even though he doesn't love her.

SOME CAME RUNNING is visually stunning, especially when the less reputable characters are on screen. Dave moves nervously through the CinemaScope image, never content, never knowing what he is searching for. 'Bama is more serene, perfectly at home in a world of bars and loose women. The alternative character of this world is underlined by Elmer Bernstein's jazzy, often dissonant music. In more middle class surroundings, the visuals are "tasteful" but bland, and the music is nondescript (as in the love theme associated with Gwen French). The film's visual tour-de-force is a carnival scene in downtown Parkman with most of the characters present. This scene and the film as a whole suggest that middle-class respectability is just too limiting, that people need the adventure of an "underworld."

IMITATION OF LIFE (1959) is another stylized melodrama directed by Douglas Sirk. The script, based on both the novel by Fannie Hurst and the 1934 film directed by John Stahl,

At the beginning of SOME CAME RUNNING (1959), Dave Hirsh
(Frank Sinatra) gets off the bus in his hometown of Parkman,
Indiana, and discovers that Ginny Moorhead (Shirley
MacLaine) has followed him from Chicago.

involves a household of four women: Lora (Lana Turner), a Broadway actress; Susie (Sandra Dee), her daughter; Annie (Juanita Moore), Lora's African-American housekeeper; and Annie's daughter, Sarah Jane (Susan Kohner). All of the characters have surface achievements but hidden failings. Lora, for example, is a successful actress who has sacrificed her personal life, at the expense of Susie and persistent beau Steve Archer (John Gavin). Much of the story focuses on the light-skinned Sarah Jane. As the daughter of an obviously black mother and a presumably white father (whom we never see), Sarah Jane is considered black within the universe of the film. But as a teenager, Sarah Jane decides she wants to "pass," to live as a white person. When a boyfriend discovers the truth and beats her, Sarah Jane runs away to Los Angeles, where she works in the chorus line of a seedy nightclub. Annie, whose health is failing, seeks out her daughter in L.A., but Sarah Jane denies their kinship and asks to be left alone. Annie dies, and the film's most emotional moment occurs at her funeral. Sarah Jane appears as the funeral procession is marching down the street, collapses on Annie's coffin, and sobs "I killed my mother!"

IMITATION OF LIFE (1959): Lana Turner as Lora Meredith and Terry Burnham as Lora's daughter Susie are in the foreground. Juanita Moore (Annie) is in the background. Later in the film, a teenaged Susie is played by Sandra Dee.

The film is basically over with this cry of anguish. Sarah Jane sits in a car with Lora and Susie, so one could say that the family has reunited, but Sirk noted that this was just a formality.[36] With Annie's death, the family has really broken apart. However, the fault does not lie entirely with Sarah Jane. One could instead blame the American system of racial discrimination, which decrees that questions of skin color and parentage have an enormous effect on individual lives. Neither of the choices presented to Sarah Jane—to accept discrimination or to deny her mother and sell her good looks—had been acceptable. A third choice—to rebel, to demonstrate, to change the world for the better—lies beyond the conventions of melodrama. However, by suggesting the huge gap between existing choices and human needs this film creates a postclassical complexity within melodrama.

In visual style, IMITATION OF LIFE is a glossy "woman's picture" full of lovely things, most of them associated with Lora's profession and her upscale suburban lifestyle. The producer was Ross Hunter, who insisted on lavish sets, beautiful stars, and old-time Hollywood glamour.[37] But Hunter's taste was subverted by his frequent collaborator Douglas Sirk, in whose films upper-middle-class opulence can look trashy and fake. Critic J. Hoberman described Sirk's visual strategy: "IMITATION OF LIFE revels in phoniness—snow-machine flurries, shiny Christmas props, a picture-perfect suburban house furnished with generic postimpressionists and unopened leather-bound books."[38] It is important to note, however, that Sirk's ironic visuals do not destroy this film's emotional range. The decors may be phony, but Sarah Jane's pain is real.

American New Realism[39]

Reacting against the mid-1950s trend toward color and widescreen spectacle, a group of fiction films stressed black and white realism instead. This set of films might be called a "cycle," indicating a short timeframe, instead of a genre. It included several much-praised films: ON THE WATERFRONT, MARTY, BLACKBOARD JUNGLE (to be discussed in the next section, "Teen Films"), THE BACHELOR PARTY, TRIAL, NIGHT AND THE CITY, TWELVE ANGRY MEN, and SHADOWS, among others.

ON THE WATERFRONT (1954) has a relatively simple crime film/social problem film plot. Dockworker Terry Malloy (Marlon Brando) unwittingly helps thugs working for his union kill a would-be reformer, Joey Doyle. Terry, a former prizefighter who at 29 is still not quite mature, is devastated by his involvement. He starts a tentative romance with Joey's sister Edie (Eva Marie Saint) and agrees to help a social activist priest (Karl Malden) clean up the corrupt dockworkers' union. Union boss Johnny Friendly (Lee J. Cobb) sends Charlie Malloy (Rod Steiger) to stop his younger brother Terry from testifying; Charlie lets Terry go. Charlie is then killed, but Terry testifies against the union,

ON THE WATERFRONT (1954): Marlon Brando and Eva Marie Saint.

and he beats Johnny Friendly in a fistfight. (For discussion of this film in political context, see Chapter 3).

Stylistically, ON THE WATERFRONT combines two distinctive influences: Italian Neo-Realism and Method Acting. Neo-Realist films of the late 1940s, including OPEN CITY (1945) and THE BICYCLE THIEF (1947), opposed Hollywood glamour and substituted simplicity and immediacy. Among the key ideas of Neo-Realism were:

1. Stories should come from the everyday lives of the working class;
2. Films should be made on real locations (exterior and interior);
3. Films should use non-actors in at least some leading roles;
4. Films should stay away from genre patterns and happy endings because reality is unpredictable.

In ON THE WATERFRONT, Budd Schulberg's thoroughly researched script comes out of the experience of New York–area dockworkers. To add authenticity, the film was made on location in Hoboken, New Jersey. The film has an impressive feel for life in a gritty, working-class community.

ON THE WATERFRONT does not, however, emulate the Neo-Realist experiments with non-actors. Instead, director Elia Kazan relies on Method Acting, which might be described as an "internal realism" to complement the external realism of location shooting. This approach, usually associated with the New York–based Actors Studio (Kazan was one of its founders), teaches an actor to develop a part based on his/her emotional experiences. Instead of creating a character out of exterior details (the more traditional approach of film acting), actors delve into their own experience of love and fear and anger and grief. In ON THE WATERFRONT, all the principal actors had been trained in the Method, but Marlon Brando is its most brilliant exponent. The Brando character is inarticulate and a bit slow but also sensitive, courageous, and instinctively fair.

Brando's love scenes with Eva Marie Saint are very good, but his tour-de-force comes in a taxicab scene with Rod Steiger. Here, the two brothers have an intimate conversation in the shadow of death. When Terry realizes his brother has been sent to stop him (and perhaps to kill him), he complains about how a fixed fight ruined his boxing career—"I coulda been a contender!"—not because he expects anything, just to set the record straight. Charlie starts by trying to manipulate his brother, then threatens him, then gives up and hands Terry a gun. Terry gets out, and the cab careens into a garage. Johnny Friendly is in a nearby window, and the implied meaning is that Charlie will be killed. According to critic James Naremore, Charlie sacrifices himself for the sake of his younger brother.[40] The taxi driver's swerve into the garage comes as a surprise, but it was set up by an earlier scene in which Johnny threatened Charlie.

MARTY (1955), another important realist film, stems from an unexpected source: American television. For a few years in the early 1950s, live drama was a staple of the emerging television industry. Hundreds of original teleplays were produced in New York, which provided wonderful opportunities for a generation of young writers, directors, and actors. *Marty*, a teleplay written by Paddy Chayefsky about a butcher living in the Bronx, caught the eye of film producer Harold Hecht (Burt Lancaster's partner). Hecht convinced United Artists to finance a film version, which became an Academy Award winner and a commercial success.

MARTY's secret was almost certainly "counter-programming": it was so different from the established cinematic norms that it drew a great deal of attention. Like the Italian

In MARTY (1955), *Ernest Borgnine plays a butcher who has trouble getting a date.*

Neo-Realists, Paddy Chayefsky decided to find his dramatic subjects in the lives of ordinary, working-class people. His butcher, played on screen by Ernest Borgnine, is a stocky, unhandsome bachelor who lives with his mother. The film is about thirty-four-year-old Marty's loneliness and shyness: his inability to find a date, let alone someone to marry. The lines exchanged by Marty and his friends on a Saturday night—"What do you feel like doin' tonight?" "I don't know, what do you feel like doin' tonight?"—still evoke the sadness of empty evenings. But on this particular Saturday night, Marty meets Clara Snyder (Betsy Blair), a twenty-nine-year-old schoolteacher, and they talk for hours. The film aims for "slice of life" realism rather than narrative closure, and so it ends with a very small decision: Marty calls Clara on Sunday.

John Cassavetes's SHADOWS (1959) draws from both Neo-Realism and the Method, but establishes its own unique approach to cinematic realism. Cassavetes, a well-known young actor of the 1950s, was also the co-founder of an acting school, and from this school came an exercise in collective creation. Over a period of three years, Cassavetes and several young actors developed characters and situations, and through a process of improvisation, the story line for SHADOWS began to form. The story focuses on three siblings and presents once again the problem of racial "passing." The oldest sibling, Hugh (Hugh Hurd), is obviously African American. He wants to be a singer, and he has a manager, Rupert (Rupert Crosse), to help him along. Unfortunately, Hugh's gig at a nightclub in Philadelphia reveals that he can't sing. The middle sibling, Ben (Ben Carruthers), is a light-skinned jazz musician who is passing for white. Ben is supposed to be a trumpeter, but we never hear him play; instead, he roams Manhattan trying to be hip, in a beatnik way. According to Ray Carney: "Ben would rather talk trumpet than play it. He goes around feeling sorry for himself and pretending to be hip, but not doing very much at all." Carney argues that posing or "masking" is a key part of Cassavetes's style, in Shadows and the films that follow it.[41] The youngest sibling, Lelia (Lelia Goldoni), is light-skinned and socializes with both whites and blacks. She takes Tony (Tony Ray), a young white man, back to the family's apartment (all three siblings live there, without parents) and has sex with him. She then becomes disturbed by his reaction to her obviously black brother. The white boyfriend is asked to leave, and not allowed to come back. In this film, unlike Imitation of Life, discrimination is a problem for the majority culture (because Tony is punished for his reaction to Hugh) as well as for the minority.

Shadows is not a mainstream film. It is set in a milieu of New York beatniks and jazz musicians, and takes their values for the norm. A musical score from jazz bassist Charles Mingus adds to the sense of time and place. The film was shot largely on the street, Neo-Realist style, but it is more fragmented and less literary than a Neo-Realist film. For Cassavetes, the key unit of meaning seems to be the scene, not the story. Every scene has its own structure and tone, and the narrative that strings them together seems to be secondary. Scenes can be intense, they can explode into quarrels, or they can be calm. Cassavetes goes beyond Method Acting by having his actors thoroughly involved in developing characters and scenes; Method actors generally were limited to interpreting a script. Cassavetes's film has high points and low points, and many viewers miss the clear structure of a three-act plot. But in its emphasis on the "now," Shadows does give a sense of bohemian New York that would be hard to duplicate by more conventional means.

Teen Films

The Hollywood studios realized in mid-decade that teenagers were the backbone of the film audience, and therefore teen-oriented movies would be good investments. The events that catalyzed these rather tardy realizations were: 1) the great success of Blackboard Jungle and Rebel Without a Cause; and 2) the emergence of rock and roll as a major force in the music industry. Both of these phenomena showed that teenage buying power had become a crucial factor in American entertainment. For the film industry, like the record industry, catering to teens was an opportunity to establish firm ties to a group that had disposable income and free time and *wanted* to spend money on entertainment.

Film historian Thomas Doherty has persuasively argued that the "teenpic" of the late 1950s actually involved a handful of genres: the juvenile delinquency film, the rock film, the horror film (sometimes with a specifically teenage angle, as in I Was a Teenage Werewolf, 1957) and the "clean teen" film (for example, anything starring Pat Boone).[42] All of these genres were aimed at teen audiences, and they often celebrated a teen point of view—with parents absent or wrong-headed, and teenagers in the foreground. Some films did look at teens from an adult perspective, but even here a reading "against the grain" was possible. For example, teenage audiences could ignore the silly main plot of The Girl Can't Help It (directed by Frank Tashlin, 1956) and concentrate on the performances by rock and roll headliners.

In narrative structure, Blackboard Jungle is not too different from other crime films or social problem films starring Glenn Ford in the 1950s. As in The Big Heat (1953), the hero played by Ford is confronted by something that is glaringly wrong. In The Big Heat, it is the corruption of organized crime; in Blackboard Jungle, it is a

Glenn Ford (standing, at left) and Sidney Poitier (right) starred in Blackboard Jungle
(1955).

vocational high school terrorized by juvenile delinquents. Ford in both films refuses to
be intimidated; instead he violently confronts the criminals and solves the problem.
There is, however, a crucial difference between the films; in Blackboard Jungle the
Ford hero is a teacher, and he manages to survive because of an alliance with some of
the kids in his class. In The Big Heat he is a policeman, concerned only with punishing
the "bad guys." So although juvenile delinquency is certainly scary in Blackboard Jungle, the film does not suggest that all the kids in a tough high school are unreachable.

Blackboard Jungle was made at MGM, but it has the "torn from the headlines" feel
of a Warner Bros. crime film of the 1930s. Juvenile delinquency was headline news in
American newspapers in the mid-1950s and was covered extensively by prestigious magazines including the *Saturday Evening Post, Colliers, Life, Time, Newsweek, Harper's* and
Atlantic Monthly.[43] Widely publicized hearings of the Juvenile Delinquency Subcommittee of the Senate Judiciary Committee were held in 1953, 1954, and 1955. MGM's program booklet for Blackboard Jungle specifically refers to this national panic, clipping
newspaper headlines ("Housewife Attacked"), citing statistics ("The F.B.I.'s report cover-
ing 1953 . . . disclosed that persons under 18 committed 53.6% of all car thefts . . ."), and
quoting from J. Edgar Hoover and President Eisenhower.[44] Yet the film also seeks to contain the hysteria in two different ways: via a disclaimer at the beginning of the film, and
more importantly via a positive conclusion. The use of a black student (played by Sidney
Poitier) as the leader of those who aid the teacher suggests that cooperation between
races, classes, and generations is possible in 1950s America.

Richard Brooks's decision to use the song "Rock Around the Clock" by Bill Haley and the Comets over the first scene of BLACKBOARD JUNGLE had important consequences. This was the first appearance of rock and roll in a major Hollywood motion picture. Within the movie, "Rock Around the Clock" suggests the separateness of the teenage culture (one of the teachers collects Bix Beiderbecke records) and invites viewers to identify with this joyous music. But rock is associated with the juvenile delinquents, so viewer sympathies are caught between the middle-aged hero and the teenagers. This complex perspective is resolved by a distinction between the "bad teen" Artie West (Vic Morrow), who pulls a knife on the teacher, and "good teen" Gregory Miller (Sidney Poitier), who defends him. "Rock Around the Clock" also showed the enormous potential for synergy between the film and popular music businesses. Before BLACKBOARD JUNGLE, the song had been released in a couple of versions to general indifference; after the film's release, "Rock Around the Clock" became a best-selling single, listed on the *Billboard* chart for twenty-nine weeks.[45]

REBEL WITHOUT A CAUSE (directed by Nicholas Ray, 1955) addresses one of the more puzzling dimensions of 1950s juvenile delinquency: the spread of teenage crime to the affluent suburbs.[46] High school student Jim Stark (James Dean) lives in a nice Los Angeles–area house and drives his own car; his parents belong to a fancy country club. Yet Jim is arrested for drunkenness, he gets in a fight the first day of school, and he participates in a "Chickie Run" (two drivers in stolen cars compete to see who will jump last as the cars race toward a cliff) that results in the death of another teen. This film is both sociological and psychoanalytic in its viewpoint. Jim's problem is that his father (Jim Backus) is a weak man and therefore not a good role model. The other teens central to the story have similar problems: Jim's girlfriend Judy (Natalie Wood) is rebelling because her father no longer shows her affection; and Plato (Sal Mineo) is the worst off because his wealthy, divorced parents have essentially abandoned him.

However, this distanced, more-or-less adult perspective on teenage problems is balanced by a teen-centered perspective. In the absence of credible adult guidance, Jim, Judy, and Plato have to work out their own ideas on honor, love, and friendship. Further, they have to respond to threats from a group of "bad teens." In one memorable sequence, the trio of friends explores an abandoned house and acts out a substitute family: Jim as the father, Judy as the mother, Plato as the child. Plato's problems with the law really begin when he wakes up and finds that Jim and Judy are gone. Plato dies, killed by the police, but Jim and Judy get the chance to reconcile with their families.

Much of this film's appeal lies with the acting and the visual style. REBEL WITHOUT A CAUSE was James Dean's most memorable film. His slouching, mumbling, perpetual motion acting accords extremely well with the character of Jim Stark. He is often reclining or partly reclining, showing that he doesn't match up with the everyday world of right angles. But Dean's unconventionally physical style can also create moments of joy. For example, when he is looking for Judy early in the film he jumps up to see over a high fence, and then almost bounces as he walks with her. These movements suggest a simple exuberance that would not be out of place in musical comedy. Natalie Wood, more conventional in her acting, is convincing as a sexy teenager not entirely separated from her daddy. And Sal Mineo, like Dean a Method actor, gives a strong performance as a twisted and desperate-for-love teen. The acting is beautifully supported by Nicholas Ray's widescreen visual style, which gives Dean and Mineo space to move while stressing off-center and sometimes tilted camera angles.

Natalie Wood and James Dean on the set of Rebel Without
a Cause *(1955). Note Dean's characteristic semi-reclining
position.*

In the wake of Blackboard Jungle, Rebel Without a Cause, and rock and roll's
assault on the pop music charts, a number of rock stars were signed to motion-picture
contracts. Of these, the most important was certainly Elvis Presley. Presley, age nineteen, made his first 45 rpm record for Sun Records in Memphis in 1954. He toured
extensively and signed with RCA, a major label, in 1955. In 1956, Elvis appeared several
times on national TV and signed his first film contract with Hal Wallis and Paramount.
There is contradictory information about the size of the contract. Wallis's files show a
three-picture contract at rates so low ($15,000 for the first film, $20,000 for the second,
$25,000 for the third) that a waiver from the Screen Actors Guild was required. How-
ever, in his autobiography Wallis remembers a Presley contract suitable for a young star
($100,000 for the first film, $150,000 for the second, $200,000 for the third).[47]

Jailhouse Rock (directed by Richard Thorpe, 1957), Presley's third and probably
best film, was made at MGM on a loan out from Wallis and Paramount. The film's script
draws on the stories and myths of Presley's two great musical influences, African American rhythm and blues and Caucasian American country music. In both traditions, musi-

cal inspiration is born from bad luck, woman troubles, and prison time. In the film, Vince Everett (Presley) is serving a prison sentence for manslaughter. His cellmate, Hunk Houghton (Mickey Shaughnessy), teaches him to play guitar. When he is released, Vince and Peggy Van Alden (who has a low-level record industry job) form their own record label. The film at this point follows Presley's rags-to-riches biography—successful records, then TV appearances, and then a Hollywood contract. But Vince quarrels with Peggy, physically fights with Hunk, and even goes through a tracheotomy. The picture ends with Vince singing again and happily reconciled with those he loves.

Despite Presley's star power, JAILHOUSE ROCK was a modestly made picture in black and white CinemaScope. The cost was $1,099,000, and the film made a profit of $1,050,000.[48] What distinguishes this film is the careful handling of Presley's bad boy (but not too bad) rock and roll image. Elvis is presented as hot-tempered; he kills a man with his fists in a bar fight (thus the charge of manslaughter). Later, he breaks a guitar in frustration and he insults people or sulks when he doesn't get his way. But he is usually soft-spoken and good-hearted, and he ends up with the girl and his musical career. The film manages to combine the juvenile delinquent, rock and roll, and clean teen genres, all in one tidy package!

Presley's singing ranges from tender ballads to a few up-tempo rockers. He was famous, or notorious, in the 1950s for a wild, hip-swinging delivery (sample headline: "6000 Kids Cheer Elvis' Frantic Sex Show").[49] JAILHOUSE ROCK features this signature style primarily in the title tune, a musical comedy–like dance number (staged for a TV broadcast, according to the film's narrative) with a stylized, two-story prison set and numerous hip-swinging dancers dressed as convicts. This is an interesting number despite a lack of precision (JAILHOUSE ROCK was made at MGM, but *not* by the Freed Unit), and it shows that Presley could have been an innovative star of film musicals. However, the film usually shows him singing in an unadorned recording studio.

Pat Boone, a wholesome, boy-next-door type, was almost as popular as Elvis Presley during this period. Another strand of clean teen films was represented by Sandra Dee, who became the leading star of films aimed at teenage girls. According to a trade press article, the characteristic problems of Sandra Dee's films "involve parental relationships and dating, and Miss Dee solves them by relying on decent instincts and common sense."[50]

GIDGET (directed by Paul Wendkos, 1959), based on the best-selling novel by Frederick Kohner, is a coming-of-age story about Francie Lawrence (Sandra Dee), who discovers surfers and surfer boys at Malibu Beach in the summer before her senior year of high school. Gidget (the nickname comes from "girl" plus "midget") is presented as a slow-to-develop teen: although she turns seventeen during the film, she wears modest swimsuits, worries about her lack of bustline, and is just beginning to get interested in boys. Gidget is adopted by the Malibu surfers as a kind of mascot, and with a summer's practice she becomes a reasonably good surfer. She also develops a friendship with Kahuna (Cliff Robertson), an older surf bum who is a role model for the teenage boys, and a crush on Moondoggie (James Darren), who is closer to her own age. Through most of the film, Gidget cannot get the surfers to take her seriously as a young woman. However, as summer ends she accepts a blind date arranged by her parents, and the unknown "Jeffrey Matthews" turns out to be her beloved "Moondoggie."

The ritual of growing up in GIDGET is unthreatening. Gidget's mother gives her lots of good advice. The surfer boys are nice kids, and when Gidget invites a seduction from the older (and presumably more dangerous) Kahuna, he tells her to forget it. Alcohol and drugs are absent except for a moment when Kahuna, alone and unhappy, takes a drink

Elvis Presley in the title number of Jailhouse Rock *(1957).*

from a bottle of cheap wine. And although boys and sex are clearly on Gidget's mind, these topics are presented in a young teen, cleaned-up way. The light, comic tone of the story is accentuated by a few moments when the characters burst into song.

Surfing is the one original feature that pulls Gidget away from complete blandness. Adolescents grow up and prove themselves by mastering the waves, and Gidget has the additional distinction of proving herself in a previously all-male pastime. The film was based on the true experiences of Kathy Kohner, daughter of novelist/screenwriter Frederick Kohner, who as a high school student surfed with the boys at Malibu. The surfing close-ups were done with back projection, but the long shots, with top California surfers doubling the actors, evoked some of the beauty of the sport. Gidget, novel and film, helped change surfing from an obscure phenomenon to a worldwide craze.

Beyond Genre?

Many Hollywood genre films of the late 1950s seem to fit the self-conscious, "postclassical" paradigm advanced by James Harvey and others.[51] Some examples from earlier sections of this chapter would be Touch of Evil, the superwesterns, and the Sirk melodramas. Another aspect of this move toward complication and self-questioning is that some of the most important movies of the period do not fit comfortably within a single genre. Movies that combine genres or work outside of genres can appear in any period—two examples would be CITIZEN KANE (1941) and SUNSET BOULEVARD (1950). But it seems that in the late 1950s the genre system lost some of its sway, and films became more individualized narratives. This tendency accelerated in the 1960s and early 1970s with the films of Robert Altman, Arthur Penn, Stanley Kubrick, and Bob Rafelson.

THE NIGHT OF THE HUNTER (1955), based on a novel by Davis Grubb, is perhaps a horror film, though it has a slow buildup and very little violence. During the Depression of the 1930s, Reverend Harry Powell (Robert Mitchum), a self-styled preacher, pursues his two stepchildren, John (Billy Chapin) and Pearl (Sally Jane Bruce), because they know where their real father hid $10,000 before he was hung. Fleeing from Powell, who has killed their mother, the children float in a small skiff down the river (the film is set in the Ohio River Valley north of Parkersburg, West Virginia). They are eventually found and taken in by the strict but good-hearted Miss Cooper (Lillian Gish), who already has a few orphans in her house. Powell comes for the kids, but Miss Cooper wounds him with a shotgun, after which he runs, weirdly screaming, into a barn. In the morning, the state police come for Powell, and John gives them the $10,000 he has hidden for so long. The film ends with Miss Cooper and her brood celebrating Christmas.

This film is uniquely and eerily atmospheric. Screenwriter James Agee and director Charles Laughton achieve an amazing feel for Appalachia in the 1930s,[52] and for a child's-eye vision. The first part of the film is more or less realistic, though the Mitchum character with his broad-brimmed hat always stands out arrestingly. When the children take off on their own down the river, their journey gains a mythic feel from striking shots of the night or dawn sky and deep focus compositions with wildlife in the foreground. Cinematographer Stanley Cortez (who also shot THE MAGNIFICENT AMBERSONS, 1942) does a marvelous job of setting the fairy tale mood.

Absolutely central to THE NIGHT OF THE HUNTER is fundamentalist Protestant religion. The film suggests that religion can be used for great evil or great good, a duality represented by the tattoos on Harry Powell's knuckles (the left hand says H-A-T-E, the right hand says L-O-V-E). Within the story, Powell is the evil one, whereas Miss Cooper personifies the good. Both are larger-than-life characters, undoubtedly because the film privileges the children's point of view. And both are tied to religion throughout the film, but never more hauntingly than when Powell starts singing a hymn outside Miss Cooper's house (he is stalking the children). Miss Cooper joins in, and they sing an astonishing duet.

SWEET SMELL OF SUCCESS (directed by Alexander MacKendrick for Hecht-Hill-Lancaster, 1957) is a combination of film noir, social realism, and black comedy. It tells a noirish story of cynical, greedy men exploiting human weakness in nighttime Manhattan. James Wong Howe's lustrous black and white photography and Elmer Bernstein's strident score add to the feeling of film noir. The film is also a New York realist film, shot on the street and in the best nightspots. It describes a unique New York subculture: the world of columnists, publicists, and publicity-seekers. SWEET SMELL OF SUCCESS has comic elements as well: nobody dies and the innocent escape at the end.

Ernest Lehman, author of the original novella and co-writer of the script, conveys this strange subculture through two wonderfully drawn characters: publicist Sidney Falco (Tony Curtis) and gossip columnist J. J. Hunsecker (Burt Lancaster). Falco is in constant motion about Manhattan, trying to make a living, trying to please Hunsecker, trying to find an angle, trying to manipulate everyone and everything. He is a ratlike character, with few if any scruples, and yet we appreciate his energy and sympathize with his problem. Falco can't get an item in Hunsecker's column until he breaks up the courtship of J. J.'s kid sister Susie (Susan Harrison) and jazz musician Steve Dallas (Marty Milner), and Susie and Steve are set to announce their engagement.

J. J. Hunsecker (the character is based on 1950s columnist Walter Winchell) is simply the god of this particular segment of Manhattan: he gets everything he wants, he lectures a U.S. Senator, he demands complete loyalty, he never picks up a check. Hunsecker expects to control Susie's life as he controls the world of publicity, and with amazing aplomb he farms out the job to Falco. Hunsecker floats through Manhattan uttering semi-profound statements, and when he has a cigarette in his mouth he commands "Match me."

At the film's end Susie escapes from her brother's control, but SWEET SMELL OF SUCCESS is not particularly about plot. It is, instead, a film of attitudes and one-liners, and a nasty portrait of a publicist's New York. Anti-glamorous and yet dependent on the star system, it may represent the producers' (Lancaster and Harold Hecht) complex feelings about the culture of celebrity.

What genre is VERTIGO (directed by Alfred Hitchcock, 1958)? Mystery? Romance? Suspense film? Horror film? This is one instance where the auteur theory may work better than genre analysis, for VERTIGO is clearly a film by the director who made the Gothic romance REBECCA, as well as many variations on the theme of trust (for example, NOTORIOUS, and TO CATCH A THIEF).

The film is based on *D'entre les morts* (literally "From Among the Dead"; in English translation this book is called *Vertigo*), a good mystery novel by Pierre Boileau and Thomas Narcejac. Hitchcock changed the location from France to San Francisco, but he retained the plot of a man attracted to a beautiful, upper-class woman—her name is Madeleine in both book and film—who seems to be "possessed" by a long-dead relative. When Madeleine dies, the hero finds a replacement for his passion, a young woman of modest origins who physically resembles her. The second woman (Judy in the film) eventually confesses to having impersonated Madeleine as part of a complex murder plot in which the real Madeleine was killed by her husband. Judy then dies as well. The film provides impressive roles for James Stewart as Scottie, a former police officer now caught up in this strange mystery/love story, and Kim Novak as both Madeleine and Judy. Another major character, the very practical Midge (Barbara Bel Geddes), does not exist in the book; Midge's presence, as Scottie's friend and potential lover, suggests that he could have avoided this strange and unattainable relationship and settled for an ordinary woman. Instead, however, Scottie plunges into the metaphysical. He wants Madeleine because she comes (or seems to come) "from among the dead."

Hitchcock has made this odd story marvelously concrete. Scottie sees Madeleine at Ernie's, an upscale San Francisco restaurant, and both he and the viewer are entranced by her restrained, classical beauty. In other scenes, Madeleine seems both part of and separated from the natural world—this effect is actually enhanced by the usually distracting technique of back projection. Judy is a more down-to-earth young woman, a salesperson at a department store. But we grasp some of the film's complexity immediately, because we *know* this is Kim Novak. Scottie's vertigo also gets a concrete manifestation; the film shows his inability to function on a roof or in a church tower with a shot combining zoom in and track out. "Vertigo" in the film has both physical and psychological/metaphysical meanings.

Kim Novak as the elegant Madeleine in VERTIGO *(1958).*

VERTIGO ends without resolving all its mysteries, and therefore the story's unique aura lingers. Judy confesses to her part in the murder plot and she falls (or jumps?) to her death—this recapitulates what supposedly happened to Madeleine. So, she is "punished" for her crime in familiar Production Code style, but we are left uncertain about what Scottie is thinking. Is he guilty? Still in love? Still clinging to an idea of transcendence? Perhaps Scottie is responsible for both deaths because he cannot love a simple, flesh-and-blood woman.

Hitchcock is a master at controlling the audience's perception, and this includes playing with the idea of genre. In VERTIGO, he never allows the viewer to get comfortable with any one genre pattern. The "mystery" of Madeleine and Judy is solved halfway through, the suspense is only intermittent, and the love story veers in strange directions because the hero does not fully understand either himself or his loved one. Perhaps the true mystery here is Scottie's twisted subjectivity, and that is never resolved.

VERTIGO was only a break-even film at the box office in 1958, but it was soon recognized by critics in France, England, and the United States as a classic. British critic Robin Wood's appreciation in *Hitchcock's Films* (1965) is representative: "VERTIGO seems to me Hitchcock's masterpiece to date, and one of the four or five most profound and beautiful films the cinema has yet given us."[53]

THE NUN'S STORY (1959) is a highly unusual subject for a $3.5 million Hollywood production—seventeen years in the life of a nun, with an emphasis on interior rather than exterior conflict. Director Fred Zinnemann notes that the major studios had no interest until Audrey Hepburn committed to the project. After this, Warner Bros. agreed to finance and distribute THE NUN'S STORY as a high-budget color film. Warners was understandably concerned about the film's commercial prospects, but it opened well at the Radio City Music Hall and went on to be a box-office success.[54]

The film was adapted from a best-selling book by Kathryn Hulme that reads like a novel but is closely based on the real life of Hulme's friend Marie Louise Habets. The story describes the life of Gabrielle van der Mal, renamed Sister Luke (Hepburn), beginning in the 1920s and ending during World War II. After a probationary period in Belgium and a first assignment in Italy, she leaves for the Congo as a nun and a trained nurse. A wonderful nurse, she struggles for years to become a perfect nun, a selfless servant of God. Unlike others in her order, she has a strongly independent nature. This is brought out by the brilliant but non-believing Dr. Fortunati (Peter Finch), who analyzes the conflicts disturbing his favorite nurse. After her return to Belgium, the Nazi occupation of Western Europe, and the death of her father at Nazi hands, Sister Luke asks to leave the order. In a sober but beautiful final sequence, she takes off her habit and her ring (as a "bride of Christ"), puts on the clothes she shed seventeen years before, and exits onto an ordinary Belgian street in wintry light.

Kim Novak as the down-to-earth Judy in VERTIGO.

American films have featured priests and nuns in a variety of contexts—consider, for example, Going My Way (1944), On the Waterfront (1954), and Heaven Knows, Mr. Allison (1957). The unique aspect of The Nun's Story is that it shows the spirituality of belonging to a religious order. In semi-documentary fashion, Zinnemann and his crew present the demanding regimen of the nuns—early prayers, long hours of work, the Grand Silence (no talking between evening and morning prayers). The nuns' habits and the halls and rooms of the convent create an extraordinary black and white pattern that dominates the film's first hour. The constant repetition and variation of black and white become the approximate equivalent of a Buddhist mandala—a limited pattern that leads via meditation to a transcendental experience. Zinnemann had hoped to shoot this part of the film in black and white but Jack Warner overruled him; however, it is hard to imagine that black and white photography would have improved the powerful first hour.

The film moves to the Congo in the second hour, an explosion of color after the ascetic convent scenes. Here Sister Luke's vocation is challenged in a variety of ways. Her pride is tested when she is assigned to the white rather than the black hospital (her dream is to minister to the African poor). She encounters the earthy and practical world-view of the Africans, who describe her as "young enough to bear children" and ask "Where is your husband, Mamma Luke?" Her relationship to Dr. Fortunati is difficult because there could be a romantic attachment between them, but her vows make this impossible. Sister Luke survives all these trials as well as a bout of tuberculosis (which Fortunati attributes to internal conflicts). However, when she returns to Belgium she renounces her vows.

Zinnemann's approach to The Nun's Story is respectful but also to some extent objective. Zinnemann, a Jew, sought out non-Catholics to play the film's most important roles (Audrey Hepburn was a Christian Scientist) because he wished to avoid "the emotional involvement a faithful believer would bring."[55] We can thus observe the seriousness and beauty of Catholic ritual while retaining independent judgment. It is not surprising that Catholic authorities were initially cool to such an enterprise, but a few Catholic institutions did eventually provide crucial help. A French order of nuns invited the lead actresses (Hepburn, Edith Evans, Peggy Ashcroft) to spend several days in a convent—each one in a different location. The filmmakers had lengthy discussions with many nuns, over a period of months. In Rome, where the convent set was built, the Dominican Order of nuns advised and assisted the production.[56]

The Nun's Story is both an atypical Hollywood film of the 1950s and evidence of the period's high level of achievement. Audrey Hepburn is magnificent as the strong-willed Sister Luke, and Peter Finch, Edith Evans, and the other cast members give her excellent support. Cinematographer Franz Planer crafts lovely images in both the convent and the Congo. Fred Zinnemann's intelligent yet unobtrusive directorial style meshes beautifully with the subject matter. The Nun's Story was nominated for eight Academy Awards but won none—1959 was the year of Ben-Hur. Nevertheless, this is a wondrous film.

Conclusion

If the early 1950s were marked by a strong and relatively stable genre system, by 1955 that system was beginning to break down. Original screen musicals were on the way out, though Jailhouse Rock and Gidget suggested the possibility of teen musicals. Film noir disappeared; Touch of Evil is sometimes described as film noir's last hurrah. A number of interesting Westerns were made, but they often added a layer of reflexivity or irony to traditional Western concerns. War was presented from a wide variety of perspectives, ranging from the cheerleading STRATEGIC AIR COMMAND to the antimilitary PATHS OF GLORY. Prestigious and high-quality melodramas seemed to be increasing. Filmmakers were scrambling to find material that would please the teenage audience. Some of the best films did not fit into any one genre.

Another sign of change was that people from outside the Hollywood system were getting involved in feature films. A "New York school" of filmmaking, including such figures as writer Paddy Chayefsky and actor/director John Cassavetes, brought a greater realism to the screen. Stanley Kubrick, another New Yorker, released his work through United Artists but was already making films that were closer to the European art film than to Hollywood norms.

Thematically, some films had moved from the blandness of the early 1950s to suggest new oppositional figures—the beatnik, the artist, the juvenile delinquent. In FUNNY FACE, Audrey Hepburn's beatnik character ultimately conforms by falling in love with the aging Fred Astaire. But SOME CAME RUNNING, BLACKBOARD JUNGLE, REBEL WITHOUT A CAUSE, and JAILHOUSE ROCK all express sympathy for the new rebels, and SHADOWS is presented entirely from the beatnik point-of-view. This broad but unfocused rebelliousness would become a crucial part of 1960s popular culture.

11

American Documentary in the 1950s

Jack C. Ellis

American documentary can be thought of as a child of the Depression that came of age during World War II. The war years marked a high point of achievement in this mode: more filmmakers made more nonfiction films for larger audiences than ever before. Given this vastly increased activity, with films being used in all sorts of new ways, it was assumed by most that the trend would continue onward and upward. And indeed production of nonfiction, nontheatrical film—educational, promotional, and industrial— did increase enormously in the postwar years. But there were severe cutbacks in key areas: in the amount of money available for the kinds of social documentary production that had existed earlier, in the number of documentary filmmakers employed, and in the quantity and quality of the documentaries produced.

Accompanying this contraction were losses in morale and leadership, and uncertainties about postwar purposes and subjects. Up to the end of the war, documentary had thrived on crisis and disaster, criticism and attack. Following the war, the great documentary causes of the 1930s (unemployment, rural poverty, conservation of land and water, housing, and urban planning) and early 1940s (the fight against fascism) were no longer relevant or popular.

Increased prosperity caused the subjects and rhetoric of the Depression to seem old-fashioned, even inapplicable. Increased conservatism and a Cold War caused the main lines of liberal and antifascist criticism to be suspect. Sponsors and filmmakers alike were unwilling to risk making a "statement" at a time when political positions were being subjected to investigation. Consequently, documentary subjects were essentially non-controversial; certainly they were not socioeconomic/political by and large, as earlier documentaries had been. Overall, they were for virtue and against vice.' Documentary had played theatrically with some of the big government films of the thirties, like THE PLOW THAT BROKE THE PLAINS and THE RIVER, and even more frequently during World War II. In the postwar years, without the drama of Depression or war, it no longer did. The newsreels ended, largely because of the new competition of television news. The innovative and highly respected filmed news magazine, *The March of Time,* ceased in 1951 after sixteen years of monthly issues, often appearing on movie house marquees above the feature. *Pathé News* stopped in 1956; *Paramount News* in 1957.

Virtually the only nonfiction films playing theatrically were the Walt Disney *True-Life Adventure* series, which began with the half-hour SEAL ISLAND in 1948 and ended with the last of the features, JUNGLE CAT, in 1960. SEAL ISLAND was followed in rapid succession by such shorts as BEAVER VALLEY, NATURE'S HALF ACRE, THE OLYMPIC ELK, and WATER BIRDS. In 1953 THE LIVING DESERT became the first feature in the series, its emphasis being on scorpions and on battles between desert creatures: tarantula and wasp, snake and kangaroo rat, hawk and rattlesnake, tortoise and tortoise. It was followed by THE VANISHING PRAIRIE in 1954. THE AFRICAN LION (1955) was shot over a period of many months by Alfred Milotte and his wife, Elma, on a plateau near Mount Kilimanjaro. About 100,000 feet of 16mm. film was edited and blown up to just over 6,000 feet of 35mm.[2]

It was generally agreed that the contents of these films were interesting and frequently absorbing; that the increasing technical proficiency, in the use of long lenses and the editing of images, was usually noteworthy and sometimes astonishing. What unfavorable reactions there were, were directed mostly at the intrusive commentary and music, particularly the anthropomorphizing of the animals, and injecting of humor in ways that distracted from rather than enhanced the inherent interest of the subject matter. Veteran British documentarian Basil Wright put the matter aptly in his observation that "in general the Disney technique tends to bring the desert to the audience instead of (as happens in films like the Soviet LIFE IN THE ARCTIC) bringing the audience to the desert. The difference is enormous, and should be noted."[3] That is, the series served nature up as entertainment rather than exploring its actuality.

Two alternatives to theatrical distribution and exhibition of documentary production became dominant during the postwar years. The first of these was the nontheatrical 16mm. field, which experienced an enormous increase in comparison with prewar years as a result of the extensive use and proven effectiveness of film by the military for all sorts of purposes—training, indoctrination, and records of battle, to name the principal categories. The second alternative was television, which emerged after the freeze in its development caused by the requirements of wartime.

In the nontheatrical field there were mainly two kinds of production: the sponsored film and the educational/classroom film. The sponsored film was by far the larger category. In this case an industrial or institutional sponsor paid for the production and the distribution, prints of the film being mailed back and forth to all sorts of audiences on a free-loan (return postage only) basis. Films selling goods or services directly were not documentaries as previously or generally conceived, of course. Documentary and documentary-type films had to work their way into the field of commercial sponsorship through films of promotion and public relations, and even then the demands of the sponsor frequently presented severe limitations on treatment of subjects being dealt with. The educational film earned back the cost of its production through sale and rental of 16mm. prints to (principally) secondary and elementary schools. Though a very large number of nontheatrical films were produced—as many as 10,000 a year—documentary as it had been conceived and practiced up to this time was not able to fit comfortably into either of the economic systems available.

As for sponsorship, the largest segment by far came from business and industry. *Film and Industry Directory* for 1951–1952 lists 1,084 individual film sponsors. Of these, about 750, or 69 per cent, represent business and industry. The others represent sponsors from the religious, educational, government, medical, and social science fields. These free films were used widely by schools but also as programs (or parts of programs) by clubs, churches, YMCAs, farm granges, labor unions, and the like. The distributor was paid a flat fee by the sponsor for every booking. As Erik Barnouw pointed out, "Many a sponsor, having spent $50,000 on the production of a short film, spent an additional $300,000 subsidizing its distribution over a period of years." Barnouw went on to say that "A 1956 brochure of Modern Talking Picture Service, specialists in business-subsidized distribution, reported that its films were being used by . . . 53,000 schools and colleges, 36,000 churches, 26,000 clubs and youth groups. Individual films—such as GREEN HARVEST, sponsored by Weyerhaeuser—received as many as 80,000 bookings."[4]

While businesses and industries became big sponsors for the first time, they also began justifying every dollar spent on a film in terms of increased sales and obvious good will. After the war, company public relations officers, given the extensive use of films and testing of their effectiveness during wartime, felt they knew very well what films should be like and could do. An increase in company profits rather than social well-being was clearly their goal. There existed virtually no industrial sponsorship of films in the general public interest, such as those sponsored by the oil and gas industries in Britain in the 1930s.

George Stoney, documentary maker, teacher, and social activist, has discussed the situation of documentarists like himself in relation to the nontheatrical field:

> In the years after the Second World War sponsorship by industry and institutions determined the nature of the bulk of the films circulated out of the 16mm. libraries. Many of these were politically "neutral" but many, including some of them made by those of us . . . tending toward the left politically, were far from neutral. Examples:
>
> Almost every child in the country saw *The American Road*, produced in 1953 by M.P.O. (a large industrial film production company) to celebrate the Ford Motor Company's fiftieth anniversary. It is as fullhearted a celebration of the free enterprise system as one could make and enshrines Henry Ford as a folk hero. . . . I directed the historical re-creations. Joe Marsh, a blacklisted Hollywood writer, did the script. Alex North, the famous Hollywood composer (then blacklisted also), did the music. We all needed the money.
>
> Almost every other documentary director active at the time has similar films to his credit. Sidney Meyers did Monsanto's *Decision for Chemistry* and lots more. Willard Van Dyke did a series for the National Rifle Association. Lee Bobker did an apology for strip mining for the Peabody Coal Company. Even Robert Flaherty's *Louisiana Story* is essentially a folksy apologia for Standard Oil's exploitation of wetlands that today we know should be protected as sources of fresh water.
>
> My hunch is that, however justified we thought we were in making these films, by doing so we lost the respect we once had as documentary filmmakers on the part of the intellectual and artistic community. . . . For, in truth, the disillusionments of the late 1940s and the intimidations of the McCarthy period that followed destroyed our political underpinnings.[5]

Nonprofit film sponsoring institutions allowed somewhat more leeway for statements closer to the filmmakers' own attitudes and interests, but there were many fewer of them. And even the large foundations and national associations were limited by growing pressure from the political Right in what they would spend their money on. This political reaction would come to be called "McCarthyism," in honor of the junior Senator from Wisconsin. Joseph McCarthy headed Senate committees—and used whatever other power he could muster—to ferret out Communists and Communist sympathizers in the Department of State and the army. At the time of his death he was about to start on the large private foundations, most notably the Ford Foundation, which he accused of sheltering "reds" and radicals.

As a result of this political climate, the foundations restricted their grants to existing and widely accepted institutions and activities. They did not sponsor films that might prove "controversial" or that might be made by filmmakers with a "past" (meaning involvement with organizations and causes on the Left). The national associations concerned with education and various health problems like tuberculosis, cancer, or heart disease, stuck to small, well-defined promotional films, or informational films used as "audio-visual aids."[6]

One maker of institutionally sponsored films who managed to do noteworthy work during this period was Charles Guggenheim, a young filmmaker from St. Louis. His A CITY DECIDES (1957), produced for the Fund for the Republic (established with Ford Foundation money), is one example. It was made in relation to the Supreme Court decision that struck down the "separate but equal" concept of educational opportunity. Regarding this documentary, Lewis Jacobs wrote:

> As with most integration films made during these years, it was aimed primarily at preparing the white community for integration. In this instance, it was school integration in St. Louis. The film was noteworthy in that it revealed, at least briefly, the fears of Negro parents in having their children attend school with white children. Production standards were high, but, typical of documentaries of the period, it used careful staging of non-actors with voice-over narration.[7]

A later film of Guggenheim's on the same subject, NINE FROM LITTLE ROCK (1963), made for the United States Information Agency (USIA), won an Academy Award as best documentary feature.

The USIA became the principal federal government sponsor of documentary film. Its forerunner, the Office of War Information, was eliminated altogether at the end of World War II. Postwar information operated out of the International Motion Picture Division (IMPD) of the Department of State, and was restricted to overseas dissemination. In 1951 information activities were greatly expanded, with the production of 400 two-reel films explaining the government's foreign policy and suggesting how the "average" American actually lived. The general idea was to celebrate those aspects of American culture thought to be most attractive abroad and, of course, attempt to counteract the portrayal of American life in many Hollywood movies as consisting mainly of sex and violence, frivolity and luxury. Soundtracks for these films were in as many as forty different languages and dialects. The State Department movies were shown in practically every country in the world; they were said to reach an audience of 10 million monthly. Every means available for showing the pictures was used, such as commercial theaters, schools, churches, and civic and fraternal organizations. Town halls or other gathering places were also rented. In addition, a vast network of 16mm. mobile projection units was operated by the IMPD to reach people in remote areas.

A large proportion of the State Department's films were a composite of stock footage and specially photographed material. The IMPD also obtained various types of pictures from large industrial concerns. All advertising was removed and they were equipped with new commentaries.[8] For example, an *Industry on Parade* series was organized with the cooperation of the National Association of Manufacturers.[9] Actual production was farmed out on a contract basis to companies producing commercial and industrial films and to various Hollywood studios.[10]

In 1953 this service was absorbed into the United States Information Agency, created to consolidate the foreign information activities in various departments and agencies of the federal government into one program. The International Motion Picture Service of the USIA operated through 135 offices in over fifty countries. Three hundred to five hundred different film titles became available through its offices abroad. They were said to reach audiences of approximately 500 million annually. Though there was some the-atrical and beginning television distribution, primary emphasis was placed on nonthe-atrical showings to community groups and organizations. As of September 1953, 214 mobile units were in operation. The vehicles generated their own electric power and carried projectors and screens.[11]

Reception of these films was evidently varied. Here is one view of the work of the traveling projectionists, written by Thomas M. Pryor, in the *New York Times* in 1951:

> Although the State Department is close-mouthed about details of its film oper-ations, reports from field representatives have made abundantly clear that this is by no means a striped-pants or kid-glove contest that is being waged between the press agents of democracy and communism. The men who carry our movies into isolated hamlets, where the people assemble in the village square and see the movies under the stars, must be prepared to face physical dangers.
>
> Reports, even from areas with sizable populations, have told of instances where the opposing forces have arranged demonstrations involving physical violence as well as costly vandalism. Theater screens have been destroyed by knife-wielding demonstrators and theater operators have been threatened with personal harm.[12]

A contrasting view was that the U.S. agents and their Soviet counterparts were rather like traveling salesmen, and anecdotes circulated about their friendly exchanges in the Middle East, for example, cautioning each other about bedbugs or overly hot spices in the town as one was leaving and the other entering. Also, the effectiveness of the U.S. propaganda approach was sometimes opened to question by reports back from the field. For instance, emphasis on our marvelous technology and high standard of living included, in one film, a kind of hymn to high-rise apartment buildings. An agent told of being approached, following a screening in Northern Greece, by an audience member who commiserated with him. It seems the local practice was that when children mar-ried, an addition was built onto the family house to accommodate the new couple, and eventually the same was done for their children, and so on, creating quite a sprawl of extended-family housing. "But we don't have it nearly so bad as you people do," the man said, "with everybody living on top of everybody else. Are they all family members?"[13]

Alas, we can know little about the nature of these films since they were prohibited by law from being distributed in the United States. This restriction grew out of the persistent and pervasive nervousness among legislators that their content would favor (serve as propaganda for) the party in power. For a film elegy to the slain President John F. Kennedy (YEARS OF LIGHTNING, DAY OF DRUMS, Bruce Herschensohn, 1968) Congress had to pass a special resolution to allow it to be released in the United States. Further, because of their primary political purpose, though some of those films may have had value as films, they were not reviewed or even described in foreign film journals.

In extreme contrast to USIA films were those produced by the Puerto Rican Division of Community Education. Its Cinema Unit was established in 1948 (with U.S. documentary veteran Willard Van Dyke assisting in setting it up). Rather than being made to be seen outside the country in an attempt to persuade others to accept certain political and economic tenets, its films were made by Puerto Ricans to improve the well-being and celebrate the culture of their own people. An outstanding filmmaker of this group was Amilcar Tirado. Of his films, the one that received most exposure in the United States (though still limited, of course, to venues frequented by critics and artists, like the Flaherty Seminar) was EL PUENTE (THE BRIDGE, 1950). In it an actual incident was reconstructed, though to some extent the film has the feel of a fiction feature. Faced with the hazard of periodic floods after heavy seasonal rain, villagers refuse to send their children to a school that lies on the other side of a river. A long, highly dramatic sequence during a storm in which a boy comes close to drowning moves the action toward solution. As a result, the community unites to build a bridge that allows the children to attend school in safety.[14]

In non-governmental filmmaking Louis de Rochemont's activities in the 1950s well represent some of the shifts occurring in the context for documentary. Founding head of *The March of Time* in the 1930s, producer of fact-based features at Twentieth Century–Fox in the 1940s (THE HOUSE ON 92ND STREET, 1945; 13 RUE MADELEINE, 1946; and BOOMERANG, 1947), he then founded Louis de Rochemont Associates. This firm made occasional semi-documentary theatrical features (LOST BOUNDARIES, 1949), sponsored films for advertising and public relations use, and classroom films. About de Rochemont's production in the last of these categories, one observer remarked that "The educational film, rescued from its stale, flat, and unprofitable past, is now assuming a more palatable form. . . . Producers of marked achievement, like Louis de Rochemont, include the educational film as a regular part of their output."[15]

De Rochemont's major educational project was *The Earth and Its Peoples*, a series of thirty-six films, each about twenty minutes in length, containing such titles as ESKIMO HUNTERS, HIGHLANDS OF THE ANDES, HORSEMEN OF THE PAMPAS, FARMERS OF INDIA, and ON MEDITERRANEAN SHORES. Reviewing one of these, entitled NOMADS OF THE JUNGLE (Malaya), British and Canadian documentarian Raymond Spottiswoode wrote:

> The first, and so far the outstanding film of the "Earth and Its People" series, is this brilliant interpretation by Victor Jurgens of a nomadic family which lives off the produce of the jungle without recourse to agriculture. The family's story is told in the first person by the son of the chief. . . . The film has been magnificently shot with a keen and humorous eye, and the sound track (recorded on location) captures the noises of the jungle and the camp. . . . Though aimed at primary-school grades, this film is so well made that any adult group would find it fascinating.[16]

On the other hand, Richard Griffith, curator of the Film Library (now Department) of the Museum of Modern Art, felt the series as a whole had been disappointing. While conceding that the films had been created by some of the top technicians in the industry—such as John Ferno, Victor Vicas, Jules Bucher, Richard Leacock, and Leo Seltzer—Griffith felt that the films in the series, "with a few exceptions like *Malaya*, tended to emerge as elementary visualisations-of-commentary little superior to the routine classroom film of weary familiarity."[17]

At Encyclopaedia Britannica Films (EBF), the largest of the educational film producer-distributors, there was a brief and limited experiment with more ambitious production, closer to the documentary tradition. Two films concerning city planning, both sponsored by the Twentieth Century Fund and produced by John Barnes, were released in 1953. THE BALTIMORE PLAN was about an interesting and evidently effective block-by-block rehabilitation of an inner-city neighborhood involving the residents as well as city employees. THE LIVING CITY, surveying city planning problems and solutions more generally, was nominated for an Academy Award. It was shot and directed by Haskell Wexler, who will appear later in this account. But it turned out that such prestige pictures "didn't pay the rent," as they said at EBF at the time, as did those fitting more neatly into K–12 curriculums.[18] One pleasant, modest example of the latter sort, with some documentary qualities, was PEOPLE ALONG THE MISSISSIPPI (1955), directed and shot by Gordon Weisenborn, an alumnus of the National Film Board of Canada.

Subjects

Films about the arts, and films that used the arts to deal with other subjects, became widely popular during the 1950s, perhaps owing to a general growth in art appreciation as prosperity and leisure increased. Sometimes they were shown as shorts in the "art theaters" specializing in European or otherwise non-Hollywood feature films, and in the film societies developing during these years. They were also shown in schools, libraries, and museums.

Many documentarians had been trained in or were attracted to the arts. Even Robert Flaherty shot material (in 1949) for a study of *Guernica*, Picasso's great painting about the Spanish Civil War, and was involved in the promotion and distribution of THE TITAN: STORY OF MICHELANGELO (a revised version, released in 1950, of a film made in Italy by the Swiss director Curt Oertel beween 1938 and 1940). The latter is a feature-length biography of Michelangelo using only contemporary architecture, interior settings, and artworks as visual material, with a highly mobile camera and editing style breathing simulated life into these static artifacts. This sort of historical compilation would become a prominent form of television documentary (to be discussed later in this chapter).[19]

Among other early films on art and artists were Erica Anderson's and Jerome Hill's GRANDMA MOSES (1950), Herbert Matter's WORLD OF CALDER (1950), Weegee's (Arthur Felig's) WEEGEE'S NEW YORK (1950), Jim Davis's JOHN MARIN (1951), Hans Namuth's and Paul Falkenberg's JACKSON POLLOCK (1951), and Lewis Jacobs's MATHEW BRADY: PHOTOGRAPHER OF AN ERA (1953).[20]

Two films on the arts were particularly interesting in that they were about jazz, which many would argue is, along with the movies themselves, America's most distinctive and important contribution to the arts. Roger Tilton's short, JAZZ DANCE (1954), a breakthrough visual-audio recording of young people jitterbugging, brilliantly shot by Richard

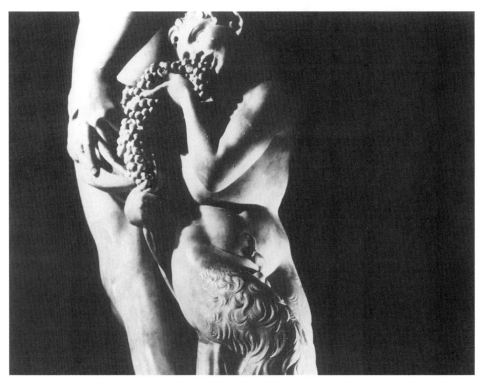

Detail of the Bacchus statue in THE TITAN: STORY OF MICHELANGELO *(1950), a documentary on the life of Michelangelo.*

Leacock, becomes a celebration of the extraordinary vigor and grace of the youthful response to this rhythmic music. The feeling of spontaneity is remarkable, requiring incredibly painstaking cutting and considerable ingenuity given the non-sync sound equipment available at the time.(The film preceded by a year the similar MOMMA DON'T ALLOW, by Karel Reisz and Tony Richardson, out of the British Free Cinema demi-movement.)

The second film about jazz, a feature, was JAZZ ON A SUMMER'S DAY (1959) by still photographer Bert Stern. Its popularity would inaugurate a documentary sub-genre of filmed pop music festivals, in this case the Newport Jazz Festival. Louis Armstrong opens the program and is featured. Among other star musicians included are Gerry Mulligan, George Shearing, Chuck Berry, Anita O'Day, Thelonius Monk, and Dinah Washington. It was one generally enthusiastic reviewer's opinion, however, that "the closing sequence of Mahalia Jackson's gospel singing is perhaps the most musically exciting part of *Jazz on a Summer's Day.*"[21]

More akin in subject and style to earlier documentary concerns than those dealing with arts and artists were documentaries about mental health. Yet there was a profound difference between them and previous documentaries: the mental health documentaries of the 1950s concentrated on persons in relation to themselves—their individual, interior lives—rather than on their relationships to society and to social problems.[22]

Spearheading production of films on psychological matters was the Mental Health Film Board (MHFB), initiated in 1949 by Alberta Altman (with the help of Irving

Jacoby, whom she later married). Its first picture, ANGRY BOY (1951), was written by Jacoby, directed by him and Alexander Hammid. It details the functioning of a guidance clinic in helping a child caught stealing to cope with the fears and hostilities that have affected his behavior. Like many of the films cited in this chapter, ANGRY BOY uses fictional techniques within a nonfictional framework—an aspect to be discussed later.

Irving Jacoby was also one of the founders of Affiliated Film Producers, Inc., in 1946 (with John Ferno, Henwar Rodakiewicz, and Willard Van Dyke). For most of its existence, Affiliated was run solely by Jacoby and Van Dyke. In addition to their own producing, writing, and/or directing of many of the noteworthy nontheatrical films of the 1950s, they employed some of the best documentarians of the day, among them (in addition to Hammid) Peter Glushanok, Sidney Meyers, Helen Grayson, Boris Kaufman, Aram Boyajian, Richard Leacock, and Francis Thompson.[23]

The second MHFB film, STEPS OF AGE (1951), deals with emotional problems of the aged. Produced for the Department of Mental Health, State of South Carolina, it was sponsored by the National Association for Mental Health. Helen Levitt was producer; Ben Maddow wrote and directed; Sidney Meyers edited. Its protagonist is a sixty-two-year-old woman living with her daughter's family after her husband's death. Her first-person voice-over narration, a sad reverie as she climbs a long flight of stairs up a hill to her daughter's house, reveals her feelings, provides the structure, and accommodates flashbacks of memories from her past. The third Mental Health Film Board film, ROOTS OF HAPPINESS (1953), directed by Henwar Rodakiewicz and made in Puerto Rico, examines the role of the father in family life. It also delineates the ways individual family members derive strength from the family unit.

Helen Levitt, well-known still photographer, came into motion-picture prominence as one of the persons responsible for the highly successful THE QUIET ONE (1948), about a troubled black youth in Harlem and his treatment at the Wiltwyck School in upper New York State. Ben Maddow had a long and distinguished career as writer of documentaries (VALLEY TOWN, 1940; NATIVE LAND, 1942) and features (INTRUDER IN THE DUST, 1949; THE ASPHALT JUNGLE, 1950; and THE SAVAGE EYE, 1960—the last to be discussed shortly). Sidney Meyers, former violinist with the Cincinnati Symphony Orchestra, entered documentary in the 1930s. He too was involved with THE QUIET ONE (as director, co-writer, and co-editor) and THE SAVAGE EYE. The daughter in STEPS OF AGE was played by Emma Agee, wife of James Agee, who wrote THE QUIET ONE's eloquent narration.

THE LONELY NIGHT (1954), made for the Mental Health Film Board by Affiliated Film, was written, directed, and produced by Jacoby. Like the other examples of mental health films discussed above, this is fiction based on common elements of many similar cases. Actress Marian Seldes plays the disturbed young protagonist. Through interviews with her psychoanalyst and flashbacks to her childhood we see the origins of her problems in her family relationships as she was growing up.

Documentaries on matters of general public health became much more plentiful and effective than before. One of these was perhaps the most accomplished and at the same time most extreme example of documentary drawing closer to fiction at this time. BENJY (1951), a short produced for the Orthopaedic Foundation of Los Angeles with the cooperation of Paramount Pictures, was directed by Fred Zinnemann and narrated by Henry Fonda. It used acted performances, studio lighting, and an opulent music score to tell an authentic story of a crippled boy.

The story begins when Benjy breaks his arm and is taken to the Los Angeles Orthopaedic Hospital. In the course of treatment a doctor discovers that he has a malformed spine. Upon inquiry it is learned that Benjy's parents have been trying to ignore their son's disability—pretending to themselves that Benjy is a physically normal boy. The film then concerns itself with the doctors' efforts to correct Benjy's spine. It received the Academy Award for documentary.

The most skillful and dedicated practitioner in the field of public health films was George Stoney, but the first film he directed, PALMOUR STREET (1950), was about mental health. Produced for the Georgia State Department of Health, it was part of a rather large-scale film program aimed at the rural and small-town African American population.

Among noteworthy Stoney films about health problems other than mental health is STILL GOING PLACES (1956), about the care and treatment of the aged. It shows in detail the practical steps that can be taken to help old people lead active lives. It was produced by the Center for Mass Communication, a division of Columbia University Press, with a grant from the pharmaceutical firm Charles Pfizer and Co. The Home for Aged and Infirm Hebrews of New York cooperated in the production, and its residents and staff comprise the "cast."

Best known of Stoney's films of the 1950s, however, is unquestionably ALL MY BABIES (1952). It began as an instructional film sponsored by the Georgia State Department of Health to demonstrate to midwives correct sanitary procedures to use in their deliveries. Stoney, himself a Southerner, became sympathetically involved with the rural black people the film is about and for. Though it is a medical film and contains all the technical information required—some 118 points—it developed a length, a scope, and an emotional intensity that lift it into the realm of art. Its protagonist, Miss Mary, is not only a consummately skillful midwife, she is a magnificent person, commanding affection and respect. The "Aunt Jemima" stereotype she might seem to represent is exploded before our eyes. Because Miss Mary's skill in delivering babies was carefully recorded, the film was shown for years in medical schools. The warm and wonderful feelings it contains—for birth, for people, for life—surely did the student doctors no harm.[24]

Films about race relations, especially between blacks and whites—referred to collectively as "brotherhood films"—were much in evidence at this time. The seminal event regarding those relations was the Supreme Court desegregation decision of May 1954.

The CBS-TV *See It Now* series, to be discussed shortly, was quick to pick up this topic. Its "Segregation in Schools," made the week following the decision, reported on reactions in two Southern towns—Natchitoches, Louisiana, and Gastonia, North Carolina. It was followed by "Clinton and the Law," depicting the problems and the ways citizens reacted when the high school in Clinton, Tennessee, attempted to admit black students.

ALL THE WAY HOME (1958), directed by Lee Bobker from a script by Muriel Rukeyser, examines the response in an all-white neighborhood when a homeowner decides to sell his house to a black family. Labor unions and churches sponsored numbers of films to promote racial understanding; examples are the feature-length BURDEN OF TRUTH (1957), from United Steel Workers, and NO MAN IS AN ISLAND (1959), originally produced for the religious television program *Look Up and Live*.[25]

In the 1950s ethnographic films began to appear in new quality and quantity. (The last noteworthy practitioners had been Gregory Bateson and Margaret Mead in Bali in the 1930s.) Beginnings of this resurgency occurred in 1951 with expeditions by the Laurence K. Marshall family to the region of the Bushmen of the Kalahari Desert in

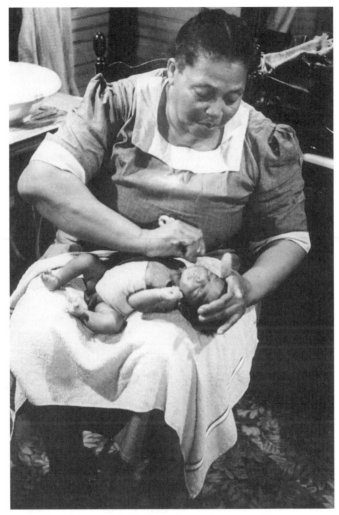

Miss Mary (Mrs. Mary Coley) and one of her babies in ALL MY BABIES (1952), directed by George Stoney. Courtesy of Robert Galbraith, photographer.

Buchanaland, South Africa. Marshall was a retired businessman and his son John's first film played a major role in the development of the ethnographic film. By 1954 John Marshall had shot hundreds of thousands of feet of film on the Bushmen. When the Marshalls contacted the Peabody Museum of Harvard University, the value of this footage was recognized and a Film Study Center was established. Robert Gardner became its director. Gardner, who had a solid background as both filmmaker and ethnographer, accompanied the Marshalls to the Kalahari in 1955, and then helped John create THE HUNTERS out of the assembled footage. It was released in 1958.[26]

The film presents life in this bitter land as a constant struggle against the hot, dry climate and an unyielding soil. The women dig all day with sticks for roots to eat. The men fashion their bows and arrows, and distill the arrow poison for hunting. The film then follows four individuals through a thirteen-day hunt for meat that ends in the killing of a giraffe.[27] THE HUNTERS became the most outstanding and influential ethnographic film of the decade,[28] preparing the way for the future work of Gardner, Timothy Asch, David and Judith MacDougall, and others. It received the 1958 Flaherty Award, an appropriate prize since its use of the drama of man-against-nature eking out a precarious existence evokes memories of Robert Flaherty's pioneering documentary NANOOK OF THE NORTH (1922) and his acclaimed MAN OF ARAN (1934). Hugh Gray, at the 1959 Flaherty Seminar, supplemented that observation by suggesting that THE HUNTERS uses "the scientist's method and the poet's vision."[29]

Forms

As for their formal aspects, documentaries of the fifties were freer and more varied in their techniques than earlier documentaries had been. More nonactuality was employed—fictional and dramatic elements—and structurally they tended to be organized as narrative or as drama. There was more location sound, especially sync sound. The latter was made possible by the availability of magnetic tape, which made recording outside the studio much more practicable than it had been with the optical system. The narrative structures and sync dialogue coincided with the tendency of these fifties documentaries to center more on individuals than had those of the thirties and forties.

ON THE BOWERY (1956) followed the models and demonstrated viability of a narrative/dramatic approach evident in LOUISIANA STORY and THE QUIET ONE (both 1948). It was Lionel Rogosin's first film, financed with his own money. (His father was a wealthy industrialist.) Rogosin conceived of the idea of a documentary film over several years investigating New York City's infamous skid row. He produced and directed it. It was written by Mark Sufrin, photographed by Richard Bagley (who had earlier photographed THE QUIET ONE), and edited by Carl Lerner. It was made for the theaters and received some theatrical distribution before going on to nontheatrical distribution.

ON THE BOWERY was an extraordinary breakthrough in a number of ways. Its subject matter had been used often enough in conventional fiction features—the ravages of alcohol on human life, the degradation of a derelict existence. What was here unusual was the taking of camera (mostly a 35mm. Arriflex with a 400' magazine) and tape recorder into the actual jungle of metropolitan life, allowing a much closer look at this particular reality than audiences were used to. This film was different, too, from conventional documentaries in that it did use a slight story and developed, to a limited degree, characters who interact with each other. Three main characters are followed; one of them in particular, an ex-lawyer who had been unable to cope with the pressures of his previous life, becomes the basis of the narrative structure.

The problems of making this kind of film, from the production standpoint, are, of course, prodigious—in terms of both human problems and technical problems. Not only are the filmmakers working in a situation that demands maximum tact and care, innumerable clearances, and cooperation which may not be volunteered, they must lead nonactors through performances, get them to deliver lines, to behave as if a camera weren't there. At the time, this film seemed to many filmmakers and critics to open up a whole new production method and range of subject matter.

Rogosin's next film, COME BACK, AFRICA (1959), which he produced, directed, and co-wrote, has an increased proportion of fictional elements and a strong polemical thrust. (ON THE BOWERY is markedly non-judgmental about the situation it deals with.) COME BACK, AFRICA is a drama of racial conflict filmed in and around Johannesburg. (The title of the film derives from the national anthem of the African Freedom movement, "Mavibuye Afrika.")

Preparation and filming took eighteen months of searching for the theme, the locations, and the cast among Africans; photographing the gold mines, the wandering street musicians, the African suburbs of Sophiatown; and concealing from the authorities the true nature of the film's social content. (Rogosin was ostensibly making a musical travelogue.) The person who plays the film's central character, a Zulu named Zachariah, was found at a railroad station. He turned out to have almost the same background as was called for in the script. Miriam Makeba, African singing star, is featured. Rogosin said of the performances that these non-actors spoke their lines "naturally" from a story treatment.

Rogosin bought a movie theater, the Bleecker Street Cinema in Greenwich Village, for the New York premiere of COME BACK, AFRICA. (He continued to operate the theater as an "art house" afterwards.) Despite good attendance there, prizes at festivals abroad, and widespread, excellent reviews in the press, he was unable to obtain nationwide distribution.[30] Like ON THE BOWERY, COME BACK, AFRICA had healthy and sustained nontheatrical distribution.

The most experimental and provocative of these fifties story-documentaries was THE SAVAGE EYE (1959) which, appearing at the end of the decade, was an anomaly in many ways. Made mostly by people who had been on the political Left, it attempted to combine a scathing view of current social ills and disorders with the new emphasis on individuals, narrative, and characterization. The initiator of THE SAVAGE EYE was Joseph Strick, who had been a cameraman with the U.S. Army Air Force during World War II. After the war he worked with Irving Lerner, jack-of-all-film-crafts, to learn how to make movies. Together they created the charming short MUSCLE BEACH (1948). Strick became a wealthy businessman, owning a controlling interest in several large electronic corporations, and was able to form a new collaboration that led to THE SAVAGE EYE.

The film is credited as being "by" Ben Maddow, Sidney Meyers, and Joseph Strick. Cinematographers are listed as Jack Couffer, Helen Levitt, and Haskell Wexler. Wexler would subsequently become a highly valued Hollywood cameraman (with Academy Awards for WHO'S AFRAID OF VIRGINIA WOOLF, 1966, and BOUND FOR GLORY, 1976); and also sometime director (MEDIUM COOL, 1969). THE SAVAGE EYE was Wexler's first feature. Two others are listed as "contributing photographers," but it was said that Strick was responsible for about half the camera work, though he took no cinematography credit.[31] Music was by Leonard Rosenman. Irving Lerner is credited as technical consultant. The film was worked on part-time for four or five years, mostly on weekends.

The visuals are made up largely of unstaged scenes of the seamier side of Los Angeles—sleazy bars, beauty and massage parlors, a wrestling match, traffic jams, animal cemeteries, addicts and transvestites, stripteasers, and faith healers. All this is seen through the eyes of a just-divorced, alienated, and angry woman (played by Barbara Baxley)—hers is "the savage eye." As she wanders through these urban settings she carries on a duologue with a subjective interlocutor, "the poet" (voice of Gary Merrill), who introduces himself to her as her "vile dreamer, conscience, ghost." (Maddow had first tried this sort of device much earlier in Van Dyke's VALLEY TOWN, released in 1940.)

Initially THE SAVAGE EYE received a great deal of attention, including festival awards. At the Edinburgh International Film Festival, instead of being shown once, as scheduled, it had to be shown eight times.[32] The review of it in the *New York Post* concluded: "*The Savage Eye* is all of one piece, masterfully, artfully wrought by its three makers, a work that must be recognized as great no matter how unlikable, a film that will be seen for many a year no matter who rejects it now."[33] The contrary proved to be the case. It soon fell into virtual obscurity, remembered only as a precursor of direct cinema, which was about to begin. Today we are more likely to agree with another critical reaction, that of Benjamin T. Jackson in a 1960 review of the film:

> The fragments of documentary film in themselves are bitterly sure-footed. They show us clearly the irresolute and pernicious side of modern American life. Personally, I would like very much to see this footage combined into another form, without the contrived story and dialogue.[34]

Along with the connections forged between documentary and fiction features in the 1950s was a tendency towards avant-garde experimentation. Some filmmakers moved away from traditional social documentary altogether into a freewheeling use of actuality footage as material for personal artistic expression.

Frank Stauffacher, a young San Franciscan, made two films of the latter sort. NOTES ON THE PORT OF ST. FRANCIS (1952) takes its title and its commentary, read by Vincent Price, from a travel essay by Robert Louis Stevenson written in 1882. This is, of course, reminiscent of Basil Wright's use of a seventeenth-century Scottish traveler's words in THE SONG OF CEYLON (1934). Stauffacher's film calls to mind two earlier "city symphony" films as well: Alberto Cavalcanti's *Rien que les heures* (1926) and Walther Ruttmann's BERLIN: SYMPHONY OF A GREAT CITY (1927), which appear in histories of both the documentary and the avant-garde. Like avant-gardists, Stauffacher was the sole creator of his films: producer, cinematographer, editor.

NOTES ON THE PORT OF ST. FRANCIS begins with waves crashing on a rocky coast and moves to earlier artwork and still photographs of San Francisco intermingled. The musical accompaniment is eighteenth-century Baroque and then nineteenth-century Romantic. The film is much freer and more personal in the choice of images and their ordering than a conventional travelogue, certainly. It is more an artist's view, or a personal essayist's (like Stevenson's)—idiosyncratic, with aspects only of the city. Even the images themselves are toyed with: lots of moving camera, and the use of long lenses, trucking, and tilting up.

SAUSALITO (1953) looks even more like an experimental film of the time. Its title is the name of the suburb on the shore of San Francisco Bay where Stauffacher lived. It offers impressions of this particular locale, from inside his own house out to the street and neighboring houses—a kind of intimate sketchbook. Its subject matter is documentary, real and everyday sights and sounds, but its style and its manner of combining miscellaneous ambient images and sounds is highly impressionistic and subjective, in the manner of imagist poetry. (Or, come to think of it, Grierson's and Cavalcanti's GRANTON TRAWLER of 1934.)

Not surprisingly, among these new city symphonies New York predominated. IN THE STREET, produced by Helen Levitt, Janice Loeb, and James Agee, consists of silent black and white footage shot in "Spanish Harlem" in the late 1940s. The shots are candid, with people unaware of the camera for the most part, and much of it was intended for but not used in THE QUIET ONE. Not released until 1952, it was shown only to small closed groups for study purposes, at least partly because clearances from the people photographed were not obtained, nor obtainable probably, given the method used. It looks ahead to direct cinema, the technology and technique for which would start to develop in the 1950s.

IN THE STREET is extraordinary in at least two ways: for the haunting individual images of children and old people, the main daytime inhabitants of Harlem's streets; and for the editing, which is following feeling rather than argument or plot. The assemblage seems on the one hand to be formless and, on the other, to have a dozen patterns which account for the exactly right arrangement and duration of each shot.

THIRD AVENUE EL was intended as a tribute to that about-to-become-defunct institution. It was made in color in 1955 with loving care by Carter Davidson, a cameraman by profession. This, too, is a film that is documentary in subject matter and impressionistic in style. Here the impressions are organized around and conditioned by perceptions of representative passengers: a photographer, a child, a drunk, young lovers. As accompaniment there is a harpsichord concerto played by Wanda Landowska, giving the whole a formal elegance and rhythm seldom associated with urban life in the twentieth century.

Francis Thompson's N.Y., N.Y. (1957), though made by a respected documentary cinematographer and director, is the film in this group most clearly working against usual expectations for a documentary. It presents the city as if it were being reflected in funhouse mirrors—a "kaleidoscopic impression of the changing moods of New York as a single day sweeps over it," Arthur Knight wrote. He went on to explain that, "here the interest is primarily in form and design. People, when they appear at all, are barely incidental. The buildings in which, and against which, they move become the raw material for myriad patterns made possible by special lenses, prisms, and distort mirrors known only to Mr. Thompson. They whirl, they blur, they stretch."

Thompson spent almost ten years in the creation of this fifteen-minute film, working on it in intervals between (and sometimes during) his commercial assignments.[35] With Alexander Hammid, he went on to apply similar techniques in TO BE ALIVE!, a multiscreen project launched at the 1964 New York World's Fair.

In the same review as N.Y., N.Y., Knight deals with Hilary Harris's five-minute HIGHWAY (1958). The images are mostly shot from a car (or cars) moving fast on the highways and expressways that encircle and move into New York City. Arthur Knight wrote of it, in part, "Cut to a jazz score provided by David Hollister, the effect is perhaps less a 'city symphony' than a 'city jam session'. . . . It is the assembly that brings the whole to life, the editing rhythms and the synchronization of the right visual to the right sound."

Among the experimental documentary filmmakers of the fifties, Shirley Clarke was the most solid and sustained in her achievement. In fact, of her films and videos, except for two fiction features shot in documentary style, all were either experimental or documentary with experimental inflections.

Clarke came to film from a career as a dancer largely, she said, because of the bad dance films she had seen. In her first films she moved quickly from using the camera primarily as a means of recording dance performances to using the techniques of cinematography, editing, and laboratory processes to create dances that never could exist on the concert stage, or in the real world, for that matter—film dances rather than dance films. From film dances, like A MOMENT IN LOVE (1956), it was a mere grand jeté to looking at nonhuman aspects of the world as if they were capable of assuming dance-like movement.

BRIDGES-GO-ROUND (1958) approaches the bridges around Manhattan Island as you would see them if you sailed under them on one of the boat excursion tours, or drove over them on your way into the city. This real (that is to say, documentary) experience is

Superimposition from Shirley Clarke's BRIDGES-GO-ROUND (1958).

infused with a great deal of style, wit, and sense of image and movement that this partic-ular filmmaker brought to film. Henry Breitrose wrote of the film:

> In actuality, the bridges become plastic materials for a highly abstract sub-jective study in structures and movements. . . . They are manipulated in a complex but extremely arresting way: the great steel girders, the taut cables, the towers and railings and roadways and abutments seem almost to dance. An exciting sense of color works with Mrs. Clarke's lively rhythmic sense.[36]

Though SKYSCRAPER (1959) credits list Shirley Clarke, Willard Van Dyke, and Irving Jacoby as producers, Van Dyke, in an interview, said of it: "First of all, let me say straight out that that's Shirley Clarke's film basically."[37] The project began when Affiliated Film Producers lined up John Tishman, builder of 666 Fifth Avenue (which would be named The Tishman Building), to sponsor a film about its construction. Footage of the destruc-tion of the old building through the construction of the new had been shot over a period of about eighteen months.

When Van Dyke ended his association with Affiliated at that time, he asked Clarke to take over the editing of the film, which really meant to create it: arrive at a conception, develop a script with a writer, supervise additional shooting.[38] The idea had been, according to Clarke, to follow the model of Steiner's and Van Dyke's celebrated THE CITY (1939). The height, the size, the significance of this massive piece of contemporary architecture would be emphasized by florid commentary.[39] Instead, Clarke created a Broadway musical. The film begins with a sort of chorus line opening; as a "hero" steps forth, an off-screen song begins "My Manhattan, lovely isle; in the twilight wears a smile." The final, romantic ending scene, in color (all of the construction footage had been in black and white), is reminiscent of ON THE TOWN (1949) or GUYS AND DOLLS (1955). (It is interesting to note that Clarke thought 666 Fifth Avenue ugly, so the only time we see a full image of it is the final shot of the lighted building taken at night from a great distance.)[40] The original score was composed by Teo Macero and sung by Gene Mumford. The musical narration is supplemented with off-screen dialogue by simulated construction workers. SKYSCRAPER won lots of festival prizes and was nominated for an Oscar. It was a fitting climax to this sort of experimental and/or poetic documentary which couldn't find a place on television and would be forced out by the pervasive direct cinema technique just beginning.

Television

During the 1950s television became the most important economic base for production and means of distribution/exhibition for documentary, adapting older forms and subjects and adding new ones. In 1946 television had been removed from the wartime freeze; in 1948 big-time TV was born. By 1950 a network out of New York linked the major cities; 100 stations telecast to four million sets. In 1951 coaxial cable and microwave relay connected the country as a whole, coast to coast.

In that 1951–1952 season on CBS-TV, Edward R. Murrow and Fred W. Friendly began their *See It Now* series, which grew out of their radio series *Hear It Now*. The 1952–1953 season on NBC-TV contained *Victory at Sea*, produced by historian Henry Salomon Jr., edited by Isaac Kleinerman, with a score by Richard Rodgers. Consisting of twenty-six half-hour films about U.S. naval warfare in World War II, it was compiled from over six million feet of combat footage. These two highly successful and seminal programs inaugurated the prevailing documentary types of the 1950s: the news documentary and the compilation documentary. One examined aspects of current concerns, the other events and personages of the past.

Victory at Sea (1952–1953), *produced by Henry Salomon Jr. for NBC.*

While dramatic and other entertainment programs shown on television came from outside producing agencies, production of documentaries was carried on primarily by the networks and local stations themselves. Both the National Broadcasting Company (NBC) and the Columbia Broadcasting System (CBS) established units for that purpose, with personnel initially drawn largely from the ranks of nontheatrical documentarians. Subsequently, television documentary makers were almost without exception journalists, with a background in radio or still photography. The main function of these units was the creation of special programs, frequently unsponsored, presented as prestige or public-service features. American Broadcasting Corporation (ABC) documentary production was later and weaker, with a news emphasis.

In 1953 what is now the Public Broadcasting Service (PBS) began as National Educational Television (NET). This noncommercial network, supported by funds from the federal government, initiated and distributed substantial quantities of documentaries and public affairs material. Its budgets tended to be smaller than those of the commercial networks, but it made up for that in part by importing many significant documentary programs from abroad.

See It Now, though a sort of news magazine of feature stories in *The March of Time* tradition, had a much quieter and more intimate tone suitable to the living room. Produced by Murrow and Friendly, it featured Murrow as the on-screen host and commentator. At first *See It Now*, like *The March of Time* and the present-day *60 Minutes*, presented several different stories in each half-hour program. In 1953 the format changed to include only one story a week. Among the *See It Now* programs most often cited are "Christmas in Korea" (1953), made during the Korean War; the several programs dealing with McCarthyism, including one in 1954 in which Senator McCarthy was afforded the opportunity to reply to what had been raised in the earlier programs (consistent with an American broadcasting concept called "the fairness doctrine"); and a visit with nuclear physicist J. Robert Oppenheimer (1955). A look at one of its more typical programs may give some sense of its distinctiveness.

"Argument in Indianapolis" (1953) presents opposing factions in that city when the American Civil Liberties Union, attempting to form a local chapter, is opposed by the American Legion post. One of the extraordinary things about this program is its balance in handling a controversial subject—which was necessary, no doubt, for it to be telecast at all. Depending on your sympathies, the Legion members become fascist monsters or upholders of true Americanism; the ACLU group, pleasant, sensitive intellectuals or dangerous radicals and subversives. At any rate the faces, speech, and manner of the protagonists are caught more or less candidly. A remarkable study is offered of diverse ideologies and personalities that exist in uneasy relationship to each other within this republic.

In 1955, when the Aluminum Company of America (Alcoa) withdrew its sponsorship, *See It Now* changed from regularly scheduled weekly half-hours to hour-long programs appearing at intervals—"specials," in effect. Media critic Gilbert Seldes quipped that it had become "See It Now—and Then." In 1958 *See It Now* was terminated, to be replaced in 1959 by occasional "CBS Reports."

NBC's response to *See It Now* was the quite different *Project XX* series, which began in 1954. It grew out of the success of *Victory at Sea*, and its production unit included many of the same creative personnel. Rather than a weekly series, however, *Project XX* offered occasional hour-long specials. Like *Victory at Sea*, its programs were compilation films devoted to re-creating aspects of the history of that century (hence XX) using existing footage—newsreel, documentary, and feature—and occasional reenactments.

Edward R. Murrow was the on-air talent and co-producer of the CBS documentary series See It Now.

Among the *Project XX* specials in the fifties that attracted most attention were "Nightmare in Red" (1955), which chronicled the rise of Soviet Communism, and "The Twisted Cross" (1956), which did the same for German Nazism.

The *Twentieth Century* weekly series, which began on CBS in 1957, was produced by Burton Benjamin and Isaac Kleinerman, and sponsored by the Prudential Insurance Company. Its programs were mostly half-hour, though a few were hour-long. At first the series was devoted entirely to compilations. The format of "From Kaiser to Fuehrer" (1959) is typical. Host Walter Cronkite introduces the program then retreats off-screen to voice-over commentary. Clips from German films of the twenties are its main basis. In addition to newsreels, extensive use is made of the documentary *Berlin: Symphony of a Great City* and the fictional feature *Variety*. The cutting pace is rapid and the editing skillful; a full orchestral score contributes much to continuity and dramatic effect.

The advantage of television as a new source of financing and distribution/exhibition for documentary, in comparison with the theatrical and nontheatrical channels, can be summed up easily. The leading attraction was the large demand for documentaries on television. It became a source of sustained sponsorship greater than any ever known, and it returned the cost of production much more quickly than theatrical or nontheatrical distribution. It also reached the large audience simultaneously—forty million individuals and small groups watching on a Thursday night, say, in their homes—rather than audiences in theaters, students in classrooms, members in club rooms and grange halls, and so on over the course of several years.

Walter Cronkite, host of the CBS documentary series Twentieth Century, *produced by Burton Benjamin and Isaac Kleinerman.*

The limitations of television for distribution-exhibition of documentaries (and other forms of art and entertainment) included its technological crudities. The image on the tube had much poorer definition—that is, it was lacking in sharpness and detail—than the projected 35mm. or even 16mm. images. Television sound had a limited dynamic range (it lacked high and low frequencies) and the three-inch speaker standard on TV sets allowed for little audio richness.

Also, TV had other kinds of limitation. Those watching television tended to be more heterogeneous and less attentive than those in theatrical and nontheatrical settings. Audiences in theaters had chosen the movie they were watching through the impression made by its promotion, the reviews it had received, and by the opinions of friends and neighbors who had already seen it. Nontheatrical audiences were generally engaged in some common undertaking involving the viewing and discussion of films. Less advance information was available to television audiences and a particular program was usually seen as one part in a flow of diverse television programming. Furthermore, there were the distractions of the television-viewing situation—for example, ringing telephones or discussion of homework in an adjoining room. And, of course, there were the commercial breaks within the television programs themselves.

Frequently in television documentaries the commentator was a star and appeared on camera. (In theatrical and nontheatrical productions the commentator was usually anonymous and unobtrusive; one heard his voice over the images and he never appeared on screen. At most he added a bit of emotional coloring.) The star commentators—Ed

Murrow, Walter Cronkite, Chet Huntley, and others—fed into and emphasized the quality of live-ness. The audience tuned in to see what Ed was offering on Friday night. He talked directly to viewers from the control room, his reporters available to come in over the monitors as he called on them. (Actually, given the technology available at the time, they were filmed beforehand with the film flown to New York, processed in the lab, and edited before being aired.) The scenes in *See It Now* were shot more as if they were being captured live and undirected than they were in non-television documentaries. And perhaps out of respect for the viewers, the commentator's own point of view in what was said and in what was chosen to show was generally withheld or balanced—or maybe the commentator was just ambivalent, and therefore, to the viewer, ambiguous.

In documentaries made for television there was an increased use of sync sound, especially talk; interviews were used much more extensively than in theatrical or nontheatrical documentaries. The sound track carried at least as much content as the visual track and the visuals tended to be less rich and interesting than in non-television documentaries. As a result of this balance between words and images, creative control of television documentaries usually was exerted by the producers, writers, and commentators rather than by directors.

Though they reached many people more quickly, in the series context and in the daily flow of television programming it was difficult for particular documentaries to offer the kind of aesthetic experience or to achieve the social impact on those they did reach that some documentaries shown in theaters and to nontheatrical audiences may have done. But perhaps, as was argued at the time by Lyman Bryson,[41] the mass media could not do very much about educating people soundly or altering their opinions on the subjects with which they dealt. Bryson thought the significance of the media in relation to their effects on social attitudes and behavior was essentially to call public attention to matters that seemed important to the media creators. Television became virtually *the* mass medium, certainly as far as documentary was concerned. It was the best qualified of any of the media of art and communication devised up to that time to quickly call large numbers of people's attention to various subjects. During the 1950s it established its ability to do just that—and sometimes documentaries made for television did it superbly.[42]

12

"Unquiet Years": Experimental Cinema in the 1950s

GREG S. FALLER

Often considered merely a transitional phase between the excitement of the avant-garde cinema of the 1940s and the alternative film culture of the 1960s, the 1950s instead deserves recognition as a crucial period in the development of a vital American experimental cinema. During the 1950s, fledgling film societies and exhibitions grew into viable organizations and venues; individual and isolated artists congregated into collective support systems; critical publications (and critics) gained a wider audience and cultural acceptance; and new stylistic approaches challenged recognized formats and ideas. In short, the 1950s saw the establishment of a fully viable experimental film "art world."

The Art World of Experimental Cinema

In his 1982 book, *Art Worlds*, sociologist Howard Becker defined an "art world" as a "*network* of people whose *cooperative activity*, organized via their joint knowledge of conventional means of doing things, produces [a popularly recognized] kind of art work."[1] Becker explored a sociology of art that de-emphasized artists and their art and stressed the complex way in which all members of the art world cooperate. He wanted to understand how these *cooperative networks* allow art to be produced and consumed. Becker also addressed issues of exhibition, critical and popular reception, and economics. As he succinctly summarized, "fully developed art worlds . . . provide distribution systems which integrate artists into their society's economy, bringing art works to publics which appreciate them and will pay enough so that the work can proceed."[2]

Art worlds must also share, by necessity, an aesthetic model. However, Becker noted that "when an established aesthetic theory does not provide a logical and defensible legitimation of what artists are doing, and more importantly, what other institutions of the art world—especially distribution organizations and audiences—accept as art . . . professional aestheticians will provide the required new rationale."[3] It is exactly this role of "professional aesthetician" that three central filmmaker-theoreticians, Amos Vogel, Maya Deren, and Jonas Mekas played, mounting during the 1950s a logical and defensible critical theory of experimental cinema. They became, according to Becker, the most specialized producers of the art world—philosophers. These three "philosophers" and their film societies, writings, and organizational efforts solidified a "cooperative network" of experimental production, distribution, exhibition, and reception that continues to this day.

Bracketing the decade in terms of exhibition and distribution were Cinema 16 and the Film-Makers Cooperative on the East Coast and the Art in Cinema series and Canyon Cinema on the West Coast. Each group succeeded in further broadening the audience for experimental films and generating more institutional support for independent filmmakers: from screenings in galleries and museums, to government grants and foundation awards, to curricula and professional associations such as the University Film and Video Association. The oldest academic media association in the United States, UFVA began in 1946 to "provide a means of communication among university production people"[4] and to champion the use of film in college education. As president of the organization Don Williams stated in 1950: "The universities can be, and we think should be, a source of films that are limited by neither the Hollywood nor the commercial traditions. We believe that documentary, educational, and experimental films can and should be used to implement the three functions of a university—teaching, service, and research."[5] In addition, the *Journal* of the UFVA began in 1948 and the *Digest* of the UFVA began in 1955.

These various organizations emerged from a steadily growing avant-garde film community initiated during the 1920s with the Amateur Cinema League, the Cinema Guild, Artkino, and the "Little Theatre" movement,[6] and during the 1930s with the Workers Film and Photo League, Nykino, the Film Forum, Frontier Films, and the formation of the Museum of Modern Art's Film Library. In his discussion of experimental cinema's postwar "revival," film historian Lewis Jacobs cited MOMA's Film Library as an important circulation effort.

The Museum's collection of pictures and its program notes on the history, art, and traditions of cinema went to hundreds of colleges, universities, museums, film-appreciation groups, and study groups. These widespread exhibitions, as well as the Museum of Modern Art's own showings in its theater in New York City, exerted a major influence in preparing the way for broader appreciation and production of experimental films.[7]

In 1947, Frank Stauffacher and Richard Foster opened an exhibit of avant-garde films under the banner "Art in Cinema." Housed at the San Francisco Museum of Art, the series became so popular that it ran as a film society with screenings, critical program notes, and post-screening discussions until 1951. These program notes, assembled as *Art in Cinema: A Symposium of Avant-Garde Film* (1947), became one of the first anthologies of experimental film criticism published. Stauffacher and Foster's strategic blend of "criticism/screening/discussion" generated what Lauren Rabinovitz described as a "prototype of experimental cinema canon formation and aesthetics"[8] that would become standardized during the 1950s.

The "Art in Cinema" series served as a venue and a catalyst to a growing number of West Coast filmmakers who envisioned filmmaking as personal expression and in opposition to Hollywood conventions.[9] Steadily growing and active during the 1950s, this loose collective of film artists coalesced, by 1961, into an informal exhibition venue, the San Francisco Cinematheque. To help support the cinematheque's screenings of avant-garde films, Canyon Cinema (so named because it began in the Canyon, California, backyard of pioneering experimental filmmaker Bruce Baillie) emerged as a non-profit distribution cooperative. By the mid-1960s, both organizations created a significant support network and an audience for local Bay Area filmmakers. The San Francisco Cinematheque still operates today and Canyon Cinema is now, according to its executive director, Dominic Angerame, "one of the principal distribution sources for independent cinema."[10]

In New York City, Amos and Marcia Vogel began Cinema 16 in 1947 employing the same "criticism/screening/discussion" combination as Art in Cinema.[11] With program notes written by such well-known film critics as Parker Tyler, William K. Everson, and Siegfried Kracauer, Amos Vogel programmed an incredibly wide spectrum of films (including many films by emerging international directors such as Yasujiro Ozu, Roman Polanski, Alain Resnais, Tony Richardson, and Agnès Varda) designed to highlight cinema's range of formal manipulation and to, in Vogel's own words, "create a disturbance in the status quo" of commercial cinema.[12] These avant-garde films—whether documentary, animation, narrative, or experimental—argued for the "appreciation of film as a medium of art, information, and education."[13] Above all, Vogel wanted to demonstrate, in Scott MacDonald's words, "that there is an alternative to industry-made cinema that is more in touch with the practical and spiritual lives of individuals."[14] This programming emphasis further developed the dominant 1950s neo-Romantic concept of the filmmaker as a social and cultural outsider channeling his/her creative energies into works of personal expression.

Cinema 16 proved so successful that it operated until 1963 and became the preeminent, most influential, and longest-lived film society in American history. At its height during the 1950s, it claimed 7,000 members, offered six to nine special events each year in addition to its regular screenings, and (in 1958) ran two children's film series. Cinema 16 not only established a showcase for avant-garde films but also (and arguably more importantly), trained American audiences in the aesthetics of experimental cinema. More than any other 1950s organization, Cinema 16, through its stated mission of creating a venue for "significant experiments in film" and providing "pleasurable, exciting education" for its patrons[15] institutionalized the "art world" of American avant-garde cinema.

In 1948, Cinema 16 became the "first organization to specialize in the distribution of avant-garde film," according to MacDonald.[16] Between 1951 and 1963, Cinema 16 published four catalogs of experimental film (which also included some documentaries and classic narratives). The catalog grew from twenty films in 1951 to 240 films in 1963. Throughout the 1950s, it circulated the films of Stan Brakhage, Kenneth Anger, Sidney Peterson, Norman McLaren, Marie Menken, Willard Maas, Maya Deren, and many others to a growing viewership. Curiously (given Cinema 16's status as a venue for personal, low budget, and even "unpopular" films), Vogel's distribution policy seemed based more on financial than on aesthetic considerations, almost equating accessibility and popularity with quality and artistic value. In short, Vogel only distributed a film if he thought it would interest enough people to cover the cost of shipping and handling and generate some profit. Vogel would then split the profit 50/50 with the filmmaker; a reasonably generous arrangement that afforded many films a much wider audience than would otherwise have been possible. But this arrangement obviously kept some films from finding an audience at all.

Vogel's autocratic approach to programming and distribution arguably precipitated Cinema 16's demise. Vogel's decision (reportedly) not to distribute Stan Brakhage's ANTICIPATION OF THE NIGHT (1958)—the film is listed in the 1963 Cinema 16 catalog—

and unwillingness to apply the new auteur approach (which also emerged during the 1950s) to Cinema 16 screenings also possibly contributed to the society's end. But the main cause of Cinema 16's shuttering was more banal: it was financial. Membership fees could no longer support the organization and Vogel did not want to solicit corporate sponsorship or wealthy benefactors (he feared the loss of programming independence). As Scott MacDonald explains:

> Cinema 16 was faced with increasing costs, and with competition: from new art theatres devoted to recently released foreign features; from TV, which was beginning to show some of the kinds of scientific film that had been a Cinema 16 staple; from college classrooms (by the 1960s many universities were developing film courses); from independent screening spaces interested in presenting avant-garde film; and even from the commercial cinema—as censorship restrictions disappeared, Hollywood was increasingly able to siphon off the interest in the risqué which had been important for some Cinema 16 members.[17]

Following André Breton's edict that the avant-garde will only survive by ceasing to exist, the death of Cinema 16 signaled the start of an even larger and stronger independent film movement (the New American Cinema Group), a better method of film distribution (the Film-Makers' Cooperative), and a longer lasting exhibition venue (the Film-Makers' Cinematheque, now Anthology Film Archives). The final years of Vogel's institution began in the late 1950s and early 1960s with the Cinema 16 premieres of three films: SHADOWS (1959), PULL MY DAISY (1959), and THE CONNECTION (1961). These "Beat Generation" films catalyzed the New American Cinema Group and its leadership of the emerging underground cinema of the 1960s. Vogel first brought these dramatic films (and their radical style and economic aesthetics) to a wide audience but oddly he was ignored during the formation of the New American Cinema Group. The group wanted a new approach to film production, distribution, and exhibition that would clearly distinguish it from Vogel's interests and method. If Vogel strove to invigorate *viewers'* interest in avant-garde film, then the New American Cinema Group would highlight the *filmmakers*, a stance which again reflected the influence of the new auteur policy. The group originally favored avant-garde narrative films (instead of Cinema 16's eclectic mix of films) and a "democratic" distribution policy (instead of a highly selective one). Ironically, the Film-Makers' Cooperative would eventually distribute mostly experimental works and Anthology Film Archives would compile a list of "essential" films, creating a highly selective canon of classics.[18]

Also contributing to the development of the growing 1950s experimental "art world" was the coordinating effort of Maya Deren. Unhappy with the artistic climate in which the independent filmmaker struggled, Deren proselytized for a collective network that would provide financial support, distribution opportunities, exhibition venues, and critical recognition for experimental cinema. Deren's call to form a community of filmmakers resulted in the Film Artists Society. Starting in 1953, the group met monthly to share information and plan for a permanent cooperative. By 1955, the group had changed its name to the Independent Film Makers Association and begun to employ the Art in Cinema model of "criticism/screening/discussion" at its meetings. In addition, the IFA hosted lectures by experimental filmmakers (such as Len Lye, Kenneth Anger, and James Broughton) and by other film societies' members, such as Amos Vogel from Cinema 16 and Cecile Starr from the Film Council of America. (The Film Council of America, founded in 1954, evolved into the American Federation of Film Societies by 1956. A nationwide society, it functioned as an "informational clearinghouse and facilitator for independent film exhibition . . . [and] offered centralized support and greater power to individual, isolated film societies," according to Rabinovitz.) By the late 1950s, Deren's vision of a vital community of artists had taken hold.

Deren also wanted to provide some organizational mechanism to help fund the production of experimental films. In 1955, she started the Creative Film Foundation to secure grants and award fellowships. Until her death in 1961, the Creative Film Foundation assisted such experimental filmmakers as Stan Brakhage, Robert Breer, Stan Vanderbeek, and Shirley Clarke. She also arranged special screenings of the fellowship recipients' work at Cinema 16 and conducted a series of symposia on the relationships between cinema and the other arts. Deren's critical interaction with Amos Vogel and Jonas Mekas also contributed to the formation of an experimental film culture. She participated in a Cinema 16 symposium on film and poetry[19] and for a few weeks in 1960 wrote as a guest columnist for the *Village Voice*'s "Movie Journal" column when Mekas took a vacation. Both venues allowed her the opportunity to impress her ideas of experimental cinema on the emerging discourse (which she initiated in 1946 with the publication of *An Anagram of Ideas on Art, Form, and Film*).[20] Deren also collaborated with Vogel to present the Creative Cinema Awards (for documentary and experimental films) annually from 1956 to 1961. Through the Creative Film Foundation and the IFA, Deren helped secure a cooperative network of, and a theoretical dialogue on, experimental cinema.

Reacting against Vogel's method of distribution and exhibition and hoping to enlarge Deren's artistic collective, Jonas Mekas began, by the late 1950s, the formation of three organizations which would dominate the avant-garde film world of the 1960s: the New American Cinema Group, the Film-Makers' Cooperative, and the Film-Makers' Cinematheque. Mekas and these organizations are more associated with the "underground cinema" of the 1960s, but their theoretical and critical genesis belongs to the 1950s. The conceptual roots of the three organizations started in 1955 when Mekas published the first issue of *Film Culture*, a journal devoted to independent and avant-garde films. In 1958, he found a larger audience for his ideas when he began writing his "Movie Journal" columns for the *Village Voice*. Both forums allowed Mekas to mount an attack against commercial Hollywood, champion the poetics of the personal film, and solidify a legitimate critical discourse regarding avant-garde cinema. Tracing some of Mekas's writings through the 1950s yields a road map of the development of the experimental art world he helped nurture.

Mekas's initial position on experimental film ("The Experimental Film in America") was infamously negative. Writing in *Film Culture* #3 (May–June 1955), he stated that "the majority of film poems made at present in America suffer from [a] markedly adolescent character." The films of Stan Brakhage, Kenneth Anger, Gregory Markopoulos, James Broughton, Maya Deren, and other "cinepoets" featured "escapism, unresolved frustrations, sadism and cruelty, fatalism and juvenile pessimism [as their] fundamental and recurrent themes." Mekas went on to observe that many experimental films of the time employed a "superexcess of unintelligible details," a shocking and persistent "conspiracy of homosexuality," and described them as "so fascinated by their personal worlds that they do not feel a need to communicate nor give to their characters or stories a larger, more human scope." He concluded that they were intellectually formal, repeated worn-out clichés and symbols, absent of artistic discipline, and were lacking what makes any art valuable: "a deeper insight into the human soul, emotions, experiences, as related to the whole rather than to exceptional abnormalities."[21]

The core of Mekas's relentless tirade was his belief that experimental film should explore the connection between nature, humankind, and society. If a film used formalist "cineplastics" in service of a solipsistic psychodrama or pure abstraction, the film contained "absolute zero value." Avant-garde film could only contain value if it fused experimental techniques with a social approach as it explored the human condition in a way accessible to all.

Mekas's early writing in *Film Culture* attempted to align four divergent tendencies in cinema: social praxis, a popular audience, personal expression, and formal experimentation. He seemed to favor a European model of modernist filmmaking that was neither empty Hollywood entertainment nor meaningless experimentation and individual catharsis, but, in David James's words, some kind of "morally responsible, aesthetically adventurous, reformed industrial cinema."[22] He wanted a type of popular narrative cinema that would challenge the cultural status quo and underline the social and political value of film.

This position became less optimistically synthetic in *Film Culture* #19 (1959) when Mekas issued his "Call for a New Generation of Film-Makers."[23] He stated that "to break the stifling conventions of the dramatic film, the cinema needs a larger movement than that of the experimental film-makers." Mekas's "larger, new cinema movement" would ideally emulate the British Free Cinema or the emerging French Nouvelle Vague. Filmmakers would create narrative films with "enthusiasm, passion, and imagination" rather than with "money, cameras, and splicers." Film would contest and agitate the Hollywood model, providing a necessary corrective to a complacent bourgeois mentality. This shift toward a more radical and subversive (yet popular) cinema brought Mekas closer to the goals of experimental filmmaking; but he wasn't willing to embrace the cinepoets yet.

"Call for a New Generation of Film-Makers" might also have been Mekas's consideration of an argument that had been forwarded by Parker Tyler in "A Preface to the Problems of the Experimental Film" published in *Film Culture* #17 in February 1958. The essay notably introduced the Independent Film Awards. The earliest winners reflected Mekas's lionizing of avant-garde films with an accessible narrative and modernist aesthetic: SHADOWS (1959), PULL MY DAISY (1959), and PRIMARY (1961). An experimental (poetic) filmmaker—Stan Brakhage—did not win until 1962, when Mekas had undergone his "conversion." The subsequent years clearly favored experimental (and non-narrative) filmmakers: Jack Smith (1963), Andy Warhol (1964), Harry Smith (1965), Gregory Markopoulos (1966), Michael Snow (1967), and Kenneth Anger (1968).

Even though Mekas acknowledged that experimental filmmakers had kept the spirit of free cinema alive in America, he observed that "film experimentation has degenerated into making experimental films." He concluded by stating that "our hope for a free American cinema is entirely in the hands of the new generation of film-makers. And there is no other way of breaking the frozen cinematic ground than through a complete derangement of the official cinematic senses."[24] Hesitant to admit that experimental filmmakers had labored towards this goal for decades, Mekas still hoped a new, modernist narrative cinema would take the lead. But after becoming a regular attendee at Cinema 16, interacting with a number of experimental filmmakers, and beginning work on his own films, Mekas started moving toward a re-evaluation of experimental cinema.[25] It is interesting to note that, in his 16 September 1959 *Movie Journal* column, Mekas claimed he had attended Cinema 16 screenings "faithfully" for eight years. Importantly, according to Scott MacDonald, Mekas applauded Cinema 16 for being open to experimentation, for breaking frontiers, and for providing a "place where the young experimentalists and film poets can still introduce their work to the general public." Four years after his attack on the experimental film, he began what he called in 1970 his "Saint Augustine conversion."

By 1962, when he wrote his "Notes on the New American Cinema" (*Film Culture* #24), Mekas fully reversed his initial outcry against experimental film with its lack of popular accessibility and inability to communicate. He by that time saw how formal experimentation, personal expression, and social praxis could work together without a prerequisite narrative structure. Experimental films might have been difficult for and unpopular with a wide audience, but their ability to forward change (both artistically and ideologically) was a power not to be denied. Mekas would take it upon himself to bring experimental cinema to everyone; to derange everyone's senses and foster a new cultural and political environment. By the mid-1960s, according to film theoretician David E. James, "*Film Culture* became the voice of the avant-garde, and Mekas its greatest and indefatigable champion."[26]

The 1950s institutionialized the "art world" of experimental cinema. Starting in the late 1940s with Art in Cinema, Cinema 16, and the University Film and Video Association, and ending in the early 1960s with the New American Cinema Group, the Film-Makers' Cooperative, and Canyon Cinema, the 1950s witnessed, as noted by Angerame, the emergence of "an infrastructure that promotes, distributes, and exhibits [experimental] work."[27] A critical and theoretical voice for a culture of experimental cinema also formalized during the 1950s from the program notes, screenings, and discussions organized by Amos Vogel and the published writings of Jonas Mekas and Maya Deren. Under their guidance, Cinema 16, the IFA, the Creative Film Foundation, and *Film Culture* (as well as the American Federation of Film Societies and the MOMA Film Library) took the seeds of the 1940s avant-garde film culture and, through the 1950s, nurtured them into a fully developed community of film artists, a viable distribution and exhibition network, an educated audience, and a critical approach for experimental cinema. Into this experimental "art world" of production, distribution, exhibition, and reception, 1950s experimental filmmakers entered as artists who worked "in the center of a network of cooperating people, all of whose work [was] essential to the final outcome."[28] With such support, these filmmakers elaborated already established film styles and initiated new ones.

Lyrical Cinema and Beyond

P. Adams Sitney said in his seminal *Visionary Film* that "the 1950s were quiet years within the American avant-garde cinema. The enthusiastic surge of the late 1940s had ended . . . [and there was no] significant influx of new artists until the very end of the decade."[29] Sitney made this claim to sanctify Stan Brakhage as the filmmaker who dominated 1950s experimental cinema and his "lyrical" filmmaking as the only valuable aesthetic development. Such reductive history focuses too much emphasis on a single, linear evolutionary path and ignores many other important filmmakers and experimental styles. Hy Hirsh created his first film in 1951. Robert Breer and Jordan Belson began making films in 1952; Shirley Clarke in 1953. In 1954 Larry Jordan, the Kuchar brothers, Peter Kubelka, and Carmen D'Avino made their first films. Stan Vanderbeek began in 1955. Ken Jacobs and Jack Smith started their work in 1956. Marie Menken returned to filmmaking in 1957. Bruce Conner released his first film in 1958; Ed Emshwiller in 1959.[30] James Broughton produced four films in the early 1950s. Mary Ellen Bute's "see-ing-sound" films of the 1940s yielded one of the first electronic abstract animations in 1952. Jim Davis's late 1940s "color reflection" films extended through the 1950s. James and John Whitney elaborated their early "film exercises" into YANTRA (1957) and CATA-LOGUE (1961). Kenneth Anger entered his "Magick Lantern Cycle" with EAUX D'ARTI-FICE (1953) and INAUGURATION OF THE PLEASURE DOME (1954). Harry Smith shifted from hand-drawn abstract color films to animated black and white collage films, culmi-nating in #12: HEAVEN & EARTH MAGIC (1957–1962). In other words, the 1950s were not quiet years, the enthusiasm had not ended, "personal expression" was achieved in ways other than abstracted lyrical cinema, and filmmakers other than Brakhage helped experimental cinema grow prodigiously. Nevertheless, Sitney correctly highlights Brakhage as a major artist; his film work—and through it, the emergence of a new form of cinematic address—is vitally important.[31]

Brakhage began his filmmaking in 1952, employing the psychodrama (or trance) model as developed in the 1940s by Maya Deren, Kenneth Anger, Curtis Harrington, Gregory Markopoulos, and James Broughton. This style of experimental film empha-sizes surreal, temporally and spatially fragmented dream narratives of psychological rev-elation in which the filmmaker typically performs as an on-screen protagonist. This protagonist experiences a literal and metaphorical journey of self-exploration built upon representational imagery that alternates between objective and subjective perspectives. As the label implies, a psychodrama enacts a Freudian examination of a filmmaker's desires, anxieties, sexuality, and mortality.

Brakhage's films from INTERIM (1952) through LOVING (1957) arguably fit within the trance model, but with hints of the new approach soon to appear. Sitney explained that this new model, the "lyrical cinema," postulates the filmmaker behind the camera as the first-person protagonist of the film. The images of the film are what he sees, filmed in such a way that we never forget his presence and we know how he is reacting to his vision. In the lyrical form there is no longer a hero; instead the screen is filled with movement, and that movement, both of the camera and the editing, reverberates with the idea of a man looking. As viewers we see this man's intense experience of seeing.[32]

This technique of expressing the extremely subjective and multiple "visions" of a film-maker (sight, memory, dreams, hallucinations) via an abstracted, first-person point of view also synthesized Romantic mythmaking with the reflexive modernism of abstract expressionism.

DESISTFILM (1954) and THE WAY TO SHADOW GARDEN (1954) began Brakhage's tran-sition from trance to lyrical. DESISTFILM demonstrated some of Brakhage's emerging lyrical techniques: hand-held moving camera; distorting reality via lenses, filters, and reflective surfaces; abstract images; plastic cutting;[33] and scratched titles (Sitney defines plastic cutting as "the joining of shots at points of movement, close-up, or abstraction to soften the brunt of montage"). Yet with neither an on-screen protagonist nor an implied off-screen subjectivity, the film operates mostly as a poetic document of five youths "hanging out." This may be why Parker Tyler called DESISTFILM "the first important beatnik film with the air of a spontaneous Happening."[34] THE WAY TO SHADOW GARDEN plays as a trance film until the final moments when Brakhage initiates his first "metaphor on vision." After the suffering protagonist (Walt Newcomb) cuts his eyes with broken glass and stumbles outside into a garden, the film switches to negative stock to suggest his "injured sight." The viewer should recognize a connection (a metaphor) between the filmic image and the expression of an interior point of view. Brakhage attempted to show the totality of the character's experience (visual, psychological, and emotional) by abandoning a third-person objectivity for a first-person subjectivity. In this film, Brakhage designed a trope he would expand over the next few years—the use, as James puts it, "of a distressed protagonist whose subjective experience the visual field more or less closely reproduced."[35] THE WAY TO SHADOW GARDEN also introduced Brakhage's continual fascination with the "untutored eye," the vision of a child not yet "infected" by laws of perspective, and the role of nature in humankind's existence.

REFLECTIONS ON BLACK (1955) continued this stylistic and thematic exploration of sight through the visions of a blind man who "sees" and experiences three incidents of erotic frustration. As the blind protagonist (Don Redlich) climbs three stories of an apartment building, we see three stories presented through increasing subjectivity. The first is purely voyeuristic; as objective observers, we see what the blind man would see from a third-person point of view. The second incorporates the blind man as a participant in an interrupted tryst. This vignette alternates between objective and subjective shots so the viewer, as in a conventional narrative film, identifies with the character while also maintaining a position of omniscience. The third story is wholly subjective; we see through the blind man's eyes. Brakhage scratches the emulsion of the film (on the blind man's eyes and on black leader) to demarcate this new interiority. In this final story, Sitney observed that Brakhage began to "transcend the distinction between fantasy and actuality, moving into the cinema of triumphant imagination."[36]

Brakhage further expanded this "cinema of imagination" in FLESH OF MORNING (1956) by casting himself, for the first time, as the film's protagonist. The "metaphors of vision" we see ostensibly represent Brakhage's psychological and emotional state of mind. One of Brakhage's overtly sexual films, it seems to explore his recollection of a lover, which leads to a masturbation fantasy. Employing the basic lyrical techniques with which he has already experimented, this film also introduces questions of gender and of childhood innocence in relationship to adult concerns of sexuality and death. FLESH OF MORNING took another important step toward linking the protagonist's vision with the filmmaker's. This shift to a first-person camera became very noticeable in another highly sexual film, LOVING (1957), and finally coalesced in what is often considered the first true example of lyrical cinema, ANTICIPATION OF THE NIGHT (1958).[37]

Working as a "diary" in which Brakhage recorded the events of his life and his feelings about them, ANTICIPATION OF THE NIGHT develops his metaphors on vision through what he calls the "eye of imagination." Consisting of three types of subjective vision—closed-eye, open-eye, and brain movies—this eye of imagination allowed Brakhage to explore the connection between his consciousness and reality/nature. (The dominant open-eye view shows a continual flux of focus and movement designed to simultaneously convey sight and impressions. The closed-eye view presents abstract graphics that represent intense psychological or highly emotional states of mind. Brain movies are images of memories, dreams, and hallucinations which briefly emerge from closed and open eye views. They appear before the visual imagination as if filmed from a fixed tripod.) Sheldon Renan noted that these three types of sight "present a rippling reality in which the photographic raw material of the film-maker's actual life is repeatedly transformed and reseen in a continual turbulence of movement, of color, of light."[38]

Brakhage's rejection of aesthetic and structural norms resulted in a very poor reception when ANTICIPATION OF THE NIGHT was first shown (reportedly causing a riot at the

FLESH OF MORNING (1956), by Stan Brakhage. Brakhage himself is shown in close-up.

1958 International Experimental Film Festival in Brussels and precipitating the formation of the Film-Makers' Cooperative). Yet according to Sitney, the great achievement of ANTICIPATION OF THE NIGHT is its new lyrical quality; its distillation of "an intense and complex interior crisis into an orchestration of sights and associations which cohere in a new formal rhetoric of camera movement and montage."[39]

In ANTICIPATION OF THE NIGHT, Brakhage created a film of self-exploration and psychological revelation that strove to communicate a "totality of vision" (what he saw, perceived, felt, imagined, and dreamed) through a complete identification between himself and a "liberated camera." Using a constantly moving hand-held camera, unfocused images, under- and over-exposure, "random" compositions, distorting lenses and filters, flash frames, varying camera speeds, fragmented time and space, and plastic cutting, Brakhage equated the process of filmmaking and the abstraction of reality with the expression of his emotions and imagination (much like the "action painting" of abstract expressionism). James Peterson referred to these techniques as a type of "personification strategy" where the film's manipulation represents the filmmaker's consciousness.[40] ANTICIPATION OF THE NIGHT "personifies" Brakhage's mental state in terms of a purely visual, subjective cinema.

In *Metaphors on Vision* (which Brakhage began writing during the 1950s), the filmmaker discusses the psychological and artistic context of ANTICIPATION OF THE NIGHT. He explains how this was to be his last film about "fulfilling the myth of myself;" that it would function as a way out from the style and themes of the psychodrama. The journey and suicide of the filmmaker/protagonist marks an end of Brakhage's early cinema and

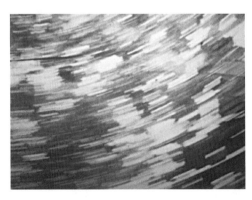

ANTICIPATION OF THE NIGHT (1958), by Stan Brakhage.

ANTICIPATION OF THE NIGHT (1958),
by Stan Brakhage.

the start of a new artistic approach (much like Godard's "end of film/end of cinema" at the close of WEEKEND, 1967).

Sitney's acclamation that ANTICIPATION OF THE NIGHT was the "first American film about and structured by the nature of the seeing experience; how one encounters a sight, how it is recalled, how it affects later vision, and where it leads the visionary"[41] may under-emphasize Marie Menken's influence,[42] but it does stress the importance of light and untutored vision in Brakhage's work. Brakhage explained this importance in the often quoted opening to *Metaphors on Vision*: "Imagine an eye unruled by man-made laws of perspective, an eye unprejudiced by compositional logic, an eye which does not respond to the name of everything but which must know each object encountered in life through an adventure of perception. . . . Imagine a world alive with incomprehensible objects and shimmering with an endless variety of movement and innumerable gradations of color."[43]

Brakhage's final films of the 1950s (CAT'S CRADLE, 1959; WINDOW WATER BABY MOVING, 1959; and SIRIUS REMEMBERED, 1959) abandoned the psychodrama formula and fully established lyrical cinema as an important model of experimental film production. By the early 1960s, with such films as THIGH LINE LYRE TRIANGULAR (1961), MOTHLIGHT (1963), and the epic DOG STAR MAN (1964), Brakhage had become the most recognized and celebrated American experimental filmmaker. His process of creating film as self-expression matched the dominant fine art discourse surrounding abstract expressionism as well as the new literary direction of the Beats (who, in their strike against the conservative sensibility and conformity of 1950s society and culture, stressed a "Romantic insistence on the moral, ethical, and spiritual potency of creative selfhood.")[44] Brakhage's critical and theoretical writings (also sharing stylistic affinities with the Beats) reinforced the notion of the solipsistic artist expressing himself with little concern for social commentary or viewers' comprehension. This convergence of lyrical cinema, the abstract expressionist art world, the Beats, and Brakhage as neo-Romantic figurehead would ultimately secure his deification in the experimental film canon. As Sitney said near the end of Jim Shedden's documentary BRAKHAGE (1998): "[There isn't] a body of work of an individual more significant in cinema than Brakhage's. . . . If you want to know what cinema is, it's Brakhage."

In an essay titled "Film: Dance" (1967) Brakhage commented on the attempts to fuse film and choreography. "I do not think there is, as of now, any cine-dance worth mentioning as such. The cine-dance . . . is at worst an attempt of one medium to put itself into another medium which will not meaningfully be put upon."[45] An "almost exception" he recognized was Maya Deren, whose four dances for the camera—A STUDY IN CHOREOGRAPHY FOR THE CAMERA (1945), RITUAL IN TRANSFIGURED TIME (1946), MEDITATION ON VIOLENCE (1948), and THE VERY EYE OF NIGHT (1955)— created a new collaborative and interdisciplinary art form.[46] Brakhage also acknowledged a "traditional sort of outgrowth" from Deren in the 1950s cine-dances of Shirley Clarke and Ed Emshwiller. As an experimental film form that started in the 1940s and grew significantly during the 1950s and as a film model radically different from lyrical cinema, an overview of the cine-dance will serve to challenge Brakhage's claims.

The first filmmaker to begin incorporating dance into his films in the 1950s was James Broughton, one of the fathers of the West Coast experimental film movement. Best known for THE POTTED PSALM (1946, with Sidney Peterson) and MOTHER'S DAY (1948), Broughton made four films between 1950 and 1953 that explore worlds of pleasure, joy, sexuality, and love unconstrained by social mores. Sometimes referred to as "the pied piper of queer experimental film" and a "Dionysian gay sage,"[47] Broughton argued for a magical cinema of transformation incorporating alchemy, silent comedy, Zen, and poetry.[48] His early films connected this philosophy with movement and dance as he challenged stifling bourgeois conventions.

THE ADVENTURES OF JIMMY (1950) and LOONY TOM THE HAPPY LOVER (1951) follow the amorous quests of the lead characters: Jimmy to find a bride; Tom to find love and kisses. Both figures are comic and, within the slapstick aesthetic of each film, both employ stylized pedestrian movement and mime as expressions of their liberating spirit. Jimmy, a woodsman, naively saunters from his mountain home to a company town and back again, changing body language and hats with each new "adventure." Tom, costumed to look like Charlie Chaplin, moves like a satyr or, in Broughton's own words, a "blissful baggy-panted Pan"[49] as he chases women through bucolic settings hoping to win a kiss. Also acting like Cupid, he brings together an artist and his model in romantic union.

THE PLEASURE GARDEN (1953) is the longest and most narrative of Broughton's films. Shot in England with the help of Basil Wright, Lindsay Anderson, and Walter Lassally, the film tells how a "fat fairy godmother routs a puritanical Minister of Public Behavior and bestows love unions on the daydreaming strangers in a public park."[50] Again using stylized pedestrian movement, slapstick comedy, mime, and tableaux vivants, THE PLEASURE GARDEN captures, according to Sitney, "the excitement of seeing and showing human bodies in action" much like early silent films.[51] The film won a special prize at the 1954 Cannes Film Festival.

FOUR IN THE AFTERNOON (1951) presents a quartet of "musical vignettes" that examine the romantic and sexual desires of men and women at different ages. The final two, "Princess Printemps" and "The Aging Balletomane," are the most obvious dance-for-the-camera works. "Princess Printemps" more or less documents choreography (a burlesque of Renaissance court dancing) in a mise-en-scène of full body wide shots and long duration takes. "The Aging Balletomane," in contrast, stands as the vital link to Deren's earlier cine-dance explorations. An elderly dancer conjures a ballerina from his imagination and from objects in his backyard. She dances; he tries to approach her many times without success. Through spatial and temporal fragmentation, Broughton develops a truly cinematic dance space. Employing montage, point-of-view shots, loops, and reverse motion, Broughton creates a pas de deux where the dancers never touch or appear in the same shot. Visually and thematically "The Aging Balletomane" conveys unrequited longing and provides concrete evidence to support Broughton's remark that "I have learned more about . . . the making of films from dance than from cinema."[52]

DANCE IN THE SUN (1953),
by Shirley Clarke.

Shirley Clarke began her academic and professional life as a dancer and choreographer. Studying at various institutions, she trained in three major schools of modern dance: Martha Graham, Doris Humphrey, and Hanya Holm. Between 1953 and 1958 she made four well-received dances for the camera[53] before turning to feature filmmaking (as part of the New American Cinema Group).

Her first film, DANCE IN THE SUN (1953), choreographed by Daniel Nagrin, followed Deren's pioneering work, A STUDY IN CHOREOGRAPHY FOR THE CAMERA (1945). Using match action and position editing, Clarke fused two different locations into a single choreographic arena. Nagrin enters a rehearsal stage and as he dances, his movements are intercut with identical movements on a beach. This spatial juxtaposition allows Nagrin to escape the confines of the stage and choreographically celebrate the freedom of an endless expanse of exterior space. A relatively simple exercise in parallel editing, DANCE IN THE SUN allowed Clarke to see, like Deren before her, that "dance as it existed on stage had to be destroyed in order to have a good film and not just a rather poor document."[54] DANCE IN THE SUN received the Best Dance Film of 1954 award by the New York Dance Film Society.

BULLFIGHT (1955), choreographed by Anna Sokolow, employed the same basic device of DANCE IN THE SUN—match action editing of a dancer's movement—but elaborated its spatial exploration by developing more abstract connections. Sokolow's performance of HOMAGE TO A BULLFIGHTER (filmed in a studio) is intercut with documentary footage of a bullfight. Matching Sokolow's stylized gestures with the matador's and the bull's actions, Clarke does not spatially link the studio dance to the stadium. Instead of DANCE IN THE

DANCE IN THE SUN (1953),
by Shirley Clarke.

SUN's unique cinematic space of stage/beach through which Daniel Nagrin dances, BULL-FIGHT isolates its locations and performances. Sokolow remains in the studio, yet graphic, narrative, and thematic connections between her and the bullfight occur as the film draws parallels between the poetry of dance and the reality of a life and death combat. BULLFIGHT won awards in 1955 at both the Edinburgh and Venice Film Festivals.

A MOMENT IN LOVE (1957), a pas de deux choreographed by Sokolow, moves its dancers (Carmela Gutierrez and Paul Sanasardo) first through idyllic locations of forest, mountain, sky, and water, and then through unsettling locations of urban decay and a remote desert. Each space is abstracted by soft-focus, exaggerated camera angles, camera movement, superimpositions, and/or color tints. The dancers' movements within and across these disparate spaces and graphic distortions are accomplished by match action and match position cutting, again creating a dance space unique to film and a performance impossible on a proscenium stage. The narrative and thematic focus of A MOMENT IN LOVE seems rather clichéd (the trajectory of romance from passion to separation to reconciliation), but the combination of film image and choreography fully exploits and impressively integrates the potentials of both mediums. With this film, Rabinovitz noted that Clarke abandoned her "dependency on stage choreography or optical realism as the raw material for a dance film [and] celebrates a high degree of line and color abstraction and movement as the formal beauty of pure dance."[55] The *New York Times* listed A MOMENT IN LOVE as one of the top ten non-theatrical films of 1957.

BRIDGES-GO-ROUND (1958), originally one of the twenty-three short film loops of American life made for the U.S. Pavilion at the 1958 Brussels World's Fair, continues Clarke's exploration of abstraction and pure dance. The film dissolves between superimposed, tinted, moving camera shots of suspension bridges, creating a choreography of still objects moving in an undefined dance space. Or as Marjorie Rosen said, "Clarke

Shirley Clarke operates the camera during production of A MOMENT IN LOVE *(1957).*

filmed Manhattan Island as a maypole. The bridges around it, detached from their moorings, execute a bewitching, beguiling dance."[56] This powerfully dynamic work proves Clarke's belief that dances for the camera are almost exclusively exercises in visual rhythm. BRIDGES-GO-ROUND became Clarke's most critically acclaimed experimental film and won a Creative Film Foundation award in 1958. (See Chapter 11 for further discussion of this film.)

Ed Emshwiller followed Clarke's graphic direction with BRIDGES-GO-ROUND by combining dance with abstract painting, investigating the tension between a flat, two-dimensional surface and three-dimensional motion. Originally known for his science-fiction illustrations, "Emsh" began to explore filmmaking during the early 1950s as a way of connecting illustration and movement. By the late 1950s and early 1960s he had created four short films that emerged from this interest.

TRANSFORMATION (1959) animates the process of abstract painting. Moving through different styles and mediums of modern painting, Emshwiller demonstrated how film could turn the development of paintings into a type of choreography. DANCE CHROMATIC (1959) and LIFELINES (1960) take this idea one step farther by integrating live human motion with the process of abstract painting. LIFELINES superimposes a nude female model (Barbara Kersey) with animated drawings. DANCE CHROMATIC (a 1959 Creative Film Foundation Award winner) most fully examines the play between two-dimensional painting and three-dimensional dance. A dancer (Nancy Fenster) struggles to emerge from the flat, still surface of a black and white canvas. When she escapes, she moves through an intricate world of depth created by camera movement, superimpositions, and the rapid application of layers of color paint. The film ends with the implication of procreation between the dancer and the painting.

THANATOPSIS (1962), the most fascinating and technically accomplished of Emshwiller's early dance films, presents an impossible mise-en-scène of a motionless man (Mac Emshwiller) and a frenetic woman (Becky Arnold) whose hyper actions cannot visually register. Adapting the animation he used for his painting films to include single frame time exposures, Emshwiller creates, according to Renan, "an eerie dynamic figure that waxes and wanes in alternately stable and vibrating environments."[57] THANATOPSIS remains one of the most complex dances for the camera and a disturbing contemplation on death. Emshwiller continued his cine-dance work through the 1960s, collaborating on a number of films with the choreographer Alwin Nikolais.

The dance for the camera work of Broughton, Clarke, and Emshwiller brought about major advances in a vital model of experimental film production. Each one expanded

THANATOPSIS (1962), by Ed Emshwiller.

THANATOPSIS (1962), by Ed Emshwiller.

Deren's approach to cine-dance: Broughton with stylized pedestrian movement, comedy, and mime; Clarke with color abstraction and the "pure" dance of objects; and Emshwiller with painting and animation. Their collaborations with choreographers produced an interdisciplinary art form that is "personally" expressive (but not egocentric like lyrical cinema) and not fully indebted to the tenets of abstract expressionism (although aspects of A MOMENT IN LOVE, BRIDGES-GO-ROUND, and Emshwiller's painting films move in that direction). Their works remain important as the core of contemporary dances for the camera.

When Stan Brakhage moved to New York City in the mid-1950s, he made two films with Joseph Cornell, WONDER RING (1955) and CENTURIES OF JUNE (1955). Cornell took WONDER RING and, in a continuation of his assemblage methods, made GNIR REDNOW (1955). GNIR REDNOW simply runs WONDER RING backwards and upside down (with an end title that reads "the end is the beginning") as a neo-Dadaist pun. Cornell's interest in assemblage not only produced his famous "boxes" (small, surreal dioramas of found objects) but also, arguably, the first "found film," ROSE HOBART (1939). The traditions of "ready made art," appropriation, and compilation started by Cornell (and Marcel Duchamp) found new expression during the 1950s in the recycled collage films of Stan Vanderbeek, Harry Smith, and Bruce Conner.

Stan Vanderbeek began his career as an animator on an early 1950s TV show, *Winky Dink and You*. After hours, he used the studio's equipment to create his first animated collages. Cutting out photographs, illustrations, and advertisements from newspapers and magazines, Vanderbeek juxtaposed the disparate images to generate dark comedy and social satire. Between 1955 and 1965 he made more than twelve animated collages developing what James Peterson called a "bricolage approach" where "consistency of style and compatibility of perspective are not concerns. Vanderbeek . . . assembles images from diverse sources utterly without regard for the relative size of the objects or the perspectives from which they are rendered."[58] Perhaps his best-known bricolage is SCIENCE FRICTION (1959).

In SCIENCE FRICTION, wrote Wheeler Dixon, Vanderbeek "manipulates twentieth century American images and idols—gadgets, rockets, satellites, television sets. He selects slick magazine illustrations and animates them, combining and recombining them with comic or satiric purpose."[59] The film, a biting commentary on technology, the arms race, and Cold War nuclear paranoia, shows in its second half President Dwight D. Eisenhower launching missiles at the Soviet Union. These missiles include the Statue of Liberty, the Washington monument, a 1950s automobile, a medieval Madonna, and

SCIENCE FRICTION *(1959), by Stan Vanderbeek.*

even a cat, as all of America helps to destroy communism and, of course, destroys itself. As a cautionary tale highly reflective of its late 1950s political context, SCIENCE FRICTION won a 1960 Creative Film Foundation award and was chosen for a special presentation at the Museum of Modern Art in New York City.

Harry Smith helped establish the West Coast experimental film movement during the 1940s but soon moved beyond such confines. He has been described as a "film-maker, anthropologist, painter, ethnomusicologist, folklorist, magician, alchemist, and legendary archivist of sediments of human activity in motion."[60] In 1951, according to his biographer, Paola Igliori, he became "one of the first American artists to exhibit at the Louvre . . . in a two man show with Marcel Duchamp."[61] In 1952, Folkway Records issued his seminal *Anthology of American Folk Music*, a very influential collection of early American blues and folk music. In the late 1950s, he built a multiplane animation system and worked with 3-D film technology. Around 1940 he made the first hand-painted films in the United States by batiking abstract animations directly on clear celluloid. His animation was impressive enough to secure him a 1951 Solomon Guggenheim Foundation grant to continue his filmmaking. Now distributed as EARLY ABSTRACTIONS (1939–1956), Smith's earliest films remain the most complex abstraction animations ever created. By the late 1950s, Smith began making fairly realistic animated collages.[62] The culmination of these labors is the surreal and occult #12: HEAVEN AND EARTH MAGIC (1957–1961).

In HEAVEN AND EARTH MAGIC, Smith uses late nineteenth-century black and white images from women's wear catalogs and elocution books as well as some original drawings to create film history's most ambitious (and certainly most bizarre) bricolage. Smith's description of HEAVEN AND EARTH MAGIC expresses some of the film's surrealism.

> The first part depicts the Heroine's toothache consequent to the loss of a very valuable watermelon, her dentistry and transportation to heaven. Next follows an elaborate exposition of the heavenly land in terms of Israel, Montreal, and the second part depicts the return to earth from being eaten by Max Mueller on the day Edward the Seventh dedicated the Great Sewer of London.[63]

Whatever the film may be about, Smith's appropriation and recycling of cut-out images provided the 1950s with a masterpiece of collage animation.

Also working in Cornell's assemblage tradition, but not as a collage animator, was Bruce Conner. Conner appropriated and recycled *film* images (like Cornell's ROSE

HOBART) producing what Peterson described as a "compilation [which] re-edits fragments of found footage from old movies, television commercials, and educational and industrial films."[64] His first two compilation films, A MOVIE (1958) and COSMIC RAY (1961), proved very successful examples of assemblage cinema. These two works succeed because Conner used montage to recontextualize images of popular culture into witty social critiques. As he explained, "All footage is found footage for a film editor. . . . The editor's role is to work with given images, put them together and, perhaps, make them do things that were never there in the original intent. There are many examples of how footage can be made to appear quite different by changing the context."[65] This recontextualization, although complex, is readily accessible to most viewers because of the familiarity of the images and the ironic humor generated by the editing. Peterson noted that A MOVIE "is probably the most widely known example of the assemblage aesthetic in the avant-garde cinema."[66]

A MOVIE emerged from the California assemblage movement to which Conner originally belonged as a sculptor. Like many compilation films (and assemblage pieces), the meaning of A MOVIE is rather ambiguous. Ostensibly about violence and sexuality in America, according to David Curtis the film also explores "the growing disorder and chaos that underlie human aspirations."[67] Moving from reflexive jokes about Hollywood filmmaking and the Romantic artist through links between sexuality and violence (the oft cited sequence of the submarine captain's sexual excitement ending with an atomic bomb orgasm) to absurd athletic events and increasingly horrifying disasters (both natural and human), A MOVIE also seems a compendium of all the banal images and clichéd narratives that constitute our media. Conner's generic title ironically implies his movie is no different than all other mainstream movies; in the final distillation, A MOVIE could be any movie. Conner's film differs of course in the criticism it provides, a criticism that surfaces by the way the film deconstructs the spatial and temporal continuity of its various shots, recontextualizes them via montage, and then reconstitutes them into a different organic whole. COSMIC RAY continues the same basic techniques as A MOVIE only faster. So fast in fact that the film is a visual and aural attack on the audience. Intercutting phallic weaponry with a nude female dancer suggests a kind of rape and again examines the links between sex and violence.

The animated collages of Vanderbeek and Smith and the compilations of Conner affirmed the status of assemblage as another major style of 1950s experimental filmmaking. Cutting out and recycling the found images of printed material or appropriating and

Links between sexuality and violence: A MOVIE (1958), by Bruce Conner.

recontextualizing old TV advertising and commercial films, these filmmakers laid the groundwork for the pop art style of the 1960s and 1970s and the postmodernism that followed it.

Another developer of Cornell's assemblage aesthetic during the 1950s was Robert Breer. Working occasionally in a mode akin to Vanderbeek's collages, Breer would ultimately generate a radical approach to animation and consequently a new form of experimental film. An outsider to both the East and West Coast experimental movements (Breer lived in Paris between 1949 and 1959 and made his groundbreaking films there starting in 1952), he employed a variety of techniques to explore the ontology of animation. Breer employed bricolage in Un Miracle (1954), colored-paper cut-outs in Form Phases I-IV (1952–1954), line drawings in A Man and His Dog Out for Air (1957), photomontage in Jamestown Baloos (1957), found objects in Recreation (1956), and used various combinations of these techniques in Cats (1956) and Eyewash (1959). In these very short films, Breer formulated a single-frame aesthetic and his work was arguably the first to demonstrate this approach. As he said in a 1959 statement published in *Film Culture* in 1963:

> Single images one after another in quick succession fusing into motion . . . this is cinema. . . . Whereas the usual intention in animation has been to represent natural movement and to do this by the gradual modification of forms permitting the eye to blend them into fluid motion, I began treating the single images as individual sensations to be experienced separately, more in counterpoint than in harmony.
>
> I find myself combining freely very disparate images and finally using continuous motion simply as a means to connect up the various fixed images.[68]

Breer's rapid montages challenge not only what a viewer sees and how, but also foreground the animation process. The most influential of these reflexive "retinal collages"[69] is Recreation.

Recreation began in 1954 as an experiment in shapes, as Breer explained: "I exposed six feet of film one frame at a time, as usual in animation, but with this important difference—each image was as unlike the preceding one as possible. The result was 240 distinctly different optical sensations."[70] Repeated viewings of this ten-second loop wore it out, requiring Breer to re-make it. The new version, made in 1956, was a re-creation of the effects seen in and ideas learned from the original. Recreation collides disparate images and objects—some still, some moving; some shown in single frame, some shown in multiple frames—into an intense play on perception. For example, one section of Recreation reveals these images: drill bits, a film reel, a newspaper, pencils, cord, hooks, tubes, pieces of colored paper, boxes, a glove, bread, clothes pins, a pen knife, a magazine ad, yarn, hands, cloth, fruit, a ruler, coins, a cat, a map, an abstract painting, and a wind-up toy chick hopping across a piece of paper. A viewer must address a number of visual tensions: between the clarity of any one image and the ambiguity of its juxtaposition to other images; between fragmentation and wholeness; between stasis and motion; between rhythmic patterns and their sudden disruptions; between the impression of different levels of three-dimensional space and flat, two-dimensional surfaces; between the illusion of a languorous superimposition and the staccato of distinct parts. This game of visual perception extends to the soundtrack as

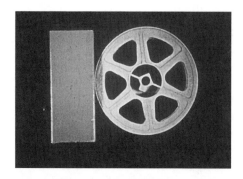

RECREATION (1956), by Robert Breer.

well. After seeing a silent version of RECREATION, Noel Burch wrote a text and recorded it for the film. An aural equivalent of the images, the text is a nonsense poem (in the Dada tradition): its words create puns on the screen objects. Speaking in French, Burch comments on "mysterious objects," how the film is "unlimited in all senses," and yet "leaves barely a trace."[71]

Contradicting Burch's voice-over, RECREATION's unique visual and aural bombardment left a very significant trace. It helped Breer win a Creative Film Foundation award in 1957 and exhibited yet another experimental filmmaking style that challenged the emerging, abstract expressionist–influenced lyrical cinema. Rejecting the neo-Romanticism of Brakhage, Breer developed the core of a reflexive minimalist/structuralist approach that would be further explored and codified in the late 1950s by Peter Kubelka. Breer met Kubelka at the 1958 Brussels Experimental Film Festival and discovered that, although working independently, they had formulated the principles of metric cinema.

Including Kubelka, an Austrian filmmaker, in a history of 1950s American experimental cinema might seem odd, but his filmmaking, critical and theoretical writings, his interaction with Jonas Mekas, and his elaboration of Breer's single-frame technique made him "one of the most influential theoreticians of the cinema in America," according to Sitney.[72] Three films he created in the late 1950s, *ADEBAR* (1957), *SCHWECHATER* (1958), and *ARNULF RAINER* (1958–1960), an interview with Jonas Mekas (published in *Film Culture* #44, 1967), and a series of lectures at New York University, form the foundation of his theory of metrical film.[73]

The fundamental principle of metric cinema, as set out by Kubelka, holds that "cinema is not movement. Cinema is a projection of stills—which means images which do not move—in a very quick rhythm. . . . Cinema is nothing but a rapid slide projection."[74] With this essential concept in place, Kubelka develops three corollaries. Like Breer, Kubelka questions the level at which montage operates, commenting, "Where is, then, the articulation of cinema? Eisenstein, for example, said it's the collision of two shots. But it's very strange that nobody ever said that it's not between shots but between frames. It's between frames where cinema speaks."[75] This is metric cinema's first corollary; that meaning occurs between frames. The second corollary is that law and order should form the basis of creation. In other words, a filmmaker must devise formal, precise, and even mathematical patterns to guide editing. The third corollary holds that content is unimportant. "Where a medium is really mirroring nature, it is valueless. . .[do not use] the qualities of the cinematographic camera to mirror the real world."[76] Value stems from building a personal image of the world radically different from everyone else's. For Kubelka, that personal image of the world meant employing a minimalist approach to filmmaking; working with little or no ostensible content.

Kubelka's and Breer's development of metric cinema remains a vital contrast to the lyrical mode of 1950s experimental filmmaking. Their challenge to the abstract expressionist art world, embodied in such concerns as structuralism, the ontology of the filmic apparatus, popular culture, and the perception of the viewer, would continue through the 1960s and 1970s in the works of Paul Sharits, Tony Conrad, Kurt Kren, Standish Lawder, and the Vasulkas.

Another important style of experimental filmmaking that developed during the 1950s from roots in the 1940s was a type of animated graphic cinema. Sometimes called "motion paintings," abstract animation, or "absolute films," this style extended into the 1960s as "cosmic cinema"[77] or "inner-eye cinema."[78] According to William Wees, by the late 1960s this style of filmmaking strove to "evoke states of mind that lie beyond the boundaries of materialist and rationalist modes of thought . . . to bypass the material demands of the medium and make direct contact with the minds of the viewer . . . to awaken dormant perceptions and encourage viewers to discover new sites of vision within themselves . . . to use images to visualize—or help induce—deep states of meditation."[79] It did this by generating hallucinations, images that do not come from external stimuli but from perceptions within the mind. The common components of this introspective cinema derive from the four basic geometrical patterns of hallucinations—lattices, cobwebs, tunnels, and spirals—and include eight colors and eight patterns of movement.[80] The earliest films of this approach made during the 1940s and 1950s may not employ many of these components or set such lofty goals, but they do include a rudimentary expression of these ideas.

Along with Harry Smith, one of the earliest American filmmakers to work in this school was Mary Ellen Bute, who made ten graphic films between 1934 and 1953. Developing what she called "seeing sound films," Bute attempted to synthesize light, movement, color, and sound in temporal, kinetic paintings.[81] Her abstract animated films increased in complexity and popularity during the 1940s, and were often programmed as shorts in theaters across the country, including Radio City Music Hall.[82] Her work culminated in the early 1950s with ABSTRONIC (1952) and MOOD CONTRASTS (1953). ABSTRONIC stands as one of the first experimental films to employ electronic designs.[83] Generating Lissajous curves (curves described by parametric equations and often drawn graphically on x/y coordinates; for example a sine wave or the patterns drawn by a pendulum) on an oscilloscope, Bute choreographed these abstract, electronic images ("abstronics") to Aaron Copland's *Hoe Down* and Don Gillis's *Ranch House Party*. In MOOD CONTRASTS, Bute combined her abstronics with hand-painted animation and used them to illustrate the music of Rimsky-Korsakov and Shostakovich. The swirling colors, movement, and implied spatial depth produced an exciting and critically acclaimed film (it won Best Short Film at the 1958 Brussels International Experimental Film Festival).

Another practitioner of this abstract movement was Jim Davis, "the pioneer filmmaker of light projections," according to Sitney.[84] Like Bute, Davis began as a painter and became interested in recording light and movement on film. Unlike Bute, Davis did not use animation; instead the abstract shapes and vivid prismatic colors of his films are produced by means of intercepting various kinds of light rays. As Davis explains, "These abstract forms are entirely artificially invented and consciously controlled by a variety of devices [reflective surfaces, distorting filters, curved plastic mobiles]. Having produced these moving, changing forms of color by the use of light—they are then recorded by the motion-picture camera."[85]

Sometimes, as in DEATH AND TRANSFIGURATION (1961), Davis would incorporate a human form using it as both a screen and as an element for distortion. Between 1946 and 1972, Davis created 113 (mostly abstract) films; only a small percentage are currently available. His work appeared at the Art in Cinema series twice (1947 and 1950), at Cinema 16 twice (1950 and 1952), and at the Museum of Modern Art in 1957, where ENERGIES was shown.[86] Davis's work influenced many filmmakers during the 1950s, including Brakhage who dedicated his film THE TEXT OF LIGHT (1974) to Davis for showing him "the first spark of refracted film light."[87]

Bute's and Davis's films explored technologies and devices that could create abstract images. This aesthetic was also explored by James and John Whitney and Jordan Belson,

 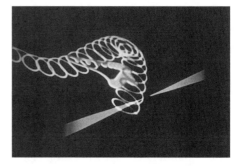

MOOD CONTRASTS (1953), by Mary Ellen Bute.

who supported their visuals with a spiritual purpose. The Whitneys' first film, FIVE FILM EXERCISES (1943–1944) reflected the films by Bute and Davis in that it tried to produce "color music," using light, abstract forms, animation, and electronic music. During the 1950s, the brothers worked separately, James taking about seven years to create YANTRA (1957) and John engaging in a number of activities (exploring the graphic potentials of analogue and digital computers, working on commercial projects like the title sequence of Alfred Hitchcock's VERTIGO [1958], collaborating with Charles Eames on a seven-screen presentation for the Buckminster Fuller Dome in Moscow in 1957, working at CBS television, and founding Motion Graphics Incorporated in 1960). John's next abstract film, CATALOGUE (1961), was one of the first computer-generated animations.

James's films seem richer and more interesting because they involve meditative goals associated with Jungian psychology, Zen Buddhism, alchemy, and yoga. The transcendental beauty and enormous spiritual power of YANTRA, HIGH VOLTAGE (1958), and LAPIS (1963) derives from their use of mandalas, geometric patterns employed during meditation. The ostensible goal of these films is to visually depict and perhaps help achieve a heightened state of consciousness, a quasi-religious union of one's "soul" with the natural world. Whitney explained that "YANTRA was basically a creation myth, an attempt to bring about a unity of cosmic happenings and inner psychic happenings, a bringing together of inner and outer realities."[88]

Jordan Belson concurrently developed a stylistic and thematic approach similar to that of his friend, James Whitney. Belson's best work actually began with ALLURES (1961) and shared a clearer historical and cultural context with the 1960s and 1970s, but his media experiments during the 1950s laid the groundwork for his more accomplished films. Like Bute and Davis, he began as a painter. After seeing the abstract animations of Hans Richter, Norman McLaren, and Oskar Fischinger at the Art in Cinema series, Belson made similar films during the early 1950s. (Belson's early animations include BOP-SCOTCH, 1952; MAMBO, 1951; CARAVAN, 1952; and MANDALA, 1953.) Between 1957 and 1960, Belson collaborated with the composer Henry Jacobs to produce nearly 100 Vortex Concerts. These multi-media presentations of abstract images and electronic music took place in San Francisco's Morrison Planetarium. The concerts synthesized films (some made by Belson) with the planetarium's machinery, which was, according to Igliori, capable of "multiple projections of geometric and polymorphous light phenomenon."[89] The concert experiences moved Belson away from animation and toward optical printing, from which his mature films would emerge. Combined with his interest in hatha yoga and meditation, Belson would create intensely spiritual and visually stunning mandala films during the 1960s: RE-ENTRY (1964), PHENOMENA (1965), SAMADHI (1967), and MOMENTUM (1968). Belson's work seems a fitting climax to a method of experimental film production that matured during the 1950s with Bute, Davis, and James Whitney.

Conclusion

The 1950s were not "quiet years." A vibrant experimental film "art world" emerged from the work of Frank Stauffacher, Amos Vogel, Maya Deren, Jonas Mekas, and others. Exhibition venues, distribution organizations, and artists' collectives grew and coalesced into a fully operational cooperative network of avant-garde cinema. Discussions and symposia held at numerous film societies and the efforts of academic associations to include film studies in university curricula generated a solid aesthetic foundation. A symbiotic theoretical discourse simultaneously materialized in critical publications such as *Film Culture* and the *Village Voice*.

Experimental filmmaking of the 1950s manifested a variety of styles. Stan Brakhage contributed a new form of cinematic address: the very personal and highly subjective lyrical film. Its connection to the dominant artistic discourse of abstract expressionism and the radicalism of the Beats pushed lyrical cinema to the forefront of the filmic avant-garde. Beyond the lyrical model, many other important filmmakers came to light during the decade. James Broughton, Shirley Clarke, and Ed Emshwiller formulated dance for the camera. Stan Vanderbeek, Harry Smith, and Bruce Conner established collage animation and compilation as media based assemblage. Robert Breer and Peter Kubelka devised a metric cinema of single-frame animation and editing. Mary Ellen Bute, Jim Davis, James Whitney, and Jordan Belson developed an abstract and meditative graphic cinema. Most of these filmmakers screened their films at Cinema 16 programs and many won Creative Film Foundation awards. Their non-lyrical styles did not ascribe to the neo-Romanticism of abstract expressionism. Instead, their work helped catalyze the minimalist, structuralist, and pop art reactions against abstract expressionism during the 1960s and 1970s.

In certain ways, the 1950s exhibited a logical and even evolutionary continuum between the 1940s and the 1960s, yet it also, and more importantly, exhibited elements that made the decade uniquely vital to the expansion of American experimental cinema.

Appendixes

NUMBER OF FEATURE FILMS RELEASED BY THE EIGHT MAJOR DISTRIBUTION COMPANIES, 1950–1960

	Columbia	MGM	Paramount	RKO	20th Century–Fox	UA	Universal	Warner Bros.	Total
1950	59	38	23	32	32	18	33	28	263
1951	63	41	29	36	39	46	39	27	320
1952	48	38	24	32	37	34	39	26	278
1953	47	44	26	25	39	49	43	28	310
1954	35	24	17	16	29	52	32	20	225
1955	38	23	20	13	29	35	34	23	215
1956	40	24	17	20	32	48	33	23	237
1957	46	29	20	1	50	54	39	29	268
1958	38	29	25	—	42	44	35	24	237
1959	36	25	18	—	34	40	18	18	189
1960	35	18	22	—	49	23	20	17	184

SOURCE: Christopher H. Sterling and Timothy R. Haight, *The Mass Media: Aspen Institute Guide to Communication Industry Trends* (New York: Praeger, 1978).

APPENDIX 2
NUMBER OF MOTION PICTURE THEATERS
IN THE UNITED STATES

	FOUR-WALL THEATERS	OUTDOOR THEATERS	TOTAL
1950	16,904	2,202	19,106
1951	16,150	2,830	18,980
1952	15,347	3,276	18,623
1953	14,174	3,791	17,965
1954	15,039	4,062	19,101
1955	14,613	4,587	19,200
1956	14,509	4,494	19,003
1957	14,509	4,494	19,003
1958	11,300	4,700	16,000
1959	11,335	4,768	16,103
1960	12,291	4,700	16,991

NOTE: As Sterling and Haight point out, there are "anomalies" in this table, including identical figures for 1956 and 1957. The overall trends described—a sharp drop in the number of traditional theaters, offset to some extent by an increase in drive-ins—are more useful than the figures for any one year.

SOURCE: Sterling and Haight, taken from *Film Daily Yearbook*.

APPENDIX 3
MOTION PICTURE BOX OFFICE RECEIPTS
IN THE UNITED STATES

	BOX OFFICE RECEIPTS IN MILLIONS OF DOLLARS	RECEIPTS AS A PERCENTAGE OF CONSUMER EXPENDITURE	RECEIPTS AS A PERCENTAGE OF RECREATION EXPENDITURE
1950	1,376	0.72	12.3
1951	1,310	0.64	11.3
1952	1,246	0.57	10.3
1953	1,187	0.52	9.3
1954	1,228	0.52	9.4
1955	1,326	0.52	9.4
1956	1,394	0.52	9.3
1957	1,126	0.40	7.3
1958	992	0.34	6.3
1959	958	0.31	5.6
1960	951	0.29	5.2

SOURCE: Joel W. Finler, *The Hollywood Story* (New York: Crown Publishers, 1988).

APPENDIX 4

AVERAGE PRICE OF A MOVIE TICKET IN THE UNITED STATES, 1950–1960

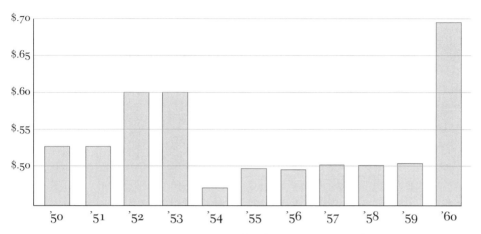

NOTE: An amusement tax on motion pictures was in effect through 1953. In 1953, this tax was 10 cents. Thus, the drop in admission prices between 1953 and 1955 is partly accounted for by the end of the tax.

SOURCE: Cobbett Steinberg, *Reel Facts* (New York: Facts on File, 1980), p. 44, based on figures published in the *Film Daily Yearbook*.

APPENDIX 5

WIDESCREEN AND 3-D RELEASES, 1952–1960

	1952	1953	1954	1955	1956	1957	1958	1959	1960
3-D	1	24	15	—	—	—	—	—	—
CINERAMA	1	—	—	1	1	1	1	—	—
CINEMASCOPE	—	4	34	72	56	64	62	56	42
REGALSCOPE	—	—	—	—	3	17	8	4	—
SUPERSCOPE	—	—	2	10	4	1	—	—	—
PANAVISION	—	—	—	—	—	—	—	—	6
TODD-AO	—	—	—	1	1	—	1	1	2
TECHNIRAMA	—	—	—	—	—	4	4	5	3
VISTAVISION	—	—	4	14	19	16	14	11	2

NOTE: Finler seems to be counting only releases from the eight largest studios. OKLAHOMA! (1955), omitted from Finler's list of Todd-AO films, is added here.

SOURCE: Finler, except for the Cinerama figures, taken from the Internet Movie Database (imdb.com).

Appendix 6
Top Ten Moneymakers Poll
(Actors and Actresses), 1950–1960

1950: John Wayne, Bob Hope, Bing Crosby, Betty Grable, James Stewart, Abbott and Costello, Clifton Webb, Esther Williams, Spencer Tracy, Randolph Scott

1951: John Wayne, Martin and Lewis, Betty Grable, Abbott and Costello, Bing Crosby, Bob Hope, Randolph Scott, Gary Cooper, Doris Day, Spencer Tracy

1952: Martin and Lewis, Gary Cooper, John Wayne, Bing Crosby, Bob Hope, James Stewart, Doris Day, Gregory Peck, Susan Hayward, Randolph Scott

1953: Gary Cooper, Martin and Lewis, John Wayne, Alan Ladd, Bing Crosby, Marilyn Monroe, James Stewart, Bob Hope, Susan Hayward, Randolph Scott

1954: John Wayne, Martin and Lewis, Gary Cooper, James Stewart, Marilyn Monroe, Alan Ladd, William Holden, Bing Crosby, Jane Wyman, Marlon Brando

1955: James Stewart, Grace Kelly, John Wayne, William Holden, Gary Cooper, Marlon Brando, Martin and Lewis, Humphrey Bogart, June Allyson, Clark Gable

1956: William Holden, John Wayne, James Stewart, Burt Lancaster, Glenn Ford, Martin and Lewis, Gary Cooper, Marilyn Monroe, Kim Novak, Frank Sinatra

1957: Rock Hudson, John Wayne, Pat Boone, Elvis Presley, Frank Sinatra, Gary Cooper, William Holden, James Stewart, Jerry Lewis, Yul Brynner

1958: Glenn Ford, Elizabeth Taylor, Jerry Lewis, Marlon Brando, Rock Hudson, William Holden, Brigitte Bardot, Yul Brynner, James Stewart, Frank Sinatra

1959: Rock Hudson, Cary Grant, James Stewart, Doris Day, Debbie Reynolds, Glenn Ford, Frank Sinatra, John Wayne, Jerry Lewis, Susan Hayward

1960: Doris Day, Rock Hudson, Cary Grant, Elizabeth Taylor, Debbie Reynolds, Tony Curtis, Sandra Dee, Frank Sinatra, Jack Lemmon, John Wayne

NOTE: These listings are in rank order, with the first name being the top box office star of the year.

SOURCE: *International Motion Picture Almanac* 2000, p. 15, also Steinberg, *Reel Facts*.

APPENDIX 7

ACADEMY AWARD NOMINATIONS AND WINNERS (IN BOLD) FOR BEST PICTURE, 1950–1960

1950 **ALL ABOUT EVE, Twentieth Century–Fox. Produced by Darryl F. Zanuck.**
BORN YESTERDAY, Columbia. Produced by S. Sylvan Simon.
FATHER OF THE BRIDE, MGM. Produced by Pandro S. Berman.
KING SOLOMON'S MINES, MGM. Produced by Sam Zimbalist.
SUNSET BOULEVARD, Paramount. Produced by Charles Brackett.

1951 **AN AMERICAN IN PARIS, MGM. Produced by Arthur Freed.**
DECISION BEFORE DAWN, Twentieth Century–Fox. Produced by Anatole Litvak and
Frank McCarthy.
A PLACE IN THE SUN, Paramount. Produced by George Stevens.
QUO VADIS?, MGM. Produced by Sam Zimbalist.
A STREETCAR NAMED DESIRE, Feldman/Warner Bros. Produced by Charles K.
Feldman.

1952 **THE GREATEST SHOW ON EARTH, DeMille/Paramount. Produced by Cecil B.
DeMille.**
HIGH NOON, Kramer/UA. Produced by Stanley Kramer.
IVANHOE, MGM. Produced by Pandro S. Berman.
MOULIN ROUGE, Romulus/UA. Produced by John Huston.
THE QUIET MAN, Argosy/Republic. Produced by John Ford and Merian C. Cooper.

1953 **FROM HERE TO ETERNITY, Columbia. Produced by Buddy Adler.**
JULIUS CAESAR, MGM. Produced by John Houseman.
THE ROBE, Twentieth Century–Fox. Produced by Frank Ross.
ROMAN HOLIDAY, Paramount. Produced by William Wyler.
SHANE, Paramount. Produced by George Stevens.

1954 THE CAINE MUTINY, Kramer/Columbia. Produced by Stanley Kramer.
THE COUNTRY GIRL, Perlberg-Seaton/Paramount. Produced by William Perlberg.
**ON THE WATERFRONT, Horizon-American/Columbia. Produced by Sam
Spiegel.**
SEVEN BRIDES FOR SEVEN BROTHERS, MGM. Produced by Jack Cummings.
THREE COINS IN THE FOUNTAIN, Twentieth Century–Fox. Produced by Sol C. Siegel.

1955 LOVE IS A MANY SPLENDORED THING, Twentieth Century–Fox. Produced by
Buddy Adler.
MARTY, Hecht-Lancaster/UA. Produced by Harold Hecht.
MISTER ROBERTS, Orange/Warner Bros. Produced by Leland Hayward.
PICNIC, Columbia. Produced by Fred Kohlmar.
THE ROSE TATTOO, Wallis/Paramount. Produced by Hal Wallis.

1956   **AROUND THE WORLD IN 80 DAYS, Todd/UA. Produced by Michael Todd.**
FRIENDLY PERSUASION, Allied Artists. Produced by William Wyler.
GIANT, Warner Bros. Produced by George Stevens and Henry Ginsberg.
THE KING AND I, Twentieth Century–Fox. Produced by Charles Brackett.
THE TEN COMMANDMENTS, DeMille/Paramount. Produced by Cecil B. DeMille.

1957   **THE BRIDGE ON THE RIVER KWAI, Horizon/Columbia. Produced by Sam Spiegel.**
PEYTON PLACE, Wald/Twentieth Century–Fox. Produced by Jerry Wald.
SAYONARA, Goetz/Warner Bros. Produced by William Goetz.
TWELVE ANGRY MEN, Orion-Nova/UA. Produced by Henry Fonda and Reginald Rose.
WITNESS FOR THE PROSECUTION, Small-Hornblow/UA. Produced by Arthur Hornblow Jr.

1958   AUNTIE MAME, Warner Bros. Jack L. Warner, studio head.
CAT ON A HOT TIN ROOF, Avon/MGM. Produced by Lawrence Weingarten.
THE DEFIANT ONES, Kramer/UA. Produced by Stanley Kramer.
GIGI, Freed/MGM. Produced by Arthur Freed.
SEPARATE TABLES, Hecht-Hill-Lancaster/UA. Produced by Harold Hecht.

1959   ANATOMY OF A MURDER, Preminger/Columbia. Produced by Otto Preminger.
BEN-HUR, MGM. Produced by Sam Zimbalist.
THE DIARY OF ANNE FRANK, Twentieth Century–Fox. Produced by George Stevens.
THE NUN'S STORY, Warner Bros. Produced by Henry Blanke.
ROOM AT THE TOP, Romulus-Continental (British). Produced by John and James Woolf.

1960   THE ALAMO, Batjac/UA. Produced by John Wayne.
THE APARTMENT, Mirisch Co./UA. Produced by Billy Wilder.
ELMER GANTRY, Burt Lancaster-Richard Brooks Prod./UA. Produced by Bernard Smith.
SONS AND LOVERS, Company of Artists/Twentieth Century–Fox. Produced by Jerry Wald.
THE SUNDOWNERS, Warner Bros. Produced by Fred Zinnemann.

Source: Robert Osborne, *70 Years of Oscar: The Official Story of the Academy Awards* (New York: Abbeville Press, 1999).

APPENDIX 8

OTHER MAJOR ACADEMY AWARDS

1950

Actor: Jose Ferrer, CYRANO DE BERGERAC.

Actress: Bette Davis, ALL ABOUT EVE.

Supporting Actor: George Sanders, ALL ABOUT EVE.

Supporting Actress: Josephine Hull, HARVEY.

Director: Joseph L. Mankiewicz, ALL ABOUT EVE.

Writing:

   (Motion Picture Story) PANIC IN THE STREETS, Edna Anhalt and Edward Anhalt.

   (Screenplay) ALL ABOUT EVE, Joseph L. Mankiewicz.

   (Story and Screenplay) SUNSET BOULEVARD, Billy Wilder.

Cinematography:

   (Black and white) THE THIRD MAN, Robert Krasker.

   (Color) KING SOLOMON'S MINES, Robert Surtees.

Art Direction:

   (Black and white) SUNSET BOULEVARD, Hans Dreier and John Meehan.

   (Color) SAMSON AND DELILAH, Hans Dreier and Walter Tyler.

Editing: KING SOLOMON'S MINES, Ralph E. Winters and Conrad A. Nervig.

Music:

   (Song) "Mona Lisa" (CAPTAIN CAREY, U.S.A). Music and lyrics by Ray Evans and Jay
      Livingston.

   (Score of Drama or Comedy) SUNSET BOULEVARD, Franz Waxman.

   (Score of Musical) ANNIE GET YOUR GUN, Adolph Deutsch and Roger Edens.

1951

Actor: Humphrey Bogart, THE AFRICAN QUEEN.

Actress: Vivian Leigh, A STREETCAR NAMED DESIRE.

Supporting Actor: Karl Malden, A STREETCAR NAMED DESIRE.

Supporting Actress: Kim Hunter, A STREETCAR NAMED DESIRE.

Director: George Stevens, A PLACE IN THE SUN.

Writing:

   (Motion Picture Story) SEVEN DAYS TO NOON, Paul Dehn and James Bernard.

   (Screenplay) A PLACE IN THE SUN, Michael Wilson and Harry Brown.

   (Story and Screenplay) AN AMERICAN IN PARIS, Alan Jay Lerner.

Cinematography:

   (Black and white) A PLACE IN THE SUN, William C. Mellor.

   (Color) AN AMERICAN IN PARIS, Alfred Gilks and John Alton.

Art Direction:

   (Black and white) A STREETCAR NAMED DESIRE, Richard Day.

   (Color) AN AMERICAN IN PARIS, Cedric Gibbons and Preston Ames.

Editing: A PLACE IN THE SUN, William Hornbeck.

Music:

    (Song) "In the Cool, Cool, Cool of the Evening" (HERE COMES THE GROOM). Music by Hoagy Carmichael, lyrics by Johnny Mercer.

    (Score of Drama or Comedy) A PLACE IN THE SUN, Franz Waxman.

    (Score of Musical) AN AMERICAN IN PARIS, Johnny Green and Saul Chaplin.

1952

Actor: Gary Cooper, HIGH NOON.

Actress: Shirley Booth, COME BACK, LITTLE SHEBA.

Supporting Actor: Anthony Quinn, VIVA ZAPATA!

Supporting Actress: Gloria Grahame, THE BAD AND THE BEAUTIFUL.

Director: John Ford, THE QUIET MAN.

Writing:

    (Motion Picture Story) THE GREATEST SHOW ON EARTH, Frederick M. Frank, Theodore St. John, and Frank Cavett.

    (Screenplay) THE BAD AND THE BEAUTIFUL, Charles Schnee.

    (Story and Screenplay) THE LAVENDER HILL MOB, T. E. B. Clarke.

Cinematography:

    (Black and white) THE BAD AND THE BEAUTIFUL, Robert Surtees.

    (Color) THE QUIET MAN, Winton C. Hoch and Archie Stout.

Art Direction:

    (Black and white) THE BAD AND THE BEAUTIFUL, Cedric Gibbons and Edward Carfagno.

    (Color) MOULIN ROUGE, Paul Sheriff.

    Editing: HIGH NOON, Elmo Williams and Harry Gerstad.

Music:

    (Song) "High Noon (Do Not Forsake Me, Oh My Darling)," (HIGH NOON). Music by Dimitri Tiomkin, lyrics by Ned Washington.

    (Score of Drama or Comedy) HIGH NOON, Dimitri Tiomkin.

    (Score of Musical) WITH A SONG IN MY HEART, Alfred Newman.

1953

Actor: William Holden, STALAG 17.

Actress: Audrey Hepburn, ROMAN HOLIDAY.

Supporting Actor: Frank Sinatra, FROM HERE TO ETERNITY.

Supporting Actress: Donna Reed, FROM HERE TO ETERNITY.

Director: Fred Zinnemann, FROM HERE TO ETERNITY.

Writing:

    (Motion Picture Story) ROMAN HOLIDAY, Dalton Trumbo (Ian McLellan Hunter served as a front for Dalton Trumbo).

    (Screenplay) FROM HERE TO ETERNITY, Daniel Taradash.

    (Story and Screenplay) TITANIC, Charles Brackett, Walter Reisch, and Richard Breen.

Cinematography:

    (Black and white) FROM HERE TO ETERNITY, Burnett Guffey.

    (Color) SHANE, Loyal Griggs.

Art Direction:

    (Black and white) JULIUS CAESAR, Cedric Gibbons and Edward Carfagno.

    (Color) THE ROBE, Lyle Wheeler and George W. Davis.

Editing: FROM HERE TO ETERNITY, William Lyon.

Music:

    (Song) "Secret Love" (CALAMITY JANE). Music by Sammy Fain, lyrics by Paul Francis Webster.

    (Score of Drama or Comedy) LILI, Bronislaw Kaper.

    (Score of Musical) CALL ME MADAM, Alfred Newman.

1954

Actor: Marlon Brando, ON THE WATERFRONT.

Actress: Grace Kelly, THE COUNTRY GIRL.

Supporting Actor: Edmond O'Brien, THE BAREFOOT CONTESSA.

Supporting Actress: Eva Marie Saint, ON THE WATERFRONT.

Director: Elia Kazan, ON THE WATERFRONT.

Writing:

    (Motion Picture Story) BROKEN LANCE, Philip Yordan.

    (Screenplay) THE COUNTRY GIRL, George Seaton.

    (Story and Screenplay) ON THE WATERFRONT, Budd Schulberg.

Cinematography:

    (Black and white) ON THE WATERFRONT, Boris Kaufman.

    (Color) THREE COINS IN THE FOUNTAIN, Milton Krasner.

Art Direction:

    (Black and white) ON THE WATERFRONT, Richard Day.

    (Color) 20,000 LEAGUES UNDER THE SEA, John Meehan.

Editing: ON THE WATERFRONT, Gene Milford.

Music:

    (Song) "Three Coins in the Fountain" (THREE COINS IN THE FOUNTAIN). Music by Jule Styne, lyrics by Sammy Cahn.

    (Score of Drama or Comedy) THE HIGH AND THE MIGHTY, Dimitri Tiomkin.

    (Score of Musical) SEVEN BRIDES FOR SEVEN BROTHERS, Adolph Deutsch and Saul Chaplin.

1955

Actor: Ernest Borgnine, MARTY.

Actress: Anna Magnani, THE ROSE TATTOO.

Supporting Actor: Jack Lemmon, MR. ROBERTS.

Supporting Actress: Jo Van Fleet, EAST OF EDEN.

Director: Delbert Mann, MARTY.

Writing:

    (Motion Picture Story) LOVE ME OR LEAVE ME, Daniel Fuchs.

    (Screenplay) MARTY, Paddy Chayefsky.

    (Story and Screenplay) INTERRUPTED MELODY, William Ludwig and Sonya Levien.

Cinematography:
  (Black and white) THE ROSE TATTOO, James Wong Howe.
  (Color) TO CATCH A THIEF, Robert Burks.
Art Direction:
  (Black and white) THE ROSE TATTOO, Hal Pereira and Tambi Larsen.
  (Color) PICNIC, William Flannery and Jo Mielziner.
Editing: PICNIC, Charles Nelson and William A. Lyon.
Music:
  (Song) "Love Is a Many-Splendored Thing" (LOVE IS A MANY-SPLENDORED THING).
    Music by Sammy Fain, lyrics by Paul Francis Webster.
  (Score of Drama or Comedy) LOVE IS A MANY-SPLENDORED THING, Alfred Newman.
  (Score of Musical) OKLAHOMA!, Robert Russell Bennett, Jay Blackton, and Adolph
    Deutsch.

1956

Actor: Yul Brynner, THE KING AND I.
Actress: Ingrid Bergman, ANASTASIA.
Supporting Actor: Anthony Quinn, LUST FOR LIFE.
Supporting Actress: Dorothy Malone, WRITTEN ON THE WIND.
Director: George Stevens, GIANT.
Writing:
  (Motion Picture Story) THE BRAVE ONE, Dalton Trumbo (written under the pseudonym
    "Robert Rich").
  (Screenplay-adapted) AROUND THE WORLD IN 80 DAYS, James Poe, John Farrow, and
    S. J. Perelman.
  (Screenplay-original) THE RED BALLOON, Albert Lamorisse.
Cinematography:
  (Black and white) SOMEBODY UP THERE LIKES ME, Joseph Ruttenberg.
  (Color) AROUND THE WORLD IN 80 DAYS, Lionel Lindon.
Art Direction:
  (Black and white) SOMEBODY UP THERE LIKES ME, Cedric Gibbons and Malcolm F.
    Brown.
  (Color) THE KING AND I, Lyle R. Wheeler and John DeCuir.
Editing: AROUND THE WORLD IN 80 DAYS, Gene Ruggiero and Paul Weatherwax.
Music:
  (Song) "Whatever Will Be, Will Be (Que Sera, Sera)" (THE MAN WHO KNEW TOO
    MUCH). Music and lyrics by Jay Livingston and Ray Evans.
  (Score of Drama or Comedy) AROUND THE WORLD IN 80 DAYS, Victor Young.
  (Score of Musical) THE KING AND I, Alfred Newman and Ken Darby.

1957

Actor: Alec Guinness, THE BRIDGE ON THE RIVER KWAI.
Actress: Joanne Woodward, THE THREE FACES OF EVE.
Supporting Actor: Red Buttons, SAYONARA.
Supporting Actress: Miyoshi Umeki, SAYONARA.
Director: David Lean, THE BRIDGE ON THE RIVER KWAI.

Writing:

(Screenplay-adapted) THE BRIDGE ON THE RIVER KWAI, Pierre Boulle, Carl Foreman, and Michael Wilson. (Only Pierre Boulle was credited in 1957, but the Academy has since recognized the contributions of blacklisted writers Carl Foreman and Michael Wilson.)

(Story and Screenplay-written for the screen) DESIGNING WOMAN, George Wells.

Cinematography: (Only one award given) THE BRIDGE ON THE RIVER KWAI, Jack Hildyard.

Art Direction: (Only one award given) SAYONARA, Ted Haworth.

Editing: THE BRIDGE ON THE RIVER KWAI, Peter Taylor.

Music:

(Song) "All the Way" (THE JOKER IS WILD). Music by James Van Heusen, lyrics by Sammy Cahn.

(Score) THE BRIDGE ON THE RIVER KWAI, Malcolm Arnold.

1958

Actor: David Niven, SEPARATE TABLES.

Actress: Susan Hayward, I WANT TO LIVE!

Supporting Actor: Burl Ives, THE BIG COUNTRY.

Supporting Actress: Wendy Hiller, SEPARATE TABLES.

Director: Vincente Minnelli, GIGI.

Writing:

(Screenplay-adapted) GIGI, Alan Jay Lerner.

(Story and Screenplay-written for the screen) THE DEFIANT ONES, Nedrick Young and Harold Jacob Smith.

Cinematography:

(Black and white) THE DEFIANT ONES, Sam Leavitt.

(Color) GIGI, Joseph Ruttenberg.

Art Direction: GIGI, William A. Horning and Preston Ames.

Editing: GIGI, Adrienne Fazan.

Music:

(Song) "Gigi" (GIGI). Music by Frederick Loewe, lyrics by Alan J. Lerner.

(Score for Drama or Comedy) THE OLD MAN AND THE SEA, Dimitri Tiomkin.

(Score for Musical) GIGI, André Previn.

1959

Actor: Charlton Heston, BEN-HUR.

Actress: Simone Signoret, ROOM AT THE TOP.

Supporting Actor: Hugh Griffith, BEN-HUR.

Supporting Actress: Shelley Winters, THE DIARY OF ANNE FRANK.

Director: William Wyler, BEN-HUR.

Writing:

(Screenplay-adapted) ROOM AT THE TOP, Neil Paterson.

(Story and Screenplay-written for the screen) PILLOW TALK, Russell Rouse, Clarence Greene, Stanley Shapiro, and Maurice Richlin.

Cinematography:
  (Black and white) THE DIARY OF ANNE FRANK, William C. Mellor.
  (Color) BEN-HUR, Robert L. Surtees.
Art Direction:
  (Black and white) THE DIARY OF ANNE FRANK, Lyle R. Wheeler and George W. Davis.
  (Color) BEN-HUR, William A. Horning and Edward Carfagno.
Editing: BEN-HUR, Ralph E. Winters and John D. Dunning.
Music:
  (Song) "High Hopes" (A HOLE IN THE HEAD). Music by James Van Heusen, lyrics by
    Sammy Cahn.
  (Score for Drama or Comedy) BEN-HUR, Miklos Rozsa.
  (Score for Musical) PORGY AND BESS, André Previn and Ken Darby.

1960

Actor: Burt Lancaster, ELMER GANTRY.
Actress: Elizabeth Taylor, BUTTERFIELD 8.
Supporting Actor: Peter Ustinov, SPARTACUS.
Supporting Actress: Shirley Jones, ELMER GANTRY.
Director: Billy Wilder, THE APARTMENT.
Writing:
  (Screenplay-adapted) ELMER GANTRY, Richard Brooks.
  (Story and screenplay-written for the screen) THE APARTMENT, Billy Wilder and I. A. L.
    Diamond.
Cinematography:
  (Black and white) SONS AND LOVERS, Freddie Francis.
  (Color) SPARTACUS, Russell Metty.
Art Direction:
  (Black and white) THE APARTMENT, Alexander Trauner.
  (Color) SPARTACUS, Alexander Golitzen and Eric Orbom.
Editing: THE APARTMENT, Daniel Mandell.
Music:
  (Song) "Never on Sunday" (NEVER ON SUNDAY). Music and lyrics by Manos Hadjidakis,
  (Score for Drama or Comedy) EXODUS, Ernest Gold.
  (Score for Musical) SONG WITHOUT END, Morris Stoloff and Harry Sukman.

SOURCE: Osborne, *70 Years of Oscar.*

Notes

Introduction

1. "One-Man Studio," *Time*, 12 June 1950, p. 64.
2. A film "package" is a story and a group of creative personnel (writer, director, producer, actors), generally put together by a producer or a talent agency.
3. Kenneth MacGowan, *Behind the Screen.* (New York: Dell, 1965), p. 315.
4. Philip Dunne, quoted by Aubrey Solomon, *Twentieth Century-Fox: A Corporate and Financial History* (Metuchen, N.J.: Scarecrow, 1988), p. 106.
5. *Ibid.*, p. 106.
6. Skouras, memo to Zanuck, 14 November 1958. Spyros Skouras Collection, Stanford University Special Collections.
7. Fredric Jameson, *Postmodernism, or The Cultural Logic of Late Capitalism* (Durham: Duke University Press, 1991), p. 280.

Chapter 1. The American Film Industry in the Early 1950s

1. John Houseman, "Hollywood Faces the Fifties, Part I. The Lost Enthusiasm," *Harper's*, April 1950, p. 52.
2. Census Bureau figures from Christopher R. Sterling and Timothy R. Haight, *The Mass Media: Aspen Institute Guide to Communication Industry Trends* (New York: Praeger, 1978), p. 352. TOA figures from an exhibit prepared for U.S. Attorney General's Conference, 10 October 1957, TOA Collection, Brigham Young University. Dept. of Commerce and Bureau of Labor Statistics figures from Ian Jarvie, *Hollywood's Overseas Campaign: The North Atlantic Movie Trade, 1920–1950* (Cambridge: Cambridge University Press, 1992), p. 216. Yet a fourth set of figures can be found in Houseman, p. 52. Houseman refers on p. 50 to "disquieting figures on weekly motion picture attendance" from "Dr. Gallup," so his numbers may stem from the Gallup Poll organization.
3. "Television! Boom!," *Fortune*, May, 1948, p. 79.
4. FCC figures, quoted in Sterling and Haight, p. 49
5. *Ibid.*, p. 361.
6. "20-30% Family B.O. Cut Via Home TV," *Variety*, 15 February 1950.
7. "TV's Impact a Puzzler," *Variety*, 22 March 1950.
8. Michael Conant has argued that Columbia, Universal, and United Artists should not have been included in the anti-trust case. Michael Conant, *Anti-trust in the Motion Picture Industry* (Berkeley: University of California Press, 1960), pp. 204–206.
9. *Ibid.*, p. 77.
10. Timothy R. White, "Hollywood's Attempt at Appropriating Television: The Case of Paramount Pictures." In Tino Balio, ed., *Hollywood in the Age of Television* (Boston: Unwin Hyman, 1990), p. 147.
11. Ian Jarvie has detailed the negotiations between Great Britain and the Hollywood film industry in *Hollywood's Overseas Campaign*. Jarvie, pp. 213–272. See also Thomas Guback, *The International Film Industry* (Bloomington: Indiana University Press, 1969), pp. 16–67.

12. "Pix Coin Nears End of Ice Age: Under $15 Million Frozen Overseas," *Variety*, 12 April 1950. See also Houseman, pp. 52–53; "Movies Come Out of the Dog House," *Business Week*, 10 November 1951, p. 141.

13. "While Sen. Johnson Puts Heat on Pix, Sen. Benton Plugs 'Em for Cold War," *Variety*, 29 March 1950.

14. Larry Ceplair and Steven Englund, *The Inquisition in Hollywood: Politics in the Film Community 1930–1960* (Garden City, N.Y.: Anchor Press/Doubleday, 1980), p. 353.

15. Tino Balio, *United Artists: The Company That Changed the Film Industry* (Madison: University of Wisconsin Press, 1987), pp. 55–61.

16. "Pix Picketing Poses Trade Dilemma; Can't Fight Local Dissident Groups," *Variety*, 19 March 1952.

17. "Kazan Warns Fear Hurts Film Industry," *New York Times*, 15 May 1952.

18. Robert Sklar, *Movie-Made America* (New York: Vintage/Random House, 1975), pp. 267–268.

19. "Films 'Struggle,' Selznick Asserts," *New York Times*, 31 March 1949.

20. "Need New Producers-Selznick," *Variety*, 22 February 1950.

21. "Enterprise Stressed by Hawks As Key to Outstrip Television," *Variety*, 17 September 1952.

22. Samuel Goldwyn, "Hollywood in the Television Age," *New York Times*, 13 February 1949; Samuel Goldwyn, "Is Hollywood Through?," *Collier's*, 29 September 1951, pp. 18–19. Goldwyn biographer Carol Easton describes a concerted publicity campaign (via ghost-written articles, for instance) to establish Goldwyn as a Hollywood elder statesman. Carol Easton, *The Search for Sam Goldwyn* (New York: William Morrow, 1976), pp. 263–265.

23. "Industry's $50,000,000 Lag," *Variety*, 8 March 1950; Thomas F. Brady, "Hollywood Warned," *New York Times*, 18 June 1950.

24. Thomas Schatz, *The Genius of the System* (Pantheon Books: New York, 1988), pp. 360–361.

25. Lillian Ross, *Picture* (New York: Avon Books, 1952), pp. 103–106, 165–167, 212–217. Ross's case study of the MGM film THE RED BADGE OF COURAGE was originally published as a series of articles in *The New Yorker*.

26. Schatz, p. 443.

27. Hugh Fordin, *The World of Entertainment: Hollywood's Greatest Musicals* (Garden City, N.Y.: Doubleday, 1975), pp. 256–257.

28. Schatz, p. 447.

29. Now available in the Howard Strickling Collection, Margaret Herrick Library, Academy of Motion Picture Arts and Sciences, Beverly Hills, Calif. (hereafter "AMPAS").

30. This explanation is given by H. Mark Glancy, "MGM Film Grosses, 1924–1948: The Eddie Mannix Ledger," *Historical Journal of Radio, Television, and Film* 12.2 (1992): pp. 1–3 of online version. Barbara Hall and Howard Prouty of AMPAS suggest that the discrepancy may be due to studio overhead (conversation with the author). However, the case of GIANT OF MARATHON (1959) makes this unlikely. For that film, production cost was $20,000 (the film was a pickup from Italian producers), earnings were $2,735,000, but profit was only $435,000. "Eddie Mannix Ledger," 1959–1960 season.

31. "Eddie Mannix Ledger."

32. Conant, pp. 120–124.

33. *Ibid.*, pp. 107, 109.

34. "Eddie Mannix Ledger"; Conant, p. 124.

35. Hugh Fordin's balance sheet for the Freed Unit shows "Total Earnings" but omits the much lower "profit" figure, and therefore greatly overstates the profits made by Freed's films. Hugh Fordin, *The Movie's Greatest Musicals Produced in Hollywood USA by the Freed Unit* (New York: Unger, 1984), pp. 567–568. This is a re-edition of *The World of Entertainment*.

36. Conant, p. 124.

37. Cobbett Steinberg, *Reel Facts* (New York: Facts on File, 1980), p. 58. The list comes from Quigley Publications.

38. Joseph C. Youngerman, *My Seventy Years at Paramount Studios and the Directors Guild of America* (Los Angeles: Directors Guild of America, 1995), p. 66.

39. Conant, p. 110.

40. Zanuck, memo to Philip Dunne, 7 May 1953, quoted in Aubrey Solomon, *Twentieth Century-Fox: A Corporate and Financial History* (Metuchen, N.J.: Scarecrow, 1988), pp. 71–72.

41. Thomas Schatz, *The Genius of the System: Hollywood Filmmaking in the Studio Era* (New York: Pantheon, 1988), pp. 437–438; Charles Higham, *Warner Brothers* (New York: Charles Scribner's Sons, 1975), p. 200.

42. Schatz, p. 437.

43. Dore Schary, *Heyday: An Autobiography* (Boston: Little, Brown, 1979), p. 156.

44. Donald L. Barlett and James B. Steele, *Empire: The Life, Legend, and Madness of Howard Hughes* (New York: Norton, 1979), p. 167; "Hughes RKO Cleanup Reported Under Way," *Los Angeles Times*, 10 July 1948.

45. An often-repeated story says that Hughes *never* set foot on the RKO lot. However, Dore Schary reports that Hughes used to screen rushes late at night at RKO in the first days of his ownership. Schary, p. 170.

46. Hal Wallis and Charles Higham, *Starmaker: The Autobiography of Hal Wallis* (New York: Macmillan, 1980), pp. 125–126.

47. "Curiosity About 'Mail Order Pic Biz' Led to Wall St. Journal's RKO Series," *Variety*, 22 October 1952; Tony Thomas, *Howard Hughes in Hollywood* (Secaucus, N.J.: Citadel, 1985), p. 107.

48. "RKO: It's Only Money," *Fortune*, May, 1953, p. 123.

49. *Ibid.*, p. 123.

50. Tino Balio, *United Artists*, p. 12.

51. Stanley Kramer and Thomas M. Coffey, *A Mad, Mad, Mad, Mad World: A Life in Hollywood* (New York: Harcourt Brace, 1997), p. 74.

52. *Ibid.*, p. 79.

53. Clive Hirschhorn, *The Universal Story* (New York: Crown, 1983), pp. 156–157.

54. Bernard F. Dick, *City of Dreams: The Making and Remaking of Universal Pictures* (Lexington: University Press of Kentucky, 1997), pp. 143–145.

55. "U Directorate Nod on Decca Merger Not Likely Without Stockholder Okay," *Variety*, 19 March 1952.

56. Dennis McDougal, *The Last Mogul: Lew Wasserman, MCA, and the Hidden History of Hollywood* (New York: Crown, 1998), p. 153, n. 6. McDougal notes that this deal was not unprecedented: Mae West, the Marx Brothers, Gary Cooper, and Howard Hawks had all had profit participation contracts.

57. "Eased Coin for Indies Ups Prod.," *Variety*, 18 January 1950.

58. Balio, *United Artists*, p. 15.

59. *Ibid.*, p. 9.

60. Janet Staiger, "The Package-Unit-System: Unit Management After 1955," David Bordwell, Janet Staiger, and Kristin Thompson, *The Classical Hollywood Cinema: Film Style and Mode of Production to 1960* (New York: Columbia University Press, 1985), pp. 330–331.

61. Janet Wasko, *Movies and Money* (Norwood, N.J.: Ablex, 1982), p. 108.

62. *Ibid.*, p. 107.

63. "'Show Me,' Say Banks to Indies," *Variety*, 13 June 1951.

64. Wasko, p. 118.

65. Quoted in Kenneth MacGowan, *Behind the Screen* (New York: Dell, 1965), p. 318.

66. *Ibid.*, p. 322.

67. David F. Prindle, *The Politics of Glamour* (Madison: University of Wisconsin Press, 1988), pp. 78, 82.

68. "From Reel Life to Real Life Headwaiter," *New York Times*, 7 August 1949.

69. "Eased Coin . . .," *Variety*, 18 January 1950.

70. "Trend to Semi-Indie Units," *Variety*, 12 July 1950.

71. "New High on Indie-Major Deals," *Variety*, 14 February 1951.

72. Balio, *United Artists*, pp. 89–91.

73. "FA (Feldman)-GAC (Rockwell) Co-Op Deal Covers Vast Talent Pool," *Variety*, 5 April 1950.

74. McDougal, especially pp. 150–151.

75. *Ibid.*, p. 212.

76. "Krim-MCA Talks Resume on Coast," *Variety*, 19 March 1952.

77. Carol Eastman, *The Search for Sam Goldwyn* (New York: William Morrow, 1976), p. 251.

78. Steven Watts, *The Magic Kingdom* (Boston: Houghton Mifflin, 1997), p. 286.

79. Watts, p. 373.

80. Todd McCarthy, *Howard Hawks, The Grey Fox of Hollywood* (New York: Grove Press, 1997), p. 443.

81. *Ibid.*, p. 465.

82. Kate Buford, *Burt Lancaster* (New York: Knopf, 2000), pp. 74–75.

CHAPTER 2. GENRES AND PRODUCTION TRENDS, 1950–1954

1. Margot Henriksen, *Dr. Strangelove's America* (Berkeley: University of California Press, 1997).

2. This poll, originally published in the *New York Times* of 24 June 1945, is reprinted in Garth Jowett, *Film: The Democratic Art* (Boston: Little Brown, 1976), p. 339.

3. This list is adapted from a longer list in Gerald Mast, *Can't Stop Singing: The American Musical on Stage and Screen* (Woodstock, N.Y.: Overlook Press, 1987), p. 246.

4. See Leo Braudy, *The World in a Frame* (Garden City, NY: Anchor/Doubleday, 1977), p. 140.

5. Claude Mauriac, "*Un Americain à Paris*" (review), *Le Figaro Littéraire*, 9 August 1952.

6. Tina Daniell and Pat McGilligan, "Betty Comden and Adolph Green: Almost Improvisation," in Pat McGilligan, ed., *Backstory 2: Interviews with Screenwriters of the 1940s and 1950s* (Berkeley: University of California Press, 1991), pp. 76–80.

7. Quoted in Peter Wollen, *Singin' in the Rain* (London: British Film Institute, 1992), p. 32.

8. Clive Hirschhorn, *Gene Kelly* (New York: St. Martin's Press, 1984), p. 192.

9. Peter Wollen, *Singin' in the Rain* (London: British Film Institute, 1992), pp. 48–51.

10. Edwin Schallert, "Kelly Says Tax Isn't Keeping Him Away," *Los Angeles Times*, 18 January 1953.

11. Richard Dyer, *Heavenly Bodies: Film Stars and Society* (New York: St. Martin's Press, 1986), pp. 31–42.

12. There is extensive correspondence on this: R. Monta to Arthur Hornblow, 1 June 1949; Hornblow to Monta, 2 June 1949; Monta to Hornblow, 9 June 1949; Hornblow to Monta, 11 June 1949; Hornblow to Monta, 8 July 1949. THE ASPHALT JUNGLE folder, John Huston Collection, AMPAS.

13. Bernard Eisenschatz, *Nicholas Ray: An American Journey*, trans. Tom Milne (London: Faber and Faber, 1993), p. 141.

14. Peter Bogdanovich, *Fritz Lang in America* (New York: Praeger, 1967), pp. 95–96.

15. *Ibid.*, p. 97.

16. Alain Silver, "KISS ME DEADLY: Evidence of a Style," in Silver and Ursini, eds., *Film Noir Reader*, p. 230.

17. Lawrence H. Suid, *Guts and Glory: Great American War Films* (Reading, Mass.: Addison-Wesley, 1978), p. 101.

18. Ron Kovic, *Born on the Fourth of July* (New York: McGraw-Hill, 1976), p. 43.

19. *Ibid.*, poem before page 1.

20. Bernard F. Dick, *The Star-Spangled Screen: The American World War II Film* (Lexington: University of Kentucky Press, 1985), pp. 136–137.

21. Most contemporary reviews of HALLS OF MONTEZUMA treated it as a realistic and patriotic war film, but Bosley Crowther commented on its pessimistic tone. Bosley Crowther, "THE HALLS OF MONTEZUMA," *New York Times*, 6 January 1951. For a conventionally patriotic review, see Frank Quinn, "'Halls of Montezuma' Blazes with the Deeds of the Marines," *New York Mirror*, 6 January 1951.

22. Dick, p. 137.

23. In a memo to Adler and Cohn, Taradash summarizes the first element as "Prew and his relationship to the Army, Warden, Captain Holmes and the Treatment." I have added Maggio because I think he is not just a sidekick; he is important to this aspect of the film. Memo, Taradash to Adler and Cohn, 8 August 1952. Zinnemann Collection, Box 28, file 358, AMPAS.

24. Letter, Joseph Breen to Harry Cohn, 4 August 1952. PCA File, FROM HERE TO ETERNITY, AMPAS.

25. Memo from Clayton Fritchey, Director, Office of Public Information, Department of Defense, to the Secretaries of the Military Departments, 20 March 1951. The subject of the memo is: "Military Cooperation or Collaboration on the Production of Commercial Motion Pictures for Either Theatrical or Television Release." Reprinted in Lawrence H. Suid, ed., *Film and Propaganda in America, A Documentary History*, vol. 4: *1945 and After* (New York: Greenwood, 1991), p. 200.

26. Suid, *Guts and Glory*, p. 123.

27. Memo, Buddy Adler, 25 February 1952. Though no recipient is stated, the intended recipient was probably Harry Cohn. Fred Zinnemann Collection, Box 28, Folder 358, AMPAS.

28. Memo, Adler, 25 February 1952; Daniel Taradash, Oral History with Barbara Hall, AMPAS, p. 216. The author read a not-quite-final version of the Taradash Oral History on 4 January 2001; therefore, pagination could change.

29. Suid, *Guts and Glory*, pp. 113–114.

30. "Regret for No Gun Ri," *Washington Post*, 13 January 2001.

31. Suid, *Guts and Glory*, p. 114.

32. Rick Worland, "The Korean War Film as Family Melodrama: 'The Bridges at Toko-Ri' (1954)," *Historical Journal of Film, Radio and Television* 19.3 (1999), pp. 361, 363.

33. Worland, pp. 359–363.

34. Peter Roffman and Jim Purdy, *The Hollywood Social Problem Film* (Bloomington: Indiana University Press, 1981), p. 289.

35. James Naremore, *More Than Night: Film Noir in Its Contexts* (Berkeley: University of California Press, 1998), pp. 123–125, 130.

36. Robert J. Corber, *In the Name of National Security: Hitchcock, Homophobia, and the Political Construction of Gender in Postwar America* (Durham: Duke University Press, 1992), pp. 61–79.

37. *Ibid.*, p. 72.

38. André Bazin, *What Is Cinema?*, v. 2, trans. Hugh Gray (Berkeley: University of California Press, 1971), p. 151.

39. Frank Manchel, "Cultural Confusion: BROKEN ARROW," Peter C. Rollins and John E. O'Connor, eds., *Hollywood's Indian: The Portrayal of the Native American in Film* (Lexington: University Press of Kentucky, 1998), pp. 96, 100.

40. *Ibid.*

41. Part of this scene is shown in the compilation film *A Personal Journey with Martin Scorsese Through American Movies* (1995).

42. Brenda Murphy, *Congressional Theatre: Dramatizing McCarthyism on Stage, Film and Television* (Cambridge: Cambridge University Press, 1999), p. 256.

43. Quoted in Fred Zinnemann, *Fred Zinnemann: An Autobiography* (New York: Charles Scribner's Sons, 1992), p. 96.

44. Stanley Kramer with Thomas M. Coffey, *A Mad, Mad, Mad, Mad World: A Life in Hollywood* (New York: Harcourt Brace, 1997), p. 73.

45. Zinnemann, *Autobiography*, p. 96.

46. *Ibid.*, pp. 95–96, 100, 108.

47. However, other Lupino films do not show a proto-feminist sensibility; see, for example, THE HITCH-HIKER (1953), a male-oriented suspense film.

48. John Houseman, "Hollywood Faces the Fifties, Part 1: The Lost Enthusiasm," *Harpers*, April 1950, pp. 50, 57.

49. Sklar, *Movie-Made America* (New York: Vintage/Random House, 1975), p. 268.

CHAPTER 3. HUAC, THE BLACKLIST, AND THE DECLINE OF SOCIAL CINEMA

1. Thomas Schatz, *Boom and Bust, The American Cinema in the 1940s* (New York: Charles Scribner's Sons, 1997), p. 307; Walter Goodman, *The Committee* (London: Secker & Warburg, 1968), pp. 173–174; on the Tenney Committee, chaired by Jack B. Tenney, see David Caute, *The Great Fear, The Anti-Communist Purge Under Truman and Eisenhower* (London: Secker & Warburg, 1978), pp. 77–78.

2. Schatz, *Boom and Bust*, pp. 307–313; Louis Pizzitola, *Hearst Over Hollywood: Power, Passion and Propaganda in the Movies* (New York: Columbia University Press, 2002), pp. 405, 409–411; on the significance of the labor disputes of 1945–1946 see Gerald Horne, *Class Struggle in Hollywood, 1930–1950, Moguls, Mobsters, Stars, Reds, and Trade Unionists* (Austin: University of Texas Press, 2001), p. 218.

3. Curt Gentry, *J. Edgar Hoover, The Man and the Secrets* (New York: W. W. Norton, 1991), pp. 353–354; John Cogley, *Report on Blacklisting, 1 – Movies* (New York: The Fund for the Republic, 1956), p. 11; Larry Ceplair and Steven Englund, *The Inquisition in Hollywood, Politics in the Film Community, 1930–1960* (Berkeley: University of California Press, 1983), pp. 209–225, 261ff.; Lee Server, *Robert Mitchum: "Baby, I Don't Care"* (London: Faber and Faber, 2001), pp. 137–138;

Variety, 26 November 1947, p. 3. Howard Suber, "The Anti-Communist Blacklist in the Hollywood Motion Picture Industry," Ph.D. dissertation, UCLA, 1968, pp. 24, 26, 285.

4. Eric Johnston, in Murray Schumach, *The Face on the Cutting Room Floor: The Story of Movie and Television Censorship* (New York: Da Capo Press, 1975), p. 139; Wyler, 26 October 1947, William Wyler Special Collection, Academy of Motion Picture Arts and Sciences, Margaret Herrick Library.

5. Carol Traynor Williams, *The Dream Beside Me: The Movies and the Children of the Forties* (Rutherford: Fairleigh Dickinson University Press, 1980), p. 203; Les K. Adler and Thomas G. Paterson, "Red Fascism: The Merger of Nazi Germany and Soviet Russia in the American Image of Totalitarianism, 1930's–1950's," *American Historical Review*, 75, April 1970, pp. 1,046–1,064.

6. See Thom Andersen, "Red Hollywood," in Suzanne Ferguson and Barbara Groseclose, eds., *Literature and the Visual Arts in Contemporary Society* (Columbus: Ohio State University Press, 1985), pp. 158–165; Paul Buhle, "The Hollywood Left: Aesthetics and Politics," *New Left Review*, 212, 1995, pp. 101–119; on the culture of the Popular Front, see Michael Denning, *The Cultural Front: The Laboring of American Culture in the Twentieth Century* (London: Verso, 1996), pp. 4–21, 26–27; Abraham Polonsky, interviewed in Eric Sherman and Martin Rubin, *The Director's Event: Interviews with Five American Film-Makers* (New York: Atheneum, 1970), p. 10; Albert Maltz to John Huston, undated, Huston Collection (1949 HUAC folder), Academy of Motion Picture Arts and Sciences; Arthur Schlesinger Jr., *The Vital Center: The Politics of Freedom* (Boston: Houghton Mifflin, 1949).

7. Richard Maltby, "Film Noir: The Politics of the Maladjusted Text," *Journal of American Studies*, 18, 1, 1984, p. 64; Capra in Lary May, *The Big Tomorrow, Hollywood and the Politics of the American Way* (Chicago: University of Chicago Press, 2000), p. 202.

8. Dore Schary, *Variety*, 5 November 1947, p. 1.

9. Morton J. Horowitz, *The Warren Court and the Pursuit of Justice*, (New York: Hill and Wang, 1998), pp. 56–59; Ring Lardner Jr., 19 June 1950, Ring Lardner Jr. Collection, Folder 239, Academy of Motion Picture Arts and Sciences; Ellen Schrecker, *Many Are the Crimes: McCarthyism in America* (Boston: Little Brown, 1998), p. 190.

10. Schrecker, *Many Are the Crimes*, p. 154; Richard Pells, *The Liberal Mind in a Conservative Age: American Intellectuals in the 1940s and 1950s* (New York: Harper and Row, 1985), p. 272.

11. Suber, p. 37; on Wayne and the Motion Picture Alliance in the early fifties see Randy Roberts and James S. Olson, *John Wayne, American* (Lincoln: University of Nebraska Press, 1995), pp. 339ff.; Harry Warner, *New York Times*, 10 September 1950; Kenneth L. Geist, *Pictures Will Talk: The Life and Films of Joseph L. Mankiewicz* (New York: Charles Scribner's Sons, 1978), pp. 173–206; Cecil B. DeMille, 18 October 1950, in Folder on Screen Directors Guild, 1950, George Stevens Collection, Academy of Motion Picture Arts and Sciences.

12. Suber, p. 38; Rossen, see Patrick McGilligan and Paul Buhle, eds., *Tender Comrades: A Backstory of the Hollywood Blacklist* (New York: St. Martin's Press, 1997), p. 377; Victor Navasky, *Naming Names* (New York: Viking Press, 1980), pp. 319–321.

13. Lewis Milestone, *New Republic*, 31 January 1949, pp. 12–17 and Lewis Milestone Collection, Folder 171/172, Academy of Motion Picture Arts and Sciences; *Alert*, 4 January 1951, 154; on Milestone, Lewis Milestone Folder, Hedda Hopper Collection, Academy of Motion Picture Arts and Sciences; Vincent Sherman, *Studio Affairs: My Life as a Film Director* (Lexington: University Press of Kentucky, 1996), pp. 246–247; *Counterattack*, undated, on Vincent Sherman; *Counterattack*, Communication 447, 2 April 1951; *Counterattack*, Communication 556 (on Schary), 3 October 1951, Box 14, Harvey Matusow Papers, 1950–1955, University of Sussex.

14. Ayn Rand, *Screen Guide for Americans*, The Motion Picture Alliance for the Preservation of American Ideals, Beverly Hills, California, undated; *Firing Line*, 15 March 1952, on DEATH OF A SALESMAN, Matusow Papers, University of Sussex.

15. J. B. Matthews, "Did the Movies Really Clean House," *The American Legion Magazine*, December 1951, pp. 13–14, 49–56; Suber, pp. 44–48; Robert B. Pitkin, "The Movies and the American Legion," *The American Legion Magazine*, May 1953, pp. 14–15, 39–44; Cogley, *Report on Blacklisting*, p. 131; on Hughes, *New York Times*, 7 April 1952.

16. "X," "Hollywood Meets Frankenstein," *Nation*, 28 June 1952, Folder 230, Ring Lardner Jr. collection, Academy of Motion Picture Arts and Sciences.

17. Jon Lewis, "'We Do Not Ask You to Condone This': How the Blacklist Saved Hollywood," *Cinema Journal*, 39, 2, (2000), pp. 4–12, 17–18. Clancy Sigal, "Hollywood During the Great Fear," *Present Tense* 9, 1982, pp. 45–48.

18. *Hollywood Reporter*, 7 April 1952; W. R. Wilkerson, "Trade Views," *Hollywood Reporter*, 25 July 1950, p. 1; Wyler's reply, *Hollywood Reporter*, 27 July 1950; Wyler to Frank Freeman, 3 May 1954, William Wyler collection, Political File, Folder 5.

19. Navasky, *Naming Names*; Lillian Hellman, *Scoundrel Time* (Boston: Little Brown, 1976). Paul Jarrico quoted in Michael S. Ybarra, "Blacklist Whitewash," *The New Republic*, 5 and 12 January 1998, p. 23; on Navasky see Andersen, "Red Hollywood," in Suzanne Ferguson and Barbara Groseclose, eds., *Literature and the Visual Arts in Contemporary Society*, pp. 158–165; Edward Dmytryk, *It's a Hell of a Life But Not a Bad Living: A Hollywood Memoir* (New York: Times Books, 1978), p. 146.

20. Dorothy B. Jones, "Communism and the Movies: A Study of Film Content," in Cogley, *Report on Blacklisting*, pp. 220, 282.

21. Richard Slotkin, *Gunfighter Nation: The Myth of the Frontier in Twentieth-Century America* (New York: Atheneum, 1992), pp. 347–348; Walter Bernstein, *Inside Out: A Memoir of the Blacklist* (New York: Alfred A. Knopf, 1996), p. 177; Farber, "Movies Aren't Movies Any More," *Commentary*, June 1952, in Farber, *Negative Space*, 1971, pp. 71–83; May, *The Big Tomorrow*, pp. 204, 273–293.

22. On the notion of film gris, see Andersen, "Red Hollywood," in Ferguson and Groseclose, pp. 183ff.

23. Michel Ciment, ed., *Conversations with Losey* (London: Methuen, 1985), pp. 90–93.

24. Breen to Robert Stillman, 3 May 1950, "The Sound of Fury," Production Code Administration collection, Academy of Motion Picture Arts and Sciences.

25. Thomas Cripps, *Making Movies Black: The Hollywood Message Movie from World War II to the Civil Rights Era* (New York: Oxford University Press, 1993), pp. 252, 259; on Garfield see Robert Sklar, *City Boys: Cagney, Bogart, Garfield* (Princeton, N. J.: Princeton University Press, 1992), pp. 203ff., and Polonsky introduction in Howard Gelman, *The Films of John Garfield*, (Secaucus, N.J.: The Citadel Press, 1975), p. 8; Paul Buhle and Dave Wagner, *A Very Dangerous Citizen: Abraham Lincoln Polonsky and the Hollywood Left* (Berkeley: University of California Press), pp. 10–11.

26. Cripps, *Making Movies Black*, p. 220.

27. David N. Eldridge, "'Dear Owen': The CIA, Luigi Luraschi, and Hollywood, 1953," *Historical Journal of Film, Radio and Television*, 20.2, 2000, p. 155.

28. Jonathan Munby, *Public Enemies, Public Heroes: Screening the Gangster from Little Caesar to Touch of Evil* (Chicago: University of Chicago Press, 1999), pp. 211, 217.

29. Bernard Vorhaus, interview with Brian Neve (BN), 15 October 1987; Endfield, interview with BN, 18 December 1989; on Endfield see Jonathan Rosenbaum, *Movies as Politics* (Berkeley: University of California Press, 1997), pp. 323–337.

30. Michael Wilson, "Hollywood and Korea," *Hollywood Review*, 1, 1 January 1953, pp. 1, 3–4; Wilson, "Hollywood's Hero," *Hollywood Review*, 1, 5, April–May 1954, pp. 1, 4; Adrian Scott, "Blacklist: The Liberal's Straightjacket and It's Effect on Content," *Hollywood Review*, 2, 2, September–October 1955, pp. 1, 3–6.

31. Thomas Schatz, *The Genius of the System: Hollywood Filmmaking in the Studio Era* (New York: Pantheon Books, 1988), p. 439; James Naremore, *More Than Light: Film Noir and Its Contexts* (Berkeley: University of California Press, 1998), p. 130.

32. W. R. Wilkerson, in *Hollywood Reporter*, 2 December 1947, cited in Joseph Foster, "Entertainment Only," *New Masses*, 66, 1948, pp. 21–22; Elia Kazan to Jack Warner, undated, Warner Bros. collection, University of Southern California.

33. Arthur Miller, *Timebends: A Life* (London: Methuen, 1987), p. 308; Elia Kazan, *A Life* (Andre Deutsch, 1988), pp. 413–415; Zanuck, Memorandum, 26 December 1950, VIVA ZAPATA!, Archives of Performing Arts, University of Southern California; Jonathan M. Schoenwald, "Rewriting Revolution: The Origins, Production and Reception of VIVA ZAPATA!," *Film History*, 8, 1996, p 120.

34. Zanuck, Memorandum, 26 December 1950, VIVA ZAPATA! Archives of Performing Arts, University of Southern California; Alex North to Elia Kazan, undated, Alex North collection, Academy of Motion Picture Arts and Sciences.

35. Slotkin, *Gunfighter Nation*, pp. 418ff.

36. Elia Kazan's testimony, 10 April 1952, and on VIVA ZAPATA! as an "anti-communist film," in Eric Bentley, ed., *Thirty Years of Treason: Excerpts from Hearings before the House Committee on Un-American Activities, 1938–1968* (New York: Viking, 1971), pp. 484–495; Kazan's letters to the *Saturday Review*, 5 April 1952, 24 May 1952.

37. John Womack Jr., *Zapata and the Mexican Revolution* (Harmondsworth: Penguin, 1972), p. 565; John Howard Lawson, *Film in the Battle of Ideas* (New York: Masses & Mainstream, 1953), pp. 38–50; Aubrey Solomon, *Twentieth Century Fox: A Corporate and Financial History* (Metuchen, N. J.: Scarecrow Press, 1988), p. 71, 86.

38. "An Interview with Budd Schulberg," *Tikkun*, 15, 3, May–June, 2000, p. 11; Navasky, *Naming Names*, pp. 239–246, 306–310.

39. John Steinbeck to Annie Laurie Williams, 17 June 1952, in Elaine Steinbeck and Robert Wallsten, eds., *Steinbeck: A Life in Letters* (London: Pan Books, 1979), pp. 450–451; Brian Neve, "The Personal and the Political: Elia Kazan and ON THE WATERFRONT," forthcoming in Joanna E. Rapf's edited collection on the film, Cambridge University Press, 2004; Elia Kazan, *New York Post*, 30 August 1954.

40. John Howard Lawson, "Hollywood on the Waterfront," *Hollywood Review*, 1, 6, November-December 1954, pp. 13–14; Lindsay Anderson, "The Last Sequence of ON THE WATERFRONT," *Sight & Sound*, 24, 3, 1955.

41. "Mankiewicz Pleads the Cause of the Liberal in the US," *Daily Variety*, 15 September 1950, p. 6.

42. See Sam B. Girgus, *Hollywood Renaissance: The Cinema of Democracy in the Era of Ford, Capra, and Kazan* (Cambridge: Cambridge University Press, 1998), pp. 155–176; see the case made by Philip C. Kolin, "Civil Rights and the Black Presence in BABY DOLL," *Literature/Film Quarterly*, 24, 1, 1996, pp. 2–11.

43. James J. Lorence, *The Suppression of SALT OF THE EARTH: How Hollywood, Big Labor, and Politicians Blacklisted a Movie in Cold War America* (Albuquerque: University of New Mexico Press, 1999), p. 54; Tim Miller, "Class Reunion: SALT OF THE EARTH Revisited," *Cineaste*, XIII, 3, June 1984, p. 33.

44. James J. Lorence, *The Suppression of SALT OF THE EARTH*, pp. 54–55; Paul Jarrico in Griffin Fariello, *Red Scare: Memories of the American Inquisition, An Oral History* (New York: W. W. Norton, 1995), pp. 281–283.

45. Lorence, *The Suppression of SALT OF THE EARTH*, pp. 91–96.

46. Congressman Donald Jackson, in Gordon Hitchens, "Notes on a Blacklisted Film: SALT OF THE EARTH," *Film Culture*, 50/51, Summer/Fall 1970, "Report on Blacklisting," pp. 79.

47. Howard Hughes, "Notes on a Blacklisted Film," *Film Culture*, pp. 80–81.

48. Pauline Kael, "Morality Plays Right and Left," in Kael, *I Lost It at the Movies* (Boston: Little Brown, 1965), pp. 331–346; Lorence, *The Suppression of SALT OF THE EARTH*, p. 130

49. Trumbo to Hugo Butler, June 1955, in Trumbo, *Additional Dialogue: The Letters of Dalton Trumbo* (New York: Bantam Books, 1972), p. 322.

50. Caute, *The Great Fear*, pp. 519–520; V. Rajakrishan, "An Interview with Arthur Miller," *Theatre Journal*, 32, 2, May 1980, pp. 196–204. Testimony of Judy Holliday, 26 March 1952, *Subcommittee to Investigate the Administration of the Internal Security Act and Other Internal Security Laws*, Committee on the Judiciary, U.S. Senate, 82nd Congress, U.S. Government Printing Office, 1952, p. 166, Matusow Papers, University of Sussex.

51. Welles was in Europe from 1947 to 1955. On the FBI interest see James Naremore, "The Trial: The FBI vs. Orson Welles," *Film Comment*, 27, 1, January–February 1991, pp. 22–27.

CHAPTER 4. CENSORSHIP AND SELF-REGULATION

1. The complete Production Code appears in the yearly editions of the *International Motion Picture Almanac*, ed. Charles A. Aaronson, a Quigley Publication.

2. Barbara Hall, "Oral History with Albert Van Schmus," Oral History Program, Margaret Herrick Library, AMPAS, 1993, pp. 99–100, 109.

3. Arthur Schlesinger Jr., "History of the Week," *New York Post*, 10 January 1954. Quigley, letter to Arthur Schlesinger, 12 January 1954. Box 1, Folder 39, Martin J. Quigley Collection, Georgetown University Special Collections.

4. Letter, Schlesinger to Quigley, 18 January 1954; Letter, Quigley to Schlesinger, 21 January 1954. Both in Box 1, Folder 39, Quigley Collection, Georgetown.

5. Schlesinger, letter to Quigley, 8 February 1954. Box 1, Folder 39, Quigley Collection, Georgetown.

6. Jack Vizzard, *See No Evil: Life Inside a Hollywood Censor* (New York: Simon and Schuster, 1970), p. 176.

7. Stephen Vaughn, "Morality and Entertainment: The Origins of the Motion Picture Production Code," *Journal of American History* 77.1 (1990): 51.

8. Vizzard, pp. 102–104.

9. Letter, Breen to Preminger, 10 April 1953, THE MOON IS BLUE folder, PCA Collection, AMPAS.

10. Bosley Crowther, "THE MOON IS BLUE," *New York Times*, 9 July 1953.

11. Quoted by Vizzard, p. 157.

12. *Ibid.*, p. 156. See also Frank Walsh, *Sin and Censorship: The Catholic Church and the Motion Picture Industry* (New Haven: Yale University Press, 1996), p. 259.

13. Tino Balio, *United Artists: The Company That Changed the Film Industry* (Madison: University of Wisconsin Press, 1987), p. 70.

14. Hall, "Oral History with Albert Van Schmus," p. 109. Permission to quote granted by Barbara Hall, Margaret Herrick Library, AMPAS.

15. Letter, Quigley to Breen, 12 October 1953, TEA AND SYMPATHY folder, PCA Collection, AMPAS.

16. Memos regarding all of these contacts are in the TEA AND SYMPATHY folder, PCA collection, AMPAS.

17. Jack Vizzard, file memo, 29 October 1953, TEA AND SYMPATHY folder, PCA Collection, AMPAS.

18. Letter, Shurlock to Schary, 25 March 1955. TEA AND SYMPATHY folder, PCA Collection, AMPAS.

19. Jerold Simmons, "The Production Code Under New Management: Geoffrey Shurlock, THE BAD SEED, and TEA AND SYMPATHY," *Journal of Popular Film and Television* 22.1 (1994), p. 8.

20. Walsh, pp. 271–274.

21. Samuel Goldwyn in the *New York Times*, 16 December 1956. Martin Quigley in the *Motion Picture Daily*, 18 December 1956. Both are quoted in "Digest of Reactions to Production Code Revision," 19 December 1956, "Production Code Administration" file, AMPTP Collection, AMPAS.

22. Thomas M. Pryor, "Hollywood Trials," *New York Times*, 16 December 1956.

23. Jack Hamilton, "Hollywood Bypasses the Production Code," *Look*, 29 September 1959, pp. 82–84.

24. *Ibid.*, p. 84.

25. For example, Arthur Schlesinger had proposed it in his correspondence with Martin Quigley. Letter, Schlesinger to Quigley, 8 February 1954, Quigley collection, Georgetown.

26. "Classification Debate On," *Variety*, 14 October 1959.

27. Fred Hift, "Kids, Sex, Films, and Tomorrow," *Variety*, 23 September 1959.

28. Walsh, pp. 217–218, 220.

29. See the voluminous correspondence between Quigley and Father Thomas Little in the Martin J. Quigley Papers, Georgetown. Gregory Black proposes that Quigley "dominated the Legion" until the mid-1950s. Gregory Black, *The Catholic Crusade Against the Movies, 1940–1975* (Cambridge: Cambridge University Press, 1997), pp. 143–144, 163.

30. Walsh, p. 263; Vizzard, pp. 227–228.

31. Black, pp. 94, 140; Walsh, p. 266.

32. Walsh, p. 274.

33. Letter, Breen to Warner, 1 August 1952, *BABY DOLL* folder, PCA Collection, AMPAS.

34. Walsh, pp. 274–275.

35. "Cardinal Scores 'BABY DOLL' Film," *New York Times*, 17 December 1956. Elia Kazan, *A Life* (New York: Knopf, 1988), pp. 563–564. Cardinal Spellman's speech had been written by Martin Quigley. Black, p. 169.

36. Walsh, p. 276.

37. Kazan, p. 564. Black, p. 172.

38. "National Legion of Decency Sermon Outline," 15 December 1957, quoted in Black, p. 181.

39. The most active state boards were in Maryland, Virginia, Pennsylvania, New York, Ohio, and Kansas. The Massachusetts board limited itself to deciding whether films were suitable for Sunday exhibition. Ira H. Carmen, *Movies, Censorship, and the Law* (Ann Arbor: University of Michigan Press, 1966), pp. 125, 131. The 1950 *Film Daily Yearbook of Motion Pictures* lists forty-nine local censorship boards; the 1950–1951 *International Motion Picture Almanac* lists ninety-three, but many of these seem to be inactive.

40. Richard S. Randall, *Censorship of the Movies* (Madison: University of Wisconsin Press, 1970), p. 81; "Balto. Sunpapers Fight to Oust Pix Censors; Cite 'Bitterness' Due to Cuts," *Variety*, 19 March 1952.

41. "Balto Sunpapers."

42. Frank Porter, "Censored," *Baltimore Sun*, 16 March 1952.

43. "The Miracle" was later released on video in the United States as part of a two-part Rossellini film entitled *L'AMORE*; the first part is "The Human Voice," the adaptation of a short play by Jean Cocteau.

44. Richard Parke, "'Miracle' Banned Throughout City," *New York Times*, 25 December 1950.

45. *New York Times*, 17 February 1951.

46. Lewis Wood, "Court Guarantees Films Free Speech; Ends 'Miracle' Ban," *New York Times*, 27 May 1952.

47. *Mutual Film Corp. v. Ohio*, 236 U.S. 230, p. 244 (1915), quoted in Randall, p. 19.

48. Wood, "Court Guarantees . . ."

49. Edward De Grazia and Roger K. Newman, *Banned Films: Movies, Censors, and the First Amendment* (New York: Bowker, 1982), pp. 84, 233, 236, 239, 240.

50. Randall, p. 33.

51. Randall, p. 35.

52. Randall, pp. 77, 80.

53. "Censorship Threat," *New York Times*, 26 March 1950.

54. Thomas F. Brady, "Hollywood Relaxes," *New York Times*, 7 May 1950.

55. Frances Stonor Saunders, *The Cultural Cold War* (New York: New Press, 1999), p. 289.

56. *Ibid.*, p. 288.

57. "U.S. Lists Movies It Limits Abroad," *New York Times*, 24 May 1959.

58. David N. Eldridge, "'Dear Owen': The CIA, Luigi Luraschi, and Hollywood, 1953," *Historical Journal of Film, Radio, and Television* 20.2 (2000): 149–196.

59. "Excerpt from an Address by the Honorable Alexander Wiley (R. Wisc.) Ranking Republican, Senate Foreign Relations Committee, In Burlington, Wisconsin at May Day-Loyalty Day" Celebration, 1 May 1955. "MoPIX Export Association" folder, AMPTP Collection, AMPAS.

60. Thomas M. Pryor, "Impact of Movies on Youth Argued," *New York Times*, 17 June 1955. Gladwin Hill, "Executives Doubt Films Hurt Youth," *New York Times*, 18 June 1955.

61. Joseph Bruce Gorman, *Kefauver: A Political Biography* (New York: Oxford University Press, 1971), p. 198.

62. "Senate Unit Hits Violence in Films," *New York Times*, 27 March 1956. "Kefauver Lauds Code," *New York Times*, 15 December 1956.

63. This was briefly discussed in Chapter 2 re: FROM HERE TO ETERNITY.

64. Fred A. Seaton (Assistant Secretary of Defense), "Policy for Extending Cooperation of the Department of Defense on Commercial Production of Motion Pictures, Including Those for Television," 17 February 1954, in Lawrence H. Suid, ed., *Film and Propaganda in America: A Documentary History, v. 4: 1945 and After* (New York: Greenwood, 1991), pp. 210–211. This volume also includes earlier versions of the cooperation policy.

65. Memo, H. D. Knight, 13 January 1956, DOD Collection, Box 2, Folder 11, Georgetown.

66. Thomas F. Brady, "Hollywood Checks," *New York Times*, 10 December 1950.

67. Walsh, pp. 251–252; "Cardinal Scores 'BABY DOLL' Film," *New York Times*, 17 December 1956.

68. Black, p. 131.

69. For a detailed study of TRIAL, novel and film, see Daniel J. Leab, "From Even-Handedness to Red-baiting: The Transformation of the Novel *Trial*," *Film History* 10.3: 320–331.

70. Jack Vizzard, "Memo for the Files," 30 March 1955, TRIAL file, PCA Collection, AMPAS.

71. Vizzard, *See No Evil*, pp. 186–188.

72. Eldridge, p. 163.

73. Dick Williams, "TRIAL Is Powerful Expose of Commies," *Los Angeles Mirror-News*, 2 September 1955; "TRIAL" (review), *Variety*, 2 August 1955; "TRIAL" (review), *Boxoffice*, 6 August 1955.

74. David Thomson, "Daniel Taradash: Triumph and Chaos" (interview), in Pat McGilligan, ed., *Backstory 2: Interviews with Screenwriters of the 1940s and 1950s* (Berkeley: University of California Press, 1991), p. 322.

75. Letter, Shurlock to Blaustein, STORM CENTER folder, PCA Collection, AMPAS.

76. This brochure also includes excerpts from an Eisenhower speech and press conference opposing book-burning; the American Library Association's Library Bill of Rights; and very positive comments from David H. Clift, the executive secretary of the American Library Association. STORM CENTER (publicity brochure), STORM CENTER folder, PCA Collection, AMPAS.

77. Thomas M. Pryor, "Rating of Movie Brings Protest," *New York Times*, 23 July 1956. James M. Skinner, *The Cross and the Cinema* (Westport, Conn.: Praeger, 1993), p. 111.

78. Black, p. 175.
79. Details of the Chasanow story are taken from Anthony Lewis, "What Happens to a Victim of Nameless Accusers," *Reporter*, 2 March 1954, pp. 10–17; and Joseph P. Blank, "Security Risk," *Look*, 17 May 1955, pp. 25–29.
80. The pseudonym "Bernard Goldsmith" was created by journalist Anthony Lewis.
81. Letter, Thomas S. Gates Jr. to Spyros Skouras, n.d. Box 11, Folder 13, DOD Collection, Georgetown.
82. Memo, Philip Dunne to Frank McCarthy, 24 August 1956. Box 11, Folder 13, DOD Collection, Georgetown.
83. Telegram, Albert Pratt to Spyros Skouras, 10 September 1956. Box 11, Folder 13, DOD Collection, Georgetown.
84. Don Baruch, Memo for Record, 14 January (1957?). Box 11, Folder 13, DOD Collection, Georgetown.
85. Philip Dunne, *Take Two: A Life in Movies and Politics* (New York: McGraw-Hill, 1980), pp. 280–281.
86. *Ibid.*, p. 282.
87. The phrase "voluntary agencies" and the discussion of "surveillance, judgment and even control" come from Father John Courtney Murray, writing in 1956 about Catholic attempts to influence literature and other communications media. John Courtney Murray, S. J., "Literature and Censorship," *Books on Trial* 14 (July 1956), p. 445, quoted in Black, p. 145.

CHAPTER 5. TECHNOLOGY AND SPECTACLE

1. Louis Pellegrine, "Developments in Color," *Film Daily Yearbook 1953*, p. 167.
2. Gorham A. Kindem, "Hollywood's Conversion to Color: The Technological, Economic, and Aesthetic Factors," *Journal of the University Film Association* 31.2 (1979): 33; Fred E. Basten, *Glorious Technicolor* (South Brunswick, N.J.: A. S. Barnes, 1980), pp. 137, 146.
3. Roderick T. Ryan, *A History of Motion Picture Color Technology* (London: Focal Press, 1977), pp. 148–149.
4. See "Chart #2" in Kindem, p. 30.
5. Basten, p. 149.
6. Kindem, pp. 30, 34.
7. Barry Salt, *Film Style and Technology: History and Analysis* (London: Starword, 1983), p. 310.
8. "Film Preservation 1993: A Study of the Current State of American Film Preservation," volume 1: "Report," Report of the Librarian of Congress, June 1993. (Accessed 16 December 2002.) Available on the World Wide Web at http://www.loc.gov/film/study.html, p. 12.
9. Gladwin Hill, "Case History of a Three-Dimensional Movie," *New York Times*, 13 January 1952.
10. Douglas Bell, "Oral History with Milton L. Gunzburg," Margaret Herrick Library, AMPAS, pp. 214, 219.
11. "Gunzburg Nets $2,500,000 Off Selling 60,000,000 Pairs of Polaroid Specs," *Variety* (daily), 29 July 1953.
12. "BWANA DEVIL" (review), *Variety*, 29 November 1952.
13. Tino Balio, *United Artists: The Company That Changed the Film Industry* (Madison: University of Wisconsin Press, 1987), p. 51. "Geo. Schaefer, in Suit, Charges Milton Gunzburg Is Trying to 'Cheat' Him," *Variety*, 28 October 1953.
14. Gunzburg Oral History, p. 201.
15. R. M. Hayes, *3-D Movies: A History and Filmography of Stereoscopic Cinema* (Jefferson, N.C.: McFarland, 1989), p. 26.
16. *Ibid.*, p. 55.
17. Frank Walsh, *Sin and Censorship: The Catholic Church and the Motion Picture Industry* (New Haven, Conn.: Yale University Press, 1996), p. 263.
18. Hayes notes an earlier reissue in 1984. Hayes, p. 42.
19. J. Hoberman, "The Stunt Men," *Village Voice*, 7 April 1999.
20. Arthur Gavin, "All Hollywood Shooting 3-D Films," *American Cinematographer* 34.3 (1953): 108–111, 134–136; "Is 3-D Dead . . . ?," *American Cinematographer* 34.12 (1953): 585–586, 608–612.
21. "Is 3-D Dead?," pp. 586, 608.
22. Salt, p. 315.

23. On Steiner's contribution to THIS IS CINERAMA, see Max Steiner, "Autobiography" (unpublished), pp. 178–179, Max Steiner Collection, Box 1, Folder 2, L. Tom Perry Special Collections Library, Harold B. Lee Library, Brigham Young University, Provo, Utah (hereafter BYU). Also Steiner, letter to Forbes, 2 July 1952, and Steiner, letter to Forbes, 7 July 1952, both in Max Steiner Collection, Box 4, Folder 19, BYU.

24. Merian C. Cooper, "Adventure in Cinerama," *Variety* (daily), 4 November 1954.

25. "Cinerama's B.O. Promise," *Variety*, 8 October 1952.

26. "Movie Revolution," *Time*, 13 October 1952.

27. *Ibid.* See also Cooper, "Adventure in Cinerama."

28. John Belton, *Widescreen Cinema* (Cambridge, Mass.: Harvard University Press, 1992), p. 106. *American Cinematographer* in 1952 estimated a much lower $25,000 to $75,000. John W. Boyle, "And Now . . . CINERAMA," *American Cinematographer* 33.11 (1952): 500.

29. Belton, pp. 105–107.

30. Merian C. Cooper, "Musts and Must Nots for Cinerama" (memo), 6 December 1954, pp. 2, 4, Merian C. Cooper Collection, Box 12, Folder 8, BYU.

31. "Cinerama-The Broad Picture," *Fortune*, January 1953, pp. 92–93.

32. Belton, p. 105; "Half of Owners Okay Cinerama Stock-Swap Idea," *Variety*, 13 August 1958.

33. Cooper, "Adventure in Cinerama"; Belton, pp. 105–106.

34. "Gunzburg Nets $2,500,000"; Cooper, "Adventure in Cinerama."

35. "What's New in 3-D," *The Exhibitor*, 15 April 1953.

36. Thomas M. Pryor, "Fox Films Embark on 3-Dimension Era," *New York Times*, 2 February 1953.

37. Zanuck, memo to Skouras, 20 June 1953, Box 37, Spyros Skouras Collection, Stanford University Special Collections.

38. Information on the Hollywood screenings is from Belton, pp. 132–133.

39. Bosley Crowther, "CinemaScope Seen at Roxy Preview," *New York Times*, 25 April 1953.

40. W. R. Wilkerson, "CinemaScope, 'ROBE' Triumph," *Hollywood Reporter*, 17 September 1953.

41. "THE ROBE," (review), *Variety*, 23 September 1953.

42. Edwin Schallert, "New Era Dawns with 'THE ROBE'," *Los Angeles Times*, 22 May 1953.

43. Lisa Cohen, "The Horizontal Walk: Marilyn Monroe, CinemaScope, and Sexuality," *The Yale Journal of Criticism* 11.1 (1998): 276–277.

44. On Zanuck and Skouras's advocacy of stereo sound, see Zanuck, letter to Skouras, 6 January 1955; Skouras, letter to Zanuck, 11 January 1955; and Skouras, letter to Zanuck, 15 April 1955. All in Box 37, Skouras Collection, Stanford.

45. Belton, pp. 133–136. Robert E. Carr and R. M. Hayes, *Wide Screen Movies* (Jefferson, N.C.: McFarland, 1988), p. 63.

46. Information on the production of A STAR IS BORN is from Ronald Haver, *A Star Is Born* (New York: Knopf, 1988), pp. 86–132.

47. My list is adapted from the dozens of formats discussed in Carr and Hayes, pp. 57–195.

48. Thomas Pryor, "Hollywood Expands," *New York Times*, 7 March 1954.

49. Belton, p. 135; Carr and Hayes, p. 146.

50. Salt, p. 321.

51. Carr and Hayes, pp. 165–166.

52. Belton, pp. 170–171.

53. Joel Sayre, "Film Process Caps His Gaudy Up-and-Down Career," *Life*, 7 March 1955, p. 144. John Belton reports that Rodgers and Hammerstein would also receive a princely 40 percent of the gross. Belton, p. 174.

54. George P. Skouras, Memo to Richard Rodgers and Oscar Hammerstein II, 27 October 1954. Zinnemann collection, Box 55, Folder 740, AMPAS.

55. Fred Zinnemann, *An Autobiography: A Life in the Movies* (New York: Charles Scribner's Sons, 1992), p. 136.

56. Letter, Zinnemann to Hammerstein, 30 September 1953, Zinnemann Collection, Box 55, Folder 737, AMPAS.

57. Letter, Oscar Hammerstein to George Skouras, 8 September 1956, Zinnemann collection, Box 55, Folder 740, AMPAS.

58. Michael Todd Jr. and Susan McCarthy Todd, *A Valuable Property: The Life Story of Michael Todd* (New York: Arbor House, 1983), pp. 134–136, 267–268.

59. Donald A. Henderson, "The Todd-AO Matter" (memo), 16 September 1963, Skouras Collection, Box 46, Stanford.

60. Information on Panavision and its products comes largely from Adrian Bijl, "The Importance of Panavision," Master's Thesis, Department of Theatre Science, University of Utrecht. Reprinted in *in7omm: The 7omm Newsletter*, March 2002. See also Carr and Hughes, pp. 173–174.
61. Andrew Dowdy, *"Movies Are Better Than Ever"* (New York: William Morrow, 1953), p. 7.
62. Belton, p. 210.
63. Belton, p. 188.

CHAPTER 6. HOLLYWOOD AND TELEVISION IN THE 1950S:
THE ROOTS OF DIVERSIFICATION

1. See Tino Balio, *Hollywood in the Age of Television* (Boston: Unwin Hyman, 1990), pp. 3–13; and, Fredrick Stuart, *The Effects of Television on the Motion Picture and Radio Industries* (New York: Arno Press, 1976).
2. This chapter is based on a variety of sources. A survey of industry and trade publications from the late 1940s and 1950s included *Variety, Broadcasting,* and *Film Daily Yearbook,* plus other publications written by industry representatives. Government and corporate documents were consulted, as well as relevant academic studies, especially those drawing on primary sources and archival material.
3. Christopher Anderson, *Hollywood TV: The Studio System in the Fifties* (Austin: University of Texas Press, 1994) p. 23.
4. See Anderson, pp. 26–33; and Michele Hilmes, *Hollywood and Broadcasting: From Radio to Cable* (Urbana: University of Illinois Press, 1990) for more discussion of Hollywood and radio.
5. Anderson, p. 33.
6. Douglas Gomery, "Failed Opportunities: The Integration of the U.S. Motion Picture and Television Industries," *Quarterly Review of Film Studies,* summer 1984, p. 224; Dennis J. Dombkowski, "Film and Television: An Analytical History of Economic and Creative Integration," Ph.D. dissertation, University of Illinois, 1982, pp. 50–51.
7. "Film Industry Advised to Grab Television," *Broadcasting,* 15 June 1937, p. 7. Also see Eric Smoodin, "Motion Pictures and Television, 1930–1945: A Pre-History of Relations between the Two Media," *Journal of the University Film and Video Association,* Vol. 34, No. 3, summer 1982.
8. "Television from the Standpoint of the Motion Picture Producing Industry," *Film Daily Yearbook* (New York: Film Daily Publications, 1939), p. 797; Timothy R. White, "Hollywood's Attempt at Appropriating Television: The Case of Paramount Pictures," in Balio, *Hollywood in the Age of Television,* pp. 150; Hilmes, p. 72.
9. Al Steen, "Television Developments of 1944," *Film Daily Yearbook* (New York: Film Daily Publications, 1945), pp. 66–68; Dombkowski, pp. 52–57.
10. See Gary N. Hess, *An Historical Study of the DuMont Television Network* (New York: Arno Press, 1979).
11. Hilmes, pp. 118–119; White, pp. 146–150; Dombkowski, pp. 31–32.
12. This section draws especially on the following discussions of Hollywood's attempts to own broadcast outlets: Hilmes, pp. 118–119; White, pp. 146–149; Gomery, pp. 219–227; Anderson, pp. 33–45; Dombkowski, pp. 29–37. See also, David Alan Larson, "Integration and Atempted Integration between the Motion Picture and Television Industries Through 1956," Ph.D., dissertation, Ohio University, 1979.
13. Al Steen, "Television Developments," *Film Daily Yearbook* (New York: Film Daily Publications, 1946), p. 75; Dombkowski, pp. 57–59.
14. Mitchell Wolfson, "Report of Theatre Owners of America Television Committee, 1950," pp. 4–5, TOA Collection, Box 41, folder 2, BYU. Wolfson, "Outmoded Theaters as TV Studios," *Film Daily Yearbook of Motion Pictures 1953* (New York: The Film Daily, 1953) pp. 717, 719.
15. Michael Conant, *Anti-trust in the Motion Picture Industry* (Berkeley: University of California Press, 1960), pp. 86–88.
16. John E. McCoy and Harry P. Warner, "Theater Television Today (Part I)," *Hollywood Quarterly,* Vol. 4, winter 1949, p. 160.
17. White, pp. 150–151. See also Orrin E. Dunlap Jr. *The Future of Television* (New York: Harper and Brothers Publishers, 1942) for a representative discussion of the enthusiasm over theater television.
18. Steen (1946), p. 75. The exhibitors' trade organization, Theatre Owners of America, published material promoting theater television, while its executive director toured the country "pushing his pet project." "TV Line Forming 'Rapidly': Sullivan," *Variety,* 31 May 1950, p. 3.

19. McCoy and Warner, p. 161.

20. Gomery, p. 221.

21. United States v. Scophony Corp., 69 F. Supp. 666 (S.D.N.Y., 1946). See also Al Steen, "Television in 1943," in *Film Daily Yearbook* (New York: Film Daily Publications, 1944), p. 65.

22. McCoy and Warner, pp. 161–163; White, p. 152.

23. White, p. 152; Hilmes, pp. 137–138; Larry Goodman, "Television," *Film Daily Yearbook 1953* (New York: Film Daily Publications, 1953), pp. 139–144.

24. Goodman, pp. 140–143; Hilmes, p. 122; Amy Schnapper, "The Distribution of Theatrical Feature Films to Television," Ph.D. dissertation, University of Wisconsin, 1975, p. 70.

25. White, p. 154.

26. White, p. 151. See also McCoy and Warner, pp. 262–266.

27. Donald La Badie, "TV's Threshold Year," *Film Daily Yearbook 1955* (New York: Film Daily Publications, 1955), pp. 23–26.

28. Hilmes, p. 125.

29. See Hilmes, pp. 187–188.

30. Stats from *Television Factbook*, cited in Christopher H. Sterling and Timothy R. Haight, *The Mass Media: Aspen Guide to Communication Industry Trends* (New York: Praeger Publishers, 1978), p. 49.

31. Gomery, p. 223.

32. *Ibid.*

33. White, p. 155.

34. Goodman, p. 141–142; Dombkowski, pp. 35–36.

35. Hilmes, p. 126.

36. Fred Hift, "Telemeter to Invade Two Cities," *Variety*, 4 May 1955, p. 1.

37. H. H. Howard and S. L. Carroll, *Subscription Television: History, Current Status, and Economic Projection* (Knoxville: University of Tennessee, 1980); "Suspension of Bartlesville Trial No Surprise to NY Execs," *Variety*, 28 June 1958, p. 23; Hilmes, pp. 127–128.

38. Howard and Carroll, pp. 44–48; White, p. 159–160.

39. See Mark Freed, "An Analysis of the Failure of Subscription Television in California in 1964," Master's thesis, University of Oregon, December 1969.

40. Hilmes, p. 133.

41. U.S. Congress, House, Committee on Interstate and Foreign Commerce, 1956; U.S. Congress, Senate, Committee on Interstate and Foreign Commerce, 1956. See also White, p. 157; "Five Bills Pend in Congress to Ban Tollvision from American Waves," *Variety*, 5 February 1958, p. 1.

42. White, p. 158.

43. Hilmes, p. 134.

44. Hilmes, p. 136.

45. Fred Hift, "Adjustment to TV Is Biggest Issue," *Variety*, 9 January 1957, pp. 7, 66.

46. U.S. Congress, Senate, Committee on Interstate and Foreign Commerce, *The Television Inquiry*, volume 4: *Network Practices, Hearings before the Committee on Interstate and Foreign Commerce*, Senate, 84th Cong., 2d sess., 1956, p. 2,280, cited in William Boddy, "The Studios Move into Prime Time: Hollywood and the Television Industry in the 1950s," *Cinema Journal*, Vol. 24, No. 4, summer 1985, p. 29.

47. Megan Mullen, *"The Revolution Now in Sight"? Cable Programing in the United States, 1948–1995* (Austin, Texas: University of Texas Press, in press).

48. See William Boddy, *Fifties Television: The Industry and Its Critics* (Urbana: University of Illinois Press, 1990), Chapters 4 and 5.

49. Hilmes, p. 150; Dombkowski, pp. 93–95. See also Robert Vianello, "The Power Politics of 'Live' Television," *Journal of Film and Video*, Vol. 37, summer 1985, pp. 26–40.

50. Boddy, "The Studios," p. 26.

51. Hift, p. 7.

52. For more discussion of these points, see Boddy, *Fifties*, pp. 65–76; Schnapper, pp. 23–30.

53. Anderson, pp. 54–56.

54. See Frederick Kugel, "The Economics of Film," *Television*, July 1951, pp. 10–15; "Hollywood Can Grind Out Film Fare for TV," *Business Week*, 24 November 1951, pp. 122–126; Bob Chandler, "TV Films: An Updated Version of Freewheeling Picture Pioneers," *Variety*, 4 January 1956, p. 157; Anderson, pp. 56–59.

55. Boddy, *Fifties,* pp. 69–70. For more on these producers, see Anderson, pp. 57–68, Dombkowski, pp. 96–105; Barbara Moore, "The Cisco Kid and Friends: The Syndication of Television Series from 1948–1952," *Journal of Popular Film and Television,* Vol. 8, spring 1980, pp. 26–33.

56. Dombkowski, p. 110.

57. Boddy, "The Studios," pp. 26–29; Boddy, *Fifties,* pp. 73–76.

58. Hilmes, p. 153.

59. Data from Dombkowski, pp. 111–123, derived from Irving Bernstein, *The Economics of Television Film Production and Distribution* (Screen Actors Guild, 1960); and Arthur D. Little, Inc., *Television Program Production* (Cambridge, Mass: Arthur D. Little, Inc., 1969), p. 113.

60. Erik Barnouw, *The Golden Web: A History of Broadcasting in the United States 1933–1953* (New York: Oxford University Press, 1968), p. 80–84.

61. "Hollywood in a Television Boom," *Broadcasting,* 26 October 1959, p. 90.

62. U.S. Congress, Senate Committee on Small Business, *Motion Picture Trade Practices-1956, Report,* 83rd Cong., 2nd Sess., 1956, p. 37.

63. Dave Kaufman, "Telefilm's Production Bill for '59 at $105,000,000 in Banner Year for Giant Biz," *Variety,* 7 January 1959, pp. 100, 174.

64. Anderson, p. 7.

65. Dombkowski, pp. 40–41.

66. *Ibid.,* pp. 164–173; "Skouras Sees Pic Future in Theatres; Big-Screen to Give That Extra Plus," *Variety,* 12 March 1952, p. 1.

67. White, pp. 158–159.

68. Conant, p. 137.

69. *New York Times,* 23 January 1958, p. 1, cited in Conant, p. 137.

70. Dombkowski, p. 180, using data from *Broadcasting Yearbook.*

71. Tim Brooks and Earle Marsh, *Complete Directory to Prime Time Network and Cable TV Shows* (New York: Ballantine Books, 1999), pp. 569–570.

72. "Will First-Run Films Be Extinct?" *Broadcasting,* 27 November 1961, p. 27.

73. See Douglas Gomery, "*Brian's Song*: Television, Hollywood, and the Evolution of the Movie Made for Television," in *American History/American Television,* ed. John E. O'Connor (New York: Frederick Ungar, 1983); Dombkowski, pp. 183, 195–216.

74. Hilmes, p. 166.

75. Even though some of the major Hollywood companies started to include television revenues on their balance sheets, accounting practices varied as to how these revenues were actually reported. For example, while MCA reported ownership of 1,657 television negatives, co-ownership of an additional 525 television negatives, and 700 pre-1948 films from Paramount, television revenues were not broken out of the revenues reported in *Moody's Industrial Manual,* 1961, p. 756. For a discussion of this problem, see Dombkowski, pp. 189–191.

76. Don Carle Gillette, "Self Deception in Diversity," *Variety,* 12 August 1959, pp. 3, 20, used these estimates as evidence that television wasn't proving to be a significant source of revenues for film companies. However, the rest of the article details the range of diversification activities already evident at the major Hollywood companies.

77. See Thomas H. Guback and Dennis J. Dombkowski, "Television and Hollywood: Economic Relations in the 1970s," *Journal of Broadcasting,* Vol. 20, No. 4, fall 1976; William Kunz, "A Political Economic Analysis of Ownership and Regulation in the Television and Motion Picture Industries," Ph.D. dissertation, University of Oregon, 1998.

78. Quoted in Jackson, *Walt Disney: A Bio-Bibliography,* pp. 49–50.

79. Balio, pp. 136–138; Bob Thomas, *Building a Company: Roy O. Disney and the Creation of an Entertainment Empire* (New York: Hyperion, 1998), p. 183.

80. Leonard Maltin, *The Disney Films* (New York: Crown Publishers, 1973), p. 122.

81. Bill Cotter, personal communication with the author, 6 September 2002; Barbara Jenkins, personal communication with the author, 16 September 2002; Bill Cotter, *The Wonderful World of Disney Television* (New York: Hyperion, 1997), pp. 185–187; Wesley Hyatt, *The Encyclopedia of Daytime Television* (New York: Billboard Books, 1997), p. 288.

82. Richard Schickel, *The Disney Version* (New York: Avon Books, 1968), p. 28.

83. *Moody's Industrial Manual,* 1961, p. 390.

84. Gillette, p. 20.

85. Much of this section is based on Janet Wasko, *Understanding Disney: The Manufacture of Fantasy* (Oxford: Polity Press, 2001). Also see Anderson's chapter on Disneyland.

86. For a detailed account of the opening of Universal City, see Richard Kozsarski, *An Evening's Entertainment: The Age of the Silent Feature Picture 1915–1928, History of the American Cinema*, v. 3 (New York: Charles Scribner's Sons, 1990), pp. 1–8.

87. "The Feature Is the Commercial," *Broadcasting*, 13 January 1958, p. 46.

88. Gillette, p. 20.

89. *Fortune*, July 1960, cited in Barnouw, p. 64.

90. This section is drawn from Universal's website, www.universalstudios.com; *Moody's Industrial Manual*, 1950–1961; Clive Hirschhorn, *The Universal Story* (New York: Crown Publishers, 1983); Dan E. Moldea, *Dark Victory: Ronald Reagan, MCA, and the Mob* (New York: Viking, 1986); Bernard F. Dick, *City of Dreams: The Making and Remaking of Universal Pictures* (Lexington: University of Kentucky Press, 1997); and Dennis McDougal, *The Last Mogul: Lew Wasserman, MCA, and the Hidden History of Hollywood* (New York: Crown Publishers, 1998).

91. Anderson, p. 5.

CHAPTER 7. HOLLYWOOD INTERNATIONAL

1. Jeremy Tunstall, *The Media Are American* (New York: Columbia University Press, 1977), p. 137.

2. Thomas Guback, *The International Film Industry* (Bloomington: Indiana University Press, 1969), Table 14, p. 53.

3. Guback, p. 71.

4. The Canadian figure was reduced from $98,699 because of taxes and an "exchange discount."All figures re: STRANGERS ON A TRAIN have been rounded to the nearest dollar. "Warner Brothers Pictures, Inc. Statement in Connection with the Photoplay STRANGERS ON A TRAIN to February 27, 1954," Schedule A. Folder 652, STRANGERS ON A TRAIN, Alfred Hitchcock Collection, AMPAS.

5. *Ibid.*

6. Freeman Lincoln, "The Comeback of the Movies," *Fortune*, February 1955, p. 131.

7. The "William Schaefer ledger," a Warner Bros. document similar to MGM's Eddie Mannix ledger, shows that STRANGERS ON A TRAIN earned $2,932,000, or slightly more than the total shown on 27 February 1954. If one uses this figure, earnings become about 1.86 times production cost. "Warner Brothers Financial Data," Microfiche Supplement to *Historical Journal of Film, Radio and Television* 15.1 (1995).

8. Guback, p. 166.

9. Ilya Lopert, "'SUMMERTIME' in the Canal City," *New York Times*, 22 August 1954.

10. Philip Dunne, *Take Two: A Life in Movies and Politics* (New York: McGraw-Hill, 1980), p. 257.

11. *Ibid.*, p. 258.

12. Irving Bernstein, *Hollywood at the Crossroads* (Hollywood: A F of L Film Council, 1957), p. 9.

13. Pryor uses the very conservative figure of twenty-five shooting days per film. Thomas M. Pryor, "34 U.S. Films Made Abroad This Year," *New York Times*, 21 December 1953.

14. Bernstein, pp. 48–49. Thomas M. Pryor, "Movies' Decline Held Permanent," *New York Times*, 7 April 1958.

15. Source for this table is Bernstein, p. 49, based on data from the *Hollywood Reporter*.

16. Romain Gary, *The Roots of Heaven*, trans. Jonathan Griffin (New York: Simon and Schuster, 1958).

17. John Huston, *An Open Book* (New York: Knopf, 1980), pp. 274–275. An earlier script by Romain Gary was not used.

18. Mel Gussow, *Don't Say Yes Until I Finish Talking: A Biography of Darryl F. Zanuck* (Garden City, N.Y.: Doubleday, 1971), p. 207.

19. Denis Gifford, *The Great British Picture Show* (New York: Facts on File, 1987).

20. Bernstein, p. 61.

21. Source for this table is Bernstein, pp. 54–55, based on data from the *Hollywood Reporter*.

22. Production information on BITTER VICTORY comes from Bernard Eisenschitz, *Nicholas Ray*, trans. Tom Milne (London: Faber and Faber, 1993), pp. 293–311. However, the interpretation is the author's.

23. Dalton Trumbo, *Additional Dialogue: Letters of Dalton Trumbo 1942–1962*, ed. Helen Manfull (New York: M. Evans, 1970), p. 209.

24. Ring Lardner Jr., *I'd Hate Myself in the Morning: A Memoir* (New York: Thunder's Mouth Press, 2000), p. 137. Trumbo, p. 286.

25. Hollis Alpert, "The Return of Carl Foreman," *Saturday Review*, 21 September 1957, p. 26.

26. Press Release, Carl Foreman Retrospective, Museum of Modern Art, 1978. Clipping File, Carl Foreman, AMPAS.

27. Ally Acker, *Reel Women: Pioneers of the Cinema* (New York: Continuum, 1991), p. 150.

28. Lardner Jr., p. 141; Stephen Farber and Marc Green, *Hollywood Dynasties* (New York: Putnam, 1984), pp. 286–287.

29. Lardner Jr. pp. 141.

30. David Robinson, *Chaplin: His Life and Art* (New York: McGraw-Hill, 1985), p. 572.

31. On the British reviews, see David Robinson, *Chaplin: The Mirror of Opinion* (London: Secker & Warburg, 1983), pp. 158–160. For American reactions, see Charles J. Maland, *Chaplin and American Culture: The Evolution of a Star Image* (Princeton, N.J.: Princeton University Press, 1989), pp. 323–324.

32. Charles Higham mentions the anti-Communist crusade in America as a reason for Welles's departure. David Thomson, in a more recent biography, says there is no evidence to support this view. Higham, *Orson Welles* (New York: St. Martin's Press, 1985), p. 282; David Thomson, *Rosebud* (New York: Knopf, 1996), p. 290.

33. Barbara Leaming, *Orson Welles* (New York: Viking, 1985), pp. 387–402.

34. Thomson, p. 307. See also p. 305 on the film's "lack of sequence."

35. Katherine Orrison, *Written in Stone: Making Cecil B. DeMille's Epic "THE TEN COMMANDMENTS"* (Lanham, Md.: Vestal, 1999), p. 20.

36. Kenneth Clark, "Confidential Notes for Mr. DeMille," 20 August 1954, DeMille Collection, Box 680, Folder 3.

37. Aeneas MacKenzie, "Search for Three Lost Decades," *New York Times*, 31 July 1955.

38. Orrison, p. 54.

39. For a good sampling of Rossetti's biblical paintings, see Russell Ash, *Dante Gabriel Rossetti* (New York: Harry N. Abrams, 1995).

40. Friburg has also painted the landscapes and historical scenes of the American West.

41. Orrison, pp. 66–67.

42. John Belton, *Widescreen Cinema* (Cambridge, Mass.: Harvard University Press, 1992), pp. 87–90.

43. Michael Wood, *America in the Movies* (New York: Dell, 1975), p. 173.

44. Edward G. Robinson (with Leonard Spigelglass), *All My Yesterdays: An Autobiography* (New York: Signet/New American Library, 1973), pp. 268–269, 288–291.

45. *Ibid.*, p. 299.

46. Charles Champlin, "Heston Revisits 'TEN COMMANDMENTS'," *Los Angeles Times*, 16 May 1990.

47. Gerald Mast, *Howard Hawks, Storyteller* (New York: Oxford, 1982), p. 347.

48. "Cardinals, Rabbis, Ministers in Praise of 'TEN COMMANDMENTS'," *Hollywood Citizen-News*, 22 October 1956.

49. See Memo, Luigi Luraschi to DeMille, "Re: THE TEN COMMANDMENTS-Asia", 25 September 1957, DeMille Collection, Box 711, Folder 18, BYU. DeMille quoted Prime Minister Ali in "An Address by Cecil B. DeMille before the Berlin League of Human Rights," 23 October 1957, DeMille Collection, Box 714, Folder 16, BYU.

50. Cecil B. DeMille, *The Autobiography of Cecil B. DeMille,* edited by Donald Hayne (New York: Prentice-Hall, 1959, released posthumously); "DeMille Itinerary," 10 October 1957, DeMille Collection, Box 714, Folder 23, BYU; "An address by Cecil B. DeMille before the Berlin League of Human Rights," 23 October 1957.

51. Bosley Crowther, "THE TEN COMMANDMENTS" (review), *New York Times*, 9 November 1956.

52. "In the Grand Tradition," *Newsweek*, 12 November 1956, pp. 113–114.

53. Arthur Knight, "Everybody Talkin' 'bout Heaven," *Saturday Review*, 10 November 1956, p. 28; John McCarten, "DeMille at the Old Stand," *New Yorker*, 17 November 1956, pp. 101–102.

54. "THE TEN COMMANDMENTS" (review), *Time*, 12 November 1956, pp. 120, 122, 124.

55. Bosley Crowther, "Screen Phenomenon," *New York Times*, 10 November 1957.

56. Jay Walz, "Movie Hits, Misses, and Trials on the Nile," *New York Times*, 20 December 1958.

CHAPTER 8. SCIENCE FICTION FILMS AND COLD WAR ANXIETY

1. Joyce A. Evans, *Celluloid Mushroom Clouds: Hollywood and the Atomic Bomb* (Boulder, Colo.: Westview Press, 1998), p. 75.
2. Other "dramatic genres were subject to direct military scrutiny and script control [and] blatant questioning of the official dominant line was impossible." Evans, p. 76.
3. Evans, p. 75.
4. Bill Warren, *Watching the Skies*, vol. 1 (Jefferson, N.C.: McFarland, 1982), p. xiv.
5. Eric Rabkin, "Science Fiction," in Eric Barnouw, George Gerbner, Wilbur Schramm, Tobia L. Worth, and Larry Gross, eds., *International Encyclopedia of Communications*, vol. 4 (New York: Oxford University Press, 1989), p. 19.
6. Vivian Sobchack, *Screening Space: The American Science Fiction Film* (New York: Ungar, 1991), p. 129.
7. Dana M. Reemes, *Directed by Jack Arnold* (Jefferson, N.C.: McFarland, 1988), p. 66.
8. Evans, p. 66.
9. Phil Hardy, ed. *The Overlook Film Encyclopedia: Science Fiction*, 3rd. ed. (New York: Overlook Press, 1995), pp. xv.
10. Paul Boyer, *By the Bomb's Early Light: American Thought and Culture at the Dawn of the Atomic Age* (Chapel Hill: University of North Carolina Press, 1994), p. 258.
11. Susan Sontag, "The Imagination of Disaster," *Against Interpretation and Other Essays* (New York: Farrar, Straus and Giroux, 1966), pp. 223–224.
12. Allan M. Winkler, *Life Under a Cloud: American Anxiety About the Atom* (Urbana: University of Illinois Press, 1999), p. 67.
13. Boyer, p. 257.
14. Hardy, p. xiv.
15. Earl Vieth, *Screening Science: Contexts, Texts and Science in Fifties Science Fiction Film* (Lanham, Md.: Scarecrow, 2001), p. 110.
16. Vieth, p. 81.
17. Barry R. Litman, *The Motion Picture Mega-Industry* (Needham Heights, Mass.: Allyn and Bacon, 1998), p. 231.
18. Vieth, p. 86.
19. Vieth, p. 86.
20. Michael Goodwin, "Heinlein on Film: DESTINATION MOON," in Danny Peary, ed., *Omni's Screen Flights/Screen Fantasies: The Future According to Science Fiction Cinema* (New York: Dolphin, 1984), pp. 102–106.
21. Untitled newspaper article on microfiche in the DESTINATION MOON clipping files at AMPAS.
22. "The Thinkers," *New Republic*, 10 July 1950.
23. Evans, p. 65.
24. *Los Angeles Times*, 8 April 1951.
25. Philip K. Scheuer, "Wail of Tortured Electrons Provides Eerie Film Score," *Los Angeles Times*, 26 February 1956.
26. J. P. Telotte, *Replications: A Robotic History of the Science Fiction Film* (Urbana: University of Illinois Press, 1995), p. 128.
27. Andrew Tudor, in *Monsters and Mad Scientists: A Cultural History of the Horror Movie* (Oxford: Basil Blackwell, 1989), p. 39, statistically analyzed the number of films in the horror/science fiction genre and found that 18 per cent of films from 1956 to 1960 were about invasion from space.
28. Hawks renamed his film from THE THING to THE THING FROM ANOTHER WORLD because a popular comedy song entitled "The Thing," sung by Phil Harris came out shortly after the shooting of the film began. Hawks wanted the public to perceive his film as serious drama, so he changed the title.
29. Todd McCarthy, *Howard Hawks: The Grey Fox of Hollywood* (New York: Grove Press, 1997), p. 482.
30. McCarthy, p. 476.
31. Perry Lieber, "'The Thing' from Another World: Vital Statistics," RKO Radio Studios, Hollywood, Calif., 1951. Production notes in AMPAS.
32. See "Interview with Howard Hawks," *Cahiers du Cinéma*, February 1956; "Interview with Kenneth Tobey," *Photon*, 1972; and McCarthy, pp. 480–481.
33. *Los Angeles Times*, 8 April 1951.

34. *Filmfax*, November 1989, p. 73.

35. Bob Thomas, "Strong UN Plea Made in Picture," *Hollywood Citizen News*, 1 May 1951.

36. Philip K. Scheuer, "Flying Saucer Film Dishes Up Choices," *Los Angeles Times*, 20 May 1951.

37. Thomas, 1 May 1951.

38. *Filmfax*, November 1989, p. 73.

39. Frank Scully, "Scully's Scrapbook," *Variety*, 3 October 1951.

40. *Los Angeles Times*, 8 April 1951.

41. Terry Christensen, *Reel Politics: American Political Movies from Birth of a Nation to Platoon* (Boston: Basil Blackwell, 1987), p. 101.

42. Peter Biskind interpreted this as a liberal film, explaining: "Like Communists, the aliens hide behind false fronts because Americans destroy what they don't understand." *Seeing Is Believing* (New York: Pantheon Books, 1983), p. 150.

43. This was the last film that William Cameron Menzies directed, and he also co-wrote it and designed the production. In 1936 Menzies had directed the science fiction film THINGS TO COME.

44. "WAR OF THE WORLDS" (review), *Variety*, 4 March 1953.

45. Taken from stock footage from ONE MILLION B.C.

46. Tom Weaver, *I Was a Monster Movie Maker* (Jefferson, N.C.: McFarland, 2001), p. 301.

47. *FilmEx Notes*, 17 March 1975.

48. *Los Angeles Weekly*, 2 June 2000.

49. Stuart M. Kaminsky, *Don Siegel, Director* (New York: Curtis, 1974), p, 104.

50. Cyndy Hendershot, *Paranoia, the Bomb, and 1950s Science Fiction Films* (Bowling Green, Ohio: Bowling Green University Press, 2000), p, 56.

51. Guy Oakes, "The Family Under Nuclear Attack: American Civil Defense Propaganda in the 1950s," in Gary D. Rawnsley, ed., *Cold War Propaganda in the 1950s* (New York: St. Martin's Press, 1999), p. 79.

52. Boyer, p. 353.

53. George Worthing Yates, who wrote the original story that the film was based on, was hired to write the script but was soon replaced by studio contract writer Russell Hughes. Hughes died after writing fifty pages, thus Sherdeman finished the script. Sherdeman's original script and other papers are held at the American Heritage Center at the University of Wyoming. *Los Angeles Times* in AMPAS.

54. Steve Rubin, "Them!" *Cinefantastique* 3.4 (Winter 1974), pp. 23–25.

55. The ending was to have been at the Santa Monica Pier, but it was too expensive to rent, thus the storm drains were chosen instead. Rubin, p. 25.

56. Weaver, pp. 261–262.

57. "Them, Suspenseful, Scary Science-Fiction Thriller," *Hollywood Reporter*, 8 April 1954.

58. "The Fly," *Newsweek*, 14 July 1958.

59. *Los Angeles Mirror News*, 23 July 1958.

60. *Los Angeles Mirror News*, 10 July 1956.

61. "The Shrinking Man's Fade-out Scary Ordeal," *Los Angeles Times*, 17 February 1957.

62. Reemes, pp. 61–62.

63. David Wilson, "The Return of Jack Arnold's Creature," *Los Angeles Weekly*, 17 February 1957.

64. *Ibid.*

65. Sara Hamilton, "Science Fiction Film Stars Carlson," *Los Angeles Examiner*, 25 February 1954.

66. In a typed handout at AMPAS (probably studio publicity).

67. *Ibid.*

68. Philip K. Scheuer, "Realism Gives Reelism Trial Filming 'WHEN WORLDS COLLIDE'," *Los Angeles Times*, 6 January 1955.

69. *Paramount News*, 11 June 1951.

70. "Atomic Age Creatures Dispense Cinema Horror," *Los Angeles Times*, 6 January 1955.

71. Correspondence between Stanley Kramer and officials of the Department of Defense, October and November 1958. Department of Defense Collection, Special Collections, Georgetown University Library, Washington, D.C.

72. Stanley Kramer, "ON THE BEACH: A Renewed Interest," in Peary, p. 118.

73. "ON THE BEACH," in *Nuclear War Films*, ed. Jack Shaheen (Carbondale: Southern Illinois University Press, 1978), p. 31.

74. Larry Glenn, "Russ OK on 'BEACH' Preem in Moscow May be Sign of Thaw," *Variety*, 30 November 1959.

75. Donald Spoto, *Stanley Kramer: Film Maker* (New York: G. P. Putnam's Sons, 1978), p. 211.
76. Spoto, p. 212.
77. Peary, p. 119.
78. *Variety,* 2 December 1959.
79. Dick Williams, "'On the Beach' Stirs Disputes," *Mirror News,* 4 February 1960.
80. Bosley Crowther, "Liable to Fallout," *New York Times,* 17 January 1960.

CHAPTER 9. THE FILM INDUSTRY IN THE LATE 1950S

1. Emmet John Hughes, "MGM: War Among the Lion Tamers," *Fortune,* August 1957, pp. 98–103, 206–208, 210, 212, 214, 216; "Vogel Still Plows Tough Loew's Row; Problems and Disputes Continue," *Variety,* 16 April 1958; "Green-Newman Plan for Splitting Loew's Stirs Wall Street; Would Spin Off Studio, Retain Theatres," *Variety,* 10 September 1958; Abel Green, "Wall Streeters See Their Own Men and Views Sure-Winning in Loew's," *Variety,* 8 October 1958.
2. Hughes, p. 101.
3. Andrew Dowdy, *Movies Are Better Than Ever* (New York: William Morrow, 1973), p. 176.
4. The Eddie Mannix ledger lists profits (or losses) for a period extending for a few years beyond a film's release date. It therefore does not match up perfectly with financial figures from annual reports.
5. See Hughes, p. 216.
6. *Ibid.,* pp. 210, 216.
7. Thomas F. O'Neil, "Why I Bought RKO," *Film Bulletin,* 8 August 1955.
8. "All R.K.O. Movies Sold for TV Use," *New York Times,* 27 December 1955; Richard B. Jewell with Vernon Harbin, *The RKO Story* (London: Octopus Books, 1982), p. 280.
9. Thomas M. Pryor, "R.K.O. to Expand; Selznick Signed," *New York Times,* 2 September 1955. Jewell and Harbin, pp. 280, 284, 290. "It'll Take up to a Year for RKO to 'Play It Off,'" *Variety,* 1 October 1958.
10. Aubrey Solomon, *Twentieth Century-Fox: A Corporate and Financial History* (Metuchen, N.J.: Scarecrow Press, 1988), pp. 122–125. Philip Dunne, *Take Two* (New York: McGraw-Hill, 1980), p. 279.
11. Solomon, pp. 105, 119.
12. *Ibid.,* p. 138.
13. Cass Warner Sperling and Cork Millner, *Hollywood Be Thy Name: The Warner Brothers Story* (Rocklin, Calif.: Prima Publishing, 1994), pp. 303–309; Neal Gabler, *An Empire of Their Own: How the Jews Invented Hollywood* (New York: Crown, 1988), p. 408.
14. Dennis McDougal, *The Last Mogul* (New York: Crown, 1998), p. 231.
15. "Box-Score on 'Indie' Producers," *Variety,* 7 January 1959.
16. Tino Balio, *United Artists: The Company That Changed the Film Industry* (Madison: University of Wisconsin Press, 1987), p. 93; "The Derring-Doers of Movie Business," *Fortune,* May 1958, p. 141.
17. Murray Teigh Bloom, "What two lawyers are doing to Hollywood," *Harper's,* February 1958, pp. 42–43; "The Derring-Doers," p. 139.
18. Balio, p. 45.
19. Thomas M. Pryor, "Republic Starts Cutback in Staff," *New York Times,* 23 May 1956. Charles Flynn and Todd McCarthy, "The Economic Imperative," in *Kings of the Bs,* ed. Todd McCarthy and Charles Flynn (New York: Dutton, 1975), pp. 31–32.
20. Mark Thomas McGee, *Fast and Furious: The Story of American International Pictures* (Jefferson, N.C.: McFarland, 1984), p. 37.
21. "Don't Kill Thrill-Chill Mill," *Variety,* 26 March 1958.
22. Balio, p. 87.
23. Balio, pp. 161–162, 165–166.
24. Thomas M. Pryor, "Rise, Fall and Rise of Sinatra," *New York Times,* 10 February 1957.
25. Information on Lancaster's independent companies comes from Kate Buford, *Burt Lancaster: An American Life* (New York: Knopf, 2000) and from Balio.
26. Buford, pp. 189–190.
27. Theater Owners of America, "Report on 1956 Convention" (brochure), National Association of Theater Owners Collection, BYU, Box 41, Folder 10.

28. Robert J. Landry called television "the big enemy and the big customer simultaneously." Robert J. Landry, "Contempt of Courtship: Production versus Exhibition," *Variety*, 7 January 1959.

29. "Bardot Is Practically a Whole Studio in Mpls.," *Variety*, 3 September 1958.

30. Balio, p. 223.

31. Fred Hift, "Put Seats Where Money Is," *Variety*, 3 September 1958.

32. *The Film Daily Year Book of Motion Pictures*, as quoted by the National Association of Theater Owners, NATO Collection, Box 9, Folder 4, BYU.

33. See Chapter 5.

34. The two technologies of most interest in 1952 were 3-D and theater TV. "TOA Angling All-Industry Research Plan; Skouras Would Ante First Cash," *Variety*, 13 December 1952.

35. Murray Schumach, "Movie Industry Flourishes in TV," *New York Times*, 31 July 1959.

36. Thomas M. Pryor, "Film Pinch Felt by Publicists," *New York Times*, 25 July 1958. Jack Gould, "TV Films Boom Hollywood Into Its Greatest Popularity," *New York Times*, 3 July 1955.

37. "Minutes of regular meeting of the board of Directors of Screen Composers Association," 6 May 1958, Screen Composers Association Collection, AMPAS.

38. Howard Kennedy, "Musicians' Union Fight Explained," *Los Angeles Times*, 20 May 1956.

39. Saxophonist Ted Nash, quoted in Jon Burlingame, *For the Record* (Los Angeles, Calif.: Recording Musicians Association, 1997), p. 22. Nash was one of the organizers of the Musicians Guild.

40. *Ibid.*, p. 21.

41. David F. Prindle, *The Politics of Glamour* (Madison: University of Wisconsin Press, 1988), p. 82.

42. Murray Schumach, "Fox Will Expand Work in Europe," *New York Times*, 4 December 1959.

43. For more detailed accounts of the SAG strike, see Paul Monaco, *History of the American Cinema*, volume 8: *The Sixties* (New York: Charles Scribner's Sons, 2001), pp. 18–19, and Prindle, pp. 82–87.

44. John Izod, *Hollywood and the Box Office* (New York: Columbia University Press, 1988), p. 146. A table showing this survey's findings is reproduced in Jowett, p. 476.

45. Izod, p. 149.

46. Milton Estrow, "Adult Films, New Comfort Revive City's Moviegoing," *New York Times*, 5 May 1958.

47. Jerry Wald, "40-Plus, 50-Plus Male Stars, Like Wine, Need Aging," *Variety*, 7 January 1959.

48. Peter Lev, *The Euro-American Cinema* (Austin: University of Texas Press) 1993, pp. 8–11; Michael Mayer, *Foreign Films on American Screens* (New York: Arco, 1965), pp. 1–2.

49. For a list of midtown Manhattan art theaters in 1958, see Estrow, *op. cit.* Information on films playing 1 October 1958 was taken from the *New York Times* movie ads.

50. Izod, p. 144.

CHAPTER 10. GENRES AND PRODUCTION TRENDS, 1955–1959

1. James Harvey, *Movie Love in the Fifties* (New York: Knopf, 2001), p. x.

2. Elaine Tyler May, *Homeward Bound: American Families in the Cold War Era* (New York: Basic Books, 1988), pp. 3–27.

3. Hugh Fordin, *The Movies' Greatest Musicals Produced in Hollywood USA by the Freed Unit*, (New York: Ungar Publishing, 1984), p. 435.

4. Rudy Behlmer, Oral History with Lela Simone, AMPAS, p. 195.

5. *Ibid.*, p. 442.

6. Gerald Mast, *Can't Stop Singing: The American Musical on Stage and Screen* (Woodstock, N.Y.: Overlook Press, 1987), p. 289.

7. *Ibid.*, p. 215.

8. The production history for SOME LIKE IT HOT is from Ed Sikov, *On Sunset Boulevard: The Life and Times of Billy Wilder* (New York: Hyperion, 1998), pp. 409–411.

9. "THE VIKINGS" (review), *New York Times*, 12 June 1958.

10. Joel W. Finler, *The Hollywood Story* (New York: Crown, 1988), p. 277; Tino Balio, *United Artists: The Company that Changed the Film Industry* (Madison: University of Wisconsin Press, 1987), pp. 158–159.

11. Libero Grandi, "The Photography of BEN-HUR," *American Cinematographer*, October 1959. Morgan Hudgins, "'BEN-HUR' Rides Again," *New York Times*, 10 August 1958.

12. Grandi, p. 605; Michael Anderegg, *William Wyler* (New York: Twayne, 1979), p. 200.

13. Lawrence H. Suid, *Guts and Glory: The Making of the American Military Image in Film*, revised ed. (Lexington: University Press of Kentucky, 2002), p. 221.

14. Memo, Maj. C. G. Forbush, HQ USAF, to Lt. Col. Tilley, Spec. Asst. to Cmdr., COMSAC, 14 December 1953. DOD Collection, Box 11, Folder 4, Georgetown.

15. Suid, p. 221.

16. Stewart was promoted to brigadier general in 1959.

17. Beirne Lay, "Original Story Outline," STRATEGIC AIR COMMAND, p. 3, n. d., DOD Collection, Box 4, Folder 4, Georgetown.

18. Balio, p. 158.

19. Whit, "*Paths of Glory*," *Variety*, 20 November 1957.

20. "Disputed Film on Again," *New York Times*, 12 March 1958.

21. Balio, p. 158.

22. Suid, p. 201.

23. Barbara Leaming, *Orson Welles* (New York: Viking, 1985), pp. 413–414. Todd McCarthy and Charles Flynn, "Albert Zugsmith" (interview), in *Kings of the Bs*, ed. Todd McCarthy and Charles Flynn (New York: Dutton, 1975) p. 420.

24. My descriptions of Menzies and Quinlan draw from Welles's comments in a 1958 interview. André Bazin, Charles Bitsch, and Jean Domarchi, "Interview with Orson Welles (II)," trans. Peter Wollen, in *Orson Welles Interviews*, ed. Mark W. Estrin (Jackson: University Press of Mississippi, 2002), pp. 50–53.

25. The DVD of this version includes, as a "bonus feature," the complete cutting memo.

26. Jim Kitses, *Horizons West* (Bloomington: Indiana University Press, 1969), p. 97.

27. The term "superwestern" was coined by French critic André Bazin. See my discussion in Chapter 2.

28. See, for example, Ivan Spear, "THE SEARCHERS," *Boxoffice*, 17 March 1956; "Vast Scope of THE SEARCHERS Indicated," *Film Daily*, 20 March 1956.

29. Brian Henderson, "THE SEARCHERS: An American Dilemma," *Film Quarterly* 34.2 (1980–81): 10–23. See also Barbara Mortimer, *Hollywood's Frontier Captives* (New York: Garland, 2000), pp. 29–48.

30. Todd McCarthy, *Howard Hawks: The Grey Fox of Hollywood* (New York: Grove Press, 1997); Robin Wood, "*Rio Bravo* and Retrospect," in Jim Kitses and Alan Rickman, *The Western Reader* (New York: Limelight, 1998), p. 173.

31. Thomas Schatz, *Hollywood Genres* (New York: McGraw-Hill, 1981), p. 222.

32. Kevin Thomas, "GIANT" (review), *Los Angeles Times*, 27 September 1996. This review was written on the occasion of the 40 year re-release of GIANT.

33. The idea of Sirk as hyperrealist comes from the painter David Salle, as quoted by J. Hoberman. J. Hoberman, "Film," *Village Voice*, 11 July 1989.

34. Todd McCarthy and Charles Flynn, "Albert Zugsmith" (interview), in *Kings of the Bs*, p. 415.

35. Jon Halliday, *Sirk on Sirk* (New York: Viking, 1972), p. 119.

36. Halliday, p. 132.

37. See James Harvey, *Movie Love in the Fifties* (New York: Knopf, 2001), pp. 371–380.

38. Hoberman, op. cit.

39. This section is indebted to James Harvey's chapter "Method Movies," in *Movie Love in the Fifties*, pp. 140–147.

40. My interpretation of this scene draws on James Naremore, *Acting in the Cinema* (Berkeley, Calif.: University of California Press, 1988), pp. 208–209.

41. Ray Carney, *The Films of John Cassavetes: Pragmatism, Modernism and the Movies* (Cambridge, UK: Cambridge University Press, 1994), pp. 35, 50.

42. Thomas Doherty, *Teenagers and Teenpics* (Boston: Unwin Hyman, 1988).

43. This list is taken from a press release signed by Richard Brooks. Richard Brooks, Press Release, BLACKBOARD JUNGLE, 4 pages, n.d., pp. 3–4. Richard Brooks Collection, AMPAS.

44. Program booklet, BLACKBOARD JUNGLE, Richard Brooks collection, AMPAS.

45. R. Serge Denisoff and William D. Romanowski, *Risky Business: Rock and Film* (New Brunswick, N.J.: Transaction Publishers, 1991), p. 17.

46. According to a segment of the TV show *Warner Brothers Presents*, REBEL WITHOUT A CAUSE, like BLACKBOARD JUNGLE, was based on the enormous amount of factual data on juvenile delinquency that was available in the mid-1950s. See the DVD for REBEL WITHOUT A CAUSE.

47. Memo, Joseph Hazen to Hal Wallis, 2 April 1956. "Elvis Presley, General" File (1 of 2), Hal Wallis Collection, AMPAS. Hal Wallis and Charles Higham, *Starmaker* (New York, Macmillan, 1980), p. 148. It is possible that the contract in Wallis's files was only a first offer. But *Starmaker* is wrong about the date of the contract (which it places in 1957), and it could be wrong about the amount as well.

   A 1958 memo in the Wallis collection showed that Presley had just signed a new, non-exclusive contract for four films at salaries ranging from $75,000 to $125,000. Memo, Joseph Hazen to Sidney Justin, 30 October 1958. Wallis Collection, AMPAS.

48. Eddie Mannix Ledger, AMPAS.

49. Dick Williams, "6,000 Kids Cheer Elvis' Frantic Sex Show," *Los Angeles Mirror News*, 29 October 1957.

50. Richard Gertner, "The Nation's Exhibitors Select the Stars of Tomorrow," *Motion Picture Herald*, 10 October 1959, quoted in Doherty, p. 196.

51. See the introduction to this chapter, and note 1. The phrases "postclassical Hollywood" and "postclassical film" are becoming fairly common in film history and criticism, but there is no consensus on when the classical ends and the postclassical begins.

52. Screenwriter James Agee reported on a similar milieu in *Let Us Now Praise Famous Men* (1941), his book collaboration with the photographer Walker Evans.

53. Robin Wood, *Hitchcock's Films* (1965), quoted in Dan Auiler, VERTIGO: *The Making of a Hitchcock Classic* (New York: St. Martin's Griffin, 2000), p. 177.

54. Fred Zinnemann, *A Life in the Movies* (New York: Charles Scribner's Sons, 1992), pp. 155, 171.

55. *Ibid.*, p. 163.

56. *Ibid.*, pp. 158, 162.

CHAPTER 11. AMERICAN DOCUMENTARY IN THE 1950S

1. Jack C. Ellis, *The Documentary Idea: A Critical History of English-Language Documentary Film and Video* (Englewood Cliffs, N.J.: Prentice Hall, 1989), p. 176.

2. John Wilcox, "The African Lion," *Sight & Sound* 26 (Summer 1956) 35.

3. Basil Wright, "The Living Desert," *Sight & Sound* 24 (July–September 1954) 35.

4. Erik Barnouw, *Documentary: A History of the Non-Fiction Film* (New York: Oxford University Press, 1993), p. 219.

5. George C. Stoney, "Appendix," in Ellis, p. 302.

6. Ellis, p. 173.

7. Lewis Jacobs, ed., *The Documentary Tradition* (New York: W. W. Norton, 1979), p. 427.

8. Thomas M. Pryor, "Films in the 'Truth Campaign,'" *New York Times*, 25 March 1951, reprinted in ibid., pp. 292–295.

9. Barnouw, p. 226.

10. Pryor, op. cit.

11. James E. Gibson, "Federal Government," *Sixty Years of 16 mm. Film* (Evanston, Ill.: Film Council of America, 1954), pp. 148–160.

12. Pryor, op. cit.

13. Former USIA agent, conversation with author at the time.

14. Colin Young and A. Martin Zweiback, "Going Out to the Subject," *Film Quarterly* 13 (Winter 1959), pp. 39–49.

15. Flora Rheta Schreiber, "New York: A Cinema Capital," *The Quarterly of Film, Radio and Television* 7 (Spring 1953) 264–273.

16. Raymond Spottiswoode, in Cecile Starr, ed., *Ideas on Film: A Handbook for the 16 mm. User* (New York: Funk & Wagnalls, 1951), p. 224.

17. Richard Griffith, "United States," in Paul Rotha, *Documentary Film* (New York: Hastings House, 1952), pp. 308–331.

18. Ellis, p. 182.

19. Ellis, pp. 177–178.

20. Richard M. Barsam, *Nonfiction Film: A Critical History* (Bloomington: Indiana University Press, 1992), p. 296.

21. Alfred Appel Jr., "Film Reviews: Jazz on a Summer's Day," *Film Quarterly* 14 (Fall 1960) 56–57.

22. Ellis, p. 178.

23. This information comes from an obituary for Jacoby the author has as a clipping, unidentified except that it is by Cecile Starr, the influential reviewer of nontheatrical films for *The Saturday Review of Literature*.

24. Ellis, pp. 180, 166–167.

25. William J. Sloan, "The Documentary Film and the Negro: The Evolution of the Integration Film," *The Journal of the Society of Cinematologists* 5 (1964) 66–69.

26. Karl G. Heider, *Ethnographic Film* (Austin: University of Texas Press, 1976), pp. 30–32.

27. Press release from Contemporary Films, distributor of THE HUNTERS.

28. Barsam, p. 295.

29. Quoted in Young and Zweiback, op. cit.

30. Most of the information on COME BACK, AFRICA is drawn from the program note for its 2 March 1962 Chicago premiere at the Documentary Film Group of the University of Chicago.

31. Benjamin T. Jackson, "The Savage Eye," *Film Quarterly* 13 (Summer 1960) 53–57. This is the fullest and best account of the film discovered, including analysis and appraisal.

32. Jacobs, *The Documentary Tradition*, p. 279.

33. Archer Winston, "Underside of a City: THE SAVAGE EYE," *New York Post*, 7 June 1960, reprinted in *ibid.*, pp. 341–342.

34. Jackson, op. cit.

35. Arthur Knight, "N.Y., N.Y. and HIGHWAY," *Film Quarterly* 12 (Summer 1959) 52–54.

36. Henry Breitrose, "The Films of Shirley Clarke," *Film Quarterly* 13 (Summer 1960) 57–58.

37. Willard Van Dyke, in G. Roy Levin, ed., *Documentary Explorations: 15 Interviews with Film-Makers* (Garden City, N.Y.: Doubleday, 1971), p. 187.

38. Ibid., pp. 187–188.

39. For THE PLOW THAT BROKE THE PLAINS (1936) prototype for this sort of epic conception, Pare Lorentz had hired a former Metropolitan Opera baritone to read the narration.

40. Shirley Clarke, in conversation with author during the time she was working on SKYSCRAPER.

41. Lyman Bryson, "Popular Art," in *The Communication of Ideas*, ed. Lyman Bryson (New York: Harper, 1948), pp. 277–286.

42. Much of the material on television documentary is drawn from Ellis, chapter 12, "A New Channel: Documentary for Television, 1951–," op. cit., pp. 184–202.

CHAPTER 12. "UNQUIET YEARS": EXPERIMENTAL CINEMA IN THE 1950S

1. Howard Becker, *Art Worlds* (Berkeley: University of California Press, 1982), p. x.

2. Becker, p. 93.

3. Becker, p. 162.

4. William Huie, "UFVA at 40: A Brief History" in *Journal of Film & Video* 38 #2 (Spring 1986), p. 22.

5. Huie, p. 23.

6. Jan-Christopher Horak, "The First American Avant-Garde, 1919–1945" in Jan-Christopher Horak, ed. *Lovers of Cinema* (Madison: University of Wisconsin Press, 1995), pp. 14–66.

7. Lewis Jacobs, *The Rise of the American Film* (New York: Teachers College Press, 1968), p. 563.

8. Lauren Rabinovitz, *Points of Resistance* (Champaign: University of Illinois Press, 1991), p. 448.

9. Dominic Angerame, "Welcome to Canyon Cinema." Available online at (www.canyoncinema.com/welcome.html), p. 1.

10. Angerame, p. 1.

11. Frank Stauffacher and Amos Vogel exchanged numerous letters between 1947 and 1951 about organizational strategies, programming, distribution, and finances. The earliest letters (September 1947) show Vogel asking Stauffacher for recommendations regarding the start of Cinema 16. A letter of condolence to Bobbie Stauffacher on Frank's death in 1955 also acknowledged Art in Cinema's influence on Cinema 16. See Scott MacDonald, ed. "Cinema 16: Documents Toward a History of the Film Society" in *Wide Angle* 19 #1 and #2 (January and April 1997).

12. Scott MacDonald, *A Critical Cinema 3* (Berkeley: University of California Press, 1998),p. 27.

13. MacDonald, *Wide Angle* 19 #1, p. 13.

14. MacDonald, *A Critical Cinema 3*, p. 14.

15. MacDonald, *Wide Angle* 19 #2, p. 14 and *Wide Angle* 19 #1, p. 13.

16. MacDonald, *A Critical Cinema* 3, p. 13.

17. MacDonald, *Wide Angle* 19 #1, p. 35.

18. P. Adams Sitney, ed. *The Essential Cinema* (New York: Anthology Film Archives, 1975), pp. xiii–xviii.

19. P. Adams Sitney, ed. *Film Culture Reader* (New York: Cooper Square Press, 2000), pp. 171–187.

20. Deren's *An Anagram of Ideas on Art, Form, and Film* was re-issued in Bill Nichols, ed. *Maya Deren and the American Avant-Garde* (Berkeley: University of California Press, 2001).

21. Sitney, *Film Culture Reader*, pp. 21–26.

22. David E. James, *Allegories of Cinema* (Princeton, N.J.: Princeton University Press, 1989), p. 104.

23. Sitney, *Film Culture Reader*, pp. 73–75.

24. Sitney, *Film Culture Reader*, p. 75.

25. MacDonald, *Wide Angle* 19 #2, p. 120.

26. David E. James, *To Free the Cinema* (Princeton, N.J.: Princeton University Press, 1992), p. 9.

27. Angerame, p. 2.

28. Becker, p. 47.

29. P. Adams Sitney, *Visionary Film* (New York: Oxford University Press, 1979), p. 137.

30. Sheldon Renan, *An Introduction to the American Underground Film* (New York: E. P. Dutton, 1967), p. 97.

31. Brakhage's importance might also be implied by the number of "essential" films *Anthology Film Archive* lists: thirty-eight between 1954 and 1971 (the list was published in 1975), roughly three times as many as any other filmmaker. Fourteen of these films were made between 1954 and 1964.

32. Sitney, *Visionary Film*, p. 142.

33. Sitney, *Visionary Film*, p. 138.

34. Parker Tyler, *Underground Film* (New York: Grove Press, 1969), p. 26.

35. James, *Allegories of Cinema*, p. 33.

36. Sitney, *Visionary Film*, p. 139.

37. In *Allegories of Cinema*, James particularly points out that ANTICIPATION OF THE NIGHT is not entirely first person. Two protagonists ground the film's visions: a baby and an adult male (and his shadow). James even compares ANTICIPATION OF THE NIGHT to Robert Enrico's acclaimed film, AN OCCURRENCE AT OWL CREEK BRIDGE (1962), in that "the entire film may be an expanded moment of redeemed vision" (p. 42), bookended by temporally contiguous moments. In other words, vestiges of the trance model (a journey metaphor, a linear narrative logic, and an on-screen protagonist) still remain.

38. Renan, p. 118.

39. Sitney, *Visionary Film*, pp. 143–144.

40. James Peterson, *Dreams of Chaos, Visions of Order* (Detroit, Mich.:Wayne State University Press, 1994), pp. 31–40.

41. Stan Brakhage, *Metaphors on Vision* (New York: Film Culture Inc, 1963), p. i.

42. In *Visionary Film*, Sitney does note the influence of Menken's VISUAL VARIATIONS OF NOGUCHI (1945) and NOTEBOOK (1943–1963) on Brakhage's ANTICIPATION OF THE NIGHT (p. 142). Also mentioned is her GLIMPSE OF THE GARDEN (1957), "in which Menken's camera sweeps through a small backyard as if imitating the point of view of a bird."

43. Brakhage, p. 1.

44. David Sterritt, *Mad to Be Saved* (Carbondale: Southern Illinois University Press, 1998), p. 2.

45. Sitney, *Film Culture Reader*, pp. 131–132.

46. Other early dances for the camera include Sarah Arledge's INTROSPECTION (1947) and Sidney Peterson's HORROR DREAM (1947) and CLINIC OF STUMBLE (1947).

47. Gary Morris, "Laughing Pan: James Broughton." Available online at (http://www.brightlights-film.com/27/broughton.html), p. 1.

48. James Broughton, *Making Light of It* (San Francisco, Calif.: City Light Books, 1992).

49. Broughton, p. 99.

50. Broughton, p. 100.

51. Sitney, *Visionary Film*, p. 80.

52. Sitney, *Visionary Film*, p. 83.

53. I am not including IN PARIS PARKS (1954) here, even though it is often presented as a cine-dance. It does explore and stylize the pedestrian movement of everyday people and objects through

music and editing tempo, but the film does not feature a choreographer and strikes me as more akin to the city symphony tradition. However, In Paris Parks might be seen as a progenitor of Clarke's Bridges-Go-Round (1958).

54. Rabinovitz, p. 97.
55. Rabinovitz, p. 100.
56. Sharon Torres, "Shirley Clarke: Bridges-Go-Round."Available online at ⟨www.ct-info.com/sharon/shirleyclarke/bridges.asp⟩, p. 1.
57. Renan, p. 145.
58. Peterson, p.149.
59. Dixon, p. 167.
60. Paola Igliori, *American Magus: Harry Smith* (New York: Inanout Press, 1996), back cover.
61. Igliori, p. 8.
62. Film-Makers' Cooperative, *Film-Makers' Cooperative Catalog #4* (1967), p. 137.
63. Film-Makers' Cooperative, p. 138.
64. Peterson, p. 146.
65. William C. Wees, *Recycled Images* (New York: Anthology Film Archives, 1993), p. 84.
66. Peterson, p. 157.
67. David Curtis, *Experimental Cinema* (New York: Dell Publishing, 1971), p. 168.
68. R. Russett and C. Starr, *Experimental Animation* (New York: DaCapo Press, 1976), pp. 134–135.
69. Scott MacDonald, *A Critical Cinema 2* (Berkeley: University of California Press, 1992), p. 16.
70. Lois Mendelson, *Robert Breer: A Study of His Work in the Context of the Modernist Tradition* (Ann Arbor, Mich.:UMI Research Press, 1981), p. 73.
71. Thanks to Peter Lev for these translations.
72. P. Adams Sitney, ed. *The Avant-Garde Film* (New York: Anthology Film Archives, 1978), p. 139.
73. Peter Kubelka, "The Theory of Metrical Film" in Sitney's *The Avant-Garde Film*, pp. 139–159.
74. Sitney, *The Avant-Garde Film*, pp. 140 and 149.
75. Sitney, *The Avant-Garde Film*, p. 141.
76. Sitney, *The Avant-Garde Film*, p. 143.
77. Gene Youngblood, *Expanded Cinema* (New York: E. P. Dutton, 1970), pp. 135–177.
78. William Wees, *Light Moving in Time* (Berkeley: University of California Press, 1992), pp. 123–152.
79. Wees, *Light Moving in Time*, p. 124.
80. Wees, *Light Moving in Time*, p. 126.
81. Mary Ellen Bute, "Statement II" in G. O'Grady and B. Posner, eds. *Articulated Light* (New York: Anthology Film Archives, 1995), p. 8.
82. Horak, p. 317.
83. William Moritz, "Mary Ellen Bute: Seeing Sound." Available online at ⟨www.awn.com/mag/issue1.2/articles1.2/moritz1.2.html⟩, p. 3. Moritz explains that Norman McLaren used oscilloscope patterns in 1950 to generate abstract images for his Around Is Around and Hy Hirsh also used oscilloscope imagery in his 1951 Divertissement Rococo.
84. Sitney, *Visionary Film*, p. 421.
85. Robert Haller, ed., *First Light* (New York: Anthology Film Archives, 1998), p. 24.
86. Robert Haller, *Jim Davis: The Flow of Energy* (New York: Anthology Film Archives, 1992), p. 9.
87. Haller, *Jim Davis*, p. 12.
88. Haller, ed., *First Light*, p. 108.
89. Igliori, p. 269.

Selected Bibliography

SPECIAL COLLECTIONS AND ARCHIVES

Academy of Motion Picture Arts and Sciences (AMPAS), Margaret Herrick Library, Special Collections: Hitchcock, Alfred; Huston, John; North, Alex; Production Code Administration, Motion Picture Association of America; Strickling, Howard (includes Eddie Mannix Ledger); Wyler, William; Zinnemann, Fred.

Brigham Young University, Harold B. Lee Library, Special Collections: Cooper, Merian C.; DeMille, Cecil B.; Steiner, Max; Theater Owners of America.

Georgetown University, Special Collections: Quigley, Martin J.; Department of Defense.

Stanford University, Special Collections: Skouras, Spyros.

University of Southern California, Special Collections: Warner Bros.

ORAL HISTORIES (ALL FROM AMPAS)

Gunzburg, Milton L. Oral History with Douglas Bell.
Simone, Lela. Oral History with Rudy Behlmer.
Taradash, Dan. Oral History with Barbara Hall.
Van Schmus, Albert. Oral History with Barbara Hall.

PRINCIPAL NEWSPAPERS, TRADE JOURNALS, YEARBOOKS, AND DATABASES

Film Daily Yearbook
Hollywood Reporter
International Motion Picture Almanac
Internet Movie Database (imdb.com)
Los Angeles Times
New York Times
Variety

BOOKS, PARTS OF BOOKS, ARTICLES

Andersen, Thom. "Red Hollywood," Suzanne Ferguson and Barbara Groseclose, eds. *Literature and the Visual Arts in Contemporary Society.* Columbus: Ohio State University Press, 1985, pp. 141–196.
Anderson, Christopher. *Hollywood TV: The Studio System in the Fifties.* Austin: University of Texas Press, 1994.

Auiler, Dan. *Vertigo: The Making of a Hitchcock Classic*. New York: St. Martin's Griffin, 2000.

Balio, Tino. *United Artists: The Company That Changed the Film Industry*. Madison: University of Wisconsin Press, 1987.

———, ed. *Hollywood in the Age of Television*. Boston: Unwin Hyman, 1990.

Barnouw, Eric. *Documentary: A History of the Non-Fiction Film*. New York: Oxford University Press, 1993.

Barsam, Richard M. *Nonfiction Film: A Critical History*. Bloomington: Indiana University Press, 1992.

Bazin, André. "The Evolution of the Western," *What Is Cinema?*, vol. 2, trans. Hugh Gray. Berkeley: University of California Press, 1971, pp. 149–158.

Bazin, André, Charles Bitsch, and Jean Domarchi, "Interview with Orson Welles (II)," trans. Peter Wollen; Mark Estrin, ed., *Orson Welles Interviews*. Jackson: University Press of Mississippi, 2002, pp. 48–76.

Becker, Howard. *Art Worlds*. Berkeley: University of California Press, 1982.

Belton, John. *Widescreen Cinema*. Cambridge, Mass.: Harvard University Press, 1992.

Bentley, Eric, ed. *Thirty Years of Treason: Excerpts from Hearings Before the House Committee on Un-American Activities, 1938–1968*. New York: Viking, 1971.

Bernstein, Irving. *Hollywood at the Crossroads: An Economic Study of the Motion Picture Industry*. Hollywood, Calif.: AF of L Film Council, 1957.

Bijl, Adriaan. "The Importance of Panavision." Master's Thesis, Department of Theatre Science, University of Utrecht, 1991. Reprinted in *in70mm: The 70mm Newsletter*, March 2002. Available on the World Wide Web at http://www.in70mm.com/newsletter/2002/67/panavision/panavision.htm

Biskind, Peter. *Seeing Is Believing*. New York: Pantheon Books, 1983.

Black, Gregory. *The Catholic Crusade Against the Movies, 1940–1975*. Cambridge, UK: Cambridge University Press, 1997.

Boddy, William. *Fifties Television: The Industry and Its Critics*. Urbana: University of Illinois Press, 1990.

Boyer, Paul. *By the Bomb's Early Light: American Thought and Culture at the Dawn of the Atomic Age*. Chapel Hill: University of North Carolina Press, 1994.

Brakhage, Stan. *Metaphors on Vision*. New York: Film Culture Inc., 1963. Originally published as *Film Culture* 30.

Breitrose, Henry. "The Films of Shirley Clarke." *Film Quarterly* 13 (Summer 1960): 57–58.

Broughton, James. *Making Light of It*. San Francisco, Calif.: City Lights Books, 1992.

Buford, Kate. *Burt Lancaster*. New York: Knopf, 2000.

Buhle, Paul, and Dave Wagner. *A Very Dangerous Citizen: Abraham Lincoln Polonsky and the Hollywood Left*. Berkeley: University of California Press, 2001.

Carney, Ray. *The Films of John Cassavetes: Pragmatism, Modernism, and the Movies*. Cambridge, UK: Cambridge University Press, 1994.

Ceplair, Larry, and Steven Englund. *The Inquisition in Hollywood: Politics in the Film Community 1930–1960*. Garden City, N.Y.: Anchor Press/Doubleday, 1980.

Cogley, John. *Report on Blacklisting, 1–Movies*. New York: Fund for the Republic, 1956.

Conant, Michael. *Anti-trust in the Motion Picture Industry*. Berkeley: University of California Press, 1960.

Corber, Robert J. *In the Name of National Security: Hitchcock, Homophobia, and the Political Construction of Gender in Postwar America*. Durham, N.C.: Duke University Press, 1992.

De Grazia, Edward, and Roger K. Newman. *Banned Films: Movies, Censors, and the First Amendment*. New York: Bowker, 1982.

Dick, Bernard F. *City of Dreams: The Making and Remaking of Universal Pictures*. Lexington: University of Kentucky Press, 1997.

———. *The Star-Spangled Screen: The American World War II Film*. Lexington: University of Kentucky Press, 1985.

Dombkowski, Dennis J. "Film and Television: An Analytical History of Economic and Creative Integration." Ph.D. Dissertation, University of Illinois, 1982.

Dowdy, Andrew. *"Movies Are Better Than Ever": Wide-Screen Memories of the Fifties*. New York: William Morrow, 1973.

Dunne, Philip. *Take Two: A Life in Movies and Politics*. New York: McGraw-Hill, 1980.

Dyer, Richard. *Heavenly Bodies: Film Stars and Society*. New York: St. Martin's, 1986.

Eisenschatz, Bernard. *Nicholas Ray: An American Journey*, trans. Tom Milne. London: Faber and Faber, 1993.

Eldridge, David. "'Dear Owen': The CIA, Luigi Luraschi, and Hollywood, 1953," *Historical Journal of Film, Radio, and Television* 20.2 (2000): 149–196.

Ellis, Jack C. *The Documentary Idea: A Critical History of English-Language Documentary Film and Video*. Englewood Cliffs, N.J.: Prentice Hall, 1989.

Evans, Joyce A. *Celluloid Mushroom Clouds: Hollywood and the Atomic Bomb*. Boulder, Colo.: Westview Press, 1998.

Finler, Joel W. *The Hollywood Story*. New York: Crown, 1988.

Fordin, Hugh. *The World of Entertainment: Hollywood's Greatest Musicals*. Garden City, N.Y.: Doubleday, 1975.

Glancy, H. Mark. "MGM Film Grosses, 1924–48: The Eddie Mannix Ledger," *Historical Journal of Radio, Television, and Film* 12.2 (1992): 127–145.

Gomery, Douglas. "Failed Opportunities: The Integration of the U.S. Motion Picture and Television Industries," *Quarterly Review of Film Studies*, Summer 1984: 219–228.

Goodman, Walter. *The Committee*. London: Secker and Warburg, 1968.

Guback, Thomas. *The International Film Industry*. Bloomington: Indiana University Press, 1969.

Haller, Robert. *Jim Davis: The Flow of Light*. New York: Anthology Film Archives, 1992.

———, ed. *First Light*. New York: Anthology Film Archives, 1998.

Halliday, Jon. *Sirk on Sirk*. New York: Viking, 1972.

Hamilton, Jack. "Hollywood Bypasses the Production Code," *Look*, 29 September 1959, pp. 82–84.

Hardy, Phil, ed. *The Overlook Film Encyclopedia: Science Fiction*, 3rd ed. New York: Overlook Press, 1995.

Harvey, James. *Movie Love in the Fifties*. New York: Knopf, 2001.

Haver, Ron. *A Star Is Born*. New York: Knopf, 1988.

Henderson, Brian. "*The Searchers*: An American Dilemma." *Film Quarterly* 34.2 (1980–1981): 10–23.

Hilmes, Michele. *Hollywood and Broadcasting: From Radio to Cable*. Urbana: University of Illinois Press, 1990.

Horne, Gerald. *Class Struggle in Hollywood, 1930–1950, Moguls, Mobsters, Stars, Reds, and Trade Unionists*. Austin: University of Texas Press, 2001.

Houseman, John. "Hollywood Faces the Fifties." Part 1, *Harper's*, April 1950, pp. 50–59; Part 2, *Harper's*, May 1950, pp. 51–59.

Hughes, Emmet John. "MGM: War Among the Lion Tamers." *Fortune*, August 1957, pp. 98–103, 206–208, 210, 212, 214, 216.

Igliori, Paola. *American Magus: Harry Smith*. New York: Inandout Press, 1996.

Jackson, Benjamin T. "The Savage Eye." *Film Quarterly* 13 (Summer 1960): 53–57.

Jacobs, Lewis, ed. *The Documentary Tradition*. New York: Norton, 1979.

James, David. *Allegories of Cinema*. Princeton, N.J.: Princeton University Press, 1989.

Jarvie, Ian. *Hollywood's Overseas Campaign: The North Atlantic Movie Trade, 1920–1950*. Cambridge: Cambridge University Press, 1992.

Jewell, Richard B., with Vernon Harbin. *The RKO Story*. London: Octopus Books, 1982.

Kazan, Elia. *A Life*. New York: Knopf, 1988.

Kindem, Gorham. "Hollywood's Conversion to Color: The Technological, Economic, and Aesthetic Factors." *Journal of the University Film Association* 31.2 (1979): 29–36.

Kramer, Stanley, and Thomas M. Coffey. *A Mad, Mad, Mad, Mad World: A Life in Hollywood*. New York: Harcourt Brace, 1997.

Lardner Jr., Ring. *I'd Hate Myself in the Morning: A Memoir*. New York: Thunder's Mouth Press, 2000.

Leab, Daniel J. "From Even-handedness to Red-baiting: The Transformation of the Novel *Trial*." *Film History* 10.3: 320–331.

Leaming, Barbara. *Orson Welles*. New York: Viking, 1985.

Levin, G. Roy, ed. *Documentary Explorations: 15 Interviews with Film-Makers*. Garden City, N.Y.: Doubleday, 1971.

Lewis, Jon. "'We Do Not Ask You to Condone This.' How the Blacklist Saved Hollywood." *Cinema Journal* 39.2 (2000): 3–30.

Lorrence, James J. *The Suppression of* Salt of the Earth, *How Hollywood, Big Labor, and Politicians Blacklisted a Movie in Cold War America*. Albuquerque: University of New Mexico Press, 1999.

MacDonald, Scott. *A Critical Cinema 2*. Berkeley: University of California Press, 1992.

———. *A Critical Cinema 3*. Berkeley: University of California Press, 1998.

———, ed. "Cinema 16: Documents Toward a History of the Film Society." *Wide Angle* 19.1 (1997): 3–48.

———, ed. "The Documents: The Cinema 16 Programs, and Selected Letters, Program Notes, and Reviews from the Cinema 16 Files." *Wide Angle* 19.1 (1997): 103–192 and *Wide Angle* 19.2 (1997): 1–203.

Mast, Gerald. *Can't Stop Singing: The American Musical on Stage and Screen*. Woodstock, N.Y.: Overlook Press, 1987.

May, Elaine Tyler. *Homeward Bound: American Families in the Cold War Era*. New York: Basic Books, 1988.

McCarthy, Todd. *Howard Hawks: The Grey Fox of Hollywood*. New York: Grove Press, 1997.

McCarthy, Todd, and Thomas Flynn, eds. *Kings of the Bs*. New York: Dutton, 1975.

McDougal, Dennis. *The Last Mogul: Lew Wasserman, MCA, and the Hidden History of Hollywood*. New York: Crown, 1998.

McGee, Mark Thomas. *Fast and Furious: The Story of American International Pictures*. Jefferson, N.C.: McFarland, 1984.

McGilligan, Pat, ed. *Backstory 2: Interviews with Screenwriters of the 1940s and 1950s*. Berkeley: University of California Press, 1991.

Mendelson, Lois. *Robert Breer: A Study of His Work in the Context of the Modernist Tradition*. Ann Arbor, Mich.: UMI Research Press, 1981.

Naremore, James. *Acting in the Cinema*. Berkeley: University of California Press, 1988.

———. *More Than Night: Film Noir in Its Contexts*. Berkeley: University of California Press, 1998.

Navasky, Victor. *Naming Names*. New York: Viking Press, 1980.

Orrison, Katherine. *Written in Stone: Making Cecil B. DeMille's Epic* The Ten Commandments. Lanham, Md.: Vestal, 1999.

Peary, Danny, ed. *Omni's Screen Flights/Screen Fantasies: The Future According to Science Fiction Cinema*. New York: Dolphin, 1984.

Pells, Richard. *The Liberal Mind in a Conservative Age: American Intellectuals in the 1940s and 1950s*. New York: Harper and Row, 1985.

Peterson, James. *Dreams of Chaos, Visions of Order*. Detroit, Mich.: Wayne State University Press, 1994.

Rabinovitz, Lauren. *Points of Resistance*. Urbana: University of Illinois Press, 1991.

Randall, Richard S. *Censorship of the Movies*. Madison: University of Wisconsin Press, 1970.

Renan, Sheldon. *An Introduction to the American Underground Film*. New York: Dutton, 1967.

"RKO: It's Only Money." *Fortune*, May 1953, pp. 123–127, 206, 208, 210, 212, 214–215.

Ross, Lillian. *Picture*. New York: Avon Books, 1952.

Salt, Barry. *Film Style and Technology: History and Analysis*. London: Starward, 1983.

Schatz, Thomas. *Boom and Bust: The American Cinema in the 1940s*. History of the American Cinema, vol. 6. New York: Charles Scribner's Sons, 1997.

———. *The Genius of the System*. New York: Pantheon, 1988.

Schrecker, Ellen. *Many Are the Crimes: McCarthyism in America*. Boston: Little Brown, 1998.

Schlesinger Jr., Arthur. *The Vital Center: The Politics of Freedom*. Boston: Houghton Mifflin, 1949.

Sikov, Ed. *On Sunset Boulevard: The Life and Times of Billy Wilder*. New York: Hyperion, 1998.

Sitney, P. Adams. *Visionary Film*. New York: Oxford University Press, 1979.

———, ed. *The Avant-Garde Film*. New York: Anthology Film Archives, 1978.

———, ed. *The Essential Cinema*. New York: Anthology Film Archives, 1975.

———, ed. *Film Culture Reader*. New York: Cooper Square Press, 2000.

Sklar, Robert. *Movie-Made America*. New York: Vintage/Random House, 1975.

Sobchack, Vivian. *Screening Space: The American Science Fiction Film*. New York: Ungar, 1991.

Solomon, Aubrey. *Twentieth Century–Fox: A Corporate and Financial History*. Metuchen, N.J.: Scarecrow, 1988.

Sontag, Susan. "The Imagination of Disaster." *Against Interpretation and Other Essays*. New York: Farrar, Straus, and Giroux, 1966, pp. 209–225.

Spoto, Donald. *Stanley Kramer: Film Maker*. New York: G. P. Putnam's Sons, 1978.

Staiger, Janet. "The Package-Unit System: Unit Management After 1955." David Bordwell, Janet Staiger, and Kristin Thompson, *The Classical Hollywood Cinema: Film Style and Mode of Production to 1960*. New York: Columbia University Press, 1985, pp. 330–337.

Steinberg, Cobbett. *Reel Facts*. New York: Facts on File, 1980.

Suber, Howard. "The Anti-Communist Blacklist in the Hollywood Motion Picture Industry." Ph.D. dissertation, University of California, Los Angeles, 1968.

Suid, Lawrence H. *Guts and Glory: Great American War Movies*. Reading, Mass.: Addison-Wesley, 1978.

———. *Sailing on the Silver Screen: Hollywood and the U.S. Navy*. Annapolis, Md.: Naval Institute Press, 1996.

———, ed. *Film and Propaganda in America: A Documentary History*, vol. 4, *1945 and After*. New York: Greenwood, 1991.

Thomson, David. *Rosebud*. New York: Knopf, 1996.

Trumbo, Dalton. *Additional Dialogue: The Letters of Dalton Trumbo*. New York: Bantam Books, 1972.

Vieth, Earl. *Screening Science: Contexts, Texts, and Science in Fifties Science Fiction Film*. Lanham, Md.: Scarecrow, 2001.

Vizzard, Jack. *See No Evil: Life Inside a Hollywood Censor*. New York: Simon and Schuster, 1970.

Wallis, Hal, and Charles Higham. *Starmaker: The Autobiography of Hal Wallis*. New York: Macmillan, 1980.

Walsh, Martin. *Sin and Censorship: The Catholic Church and the Motion Picture Industry*. New Haven, Conn.: Yale University Press, 1996.

Wasko, Janet. *Movies and Money*. Norwood, N.J.: Ablex, 1982.

———. *Understanding Disney: The Manufacture of Fantasy*. Oxford: Polity Press, 2001.

Watts, Steven. *The Magic Kingdom*. Boston: Houghton Mifflin, 1997.

Wees, William. *Light Moving in Time*. Berkeley: University of California Press, 1992.

Wollen, Peter. *Singin' in the Rain*. London: British Film Institute, 1992.

Youngblood, Gene. *Expanded Cinema*. New York: Dutton, 1970.

Zinnemann, Fred. *Fred Zinnemann: An Autobiography*. New York: Charles Scribner's Sons, 1992.

Picture Sources

Academy of Motion Picture Arts and Sciences. Pages: 17, 32, 41, 158.

Brigham Young University, Photographic Archives, Harold B. Lee Library. Page: 11.

CBS. Pages: 275, 276.

Jerry Ohlinger's Movie Material Store (New York) Pages: 4, 36, 40, 79, 115, 117, 122, 143, 159, 160, 161, 165, 166, 210, 221, 224, 230, 231, 236, 237, 241, 245, 247, 249, 252, 253.

Larry Edmunds Cinema Bookshop (Hollywood). Pages: 19, 23, 39, 45, 48, 49, 52, 56, 57, 59, 61, 73, 75, 76, 81, 90, 91, 93, 96, 103, 111, 118, 119, 121, 123, 136, 145, 151, 152, 155, 156, 175, 176, 178, 181, 185, 187, 189, 190, 199, 201, 203, 208, 233, 239, 240, 243.

Museum of Modern Art, Film Stills Archive. Page: 264.

National Film Archive, London. Page: 273.

Photofest. Pages: 3, 24, 30, 84, 113, 140, 153.

Robert Galbraith. Page: 267.

Wisconsin Center for Film and Theater Research/Wendy Clarke. Pages: 272, 292.

The photographs in Chapter 12 are frame enlargements, with one exception.

General Index

Italic numerals signify illustrations.

Index of Films

Italic numerals signify illustrations.

DATE DUE